QUALITATIVE ORGANIZATIONAL RESEARCH

GILLIAN SYMON & CATHERINE CASSELL

QUALITATIVE ORGANIZATIONAL RESEARCH

CORE METHODS AND CURRENT CHALLENGES

Los Angeles | London | New Delhi
Singapore | Washington DC

SAGE Publications Ltd
1 Oliver's Yard
55 City Road
London EC1Y 1SP

SAGE Publications Inc.
2455 Teller Road
Thousand Oaks, California 91320

SAGE Publications India Pvt Ltd
B 1/I 1 Mohan Cooperative Industrial Area
Mathura Road
New Delhi 110 044

SAGE Publications Asia-Pacific Pte Ltd
3 Church Street
#10-04 Samsung Hub
Singapore 049483

Library of Congress Control Number: 2011936798

British Library Cataloguing in Publication data

A catalogue record for this book is available from the British Library

ISBN 978-0-85702-410-7
ISBN 978-0-85702-411-4 (pbk)

Typeset by C&M Digitals (P) Ltd, Chennai, India
Printed by MPG Books Group, Bodmin, Cornwall
Printed on paper from sustainable resources

Contents

Notes on Contributors

Eva A. Alfoldi is a Lecturer in International Business at Manchester Business School, University of Manchester. Her research focuses on multinational subsidiary management, knowledge transfer and research methods in international business. She received her PhD from the University of Leeds where she was the recipient of a Society for the Advancement of Management Studies (SAMS) scholarship. She is currently working on publications from her thesis as well as on new projects, targeting journals such as the *Journal of Management Studies*, *Management International Review*, the *Journal of World Business* and the *British Educational Research Journal*. She has a strong focus on developing and delivering innovative materials for qualitative research methods teaching. She was born in Hungary and now lives and works in Manchester.

Mats Alvesson is Professor of Business Administration at the University of Lund, Sweden, and at the University of Queensland Business School, Australia. He is also a Visiting Professor at Exeter University. His research interests include critical theory, gender, power, management of professional service (knowledge intensive) organizations, leadership, identity, organizational image, organizational culture and symbolism, qualitative methods and philosophy of science. Recent books include *Theory Development and Qualitative Research* (Sage, 2011, with Dan Kärreman), *Interpreting Interviews* (Sage, 2011), *Metaphors We Lead By: Understanding Leadership in the Real World* (Routledge, 2011, edited with Andre Spicer), *Oxford Handbook of Critical Management Studies* (Oxford University Press, 2009, edited with Todd Bridgman and Hugh Willmott), *Understanding Gender and Organizations* (Sage, 2009, 2nd edn, with Yvonne Billing), *Reflexive Methodology* (Sage, 2009, 2nd edn, with Kaj Sköldberg), *Changing Organizational Culture* (Routledge, 2008, with Stefan Sveningsson), and *Knowledge Work and Knowledge-Intensive Firms* (Oxford University Press, 2004).

Karen Lee Ashcraft is a Professor in the Department of Communication at the University of Colorado at Boulder, USA, and an Associate Editor for *Human Relations*. Her research examines organizational forms and occupational identities, with a particular emphasis on gender and race relations. Her work has appeared in such venues as *Administrative Science Quarterly*, the *Academy of Management Journal*, *Communication Theory* and *Communication Monographs*. Her co-authored book with Dennis Mumby, *Reworking Gender*, received the 2004 Book of the Year Award from the Organizational Communication Division of the National Communication Association.

Matthew J. Brannan is a lecturer in Management at the School of Management at Keele University. He has also held a post at the Centre for Labour Market Studies, University of Leicester. His research focuses upon the growth of the service sector and the contemporary experience of work using ethnographic techniques to gain an immersive insight into the world of work. His work has included the use of role play in call centre recruitment and selection processes, the engagement of workers' sexuality in customer service environments, the career path of female junior managers and employee branding.

David A. Buchanan is Professor of Organizational Behaviour at Cranfield University School of Management, specializing in change management, change agency and organization politics. He has a Doctorate in Organizational Behaviour from Edinburgh University and is the author/co-author of over two dozen books, one of which has been a bestseller since 1985: *Organizational Behaviour* (FT Prentice Hall, 2010, 7th edn, with Andrzej Huczynski). He is co-editor (with Alan Bryman) of *The Sage Handbook of Organizational Research Methods* (2009) and has written numerous book chapters, papers and articles on organizational behaviour, change and research methods. Current projects include a study of the realities of management in healthcare and managing change in extreme contexts – including incidents that adversely affect patient safety in hospital.

Catherine Cassell is Professor of Organizational Psychology at Manchester Business School, University of Manchester, where she heads up the School's People, Management and Organizations Division. Catherine has spent many years working with Gillian Symon on promoting the use of qualitative methods in organizational, management and work psychology research, and this is their fourth edited book for Sage on this topic. They also jointly edit *Qualitative Research in Organizations and Management: An International Journal*. Catherine's research interests are in the areas of organizational learning, change and fairness at work. She is an Associate Editor of the *British Journal of Management* and also edits their *Methodology Corner*.

Timothy Clark is Professor of Organizational Behaviour at Durham Business School, Durham University. In the last decade he has conducted a series of research projects into consultancy work and speaker–audience interaction during management guru lectures. The publications emanating from these projects include *Critical Consulting: New Perspectives on the Management Advice Industry* (Blackwell, 2002, with Robin Fincham), *Management Speak* (Routledge, 2005, with David Greatbatch) and most recently *Management Consultancy: Knowledge and Boundaries in Action* (Oxford, 2008, with Andrew Sturdy, Robin Fincham and Karen Handley). He is currently working on a multidisciplinary project examining the emergence and nature of 'Tipping Points'.

Laurie Cohen is Professor of Organization Studies and Director of the Centre for Professional Work and Careers at the School of Business and Economics, Loughborough University. Her research interests include changing careers of professional workers, careers in emerging forms of organization and research methods in the study of career, focusing in particular on interpretive approaches and the use of narrative. Her work has been supported by grants from the Economic and Social Research Council and the British Academy. Laurie has published in a wide range of international journals, including *Human Relations*, *Organization Studies*, *Organization*, *Work, Employment and Society*, *Journal of Vocational Behaviour* and the *Journal of Management Inquiry*, as well as contributing chapters to many edited collections. She is also on the editorial boards of the *Journal of Vocational Behavior, Human Relations Journal of Management Inquiry* and *Management Learning*.

Joep Cornelissen is Professor of Communication and Organization Theory at VU University Amsterdam and the University of Leeds. He has taught courses on communication, strategic change and organization theory at universities across Europe. His much-loved textbook, *Corporate Communication: A Guide to Theory and Practice,* was published in its third edition in March 2011, fully revised, extended and updated to take into account recent developments in strategic and corporate communication. Besides his writing and teaching commitments, Joep is also an active researcher within the fields of communication and management and a general editor for the *Journal of Management Studies*. His own current research focuses on the role of framing and narration in strategic change, entrepreneurial and innovation contexts.

Joanne Duberley is a Reader in Organization Studies at Birmingham Business School, University of Birmingham. Her recent research interests focus upon the study of careers in a wide variety of settings including academic scientists, self-employed women and NHS managers. She also maintains an interest in the philosophical underpinnings of management research.

Hanna Gajewska-de Mattos is Lecturer in Business Development in Emerging Markets at the Centre for International Business University of Leeds (CIBUL). She was a European Union Phare ACE Scholar at the University of Leeds from which she obtained her doctorate. She was also a Foundation for Management Education Research Officer in CIBUL and she worked on International S&T Cooperation Policy issues in the Director General for Research in the European Commission. Her current research interests centre on the role of cultural distance within international management relationships, the role of language in international business, qualitative research methodology and pedagogy in international business.

David Greatbatch is a Visiting Professor at Durham Business School, Durham University. He specializes in video-based studies of social interaction in organizational settings, drawing on conversation analysis and ethnomethodology. He has under-taken research in a wide variety of contexts including management consultancy, live corporate events, broadcast journalism, general practice and telemedicine. He has also published articles in journals such as the *American Sociological Review, American Journal of Sociology, Language in Society, Human Relations, Leadership Quarterly* and *Law and Society Review*. He co-authored *Management Speak* (Routledge, 2005, with Timothy Clark) and is currently completing a book on the social organization of conflict talk in family mediation sessions.

Kathryn Haynes is Northern Society Professor of Accounting and Finance at Newcastle University Business School. Previously she worked at Aston Business School and the University of York. She is also an Advanced Institute of Management (AIM) Services Fellow. Her research interests include identity and its relationship with gender; the body and embodiment within organizations; the juxtaposition of professional and personal identities; social and environmental accounting; sustain-ability and responsibility; issues of governance and accountability; and the conduct of the professions and professional services firms. She is also interested in reflexive research methodologies, including narrative, autoethnography, oral history and ethnography. Kathryn is associate editor of the *International Journal of Management Reviews* and *Gender, Work and Organization*.

Robin Holt is a Professor at the University of Liverpool Management School. He has enjoyed a serpentine academic career, working in departments of politics and philosophy as well as business and management, and at a number of universities. Throughout he has been interested in basic questions of meaning associated with words such as value, production, knowledge, good and wealth, and continues to be curious about these, currently through research work on judgement, on entre-preneurial activity and on strategic practice.

Merlijn van Hulst was trained in cultural anthropology at Utrecht University and received his PhD from Erasmus University, Rotterdam. Currently, he is Assistant Professor at the Tilburg School of Politics and Public Administration. He is inter-ested in the role of sensemaking in (local) governance and specializes in interpretive methods. His current research includes an analysis of storytelling in police practices, the work of excellent practitioners in neighbourhood governance and the concept of framing in policy analysis.

Michael Humphreys is Professor of Organization Studies at Nottingham University Business School. His current research interests include: studies of organizational identity, narrative and change, innovation and improvisation in teams, public sector management and qualitative research methodology. He has published in a range of journals including the *Journal of Management Studies, Organization Studies, Human*

Relations, Organization, the *Journal of Applied Behavioral Science,* the *British Journal of Management* and *Public Administration.* He is a member of the editorial boards of the *Journal of Management Studies, Organization Studies* and the *Journal of Vocational Education and Training.*

Phil Johnson is currently Professor of Organization Studies and Head of the OB/HRM Division at the Management School, Sheffield University. His research interests include methodologies and epistemologies in organization studies as well as current developments in HRM praxis and organizational forms.

Binna Kandola OBE is a chartered psychologist. He is the senior partner and co-founder of Pearn Kandola, a practice of business psychologists. Professor Kandola has published research books, one of which, *Diversity in Action: Managing the Mosaic* (CIPD, 1998), won a special commendation at the Management Book Awards in 1995. His latest book on unconscious bias in the workplace, *The Value of Difference* (Pearn Kandola Publishing, 2009), has received widespread critical acclaim. He is also Visiting Professor at Leeds University Business School.

Graham J.J. Kenealy is an independent consultant and researcher. He is an experienced change professional who uses grounded theory as an instrument for his daily work, enabling him to deliver change programmes for both UK government and global blue chip organizations. His interest in classic grounded theory, which developed during his period of PhD study at the University of Manchester, has continued to grow and he is currently a peer reviewer for *The Grounded Theory Review.* Dr Kenealy also acts as a troubleshooter at grounded theory seminars for the Grounded Theory Institute. These seminars are designed to help PhD students and supervisors using classic grounded theory.

Nigel King is Professor in Applied Psychology and Director of the Centre for Applied Psychological Research at the University of Huddersfield. He has a long-standing interest in the use of qualitative methods in 'real world' research, especially in community health and social care settings. Recently, he has carried out several projects in community palliative care, focusing especially on roles, relationships and identities. Other interests include the experience of chronic illness, psychological aspects of contact with nature and ethics in qualitative research. He is well known for his work on the 'template' style of thematic analysis and more recently the development of a visual technique known as 'Pictor'.

Ann Langley is Professor of Management at HEC Montréal and Canada Research Chair in Strategic Management in Pluralistic Settings. Her research focuses on strategic change, leadership, innovation and the use of management tools in complex organizations with an emphasis on processual research approaches. She has published over 50 articles and two books, most recently *Strategy as Practice: Research Directions and Resources* (Cambridge University Press, 2007, with Gerry Johnson, Leif Melin and Richard Whittington).

Mark Learmonth is Professor of Organization Studies at Durham University. He spent the first 17 years of his career in management posts within the British National Health Service and still conducts research in healthcare, though with increasingly regular forays elsewhere. Prior to taking up his post in Durham he has worked at the universities of Nottingham and York.

Bill Lee is Professor and Head of Accounting at Keele Management School, having recently moved from a position as senior lecturer in accounting and financial management in the Management School at the University of Sheffield. His research interests include accountability in the workplace and accounting issues that are relevant to learning initiatives. He also has a long-term interest in research methods and research practice and has been active in the broader academic community in establishing conference tracks and networks in which such issues may be discussed.

Sally Maitlis is an Associate Professor of Organizational Behavior in the Sauder School of Business, University of British Columbia. Her research interests include organizational sensemaking, post-traumatic growth at work and narrative and discursive approaches to the study of emotion. Her work has been published in journals such as the *Academy of Management Journal, Human Relations*, the *Journal of Management Studies*, the *Journal of Organizational Behavior, Organization Science* and *Organization Studies*. She serves on the editorial boards of the *Academy of Management Journal*, the *Academy of Management Review* and *Organization Studies*, and is a former associate editor for non-traditional research at the *Journal of Management Inquiry*.

Cliff Oswick is Professor of Organization Theory and Head of the Faculty of Management at Cass Business School, City University London. Cliff's research interests focus on the application of aspects of discourse to the study of organizations, organizing and organizational change. He has published over 120 academic articles and contributions to edited volumes, including contributions to the *Academy of Management Review, Human Relations*, the *Journal of Management Studies, Organization* and *Organization Studies*. He is European editor for the *Journal of Organizational Change Management*, associate editor for the *Journal of Change Management* and co-director of ICRODSC (International Centre for Research on Organizational Discourse, Strategy and Change).

Teresa Oultram received her PhD from Keele University. Her thesis on 'Exploring the identities of the young male worker: a case study of English apprenticeship schemes' focuses on how an official government discourse of enterprise competes with localized, workplace discourses, in particular, that of working-class masculinity.

Rebecca Piekkari is Professor of International Business at the Aalto University, School of Economics (formerly Helsinki School of Economics), in Finland. She has published on qualitative research methods, particularly on the use of case studies in international business. Her most recent book, entitled *Rethinking the Case Study in International Business and Management Research*, was co-edited with Catherine Welch (Edward Elgar, 2011). Rebecca's teaching and research focus on international management, particularly on control, coordination and communication issues in multinational corporations. During the past few years, she has developed a special interest in multilingual organizations and the challenges associated with managing people in such organizations. Rebecca has worked as Visiting Professor and researcher at several well-known business schools and universities, such as INSEAD, the University of Leeds, University of Sheffield, University of Sydney and Copenhagen Business School.

Katrina Pritchard is a lecturer in the Organizational Psychology Department of Birkbeck, University of London. While her teaching is primarily in the area of Organizational Behaviour and HRM, she also teaches research methods to both Master's and PhD students, covering topics ranging from data management to dissemination. Her research interests lie in the social construction of knowledge, particularly notions of professional knowledge, and in the relationships between knowledge and identity in a variety of organizational contexts. Katrina is interested in a broad range of methodological issues encountered in qualitative research in organizational studies including, as discussed here, combining qualitative methods.

M. N. Ravishankar is a senior lecturer in International Business and Strategy at the School of Business and Economics, Loughborough University. His research interests span the offshore outsourcing of work and culture in global organizations. Ravi's approach to the collection and analysis of empirical material draws inspiration from the interpretive world-view and typically he adopts the case study and ethnography methods in his work. His recent research has appeared in leading international journals such as *Information Systems Research*, *Omega* and the *Industrial Relations Journal*.

Mark N.K. Saunders is Professor in Business Research Methods at the Surrey Business School, University of Surrey. His research interests focus on two themes. The first, research methods, includes the development of tools to learn about, understand and improve organizational relationships within a process consultation framework, online research methods and methods for researching trust. The second, human resource aspects of the management of change, is concerned particularly with trust and justice. Mark's research findings have been published in a range of academic and practitioner journals. Recent books include: *Research Methods for Business Students* (FT Prentice Hall, 2009), now in its fifth edition, and co-authored with Phil Lewis and Adrian Thornhill; and *Handbook of Research Methods on Trust (Edward Elgar, 2012)* co-edited with Fergus Lyon and Guido Möllering.

Rudolf R. Sinkovics is Professor of International Business at Manchester Business School, University of Manchester. His research centres on inter-organizational governance, the role of ICT and research methods in international business. Recent work is geared towards rising powers, emerging markets and drivers of economic change. He received his PhD from Vienna University of Economics and Business (WU-Wien), Austria. His work has been published in journals such as the *Journal of International Business Studies*, *Management International Review*, the *Journal of World Business*, *International Business Review* and *International Marketing Review*. Born in Austria, he now lives and works in Manchester.

Inger Stensaker is Associate Professor of Strategy at NHH Norwegian School of Economics and Business Administration. Her research interests are within strategic change implementation, focusing on the dynamics between change management and change recipients using cognitive and sensemaking perspectives and qualitative methods. Her work has been published in journals such as *Human Relations*, the *British Journal of Management*, the *Journal of Applied Behavioral Science*, *Organizational Dynamics* and the *Journal of Change Management*.

Gillian Symon is Reader in Organizational Psychology at Birkbeck, University of London. With Catherine Cassell, she has edited three previous books on qualitative methods in organizational research (published by Sage) and they have also, together, written a number of journal articles and book chapters on this topic. They jointly edit the journal *Qualitative Research in Organizations and Management: An International Journal*. Gillian also has research interests in the wider issue of academic research practices and identity, and in the relationship between technology, work and identity.

Susanne Tietze is Professor of Organization Studies at Sheffield Hallam University, Sheffield Business School. Her research focuses on language and discourse as used in work contexts and, more recently, on the role of the English language in knowledge production processes in the management academy. She has also conducted studies on emergent forms of work organization and worked for several UK and European universities, as well as consulted on topics such as home-based telework, management and career development. She has published in leading scholarly journals such as *Organization Studies*, *English for Specific Purposes*, the *Scandinavian Journal of Management* and the *Journal of Business Ethics*.

Russ Vince is Associate Dean, Research and Professor of Leadership and Change in the School of Management, University of Bath. His research interests are in management and organizational learning, leadership and change. His most recent books are: *The Handbook of Experiential Learning and Management Education* (Oxford University Press, 2007), *Rethinking Strategic Learning* (Routledge, 2004) and *Organizing Reflection* (Ashgate, 2004). Russ is a former editor-in-chief of the international academic journal *Management Learning* (2005–2010). He is also one of six founding members of the International Network for Visual Studies in Organizations (http://in-visio.org/).

Samantha Warren is Professor in Management at Essex Business School, University of Essex. Her research interests centre on the aesthetic dimension of organizational life and more specifically, objects, space, materiality and their implications for people's workplaces and professional lives. Her early work explored the role of the material in organizational 'fun cultures' and through this she became intrigued as to the possibilities offered to organization studies by visual research. She has remained fascinated by sensory research methods and is currently undertaking a project with Dr Kathleen Riach to explore the role of smell in the workplace. She is a longstanding board member of the Standing Conference on Organizational Symbolism (SCOS) and a founder member of the International Network for Visual Studies in Organizations (http://in-visio.org/).

Catherine Welch is a senior lecturer in International Business at the University of Sydney, Australia. Her current research interests lie in the areas of qualitative research in international business, particularly the use of the case study, and process theories of firm internationalization. Together with Rebecca Piekkari, she has edited two volumes on qualitative research published by Edward Elgar: *Handbook of Qualitative Research Methods for International Business* (2004) and *Rethinking the Case Study in International Business and Management Research* (2011). She is part of a Linked In network of qualitative researchers (Qualitative Research in IB) coordinated by Daniella Fjellström at the University of Leeds; anyone interested in joining the network is welcome to contact her.

Julie Wolfram Cox is Professor of Management (Organization Studies) at Monash University, Australia. She received her PhD in organizational behaviour from Case Western Reserve University in Cleveland, Ohio, and is interested in critical and aesthetic perspectives in organization theory, particularly in the area of organizational change. In 2005 she co-edited the four volume collection *Fundamentals of Action Research* (Sage) with Bill Cooke. Her other publications include *Disorganization Theory: Explorations in Alternative Organizational Analysis* (Routledge, 2008, with John Hassard and Mihaela Kelemen) and articles in *Organization Studies*, the *Journal of Management Studies*, *Organization*, the *Journal of Applied Behavioral Science*, the *Journal of Organizational Change Management, Culture and Organization*, and the *International Journal of Management Reviews*.

Dvora Yanow is a policy and organizational ethnographer and interpretive methodologist whose research and teaching are shaped by an overall interest in the communication of meaning in organizational and policy settings. Holder of the 2005–2010 Strategic Chair in Meaning and Method in the Faculty of Social Sciences, VU University, Amsterdam, she is presently Visiting Professor in the Faculty of Social and Behavioural Sciences, University of Amsterdam, in the Department of Sociology and Anthropology, and at Wageningen University's Faculty of Social Sciences in the Communication Science Department. Her research investigates state-created categories for race-ethnic identity, immigrant integration policies and citizen-making practices, and research regulation policies and practices, on the policy side; science/technology museums and the meaning of 'science', on the methodological side; and spatial and practice studies, on the organizational side.

Sierk Ybema is Associate Professor, Department of Culture, Organization and Management, VU University, Amsterdam. His ethnographic research centres on processes of politics, identity and sensemaking, with empirical settings ranging from amusement parks to newspaper offices to multinational corporations. He has published widely on culture and conflict, relational and temporal identity talk, managerial discourse and 'postalgia', intercultural communications, interorganizational relationships, and organizational change and crisis, in such journals as *Human Relations*, the *International Journal of Cross-Cultural Management*, *Organization Studies* and the *Journal of Managerial Psychology*. He is co-editor of *Organizational Ethnography: Studying the Complexities of Everyday Life* (Sage, 2009, with Dvora Yanow, Harry Wels and Frans Kamsteeg) and *Organizational Culture* (Edward Elgar, 2011, with Dvora Yanow and Ida Sabelis), as well as, among others, a 2009 *Human Relations* Special Issue on 'Constructing identity in organizations'.

1 Introduction: The Context of Qualitative Organizational Research

Catherine Cassell and Gillian Symon

Introduction

This is the fourth collection we have put together on qualitative methods in organizational research. There have been some changes since our first book in 1994. Certainly, qualitative methods are now far more widespread within organizational research than they were at that time. Additionally it would seem that there is now less of a need to document the wide variety of methods available to the qualitative researcher as this has been done by ourselves and others elsewhere during recent years (Cassell and Symon, 1994; Symon and Cassell, 1998; Cassell and Symon, 2004; Thorpe and Holt, 2008; Eriksson and Kovalainen, 2008).

In the introduction to our last book, *Essential Guide to Qualitative Methods in Organizational Research*, published in 2004, we suggested that this was 'our last venture into this particular genre' (Symon and Cassell, 2004: 1), so why another text now? Three things have influenced the development of this collection. Firstly, together with our colleagues Phil Johnson, Vicky Bishop and Anna Buehring, an ESRC project entitled *Benchmarking Good Practice in Qualitative Management Research* (grant number H333250006) enabled us to discuss with a range of different stakeholder groups the processes that went into the production of good qualitative research. It also enabled us to devise a range of training materials for qualitative researchers (see www.restore.ac.uk/bgpinqmr/). From this project we learned a lot, notably about the complexity of criteria for qualitative organizational research and the criteriological debates associated with discussions of quality criteria (see Symon and Cassell, in this volume). Secondly, we set up a new journal in 2006 entitled *Qualitative Research in Organizations and Management: An International Journal* (QROM). The aim of the journal is to publish exemplars of excellent qualitative empirical work. Through our experiences of the editorial process and our interactions with our informed and constructive editorial board and contributors we have developed more insights into the struggles that qualitative researchers experience in turning their empirical work into high quality output. Thirdly, we have taught many different groups of students the joys of qualitative methods over recent years. These include undergraduates; postgraduates in work psychology, HRM and other management disciplines; doctoral students; MBAs and DBAs. With all of these groups we have seen the demands made upon them in encountering qualitative methods and using them in their dissertations for what in many cases is the first time.

From these experiences we have become more aware that the processes that go into the production and practice of high quality qualitative research are both complex and context bound. Therefore we believe there is a need for a text that not only covers key methods but also addresses the issues of research practice faced by the qualitative organizational researcher. This is what we seek to do in this book. We see it as a companion text to the *Essential Guide*, which focuses more exclusively on detailing the range of methods available. However, there have been some changes in the field of qualitative organizational research since we published the *Essential Guide* eight years ago. Indeed the context in which qualitative organizational research is conducted and assessed seems to be forever changing. In the remainder of this introductory chapter we outline what we see to be some of the key dynamics in the current context as a way of setting the scene for the chapters that follow.

Current Concerns in Research Practice

In the introduction to the *Essential Guide* we stated that: 'our intention has always been to influence research practice within our own discipline' (Symon and Cassell, 2004: 4). There are four particular things that concern us about research practice at the current time and looking towards the future: the teaching training of qualitative researchers; the impact of a variety of institutional pressures on the conduct of qualitative research; the potential standardization of qualitative research; and contemporary concerns with ethics and evidence. It is to these issues that we now turn.

Teaching and training qualitative researchers

In regard to the teaching and training of qualitative researchers, there are now clearly more resources available in terms of textbooks which outline the potential uses of qualitative research. Previously we mentioned the training materials we developed through our ESRC project (see www.restore.ac.uk/bgpiqmr/). From the empirical research we conducted for that project we investigated what kinds of knowledge and skills were perceived as necessary to conduct good qualitative research. Our analysis suggested that novice researchers needed to learn a range of skills including those of data collection; data analysis; writing; and critique and evaluation. They also needed to acquire knowledge about the various different methods of qualitative research available and the philosophical methods that underpin method use. Hence the inclusion in this collection of a chapter by Joanne Duberley, Phil Johnson and Catherine Cassell about the different philosophies that underlie qualitative research. Finally, we suggested that qualitative researchers also needed to develop three types of research practices for the accomplishment of good qualitative research: reflective practice, reflexive practice and phronesis (Cassell et al., 2009). The term 'reflection' as used here draws upon the work of Schön (1983) and refers to when the researcher explores the impact of their research in a problem-solving manner with the intention of generating some form of learning upon which future action can be based. Reflexivity (see Haynes, in this volume) encourages the researcher to understand and make sense of their research by challenging and critiquing their assumptions and research practices throughout the research process. Phronesis was originally a term used by Aristotle to describe a form of value-laden knowledge that we could draw upon to respond appropriately within a given – in this case, research – context. The experienced qualitative researcher can, for example, respond to a difficulty in an interview situation in a way that is informed by their previous understanding of how they should act within that situation given the particular set of values that inform it. This is something the qualitative researcher learns through the experience of conducting qualitative research. Clearly this is a somewhat demanding set of requirements, not all of which can be learned in the classroom. Further details of what can be achieved in the classroom can be found in Learmonth and Humphreys (Chapter 13 in this volume).

A further issue here is the extent to which students have access to training in qualitative methods in business schools. Indeed a number of our respondents in our ESRC project mentioned that the inclusion of qualitative research methods in a doctoral training programme was often dependent upon having an enthusiast on the faculty rather than upon such training being viewed as part of the mainstream curriculum. The complex nature of the research questions we face adds another dimension. For example, Lowery and Evans (2004: 307) in reviewing the changing standing of qualitative research in the discipline suggest that the big questions we face require 'the rigorous use of a broader range of research strategies and tools than those usually taught' in business schools. Indeed they raise the question 'Do we teach quants and stats because they lead to useful outcomes or because they are the only ones we know how to teach?' (2004: 318). Therefore there still seems to be need for greater provision of learning opportunities for researchers who want to use qualitative techniques. This is interesting given that the debates within the UK recently about the skills of graduates of UK doctoral programmes have focused upon highlighting concerns regarding the lack of doctoral students sufficiently trained in quantitative skills (e.g. Wiles et al., 2009).

Institutional concerns

Our experience thus far has been that our academic lives are being increasingly measured and audited in line with the moves towards an audit society (Power, 1997). Elsewhere we have highlighted some of the institutional pressures faced by academics and qualitative researchers in this climate (Symon et al., 2008). The increased emphasis on research audit (for example through the Research Assessment Exercise/Research Excellence Framework in the UK) means that successful academic careers rely upon publishing in what are considered to be the top journals in the field. However, it may be difficult for qualitative researchers to publish in those journals which are dominated by the North American research community and positivist traditions (Singh et al., 2007). Although Buchanan and Bryman (2007: 485) suggest that the organization and management field 'is no longer dominated or constrained by positivist or neo-positivist epistemology and its extended family of primarily quantitative hypothetico-deductive methods', publishing in these journals is still challenging for the qualitative researcher (see Cornellissen, Gajewska-de Mattos, Piekkari and Welch, in this volume). This is despite the attempts by editors of those journals to signify their openness to qualitative research (e.g. Gephart, 2004; Pratt, 2009; Bansal and Corley, 2011). It would seem therefore that despite our best efforts and those of others, there still seems to be a long way to go before we reach the stage where qualitative methods are accepted as part of the mainstream. Further discussion on this can be found in the chapter on writing up and publishing qualitative research by Joep Cornellissen, Hanna Gajewska-de Mattos, Rebecca Piekkari and Catherine Welch.

A parallel development is the growing significance in UK business schools and in other organizations of journal ranking lists such as the *Financial Times* list of journals and the Association of Business Schools' journal quality ranking guide. These seem to be used increasingly as shorthand indicators of quality research with potentially devastating consequences for new journals and more diverse or non-traditional methodological approaches. Indeed we experience this with our own journal *QROM* where as editors we feel the pressure to enhance the profile and ranking of the journal on the various quality lists so that people will want to submit their best work to it. We are not alone in noting these trends and expressing concern about their implications. Indeed numerous authors have paid attention to the impact of the increased culture of performativity on academic researchers (e.g. Sparkes, 2007; Bell, 2011; Willmott, 2011). Here our key concern is the implications that such institutional pressures will have upon people's desire to conduct qualitative research. Indeed we have met early-career researchers who have been advised against conducting qualitative research because of the potential career costs in terms of publication.

The standardization of qualitative research

A further concern is that these kinds of developments lead to an increased standardization in what is viewed as good qualitative research. In seeking to address the difficulties in publishing qualitative research, a number of editors have produced guidelines and editorial advice regarding what it is that makes a piece of qualitative research publishable (e.g. Gephart, 2004; Pratt, 2009; Bansal and Corley, 2011). Although we recognize that these guides can be valuable to qualitative researchers, journal editors are important 'epistemological gatekeepers' (Symon and Cassell, 1999) and it is potentially a formulaic kind of qualitative research that follows a standardized route which gets published (Bansal and Corley, 2011; see also Cornellissen, Gajewska-de Mattos, Piekkari and Welch, in this volume). Hence more diverse or alternative accounts of qualitative research are potentially marginalized. Perhaps it is not surprising that as Gephart (2004) suggests, a large proportion of the qualitative submissions to the *Academy of Management Journal* have a positivist or post-positivist orientation and seek to mirror quantitative techniques.

It is important to recognize here that definitions of the 'top' journals are often equated with North American outlets, yet as numerous authors have noted there are different international traditions of qualitative research and internationally prestigious – yet European based – journals such as *Organization Studies* and *Human Relations* which do publish qualitative and interpretivist studies (Prichard et al., 2007; Yanow and Ybema, 2009; Bell, 2011). We are keen not to engender some self-fulfilling failure prophecy here and would not want to deter our readers from submitting their work to top international outlets. Rather our concern is that in what seems to be an increased move towards standardization, the diversity and consequent richness of different qualitative methodological approaches are potentially compromised.

The emphasis on ethics and evidence

There are two other areas of concern regarding the potential standardization of qualitative research designs: those of ethics and evidence. Our recent explorations into the world of our US colleagues have highlighted the concerns that they have about the increased ethical regulation of research more generally and the potential impact of this for qualitative researchers. For example, North American based qualitative researchers from other disciplines have drawn attention to the impact and pressure of Institutional Review Boards on the design and funding of qualitative research (e.g. Lincoln and Cannella, 2004). Elsewhere management researchers have commented that ethical governance structures tend to be devised to work with clear pre-determined research strategies that are more suitable to quantitative research (Bell and Wray-Bliss, 2009). Given that qualitative research is more messy and that 'consent is contingent and situated' (Bell, 2011: 129) it is potentially difficult for qualitative researchers to meet the demands of these ethical procedures.

A similar concern lies with the arguments regarding the utility of evidence-based practice that have emerged in the organization and management field in recent years. Within our own discipline of organizational psychology, for example, evidence-based practice has been hailed as something that can develop and enhance the discipline so that it is in a better position to speak to practitioners and have a more meaningful impact on the world of work more generally (Briner and Rousseau, 2011). However, a concern we have with this movement is again the potential it offers for methodological standardization. This potential move towards uniformity in research methods has also been noted in other areas where there has been the advocacy of evidence-based practices, ranging from Denzin and Lincoln's (2005) critique of the threats of evidence-based methodologies to qualitative health and education research to the critical voices that have emerged within the management field (e.g. Learmonth and Harding, 2006; Learmonth, 2011). Examples of such uniformity can be found in some of the systematic reviews advocated by evidence-based researchers, where any research that is not informed by randomized control trials or based upon experimental designs is ruled out of consideration (Cassell, 2011).

In summary then, our key concerns at the current time for the future of qualitative research focus upon the pressures that arise from a variety of institutional sources. The reader will see that these challenges provide the context for the chapters that follow. Having outlined our concerns, we do not want to leave the impression that we are somewhat depressed about the prospects for qualitative research in this field. As we suggested earlier, the current context seems to be continuously shifting and the history of qualitative research tells us that qualitative researchers have always had to face challenges to the legitimacy of their research along the way. We remain optimistic that the prospects for qualitative researchers are rosy and that the distinctive insights that qualitative research can provide into the organizational arena are increasingly being recognized (Bansal and Corley, 2011).

Core Methods and Key Challenges in Qualitative Inquiry

The book is divided into core methods and key challenges. We realize that suggesting that some methods are core implies that others may be peripheral, therefore this is somewhat controversial. However, our intention in providing these chapters is to offer the reader an overview of what are the most well-used methods of qualitative data collection and analysis. In choosing these methods as core we also wanted to display methods that could be used from a range of philosophical viewpoints. The core methods of data collection covered are interviews (Mats Alvesson and Karen Lee Ashcraft); focus groups (Binna Kandola); participatory visual methods (Russ Vince and Sam Warren); participant observation (Matthew Brannon and Teresa Oultram); autoethnography (Michael Humphreys and Mark Learmonth); and ethnography (Dvora Yanow, Sierk Ybema and Merlijn van Hulst). We then have case studies (David Buchanan); action research (Julie Wolfram Cox); and document analysis (Bill Lee), which comprise both data collection and analysis. In regard to different methods for the analysis of qualitative data, we have grounded theory (Graham Kenealy); template analysis (Nigel King); conversation analysis (David Greatbatch and Timothy Clark); discourse analysis (Cliff Oswick); and narrative analysis (Sally Maitlis). We believe this to be a comprehensive overview of what can be seen as the core methods currently in use in our field. As highlighted earlier we envisage that readers will still refer to the *Essential Guide* for details of other methods.

This book also covers issues of research practice, which we consider to be important for qualitative organizational researchers. Some of these issues have particularly come to the fore more recently since our last book. In our own teaching experience we increasingly encounter students who are conducting research in their own organizations. This raises a distinctive set of concerns, which Susanne Tietze addresses in her chapter. Another matter commonly raised in the classroom and one that concerns novice qualitative researchers particularly is the ideal sample size for qualitative research. This is particularly a challenge for those who may be more familiar with the demands of quantitative research where there are clear prescriptive guidelines for sample size. Mark Saunders's chapter on choosing research participants seeks to address this topic. Furthermore, there is an increased use of software to support the analysis of qualitative data and data management, something addressed by Rudolf Sinkovics and Eva Alfoldi in their chapter. We have also noticed that there is little work published providing advice for qualitative researchers regarding how to combine different methods of data collection. The terms 'mixed methods' and 'hybrid methods' seem to imply mixing the qualitative with the quantitative, yet there are also challenges that occur when seeking to combine different types of qualitative methods in a single investigation, hence Katrina Pritchard's chapter on mixing methods. In a similar vein there are the distinctive issues associated with conducting qualitative research longitudinally, which is something that Ann Langley and Inger Stensaker consider in their chapter. Increasing globalization also draws attention to the dynamics associated with conducting qualitative research across cultural boundaries, which is the subject of Laurie Cohen and M.N. Ravishankar's contribution. Whereas we expect that authors will highlight any distinctive ethical issues in their individual chapters we also thought it would be useful to include a chapter that provides a basis for a philosophical understanding of ethical issues in qualitative research. This is the focus of Robin Holt's chapter.

Conclusion

Clearly any edited collection will reflect how the authors understand and construct the field and their own place within it. Our issues as qualitative researchers are different now from what they were when we edited the first book in 1994. Although our commitment to raising the profile of qualitative methods in organizational research still remains, we are now far more experienced in using qualitative methods and in teaching, editing and publishing. Our intention is that this book covers what we think the qualitative organizational researcher needs to know regarding methods and also some of the issues they may encounter within the contexts in which qualitative research is conducted. The aim then is that this book will become a key resource for qualitative organizational researchers. Although we can never replace what is gained from the actual experience of doing qualitative research, our contributors generously share the expertise they have gained through doing their own qualitative research and showcase examples of the rich research opportunities offered by qualitative approaches. Gaining insights into organizing and organizations through qualitative research methods is something that has inspired us for many years. We hope that we can encourage our readers to be just as enthused as we are about the prospect.

References

Bansal, P. and Corley, K. (2011) 'From the editors: the coming of age of qualitative research: embracing the diversity of qualitative methods', *Academy of Management Journal*, 54 (2), 233–237.

Bell, E. (2011) 'Managerialism and management research: would Melville Dalton get a job today?', in C.M. Cassell and B. Lee (eds), *Challenges and Controversies in Management Research*. London: Routledge.

Bell, E. and Wray-Bliss, E. (2009) 'Research ethics, regulations and responsibilities', in D. Buchanan and A. Byman (eds), *The Sage Handbook of Organizational Research Methods*. London: Sage.

Briner, R. and Rousseau, D. (2011) 'Evidence-based psychology: not there yet', *Industrial and Organizational Psychology: Perspective on Science and Practice, 4 (1), 3–22*.

Buchanan, D.A. and Bryman, A. (2007), 'Contextualising methods choice in organizational research', *Organizational Research Methods*, 10, 483–501.

Cassell, C.M. (2011) 'Evidence-based I-O psychology: what do we lose on the way?', *Industrial and Organizational Psychology: Perspectives on Science and Practice, 4 (1), 23–26*.

Cassell, C.M., Bishop, V., Symon, G., Johnson, P. and Buehring, A. (2009) 'Becoming a qualitative management researcher', *Management Learning*, 40 (5), 1–21.

Cassell, C.M. and Symon, G. (1994) *Qualitative Methods in Organizational Research*. London: Sage.

Cassell, C.M. and Symon, G. (2004) *Essential Guide to Qualitative Methods in Organizational Research*. London: Sage.

Denzin, N.K. and Lincoln Y.S. (2005) 'Introduction: the discipline and practice of qualitative research', in N.K. Denzin and Y.S. Lincoln (eds), *The Sage Handbook of Qualitative Research*. Thousand Oaks, CA: Sage.

Eriksson. P. and Kovalainen, A. (2008) *Qualitative Methods in Business Research*. London: Sage.

Gephart, R.P. (2004) 'Qualitative research and the *Academy of Management Journal*', *Academy of Management Journal*, 47 (4), 454–462.

Learmonth, M. (2011) 'The relationship between evidence and theory in management research', in C.M. Cassell and B. Lee (eds), *Challenges and Controversies in Management Research*. London: Routledge.

Learmonth, M. and Harding, N. (2006) 'Evidence-based management: the very idea', *Public Administration*, 84, 245–266.

Lincoln, Y.S. and Cannella, G.S. (2004) 'Qualitative research, power, and the radical right', *Qualitative Inquiry*, 10 (2): 175–201.

Lowery, D. and Evans, K.G. (2004) 'The iron cage of methodology. The vicious circle of means limiting ends limiting means', *Administration and Society*, 36 (3), 306–327.

Power, M. (1997) *The Audit Society: Rituals of Verification*. Oxford: Oxford University Press.

Pratt, M.G. (2009) 'For the lack of a boilerplate: tips on writing up (and reviewing) qualitative research', *Academy of Management Journal*, 52, 856–62.

Prichard, C., Sayers, J. and Bathurst, R. (2007) 'Franchise, margin and locale: constructing a critical management studies locale in Aotearoa New Zealand', *New Zealand Sociology*, 22 (1), 22–44.

Schön, D.A. (1983) *The Reflective Practitioner*. New York: Basic Books.

Singh, G., Haddad, K.M. and Chow, C.W. (2007) 'Are articles in top management journals necessarily of higher quality?', *Journal of Management Inquiry*, 16 (4): 319–331.

Sparkes, A. (2007) 'Embodiment, academics and the audit culture: a story seeking consideration', *Qualitative Research*, 7 (4): 521–550.

Symon, G., Buehring, A., Johnson, P. and Cassell, C.M. (2008) 'Positioning qualitative research in the academic labour process', *Organization Studies*, 29 (10): 1315–1336.

Symon, G. and Cassell, C.M. (1998) *Qualitative Methods and Analysis in Organizational Research*. London: Sage.

Symon, G. and Cassell, C.M. (1999) 'Barriers to innovation in research practice', in M. Pina e Cunha and C.A. Marques (eds), *Readings in Organization Science: Organizational Change in a Changing Context*. Lisbon: ISPA.

Symon, G. and Cassell, C.M. (2004) 'Promoting new practices in organizational research', in C.M. Cassell and G. Symon (eds), *Essential Guide to Qualitative Methods in Organizational Research*. London: Sage.

Thorpe, R. and Holt, R. (2008) *The Sage Dictionary of Qualitative Management Research*. London: Sage.

Wiles, R., Durrant, G., De Broe, S. and Powell, J. (2009) 'Methodological approaches at PhD and skills sought for research posts in academia: a mismatch?', *International Journal of Social Research Methodology*, 12 (3), 257–269.

Willmott, H. (2011) 'Journal list fetishism and the perversion of scholarship: reactivity and the ABS list', *Organization*, 18 (4): 429–442.

Yanow, D. and Ybema. S. (2009) 'Interpretivism and organizational research: on elephants and blind researchers', in D. Buchanan and A. Byman (eds), *The Sage Handbook of Organizational Research Methods*. London: Sage.

PART I

THE ISSUES AND CHALLENGES OF QUALITATIVE INQUIRY IN ORGANIZATIONAL RESEARCH

2 Philosophies Underpinning Qualitative Research

Joanne Duberley, Phil Johnson and Catherine Cassell

Introduction

As the range of chapters in this book would suggest, there is considerable diversity in the different methods available to the researcher seeking to access the organizational world qualitatively. However, any process of methodological engagement inevitably articulates, and is constituted by, an attachment to particular philosophical or metatheoretical commitments that have implications for research design. As Cunliffe (2010) highlights, 'Our metatheoretical assumptions have very practical consequences for the way we do research in terms of our topic, focus of study, what we see as "data", how we collect and analyse the data, how we theorize, and how we write up our research accounts'. Therefore they are a key part of the methodology within which our methods of data collection and analysis are located. Accordingly, methodology comprises both our philosophical assumptions and our methods. Qualitative research is particularly challenging in this respect, because such methods are used in a range of epistemological and ontological approaches within the management field (Johnson and Duberley, 2000; Johnson et al., 2006; Kelemen and Rumens, 2008; Alvesson and Sköldberg, 2009; Gill and Johnson, 2010). Therefore the qualitative researcher needs to be aware of these commitments and the options available to them, hence the significance of a chapter on the philosophies of qualitative research.

The primary aim of this chapter is to explore how qualitative organizational research methods may be deployed differently given the various modes of philosophical engagement. For the novice researcher, engaging in philosophical debates for the first time can be somewhat bewildering. However, one intention of this chapter is to provide the reader with an overview of the various philosophical stances within which qualitative research sits so the researcher can be aware of the various consequent methodological assumptions underpinning their research. The chapter is structured in the following way. First we shall attempt to establish how qualitative research initially arises under the umbrella of a shared philosophical critique of certain assumptions deployed by the positivist mainstream – assumptions primarily to do with the nature of human behaviour. Having established this initial philosophical break we shall then proceed to explore some of the other different traditions underpinning qualitative research. These include neo-empiricist qualitative research; interpretivism; critical theory; postmodernism and poststructuralism; and other post traditions. We realize that each of these categorizations will have variation within them, and it is not always possible to draw neat lines around particular approaches; however, they can be seen as useful heuristic devices in structuring our understanding. The chapter concludes by summarizing the key philosophical issues that qualitative researchers should pay attention to in their work.

Before presenting an overview of some of the different philosophical stances that underpin qualitative research, it is useful to define the key terms encountered in these philosophical discussions, notably epistemology and ontology.

Epistemology

As has been argued elsewhere (Johnson and Duberley, 2000: 3) that the philosophical term 'epistemology' derives from two Greek words: *episteme* which means 'knowledge' or 'science'; and *logos* which means 'knowledge', 'information', 'theory' or 'account'. Therefore epistemology is usually understood as being concerned with knowledge about knowledge. In other words, epistemology is the study of the criteria by which we can know what does and does not constitute warranted, or scientific, knowledge. That is, what do we mean by the concept 'truth' and how do we know whether or not some claim, including our own, is true or false? Usually people think that such processes of justifying knowledge claims are in principle straightforward: – in judging the truth or falsity of any such claim surely 'the facts speak for themselves'? All we need to do is look for the relevant evidence whose content will either support or refute any claim. Thus it is often thought that what is true is something that corresponds with the given facts: empirical evidence is the ultimate arbiter. Perhaps this view of warranted knowledge initially seems harmless and unproblematic. However, it has been subject to much dispute in both the natural and social sciences: a dispute that has had a direct influence on the evolution of qualitative research.

The positivist epistemological commitment that it is possible to objectively, or neutrally, observe the social world in order to either test theoretical predictions, or to describe cultural attributes, has been considerably undermined by those who think that in observing the world we inevitably influence what we see and that notions of truth and objectivity are merely the outcomes of discursive practices which mask rather than eliminate the researcher's partiality (see Willmott, 1998). In other words there is an epistemological choice here which influences the form that qualitative research takes between an objectivist (realist) and a subjectivist (relativist) epistemological stance. If we reject the possibility of neutral observation, we have to admit to dealing with a socially constructed reality that may entail a questioning of whether or not what we take to be reality actually exists 'out there' at all? This leads us to the philosophical issue that revolves around our ontological assumptions.

Ontology

Like the term 'epistemology', the term 'ontology' also is a combination of two Greek words – but in this case they are *ontos* and *logos*. The former refers to 'being' while the latter refers to theory or knowledge, etc. Ontology is a branch of philosophy dealing with the essence of phenomena and the nature of their existence. Hence to ask about the ontological existence of something is often to ask whether or not it is real or illusory. Ontological questions concern whether or not the phenomenon that we are interested in actually exists independent of our knowing and perceiving it – or is what we see and usually take to be real, instead, an outcome of these acts of knowing and perceiving? Here it is useful to differentiate between realist and subjectivist assumptions about the status of social reality. Realist assumptions entail the view that it exists, 'out there', independent of our perceptual or cognitive structures. We might not already know its characteristics, indeed it may be impossible for us ever to know those characteristics, but this reality exists, it is real and it is there potentially awaiting inspection and discovery by us. Taking occupational stress as an example, an objectivist ontological stance would see stress as a real phenomenon that exists within oneself. It is there to be accessed and measured. A subjectivist ontological stance would, however, position occupational stress somewhat differently. From this perspective stress would be something that does not exist in individuals and groups, rather it would be something created through our everyday talk. That is, subjectivist assumptions about the ontological status of the social phenomena we deal with – such as stress – entail the view that what we take to be social reality is a creation, or projection, of our consciousness and cognition. What we usually assume to be 'out there' has no real, independent, status separate from the act of knowing. In perceiving or knowing the social world we create it – we are just not usually aware of our role in these creative processes.

By combining the above ontological assumptions with the competing assumptions regarding epistemology that we have already discussed, we can see some of the different philosophical positions which impact qualitative research. These philosophical assumptions about ontology and epistemology are always contentious and debatable. Indeed we cannot operate without adopting some epistemological and ontological position. Therefore it is important that we are aware of them; are prepared to defend them; and also prepared to consider their implications. It is the variation in these assumptions that leads to some of the different methodological approaches we can identify within qualitative organizational research. It is to these different approaches we now turn.

Positivism

As many authors have highlighted, the development of management and organizational research has been characterized by the domination of positivism as an underlying philosophy. According to some (e.g. Keat and Urry, 1982) two of the most significant characteristics of positivist epistemology concern, firstly, the claim that science should focus on only directly observable phenomena, with any reference to the intangible or subjective being excluded as being meaningless; and secondly, that theories should be tested, in a hypothetico-deductive fashion, by their confrontation with the facts neutrally gathered from a readily observable external world.

A key aspect of positivism is the tendency to reduce human behaviour to the status of automatic responses excited by external stimuli wherein the subjective dimension to that behaviour is lost, intentionally or otherwise. This reduction is achieved by positivists attempting to follow what is presumed to be the methodological approach taken in the natural sciences. This entails ignoring the subjective dimensions of human action. Instead, human behaviour is conceptualized and explained deterministically: as necessary responses to empirically observable, measurable, causal variables and antecedent conditions. The resultant approach, often called *erklaren* (see Outhwaite, 1975), usually investigates human behaviour through the use of Popper's (1959) hypothetico-deductive method. Here the aim is to produce generalizable knowledge through the testing of hypothetical predictions deduced from a priori theory. As such it entails the researcher's a priori conceptualization, operationalization and statistical measurement of dimensions of actors' behaviour rather than beginning with their socially derived (inter)subjective perspectives. This is based on an allegiance to methodological monism: the notion that only natural science methodology can provide certain knowledge and enable prediction and control: it follows that it must be emulated by social scientists (Ross, 1991: 350).

Although positivism and the resultant use of quantitative methods have typically dominated organizational research, concern about the lack of attention given to the subjective nature of human thoughts and actions has led to the promotion of a variety of different philosophical stances aimed at addressing the dominance of positivism within the organizational and management field.

Qualitative Neo-positivism

Even those who reject key aspects of positivism regarding the use of hypothetico-deductive methodology, and the exclusion of the subjective as meaningless, will sometimes retain a commitment to being able to objectively investigate human intersubjective cultural processes by gathering the facts from a readily observable external world. The result is a kind of 'qualitative positivism' (see Knights, 1992; Van Maanen, 1995; Schwandt, 1996; Prasad and Prasad, 2002) or 'neo-empiricism' (Alvesson and Sköldberg, 2009) which, although different from mainstream positivism, shares its commitment to a theory-neutral observational language: that it is possible to neutrally apprehend the facts 'out there'. Therefore although positivism is generally linked with quantitative methods, there are some elements of positivism that continue to exert an influence in certain approaches towards qualitative research. As we have discussed, the belief that science can produce objective knowledge rests on two assumptions: first the assumption of ontological realism – that there is a reality 'out there' to be known – and second that it is possible to remove subjective bias in the assessment of that reality. These assumptions can be seen to underpin certain approaches towards ethnography, for example. Hammersley and Atkinson (1995) discuss how ethnography is often wedded to the notion of realism, which means that while ethnographers may discuss how the subjects of their study socially construct their realities, they do not apply this constructivism to the ethnographic process (for more on ethnography, see Yanow, Ybema and van Hulst, in this volume). Indeed it was a classic ethnographer Malinowski who argued that 'ethnography's peculiar character is the production of ostensibly "scientific" and "objective" knowledge based on personal interaction and subjective experience' (cited in Yanow and Schwartz-Shea, 2006: 261). Thus what is 'out there' is presumed to be independent of the knower and is accessible to the trained observer or ethnographer following the correct procedures. This leads to a situation where tension exists between a subjectivist attention to actors' meanings and an objectivist treatment of them as phenomena that exist 'out there' independent of observer's identification of them (Weiskopf and Willmott, 1996).

Alvesson (2003) further discusses how the qualitative research interview is used by neo-positivists to attempt to access a context-free truth about reality by rigidly following a research protocol and minimizing researcher influence and other potential sources of bias (for more on interviews see Alvesson and Ashcraft, in this volume). He sees the ideal for neo-positivist qualitative research interviewers as being 'a maximum, transparent research process, characterized by objectivity and neutrality' (Alvesson, 2003: 16) with the interview conversation being viewed as 'a pipeline for transmitting knowledge' (Holstein and Gubrium, 1997: 113 cited in Alvesson, 2003: 15). Here researchers attempt to remove themselves from the process, presenting instead an objective picture, free from the potential taint of their assumptions and values. Thus although qualitative researchers may seek to distance themselves from positivism – the reliance on tools and techniques – the assumption that bias can be removed, and that with the right tools and techniques peoples' subjective realities can be accessed, shows some continuity with the past.

Interpretivism

A variety of different philosophical approaches are covered by the loose term 'interpretivism'. Prasad (2005: 13) suggests that 'all interpretive traditions emerge from a scholarly position that takes *human interpretation* as the starting point for developing knowledge about the social world'. Particularly important in this tradition is a commitment to *verstehen* (Outhwaite, 1975), which entails accessing and understanding the actual meanings and interpretations actors subjectively ascribe to phenomena in order to describe and explain their behaviour through investigating how they experience, sustain, articulate and share with others these socially constructed everyday realities (see Van Maanen, 1979, 1998; Patton, 1990; Guba and Lincoln, 1994; Schwandt, 1996; Denzin and Lincoln, 2005). Examples include qualitative work that is informed by symbolic interactionism, ethnomethodology and hermeneutics.

It is more complicated to locate this whole body of work. Some of these traditions can be seen as similar to that of neo-positivism, in that a realist ontology is utilized – that is, there is a real world with real phenomena to explore – and a subjectivist or constructionist epistemology, in that our understanding of that reality is socially constructed. However, some interpretivist traditions such as ethnomethodology are more subjectivist in their ontological stance. One point of connection, however, is that interpretivists are less likely to be concerned with mirroring the tenets of positivism, in that their search for the understanding of interpretation offers different approaches to how empirical work is conducted and the role of the researcher within it. Indeed the researcher becomes a focal point of interest in some interpretivist traditions. Prasad (2005: 16) suggests that 'although a variety of perspectives come under the banner of interpretivism ideas of social construction, verstehen, intersubjectivity and reification are all integral to the different interpretive traditions ... Yet each tradition appropriates and extends these central tenets quite uniquely'. It is impossible to provide a review of them all here but a brief exploration of hermeneutics and ethnomethodology highlights some of the underlying principles.

Hermeneutics is informed by the European social science traditions of Dilthey, Heidegger and others and initially emerged when the techniques used to interpret biblical works were applied to other texts (Murray, 2008). Alvesson and Sköldberg (2000: 53) suggest that the key principle underlying hermeneutics is that the meaning of a part can only be understood if it is related to the whole. The key heuristic device for understanding and interpretation is the hermeneutic circle. Within the hermeneutic circle the link between pre-understanding and understanding is made. No one comes to interpretation with an open mind, rather there is the pre-understanding of the phenomenon that we already have. Hence the hermeneutic circle focuses upon the iteration of interpretation where pre-understanding informs understanding and so on, leading to a greater understanding of both. Within qualitative research the development of hermeneutic interpretation forms the basis of some approaches to qualitative data analysis, for example where patterns of interpretation of themes from interview transcripts start to shape our understanding of interviewee accounts (McAuley, 2004).

Ethnomethodology builds on the philosophy of phenomenology to seek to understand and interpret how individuals make sense of their lifeworlds. The key principles are informed by American sociological traditions and particularly the work of Garfinkel (1967) who was interested in the everyday ways in which individuals construct and make sense of complex social situations. Ethnomethodology is thus more interested in the ways in which interpretive schemas are put into practice and accepted, altered or rejected (Prasad, 2005). The methods that tend to be associated with this tradition focus upon examining the social minutiae of happenings in acute detail. For example, various linguistic approaches to qualitative data analysis such as conversational analysis (see Greatbatch and Clark, in this volume) can be located within this approach. Within the business and management field a key use of ethnomethodology is the concept of sensemaking (Weick, 1995). Qualitative research in this tradition has focused upon paying attention to how individuals or groups retrospectively make sense of events such as disasters or crises (Weick, 1993; Brown, 2006). Throughout, these accounts draw upon the documentary method highlighted by Garfinkel (Fox, 2008) with a view that reality is an ongoing and skilful social accomplishment.

Critical Theory

Critical theory focuses on the inherent connection between politics, values and knowledge and thereby provokes a deeper consideration of the politics and values that underpin and legitimize the authority of scientific knowledge (Alvesson et al., 2009). The aim of critical theory-based approaches towards organizational research is to understand how the practices and institutions of management are developed and legitimized within relations of power and domination such as capitalism. Yet critical theory also asserts that systems can and should be changed, thus qualitative research from this perspective tends to have an orientation towards investigating issues such as exploitation, asymmetrical power relations, distorted communication and false consciousness.

Fundamental to this perspective is the belief that these systems can be transformed to enable emancipation, which involves a continuing process of critical self-reflection and associated self-transformation. Prasad and Caproni (1997: 3) identify four broad themes that are integral to research from the perspective of critical theory: an emphasis on the social construction of reality; a focus on issues of power and ideology; the need to understand any social or organizational phenomenon with respect to its multiple interconnections and its location within holistic historical contexts; and the importance of praxis – the on-going construction of social arrangements that are conducive to the flourishing of the human condition.

The presupposition of a theory neutral observational language is rejected by critical theorists who see knowledge as contaminated at source by the influence of socio-cultural factors upon sensory experience (see Habermas, 1974). The researcher is no longer the neutral observer. Instead, for emancipation to take place, there is a need to counter the influence of 'scientism', which occurs when scientific or 'objective' knowledge can lead to domination and dehumanization. Examples from the management and organization arena are highlighted by Willmott (2008: 67) who points out that 'a positivist conception of objective knowledge has filtered into the field of management through the processes of quantification and the development of seemingly impartial means of legitimising instrumental rationalizations [sic] – from scientific management through human relations to BPR'. The role of the critical theorist is to critique these forms of scientism and create opportunities for change. The outcomes of research are influenced by the subjectivity of the social scientist and his or her mode of engagement, which leads to the production of different versions of an independently existing reality that we can never fully know. For Habermas (1974), it is only through reference to fundamental interests that it becomes possible to understand first the criteria that are applied in identifying what are taken to be 'real' and second the criteria by which the validity of such propositions may be evaluated.

In order to escape the dangers of relativism where any interpretation would potentially have equal value, Habermas stresses the need for interpretations to be agreed democratically. Thus for knowledge to be legitimate it must be grounded in the consensus achievable in an ideal speech situation where discursively produced agreement results from argument and analysis without any resort to coercion, distortion or duplicity. However, it is evident to Habermas that such a consensus is not attained in everyday social interaction due to the asymmetrical operation of power relations which systematically distort communication. Therefore it must remain a regulative epistemic ideal against which extant organizational practices may be assessed (Deetz, 1992; Forrester, 1993). Here reflexivity (see Haynes, in this volume) is construed as emancipatory since it sanctions the investigation and problematization of the taken-for-granted social constructions of reality which are located in the varying practices, interests and motives that constitute different communities' sensemaking.

Forrester (1993) argues that doing fieldwork in a Habermasian way enables researchers to examine the processes and the outcomes of relations of power. Thus from a critical theory perspective, qualitative researchers should be concerned to develop new modes of engagement that allow participants to pursue interests and objectives that are currently excluded by the dominant management discourses. As expressed in various forms of participatory management research (e.g. Power and Laughlin, 1992; Reason and Bradbury, 2001), through dialogue participants should democratically co-determine and co-develop the substantive basis of that knowledge so that their interests and objectives become metaphorically permitted and encoded into its 'gaze'.

Given the various commitments of critical theory, a range of different traditions has developed that seeks to apply these principles, so qualitative research within these traditions uses a range of different methods. For example, participant observation and ethnographies are used to highlight the subjective experiences of how dominance and control are exercised in the workplace (see Rosen's (1985) study of an advertising agency and Jackall's (1988) tales of managers and ethics). A commitment to emancipation can also be seen in various forms of participatory action research (e.g. Power and Laughlin, 1992; Reason and Bradbury, 2001).

A range of other perspectives has drawn upon critical theory, for example the development of critical management studies (Alvesson and Deetz, 2000; Kelemen and Rumens, 2008; Hassard and Rowlinson, 2011) and feminism. In feminist and radical feminist epistemologies concepts of sex, sexuality, gender and the enduring nature of patriarchy come to the fore. There has been an ongoing tradition within organization studies of challenging the dominance of patriarchy and its implications for both women and men in the workplace (though it is important to point out that feminist approaches are informed by a range of different epistemological perspectives and not only critical theory; see Calás and Smircich, 1996; Gheradi et al., 2003). Given that the primary objective of feminist informed studies is to understand the subjective life-worlds of women (and liberate them from patriarchal ideals), the methods of choice in these studies usually require in-depth interviews (see Alvesson and Ashcraft, in this volume) or other methods that require immersion in women's experience (Prasad, 2005). A focus upon the role of the researcher (see Tietze, in this volume) and reflexive critique is also important within this tradition (see Haynes, in this volume).

Postmodernism and Poststructuralism

There is considerable debate within the literature about whether postmodernism and poststructuralism can be seen as having unique identities, or whether poststructuralism is another variant of postmodernism. Given that they share similar concepts such as a focus upon language, discourse and deconstruction, we will treat them together here, though as Prasad (2005) suggests, poststructuralism does have some distinctive features of its own, particularly relating to the focus upon language as it relates to institutions and power. It is important to recognize that these approaches emerged as a response to what were seen as the constraints and excesses of modernism, and are therefore, as Chia (2008: 162) suggests, 'experimental and reactionary'.

Qualitative researchers from these traditions favour a position where subjectivist ontology is combined with a subjectivist epistemology. This involves abandoning 'the rational and unified subject in favour of a socially and linguistically decentred and fragmented subject' (Best and Kellner, 1991: 4). Postmodernist epistemology dismisses the positivist rational certainty in the attainability of epistemic privilege and replaces it with a relativist view of science and knowledge. From a postmodern perspective any attempt to develop a rational and generalizable basis to scientific enquiry that explains the world from an objective standpoint is flawed. Lyotard (1984: xxiv) calls this 'an incredulity towards metanarratives'. Instead postmodernists put forward a perspective where all knowledge is indeterminate: what we take to be reality is itself created and determined by those acts of cognition. The social world is not seen as external to us, waiting to be discovered; everything is relative to the eye of the beholder.

A key element of postmodern research has been a renewed focus on language. The 'linguistic turn' suggests that language is never innocent; that no meaning exists beyond language; that knowledge and truth are linguistic entities and constantly open to revision (Lyotard, 1984). There is an emphasis in postmodernism on the role of discourses. These are subjective, linguistically formed ways of experiencing, acting and constituting phenomena which we take to be 'out there'. These discursive conceptions are 'collectively sustained and continually renegotiated in the process of making sense' (Parker, 1992: 3). Thus what we take to be knowledge is constructed in and through language. The language of science cannot represent or illuminate some external reality – there is no discoverable true meaning, only a variety of different interpretations. Hence for postmodernists reality can have an infinite number of attributes, since there are as many realities as there are ways of perceiving and explaining. Influential upon our linguistically derived sensemaking are our social interactions in various milieux, which bias us towards particular ways of viewing the world. Usually we remain unaware of these constructive socio-linguistic processes, thus although we may perceive things as objective and separate from ourselves, as 'out there', through language we are active participants in creating what we apprehend (Chia, 1995).

However, people are not free to make their own interpretations. Instead the decentring of the subject that is associated with postmodern writings places emphasis on the development of shared discourses through exposure to which the individual is constituted. Human beings therefore make sense of the world through particular historical and socially contingent discourses. These discursively produced hyper-realities can be mistaken for an external reality. Postmodernists counter this through the use of deconstruction, which is a key element of poststructuralist approaches informed by the work of writers such as Derrida, Foucault and Lacan. This originally derives from literary criticism where texts are analysed in order to reveal their inherent contradictions, assumptions and layers of meaning. In organization studies, deconstruction attempts to show how any claim to truth, whether made by social scientists or practising managers, is always the product of social construction and therefore always relative (Johnson and Duberley, 2000). This is attempted by showing how texts contain taken-for-granted ideas which depend upon the exclusion of other things. Often this will involve identifying the assumptions that underpin any truth claim and the identification of the absent alternatives whose articulation may produce an alternative rendition of reality. Thus deconstruction denies that any text is ever settled or stable. However, it does not offer a tool to find 'the truth'. At most it offers alternative social constructions of reality within a text, which are themselves then available to deconstruction and thereby not allowed to rest in any finalized truth. Thus there is a strong strand of postmodern writing focusing on the deconstruction of existing works in organization studies (see for example Kilduff's (1993) deconstruction of March and Simon's work and Carter and Jackson's (1993) examination of motivation theory), which focuses on the logics and contradictions of existing theories, examining gaps and instabilities in time, space and text (Cooper, 1989).

While there is a degree of scepticism about empirical work and a recognition that scientific methodology 'loses its status as the chief arbiter of truth' (Gergen and Thatchenkerry, 1996: 12), postmodernism offers some important insights into research methodology. Qualitative research from this perspective focuses upon gaining an understanding of a situation at a particular point in time, recognizing that this is only one of a number of possible understandings. There is no reliance on particular methods to provide an accurate correspondence with reality and while there appears to be a preference for qualitative approaches in much postmodernist work, research methods are viewed as embodied in cultural practice and no particular approach is considered to have a privileged status. Thus some management researchers have focused on the liberating potential of the postmodern perspective, arguing that it frees researchers to mix and match various perspectives or research styles in order to challenge conventional wisdom (Kilduff and Mehra, 1997; Gergen and Thatchenkerry, 1996).

Others, however, see postmodernist perspectives as aligned with qualitative methods (Kondo, 1990), in particular ethnography, which Linstead claims is '*the* language of postmodernism' (Linstead, 1993: 98) because it has the ability to evoke rather than just describe. This, according to Linstead, requires both poetic and conceptual rigour from the author in order to produce an account 'poised in the space between fact and fiction' (1993: 70). Other methods informed by these perspectives are the analysis of stories, for example Boje's (1991, 1995) explorations of the multiple stories in use at Disney, and the analysis of narratives in relation to how identities are constructed (e.g. Brown, 2006; Beech, 2008; and see Maitlis, in this volume). An important method is also discourse analysis (see Oswick, in this volume), which has been used to explore a range of organizational phenomena. Oft-quoted examples of this kind of work include Linstead's (1985) study of shopfloor discourse, Kondo's (1990) examination of the production of identity in Japanese workplaces, and Ely's (1995) study of sex roles in organizations. More recent examples are studies of HRM (Harley and Hardy, 2004), entrepreneurship (Perren and Jennings,

2005), public policy (Motion and Leitch, 2009), and management strategy (Greckhamer, 2010).

As has been discussed in detail elsewhere (Johnson and Duberley, 2000), postmodernism demands that researchers are sceptical about how they engage with the world, the categories they deploy, the assumptions they make, and the interpretations they impose. It encourages irony and humility as well as rebellion against the imposition of any unitary scientific discourse (Cooper and Burrell, 1988). It elevates the role of both the producer of research accounts and the reader of them. Authors from this perspective recognize that their work may be interpreted in a multitude of different ways depending on the perspective of the reader (Parker, 1992; Burrell, 1997). Thus it has been argued that postmodernist approaches enable us both to know more and yet doubt what we know (Richardson, 1998: 358).

Postcolonialism and Indigenous Epistemologies

Recent years have seen the development of further epistemological approaches which may encompass qualitative research. These encourage the framing of research questions in different ways. For example, postcolonialism has surfaced within business and management research (Prasad and Prasad, 2002; Prasad, 2005). As Prasad (2005: 263) suggests: 'postcolonialism is extraordinarily relevant to management and organization studies because it offers an alternative historical explanation for many commonplace business practices that have their origins in colonial structures'. Indeed she argues that the intensification of globalization makes postcolonialism especially pertinent in that it becomes 'particularly important in understanding some of its [globalization] less visible and more unsavoury facets' (2005: 263). Such colonial practices include epistemic coloniality (Ibarra-Colado, 2006: 464) where 'the processes by which the institutionalization of knowledge as scientific knowledge permitted the integration of native elites into the dominant Anglo-Euro-Centric ideology of modernity' (Florescano, 1994: 65).

Alongside the challenges of postcolonial approaches to accepted perspectives, indigenous scholarship has become apparent within the literature on qualitative research (e.g. Smith, 1999), and more recently within qualitative management research (e.g. Ruwhiu and Cone, 2010; Stablein and Panoho, 2011). Stablein and Panoho (2011: 78) outline how Kaupapa Maori epistemology and methodology are examples of how 'throughout the world the relationship between indigenous peoples and academic research is being challenged'. Rather than the traditional route of indigenous people being studied as different by those on the outside, Maori epistemology starts from their inside knowledge and worldview (Smith, 1999). For qualitative management and organizational researchers, such epistemological approaches offer new ways of critiquing management processes and practices and the possibility of framing research questions in innovative ways. Traditional ways of constructing questions about groups must be questioned. A further example here is the lens of queer theory, which is relatively new to management research (e.g. Parker, 2002; Butler, 2004; Tyler and Cohen, 2008). Parker (2002: 164) suggests that queer theory questions knowledge claims, ethics and language and also that it 'endangers a nervousness about categories' because from this perspective identities consist of many different elements; therefore to assume that people can be viewed collectively on the basis of one shared characteristic (for example being a woman) is flawed.

Conclusion

In this chapter we have tried to outline the variety of philosophical debates and commitments that implicitly and explicitly underpin different approaches to undertaking qualitative organizational research. Qualitative researchers are increasingly being called upon to reflexively think through their own beliefs and how those beliefs will have repercussions for our engagements with areas of interest (Willmott, 1998; Prasad, 2005; Alvesson and Sköldberg, 2009). This involves reflecting upon how those often tacit, unacknowledged pre-understandings impact upon: how those 'objects' of research are conceptually constituted by the researcher; what kinds of research question are then asked by the researcher; and how the results of research are arrived at, justified and presented to audiences for consumption (e.g. Holland, 1999; Chia, 1995; Alvesson and Sköldberg, 2009). Caelli, Ray and Mill (2003) argue that to have credibility, qualitative research papers must address the following four areas (see also Symon and Cassell, in this volume):

1   The theoretical positioning of the researcher, including motives, presuppositions and personal history, which leads them towards and shapes a particular inquiry.

2   The congruence between methodology, reflecting the beliefs about knowledge that arise from the philosophical framework being employed, and the methods or tools of data collection and analysis.

3   Strategies to establish rigour – in other words they must evaluate their research in a way that is philosophically and methodologically congruent with their enquiry.

4   The analytical lens through which data are examined, in terms of the epistemological and ontological assumptions researchers make in engaging with their data.

This seems a useful starting point to ensure that researchers at least consider the philosophical assumptions they are making when undertaking qualitative research. Of course, it may not be possible to draw neat lines around particular approaches. As we mentioned at the beginning of this chapter, these categorizations are a useful heuristic. Each contains within it a variety of alternative approaches and reality is always far messier, where qualitative researchers face contested ideas and multiple ongoing influences. The challenge is not to be able to fit one's research approach neatly into any particular category but to ensure self-reflexivity and an awareness of the various ways in which our philosophical assumptions have influenced our research.

Further Reading

For a more in-depth discussion of the philosophical underpinnings of qualitative research, see Denzin and Lincoln's (eds) (2007) *The Landscape of Qualitative Research* (3rd edn), which examines the competing paradigms that underpin qualitative research and their implications for methods. Prasad's (2005) *Crafting Qualitative Research: Working in the Postpositivist Traditions* similarly provides a clear and concise view of alternative traditions that exist within the qualitative field. Marshall's (2006) *Designing Qualitative Research* gives a useful overview of the implications of various philosophical positions for methodology and also provides interesting vignettes to illustrate the methodological challenges of qualitative research. Finally, Alvesson and Sköldberg's (2009) *Reflexive Methodology* (2nd edn) gives a thought provoking analysis of the linkages between philosophical assumptions and methods employed, which they see as both an 'intellectualization of qualitative method' and 'a pragmatization of the philosophy of science' (p. vii). It is to be recommended for those wishing to explore the underpinning assumptions of qualitative research in more depth.

References

Alvesson, M. (2003) 'Beyond neopositivists, romantics and localists: a reflexive approach to interviews in organisational research', *The Academy of Management Review*, 28 (1): 13–33.

Alvesson, M., Bridgman, T. and Willmott, H. (2009) 'Introduction', in M. Alvesson, T. Bridgman and H. Willmott (eds), *The Oxford Handbook of Critical Management Studies*. Oxford: Oxford University Press, pp. 1–28.

Alvesson, M. and Deetz, S. (2000) *Doing Critical Management Research*. London: Sage.

Alvesson, M. and Sköldberg, K. (2000) *Reflexive Methodology: New Vistas for Qualitative Research* (1st edn). London: Sage.

Alvesson, M. and Sköldberg, K. (2009) *Reflexive Methodology: New Vistas for Qualitative Research* (2nd edn). London: Sage.

Beech, N. (2008) 'On the nature of dialogic identity work', *Organization*, 15: 51–74.

Best, S. and Kellner, D. (1991) *Postmodern Theory: Critical Interrogations*. London: Macmillan.

Boje, D. (1991) 'The storytelling organization: a study of story performance in an office supply firm', *Administrative Science Quarterly*, 36: 106–126.

Boje, D. (1995) 'Stories of the storytelling organization: a postmodern analysis of Disney as "*Tamara*-land"', *Academy of Management Journal*, 38 (4): 997–1035.

Brown, A. (2006) 'A narrative approach to collective identities', *Journal of Management Studies*, 43: 731–753.

Burrell, G. (1997) *Pandemonium: Towards a Retro-organization Theory*. London: Sage.

Butler, J. (2004) *Undoing Gender*. New York: Routledge.

Caelli, K., Ray, L. and Mill, J. (2003) 'Clear as mud: toward greater clarity in generic qualitative research', *International Journal of Qualitative Methods*, 2 (2), Article 1. Available at www.ualberta.ca/~iiqm/backissues/2_2/html/caellietal.htm (last accessed 21 September 2010).

Calás, M. and Smircich, L. (1996) 'From "the woman's" point of view: feminist approaches to organisation studies', in S. Clegg, C. Hardy and W. Nord (eds), *Handbook of Organization Studies*. London: Sage.

Carter, P. and Jackson, N. (1993) 'Modernism postmodernism and motivation, or why expectancy theory failed to live up to expectations', in J. Hassard and M. Parker (eds), *Postmodernism and Organizations*. London: Sage.

Chia, R. (1995) 'From modern to postmodern organizational analysis', *Organization Studies*, 16 (4): 579–604.

Chia, R. (2008) 'Postmodernism', in R. Thorpe and R. Holt (eds), *The Sage Dictionary of Qualitative Management Research*. London: Sage.

Cooper, R. (1989) 'Modernism, postmodernism and organizational analysis: an introduction', *Organization Studies*, 10 (4): 479–502.

Cooper, R. and Burrell, G. (1988) 'Modernism, postmodernism and organisational analysis: an introduction', *Organization Studies*, 9: 91–112.

Cunliffe, A.L. (2010) 'Crafting qualitative research: Morgan and Smircich 30 years on', *Organizational Research Methods*, OnlineFirst, 26 July. DOI: 10.1177/1094428110373658.

Deetz, S. (1992) *Democracy in the Age of Corporate Colonialism: Developments in Communication and the Politics of Everyday Life*. Albany: State University of New York Press.

Denzin, N.K. and Lincoln, Y.S. (eds) (2005) *The Sage Handbook of Qualitative Research* (3rd edn). London: Sage.

Denzin, N.K. and Lincoln, Y.S. (eds) (2007) *The Landscape of Qualitative Research* (3rd edn). London: Sage.

Ely, R.J. (1995) 'The power in demography: women's social construction of gender identity at work', *Academy of Management Journal*, 38: 589–634.

Florescano, E. (1994) *Memory, Myth and Time in Mexico: From the Aztecs to Independence*. Austin, TX: University of Texas Press.

Forrester, J. (1993) *Critical Theory, Public Policy and Planning Practice*. Albany, NY: University of New York Press.

Fox, S. (2008) 'Ethnomethodology', in R. Thorpe and R. Holt (eds), *The Sage Dictionary of Qualitative Management Research*. London: Sage.

Garfinkel, H. (1967) *Studies in Ethnomethodology*. Cambridge: Polity Press.

Gergen, K. and Thatchenkerry, T.J. (1996) 'Organization science as social construction: postmodern potentials', *Journal of Applied Behavioural Science*, 32 (4): 356–377.

Gheradi, S., Marshall, J. and Mills, A. (2003) 'Theorizing gender and organizing', in R. Westwood and S. Clegg (eds), *Debating Organization: Point-counterpoint in Organization Studies*. Blackwell: Malden.

Gill, J. and Johnson, P. (2010) *Research Methods for Managers* (4th edn). London: Sage.

Greckhamer, T. (2010) 'The stretch of strategic management discourse: a critical analysis', *Organization Studies*, 31 (7): 841–871.

Guba, E.G. and Lincoln, Y.S. (1994) 'Competing paradigms in qualitative research', in N.K. Denzin and Y.S. Lincoln (eds), *Handbook of Qualitative Research*. Newbury Park, CA: Sage.

Habermas, J. (1974) *Theory and Practice*. London: Heineman.

Hammersley, M. (1992) *What's Wrong with Ethnography?* London: Routledge.

Hammersley, M. and Atkinson, P. (1995) *Ethnography: Principles in Practice* (2nd edn). London: Routledge.

Harley, B. and Hardy, C. (2004) 'Firing blanks? An analysis of discursive struggle in HRM', *Journal of Management Studies*, 41 (3): 377–400.

Hassard, J. and Rowlinson, M. (2011) 'The potential of radical research: Marxism, labour process theory and critical management studies', in C.M. Cassell and B. Lee (eds), *Challenges and Controversies in Management Research*. London: Routledge.

Holland, R. (1999) 'Reflexivity', *Human Relations*, 52 (4): 463–483.

Ibarra-Colado, E. (2006) 'Organization studies and epistemic coloniality in Latin America: thinking otherness from the margins', *Organization*, 13 (4): 463–488.

Jackall, R. (1988) *Moral Mazes: The World of Corporate Managers*. Oxford: Oxford University Press.

Johnson, P., Buehring, A., Cassell, C.M. and Symon, G. (2006) 'Evaluating qualitative management research: towards a contingent criteriology', *International Journal of Management Reviews*, 8 (3): 131–156.

Johnson, P. and Duberley, J. (2000) *Understanding Management Research: An Introduction to Epistemology*. London: Sage.

Keat, R. and Urry, I. (1982) *Social Theory as Science*. London: Routledge

Kelemen, M. and Rumens, N. (2008) *An Introduction to Critical Management Research*. London: Sage.

Kilduff, M. (1993) 'Deconstructing organizations', *Academy of Management Review*, 18 (1): 13–31.

Kilduff, M. and Mehra, A. (1997) 'Postmodernism and organizational research', *Academy of Management Review*, 22 (2): 453–481.

Knights, D. (1992) 'Changing spaces: the disruptive impact of a new epistemological location for the study of management', *Academy of Management Review*, 17 (3): 514–536.

Kondo, D. (1990) *Crafting Ourselves: Power, Gender and Discourses of Identity in a Japanese Workplace*. Chicago: University of Chicago Press.

Linstead, S. (1985) 'Breaking the purity rule: industrial sabotage and the symbolic process', *Personnel Review*, 14 (3): 12–19.

Linstead, S. (1993) 'From postmodern anthropology to deconstructive ethnography', *Human Relations*, 46 (1): 97–120.

Lyotard, J.-F. (1984) *The Postmodern Condition: A Report on Knowledge*. Manchester: Manchester University Press.

Marshall, C. (2006) *Designing Qualitative Research*. London: Sage.

McAuley, J. (2004) 'Hermeneutics', in C.M. Cassell and G. Symon (eds), *Essential Guide to Qualitative Methods in Organizational Research*. London: Sage.

Motion, J. and Leitch, S. (2009) 'The transformational potential of public policy discourse', *Organization Studies*, 30 (10): 1045–1061.

Murray, A. (2008) 'Hermeneutics', in R. Thorpe and R. Holt (eds), *The Sage Dictionary of Qualitative Management Research*. London: Sage.

Outhwaite, W. (1975) *Understanding Social Life: The Method Called Verstehen*. London: George Allen Unwin.

Parker, M. (1992) 'Postmodern organisations or postmodern organisation theory', *Organisation Studies*, 13: 1–17.

Parker, M. (2002) 'Queering management and organization', *Gender, Work and Organization*, 9 (2): 146–166.

Patton, M. (1990) *Qualitative Evaluation and Research Methods*. London: Sage.

Perren, L. and Jennings, P. (2005) 'Government discourses of entrepreneurship: issues of legitimation, subjugation and power', *Entrepreneurship Theory and Practice*, 29 (2): 173–184.

Popper, K. (1959) *The Logic of Scientific Discovery*. London: Hutchinson.

Power, M. and Laughlin, R. (1992) 'Critical theory and accounting', in M. Alvesson and H. Willmott (eds), *Critical Management Studies*. London: Sage, pp. 113–135.

Prasad, A. and Prasad, P. (2002) 'The coming age of interpretive organizational research', *Organizational Research Methods*, 5 (1): 4–11.

Prasad, P. (2005) *Crafting Qualitative Research: Working in the Postpositivist Traditions*. New York: M.E. Sharpe.

Prasad, P. and Caproni, P. (1997) 'Critical theory in the management classroom: engaging power, ideology and praxis', *Journal of Management Education*, 21 (3): 284–291.

Reason, P. and Bradbury, H. (2001) 'Introduction', in P. Reason and H. Bradbury (eds), *Handbook of Action Research: Participative Inquiry and Practice*. London: Sage, pp. 1–14.

Richardson, L. (1998) 'Writing: a method of inquiry', in N.K. Denzin and Y. Lincoln (eds), *Collecting and Interpreting Qualitative Materials*. Thousand Oaks, CA: Sage, pp. 516–529.

Rosen, M. (1985) 'Breakfast as Spiros: dramaturgy and dominance', *Journal of Management*, 11 (2): 31–48.

Ross, D. (1991) *The Origins American Social Science*. New York: Cambridge.

Ruwhiu, D. and Cone, M. (2010) 'Advancing a pragmatist epistemology in organisational research', *Qualitative Research in Organizations and Management: An International Journal*, 5 (2): 108–126.

Schwandt, T.A. (1996) 'Farewell to criteriology', *Qualitative Inquiry*, 2 (1): 58–72.

Smith, L.T. (1999) *Decolonizing Methodologies: Research and Indigenous People*. London and Dunedin, NZ: Zed Books/University of Otago Press.

Stablein, R. and Panoho, J. (2011) 'Comparative research epistemology and methodology: past, present and promising', in C.M. Cassell and B. Lee (eds), *Challenges and Controversies in Management Research*. London: Routledge.

Tyler, M. and Cohen, L. (2008) 'Management in/as comic relief: queer theory and gender performativity in the office', *Gender, Work and Organization*, 15 (2): 113–132.

Van Maanen, J. (1979) 'Reclaiming qualitative methods for organizational research: a preface', *Administrative Science Quarterly*, 24: 520–526.

Van Maanen, J. (1995) 'An end to innocence: the ethnography of ethnography', in J. Van Maanen (ed.), *Representation in Ethnography*. London: Sage, pp. 1–36.

Van Maanen, J. (1998) 'Different strokes: qualitative research in the administrative science quarterly from 1956 to 1996', in J. Van Maanen (ed.), *Qualitative Studies of Organizations*. London: Sage.

Weick, K. (1993) 'The collapse of sensemaking in organizations: the Mann Gulch disaster', *Administrative Science Quarterly*, 38 (4): 628–652.

Weick, K. (1995) *Sensemaking in Organizations*. Thousand Oaks, CA: Sage.

Weiskopf, R. and Willmott, H. (1996) 'Turning the given into a question: a critical discussion of Chia's organisational analysis as deconstructive practice', *European Journal of Radical Organisation Theory*, 3 (2): 1–10.

Willmott, H. (1998) 'Re-cognizing the other: reflections of a new sensibility in social and organization studies', in R. Chia (ed.), *In the Realm of Organization: Essays for Robert Cooper*. London: Routledge, pp. 213–241.

Willmott, H. (2008) 'Critical theory', in R. Thorpe and R. Holt (eds), *The Sage Dictionary of Qualitative Management Research*. London: Sage.

Yanow, D. and Schwartz-Shea, P. (2006) *Interpretation and Method: Empirical Research Methods and the Interpretive Turn*. Armonk, NY: M.E. Sharpe.

3 Choosing Research Participants

Mark N.K. Saunders

Introduction

Within qualitative research choice of research participants is, invariably, constrained by what is practicable. While in an ideal world we may wish to collect data from participants in a particular organization or a number of organizations, our abilities to do this are dependent upon gaining access to these organizations and our intended participants, as well as being granted permission to collect the data we require. Once physical access has been granted and permission obtained (Gummesson, 2000), it may occasionally be possible to collect data from the total population, for example all of an organization's employees, but for most research projects this will be impossible. As a condition of our access, our potential population of research participants may be constrained to a smaller sub-group. The resources we have available to support our research may also constrain the amount of data we can collect and analyse, almost invariably resulting in it only being practicable to collect data from a sample of our population of research participants (Fink, 2003; Saunders et al., 2009b). Consequently for virtually all qualitative research it will be necessary to consider carefully how we will choose those research participants, our sample, from whom we will collect data to answer our research question and meet our research aim.

This chapter takes as its starting premise that there is a clear connection between our research aim and our research design (Kvale and Brinkmann,

2009). Our choice of research participants should be determined by the focus of our research, thereby enabling us to meet our research aim and answer our research question. Choosing research participants is likely to be difficult until we are clear regarding the focus of our research. The chapter commences with a discussion of the main concerns and debates associated with choosing participants for qualitative organizational research. Within this I consider the importance of gaining access, the need for the sample to enable collection of appropriate data, the use of different non-probability sample selection techniques and the number of participants needed. These are illustrated subsequently by two examples drawn from my own and colleagues' research experiences. The first focuses on the selection of a single case study, issues of access and purposive sampling techniques. The second explores the use of a self-selection sample to choose participants drawn from a variety of organizations and the issues associated with sample size. The chapter closes with guidelines for new qualitative researchers when choosing participants and suggestions for further reading.

Main Concerns and Debates

Gaining access

Like all organizational researchers, when undertaking qualitative research we are dependent upon gaining access. Without paying careful attention to how we will gain access, interesting research aims may flounder, proving impractical or problematic when we attempt to gain permission to collect data. Inevitably as researchers our position is weak compared to that of organizations as we have relatively little to offer (Lee, 1993). Many organizations receive frequent research requests for access and would find it impossible to agree to all or even some of these. Equally our requests may fail to interest the gatekeeper who controls research access, resulting in a refusal. This may be for a number of reasons such as a lack of perceived value of the research to the organization, the time required of participants (who are first and foremost employees), the intrusive nature or sensitivity of the research and associated confidentiality issues, scepticism regarding the role of outsiders, or even concerns about the competence of the researcher (Coleman, 1996; Laurila, 1997; Saunders et al., 2009b). Finally, even when access has been promised, often through an existing contact who has agreed to act as broker for our request, this initial agreement can still be overruled at a higher level in the organization.

Difficulties associated with gaining access mean that many organizational researchers, including myself, will often adopt what Buchanan et al. (1988: 53) refer to as an 'opportunist approach' both to gaining access and choosing research participants. Access to organizational gatekeepers is usually brokered by friends and colleagues. While this may involve some luck (Okumus et al., 2007), for example friends working in organizations that might prove suitable research sites, such 'luck' is invariably assisted by careful preparation. Before seeking access I have found it is important to develop a clear research design, part of which will be concerned with how research sites will be selected and research participants will be chosen. Discussions with the broker can reveal if my design is unfeasible, necessitating changes in either the participants or the data collection method. For example, in work to explore how public sector organizations' employees were responding subsequent to the changes brought about by the 1998 reorganization of local government in England and Wales, Adrian Thornhill and I were informed by our broker that we would be asked to exclude school-based employees (mainly teachers) from our sample (Thornhill and Saunders, 2003). In such situations being forewarned allows time to amend the research design and minimize any negative impact on collecting data that will enable the research aims to be met; recognizing slight amendments to the research focus may sometimes also be required.

Initial discussions with the broker, along with information gleaned from secondary sources such as organization web sites, are also helpful in developing an understanding of the organization prior to formally meeting the organizational gatekeeper. Such discussions can be used to explore likely organizational concerns regarding confidentiality, internal political sensitivities and time requirements so these can be respected subsequently. I have also found it helpful when meeting the gatekeeper to offer to collect additional data, even if not directly relevant to my research, where this is clearly of particular interest to the organization (Saunders, 2011). In some cases compromises may be necessary regarding the choice of participants, especially if the research addresses sensitive topics. This does not detract from or negate the importance of theoretical and epistemological concerns, emphasized rightly by many of the rigour and relevance debate commentators (for example, Hodgkinson et al., 2001; Bartunek et al., 2006; Huff et al., 2006). Rather, while organizational pressures can compromise methodological rigour (Van De Ven and Johnson, 2006), like Buchanan and colleagues I believe it is better to compromise to a limited extent and be able to collect data that will help address the research aim. The alternative, if refusing to deviate from the ideal method, is being unable to collect any data due to access being denied.

Even when entry has been negotiated, continued access needs to be actively managed and the relationship with the gatekeeper maintained (Okumus et al., 2007). Despite physical access having been formally granted, it will still be necessary to gain acceptance and consent from the intended participants (cognitive access). Each participant's refusal or non response reduces the likelihood that we will be able to collect those data we need the intended participants to share with us in order to be able to address our research aim (Robson, 2002). Ethical considerations (see Holt, in this volume) rightly emphasize that we should not use coercion to ensure that participants take part. Participants should be given the opportunity to make an informed choice regarding whether to consent; ethical codes emphasizing forms of deception are rarely considered acceptable (Bell and Bryman, 2007). Whereas in the past many of my participants appeared unconcerned about these rights, for example considering reading a participant information sheet and signing a consent form unimportant, I have found this is no longer the case. Simply obtaining physical access to an organization and expecting its members to take part on the basis of this is rarely adequate. Rather discussion of the research with participants and gaining their informed consent can allow us to begin to gain their trust. While this is crucial to the collection of data, it is of little value unless we establish precisely from whom we need to collect data and how these participants will be chosen. This raises three specific concerns with regard to choosing participants to answer our research question and meet our aim: firstly, the need to ensure our sample enables us to collect data that are appropriate; secondly, the use of specific sampling techniques to choose participants who are appropriate to meeting the research aim; and, thirdly, the number of participants that are required to provide sufficient data. It is these that I now consider.

Enabling the collection of appropriate data

Choosing a sample is based on the premise that the choice will enable appropriate data to be collected, thereby allowing us to meet our research aim. While 'appropriate' is often discussed in terms of the data collected representing the population from which they are drawn in some specified way (Becker, 1998), for some ontological positions representation may be considered an inappropriate concept. What is important is that the sample meets the needs of our research. The word 'appropriate' has distinct but different connotations dependent upon whether non-probability (non-random) or probability (random) sampling techniques are used. Although non-probability samples are used far more widely than probability samples in qualitative research, I will contrast briefly both categories. The reasons for this are two-fold. Firstly, to emphasize that, despite it rarely being feasible to collect sufficiently large samples of qualitative data for statistical analysis, it is possible to collect data for qualitative analysis from participants who have been selected at random (Kvale and Brinkmann, 2009). Secondly, it will allow a consideration of any epistemological differences between the two types of sampling techniques and of concerns raised regarding the ability of non-probability samples to provide appropriate data. In particular I will contrast the way in which the categories of sampling techniques differ in their specification of the population, the sample, the basis of generalizing from the sample and, as a consequence, the nature of the research aims to be addressed (Table 3.1). More detailed aspects such as criteria for the use of selected non-probability sampling techniques and the number of participants required (sample size) will be discussed in subsequent sections.

When a non-probability sampling technique is used, choice is based on the researcher's judgement regarding those of the population's characteristics that are important in relation to the data required to address the research aim. This means we actively choose appropriate cases to be in our sample while actively excluding others. As a consequence some of the population will have a chance of being chosen as participants, while others will not (Table 3.1). For non-probability samples, 'appropriate', as we will see in both examples, is concerned with ensuring the sample chosen will enable us to gain understandings

Table 3.1 Differences between non-probability and probability sampling

Difference	Non-probability	Probability
Specification of population	not necessary	essential as is a sampling frame
Basis of sample choice/selection	researcher's judgement	random
Basis of generalizing from sample	if undertaken theoretically, findings may be transferable	statistical representation
Nature of aim usually addressed	exploratory, answered utilizing rich understandings	explanatory, answered utilizing statistical inferences
Sample size	relatively small (other than for quota sampling)	relatively large

and insights (Patton, 2002) and the justification we provide for this. This is crucial for exploratory research where the aim is to garner new insights into phenomena or for phenomena to be assessed in a new light, and for research aims that require the development of rich understandings upon which theoretical generalizations may be based (Table 3.1). Such generalizations involve reasoned judgement regarding how the research findings might apply to other situations through the use of supporting evidence and clear argument (Kvale and Brinkmann, 2009). This is often referred to as the 'transferability' of findings. Advocates of probability sampling quite rightly argue that choosing a sample using a non-probability technique means we will not be able to estimate statistically the characteristics of a population from our sample. For many non-probability samples the number of participants will be less than the often quoted minimum number for statistical analysis of 30 (Stutely, 2003). However, while a small sample prevents us from generalizing about a population statistically, it is still possible to generalize theoretically providing the participants chosen are appropriate for our research aim (Saunders et al., 2009b).

In contrast, probability sampling techniques select each participant at random. This eliminates the researcher's judgement from the choice of actual participants. Instead we specify the population, the sampling technique through which participants will be selected and the probability of each participant being chosen (Table 3.1). Unlike non-probability sampling, probability sampling techniques require a complete, accurate and up-to-date list of all the cases in the population (sampling frame) from which to select the sample. Consequently, if it is not possible to obtain such a list, probability sampling cannot be used. The utility of data depends, in part, upon the accuracy with which the sample selected represents or mirrors this population (Fink, 2003); probability sampling techniques provide the basis for arguing that the sample statistically represents the population (Barnett, 2002). It also means that if data are collected using a probability sample drawn from a population of a single organization's employees, although it is possible to generalize theoretically beyond this population, strictly we should not generalize statistically to other organizations (Saunders et al., 2009b).

Inevitably, given the nature of associated research aims, probability sampling is more likely to be driven by a positivist epistemology and quantitative research. In contrast non-probability sampling is associated principally with the range of non-positivist epistemologies and qualitative research, being based on judgement rather than statistical probability. Drawing upon the reasoning for such judgements, I now consider how the use of particular non-probability sampling techniques differs, depending upon the research aim.

Use of non-probability sampling techniques

Despite the broad range of non-probability sampling techniques available, with the exception of quota sampling, these tend to receive less prominence than probability sampling techniques in the majority of research methods texts. Non-probability sampling techniques can be divided into four groups: those used as a substitute for a probability sample to select participants when a sampling frame is not available (quota sampling); those where participants are chosen on the basis of judgement (purposive sampling); those where participants volunteer (snowball and self-selection sampling); and those where participants are included for convenience (haphazard) (Table 3.2). Of these, I will not discuss quota sampling further, as it is used mainly in quantitative research for selecting large samples, often of between 2,000 and 5,000 cases (for further details see Saunders et al., 2009b).

Purposive samples are the most frequently used form of non-probability sampling in qualitative research (Miles and Huberman, 1994). These techniques require our judgement in choosing cases that will best enable us to answer our research question and meet our aim. They are normally used to choose a relatively small number of participants, such as those that are particularly informative (Neuman, 2005). Patton (2002) outlines 16 different varieties, with all participants being chosen according to predetermined common criteria that are relevant to meeting the research aim. The most widely used of these, along with other non-probability sampling techniques frequently used by qualitative researchers, are summarized in Table 3.2.

Table 3.2   Justifications for frequently used non-probability samples

Group	Sampling technique	Criteria in relation to research aim	Researcher's control
Quota	Quota	proportionally represents population	specifies quota selection criteria
Purposive	Typical case	illustrate	specifies selection criteria
	Critical case	important	specifies selection criteria
	Extreme case	unusual or special	specifies selection criteria
	Heterogeneous	reveal/illuminate key themes	specifies selection criteria
	Theoretical	inform emerging theory	selects cumulatively on basis of emerging codes and categories
Volunteer	Snowball	cases difficult to identify	selects only initial participant, remainder likely to be similar
	Self-selection	access difficult, research exploratory	offers only general invitation, participants identify themselves
Haphazard	Convenience	ease of access (often lacks credibility)	haphazard

Typical case purposive samples are usually chosen to provide an illustrative profile that is considered representative, albeit not statistically. Such non-probability samples are justified by their typicality of the wider populations such as a 'typical' production line employee or call centre operative. In contrast, as we will see in Example 1 below, critical case purposive samples are chosen on the basis of either their ability to make a point dramatically or their importance to addressing the research aim. Their purpose is to understand what is happening in each case so that logical generalizations can be made. Patton (2002) offers clues regarding how to discern those cases that are likely to be critical to our research. These have been phrased as a number of questions by Saunders et al. (2009b): if it happens here, will it happen everywhere? If they are having problems, can you be sure that everyone will be having problems? And, are they essential to the operation of the process in which you are interested? Extreme case purposive sampling chooses unusual or special participants on the basis that the data collected from such cases will enable us to find out the most. This is based on the premise that findings from extreme cases will be relevant in understanding or explaining more typical cases (Patton, 2002). If our research was concerned with exploring and understanding the reasons for differences in employee performance, such cases might include some employees who consistently performed extremely well and others who performed extremely poorly.

Heterogeneous purposive sampling uses our judgement to choose participants with sufficiently diverse characteristics to provide the maximum variation possible in the data collected (Example 1). This can include what is sometimes referred to as 'taking a diagonal slice' through an organizational chart, thereby ensuring participants are included from all departments and across all levels of the hierarchy. Although such samples are likely to contain participants who are different, Patton (2002) argues that this is a strength, as any patterns that do emerge are likely to be of particular interest and value, representing key themes. In direct contrast, homogeneous purposive sampling focuses on choosing one particular sub-group, such as a particular occupation or level in an organization's hierarchy. The characteristics of such participants are similar, thus allowing these to be explored in greater depth and minor differences to be more apparent.

Theoretical sampling represents a special case of purposive sampling, being particularly associated with grounded theory (Coyne, 1997; see also Kenealy, in this volume) and analytic induction. Corbin and Strauss (2008: 195) define theoretical sampling as 'data collection based on concepts that appear to be relevant to the evolving story line' and derived from the data. Initially researchers will need to have some idea of where to sample, although not necessarily what to sample for, with participants being chosen as they are needed. Subsequent sample selection is dictated by the needs of the emerging theory, with participants being chosen purposively to inform this. A theoretical sample is therefore cumulatively chosen according to the developing categories and emerging theory based upon a simultaneous collection, coding and analysis of the data.

Snowball sampling is the first of two techniques we must consider where participants are volunteered to be part of the research rather than being chosen. This is commonly used when it is difficult to identify members of the desired population. For these populations, such as people who are working in the informal economy while claiming unemployment benefit, snowball sampling may provide the only possibility for finding potential participants. Alternatively where participants are easily identifiable but difficult to access, such as organizations' chief executives, using snowball sampling can allow these people to be reached. Once we have made contact and collected data from an initial participant she or he identifies a number of other participants from the same population and supports our gaining access. They in turn will identify further participants and so the sample snowballs (Saunders et al., 2009b). Invariably participants are most likely to volunteer other potential participants who are similar to themselves, resulting in a homogeneous sample (Lee, 1993).

The second technique where the participants volunteer, self-selection sampling (Example 2 below), occurs where potential participants identify their desire to take part in the research. Usually we, as researchers, will publicize our need for participants perhaps by advertising using appropriate media or inviting them to take part in the research. Increasingly, organizational researchers are using a variety of electronic media such as intranets, blogs and bulletin boards alongside invitations through general letters or all user emails (Hookway, 2008). Participants who self-select by responding will often do so because they have strong feelings or opinions about the research, consider it important or interesting and so are willing to devote their time.

Finally, convenience sampling involves using those participants that are easiest to obtain for our sample, for example choosing MBA students for research about managers. However, samples ostensibly chosen for convenience will often meet purposive sample selection criteria that are more relevant to the research aim. It may be that two organizations you intend to use as comparative case studies are 'convenient' because you have been able to negotiate access through existing contacts. Where these two organizations also represent extreme or unusual cases they offer appropriate contrasting scenarios, providing justification regarding their purpose when addressing the research aim. Alternatively, while a sample of operatives in another division of an organization for which you work might be easy to obtain and are consequently 'convenient', the fact that such participants allow you to address a research aim necessitating an in-depth focus on a particular homogenous group is more crucial. Where the reasons for using a convenience sample have little if any relevance to the research aim, they are considered haphazard. In such situations, participants appear in the sample only because of the ease of obtaining them rather than because of their appropriateness. While this may not be problematic if there is little variation in the population, where the population is more varied it can result in participants that are of limited use in relation to the research question.

The number of participants needed

Unlike probability samples (for example see Barnett, 2002), the issue of a suitable sample size for non-probability samples often appears ambiguous, there being no hard and fast rules. Rather sample size is dependent upon what we need to find out, what will be helpful, what will have credibility and what we can do within the resources we have available (Patton, 2002). Although the validity of the qualitative data we collect and the understanding we gain will be more to do with our data collection skills (for example observation or interviewing) than with the size of our sample (Patton, 2002), a crucial concern is, invariably, the number of observations or interviews that will be sufficient.

Despite the importance of estimating the required sample size when designing qualitative research, compared to probability samples there is very little advice regarding the likely number of participants needed. Writing in the first edition of the *Handbook of Qualitative Research*, Morse (1994: 147) commented, 'saturation is the key to excellent qualitative work', noting that 'there are no published guidelines or tests of adequacy for estimating the sample size required to reach saturation'. Yet, many texts still simply recommend establishing the size of a non-probability sample inductively – namely continuing to collect data until there is data saturation, the point at which no new information or themes are observed in the data. This is problematic as it is often necessary to have an idea of the number of participants likely to be involved in the research at the design stage. Fortunately, Guest et al. (2006) summarized the limited guidance available from their own and other studies, which is aggregated along with other advice

Table 3.3 Minimum non-probability sample size

Original source	Nature of study	Minimum size (range)
Bertaux (1981)	Qualitative	15
Kvale and Brinkmann (2009)	Interviews	5–25
Bernard (2000); Morse (1994)	Ethnographic	35–36
Creswell (1998); Morse (1994)	Grounded theory	20–35
Creswell (1998); Morse (1994)	Phenomenological	5–25
Guest et al. (2006); Kuzel (1992); Romney et al. (1986)	Considering an homogeneous population	4–12
Kuzel (1992); Creswell (2007)	Considering a heterogeneous population	12–30

in Table 3.3. As illustrated in both Examples 1 and 2, colleagues and I have found this advice to be applicable for both homogeneous and heterogeneous samples when collecting qualitative data using interviews.

Advice offered indicating sample size is likely to differ between research strategies and be dependent upon the nature of the population from which the sample is selected (Table 3.3). For research where the aim is to understand commonalities within a fairly homogeneous population, Guest et al. (2006) suggest that a carefully selected purposive sample of 12 participants is likely to suffice (Table 3.3). However, they also note where the data quality is poor, the area being researched is diffuse or vague, or the population is more heterogeneous (Example 2), this number is unlikely to be sufficient. In such situations, although higher than other advice, Cresswell's more recent (2007) suggestion of between 25–30 participants for a general study provides a conservative estimate. Additionally, Guest et al. (2006) advise, where the research requires a comparison between distinct groups (Example 1), the sample size will need to be larger, with each group being treated as a separate homogeneous population. Consequently, for a comparison of two homogeneous groups, two samples each of 12 participants would appear likely to be sufficient.

Examples From My Own Experience

Example 1: purposive sampling

My first example focuses on issues of access alongside choosing a purposive sample using both critical case and subsequently, within the case, heterogeneous sampling techniques. It is taken from recent research with Levent Altinay and Katharine Riordan, which was concerned with employees' reactions to the management of post-merger cultural integration in the service sector. Our aim was 'to explore reactions to an acquiring organisation's approach to the management of post-merger cultural integration of two international hotel organisations from the perspectives of both acquiring and acquired employees' (Saunders et al., 2009a: 1360).

To meet our aim, we needed to gain access to a recently merged hotel organization. We decided the case study organization should be a leading operator within the hotel industry with considerable experience of mergers. It could therefore be considered a single critical case due to this experience, as well as its significance to the industry. Fortunately, one of our research team had a close friend who worked for a deluxe global hotel chain, referred to as 'Global Hotels' to preserve anonymity, which had recently undergone a merger and acquired another hotel chain in the United Kingdom. This hotel chain was the acquiring organization and had significant involvement in mergers, being one of the world's largest branded hotel operators. Initial access to the acquiring hotel operator was brokered through the close friend.

Further discussion with our broker highlighted the importance of head office employees to this organization in relation to cultural integration. These employees were viewed by the organization as 'custodians of the brand and the [Global Hotels] Inc. culture' (Saunders et al., 2009a: 1363) and were considered critical to the success of the post-merger cultural integration. We defined them as the population to whom we wished to gain access. At the same time, their head office location meant the travel and time costs associated with our interviewing could be kept to a minimum. Discussions with our broker and other senior Global Hotels managers during access negotiations indicated the post merger integration process might not have been managed well, suggesting a need for sensitivity. The head office employee turnover rate was the highest for seven years with increasing numbers of acquired middle and senior managers leaving, often to work for competitors. Consequently, during negotiations we continued to emphasize that we would ensure the anonymity of Global Hotels as well as that of all participants.

Eventually we were granted full access to interview (see Alvesson and Ashcraft, in this volume) a sample of up to 30 head office employees. Although senior management considered these employees an homogeneous group, our need to compare acquiring and acquired employees' perspectives meant we chose our sample as matched pairs, with one member of the pair being drawn from those originally employed by the acquiring organization and the other coming from the acquired organization. These were chosen purposively from a full list of head office employees by matching them across the two discrete strata. As previous research had indicated that reactions to mergers were likely to differ between employees (for example, Child et al., 2003), we ensured these pairs were drawn from different levels within the organization structure. Our heterogeneous sample therefore consisted of board members (one pair), senior managers (two pairs), middle managers (seven pairs) and non-management staff, including administrative and technical employees (five pairs). Subsequently data were collected through individual interviews with these participants.

Our use of matched pairs ensured that direct comparisons could be drawn between acquiring and acquired participants employed within the same role. Subsequent data analysis revealed that within the two groups of acquiring and acquired employees, the sample size of 15 was sufficiently large to reveal key patterns. These patterns differed between these two groups (Saunders et al., 2009a).

Example 2: self-selection sampling

My second example focuses particularly on the use of self-selection sampling and issues of sample size. It is drawn from work undertaken with Almuth McDowall (McDowall and Saunders, 2010) exploring how managers responsible for training and development conceptualized these activities in practice. The aims were to investigate the factors that guided their decision-making, how they evaluated the outcomes of these activities and the extent to which they perceived a relationship between training and development. Within this we sought to obtain a sample that represented a range of contemporary experiences from those managing training and development within organizations.

Using a list of human resource (HR) contacts from an existing subscription database, *The Personnel Manager's Yearbook*, UK managers were contacted using an invitation letter or email. This outlined the purpose of our research, explained why we would value their involvement and invited potential participants who fitted specified inclusion criteria and wished to be involved to volunteer. These criteria specified, firstly, that volunteers should be in managerial roles that included a responsibility for identifying the development and training needs of employees. Secondly, they should be making decisions on the basis of these identified needs such as recommending attendance at a particular training course or development activity following a staff appraisal. Finally, we specified that our participants should have been undertaking this role for at least a six month period.

Following our invitation, we received responses from managers located in 20 different organizations dispersed throughout the UK. Of these, 26 met our criteria. Although our sample could not be statistically representative, having not been selected at random, participants were from a variety of organizations and had a range of different managerial roles. These self-selecting managers, like those we had originally contacted, were working in public sector organizations, such as local authorities, the emergency services and education, and private sector organizations across a range of sectors including finance, retail and publishing. Of these participants 16 were male and 10 female, their ages ranging from 28 to 59 years. The nature of their managerial responsibilities varied from senior managers (with active line management for up to 50 staff) to those with specific responsibility for specialist training and development functions.

All participants were sent a short information sheet outlining the nature of the research in advance via email. Subsequently individual interviews were conducted during working hours by telephone at a mutually agreed time, thereby ensuring minimal disruption. At the outset of each interview we checked that the inclusion criteria outlined earlier were met. All participants were assured that their identities and those of their organizations would be anonymized. This was particularly important as the majority of respondents had strong, albeit varied, opinions regarding training and development (McDowall and Saunders, 2010).

Subsequent analysis of the interview transcripts was undertaken using template analysis (see King, in this volume). Coding was therefore undertaken in a hierarchical manner, using meaningful themes to encompass successively narrower and more specific second and third level codes. We developed our initial template of meaningful themes (first level codes) using our first six interviews. Through a process of constant revision this template provided the basis for analysing all remaining interview transcripts. As we worked through these transcripts, definitions were refined, new codes were added and redundant codes were removed, with more salient themes being moved to higher level codes and less salient themes to lower level codes. Relatively few alterations to the template were made after 13 interviews had been coded, although full 'saturation' was not reached until 19 transcripts had been analysed fully. Analysis of the remaining seven interview transcripts resulted in no additional changes to the template or further insights.

Guidelines for New Qualitative Researchers

Within this chapter I have highlighted a range of aspects relating to choosing research participants. These have been illustrated through two examples and are now summarized as guidelines for new qualitative researchers:

When choosing participants for qualitative research the subject matter of the research, as expressed by the research question and the research aim, should be the main factor influencing the technique used to choose the sample and the criteria on which this is based.

Choice of participants will invariably depend upon whether access is granted. Choice can also be constrained by the precise access granted by the organizational gatekeeper and, subsequently, participants' willingness to consent to be involved. It is therefore important to have prepared fully prior to negotiating access through developing good background knowledge of the organization alongside topics that have the potential to prove contentious or sensitive. In addition it is vital to have planned the research design, including how the sample will be chosen and the likely number of participants. This will allow an identification of those aspects of the research focus and the method where compromises may be made to address organizational concerns, while still meeting the research aims and maintaining methodological rigour.

Use of particular sampling techniques is, invariably, based on whether or not a particular technique will select participants who can provide data that will enable the research question to be answered. Although most qualitative research is likely to use non-probability sampling techniques, where statistical representativeness is required, one or more probability sampling techniques will have to be used. This will only be feasible where it is possible to construct a sampling frame.

Criteria for using purposive non-probability sampling techniques include whether the resultant sample is required to be illustrative (typical case), important (critical case), unusual (extreme case), revealing of key themes (heterogeneous), in-depth (homogenous) or useful in developing grounded theory (theoretical). Where cases are difficult to identify or access is difficult, snowball or self-selection sampling should be considered. While convenience samples can provide easy access, their use should normally be avoided as they provide limited control over participant selection.

The number of participants needed is a function of the relationship between the research aim and the sampling technique used. While clear rules are available for probability samples, this is not the case for non-probability samples. Rather, sample sizes are dependent upon data being collected until no new themes or information are observed, that is until saturation is reached. Where the population are homogeneous, data saturation is likely to be reached having collected data from between 4 and 12 participants. In contrast, for heterogeneous populations, data will likely need to be collected from between 12 and 30 participants before saturation is reached. Such saturation is also likely to be influenced by the kind of research strategy adopted.

The choices made when following these guidelines will invariably need to be justified fully. It is therefore imperative that, along with the choices made, the reasons for these are noted in full as the research unfolds. If this is left until the later stages of research the precise justification for a particular choice may prove unclear or have been forgotten.

Further Reading

Despite the proliferation of books on research methods over the past decade, few have considered in any depth the use of non-probability sampling techniques to choose participants. Two qualitative methods texts that both contain useful discussions and examples of non-probability sampling techniques and how to use them are Chapter 2 of Miles and Huberman's (1994) *Qualitative Data Analysis* and Chapter 5 of Patton's (2002) *Qualitative Research and Evaluation Methods*. A clear discussion with examples of both non-probability and probability sampling techniques with examples of how to use them can be found in Chapter 7 of Saunders, Lewis and Thornhill's (2009b) *Research Methods for Business Students*. Chapter 6 of deVaus's (2002) *Surveys in Social Research* offers a useful overview of both non-probability and probability sampling. Finally, interesting insights into the use of non-probability samples and the issue of sample size can be found in the (2006) paper by Guest, Bunce and Johnson, 'How many interviews are enough?' in *Field Methods*.

References

Barnett, V. (2002) *Sample Surveys Principles and Methods* (3rd edn). Oxford: Wiley-Blackwell.

Bartunek, J.M., Rynes, S.L. and Ireland, R.D. (2006) 'What makes management research interesting and why does it matter?', *Academy of Management Journal*, 49 (1): 9–15.

Becker, H.S. (1998) *Tricks of the Trade.* Chicago: University of Chicago Press.

Bell, E. and Bryman, A. (2007) 'The ethics of management research: an exploratory content analysis', *British Journal of Management*, 18 (1): 63–77.

Bernard, H.R. (2000) *Social Research Methods*. Thousand Oaks, CA: Sage.

Bertaux, D. (1981) 'From the life-history approach to the transformation of sociological practice', in D. Bertaux (ed.), *Biography and Society: The Life History Approach in the Social Sciences*. London: Sage, pp. 29–45.

Buchanan, D., Boddy, D. and McCalman, J. (1988) 'Getting in, getting on, getting out and getting back', in A. Bryman (ed.), *Doing Research in Organisations*. London: Routledge, pp. 53–67.

Child, J., Faulkner, D. and Pitethly, R. (2003) *The Management of International Acquisitions*. Oxford: Oxford University Press.

Coleman, S. (1996) 'Obstacles and opportunities in access to professional work organizations for long-term fieldwork: the case for Japanese laboratories', *Human Organization*, 55: 334–343.

Corbin, J. and Strauss, A. (2008) *Basics of Qualitative Research* (3rd edn). Thousand Oaks, CA: Sage.

Coyne, I.T. (1997) 'Sampling in qualitative research, purposeful and theoretical sampling: merging or clear boundaries?', *Journal of Advanced Nursing*, 26: 623–630.

Creswell, J. (1998) *Qualitative Inquiry and Research Design: Choosing Among Five Traditions*. Thousand Oaks, CA: Sage.

Creswell, J. (2007) *Qualitative Inquiry and Research Design: Choosing Among Five Approaches* (2nd edn). Thousand Oaks, CA: Sage.

deVaus, D.A. (2002) *Surveys in Social Research* (5th edn). London: Routledge.

Fink, A. (2003) *How to Sample in Surveys* (2nd edn). Thousand Oaks, CA: Sage.

Guest, G., Bunce, A. and Johnson, L. (2006), 'How many interviews are enough?', *Field Methods*, 18: 59–82.

Gummesson, E. (2000) *Qualitative Methods in Management Research* (2nd edn). Thousand Oaks, CA: Sage.

Hodgkinson, G.P., Herriot, P. and Anderson, N. (2001) 'Re-aligning the stakeholders in management research: lessons from industrial, work and organizational psychology', *British Journal of Management*, 12, Special Issue: S41–S48.

Hookway, N. (2008) 'Entering the blogosphere: some strategies for using blogs in qualitative research', *Qualitative Research*, 8: 91–113.

Huff, A.S., Tranfield, D. and Van Aken, J.E. (2006) 'Management as a design science mindful of art and surprise', *Journal of Management Inquiry*, 15 (4): 413–424.

Kuzel, A. (1992) 'Sampling in qualitative inquiry', in B. Crabtree and W. Miller (eds), *Doing Qualitative Research*. Newbury Park, CA: Sage, pp. 31–44.

Kvale, S. and Brinkmann, S. (2009) *InterViews: Learning the Craft of Qualitative Research Interviewing*. Thousand Oaks, CA: Sage.

Laurila, J. (1997) 'Promoting research access and informant rapport in corporate settings: notes from research on a crises company', *Scandinavian Journal of Management*, 13: 407–418.

Lee, R. (1993) *Doing Research on Sensitive Topics*. London: Sage.

McDowall, A. and Saunders, M.N.K. (2010) 'UK managers conceptions of training and development', *Journal of European Industrial Training*, 34 (7): 609–630.

Miles, M. and Huberman, A. (1994) *Qualitative Data Analysis* (2nd edn). Thousand Oaks, CA: Sage.

Morse, J. (1994) 'Designing funded qualitative research', in N. Denzin and Y. Lincoln (eds), *Handbook of Qualitative Research*. Thousand Oaks, CA: Sage, pp. 220–235.

Neuman, W.L. (2005) *Social Research Methods* (6th edn). London: Pearson.

Okumus, F., Altinay, L. and Roper, A. (2007) 'Gaining access for research: reflections from experience', *Annals of Tourism Research*, 34 (1): 7–26.

Patton M.Q. (2002) *Qualitative Research and Evaluation Methods* (3rd edn). Thousand Oaks, CA: Sage.

Robson, C. (2002) *Real World Research* (2nd edn). Oxford: Blackwell.

Romney, A., Batchelder, W. and Weller, S. (1986) 'Culture as consensus: a theory of culture and informant accuracy', *American Anthropologist*, 88: 313–338.

Saunders, M.N.K. (2011) 'The management researcher as practitioner', in C. Cassell and W.J. Lee (eds), *Challenges and Controversies in Management Research*. London: Taylor and Francis, pp. 243–256.

Saunders, M.N.K., Altinay, L. and Riordan, K. (2009a) 'The management of post-merger cultural integration: implications from the hotel industry', *Service Industries Journal*, 29 (10): 1359–1375.

Saunders, M.N.K., Lewis, P. and Thornhill, A. (2009b) *Research Methods for Business Students* (5th edn). Harlow: FT Prentice Hall.

Stutely, M. (2003) *Numbers Guide: The Essentials of Business Numeracy*. London: Bloomberg Press.

Thornhill, A. and Saunders, M.N.K. (2003) 'Exploring employees' reactions to strategic change over time: the utilisation of an organisational justice perspective', *Irish Journal of Management*, 24 (1): 66–86.

Van De Ven, A.H. and Johnson, P.E. (2006) 'Knowledge for theory and practice', *Academy of Management Review*, 31 (4): 802–821.

4 Researching Your Own Organization

Susanne Tietze

Introduction

The purpose of this chapter is to introduce and discuss the involvement of the researcher in the research scene and with the research participants in a specific scenario, i.e. where the researcher's employing organization provides the context for the research project. Such contexts also include settings where the researcher might be the owner of a small business, in particular where family businesses are at the core of the research venture. It has always been of interest to academic researchers and scholars to understand researchers' involvement in the research scene. Yet recent trends, in particular in doctoral studies, have made an exploration of the ties of researcher and researched in the context of researchers exploring their employing organization more prevalent. Here, the emergence and continued growth of professional doctorates (Doctor of Business Administration) degrees in the UK and Europe (Fisher and Tietze, 2010) has also seen an increasing number of research projects where managers and practitioners will bring the problems and issues of their employing organization to the research agenda and articulate research plans that are set in the context of their employing organization. While there is a body of literature exploring the notions and processes of auto-ethnography and writing the self into the research texts (Reed-Danahay, 1997; Watson, 1995; and see also Humphreys and Learmonth, in this volume), there is not much literature and guidance available for students who are researching their own and colleagues' practices in the context of their employing organization (Costley et al., 2010). The chapter therefore presents some ideas about the nature and dynamics of the researcher–researched relationship when research is located in the employing organization.

Any research project is, of course, situated in particular contexts, which will shape and inform the parameters and questions a researcher might venture to address. Researchers, too, are 'situated', i.e. they will bring a particular socio-political, historical, gendered, generational, ethnic and racial background to their research projects. In this regard research questions, research interests, choice of method and research instruments are interlinked with the researcher herself, with her life experience, and her development, background and values. Thus, becoming aware of the researcher's role in the research process is vital to understanding how such involvement shapes the generation of knowledge. In other words, the researcher 'is the research instrument par excellence' (Hammersley and Atkinson, 1995: 19) and appreciating his or her role in the research process is also vital to appreciating the trustworthiness and authenticity of qualitative research and accounts produced by the researcher (Guba and Lincoln, 1981; Lincoln and Guba, 1985).

Understanding the relationships between researchers and those they research is therefore a key part of appreciating the situatedness of all knowledge. Yet in contexts of researching one's employing or own organization issues of researcher involvement are particularly pertinent, as the boundaries between researcher and researched, as well as the spatial and temporal confines of where and when data are collected and when the research project is completed, become more ambiguous and open-ended.

My experience of conducing a social science research project set in my employing organization informs much of this chapter, as coping with the ambiguity of roles and boundaries turned out to be a conflict-ridden personal experience. As a researcher defined by the interpretive tradition, which stresses the importance of meaning in all social processes, I have put great value on understanding how meaning is generated in organizational contexts and in the interplay between social actors (see Tietze et al., 2003: 17–31). Writing this chapter is therefore a way of (re)articulating for its readers as well as for myself how the relationships and bonds between researcher and researched are part of the 'meaning' researchers make of their findings and of the research accounts they write and make available to a wider audience.

In the following, I will first discuss the relationship between the researcher and the researched, focusing on the issues that arise when researching one's employing organization. This includes a commentary on field roles and ethical involvements (see also Holt, in this volume). A section on 'reflexivity' (see also Haynes, in this volume) as central to qualitative-interpretive research then follows, and again, the discussion focuses on issues that are particularly pertinent when researching contexts one is familiar with. These discussions include a commentary on the precariousness, dilemmas and emotions that inform such 'bonds' of researcher and the researched in the context of researching one's own organization. From there on there follows an account of my own experience of conducting an ethnographic study set in an organization where I was both researcher and employee. This account will focus in particular on relationships with colleagues.

The Researcher–Researched Relationship

Work by scholars such as Becker (1967) and Berger and Luckman (1966), as well as the increasing involvement of women in academic research projects, had contributed to the dismantling of 'impartiality' and 'objective neutrality' as the only basis for investigating the social world. Instead, this had been increasingly seen as an intersubjective creation (Burr, 2003). This now being accepted, it is no longer possible to treat people as 'research objects', as 'mere mines of information' to be exploited by the researcher as the neutral collector of facts. Arendell (1997), for example, reports from her experience of interviewing men and argues that the relationship that evolved during the research process was influenced by the identities and histories of those involved and was activated as the researched asserted gendered hierarchies during the interview process. Cotterill (2002) also recounts issues of friendship, vulnerability and power as part of the process of interviewing women. In other words, these researchers started to pay attention to the notion that researching 'the other' always involves reflections on one's own position, purpose and sources of power as pre-knowledge and presuppositions are activated in establishing relationships with the researched. Imbued in such a stance *vis-à-vis* the researched is an ethics of involvement, which attempts to avoid potentially exploitative relationships; rather the researcher lays open to the respondents her/his dependence to provide access to their meaning-worlds and interpretations of circumstance. Establishing a deep relationship with the researched as people and agents in their own right is therefore a key task of qualitative reflexive researchers. Watson (1994), for example, begins his ethnography of managerial work by reproducing a piece of banter between himself and a manager who was employed by the organization Watson observed. This piece of banter is used as a rhetorical device to introduce the reader to the characters and people within the ethnography. In particular, the author, Watson, introduces himself as an active agent in the research process and uses the authorial voice 'I' and also refers to the person he exchanged banter with as 'my management friend' (Watson, 1994: 1) – pointing to the different roles and identities people take on or are given in such involved research.

The issues of involvement and establishing relationships with the researched are a key topic for all qualitative-interpretive research projects – one that comes more clearly and urgently to the fore when researching one's own organization or social context. In other words, it magnifies the issues that all qualitative researchers face when seeking close, sometimes even intimate involvement with the people whose meaning worlds they want to access and understand. Frequently, researchers will indeed focus their inquiry on aspects of their own work organization or professional setting – this is particularly so for (junior) researchers who may conduct empirical research for their thesis or dissertation in the context of their employing organization. In this regard they will bring their pre-understanding and pre-conceptions of organizational issues to the research scene. Importantly, they will have also already established a relationship with their potential respondents, i.e. their colleagues, because as researchers/employees they will carry particular organizational roles and positions in the organizational hierarchy. They will be – sometimes deeply – embedded in the organizational context they research. One could argue that this position makes it difficult to research one's own organization, as it has been argued that (qualitative) researchers should be like 'professional strangers' (Agar, 1980) – yet researchers who research their own organizations are already aware of their routines and practices, people and processes. They are not strangers. In this regard researching one's own organization, inclusive of pre-formed relationships, is a precarious balancing act between 'strangeness' and 'familiarity'. Researchers will have to find the means to render strange what is established as 'normal', that will find mechanisms that will distance themselves from what they already know. Such close engagement with the research scene and the researched can be an advantage, of course, as pre-existing ties could ensure access to organizational niches and nooks, which may remain hidden otherwise. Having a good network of accessible colleagues and (work) friends can also provide depth and colour to a research project. While not all projects focusing on one's own organization are necessarily auto-ethnographic in character (making the life experience of the ethnographer central to the ethnographic work; Coffey, 1999), all fieldwork conducted in a setting the researcher is familiar with evokes emotional and intellectual work, which is different from the emotional-intellectual work associated with 'normal' research projects (i.e. researching a 'strange' setting). As the engagement

of the researcher with the researched is likely to last beyond the temporal boundaries of the research project, the stakes of the relationship between the two parties
are higher than in more detached modes of engagement.

Reflexivity

Reflexivity challenges the notion that it is possible for researchers to be neutral
automatons and implies that the orientations of researchers are shaped by their
socio-historical location and in this regard the biography of the researcher
informs the research. This is inclusive of the values and emotional dispositions
that they bring to the research setting – indeed, some scholars would argue that
research projects pose serious questions of 'identity' and 'self' for the researcher
(Etherington, 2004). In this regard, part of the research process is to ask questions about one's own personal interest in the topic, one's presupposition and
pre-knowledge; how do gender, class, ethnicity and nationality influence one's
positioning in relation to the topic and the respondents? Cohen et al. (2009)
provide a recent example of how researchers' sensibilities and circumstance
inform the topic choice, reflection and theorizing on an issue of topical relevance, i.e. the relationship between home and work. The authors use their own
lives and conversations they have with each other as fellow academics and
friends to conduct a metaphorical analysis of their circumstances. Of interest
here is the way the authors break traditional academic conventions about how
to integrate examples and experiences from one's own life to make sense – and
even theorize – institutional relationships (between home and work) from a
personal yet also a theoretical perspective.

   In work contexts, one might consider the impact of one's hierarchical position,
one's degree of technical expertise, subject specialism or occupational knowledge as aspects that may influence how one is perceived as a researcher by the
researched and how this might influence the interactions of the research process.

Ethics

The intersubjective nature of social and organizational life means that the
researcher and the researched have shared meanings and that the researcher
brings her methodological understanding to the research scene to develop this

shared meaning into collective knowledge. Meaningful engagement and understanding between the two parties involved in academic inquiry can only happen if a degree of closeness, understanding, trust and openness is developed. Yet in this there also lies a danger or at least a dilemma: fieldwork, in particular ethnographic studies set in one's employing organization or such like, is 'up close and personal'. It has to be in order to be successful and meaningful. Yet, such 'closeness' breeds complications and conflict and poses some serious ethical dilemmas.

Fieldwork is a deliberate interruption of the respondents' lives with a view to generating understanding and knowledge. Indeed some anthropological scholars speak of the 'violence' of fieldwork, even if that violence is symbolic (e.g. Hastrup, 1992, quoted in England, 1994: 249; Okely and Callaway, 1992). In particular if relationships between researcher and researched are pre-established, friendly and personal, the greater the risk is for them to be potentially even more exploitative compared to more traditional methods, as such relationships are more open to manipulation and betrayal – by the researcher as well as by the researched. The line between gossip, chat, a research interview, the exchange of information and opinions melts into 'data'; the formal parameters of the research interview can burst boundaries as interviews are continued via chats by the coffee or photocopy machine. These encounters provide an opportunity to achieve genuine insights into the unfolding nature of organizational processes and human projects. Yet, ultimately, such words and talk become 'data', in that the 'lives, loves, and tragedies that fieldwork informants share with a researcher are ultimately data, grist for the ethnographic mill, a mill that has a truly grinding power' (Stacey, 1988: 23). The opportunities to blur relational and spatial boundaries in a research setting where the researcher is already an established member are manifold and tempting.

In other words, the researcher's task is to 'appropriate' the words and meanings of 'other people' with a view to turning them into written texts (thesis, reports, papers, articles). In my own experience, I have (not in my own organization) researched the consequences of flexible working from the perspectives of flexible workers and their families, their team leaders, senior managers and a host of other organizational stakeholders. There were occasions during this research project when, while listening sympathetically to the stories of flexible workers, I found myself thinking: 'this is a great quote for the paper on the hidden consequences of flexible work'. It is, in my view, inevitable that a researcher will 'objectify' a research participant at the very latest when 'data' are turned into written texts. As researchers who are researching their own organizations, such appropriation and objectification can be even more problematic as relationships continue to exist beyond the end of the research project, i.e. 'exiting the field' is not an easy option to evade potential conflicts and the complexities of 'tangled' relationships. On the contrary, the political and emotional dimensions of fieldwork and writing up fieldwork (Atkinson, 1990) become highlighted as the 'detachment' of the researcher from the research scene and its inhabitants is non-existent. Also, in transforming one's observations and interview data into written texts, the thoughts and meanings of the researched are opened up to public gaze and the scrutiny (and not even in 'their own words' and on 'their own terms', but through the interpretive filters of the researcher) not only of scholars and academics, but potentially also of their managers and bosses, their peers and (work) friends. This exposure is inevitable as the purpose of research will be to produce permanent, systematic and written accounts of the (empirical) study.

Field Roles – Between Familiarity and Strangeness

The question of which role to take on when conducting empirical research is of crucial importance for the researcher as this choice will influence how to engage with the researched or which parts of the organization one has access to or not. For researchers whose inquiry is set in their own organizational contexts, there are automatically several roles to be considered here. They are researchers as well as employees, managers, bosses, occupational experts, colleagues and friends. These different roles are sometimes hard to keep apart and in terms of conducting research in one's own setting it is not possible to enter and exit the field in the same way as an 'outsider' could do. Typologies for field roles for the researcher have been identified and discussed for many years (Gold, 1958; Junker, 1960; Adler and Adler, 1987). It is still useful to consider which role is appropriate along a continuum of conducting covert/overt research, to assess degrees of engagement/detachment from the research scene and subjectivity/objectivity in the production of research accounts (see Hammersley and Atkinson, 1995: 80–124 for an in-depth discussion). These roles can be dotted along a continuum between 'complete participant', 'participant-as-observer', 'observer-as-participant' and 'complete observer'. Scholars researching their own organization may be complete participants in terms of their employee roles and in this regard they will bring their experiences and perspectives to the scholarly inquiry. Indeed, in many instances there will have been a public announcement or acknowledgement that they are conducting a research project in the organization, so that a complete (and thus covert) participation is not possible. As researchers they are therefore more likely to 'participate and observe'. This juggling of an employee role with a researcher role requires a degree of emotional and intellectual flexibility in terms of handling researcher engagement with the research scene. Yet such flexibility needs to be balanced with having a firm stance about modes of engagement with the researched who may have developed different perspectives of what it means to be both a colleague and a research participant. They, for example, might differentiate between information provided in a research interview that can be used for research purposes, and informal exchanges over a cup of tea or coffee that they assume are 'personal' and not meant to be reproduced as 'quotes' in papers and texts.

Returning to Agar's (1980) notions of familiarity and strangeness, these can be drawn on to appreciate the precarious balancing act researchers in their own organizations have to maintain in order to gain access to the information/ data/meaning they require so that they can address their research concerns while maintaining good relationships with their respondents. Familiarity is linked to a pre-engagement with the research scene and its inhabitants, with perceptions, perspectives and views that have been acquired through processes of occupational and organizational socialization. Strangeness is usually associated with entering the research setting as an outsider and the research process is seen as a process to render what is puzzling, new and 'strange' into something that is understood, meaningful and to be made sense of within selected academic conventions and traditions. Being both employee and researcher this process is somewhat different and less linear compared to entering a field as an 'outsider-researcher'. Researching one's own organization requires managing a simultaneous familiarity and strangeness in a way that focuses on addressing research issues. The researcher process entails asking questions about what is familiar and why; and how to render the familiar strange and novel in order to deepen the understanding of organizational processes. If the 'normal' (researcher entering research scene as stranger) process of research is to transform the 'unfamiliar' and 'strange' into the 'known' and 'familiar', the research process for the researcher-employee is reversed: the challenge is to transform the 'familiar' and 'known' into the 'strange' and 'unknown', with a view to generating a different and more informed understanding of the issues under investigation.

Isn't This a Bit Too Close to Home?[1] Experiences of Researching One's Own Organization

'Isn't it a bit close too home?' was a comment a colleague made when it had been announced via the email system that I was going to conduct research work for my doctoral thesis within my then employer, a university in the UK. This was uttered in passing as part of a corridor conversation; it nevertheless made me reflect about my involvement with the research scene and the organization I was about to explore in depth.

The background and rationale for my research were based on a deeply personal purpose, which was to resolve the 'linguistic confusion' I experienced at the time of entry into the organization and for many years afterwards. Both private and professional reasons had brought me, a German national steeped in the traditions of the humanities and the arts, to the UK, and my professional socialization fell into a period of change in the UK higher education sector as it expanded from an elite system to a mass education system. I experienced my socialization time as long and difficult as I could not make sense of certain words such as 'the student-customer', 'internal markets' or 'portfolio of activities'. Today I can theorize such introduction of new words and concepts as a discursive shift concomitant with a redefinition of the purpose of higher education and universities. However, back then I was not able to 'theorize' my confusion, despite being technically competent in the use of the English language and functioning well at work. Thus, my experience of trying to make sense of my own sector and circumstances provided the motivational basis for the selection of my broad research topic, which was to find out how 'language work' was essential to an understanding of organizational and cultural processes. My aim was to observe and record language use over a prolonged period of time. In the early stages, my main intent was to combine the pursuit of doctoral studies with the resolution of my 'puzzlement' and 'linguistically confused state'. In doing so, I also intended to make a contribution to the then expanding field of language-sensitive studies set in the context of work organizations.

---

[1]No talk data that are directly related to my PhD thesis will be used in this chapter. Narrating my account of the research process, I draw on memory only. This does reflect the meaning of what was said, rather than using the words that were uttered. This is partly to protect my former colleagues, but also to make the point that much of what we write about we retrieve from memory.

Initial perceptions of research

Following the announcement of my intent to research language-based organizational processes colleagues commented on my project. These remarks were
mainly expressing interest and support, with some 'mild fun' being dispensed
at times as my research interest in language was seen to be curious and intriguing as well as a little bit 'odd' and 'unworldly'. My position as a junior member
of the faculty, together with my choice of research which was seen as slightly
out of sync with the faculty's ambition and strategic drive, resulted in my being
perceived as 'non-threatening' in terms of the information I might require. In
many regards this worked to my advantage as observing quite senior management meetings, gaining access to documentation and arranging to talk to colleagues were easy to organize. In making field notes and conducting my
research, my data collection proceeded nicely. Concomitant with the empirical
work, my reading of the literature progressed and in particular David Lodge's
(1977) *The Modes of Modern Writing* and Lakoff and Johnson's (1980) *Metaphors
We Live By* provided theoretical trajectories that proved invaluable for the latter
stages when I began to theorize my experiences and findings in terms of metaphorical (learning, developing, changing) and metonymical (ordering, categorizing, normalizing) processes.

Relationship with the researched

I want to use three examples that brought to the fore some dilemmas I faced
in conducting my research. Partly, these experiences – and some difficulties –
reflect a degree of naivety when I embarked on my project as I genuinely
thought of my doctoral work as 'only' seeking understanding and developing conceptual advancement, rather than being embedded in political and
power structures. However, let it be stated here that overall the experience of
conducting research into my own organization was a positive one and colleagues were generous with their time, their willingness to speak freely, and
also their desire to be quoted and 'heard'.

Relationship with senior managers

I sat in and observed senior management meetings in order to understand
how 'words and meanings' were used and generated, by whom and in which
contexts. Here, the relationship worked quite well. Being a junior member of
staff (and female as opposed to the all male senior management team at the

time) was helpful as colleagues liked to chat before or after meetings; sometimes they offered their particular interpretation of events or people or even added further comments and views. In one instance, it was expressed to me that my work ought to contribute to 'getting the message across' (i.e. how faculty needed to change), which I saw as a mild form of using my research to suit a particular interest. However, in my view no stronger or more direct attempts to influence my research were made.

At the stages of writing up my research and consequent publications however there was more interference, as I had to provide, for example, papers to a particular senior manager to be inspected. There was never a direct attempt to change or even comment on my papers, yet I was also asked to ensure that my written thesis would remain confidential for a period of two years as a minimum. Towards the end and nearer the writing-up period of my research, a degree of 'edginess' surrounding my research became more tangible and my realization grew that a language-focused project was no longer perceived as innocent and harmless as it had been in its early stages. At a 'PhD student conference' at which I presented some findings, the attending professors commented about the academic merit of the work. Afterwards I remember being advised to be careful about how I would handle the data and how I would use these. While relations with senior managers I met with at other times to discuss the written outputs remained cordial, there was also an undertone of wariness and nervousness in the conversations I had with them.

Peer relationships

Mainly, I worked with colleagues and peers; happily drifting between my research and employee identity, both developing and changing in the light of their mutual enactment.

There were two such relationships with colleagues, which triggered in me feelings of unease and tension. The first instance relates to two colleagues who were of similar age to me, yet much more advanced in career terms, as they had achieved senior and strategic positions in the faculty. They were using 'words' in different ways from other colleagues and therefore I wanted to understand their perspectives on the faculty and the university. My internalized norms required me to see them as peers and equals, friendly colleagues with whom I shared a certain socialization experience. Yet, mainly I felt inadequate and somehow 'not up to scratch' when comparing myself to them. In one case I decided not to seek this colleague out for a further interview – although she clearly symbolized a new model of career and 'talk' in the newly emergent faculty structures. I can now look at my choice and see it as an unease about or inability to deal with the simultaneous existence of hierarchical differences, peer relationships, gender and age dimensions. Yet, at the time I simply decided 'not to go there' and in research terms my decision implied the exclusion of particular perspectives and interpretations from my work.

Another emotionally fraught relationship concerned a colleague with whom I taught on a module. My 'problem' was that I did not respect this colleague very much, as the teaching relationship was difficult and characterized by differences about assessments. However, this colleague was helpful to the extent of volunteering himself as a potential interviewee. I felt unable to decline his offer. The specific interview with him was long and long-winded, in my view. Yet from this interview I used many of his interpretations and views later on when revisiting my scripts and when theorizing this experience, as some of his views entailed almost poetic comments and summaries on his painful experiences of changing contexts and meanings in the context of higher education.

Peer relationships: betrayal

In the final stages of my research I asked some female colleagues whether they would work with me to capture the particular view of women on the change process in higher education and the university. I had made it clear to them that I intended to take notes and write a conference paper based on my findings. The meeting went well, it was cordial and chatty, many a story was told and views were exchanged freely. Having turned my interpretation of this event into a conference paper and before submitting it to the conference convenors, I sent it to these colleagues for their perusal. Not expecting much in terms of comments, I was taken by surprise by some of the reactions, which were bordering on the fierce and requested changes to the paper or for particular contributions and involvements to be completely removed. There were also arguments pointing out that the paper was 'only' my interpretations and therefore not a 'true' account of what my colleagues had said and in particular what they had meant by their words. While relationships did not break down in the context of the 'group interview', there was a definite 'cooling off' and a general increase in wariness between colleagues and myself. I remember having to work hard at the time in order to appease and alleviate their fears, while feeling at the same time misunderstood and hard done by. Ultimately, this paper was never made publicly available.

Reflections

Overall and with hindsight these events point to the emotional, gendered and political nature of fieldwork – a fact I had read about as part of my literature review, but that I had not associated with my 'harmless' study of words and meanings.

First, my 'juniority' in the hierarchy of the faculty helped me to gain access to meetings, information and participants' perspectives. Here, my relatively junior status was overall helpful and in particular for capturing the views of senior management. Yet, the insecurities related to my junior status when talking to two particular colleagues similar in age, yet much senior in terms of their hierarchical position, resulted in my decision not to seek a closer collaborative relationship with one of them – thus potentially limiting a source of useful and meaningful information. It is only in writing this chapter, many years after the completion of my doctoral thesis, that I have realized it was the female of these two colleagues whom I found more troublesome to work with – a reflection of gendered relationships, perhaps, in particular the female–female ones?

Second, the further my work proceeded and took shape, and the nearer thoughts and ideas came to be expressed in a thesis and papers, the more complicated and precarious the research process became. Writing research accounts is part of the scholarly project and it renders permanence, consequence and substance to 'insubstantial talk' and 'ideas'. This transformative process makes research potentially dangerous to participants as their words and speech translate into interpretations and written accounts. They become re-appropriated in contexts that are embedded in political and power structures. Frequently, issues of the re-appropriation of meaning come to the fore at the early stages of research when access is negotiated (and frequently declined). Yet in my particular case, it was at the later stages of the research process when the 'permanence' and 'consequence' of the written text provoked reactions. Also, these reactions at the time appeared to me exaggerated, unfair even, because after all I had informed all participants that I was working as a researcher and that therefore their spoken words might be turned into written accounts. Yet writing today, I can see colleagues' reactions as being informed by a different rationality: when reading my written interpretation of their words, they responded within their particular contexts, which went far beyond the confines of the chatty, animated meeting with colleagues as the written account evoked the political, ongoing and precarious contexts of their everyday lives. They also responded epistemologically by pointing to the notion of my account 'only' being my interpretation and as such 'not true'. The reactions were emotional, possibly driven by nervousness, yet they also indicated a sense of the betrayal my interpretation had caused, as colleagues felt that I had used their personal involvement and friendly relationships for academic gain without taking their positions and contexts into account.

Third, emotions, my own and those of colleagues, played a continuous part in the research process. In this regard the research process is an emotional process, which using reflective hindsight is related to the blurring of boundaries between myself as researcher and as employee, each of which required different dispositions and modes of engagement with the researched. At the same time the researched made themselves available as informants and participants, but they also remained colleagues, allies, friends or foes. In blurring such boundaries interesting data may be collected – albeit too easily at the expense of relationships that will have to last beyond the temporal parameters of a research project.

In addition, my own emotional disposition *vis-à-vis* colleagues was laid bare as the research process forced me to face some home truths about my own gendered behaviour and my sometimes contradictory position about balancing my academic and organizational ambition with a tempered view of preserving some scepticism and distance about career advancement. With hindsight, I can see myself now at a crucial stage of my career and life, where I had to decide what kind of academic I wanted to become and at what cost. Thus, my own precarious sensibilities were played out through the enactment of the dual role of researcher/colleague for a while.

In my view the greatest challenge of this mode of engagement is to establish and protect meaningful and authentic relationships in the light of the possibility of exercising 'symbolic violence' that implies the manipulative engagement of those one involves in the research.

Generating Knowledge: Experiences Recollected in Tranquillity

In my work, past and present, acts of theorizing have helped me to achieve a degree of detachment from the emotional dilemmas and encounters of fieldwork.

In the case of my doctoral work, theorizing was not only a necessity to make sense of the data, it also removed me from the research setting, from colleagues, from politics, and an emotional entanglement with people. The process of developing conceptual understanding requires abstracting oneself from the immediate context, so that in writing one oscillates between experience, pure and raw, and reflection, pure and calm. In my doctoral work, I experienced an aloofness when analysing my fieldwork notes. To an extent, the analytic process was a more peaceful period in which the emergence of conceptual understanding replaced the immediate experience of relationships and vested interests. Briefly, my theorizing addressed the budding interest of organizational scholars in rhetorical figures, in particular metaphors, but also in metonymy and irony. Thus the development of a 'tropological approach' in order to understand language use and meaning making in one organizational setting was my theoretical contribution to knowledge. Personally, at the end of my doctoral thesis, my initial experience of linguistic confusion had been addressed. I could now describe my confusion more concisely and in terms that allowed me to resolve it. A year after my completion of the thesis, I left the organization as part of a career move. Most of the relationships I formed in these early and difficult years have remained cordial and conflicts and tensions have become part of a mutually shared past.

Guidelines for Qualitative Researchers

Following on from the lessons learned, there is some advice I can offer to researchers embarking on a project set in the context of their employing organization. It mainly entails aspects for developing awareness of the emotional aspects of relationships, their management over time and beyond the research project's temporal boundaries. It also relates to the acknowledgement of one's own views, as well as emotional and social dispositions.

- Your research is informed by your background and situation and these form the bedrock of your research from the articulation of themes, topics and questions to the design and execution of the empirical work and also to writing your accounts. As you are the research instrument par excellence, you form part of your own inquiry. Be aware and honest about how such involvement may frame how you formulate and execute your research and also how you write about it.

- Researching includes the production of written accounts and making them available to the world. There are two issues to consider here: a) which authorial voice you will adopt, i.e. from which position will you write your account; b) how any written account bestows permanence to your research and is subject to readers' interpretation. This renders a written account potentially dangerous to participants and to yourself. Other than adhering to the ethical guidelines of your employer/professional body (e.g. adhering to the rules about confidentiality and anonymity), how will you protect those involved in the research (see also Holt, in this volume)?

- Following on from there, your engagement with the researched will bring into play dual identities played out by yourself, the researcher-employee, and the researched colleagues. The blurring of boundaries between roles and identities is perhaps the most beneficial aspect of researching one's own organization. At the same time it is also the most difficult one as such blurring may lead to unclear situations, implicit expectations and assumptions about the research process and outcome.

- Emotions form part of the research process. At times the 'emotionality' of engagement may take forms that can be both highly conducive or highly detrimental to the achievement of your research aims. In the first instance, you need to be aware of your own emotions and manage them as a normal and sensitizing process of your research.

- The role of theory and conceptual work is part and parcel of the academic project. In addition, the abstracting and analytical framing of data in the vocabularies and meaning systems of particular traditions can assist in rendering 'strange' the 'all-too-familiar' and the 'all-too-emotional'. The use of theory can be activated almost as a Brechtian alienation effect to counter-balance the familiarity and closeness concomitant with researching one's own organization with a measure of intellectual detachment.

Conclusion

Research enquiry is positioned in the tension between what is 'familiar' and what is 'strange'. Much of our understanding of what good research is about centres on the assumption that good research makes the 'strange' more 'familiar' and known. This assumption is, perhaps, in itself debatable as one always brings pre-supposition and pre-knowledge to the research scene, so that what the researcher already knows and assumes is an intrinsic part of any enquiry. Yet, in cases where researchers investigate their own (employing) organization, the research process is to an extent reversed, i.e. it is about making the 'familiar' 'strange'. In doing so, research questions, issues and objectives become entangled in blended identities and relationships within social, emotional and gendered contexts of hierarchy and power. Developing the reflective awareness and ability to address such contexts is part of becoming a researcher and is particularly so in the context of researching one's own organization.

Further Reading

In his (1994) book *Language Shock: Understanding the Culture of Conversation* Michael Agar proposes that language and culture are inseparably linked. Understanding one's own assumptions about language use, conversation and knowledge is linked to an understanding of language use as a social and cultural practice. The book is helpful in introducing different theoretical approaches to understanding language and developing language-sensitive, theoretically grounded approaches to research projects.

Paul Atkinson's (1990) *The Ethnographic Imagination* points to the importance of writing research accounts and the construction of texts as deliberately shaped knowledge accounts. This includes the conventions and expectations of audiences who might read these accounts. It is helpful to appreciate the importance and processes of writing research accounts.

Howard Becker's volume of essays, *Sociological Work* (1970), contains one essay titled 'Whose side are you on?'. Here, Becker proposes that every researcher takes sides and that this is a normal, but often denied part of social science research. This essay helped me to acknowledge and accept my involvement and the perspectives in my research.

In Bridge and Baxter's (1992) 'Blended relationships: Friends as work associates', the authors provide interesting examples, based on their empirical research, about working with friends, who are also research respondents.

Jennifer Moon's (2004) *A Handbook of Reflective and Experiential Learning* is an instructive text on learning and reflection and can be related easily to the researcher's experience. It also provides useful inputs on reflective writing, including the use of diaries and logs – these may be techniques that can be drawn upon to keep a record of the research process.

For a good variety of chapters on different aspects of the researcher and author-self and their involvement in auto-ethnographic writing, see Deborah Reed-Danahay's (1997) edited volume, *Autho/Ethnography: Rewriting the Self and the Social*.

John Van Maanen's (1988) *Tales of the Field: On Writing Ethnography* offers different approaches to writing ethnographic accounts, based on different epistemological positions and therefore employing different rhetorical means of persuasion. It is a stimulating text to read and helpful in providing ideas about how writing research accounts, and how to cope, rhetorically, with issues of researcher involvement.

T.J. Watson's (1995) 'Rhetoric, discourse and argument in organizational sense making: a reflexive tale' is a research account based on an ethnographic study of a company in the UK. The author worked there for a long period of time and the account is a good example of a style of writing which makes the author's voice central to the account and also 'reveals' how his thinking shaped the interpretation and analysis of data.

References

Adler, P.A. and Adler, P. (1987) *Membership Roles in Field Research*. Newbury Park, CA: Sage.

Agar, M. (1980) *The Professional Stranger.* Chicago: University of Chicago Press.

Agar, M. (1994) *Language Shock. Understanding the Culture of Conversation.* New York: William Morrow and Company, Inc.

Arendell, T. (1997) 'Reflections on the researcher-researched relationship: a woman interviewing men', *Qualitative Sociology*, 20 (3): 341–368.

Atkinson, P. (1990) *The Ethnographic Imagination: textual constructions of reality*. London: Routledge.

Becker, H. (1967) 'Whose side are you on?', *Social Problems*, 14 (3): 239–247.

Becker, H. (1970) *Sociological Work.* London.

Berger, P.L. and Luckman, T. (1966) *The Social Construction of Reality: A Treatise in the Sociology of Knowledge.* London: Penguin.

Bridge, K. and Baxter, L.A. (1992) 'Blended relationships: Friends as work associates', *Western Journal of Communication*, 56: 200–225.

Burr, V. (2003) *An Introduction to Social Constructionism* (2nd edn). Hove: Routledge.

Coffey, A. (1999) *The Ethnographic Self: Fieldwork and Representation of Identity.* London: Sage.

Cohen, L., Duberley, J. and Musson, G. (2009) 'Work-life balance? An autoethnographic exploration of everyday home-work dynamics', *Journal of Management Inquiry*, 18 (3): 229–241.

Costley, C., Elliott, G. and Gibbs, P. (2010) *Work-based Research: Approaches to Enquiry for Insider-Researcher*. London: Sage.

Cotterill, P. (2002) 'Interviewing women: issues of friendship, vulnerability and power', *Women's Studies International Forum*, 15: 593–606.

England, K.V.L. (1994) 'Getting personal: reflexivity, positionality, and feminist research', *The Professional Geographer*, 46 (1): 80–89.

Etherington, K. (2004) *Becoming a Reflexive Researcher: Using Our Selves in Research.* London and Philadelphia: Jessica Kinsley.

Fisher, C. and Tietze, S. (2010) 'Doctor of Business Administration: DBA Programmes in the UK', in T. Fell, K. Flint and I. Haines (eds), *Professional Doctorates in the UK*. Staffordshire: UK Council for Graduate Education, pp. 40–45.

Gold, R.L. (1958) 'Roles in sociological fieldwork', *Social Forces*, 36: 217–223.

Guba, E.G. and Lincoln, Y.S. (1981) *Effective Evaluation: Improving the Effectiveness of Evaluation Results through Responsive and Naturalistic Approaches*. San Francisco, CA: Jossey-Bass.

Hammersley, M. and Atkinson, P. (1995) *Ethnography: Principles in Practice* (2nd edn). London and New York: Routledge.

Hastrup, K. (1992) 'Writing ethnography', in J. Okely, and H. Callaway, (eds), *Anthropology and Autobiography*. London: Routledge, pp. 115–132.

Junker, B. (1960) *Field Work*. Chicago: University of Chicago Press.

Lakoff, G. and Johnson, M. (1980) *Metaphors We Live By*. London and Chicago: University of Chicago Press.

Lincoln, Y.S. and Guba, E.G. (1985) *Naturalistic Inquiry*. Beverly Hills, CA: Sage.

Lodge, D. (1977) *The Modes of Modern Writing: Metaphor, Metonymy and the Typology of Modern Literature*. London: Arnold.

Moon, J. (2004) *A Handbook of Reflective and Experiential Learning: Theory and Practice*. Oxford: Taylor and Francis.

Okely, J. and Callaway, H. (eds) (1992) *Anthropology and Autobiography*. London: Routlege.

Reed-Danahay, D. (ed.) (1997) *Autho/Ethnography: Rewriting the Self and the Social*. Oxford: Berg.

Stacey, J. (1988) 'Can there be a feminist ethnography?', *Women's Studies International Forum*, 11: 21–27.

Tietze, S., Cohen, L. and Musson, G. (2003) *Understanding Organizations Through Language*. London: Sage.

Van Maanen, J. (1988) *Tales of the Field: On Writing Ethnography*. Chicago: University of Chicago Press.

Watson, T.J. (1994) *In Search of Management: Culture, Chaos and Control in Managerial Work*. London: Routledge.

Watson, T.J. (1995) 'Rhetoric, discourse and argument in organizational sense making: a reflexive tale', *Organization Studies*, 6 (3): 805–821.

5 Reflexivity in Qualitative Research

Kathryn Haynes

Introduction

The term *reflexivity* is widely used in organizational research. The concept of reflexivity has been part of qualitative research methods in organizational research for a number of decades, so it is not a new phenomenon. However, as qualitative methods have become more prominent and more accepted within social science, reflexivity has increased in significance and has become embedded in debates about the nature of knowledge.

But what does reflexivity actually mean? How does it affect the way we approach research? And how is it applied in practice? This chapter will address these questions with a discussion of the meaning of reflexivity and its significance in organizational research, together with some examples of reflexive research practice.

What is Reflexivity?

In simple terms, reflexivity is an awareness of the researcher's role in the practice of research and the way this is influenced by the object of the research, enabling the researcher to acknowledge the way in which he or she affects both the research processes and outcomes. It is often termed as the process by which research turns back upon and takes account of itself (Weick, 2002; Alvesson et al., 2008), described by Clegg and Hardy (1996: 4) as 'ways of seeing which act back on and reflect existing ways of seeing'. Reflexivity involves an aware-ness that the researcher and the object of study affect each other mutually and continually in the research process (Alvesson and Sköldberg, 2000). In other words, researcher reflexivity involves thinking about how our thinking came to be, how a pre-existing understanding is constantly revised in the light of new understandings and how this in turn affects our research.

Some researchers may query the difference between reflection and reflex-ivity. Hibbert et al. (2010) provide a useful distinction between the two: that reflection suggests a mirror image which affords the opportunity to engage in an observation or examination of our ways of doing, or observing our own practice, whereas reflexivity is more complex, involving thinking about our experiences and questioning our ways of doing. Alvesson and Sköldberg (2000) suggest there are two key elements embedded within reflexive research – interpretation *and* reflection. The interpretive element recognizes that interpretation is not just based on a simple analysis of facts or data, which reflects some kind of 'reality'; instead it is aware that interpretation is influenced by the assumptions of the researcher doing the research, their values, political position, use of language. They suggest it calls for the utmost awareness of theoretical assumptions, the importance of language and of pre-understandings brought to the research. The second element is reflection – where the researcher turns the attention onto themselves, their research community and their intellectual and cultural conditions and tradi-tions informing the research. Reflection becomes a form of interpretation of the interpretation and this is what makes the research reflexive. We reflect on how our intellectual, perceptual, theoretical, ideological, cultural, textual and cognitive principles and assumptions inform the interpretation. For Cunliffe the distinction between a reflective analysis and critical reflexive questioning relates to assumptions about the nature of reality: 'a reflective analysis draws on traditional assumptions that there is an objective reality that we can analyse using logic and theory, whereas reflexivity draws on social constructionist assumptions to highlight subjective, multiple con-structed realities' (2004: 414).

Hence, reflexivity goes beyond a simple reflection on the research process and its outcomes, to incorporate multiple layers and levels of reflection within the research. These would include considering the complex relation-ships between the production of knowledge (epistemology), the processes of knowledge production (methodology), and the involvement and impact of the knowledge producer or researcher (ontology). Reflexivity enables the research processes and outcomes to be open to change and adaptive in response to these multiple layers of reflection.

Conceptualizing Reflexivity

Conceptualizations of reflexivity will therefore vary according to the researcher's own epistemological and ontological assumptions (see also Duberley, Johnson and Cassell, in this volume).

An objectivist view assumes a form of pre-existing social reality, which can be researched by an independent researcher, where what is described exists independent of the researcher's description of it. An account of reality mirrors reality. Hence, reflexivity may be used as a technique or tool for evaluating the role of the researcher in the research process, often with a view to eradicating bias in research design and analysis, in order to maintain the objective position of the researcher. Often, fieldwork confessions are utilized to account for the field roles adopted by the researcher in the research, and as a means of ensuring analytical distance by avoiding over familiarity and maintaining sufficient detachment. The self (researcher) and the other (researched) are considered as independent entities. However, this view might be deemed to consider only the method and not the ontological and epistemological assumptions that underlie it.

A subjectivist view questions the independent existence of reality and the researcher's role in researching it, suggesting that knowledge is socially constructed. The researcher's interpretation and representation of reality through their research therefore actively creates reality. Hence, reflexivity is used here to question knowledge claims and enhance understanding by acknowledging the values and preconceptions the researcher brings to that understanding. Within ethnomethodological approaches, such as interpretative research, insights can be drawn from 'pre-understanding', i.e. 'knowledge, insights, and experience before [engaging in] a research program', and 'understanding', i.e. 'knowledge that develops during the program' (Gummeson, 1991: 50), such that prior knowledge, experience and new knowledge interact. For postmodernists, the social construction of reality is constituted within discursive and textual practices, where no fixed truths are privileged and a number of fluid, emergent and multiple truths may emerge. Hence, reflexivity is often centred on the process of writing and interpreting text, in all its various and multiple forms.

Cunliffe's conceptualization of 'radical-reflexivity' suggests that researchers 'need to go further than questioning the truth claims of others, to question how we as researchers (and practitioners) also make truth claims and construct meaning' (2003: 985). Such a view of reflexivity goes beyond advocating reflexivity as a 'tool' for more effective research and tends more towards a lived moral or ethical project (Cunliffe, 2003; 2004). So for Cunliffe (2003: 991), a construction of radical-reflexivity comprises:

- 'Questioning our intellectual suppositions.

- Recognizing research is a symmetrical and reflexive narrative, a number of "Participant" stories which interconnect in some way.

- Examining and exploring researcher/participant relationships and their impact on knowledge.

- Acknowledging the constitutive nature of our research conversations.

- Constructing "emerging practical theories" rather than objective truths.

- Exposing the situated nature of accounts through narrative circularity.

- Focusing on life and research as a process of becoming rather than an already established truth'.

Processes of Reflexivity

A number of researchers have considered the process of reflexivity. Hibbert et al. (2010) evaluated the importance of recursion, or a sense of return, in the process of reflexivity, whereby questioning the basis of our reflections reflexivity necessarily brings about change in the process of reflection and is therefore recursive. They describe four steps that collectively encapsulate a meta-process of reflexivity, which integrates reflection and recursion. The initial step is *repetition*, in which an individual reflects in a relatively self-focused manner and recursivity occurs passively. This is followed by *extension*, where there is 'some building of new principles or understandings that connect with well-known principles' (2010: 53) with a conscious involvement in change. There then follows *disruption*, which captures the doubting, unsettling element of reflexive research, as opposed to the routine or confirmatory modes of repletion and extension. Finally, *participation* describes 'the situation where the researcher engages with a particular community and [is] transformed by it' (2010: 56). Not every conceptualization of reflexive research would go so far as the disruptive, but the notion of self-critique and an unsettling effect is common in many reflexive accounts, as basic assumptions and values are challenged and ultimately potentially transformed. It is in such moments that ontology and epistemology interact, questioning both the self and knowledge. Reflexivity forces the researcher to re-examine his or her positioning in relation to methodology, theory, participants and the self. Moreover, in participatory research, especially co-produced research between researchers and practitioners, the significance of politics, hierarchy and authority in co-production is central to reflexive understandings of the dynamics in play (Orr and Bennett, 2009).

Tensions and Limitations in Reflexivity

Notwithstanding, or perhaps because of, the variety of approaches to conceptualizing reflexivity, there are tensions within and criticisms of reflexive research. Lynch (2000), for example, argues against reflexivity as an academic virtue and source of privileged knowledge, questioning the way reflexivity is used to promote a theoretical and methodological advantage. Others have noted the tendency for reflexivity to be perceived as narcissism or naval-gazing (Weick, 2002; Cunliffe, 2004; Tomkins and Eatough, 2010). In reflexive practice, the occasional confessional nature of reflexivity may stand in a tension with self-indulgence, such that Fournier and Grey have argued that there is a tendency 'to privilege the voice of the author, while the subjects of organizational life are effaced, or kept at a distance' (2000: 22). Similarly, the *process* of conducting reflexive research may become more central than the content of the research itself. Cunliffe notes that the danger of 'talking about reflexivity while being unreflexive' lies in not recognizing the situatedness of our position as researchers, an issue that she argues can be overcome through the use of radical reflectivity which highlights the tentative nature of theories and explanations and surfaces our fallibility as researchers (2003: 986).

Alvesson et al. (2008) provide a comprehensive critique of four sets of reflexive practices that they find commonly appear in organization and management literature, together with their limitations. Firstly, *multi-perspective practices* occur when the researcher uses tensions among different perspectives to expose assumptions and open up new ways of thinking, using reflexivity to complement 'incomplete' research. However, the strategies for selecting particular perspectives may be unclear, and the particular ways in which the perspectives are juxtaposed remain contested. Secondly, *multi-voicing practices* focus on the authorial authority of the researcher and their relation to the 'other', the research subject, in the interests of reflexivity being used to redress the balance between research and subject. However, Alvesson et al. suggest that there is a paradoxical danger where attempts to 'downplay' the researcher actually draw all the attention towards the researcher. Thirdly, *positioning practices* draw attention to the various political, cultural and institutional constraints embedded in the academic community, in the interest of using reflexivity to reveal the role of institutional forces. However, in showing how reflexive researchers can navigate supposedly inescapable social forces, Alvesson et al. suggest that these practices help construct the heroic researcher that they are trying to repudiate, which leads to a highly individualistic explanation of knowledge production. Fourthly, *destabilizing practices* occur when the researcher is 'disruptive', often using reflexivity to cross-examine or point out a lack of reflexivity on the part of others, in order to unsettle or undermine the foundations of research. However, such practices may be limited in their ability to generate new knowledge (Alvesson et al., 2008). Nonetheless, in critiquing reflexivity, Alvesson et al. call for its use in a 'route to more thoughtful and interesting research' (2008: 498).

Hence, a researcher engaging in reflexive research may encounter tensions in the extent of self-disclosure and focus on processes of research. Nevertheless, reflexivity enables research to be insightful, questioning, intersubjective and transparent on a number of different levels. Having defined reflexivity and discussed its conceptualization, processes and tensions, the following sections will put some of these ideas into focus through the use of examples drawn from research practice. I shall draw upon my own research projects on the gendered experience and embodiment of women in the accounting and professional services context, to illustrate some of the ways of doing and writing reflexive qualitative research.

Conducting Reflexive Research

While the importance of *being* reflexive is acknowledged, and indeed promoted, in qualitative research into organizations and management, the actual practice of reflexive research is less clear. So how do we actually go about it in practice?

There are some choices to be made about how reflexivity is enacted in practice. We might, for example, be aware of 'seeing oneself in the data' (Weick, 2002: 894) at a number of different levels. As researchers we should try to be aware of how our ontological, social and political positioning affects the work that we do by informing the choices we make about research topics, questions, approaches, methodologies and outcomes. We might ask ourselves:

- What is the motivation for undertaking this research?

- What underlying assumptions I am bringing to it?

- How am I connected to the research, theoretically, experientially, emotionally? And what effect will this have on my approach?

Example – motivations for research

My research project attempted to examine the identity politics of women accountants in the UK, particularly the social organization of the accounting profession and its interaction with their experiences of motherhood (Haynes, 2005). It considered three interconnected areas, identity, motherhood and accounting, to explore whether interrelations between these were embedded within gendered processes, and the implications of these for women's identity construction. Accordingly, it also aimed to contribute to theoretical understandings of personal and professional identity, and the social structures of motherhood and accounting, with potential implications for the cultural and political practices within them.

Despite these theoretical, academic aims, I actually had some much more personal aims. I wanted to try to understand, as part of a personal process of self-discovery, how I came to be myself, as a woman, mother, accountant and academic, with the myriad sensibilities that all these beings entail. The very nature of being human enables most of us at some time to speculate about who and what we are. How did I become myself? Is what I take to be myself my *real* self? Is there any such thing as a real self? What is the essence of my being and how has it been shaped by cultural and political forces? Why do I feel I want to be a 'good' mother? How important is my career to my sense of self? It was the desire to try to gain a better understanding of myself, or rather all the selves described above, that was the personal impetus behind the research.

In my project, the academic and personal aims were very much intertwined. Not all research projects have such a personal motivation as this did, nor do they need to. Reflexive research does not require a desire for personal or individual understanding, but it does require sensitivity on the part of the researcher as to how their self, preconceptions and sensibilities will influence the research. It is important to acknowledge and articulate the varied motivations, theoretical and/or personal, underpinning any research, as these are likely to shape the way the research is conceived, carried out, interpreted and produced. Such issues reflect the ontological position and identity of the researcher, which will influence the choice of theoretical position, methodological approach and interpretive rationale.

Strategies for Reflexive Awareness

There are a number of strategies for enabling this process of reflection, which then becomes a reflexive process, incorporating the reflections into reflexive knowledge production:

- Write down any theoretical assumptions and presuppositions about the subject of the research and revisit these throughout the research process, noting how these may have shifted.

- Consider if or how this has revised the research question, focus or findings.

- Keep a research diary noting down thoughts and feelings about the research process.

- Keep fieldwork notes of observations, interactions, incidents, conversations, emotions and responses.

- Listen to tape recordings or watch video clips of your qualitative data gathering (interviews, focus groups, life histories, etc.) noting how your presence or interaction as the researcher affected the process.

- Discuss and evaluate responses to the research subject, participants and process with fellow researchers.

The following example draws upon the use of fieldwork notes and a reflexive account of the process of conducting a research interview.

Example – managing oral history interviews

My research project used an oral history methodology to explore the detailed life experiences of women accountants (Haynes, 2005). One of the participants, Deborah, was an audit partner in an accounting firm, who initially gave me what seemed like some kind of sales pitch about the value of accounting and the nature of her firm, such as might be given to a prospective client. Deborah appeared to be reluctant to speak about herself in any depth and I began to think that the meeting was not going to be particularly worthwhile for my research. As I explained that I was interested in the experiences of women who, like myself, were accountants and mothers, Deborah took a deep breath and interrupted me forcefully. The tone and pace of the conversation changed dramatically, being much less measured and far more personal. Deborah then gave a frank and somewhat heart-rending account of her experiences and her struggles managing her new identity as a mother and her pre-existing identity as an audit partner, between her unanticipated passion for caring for her child and her loyalties to her clients. Deborah's emotional account left us both moved and near to tears at times. I felt that she saw me as another mother to whom she could unburden herself rather than as a researcher. She appeared to value the opportunity to discuss some of her problems with someone from outside the accounting firm or her family, all of whom appeared to be implicated in any decisions about how she conducted her life and working arrangements. I noted in my fieldwork diary immediately afterwards:

> Despite her apparent primness at first, I liked Deborah and genuinely wished her well. This was much more like a conversation than an oral history interview and I wonder whether she will regret saying any of this later. But she seemed to value the opportunity to get it all off her chest … This was definitely a therapeutic opportunity for her. She is so raw and emotional and needing to talk things through.

Deborah also probed me quite hard about my own experiences, as if she were eager for knowledge about ways of coping with what she saw as a problematic situation, being a working mother, as this further extract from my fieldwork diary illustrates:

> Deborah wanted to know a lot about what *I* thought and how *I* coped, and what other issues had derived from other women's experiences … I felt guilty that I could not help her more.

Deborah's probing went on to feel more like an interrogation of me at one stage, to the extent that she asked some deeply personal questions of me. For example, although she stated that she did not intend to have any more children, she was very interested in my account of having more than one child and whether I desired to have more, as if she were still affirming her own decisions. As I was trying to follow a feminist research paradigm, in which it is often argued that self-disclosure during the research is good practice because it puts women participants at their ease (Reinharz, 1992), and as she had been so open with me, I felt some sense of obligation to respond and reciprocate. However, my disclosures here impinged on my unresolved sense of self, and left me feeling emotionally vulnerable. I did not want to discuss some of the issues she was confronting me with, as they left me feeling emotionally raw, just as she was. I was concerned about the implications of becoming too self-analytical myself, not only from the perspective of how it made me feel on a personal level, but also in my role as a researcher with the need to remain in control of myself and my conduct. Whereas Deborah appeared to find the meeting therapeutic, contacting me afterwards to say how helpful she had found it to talk through her life history, decisions and doubts, I found myself weeping after leaving our meeting (Haynes, 2006).

Given that reflexivity means interpreting one's own interpretations, the field notes, diary, observations and subsequent listening to tape recordings all facilitated this process.

Multiple Levels of Reflexivity

Reflexivity occurs on a number of levels and on several different themes within, and arising from, these two accounts.

Theoretical reflexivity

Theoretical assumptions may be revised as a result of research practice and engagement. Reflexive research does not assume a social reality simply exists 'out there' waiting to be discovered by the researcher; rather, it recognizes that all research is affected by the preconceptions, theoretical, methodological or ontological, which the researcher brings to the research and its interpretation. More importantly, our theoretical assumptions and understandings will be revised by the new understandings gained during the process of research, which will then go on to inform new theoretical knowledge. This is what has been termed a 'double hermeneutic' or the interpretation of interpreting subjects (Giddens, 1976, cited in Alvesson and Sköldberg, 2000: 247). In my example, engaging with theoretical perspectives on identity, the politics of motherhood and the sociology of the accounting profession gave me some new insights into my own identity and that of the research participants, which in turn informed new theoretical understandings.

Methodological reflexivity

Methodological position and detailed methods may be revised as researchers engage reflexively with the research process. By considering the effectiveness, conduct and process of data collection, researchers may reinterpret and revise their methodological position to take account of such issues as ethics, power relations or the use of language. In my example, if I felt as if I were being interrogated, how did the participant in the research feel about the process? What ethical issues arise from this situation and how can they be dealt with? How far is the research embedded in a series of complex power relations? Reflexivity enables the power relations in the research process to be more explicit and the researcher to be more aware of how he or she may be affecting or affected by the research process (Haynes, 2006). In my case, a feminist perspective informed the research and its methodological approach (Haynes, 2008). A theoretical position or paradigm may underpin the research, informing a particular methodological approach, but a reflexive researcher will always reflect on the interaction of theory and methodology to evaluate whether each should revise the other.

Ontological reflexivity

As researchers all of us will have our own ontological position, comprising of our perception of the nature of reality, our sense of reality, or the way we see the world. A reflexive research approach engages with our ontological position as well as our values and choices. As Calás and Smircich (1999: 664) argue:

> Whether we are involved in ethnography, or heavy statistics research, whether we are writing about institutional theory, population ecology,

organizational justice corporate mergers – whatever, no matter what topic or area or what methods we use – we are all … picking and choosing to pay attention and ignore … excluding, including, concealing, favoring some people, some topics, some questions, some forms of representation, some values. Can we do our writing in a way that is 'self-conscious' of our choices?

Being reflexive requires analysis of our ontological position, or view of reality, to make explicit these choices and the researcher's relationship with the research object. Hence, in my example, through the empirical fieldwork and listening to the oral history narratives, I came to know myself better by observing and reflecting on the experiences presented by others, and by reflexively reviewing my own experiences in the light of other's narratives. My aim to come to a deeper understanding of myself through the project was informed by the understandings I gained of others from the oral histories, and my greater understanding of myself informed those understandings of others, in an intersubjective analysis. The researcher's ontology links to, will influence and is influenced by theoretical positioning and methodology as he or she both acts within the research and is acted upon by it.

Emotional reflexivity

Emotion is also a valuable source of reflexive insight. The emotionalization of reflexivity refers to the process whereby individuals are increasingly drawing on emotions in assessing themselves and their lives, recognizing that emotions are crucial to how the social is reproduced and to enduring within a complex social world (Holmes, 2010). In my example, I could not gather and analyse the oral histories, where participants are being asked not only to relate facts about their lives but also to explore the very essence of their being, without engaging with emotional hurdles, whether my own or those of the participants. Not all research may provoke such an emotional response as this, but all researchers will feel some kind of response towards their research and/or their research participants. Whether it is frustration, sadness, fear, liking or loathing, it is undeniable that the research process engenders emotional responses. These can be used as a source of reflexive intellectual inquiry where the emotional sensibilities of the researcher can be used creatively and analytically to enhance the research process and outcomes. Thus, this methodological, reflexive approach recognizes the strong relationship between the process of research and the resultant product.

Cultural, social and political reflexivity

Reflexivity is also about understanding the relationship between individual practice and social structure, not only relating selves to social collectivities, but also recognizing the part that selves play in constructing structures as well as being mediated by them (Stanley, 1993), so that the researcher is aware of how he or she may 'inadvertently realign the issues that concern us with those of the relations of ruling' (Smith, 1992: 96). In other words, the very cultural, social and political discourse of the subject being researched could affect the way that the researcher treats and analyses the data derived on that subject. In my example, the discourses and ideologies of being a 'working mother', both positive and negative, are implicated in any interpretation I make of the oral history interview, which could either challenge or maintain those discourses. Researchers, therefore, need to maintain a reflexive awareness of whether their research interpretations make use of dominant cultural, social and political discourses, which in turn would perpetuate those dominant discourses.

Subjective reflexivity

A final level of reflexivity is related to this point. In many qualitative research projects, the researcher may effectively be both the subject and object of the research. In my case, this was explicitly expressed: I was a researcher investigating accountants who were mothers, and I was both an accountant and a mother. In other research projects this may not be so explicit, but organizational researchers may often research aspects of organizational life that they have experienced or observed. We may experience the tension of being both the subject and object of the research, and of working between the dualities of public social knowledge and private lived experience, by simultaneously serving an academic audience while also remaining faithful to forms of knowledge gained in domestic, personal and intimate settings (Haynes, 2008). We may also find ourselves on the margins of academic discourse, as part of the 'other', the group we want to explore, perhaps because of their underrepresentation in academic analysis, while at the same time, we may be part of the academic social world that can potentially silence this 'other'. Our research opens up, extends, limits or constrains our understanding of particular groups or particular forms of knowledge. Hence, we need to maintain a reflexive awareness of our shifting sense of self as both the subject and object of the research, of belonging to the research and being outside it. We may even question whether this distinction between subject and object is meaningful at all, given that it could be argued reality is constructed intersubjectively through the process of research and does not represent some pre-defined existing reality or 'truth'.

So instead of discussing reflexivity, we might instead talk of 'reflexivities' as there may be multiple forms of reflexivity. Of course, there may be additional reflexivities not noted here in relation to my own project, and, in practice, all these various forms, levels and themes of reflexivity are interconnected and mutually related, not necessarily separate and discrete facets of reflexivity. They may have different emphases depending on what the research entails, includes or questions. These all have a part to play in the relationship between knowledge production, methodological processes and the role of the researcher, enabling the research processes and outcomes to be open to change and adaptive in response to these multiple layers of reflexivity.

Applying Theoretical Processes and Perspectives to Practicing Reflexivity

In this section I make use of my example to return to some of the theoretical approaches to reflexivity outlined earlier in this chapter to illustrate how the sometimes quite complex concepts that are the focus of the literature can be operationalized and applied to our own research practice.

Firstly I apply Hibbert et al.'s (2010) conceptualization of reflexive processes to my research encounter with Deborah illustrated above. Hibbert et al. suggest that recursion, or a sense of return, occurs in a four-stage meta-process of reflexivity, which brings about change in the process of reflection and is therefore recursive. The initial step of *repetition* occurs when an individual reflects in a relatively self-focused manner and recursivity occurs passively, and benignly, so that the individual stays within the accepted boundaries of thought for addressing a particular issue or, in my case, role. In the case of Deborah, illustrated in the example above, my attitude towards her as a research participant was limited by my initial assumptions about her role as an audit partner and her portrayal of herself as a spokesperson for the audit firm. During the first part of my meeting with Deborah she treated me as if I were a potential client, relating to me a promotional sales pitch on the attributes of her firm. I was more closed than I should have been to subtle alternative conceptions of her identity, to the point where I had even wondered whether the research interview was going to yield any useful information, as my processes of recursive change merely supported an initial reinforcement of existing assumptions.

However, as Deborah unburdened herself in an emotive account, my processes of reflexivity turned towards *extension* and the building of new understandings. My initial conceptions and transition to this mode of extension were overturned by failure or exogenous shock, with a sensation that existing notions are inadequate, promoting a more active form of reflexive engagement (Hibbert et al., 2010). Hence I was forced to engage in self-reflexivity to question my own practices, assumptions and role in the creation of social life, though still on my own terms (Cunliffe and Jun, 2005).

It was at the next stage in the recursive process that *disruption* occurred, leading to a more critical reflexivity that caused me to question my own ideologies and hidden assumptions, in what was an unsettling and disorientating process. Hence at the time of the interview my own emotional response challenged not only my sense of self as a researcher but also my understanding of the research participant as 'other', as separate from and outside the research process. Through this form of critical reflexivity, my understandings were problematized through interacting with the inputs of others. This continued on to a more disruptive form of recursion leading me to evaluate and problematize some of my fundamental ideological and methodological assumptions about ethical issues within an oral history methodology, arising from power relations in the research, the interpretation and ownership of research, disclosure and reciprocity within the research relationship, and what can be avowed as a 'feminist' methodology (Haynes, 2010). While these were resolvable, they shifted my relationship with the research participants and the research to a more nuanced reflexive level. Finally, *participation* might be said to have occurred as a consequence of choosing to trust the other and engage seriously with their view, to engage with a community and be transformed by it. Hence, my example illustrates Hibbert et al.'s (2010) call for a consideration of reflexivity as change in the researcher as well as in the research activities, demonstrating the temporal dimension and transformative nature of the organizational researcher's practice.

It also has resonance with some of Alvesson et al.'s (2008) conceptualization of reflexive practices. I would position my example as partly reflexivity as a *multi-voicing* practice, focusing on the relationship between the researcher and the 'other', which recognizes how the researcher forms part of the research project and is actively constructed through the process of research. In addition, as the research moved on it also became more embedded in reflexivity as a *positioning* practice, emphasizing how research takes place within an academic field, within broader social processes that shape knowledge within a particular community.

Conclusion

Reflexivity is an important and pervasive concept that permeates much organizational research, enabling us to 'think about thinking'. Reflexivity allows for a form of conversation through which we come to know ourselves and others, the positions from which we speak, and the political and social context in which these conversations take place. It questions the relationship between knowledge and the production of that knowledge, problematizing how social, ethical and political issues come to be embedded in the way that we produce and value knowledge, from defining research, data gathering, analysis and interpretation, through to writing up and publication. In doing so, reflexivity allows us to think 'through what one is doing to encourage insights about the nature of social science, especially the role that language, power/knowledge connections, social interests and ideologies, rhetorical moves and maneuvering in the socio-political field play in producing particular accounts' (Alvesson et al., 2008: 497).

Reflexivity questions the processes and practice of research, in terms of how our methodological conduct and theoretical pre-understandings as researchers transform and influence new understandings. It also questions the product of that research, in terms of how our philosophical or ontological positioning influences what counts as 'knowledge' or social reality. When researching and writing reflexively, therefore, we need to be aware of how the traditions of our particular field influence the way that research is carried out, by constraining or enabling, valuing or rejecting, particular forms of knowledge. Reflexive methodologies link with ontology and epistemology to integrate ethical, social and political judgements on the research process and increase accountability for the knowledge that is produced.

Further Reading

The *International Journal of Social Research Methodology* and *Qualitative Research in Organizations and Management: An International Journal* are both useful as they contain a number of reflexive accounts using different research methodologies. In addition the following publications provide a range of perspectives on reflexivity:

Bourdieu, P. and Wacquant, L. (1992) *An Invitation to Reflexive Sociology*. Chicago: University of Chicago Press.

Hines, R.D. (1988) 'Financial accounting: in communicating reality, we construct reality', *Accounting, Organizations and Society*, 13 (3): 251–261.

Johnson, P. and Duberley, J. (2003) 'Reflexivity in management research', *Journal of Management Studies*, 40 (5): 1279–1303.

Rhodes, C. (2009) 'After reflexivity: ethics, freedom and the writing of organization studies', *Organization Studies*, 30 (6): 653–672.

Woolgar, S. (1988) 'Reflexivity is the ethnographer of the text', in S. Woolgar, (ed.), *Knowledge and Reflexivity*. London: Sage, pp. 14–34.

References

Alvesson, M., Hardy, C. and Harley, B. (2008) 'Reflecting on reflexivity: reflexive textual practices in organization and management theory', *Journal of Management Studies*, 45 (3): 480–501.

Alvesson, M. and Sköldberg, K. (2000) *Reflexive Methodology*. London: Sage.

Calás, M. and Smircich, L. (1999) 'Past postmodernism? reflections and tentative directions', *Academy of Management Review*, 24 (4): 649–671.

Clegg, S. and Hardy, C. (1996) 'Introduction', in S. Clegg, C. Hardy and W. Nord (eds), *Handbook of Organizational Studies*. London: Sage, pp. 1–28.

Cunliffe, A. (2003) 'Reflexive inquiry in organizational research: questions and possibilities', *Human Relations*, 56 (8): 983–1003.

Cunliffe, A. (2004) 'On becoming a critically reflexive practitioner', *Journal of Management Education*, 28 (4): 407–426.

Cunliffe, A. and Jun, J. S. (2005) 'The need for reflexivity in public administration', *Administration and Society*, 37: 225–242.

Fournier, V. and Grey, C. (2000) 'At the critical moment: conditions and prospects for critical management studies', *Human Relations*, 53 (1): 7–32.

Gummeson, E. (1991) *Qualitative Methods in Management Research*. Beverly Hills, CA: Sage.

Haynes, K. (2005) '(Sm)othering the self: an analysis of the politics of identity of women accountants in the UK'. Unpublished PhD thesis, School of Management, University of St Andrews.

Haynes, K. (2006) 'A therapeutic journey? reflections on the impact of research on researcher and participant', *Qualitative Research in Organizations and Management: An International Journal*, 1 (3): 204–221.

Haynes, K. (2008) 'Moving the gender agenda or stirring chicken's entrails? Where next for feminist methodologies in accounting?', *Accounting, Auditing and Accountability Journal*, 21 (4): 539–555.

Haynes, K. (2010) 'Other lives in accounting: critical reflections on oral history methodology in action', *Critical Perspectives on Accounting*, 21 (3): 221–231.

Hibbert, P., Coupland, C. and MacIntosh, R. (2010) 'Reflexivity: recursion and relationality in organizational research processes', *Qualitative Research in Organizations and Management: An International Journal*, 5 (1): 47–62.

Holmes, M. (2010) 'The emotionalization of reflexivity', *Sociology*, 44 (1): 139–154.

Lynch, M. (2000) 'Against reflexivity as an academic virtue and source of privileged knowledge', *Theory, Culture and Society*, 17 (3): 26–54.

Orr, K. and Bennett, M. (2009) 'Reflexivity in the co-production of academic-practitioner research', *Qualitative Research in Organizations and Management: An International Journal*, 4 (1): 85–102.

Reinharz, S. (1992) *Feminist Methods in Social Research*. Oxford: Oxford University Press.

Smith, D.E. (1992) 'Sociology from women's experience: a reaffirmation', *Sociological Theory*, 10: 88–98.

Stanley, L. (1993) 'On auto/biography in sociology', *Sociology*, 27 (1): 47–52.

Tomkins, L. and Eatough, V. (2010) 'Towards an integrative reflexivity in organisational research', *Qualitative Research in Organizations and Management: An International Journal*, 5 (2): 162–181.

Weick, K. (2002) 'Real-time reflexivity: prods to reflection', *Organization Studies*, 23 (6): 893–898.

6 Ethical Research Practice

Robin Holt

Introduction

Understanding how research effects and affects those it touches, and attending to the rights and wrongs of this influence and the possible harms or benefits that might accrue, has become an increasingly explicit, even formalized concern. As social science has matured so has awareness of 'proper' research conduct. Many social science researchers will now blanche, even recoil, when witnessing early studies such as psychologist Harry Harlow's investigation of the devastating emotional effects of prolonged isolation using rhesus monkeys held and observed in the provocatively titled 'well of despair'. Similar reactions are evoked on reading about Laud Humphries' 'tearoom sex' studies in which the sociologist gained the trust of homosexual men by posing as a 'lookout' for their trysts, only after which he confessed to being a researcher interested in their lives and motives. Research practice has 'moved on' it seems. The ethical permission required for such studies would probably not be granted. Yet both these studies can claim to have had done good. Harlow's defenders claim without his abuse of monkeys the possible harm to children isolated in institutional care would be less well understood, and Humphries' findings that many of the men had nicely functioning families and regular jobs challenged prevailing prejudices associating homosexuality with deviancy. What is apparently bad from one spatial and temporal perspective, is not so from another. Research ethics is the thoughtful activity of negotiating this shifting sense of the good. Can there be an absolute right and wrong way of doing things? Is research compromised by ethical formalities? Is method amoral? This chapter has been written to consider such questions, attempting to make sense of how researchers might make sense of the demands to be ethical in ways that formalities of procedure cannot readily confine.

The chapter begins with a discussion of Immanuel Kant for whom ethics is 'a science of inner duties' (1997 [1762–64]: 3), by which he means a capacity to judge our own actions and thoughts. Why Kant? Well because he was possessed by questions of ethics. If philosophy is a concern first with what 'is' the case, and second with what one 'ought do', he found the intractability of the former (to make something appear as fact requires a lot of unapparent scene setting concerning the schemes by which facts can be established) would give way to the lure of the latter. If we cannot, once and for all, state what 'is' the case because of an often indifferent and recalcitrant world, we can nevertheless consider what ought be the case with that part of the world we know best: ourselves. And this is the other reason for starting with Kant; he remained medieval enough in his thought to be sceptical about claims to what we now call full objectivity, and so keenly attuned to the intimacy between knowledge and human conduct. Self-awareness of conduct emerges from our capacity for reason, of which universal condition we are imperfect and particular exponents. Reason affords us a perspective on immediate perceptions and self-interested feelings (concerning our interests and their gratification), provoking in us (potentially) a disinterested concern for the nature of what pursuing interests involves and entails. This disinterestedness becomes a science if we organize our thought and activity in ways that expose us persistently to questioning scrutiny. This scrutiny is only possible, though, if we appreciate ourselves from beyond ourselves. So to talk of ethics we have to begin by talking about what is beyond us: 'the other'. So in starting with Kant the chapter starts with a discusssion of 'the other'. It then takes in discussions on social science generally and the nature of knowledge being produced, before considering the particular quality of phenomena arising through qualitative methods and whether these methods can ever be called 'good'. It ends with a hesitant list of virtues by which research practice might constitute itself.

The Other

For Kant ethical concern arises from the scrutiny of our thought and action made possible through comparative association with what is distinct from, or other than, it. There are two sources of otherness. First reason itself, because no matter how rational we are, we are never perfectly so (Kant likened humans to 'crooked timber'). Reason becomes an ideal that goads us into requiring yet more autonomous consideration of our particular thoughts and actions. Second, reason enables us to compare and so acknowledge others' thoughts, actions and interests alongside our own, insofar as they too are (potentially) rational. So while ethics apparently begins with the critical experience of judging our own thoughts and actions, Kant reminded us individuality is a relational condition, both with respect to the idealized condition of reason itself and to the empirical condition of living in others' company.

It is, Kant believed, a boon and curse of being human that experience is inherently relational. It offers both the excitements and fulfilments associated with judgement, as well as the inaccessibility of final truths. Life is under-determined because we are always taking perspectives on things, including ourselves. So what belongs to 'the self' does so because it is in relief from what is distant from, and hence other to, it. Ethics (the normative codes associated with being-in-the-world) gives voice to this grounding condition, involving the creation of a kind of personal atmosphere in which what interests us as desiring beings is shadowed by an awareness of what is beyond those interests, enabling us to judge desires against the inevitability of other conflicting desires, both one's own and those of others. This awareness might begin by putting oneself in others' shoes, imagining how thoughts and actions might appear to those who witness and are implicated by them. Hence we become wary about treating others as means to our ends. How would we feel if we were treated similarly? But for Kant ethical concern should not stop until it unfolds into an acceptance that, no matter how accomplished and knowledgeable we become about our own interests and those of others, we recognize two related tendencies common to all human beings. First, we accept our urge for infinite knowledge (and so for control over otherness) to be the fantasy it is; otherness is always with us. Second, we accept that to speak the truth we must sometimes do so to our apparent disturbance and even disadvantage. As a science, then, ethics is peculiar in that it advocates insight through knowledgeable self-discipline and reticence. For all his sober and demanding talk of moral imperatives, Kant remains alive to ethics being grounded as much in hesitation as claims of right and wrong.

Research Practice

On the etymological face of it, the admission and acceptance of otherness will not sit easily with social science research. Research submits the unknown – what is 'other' – to the known. The isolation of variables and patterns in social phenomena and their distillation into testable theories by which these identities and regularities might be explained are activities in which the social lives of people are gradually uncovered and otherness is sidelined; research practice seems to pursue what François Jullien (2005: 130) calls 'the obliteration of the negative'. If we equate social science research with making aspects of the world clear 'as fact', then to admit otherness is also to admit to limitations. Good social science overcomes limitations. Even where it is accepted that the search for absolute knowledge is just so much tilting at windmills, there remains an expectation of a steadying generalization in which propositional statements concerning persisting relations between entities provide deeper and deeper insight. It was this expectation that Kant surfaced and questioned. He likened knowledge to a land that we have walked over again and again, steadily defining everything in its place: 'However this land is an island', he goes on, 'surrounded by a wide stormy ocean … where many banks of fog and a great deal of ice beginning to melt pose as new lands, and by incessantly fooling the sailor who is eagerly moving about filled with false hopes in quest of discoveries, entangles him in adventures from which he will never desist and yet will never be able to complete' (quoted in Safranski, 1998). What lies beyond the island, what Kant called 'the thing in itself', is never graspable because it is beyond our experience and it is with our empirically filled self-consciousness that knowledge of what is out there stops (Kant, 1981 [1781]: B276 = 255). Hence his exhortation that we acknowledge our limits to know things and we accept feelings of disturbance, because this affords us a sense of our active complicity with the world we are trying to understand. Ethics as science makes this complicity apparent.

Kant's idea of otherness is not an a-human otherness, something occult, but a persisting sense of absence and puzzlement. He recognizes how science – the pursuit of knowledge – tends to encroach on this sense, sometimes tentatively, sometimes swiftly. Human intellect, like Nature, abhors a vacuum, and as human beings we want to fill in spaces, to announce ourselves. In his essay 'The Poet', Ralph Emerson (1990 [1847]: 216) wrote, 'The man is only half himself … the other half expression'. If this is so, then social science research is the public disciplining of such expression. And here we can bring ethics and research back into sympathy. This disciplining of expression need not be about content, or final laws, and indeed it rarely is. Kant noticed how the incursion of science into 'the other' was both knowledge and the means or methods by which inquiry was undertaken. While ethics demands our being humble in the pursuit of the former, we might nevertheless be ambitious in the practice of the latter. The disciplining of expression is less any conclusion about the 'painful mystery' of Kant's stormy sea, and more an attentiveness to the manner of investigation into it. Kant likened this attentiveness to the 'public use of reason': arguments are placed publicly, read and tarried with anew and without end, outside of the influence of any specific set of vested interests or authority. The grounding quality is one of disinterest, an ability to remove oneself from the phenomena of concern sufficiently to gain a perspective upon its own nature, rather than upon how it might appear to us ordinarily, cleaved to our conceits and self-concern. To go back to Emerson (1990 [1847]: 188), by making facts the subject of public reason they are raised up and separated from the mass of everyday empirical happenings to take on the quality of truths, becoming temporarily immune to the vagaries of upset and decay. In Emerson's words they are addressed to us for our contemplation, which in turn makes us intellectual beings, allowing us to grow in every direction. Given, however, we cannot hope to arrive at settled conclusions as to the nature of things outside of our interest in them, Kant's (1991 [1784]: 57) insistence on public reason amounts to a methodological commitment through which we strive towards knowledge, rather than ever attain it. Hence: 'If it is now asked, "Do we presently live in an enlightened age?" the answer is, "No, but we do live in an age of enlightenment." Methodologically this age is defined by epistemological values associated with predictive and explanatory power, with the reach and relevance of the findings, the simplicity of approach, with characteristics of insightfulness, practicality and persistence. It seems the content of truth is beginning to take a back seat' (Kuhn, 1977: 338).

Move onwards a few hundred years and the sense that what defines research practice is less truth-content than methodological commitment accelerates, and with this what constitutes method has changed. The philosopher of science Hans Rheinberger (1997: 17) puts it well in his study of laboratory work. He finds research averring from final conclusions, and that as a practice it is distinguished through the experience of challenge, the character of persistence and the politics of opportunism. Where the science of Kant's period involved a reaching after essences (that would never be found) the laboratory work noted by Rheinberger veers between clean, dispassionate objectivity (recording what is found, neutrally) and imaginative flights. Either way, the purposeful accumulation of fact is accompanied by purposive processes of experimentation, and the feel of the latter governs the form of the former. Research practice becomes a conscious concern with, and ordering of, the conversations, disputes, challenges and skills by which truths are arrived at, rather than the invariant content of those truths.

Though not voiced directly in ethical terms, the resonance with Kant's 'science of inner duty' remains striking: research is good research if as a process the dominant authority is the self-discipline manifest in the researchers' methodological commitment. Kant's motto of the Enlightenment – dare to know (*sapare aude*) – appears to be alive and well. Perhaps the closest overt expression of the ethical resonance of such commitment comes with the sociologist Robert Merton's (1942) CUDOS norms. First is Communalism – where the findings of science are a common product and assigned to the common stock of goods for all to use equally and openly, making quick and open publication a duty and allowing others to benefit from findings without protecting property rights. Then comes Universality – wherein all truth claims are subject to objective assessment irrespective of the status of claimants or context of expression, so meritocracy reigns and influences of class, ethnicity gender, wealth and the like are sidelined. Next comes Disinterest – in which the bias of personal and social gain dissolves, hence a Weberian concern for disclosing vested interests and funding sources out of which admission sentiments are discounted. Finally comes Organized Scepticism – by which knowledge is continually subject to scrutiny, repeat testing, highlighting the importance of clear and comprehensive record keeping and exposure to peer review.

With its commitment to methodological integrity and tireless experiment, research practice seems to have much to say about ethics, or more accurately, a certain kind of ethics associated with personal disciplines of detachment sufficient to test the value commitments for internal consistency, practical implication and possible alternatives (Blaug, 1980: 135; Post, 2009). The standards and procedures sustaining this commitment include: techniques for gathering and analysing evidence; ways of ordering and working with questions and behaviours associated with demonstration; and proof and archiving, all of which afford researchers entrance into an institutional condition of academic expertise (Chandler, 2009).

Qualitative Research Practice

To define research and its ethical resonance through method is not without problems. To echo Nietzsche in *Beyond Good and Evil* ([1886]/2003), fixing on method suggests researchers are indifferent whether they study famine or families, when most would passionately resist such a conclusion. Researchers care about what they study, and their practice is not a passive contemplation of what exists, but giving form to phenomena through action and educated attention to which they are committed in some way (Winch, 1964). It is here that qualitative social science research becomes interesting. Typically qualitative research is distinguished by its proximity to what is being studied. Researchers evaluate what is of significance and engage with this, speaking and influencing subjects and even discussing findings. Method and content bleed into one another irretrievably and through such face-to-face relationships inquiry might more readily acknowledge the limits of knowledge and discomforting truths (*sic* Kant) than quantitative work. These limits and discomforts are considered in George Perec's (2008 [1978]) *The Tale of the Misunderstood Anthropologist* in his *Life: A User's Manual*. The central character, Marcel Appanzzell, is found deep in the jungle, researching a secretive tribe. Despite intense efforts at engagement his approaches meet with silence, as though he didn't exist. Waking one morning he finds the tribal village deserted. Undaunted he pursues and finds the villagers, now living in insect-infested swamps. He stays, renewing unsuccessfully attempts at communication, while theorizing on why they have suddenly become mobile, and willing to tolerate harsher living conditions. They leave again, and he follows, deeper into the jungle, before suddenly realizing the tribe are leaving solely to avoid him. His distinctiveness as an expert dissolves and, profoundly disturbed, he relinquishes 'the field', wandering the jungle until he is found some years later, barely able to function, without language. Perec's fiction is salutary, reminding us of the reticence through which subjects might protect themselves, and the fragilities of any research project. It is also humane. Appanzzell is patient, persistent, skilled, does everything correctly, and yet suffers an extreme epistemological anxiety that induces a collapse of the self. The irony being that the only causal influence he successfully isolates is himself, and in doing so he induces his own breakdown, so stark and alien is such a solitary phenomena. Perec, like Kant, realizes that science, ethics and our very identity are indistinct: without the possibility and experience of contact with one another and the world (and hence otherness) we are nothing. Qualitative research remains close to this understanding.

Being close does not make qualitative research more ethical of course. Indeed it invokes perhaps a duty to acknowledge the difficulties of complicity and involvement more directly than other, apparently less invasive forms. Appanzzell realizes his attempts to theorize the tribe's mobility and tolerance of discomfort are, in fact, corrupt, a case of his language inferring nonexistent meanings. His mistake stems from what de Certeau (1988: 67) calls a process of 'linguistic inversion'. Rather than thinking about himself and his influence, Appanzzell explains by analysing objects and events through a principle of extension, in either space (filled by extended material) or time (flowing in extended lapses). For Appanzzell the village exists because it has a distinct extension at any one instant, and it relates to other such things (the people, the wider forest) through a causal transmission of stresses. This measuring involves a 'flattening out' that transforms the temporal articulation of places into a spatial sequence of points: 'a graph takes the place of an operation' (de Certeau, 1988: 35). This identification of entities and relations between them allows researchers to divide and compare states of affairs; but what is being divided and compared are selections, or incisions, that presume the world a neater place than it really is. The fact that the tribe were leaving solely to avoid Appanzzell himself had not occurred to him. It was too disruptive, too disturbing, yet ethically quite profound.

The Importance of Questionability

Research, even qualitative research, has a tendency to regard the world as always amenable to study. The risk is that in this 'ethnological colonization' of everyday social activity the direct experiences of social life have become mediated by the established concepts, scientific expectations and dispositional values of the researcher and research community (de Certeau, 1988: 43–44; Bourdieu, 1998: 130). What can be lost is an awareness that, as well as being distinct as spatially bounded and persisting across time, things, whether material or immaterial, also exist *in* space and time and can change through them. The psychiatrist Elisabeth Kübler-Ross, for example, spent many years working with terminally ill patients, persuading the medical establishment (including students) to confront and learn from these often ignored 'cases'. Through her tireless research, Kübler-Ross (2005) identified five phases (denial, anger, bargaining, depression and acceptance) through which people 'pass' on hearing of their terminal illness, phases that have subsequently been applied to other forms of human loss/hurt/grief. It might seem churlish to find this work wanting, yet following Bourdieu we might take issue, less with its spirit and insight than its generalization. What do the phases tell us about grief? To say grief involves anger before depression and after denial seems to foreclose on those experiencing it differently. Moreover, what of our insight into the disease, love, care, anxiety or indifference out of which grief precipitated? Phases tighten and clarify experience, but they also distance us from it. We assume, for example, the same person persists through the different phases, but the feeling might be so intense as to admit a fundamental change: they cease to become the person they were. We also assume the meaning of grief is enriched through the addition of multiple, related concepts (grief is denial, then anger, then bargaining, and so on), but then what are denial and anger? What is the 'other' being listened to here if one concept is simply being explained by extensions into others? The same issues go for other social phenomena parsed into phases; the growth from smaller to larger firms, say, or the maturing of democratic politics in a nation state, or even the stages of development of morality itself, as in Kohlberg's (1981) work and Carol Gilligan's trenchant (1982) critique. Research can mark the passage of grief, growth, democracy or moral capacity without getting at what goes on 'in between' the phases so to speak (for a fuller discussion of this see Tsoukas and Chia, 2002; as well as work by Alfred Whitehead, 1919: 19; 1985 [1926]: 248).

All researchers have a methodological interest in rendering social phenomena immobile, in order that the subsequent representations carry sufficient authority to be added to, or challenged, or refuted by others. In not being critically aware of this, however, research practice has a tendency to reside within its own disciplinary conceits. So what matters ethically is not just that methodological norms allow researchers to bring knowledge into view through public questioning, but also that methodological standards and established concepts are themselves subject to what Bourdieu calls 'epistemic reflexivity'. This entails the systematic exploration of the 'unthought categories of thought that delimit the thinkable and predetermine the thought' (Bourdieu, 1990: 178), allowing social agents – like researchers – to acquire a heightened awareness of their performative roles and to realize that their ways of thinking are irretrievably the products of socio-historical conditions. To understand how this reflexivity might develop, more might be said about the nature of research practice.

The Goods of Research Practice

Alasdair MacIntyre (1981: 175) defines a practice as human activity, the key features of which are the pursuit and institutional arrangement of internal and external goods under the governance of 'collectively established standards of excellence'. External goods include assets, status and power, and these are possessed exclusively (if some have more, others have less) and traded within and across practices. They are often material in nature and form the main objects of concern for organized social institutions. Internal goods are associated with the learning and realization of standards into which an adherent of a practice is initiated. The standards describe the criteria by which the practice is undertaken well, or badly, meaning it is internal and not external goods that will distinguish practices from one another.

Research practice is the organized pursuit and production of knowledge. The external goods involve status (academic titles, guru status, prestigious awards, publications), power (positions in academies, policy and advisory communities, grant funding bodies) and rewards (income, prizes). These are institutionally supported. For example, research bodies such as universities encourage the acquisition of external goods through the overt organization of career paths (tenure); they measure performance through benchmarks of research income; and they covet associations with notable employees, alumni, officers and advisors. Status and income, however, do not constitute research practice. What defines research are the internal goods associated with methodological apprenticeship, a skilled engagement with phenomena under investigation and a theoretical advance. These internal goods emerge by disclosing one's judgement within historically configured communities in which standards have emerged through the successive efforts of generations. Following Merton, this requires from researchers a diligent command of appropriate methods, an honest self-appraisal of limits, a willingness to trust others, the ability to recognize the possible validity of alternate points of view, and a resistance to forces repressing such qualities of character. Without these qualities the internal goods of research are foreclosed and what is left is the empty pursuit of external goods.

The academic norms associated with methodological skill and integrity are acknowledged through learning and then enforced through scholarly practice. The standards enable and foster the trust by which the free pursuit and expression of knowledge is sustained (Butler, 2009). The problem of their passive acceptance however beckons what MacIntyre recognizes as an inherently ethical question:

how can we distinguish the goods that we want to pursue from the goods that it is good for us to pursue? In respect of the former the individual is the authority, whereas the latter involves us looking beyond our own self-interested sense of good. MacIntyre (1999a: 70–78) describes this as moving from having reasons to having good reasons, whereby researchers consider the goods realized by research practice not only because they are established objects of directed activity and desire, which when satisfied bring about a summation of the activity, but also because they contribute in some way to human flourishing. Thus researchers will be aware of the uses to which research is put and will imagine different futures for research practice, with different goods and modes of flourishing, allowing an enriched sense of possibility; hence standards have to be worked at so as to ensure the practice remains significant and functional as new empirical situations arise. Part of the distinctiveness of a practice stems from the ways in which perceptions of ends and internal goods (which technical skills help to achieve) are 'transformed' and 'enriched' by imagined extensions of their constraints (MacIntyre, 1981: 190–209).

Cultivating Research Practice

Having good reasons evokes what MacIntyre calls the necessary conditions of independent practical reasoning by which a practice can be said to be ethical. Under the impress of such reasoning, the practice balances internal and external goods. Too much of an emphasis on the trappings of status, the material conditions and equipment, and the often competitive creation of research outputs creates a rationalizing calculus whereby research and associated learning become factors of production. Internal goods associated with curiosity, wonder, the struggle of apprenticeship and the recognition of well-crafted work risk getting squeezed out. Practical reasoning acts as a check on this institutional tendency to skew attention towards the external and visible elements of practice. It also ensures the practice is on-going. The standards of the practice (the rules, the purposes, the norms) are appreciated as pre-conditions by which researchers can develop and fulfil potential, yet they are not inviolable, and experimenting with methodology remains possible. Along with learning, preserving and experimenting with the standards associated with methodological goods comes an equally important consideration of how research can be performed 'sometimes to clarify, sometimes to intervene, sometimes to generate new perspectives, and always to serve as eyes and ears in ongoing efforts to understand the present and deliberate about the future' (Flyvbjerg, 2001: 357). Practical reasoning, this public willingness to expose research to public challenge, becomes versed in a certain form of conduct that acknowledges its debt to the wider practice (research apprenticeship incurs an asymmetric debt insofar as reciprocity is not demanded by those being researched, yet those being researched are part of a public that expects research to matter) without slavishly falling into established relationships of power and habit.

The possibility for practical reasoning arises from our actions having intentional aspects (they are our actions) and also from our ability to appreciate their potential effects and incidental aspects. Take, for example, a researcher who releases data incriminating a company in an environmentally damaging activity. She knows this company has a long tradition of sound community work and has good employment conditions, yet it has not extended this sense of responsibility to the natural world. She knows the company might suffer, possibly even be forced into a temporary shutdown, threatening jobs and the community livelihood. Another researcher demurs, instead advising the company of the breach, to which the company's management listen and respond with effective remedies. In the first case, though the researcher realizes the potential harms in disclosure, she decides these do not override first the methodological duty to publish data as they have been found, second the academic duty to discuss openly what is being studied, and third the duty humans have to the wider environment. In the second case, the researcher feels that the potentially adverse economic and social costs associated with the release of these data trump the duty to methodological and academic standards, as well as to nature, and he resists publication. The two cases reveal an intimacy between discrimination and research to which there is no calculable end point; it is a condition of making a judgement. Moreover, it involves researchers considering the standards by which such reasonable discrimination is learnt. In the second case, for example, reasonableness is itself informed by wider social standards that deem a concern for job preservation as legitimate, thereby involving a researcher considering not only the legitimacy of his actions in terms of their conformity to methodological standards, but also the appropriateness of the standards themselves. Should the smooth running of an economic enterprise trump the protection of environmental bio-diversity?

In the above examples, amended from similar examples given by MacIntyre (1999b), the responsibility for action stems from a consideration of the intentional involvement, a consideration of the effects set against the established normative standards, and finally a consideration of the legitimacy of those standards themselves. Hence ethical research will involve disputes as to what constitutes a sound piece of writing; queries as to the soundness of methodological applications; and equivocation as to how any results will implicate themselves within wider senses of the human good; and throughout all of this researchers, as potentially ethical beings, will have to exercise appropriate judgement. Personal views of the good will always be contested, both in terms of acts that infringe upon the good (the clash of loyalties when, for example, deciding whether to support those publishing potentially inflammatory conclusions or those potentially offended by such) and acts that interfere with the full acknowledgement of the good (such as the weakness of will that steers you towards easily reached conclusions or thoughtlessly used academic cant) (Nussbaum, 2003). So this judgement will never be absolutely right, nor wholly wrong. It will always be a question of degree. As practical reasoners, researchers learn which actions are appropriate, when and where, and for what reasons, without presuming there is a right or wrong answer. Their theoretical judgement takes place from within any situation, and what is being judged here is always in relation to its own potential rather than to external standards of right and wrong, eliciting corrective analysis and absorption rather than damning judgement and exclusion (Jullien, 2005). So rather than reaching a pre-defined threshold (and identifying such in research terms), performance becomes a condition of readiness, an awareness not of what the case is, but of what it might be. Without this ability to judge the appropriateness of actions beyond simply a strict application of the rules, the purposive structures and standards of the practices can unravel. For example, if the public disclosure of research findings is simply asserted as a duty, then it is indistinct from serial truth-telling, no matter how intimate the details are. Such openness can undermine trust in the very academic institutions that sustain this sort of research practice in the first place. Being open with disclosure requires that a range of goods and interests is being imagined and deliberated, collectively. It is not sufficient to simply assert a rule.

The Virtues of Research Practice

In summary, then, ethical research practice involves both an apprenticeship in and a commitment to establishing the methodological norms associated with investigating phenomena and the theories established around them. In taking on such standards, however, an ethical sensibility arises from the development of independent practical reason. Here researchers acknowledge relationships of dependence (for example those within a university, or funding body, or scientific cannon) and then explore beyond these relationships, exploiting the trust and reliance in order to create new spaces of possibility. This experience of working beyond conditions of comfort allows researchers to distinguish between the subjective motivations associated with their individuality and their research role (what satisfies desires) and what it would be good to do in a situation as someone else, either a different member of the research practice including a participant, an exponent of a different practice, or even simply *qua* human being.

While there is no readily available set of duties by which researchers might consider their practice as ethical, we might hazard at a number of virtues by which the use of practical reason can arise.

Deliberative conversation. Whether in seminars and symposia, or in written exchanges through essays, studies and comments, or in explaining research to participants or giving them feedback, researchers are required to talk clearly and openly about the ideas, but not to linger in such a way that others' voices are excluded. This might involve researchers thinking about the rules or conventions for engagement. For example, when organizing focus groups or interviews, allowing silences and room for people to speak can be important, as can the choice of venues in which their conversations cannot be overheard or interrupted.

Constancy of language and behaviours within different institutional settings and through time. This is not a call for repetition, but a pragmatic awareness that concepts and signifiers need to be used carefully and consistently, with an awareness of how these might be interpreted by others. It is also an awareness of the value of consistent approaches in different spatial and temporal settings; using similar techniques, questions and even dress codes in a set of interviews common to a single study, for example. More profoundly, constancy delivers a humane form of Merton's disinterest, insofar as the personal commitment to ways of proceeding acts as a bulwark against the changeability of approach that can undermine academic independence.

Sensitivity in handling participant relationships/data. Information is not a mute possession, but the residue of others' lives that will often warrant confidentiality or anonymity. There is also a sense in which it elicits from the researcher a sense of solicitude and involvement, that while it cannot trump all other relationships (with the discipline itself, say) or other virtues (such as honesty) it is worthy of acknowledgement as a relationship of mutual dependency and exposure in some way. Here the interests of participants must be acknowledged as potentially being in tension with one's own as a researcher, and in some cases trumping one's own. So procedurally participants should be informed about the purpose of the research being proposed, the level of their expected involvement and duration; they should be given the opportunity to withdraw; they should be told about the implications of withdrawing; and finally the possible effects and affects of any involvement should be discussed.

Honesty. A willingness to disclose intentions to participants and employers, as well as all data and thoughts germane to the objects of inquiry. As academics, researchers' practice is in part defined by an internal good of realizing the fullest disclosure of 'facts'. Full disclosure can militate against access, so agreeing to temporary suspensions in the release of data, for example, might in the long run allow for a fuller public discussion than a rigid adherence to immediate, full disclosure. Moreover, dishonesty and deception can work in some contexts, for example in covert ethnography in places otherwise untouched by academic inquiry (see the 1996 debate between Richard Leo and Kai Erikson in *American Sociologist* (Leo, 1996) for an interesting discussion of the nuanced right and wrong).

Learning from mistakes. An acceptance of mistakes being integral to good research, insofar as insight comes from working along the edges of acquired skill, coupled to a willingness to engage in retrospective reasoning as to why the mistakes occurred. If, for example, there has been a misunderstanding as to the nature of the research, the researcher might consider in what ways they were dependent on others and vice versa, and hence under what conditions of asymmetry the misunderstanding might have arisen and so could be avoided in the future.

Maturity. Awareness that methods are far from innocent, and that in making an incision into the world, human lives are being effected and affected in some way, no matter how small. This requires what Nussbaum (2003) calls narrative imagination, a capacity to acknowledge one's own traditions while refusing to accept the superiority of these, thereby allowing researchers to make imaginative leaps into the conditions of others and otherness. Maturity is particularly important in thinking about the evaluative aspects of research. In recommending certain organizational behaviours or out-comes as desirable, for example, to what extent is the idea of this desirability contested, and in whose interests is it being pursued? Even basic evalua-tions such as a firm earning sustainable revenues or creating stable family conditions can be considered otherwise, for example showing concern for the manner in which customers are persuaded to part with money or the implications of promoting family stability over mobility.

Amateur (*amatore*). In its original sense, a person who cultivates a body of knowledge through inquiry in the spirit of affinity rather than utility, though of course utility might arise. Without the pressure of vested interests (often commercially configured), the amateur flourishes. The inevitability of vested interests, however, means an amateur requires judgement. For an often profound discussion of the use of research for practical ends, Michael Frayn's 1988 play *Copenhagen* dramatically replays conversations between the physicists Werner Heisenberg and Neils Bohr. Mired in the employ of governmental institutions concerned with the external goods of power and repute, their science has lost its wonder and sense of innocent disclosure. It is traduced in spirit yet its effects are utterly profound. A lack of easy answers and the requirement for complex and thoughtful judgement in the face of those demanding one's findings be used in a certain way retain com-pelling relevance for any researcher.

Listening. The willingness to hear as well as say, and in hearing to admit, first, that there are different ways of measuring the social world, and second, that measurement of the world is not the only way of approaching it, and that too readily approaching the world as something amenable to measurement forecloses much of the world to us. The former is found, for example, in the emerging and often incompatible ways in which wealth is assessed. Something of the latter is revealed in Michel Foucault's (1977: 171) sustained analysis of practices of incarceration, warning us that if it were not for the presence of prisons as objects of use and study, we would all of us realize we were already imprisoned by a power (pouvoir) that sees without being seen.

Irony. Appreciating how research practice involves the self-production of knowledge, while avoiding the pull towards self-promotion. Favourable and populist citations are often worthwhile external goods, yet their pursuit might exclude interesting, if unpopular, elements of study. If we take irony as the capacity to absorb the possible contingency of all truth content, this enables the researcher not only to follow Merton in suspending belief awhile, but also to stand aside from the conceits of the dogmatic and narcissistic.

Further Reading

Hannah Arendt's 1950 paper gives a moving, trenchant and provocative critique of how social science is parasitical of 'the social', notably the behavioural sciences and their emphasis on conformity and typification (with human beings read as 'a bundle of reliable reactions').

John Law's (2004) *After Method* is a provocative and insightful book which argues that things are ephemeral and vague methods might expand the criteria of relevance by which these things are made sense of. So the 'good' by which research can be assessed might begin with truth-value, but extend to cover a concern for just effects, aesthetics and imaginative vision. We thus arrive at a view of research practice that is both varied and humble.

Charles Taylor's 1971 paper is a sustained consideration of whether social science can be a naturalist science and its implications for the neutrality of practice.

For an overview of practical issues, though with a slight UK bias, the UK's Economic and Social Research Council (ESRC) funded a three-year project on Ethics and Ethical Practice in Social Science. Based at Lancaster University, the research team have collected their findings, case studies and recommendations at: www.lancs.ac.uk/researchethics. A PDF file incorporating these findings and used by the ESRC is available at: www.esrc.ac.uk/about-esrc/information/research-ethics.aspx

References

Arendt, H. (1950) 'Social sciences and the concentration camps', *Jewish Studies*, 12: 49–64.

Blaug, M. (1980) *The Methodology of Economics*. Cambridge: Cambridge University Press.

Bourdieu, P. (1990) *The Logic of Practice*. Cambridge: Polity Press.

Bourdieu, P. (1998) *Practical Reason*. Cambridge: Polity Press.

Butler, J. (2009) 'Critique, dissent, disciplinarity', *Critical Inquiry*, 35 (4): 773–797.

Certeau, M. de (1988) *The Practice of Everyday Life*. Berkeley: University of California Press.

Chandler, J. (2009) 'Doctrines, disciplines, discourses, departments', *Critical Inquiry*, 35 (4): 729–748.

Emerson, R.W. (1990 [1847]) *Essays: First and Second Series*. Vintage/Library of America

Flyvbjerg, B. (2001) *Making Social Science Matter*. Cambridge: Cambridge University Press.

Foucault, M. (1977 [1975]) *Discipline and Punish*, trans. Alan Sheridan. London: Allen Lane.

Gilligan, C. (1982) *In a Different Voice: Psychological Theory and Women's Development*. Cambridge, MA: Harvard University Press.

Jullien, F. (2005) 'The shadow on the picture: of evil or the negative', *Critical Inquiry*, 32: 130–150

Kant, I. (1981 [1781]) *Beiträge zur Kritik der reinen Vernunft*, edited by I. Heidemann and W. Ritel. Berlin and New York: De Gruyter.

Kant, I. (1991 [1784]) 'An answer to the question: 'What is enlightenment'?', in H. Reis (ed.), *Kant: Political Writings*. Cambridge: Cambridge University Press, pp. 54–60.

Kant, I. (1997 [1762–64]) *Lectures on Ethics*. From notes taken by J.G. Herder, edited by J.B. Schneewind. Cambridge: Cambridge University Press.

Kohlberg, L. (1981) *Essays on Moral Development*. San Francisco, CA: Harper Row.

Kübler-Ross, E. (2005) *On Grief and Grieving*. New York: Charles Scribner.

Kuhn, T. (1977) *The Essential Tension*. Chicago: University of Chicago Press.

Law, J. (2004) *After Method*. Abingdon: Routledge.

Leo, R.A. (1996) 'The ethics of deceptive research roles reconsidered: a response to Kai Erikson', *American Sociologist*, 27 (Spring): 122–128.

MacIntyre, A. (1981) *After Virtue* (2nd edn). London: Duckworth and Co.

MacIntyre, A. (1999a) *Dependent Rational Animals*. London: Duckworth and Co.

MacIntyre, A. (1999b) 'Social structures and the threats to moral agency', *Philosophy*, 74: 311–329.

Merton, R. K. (1942) 'The normative structure of science', in R. Merton (ed.), *The Sociology of Science: Theoretical and Empirical Investigations*. Chicago: University of Chicago Press.

Nietzsche, F. ([1886]/2003) *Beyond Good and Evil*. R. J. Hollingdale (Trans.). London: Penguin.

Nussbaum, M. (2003) 'Cultivating humanity in legal education', *University of Chicago Law Review*, 70: 265–279.

Perec, G. ([1978] 2008) *Life: A User's Manual* (trans. D. Bellos). London: Vintage.

Post, R. (2009) 'Debating disciplinarity', *Critical Inquiry*, 35 (4): 749–772.

Rheinberger, H. (1997) *Towards a History of Epistemic Things: Synthesising Problems in the Test Tube*. Stanford: Stanford University Press.

Safranski, R. (1998) *Marin Heidegger: Between Good and Evil*, trans E. Osers. Cambridge, MA: Harvard University Press.

Taylor, C.(1971) 'Interpretation and the sciences of man', *Review of Metaphysics*, 25 (1): 3–51.

Tsoukas, H. and Chia, R. (2002) 'On organizational becoming: rethinking organizational change', *Organization Science*, 13: 568–582.

Whitehead, A.N. (1919) *An Inquiry Concerning the Principles of Natural Knowledge*. Cambridge: Cambridge University Press.

Whitehead, A.N. (1985 [1926]) *Science and the Modern World*. London: Free Association.

Winch, P. (1964) 'Understanding a primitive society', *American Philosophical Quarterly*, 1: 307–324.

7 Facilitating the Interaction Between Theory and Data in Qualitative Research Using CAQDAS

Rudolf R. Sinkovics and Eva A. Alfoldi

Introduction

It is generally acknowledged in the business and management literature that qualitative research tends to be 'messy'. In contrast to the typical linear structure of the quantitative research task (find or develop a theory, gather empirical data, confirm or disconfirm the theory), qualitative findings often emerge through a complex process of gradual evolution, driven by the interaction between theory and data. This iterative, cyclical process can be considered a hallmark of qualitative research. It lies at the heart of terms such as *evolution of perspective* (Peshkin, 1985), *zipping* (Orton, 1997), *systematic combining* (Dubois and Gadde, 2002), *cycles of deliberation* (McGaughey, 2004; 2007) and the term we adopt in this chapter, *progressive focusing* (Parlett and Hamilton, 1972; Stake, 1981; 1995). Our aim is to demonstrate how such an inherently 'messy' process can be made more manageable and rigorous through the use of CAQDAS. We would also acknowledge potential dangers in the indiscriminate and overly mechanistic use of CAQDAS (Hesse-Biber, 1996; Marshall, 2001). However, drawing on the example of a research project carried out by one of the authors, we illustrate ways to use CAQDAS fruitfully to make non-linear research processes more systematic and add to both flexibility and rigour (Sinkovics et al., 2008).

First, we must define what we mean by progressive focusing. The term was initially noted by Parlett and Hamilton in 1972, who advocated an approach where 'researchers systematically reduce the breadth of their enquiry to give more concentrated attention to the emerging issues' (Parlett and Hamilton, 1972: 18). This perspective was taken up and refined by Stake (1981; 1995) who described progressive focusing as follows:

> Progressive focusing requires that the researcher be well acquainted with the complexities of the problem before going to the field, but not too committed to a study plan. It is accomplished in multiple stages: first observation of the site, then further inquiry, beginning to focus on the relevant issues, and then seeking to explain. (Stake, 1981: 1)

With its emphasis on pre-fieldwork preparation and openness to emergent issues from the field, we find this description sets a useful example for qualitative research. We use the concept of progressive focusing to extend and refine the linear model of the qualitative research process commonly depicted in the literature (see Eisenhardt, 1989; Yin, 2003; Sinkovics et al., 2008; Iacobucci and Churchill, 2010). Hence, the key distinguishing feature of our model (shown in Figure 7.1) is the iterative and repeatable nature of its component steps.

Step 1 of the research task encompasses several key tasks facing the researcher at the start of a new research project: choosing a topic and conducting a literature review, in order to build the theoretical and conceptual foundations of the research. This step includes the articulation of basic assumptions, logic and expectations, as well as developing the research questions – a task that is closely intertwined with the literature review, since research questions should be clearly rooted in the theoretical foundations and literature gaps identified through a review of the existing research.

Step 2 focuses on the logic behind operationalizing the research questions. The researcher draws up a 'blueprint', seeking a good fit between theoretical foundations, epistemological assumptions and practical feasibility issues. Building sound logic and coherent ideas, with input from fellow academics, forms an essential part of this step.

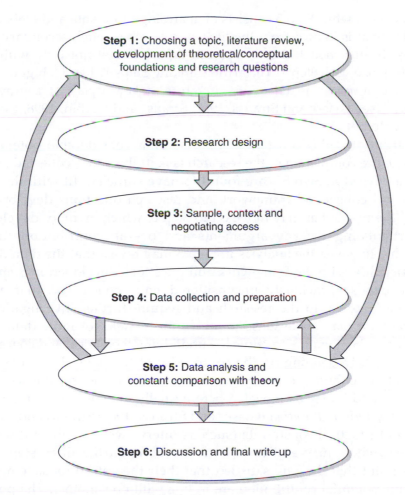

Figure 7.1   A progressive focusing model of the qualitative research process

Building on the first two steps, Step 3 is concerned with moving the research 'out of theory and into the field' by carefully choosing a sample and a context (see Saunders, in this volume). Admittedly, in many cases, sampling and context are influenced by pragmatic issues such as pre-existing contacts or the ease and level of access – as a result, Step 3 could involve prolonged negotiations, or alternatively even precede Step 1.

Once the first three steps have been taken, it is time for the researcher to enter the field in earnest. Step 4 contains the task of collecting and preparing primary data, while Step 5 consists of analysing those data and embedding these in what is known from the literature or other (often secondary) data sources. In our model, these steps are tightly linked not only with each other, but also with Step 1. The arrows linking Steps 1, 4 and 5 highlight the *constant comparison* of data with literature, a key aspect of a grounded approach (see Glaser and Strauss, 1967; Strauss and Corbin, 1998; Kenealy, in this volume).

We argue that this constant comparison has considerable potential to influence the completion of the research task. If the data – collected in Step 4 and analysed in Step 5 – are found to have sufficient fit with the theoretical and conceptual framework and research questions developed in Step 1, the researcher may move on to Step 6, which involves developing and articulating the key arguments and overall contributions of the research. However, the analysis in Step 5 may reveal that the data do not fit sufficiently with the framework and questions developed in Step 1; or it may expose previously unconsidered emic constructs[1] that are of particular interest to the research and require further investigation. In such cases, it may make sense to return to the field for more data, and/ or return to the literature to refine the underlying theoretical and conceptual foundations. Depending on the complexity of the data, the researcher's interpretations and the emergent theoretical framework, any or all of Steps 1, 4 and 5 may be repeated before finally moving on to Step 6. The goal of *theoretical saturation* (Glaser and Strauss, 1967; Strauss and Corbin, 1998) and practical constraints (such as interviewees' availability) mean that researchers may end up alternating between the three steps until such a point that they are satisfied that their theoretical focus, empirical data and potential contribution are in line with one another. The point at which this is achieved – and thus the number of iterations between Steps 1, 4 and 5 that are required – may differ widely across research projects. While the optimal number of iterations cannot be prescribed *ex ante*, the process can be managed in a systematic manner through the use of CAQDAS.

---

[1]In our terminology, etic refers to constructs that are developed by the researcher and take an outside view of the phenomenon under investigation, while emic refers to native constructs emerging from inside the research setting and reflecting the insider's view of reality (see Buckley and Chapman, 1997; Sinkovics et al., 2008).

The Role of CAQDAS in the Qualitative Research Process

We believe that the research model described above is helpful in capturing the 'true' nature of qualitative research and makes a contribution to increasing the legitimacy and acceptance of the 'messiness' of qualitative research (Mellor, 2001). However, we also recognize the inherent danger that a call for acknowledging flexibility and progressive focusing in qualitative research may be misinterpreted as a call for leniency towards unsystematic research, at a time when qualitative research is rife with accusations of a lack of rigour, the apparent misuse of concepts such as grounded theory and opacity in describing research methodology (Suddaby, 2006; Jones and Noble, 2007). In order to tackle these kinds of criticism, we encourage the use of CAQDAS during each of the six steps in our model. We believe that using CAQDAS can accommodate the non-linear and evolving process of interaction between qualitative data and the theoretical and conceptual backbones of research, while also helping in the operational management and formalization of the research.

The term CAQDAS can refer to various types of software designed to facilitate the analysis of qualitative data. Weitzman and Miles (1995) originally developed a typology concerning the handling and management of qualitative (then, mostly textual) data, formerly labelled code and retrieve software, and the more extensive functionality in code-based theory builders. However, the boundaries between these types of software have become increasingly blurry and nowadays most modern CAQDAS packages can handle data beyond text, i.e. graphics, audio and video, and offer tools that will enable content searching tools, linking, coding, querying, writing and annotation, and often also mapping and networking (Lewins and Silver, 2007; 2009).

We believe that the acronym CAQDAS is something of a misnomer: to the untrained ear, Computer-Assisted Qualitative Data Analysis Software may convey an inappropriate sense of the software taking over the analytical process. It has long been recognized that such software was never intended to replace the researcher's unique skills in analysing and interpreting complex data (Catterall and Maclaran, 1998; Gordon and Langmaid, 1988; Gummesson, 2005). Instead, CAQDAS is designed to facilitate the organization and processing of data and enhance the dialogue between researcher and data. As such, it is a meritorious tool that helps in legitimizing the acknowledgement of complexity and 'messiness' in the reporting of qualitative research, while also encouraging greater transparency, credibility and trust-worthiness (Sinkovics et al., 2005; Sinkovics et al., 2008; Ghauri and Firth, 2009; Symon and Cassell, in this volume).

CAQDAS provides a toolset for the analysis of abundant qualitative data that can be understood as similar to the *decision support systems* used by practitioners (Shim et al., 2002). Following Little's *decision calculus*, we believe qualitative research can benefit from a 'set of procedures for processing data and judgements to assist [...] in decision making' (Little, 1970). These procedures are to be 'simple, robust, easy to control, adaptive, complete on important issues and easy to communicate' (Little, 2004: 1855). When used appropriately, CAQDAS allows qualitative researchers to have a 'dialogue with the computer' and develop a greater degree of effectiveness and rigour at each step of the research process. This is achieved through documenting the interactive process of going forwards and backwards between theory and the field.

By creating an auditable 'footprint' of the progressive dialogue between the researcher and their data, CAQDAS can help researchers define the space in between the two opposing views that dominate qualitative research debates: the highly inductive grounded theory approach promoted by Glaser (Glaser and Strauss, 1967; Glaser, 1992), and the highly structured, deductively oriented qualitative analysis advocated by Eisenhardt (1989) and Yin (2003). In essence, the debate between these opposing views is a debate about the relative importance of creativity versus formalization, of meaning versus validity. We believe that the two are equally important and achievable through an emphasis on strong research logic, flexibility and thorough documentation. In particular, CAQDAS can assist qualitative researchers in managing each step of the research process and in making their methodology more accessible to peers and reviewers.

As a caveat, it should be noted that, like any other tool, CAQDAS can be used well or badly. It is up to the individual researcher – and those involved in their training and guidance – to ensure that any expectations are appropriate and realistic. CAQDAS is neither a shoehorn for forcing grounded research into a set of mechanistic criteria, nor a cover-all for superficial research. We urge researchers to acknowledge the fluidity and 'moving goalposts' that characterize qualitative research, but we also encourage careful and detailed documentation of this process. Many qualitative researchers – particularly those new to academia – fear that by closely documenting the unexpected twists and turns of their research, they are laying themselves open to criticism. Nonetheless, it should be recognized that in qualitative research, the realistic purpose of a systematic audit trail is not to *ensure replicability*, but precisely to explain the idiosyncrasies of each qualitative research project that *preclude replicability*. As such, we argue that CAQDAS can enable the production of robust and defensible qualitative research that can stand up to close scrutiny.

Methodology and Application to Data

In this section, we use the example of case study research conducted by one of the authors (Alfoldi, 2008) to illustrate the practical application of CAQDAS (in particular, the NVivo software)[2] during each step of the progressive focusing model in Figure 7.1. The research consisted of a single in-depth case study (see Buchanan, in this volume) of knowledge transfer and regional governance in a large multinational firm, and is briefly described next.

Timeline of the qualitative research project

The research project started with a 'preparatory' phase that encompassed Steps 1, 2 and 3 of the model presented in Figure 7.1. Step 1 began with a thorough review of theories of the multinational enterprise, subsidiary management, knowledge transfer and management and organizational learning. Based on this, research questions were developed concerning the nature of knowledge transfer in multinational companies, with a particular focus on two constructs: *reverse knowledge transfer* (knowledge created at the subsidiary, then transferred to headquarters (HQ)) and *secondary knowledge transfer* (subsidiaries adapting knowledge received from HQ and transferring it to other subsidiaries in the intra-company network). Given the scarcity of extant research on these types of knowledge transfer and the exploratory nature of the research questions, a qualitative case study methodology was designed in Step 2, based on a social constructionist epistemology (see Duberley, Johnson and Cassell, in this volume). In Step 3, pilot interviews were conducted at the Hungarian subsidiaries

---

[2]As noted before, several different kinds of CAQDAS tools are available for qualitative researchers. We use NVivo (Richards, 2005) for pragmatic reasons, rather than to advocate the utilization of a specific software package over alternative software. Nonetheless, NVivo offers a number of features (such as collaborative and merge features) that are particularly helpful in the coordination of international fieldwork.

of three multinational companies that the researcher had negotiated access to. Only one of the three subsidiaries indicated extensive ongoing links with other subsidiaries, which was a vital prerequisite for the research topic, so a single in-depth case study was chosen as the research method.

Step 4 of the research process involved conducting several interviews at the Hungarian subsidiary of the focal company. Faced with the considerable size and complexity of the subsidiary's overall operations, the empirical focus was narrowed down to a specific functional division, *trade marketing*, which concentrated on marketing the company's products and services to retail customers rather than consumers. In Step 5, the rich data generated from these interviews were analysed in depth, which revealed a complex, formal regional hierarchy between the company's Hungarian unit and two other subsidiaries in Slovenia and Croatia. These findings inspired a return to Step 1 of the research process: and conducting a literature review of previously unexamined theoretical areas such as *regional integration and responsiveness* (Lehrer and Asakawa, 1999) and *subsidiary mandates* (Birkinshaw, 1996). It also fostered theorizing about new constructs such as *regional administrative mandates*.

This was followed by a return to Step 4, in the form of a second set of interviews at the company's units in Slovenia and Croatia. The analysis of these new data (Step 5) not only provided an alternative empirical perspective on the issues investigated so far, but also highlighted the relevance of related constructs such as *inter-unit ties* (Hansen, 1999), *corporate socialisation* (Björkman et al., 2004) and the *motivation for knowledge sharing* (Osterloh and Frey, 2000). This in turn triggered going back to Step 1 again to conduct a literature search for conceptual links with knowledge transfer and regional management.

Inspired by the findings and constructs emerging from the data as well as from the newly explored strands of literature, a third and fourth set of interviews were carried out face-to-face and over the telephone (repeating Step 4 twice more). These interviews followed up and extended the findings to another division, *marketing*, which was emerging as a useful contrast to the trade marketing division in terms of its reporting structure and knowledge transfer links. The new data also provided insights suggesting the presence of *role stress* (see Wong et al., 2007) as a factor in the units' difficulties in sharing knowledge effectively. This prompted an investigation of the role stress literature and its links to knowledge transfer (Step 1), as well as a careful re-examination of previously collected data for references implying role stress (Step 5). There was also some hard-won input from the company HQ on wider regional perspectives, but not enough to justify a continued focus on HQ–subsidiary knowledge transfer without the danger of biased representation. As such, the research had to be refocused entirely on the subsidiary perspective, necessitating another return to Step 1, as the 'natural boundaries' of the case were discovered (and to a certain extent, imposed) in a progressive manner. By this point, the theoretical and empirical analysis was finally indicating a degree of theoretical saturation that was deemed sufficient to embark on Step 6: a final write-up articulating and synthesizing the arguments and contributions of the research.

This account illustrates the emergent and idiosyncratic nature of the typical qualitative research process, highlighting the repeated interaction between theory and data that is the hallmark of progressive focusing. Next, we address each step in turn to show how CAQDAS can be used to facilitate this complex process of interaction.

Application of CAQDAS during each step of the research process

In this section, we use specific examples from the project described above to illustrate how CAQDAS may be used to manage and document rich data and complex analytical processes during each of the six steps of the progressive focusing model.

Step 1: choosing a topic, literature review, development of theoretical and conceptual foundations and research questions

One of the first tasks facing a researcher embarking on a new project is creating a title for the intended contribution. A good title serves a dual purpose: it communicates the researcher's intent to others, but more immediately, it also shapes the researcher's own thinking by temporarily demarcating the boundaries of the core topic (Peshkin, 1985). As we have argued, the focus and perspective of qualitative research will evolve progressively, so the title of a qualitative study will rarely stay constant throughout the research process. Peshkin (1985) recommends filing and dating each version of the title, in order to allow the researcher to reconstruct the evolution of key perspectives and conceptual drivers and to aid as well as evaluate progress. Although this may be achieved by saving several word-processed drafts of the research, the evolution of the title can be more formally and reliably documented via the use of CAQDAS such as NVivo (Richards, 2005). We advocate filing and dating successive versions of the title as well as the evolving research questions (see Andersen and Skaates, 2004) in the form of a *project memo*, which allows the progression of the researcher's thinking and intended contribution to be documented and tracked.

During the first step of the qualitative research process, the researcher's principal task is to conduct a thorough, critical and rigorous literature review. Such a review is crucial for building up a robust theoretical basis for the study, accurately defining a gap in the literature and developing the core topic and research questions of the study. In the business and management discipline, *narrative reviews* are the norm, which are 'singular descriptive accounts of the contributions made by writers in the field, often selected for inclusion on the implicit biases of the researcher' (Tranfield et al., 2003: 208). Narrative reviews can appear subjective and arbitrary when compared with the *systematic reviews* found in medical science and healthcare. Systematic reviews observe a strict 'hierarchy of evidence' (Davies and Nutley, 1999; Tranfield et al., 2003) and use explicit procedures for including or excluding previous studies, in order to minimize bias and error. However, the *soft, applied, rural* and *divergent* nature of business and management research (Tranfield and Starkey, 1998) often precludes this kind of systematic approach. While quantitative studies in business and management may lend themselves to meaningful meta-analysis, qualitative studies are generally ill-suited to this purpose – the sheer diversity of methodologies and contextual idiosyncrasies makes reliable comparisons and quality assessments very difficult.

Nonetheless, even if fully systematic literature reviews are not achievable in qualitative business and management research, we feel there is room for enhancing the credibility of narrative reviews. Greater rigour can be achieved by meticulously documenting literature searches, keeping a record of keywords and key arguments, and systematically extracting information to build a *casebook* of references, through a process of *descriptive coding* (Richards, 2005). For example, during the research project we described above, a list of the key journal articles related to regional management in multinational companies was compiled by importing abstracts and document links into NVivo and coding them as individual cases. A number of key attributes were defined (journal star rating, study methodology, etc.) and values were assigned for each case. This approach not only allowed the researcher to keep a reliable, searchable record of the literature used, but also enabled a matrix data display (see Miles and Huberman, 1994) of the articles in NVivo and filtering by attributes.

Attributes		
Name	Type	Description
⊞ 1 - Area	String	Regional or country context of the research (if applicable)
⊞ 2 - Industry	String	Industry context of the research (if applicable)
⊞ 3 - Method	String	Qualitative, Quantitative or Mixed (if applicable)
⊞ 4 - Data source	String	Survey, Case study (single/multiple), Panel data, Survey + Interview etc. (if applicable)
⊞ 5 - No. of respondents	String	Number of respondents (if applicable)

⊞ Casebook				
	A : 1 - Area ▽	B : 2 - Industry ▽	C : 3 - Method ▽	D : 4 - Data source ▽ ▽	E : 5 - No. of resp... ▽
1 : Rugman & Verbeke (2004)	General	General/Mixed	Quantitative	Panel data	300+
2 : Schlie & Yip (2000)	General	Automotive	Mixed	Survey + interview	Not Reported
3 : Enright (2005a)	Asia-Pacific	General/Mixed	Quantitative	Survey + interview	300+
4 : Enright (2005b)	Asia-Pacific	General/Mixed	Quantitative	Survey + interview	300+
5 : Lasserre (1996)	Asia-Pacific	General/Mixed	Mixed	Survey + interview	Not Reported
6 : Morrison et al (1991)	North America	General/Mixed	Mixed	Survey + interview	100-199
7 : Sullivan (1997)	Europe	Manufacturing	Mixed	Survey + interview	20-29
8 : Paik & Sohn (2004)	General	Manufacturing	Qualitative	Case study (single)	1-9
9 : De Koning et al (1997)	Europe	FMCG	Qualitative	Case study (single)	20-29
10 : Quelch & Bloom (1996)	General	General/Mixed	Qualitative	Case study (multiple)	30-99
11 : Schuh (2007)	CEE	General/Mixed	Qualitative	Case study (multiple)	1-9
12 : Roure et al (1993)	General	General/Mixed	Qualitative	Case study (multiple)	1-9
13 : Daniels (1987)	Europe	General/Mixed	Qualitative	Case study (multiple)	10-19
14 : Lehrer & Asakawa (1999)	Multiple regions	General/Mixed	Qualitative	Case study (multiple)	30-99
15 : Schuh (2000)	CEE	General/Mixed	Qualitative	Case study (multiple)	1-9

Figure 7.2 Example of a literature review casebook

Looking at Figure 7.2, qualitative case studies appear to be the dominant empirical research method in the area of regional management. Insights such as this can facilitate more robust and credible arguments about the state of the art in the field than anecdotal citations alone. In addition to enhancing credibility, casebooks also make it easier to find pre-existing measurements and remain alert to the background assumptions of the research (see Potter, 1996). The initial time outlay on importing abstracts and assigning attributes can be more than compensated for by the benefits of an organized, searchable database of theoretical inputs, which can be coded and constantly compared with the empirical data. We recommend using Endnote (Thomson Reuters, 2010) and NVivo concurrently to manage references and document the development of the theoretical foundations of the study.

Step 2: research design

The aim of Step 2 is to develop a robust research design that fits the underlying research questions and logic. This should be underpinned by a sound understanding of the relevant epistemological conventions and the explicit articulation of what the study is trying to achieve (see Duberley, Johnson and Cassell, in this volume). Source materials on methodology can be catalogued in NVivo in much the same way as items in the theoretical literature review (Step 1). This makes it easier to search for specific references, keywords or arguments when discussing the suitability of, and justifications for, a particular research design. Importing abstracts of methodological and empirical papers within the same NVivo project file and filtering them by attributes also allows quick and systematic access to exemplars, i.e. a side-by-side comparison of how other researchers have applied a specific methodology or technique in a given context. This facilitates comparisons and encourages an ongoing awareness of how the developing research design fits in with the designs used in previous research. In addition, NVivo's modelling function can be used to visualize various aspects of the research design, and external documents such as drawings and sketches can be linked to a central 'hub'. All of these can help the researcher to keep more reliable records and cultivate a clearer and more rigorous approach to methodology.

Step 3: sample, context and negotiating access

Although theoretical sampling, choosing a suitable research context and negotiating access tend to be largely 'hands-on' tasks, the organizing capabilities of CAQDAS such as NVivo may also prove useful during this step. In particular, first impressions and observations during access negotiations and initial rapport-building with specific companies or respondents can prove to be a rich source for useful data later on (Lee, 1999). NVivo allows observations, notes and e-mail conversations to be recorded in memos, which can then be linked to documents and coded alongside other items. For example, if a gatekeeper at a company expresses a specific concern or attitude during the initial access negotiations, or offers an insight into the organizational structure of the company, this can be noted and stored in memos and linked to other materials. Such memos may inform the approach taken during a subsequent data collection, or provide vital clues and insights during data analysis. In this sense, we argue that by helping the researcher capture and file away potentially important details from the outset, the data storage and organization capabilities of CAQDAS can even facilitate 'Eureka!' moments.

With regard to choosing and managing the context of the research, NVivo can be particularly useful for cross-cultural or inter-industry comparative studies where empirical data are collected from different sources (see Cohen and Ravishankar, in this volume). Firstly, it allows the researcher to collate and code information about multiple contexts (e.g. country or company statistics from secondary sources) and document the selection of context(s) in a transparent manner, e.g. by using the modelling function to build decision trees. Secondly, once a particular research context has been chosen, the existing materials stored in NVivo can be regularly updated or supplemented with new information (such as press cuttings, company press releases or industry analysis reports).

Step 4: data collection and preparation

During this step, Andersen and Skaates (2004) advocate creating a diary for tracking emergent themes and changes in the theoretical focus, a task that can be greatly assisted by the use of CAQDAS. There are a number of ways to collate data from primary sources in a single place using NVivo. Word-processed data such as interview transcripts can be directly imported into the project file; observations can be recorded in memos; and visual or aural data (sketches drawn by interviewees, photographs, voice files, etc.) can be linked to the project file externally. Data sources such as interviews can also be coded as cases and directly compared in a data matrix (noted above). Figure 7.3 shows an example of creating and assigning key attributes (such as respondent nationality, functional division, etc.) to each interview and charting the cases according to certain attribute values.

In Figure 7.3, the chart shows the overall distribution of respondents according to their official work level in the company. It can be seen that most interviews were conducted with respondents at the middle manager level (WL3 in the case company), followed by operational-level managers (WL2), country group-level directors (WL4), junior employees (WL1) and finally regional or HQ-level directors (WL5). Since middle managers are often seen as critical 'roadblocks' for transferring knowledge within multinational companies (Mäkelä and Seppälä, 2005), charts like these were used as a gauge between periods of data collection to decide on which 'snowballing' leads (Patton, 1990; and see Saunders, in this volume) to follow and what level of respondents to approach next, given resource and access constraints. The ability to keep track of the balance of respondents, maintain searchable descriptive casebooks and chart them according to researcher-defined attributes using CAQDAS can be especially useful for large projects with a considerable diversity among respondents.

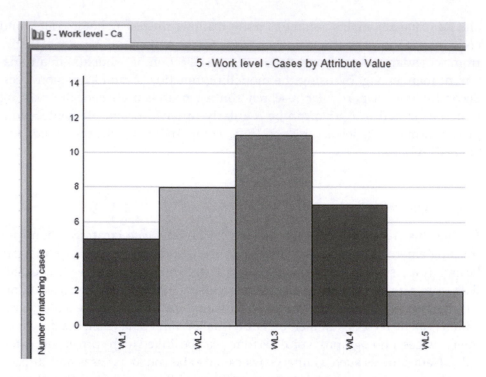

Figure 7.3   Example of charting cases by attribute value

Step 5: data analysis

Out of all six steps of the qualitative data analysis process, data analysis is perhaps the most obvious task to benefit from the application of CAQDAS such as NVivo, and a lot has been written about the use of CAQDAS for data analysis (see e.g. Maclaran and Catterall, 2002; Lindsay, 2004; Sinkovics et al., 2005; Ghauri and Firth, 2009). During this step, the competent and systematic use of software such as NVivo can strengthen trustworthiness by establishing a chain of evidence (Yin, 2003) that truthfully represents the formalized tasks contained in the process of data analysis: organizing and coding the data, searching for patterns and modelling emergent frameworks. By systematically linking and organizing multiple sources of data, it can also assist in tackling the problem of *anecdotalism* that qualitative research often suffers from (Silverman, 2005). As noted already in Step 1, NVivo can greatly assist the constant comparison or triangulation between theory and data (Denzin, 1989; Strauss and Corbin, 1998) and allow the researcher to effectively manage the alternating sequences of data collection and analysis that are the hallmarks of progressive focusing. Using CAQDAS enables the documentation of the ongoing evolution of complex and closely interlinked components of the study, such as the interview protocol and the study's key constructs and themes, be they etic or emic. Perhaps most importantly, NVivo is a useful platform for formally articulating and defining the codes and themes that form the backbone of qualitative data analysis.

There are two basic strategies for analysing qualitative data: *topic coding* and *analytical coding* (also known as axial coding, see Strauss and Corbin, 1998). Topic coding refers to the coding of material into a *subject-based* structure and is recommended as the first step in the formal analysis of newly gathered data (Richards, 2005). It follows a primarily grounded, data-driven logic: its main purpose is to allow the researcher to make sense of the rich, complex data collected during fieldwork and create an organized record of all the themes in the data that are considered (potentially) illuminating. By contrast, analytical coding refers to coding the data into an evolving structure based upon the analyst's *ongoing interpretation* of the action (Richards, 2005). As such, analytical coding relies heavily on the theoretical and conceptual inputs into the research, in addition to the empirical data. Since analytical coding is structured around the intended contribution of the study, its purpose is to generate a refined, integrated and theorized coding scheme, building on the outputs of the topic coding process and the progressive interaction between theory and data. Therefore, both of the above coding strategies form an integral part of qualitative data analysis (Richards, 2005).

In our example, the cyclical process of going back and forth between the theoretical foundations of the study and the field yielded emergent themes and constructs that were significant both because of their number and their influence on the study (a number of these constructs were noted above). Figure 7.4 shows abridged versions of the evolving *topic coding* scheme from different phases of the research process. The first version consists of 37 codes, which include contextual information about the company (operations, trade marketing function, reporting lines), and focus primarily on the construct of knowledge transfer, the main theoretical driver of the research. There is also an early conceptualization of subsidiary mandates, broken down into management mandates and knowledge transfer-related mandates.

Tracing these constructs to the second version of the coding scheme, created several months later, we find not only more references (thanks to the growing number of interviews conducted) but also more codes (93 in total). Subsidiary

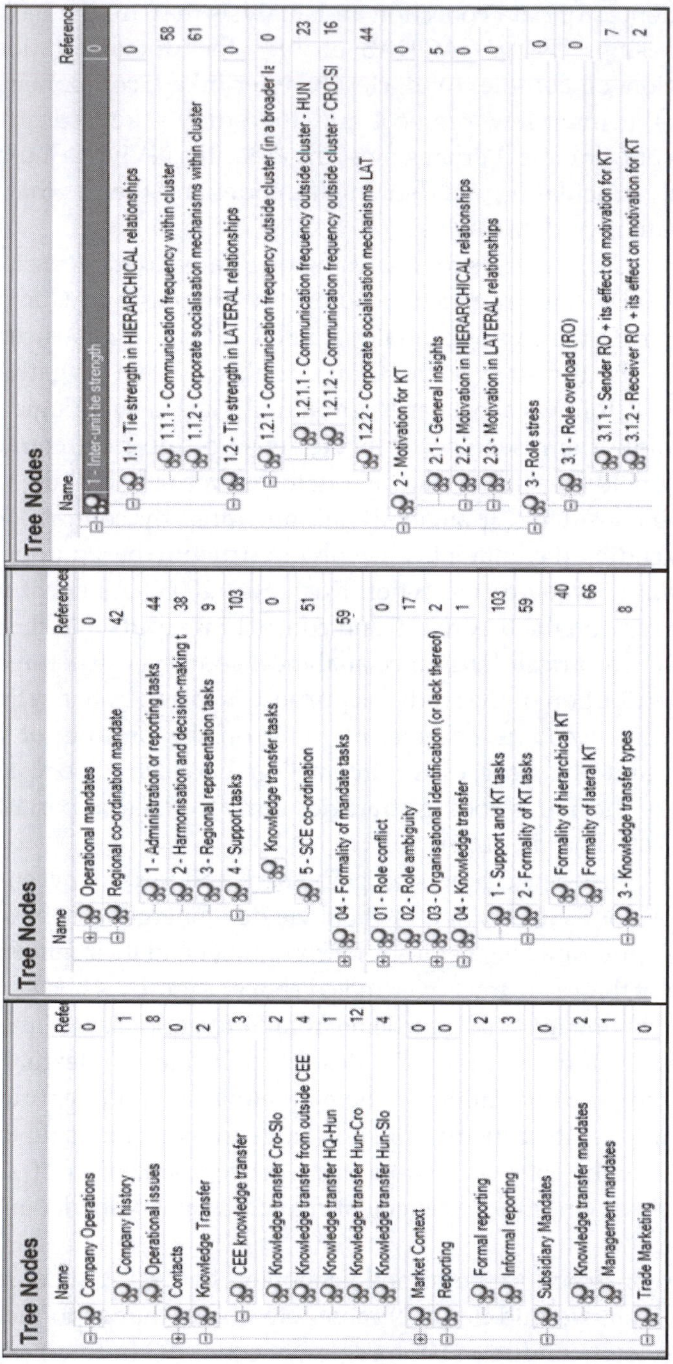

Figure 7.4 Topic coding schemes (2006, 2007) and the analytical coding scheme (2008), (abridged)

mandates are now conceptualized in more detail, incorporating formal task classifications from the literature. The construct of knowledge transfer is elaborated in detail and while the codes are still primarily descriptive (making sense of the data), they also include new conceptual aspects such as the level of formality. Meanwhile, contextual codes such as company operations no longer occupy a prime position – nonetheless, having captured them in the early version of the topic coding scheme allowed the researcher to build a thorough company introduction section in the finished piece.

The final column in Figure 7.4 shows the analytical coding scheme developed during the latter stages of the research project, which consists of 30 final codes. These codes are built on the previous topic codes, but structured around the intended contribution of the research: as such, they no longer include certain emergent constructs such as subsidiary mandates (which subsequently formed the basis of a different publication) but expand on other emic constructs such as types of role stress. Descriptive constructs such as knowledge transfer types (originating from the data) have been absorbed into constructs such as communication frequency, corporate socialization and the motivation for a knowledge transfer (embedded in the literature). As such, the final analytical coding scheme represents an intricately fused version of etic and emic insights, of theory and data, formed through repeated interactions between newly acquired data and newly explored literature streams during the project.

The ability to save these evolving versions of the coding scheme within NVivo provided crucial assistance in documenting the ongoing development of the analysis and interpretation of empirical data, signposting as well as facilitating the progressive focusing approach taken in this study. Our example demonstrates the major role that CAQDAS can play during this step of the qualitative research process.

Step 6: discussion and final write-up

It has been argued that the central problem of presenting qualitative findings is the lack of accessibility to the interpretation process itself (Andersen and Skaates, 2004: 479). To an extent, this problem can be alleviated by paying careful attention to the explanation and illustration of the research methodology in the final output. The inclusion of examples of data displays and coding schemes, as well as a clear and consistent explanation of the procedures followed during each step of the research process, can go a long way to enhancing the credibility and authenticity of the research, without obscuring or distorting the nonlinear nature of the process. To this end, CAQDAS can play a significant role in constructing the methodology section of the final research report. In addition, the logic and contribution of the study must be explicitly summarized and embedded within the literature, with a special focus on any contradictions between the study's findings and previous research (Andersen and Skaates, 2004). During this step, having a well-documented, searchable record of each step of the research process can be a vital tool for an insightful discussion and thoughtful evaluation of the research findings. In the case of cross-border research teams, NVivo's merge function can facilitate and simplify the writing-up task by synchronizing research materials (Sinkovics et al., 2008).

Conclusion

This chapter argues that the use of CADQAS such as NVivo can facilitate the qualitative research process and enhance the trustworthiness of qualitative research (Sinkovics et al., 2008; Sinkovics, 2009). This can be achieved in two ways: (1) by assisting the interaction of theoretical and empirical inputs into the research; and (2) by laying down an *audit trail* or *chain of evidence* (Yin, 2003). Our experience has been that, if used appropriately, CAQDAS can enable a logical and systematic approach without constraining the emergent nature of qualitative data collection and analysis. Through systematizing and documenting the research process, CAQDAS may be seen as a way to strengthen the trustworthiness and rigour of reporting qualitative research, without constraining its flexibility.

Despite concerns about CAQDAS fostering a temptation to quantify, fragment or over-simplify qualitative research (Bryman and Bell, 2003; Jack and Westwood, 2006), our experience leads us to concur with Kelle (1997) that these dangers have been exaggerated. Through the empirical example provided in this chapter, we have not only demonstrated the progressive focusing process of a typical qualitative research project, but also showed how CAQDAS can be used to open up dialogues and an interaction between human and computer (Little, 2004) and enhance the credibility of research through systematization and record-keeping (Sinkovics et al., 2005; 2008; Ghauri and Firth, 2009). We argue that, far from obscuring the inherently 'messy' and constantly evolving nature of qualitative research, CAQDAS can be used to facilitate the analysis of large volumes of data through a systematic comparison with theory. The role of CAQDAS in this fluid and dynamic interaction between theory and data is to aid a more formalized process that potentially makes qualitative inquiry more logical, transparent and trustworthy. To this end, we hope that this chapter contributes to overcoming the artificially linear reporting of qualitative research towards a more 'real-world' presentation, while also observing the requirements of rigour and trustworthiness in data and reporting.

Further Reading

For researchers wishing to use CAQDAS for qualitative research, the works of Bazeley (2007), Richards (2000), Weitzman and Miles (1995) and Kelle et al. (1995) provide a comprehensive introduction and practical guide. Séror (2005) and Gilbert (2002) present helpful perspectives on the advantages and dangers of CAQDAS, while Wickham and Woods (2005) and DiGregorio (2000) discuss their reflections and strategies regarding the use of CAQDAS for literature reviews in particular.

Acknowledgements

The authors gratefully acknowledge the editorial guidance and support of Gillian Symon and Catherine Cassell, who significantly helped to sharpen and focus this contribution. We are also indebted to L. Jeremy Clegg and Sara McGaughey, both of whom have helped to uplift the execution of the empirical project. Finally, insightful comments from Brandon Charleston have triggered some of the systematization arguments, upon which this chapter hinges.

References

Alfoldi, E.A. (2008) 'Knowledge transfer in the multinational enterprise: The impact of inter-subsidiary hierarchy and role stress', PhD dissertation. Leeds: University of Leeds.

Andersen, P.H. and Skaates, M.A. (2004) 'Ensuring validity in qualitative international business research', in R. Marschan-Piekkari and C. Welch (eds), *Handbook of*

Qualitative Research Methods for International Business. Cheltenham: Edward Elgar, pp. 464–485.

Bazeley, P. (2007) *Qualitative Data Analysis with NVivo*. London: Sage.

Birkinshaw, J. (1996) 'How multinational subsidiary mandates are gained and lost', *Journal of International Business Studies*, 27 (3): 467–495.

Björkman, I., Barner-Rasmussen, W. and Li, L. (2004) 'Managing knowledge transfer in MNCs: The impact of headquarters control mechanisms', *Journal of International Business Studies*, 35 (5): 443–455.

Bryman, A. and Bell, E. (2003) *Business Research Methods*. Oxford: Oxford University Press.

Buckley, P.J. and Chapman, M. (1997) 'The use of native categories in management research', *British Journal of Management*, 8 (4): 283–299.

Catterall, M. and Maclaran, P. (1998) 'Using computer software for the analysis of qualitative market research data', *Journal of the Market Research Society*, 40 (3): 207–222.

Davies, H.T.O. and Nutley, S.M. (1999) 'The rise and rise of evidence in health care', *Public Money and Management*, 19 (1): 9–17.

Denzin, N. (1989) *The Research Act*. Englewood Cliffs, NJ: Prentice Hall.

DiGregorio, S. (2000) 'Using NVivo for your literature review: Strategies in qualitative research: issues and results from analysis using QSR NVivo and NUD*IST'. London: Institute of Education, September.

Dubois, A. and Gadde, L.-E. (2002) 'Systematic combining: An abductive approach to case research', *Journal of Business Research*, 55 (7): 553–560.

Eisenhardt, K.M. (1989) 'Building theories from case study research', *Academy of Management Review*, 14 (4): 532–550.

Ghauri, P.N. and Firth, R. (2009) 'The formalization of case study research in international business', *der Markt*, 48 (1): 29–40.

Gilbert, L.S. (2002) 'Going the distance: "closeness" in qualitative data analysis software', *International Journal of Social Research Methodology*, 5: 215–228.

Glaser, B. (1992) *Basics of Grounded Theory Analysis: Emergence vs Forcing*. Mill Valley, CA: Sociology Press.

Glaser, B.G., and Strauss, A. (1967) *The Discovery of Grounded Theory: Strategies of Qualitative Research*. London: Wiedenfeld and Nicholson.

Gordon, W. and Langmaid, R. (1988) *Qualitative Market Research: A Practitioner's and Buyer's Guide*. Aldershot: Gower.

Gummesson, E. (2005) 'Qualitative research in marketing: Road-map for a wilderness of complexity and unpredictability', *European Journal of Marketing*, 39 (3/4): 309–327.

Hansen, M.T. (1999) 'The search-transfer problem: The role of weak ties in sharing knowledge across organization subunits', *Administrative Science Quarterly*, 44 (1): 82–111.

Hesse-Biber, S. (1996) 'Unleashing Frankenstein's monster?', in R. Burgess (ed.), *Studies in Qualitative Methodology: Computing and Qualitative Research*, vol. 5. London: JAI Press, pp. 25–41.

Iacobucci, D. and Churchill, G.A. (2010) *Marketing Research: Methodological Foundations* (10th edn). Mason, OH: South-Western Cengage Learning.

Jack, G. and Westwood, R. (2006) 'Postcolonialism and the politics of qualitative research in international business', *Management International Review*, 46 (4): 481–500.

Jones, R. and Noble, G. (2007) 'Grounded theory and management research: A lack of integrity?', *Qualitative Research in Organizations and Management*, 2 (2): 84–103.

Kelle, U. (1997) 'Theory building in qualitative research and computer programs for the management of textual data', *Social Research Online*, 2 (2). Available at www.socresonline.org.uk/2/2/1.html (last accessed 5 October 2011).

Kelle, U., Prein, G. and Bird, K. (1995) *Computer-aided Qualitative Data Analysis: Theory, Methods and Practice*. London: Sage.

Lee, T.W. (1999) *Using Qualitative Methods in Organizational Research*. Thousand Oaks, CA: Sage.

Lehrer, M. and Asakawa, K. (1999) 'Unbundling european operations: Regional management and corporate flexibility in American and Japanese MNCs', *Journal of World Business*, 34 (3): 267.

Lewins, A. and Silver, C. (2007) *Using Software in Qualitative Research: A Step-By-Step Guide*. London: Sage.

Lewins, A. and Silver, C. (2009) 'Choosing a CAQDAS package'. Available at http://eprints.ncrm.ac.uk/791/1/2009ChoosingaCAQDASPackage.pdf (last accessed 21 October 2010).

Lindsay, V.J. (2004) 'Computer-assisted qualitative data analysis: Application in an export study', in R. Marschan-Piekkari and C. Welch (eds), *Handbook of Qualitative Research Methods for International Business*. Cheltenham: Edward Elgar, pp. 468–506.

Little, J.D.C. (1970) 'Models and managers: The concept of a decision calculus', *Management Science*, 16 (8): B466–B485.

Little, J.D.C. (2004) 'Comments on "models and managers: The concept of a decision calculus": managerial models for practice', *Management Science*, 50 (12): 1841–1853.

Maclaran, P. and Catterall, M. (2002) 'Analysing qualitative data: Computer software and the market research practitioner', *Qualitative Market Research: An International Journal*, 5 (1): 28–39.

Mäkelä, K. and Seppälä, T. (2005) 'Knowledge sharing in interpersonal cross-border relationships within the MNC', 32nd AIB UK Chapter Conference, Bath.

Marshall, H. (2001) 'Rigour or rigidity? The role of CAQDAS in qualitative research', paper presented at the Association for Qualitative Research (AQR), Melbourne, Australia, 5–7 July.

McGaughey, S.L. (2004) 'Writing it up: The challenges of representation in qualitative research', in R. Marschan-Piekkari and C. Welch (eds), *Handbook of Qualitative Research Methods for International Business*. Cheltenham: Edward Elgar, pp. 529–550.

McGaughey, S.L. (2007) *Narratives on Internationalisation: Legitimacy, Standards and Portfolio Entrepreneurs*. Cheltenham: Edward Elgar.

Mellor, N. (2001) 'Messy method: The unfolding story', *Educational Action Research*, 9 (3): 465–484.

Miles, M.B. and Huberman, A. (1994) *Qualitative Data Analysis: An Expanded Sourcebook*. Thousand Oaks, CA: Sage.

Orton, J.D. (1997) 'From inductive to iterative grounded theory: Zipping the gap between process theory and process data', *Scandinavian Journal of Management*, 13 (4): 419–438.

Osterloh, M. and Frey, B.S. (2000) 'Motivation, knowledge transfer, and organizational forms', *Organization Science*, 11 (5): 538–550.

Parlett, M. and Hamilton, D. (1972) 'Evaluation as illumination: A new approach to the study of innovatory programs', occasional paper, Centre for Research in the Educational Sciences, University of Edinburgh, Edinburgh.

Patton, M.Q. (1990) *Qualitative Evaluation and Research Methods* (2nd edn). Thousand Oaks, CA: Sage.

Peshkin, A. (1985) 'From title to title: The evolution of perspective in naturalistic inquiry', *Anthropology & Education Quarterly*, 16 (3): 214–224.

Potter, W.. (1996) *An Analysis of Thinking and Research about Qualitative Methods*. Mahwah, NJ: Lawrence Erlbaum Associates.

Richards, L. (2000) *Using NVico in Qualitative Research* (2nd edn). Victoria, Australia: QSR International.

Richards, L. (2005) *Handling Qualitative Data – a Practical Guide*. London: Sage.

Séror, J. (2005) 'Computers and qualitative data analysis: Paper, pens and highlighters vs screen, mouse and keyboard', *TESOL Quarterly*, 39: 321–328.

Shim, J.P., Warkentin, M., Courtney, J.F., Power, D.J., Sharda, R. and Carlsson, C. (2002) 'Past, present, and future of decision support technology', *Decision Support Systems*, 33 (2): 111–126.

Silverman, D. (2005) 'Instances or sequences? Improving the state of the art of qualitative research', *Forum: Qualitative Social Research*, 6 (3). Available at www.qualitative-research.net/index.php/fqs/article/viewArticle/6/13 (last accessed 5 October 2011).

Sinkovics, R.R. (2009) 'Special issue: Qualitative marketing forschung – konzeptionelle entwicklungen und methodische trends', *der Markt*, 48 (1): 3–5.

Sinkovics, R.R., Penz, E. and Ghauri, P.N. (2005) 'Analysing textual data in international marketing research', *Qualitative Market Research: An International Journal*, 8 (1): 9–38.

Sinkovics, R.R., Penz, E. and Ghauri, P.N. (2008) 'Enhancing the trustworthiness of qualitative research in international business', *Management International Review*, 48 (6): 689–714.

Stake, R.E. (1981) 'The art of progressive focusing', 65th Annual Meeting of the American Educational Research Association, Los Angeles.

Stake, R.E. (1995) *The Art of Case Study Research*. Thousand Oaks, CA: Sage.

Strauss, A.L. and Corbin, J.M. (1998) *Basics of Qualitative Research: Grounded Theory Procedures and Techniques*. Thousand Oaks, CA: Sage.

Suddaby, R. (2006) 'From the editors: What grounded theory is not', *Academy of Management Journal*, 49 (4): 633–642.

Thomson Reuters (2010) 'Endnote'. Available at www.endnote.com (last accessed 6 June 2010).

Tranfield, D., Denyer, D. and Smart, P. (2003) 'Towards a methodology for developing evidence-informed management knowledge by means of systematic review', *British Journal of Management*, 14 (3): 207–222.

Tranfield, D. and Starkey, K. (1998) 'The nature, social organization and promotion of management research: towards policy', *British Journal of Management*, 9 (4): 341–353.

Weitzman, E.A. and Miles, M.B. (1995) *Computer Programs for Qualitative Analysis*. Thousand Oaks, CA: Sage.

Wickham, M. and Woods, M. (2005) 'Reflecting on the strategic use of CAQDAS to manage and report on the qualitative research process', *The Qualitative Report*, 10: 687–702.

Wong, S.-S., DeSanctis, G. and Staudenmayer, N. (2007) 'The relationship between task interdependency and role stress: A revisit of the job demands-control model', *Journal of Management Studies*, 44 (2): 284–303.

Yin, R.K. (2003) *Case Study Research: Design and Methods* (3rd edn, vol. 5). Thousand Oaks, CA: Sage.

8 Combining Qualitative Methods

Katrina Pritchard

Introduction

In this chapter I explore the practice of combining qualitative methods, drawing specifically on my own experience in organizational research. I aim to deal with both the pragmatic issues of combining qualitative methods across different types and stages of research practice, while also unpacking broader methodological concerns. This is particularly pertinent since typically discussions of methodological combination focus on quantitative-qualitative ('quan-qual') blends, often under the heading of 'multi-method' or 'mixed-methods' research (Creswell, 2003; Tashakkori and Teddlie, 2003). In contrast, despite the representation of qualitative research as 'bricolage' (Kincheloe, 2005), the actual practice of working with qualitative-qualitative ('qual-qual') combinations receives much less attention within the literature and can remain inaccessible, particularly to new researchers (Hesse-Biber, 2010).

This lack of focus on 'qual-qual' combinations may in part be due to the increasing 'brand identity' of individual methods which, along with the usual chapter per method structure of many textbooks, gives an impression of separation and incompatibility. Indeed, researchers may feel the need to adopt a clear and specific label for their research so as to secure legitimacy and credibility with reviewers or examiners. However, such labels are not necessarily indicative of a definitive methodological commitment or of the specific way in which methods have been applied. For example, Broadfoot et al. (2004: 200) observe in respect to Critical Discourse Analysis (CDA) that 'there are as many kinds of CDA as there are analysts' (see also Oswick, in this volume).

At the same time, there is a shared and somewhat generic language of qualitative research (for example, of coding frameworks and themes), which hints at common concerns across methods. Indeed, informal discussions with other qualitative researchers suggest that many do experiment with different approaches and ideas during the course of a research project but that these practices may not be reflected in the final published accounts (Bryman, 2008).

However, there is a broader methodological perspective at stake here. That is to say, methodological decisions often entail more than the simplistic selection of a means by which data are collected, analysed and reported. Rather, such decisions imply overarching (and hence potentially incompatible) ontological and epistemological commitments (Bryman, 1984). Qualitative researchers cannot side step such issues when investigating the potential to combine different approaches, but there is little within the broader 'quan-qual' mixed-methods literature to guide us through such debates. Further, engaging in debates regarding the ontological and epistemological foundations of qualitative research, both more broadly and when considered in respect to individual approaches, might be a potentially paralysing process since, as Shotter and Lannamann (2002: 578) suggest, 'the possibilities for continued disagreement seem endless'. Therefore an important consideration for the researcher exploring the potential of combining qualitative methods is the extent to which they can tolerate the resulting ontological insecurity (Giddens, 1990) and engage in productive ontological oscillation (Weick, 1995) when required. There is unfortunately no 'one size fits all' solution to this challenge, but a key requirement is a strong sense of reflexive engagement throughout the research process.

My aim here is not to catalogue every potential combination of methods but rather I explore three examples from my own research to illustrate different approaches to (and challenges of) combining qualitative methods:

- *An instrumental approach:* using a twenty statements test (TST) as a primer for qualitative research interviews.

- *An integrative approach:* using a tracer study within the preliminary fieldwork stage of an ethnographic project.

- *A dialogic approach:* using ethnography and discourse analysis together across all stages of a research project.

The above labelling is not intended as a definitive classification of a methodo-logical combination (Denzin, 2010) but rather is a purposive categorization proposed to highlight the range of approaches that may be considered. In the instrumental combination, a second method is used to facilitate the first (here as an interview primer) but remains marginal in the broader research process. An integrative approach sees an increased methodological and practical com-bination, with a closer interaction between the research methods (here, a tracer study and the preliminary fieldwork phase of ethnography) as they are imple-mented. The dialogic approach represents a more complex means of combin-ing qualitative methods in which the researcher engages in a dialogue with emerging methodological and practical tensions (here between discursive and ethnographic approaches) in order to facilitate a reflexive research process. In the examples presented later, there are elements of both a pre-planned and more opportunistic combination, though all are more characteristic of simulta-neous rather than sequential approaches to mixed-methods research.

The Broader Context of Mixed-Methods Research

As highlighted above, the notion of methodological combination and the asso-ciated term mixed-methods research is most commonly used when referring to a combination of qualitative and quantitative methodologies within a single research project (Creswell, 2003; Tashakkori and Teddlie, 2003). Methods may be applied in parallel (simultaneously) or sequentially and include different forms of 'mixing' such that data may be converted to a single (usually quanti-tative) form before analysis, applied to different levels of research question or used as a means of triangulation around a single research question (Lewis and Grimes, 1999; Cox and Hassard, 2005).

There are many resources concerned with the different applications and com-binations of mixed-methods (including in the *Journal of Mixed Methods Research* and in a recent special issue of *Qualitative Inquiry*). However, much of this debate glosses over both the potential for, and challenges of, 'qual-qual' combinations (Burke Johnson et al., 2007; Morse, 2010), focusing instead on the more visible divide assumed in 'quan-qual' approaches. Moreover, as Greene and Caracelli (2003: 107) comment, there is a broader concern that 'mixed-methods inquirers are insufficiently reflective and their practice is insufficiently problematized'. Certainly it appears that the challenges discussed within the existing literature focus on technical research topics related to the time and manner in which methods are to be 'mixed'. Here, even in the relatively rare discussions of qualitative method combinations, there is primarily attention being paid to the research design (as a period of planning) and to analysis (as the point at which the methods are 'mixed') (Waddington, 2005; Frost et al., 2010; Morse, 2010). But even in respect to those areas that do receive attention in the literature, there is still much more work to be done: 'the key idea that mixed methods research requires some form of integration is clear; still however additional research is needed to further explicate this process' (Burke Johnson et al., 2007: 125). Indeed Bryman's (2008) content analysis of mixed-methods articles suggests that it is often difficult to detect why and in what ways methods have been combined, since the actual research practices remain hidden from view (Hesse-Biber, 2010).

Further, the focus on differences between quantitative and qualitative perspectives results in insufficient attention being given to the 'paradigm soup' (Buchanan and Bryman, 2007: 486) of qualitative research itself. Moreover, the researcher is largely absent from accounts of mixed-methods research or appears to move easily and silently between methods, selecting from a menu of combinations and 'mixing' only when desired. There is little attention paid to the impact of adopting a mixed-methods research approach across the life-cycle of the research process which, as qualitative researchers, we would expect to see reflexively unpacked (Pritchard and Symon, 2009). Some, however, might suggest that in itself this is not a bad thing and that the qualitative researchers' tendency for navel gazing also often stems more from a broader concern with (ontological and epistemological) inadequacy than a genuine concern for openness (Finlay, 2002; Knights, 2006). Yet for the researcher wishing to combine qualitative methods, a lack of detailed accounts and guidelines might be frustrating. Overall then, while the mixed-methods literature provides a useful backdrop for qualitative researchers to examine when considering the issues associated with combining qualitative methods, the discussions do not address directly those areas of most concern (Hesse-Biber, 2010).

Combining Qualitative Methods: Examples of Instrumental, Integrative and Dialogic Approaches

Based on the discussion above it is clear that we need to unpack what 'combining qualitative methods' might imply by considering both the notion of 'combining' and that of 'method'. It is also important to consider what prompts a researcher to utilize different methods or methodologies in a particular research project (Kincheloe, 2005). For example, are there strong influences within the field of research, the academic institution or the site of investigation? Further, we should attend to how (when and with whom) the decision was made. For example, was it a planned approach or adopted in response to a problem encountered during the research process? Finally, we need to think about the degree of combination that results, and the different issues that arise depending on the degree of methodological *vs* technical combination attempted. The approach taken to examining these issues below is a broadly confessional account based on my own research practice. In developing this, I have drawn on official accounts of my own research practice (e.g. in conference papers and my PhD thesis), reflexive research diaries and logs maintained during these undertakings, and various communications with others researchers (including emails and seminar presentations). These sources are inevitably partial and incomplete, but have proved useful in prompting the recall of, and reflection on, these research projects. Such accounts, developed either solely by a single researcher or jointly by co-researchers and potentially even participants, are not only useful in a retrospective summary such as this chapter but also may prove invaluable in working through the many and varied challenges of combining qualitative methods during the various times and places of the research undertaking (Richards, 2009). The examples discussed below have been deliberately selected to highlight different modes of combination and represent a chronological development of my own research exploring different aspects of the professional identity of HR (Human Resources) practitioners.

Instrumental approach: using a twenty statements test (TST) as a primer for qualitative research interviews

In this study, my focus was on the role of HR practitioners and their perception of professional knowledge (Pritchard et al., 2004). Initially, following a standard process, I identified specific research questions, which I used to develop a semi-structured interview protocol. However, at this point I encountered two key challenges. Firstly, I wanted to unpack participants' own understandings and constructions of professional knowledge, rather than impose my own definitions. Secondly, I was keen to avoid any sense of assessment within the interview.

Rather than extend the length of the interview, I developed a 'primer' for participants to complete in advance, which would then form the basis for the topics explored during the interview discussion. I considered a range of options (including a pre-interview questionnaire and the use of visual methods) but determined that the TST would provide a useful and practical (from the perspective of both participants and researchers) primer. Further, the original application of the TST, to look at relationships between self-concept and role, fitted with the broader aims of my own research (Rees and Nicholson, 1994) in respect of concerns with professional identity. After pilot testing several options, the statement set for the test was 'I believe an HR professional should be ...' and this was given to individuals along with 20 blank lines on which to write their responses. This was described as 'a form to collect some initial views' in the accompanying email sent to participants.

The resulting TSTs were used in the interviews as a spring-board to explore participants' views and perceptions regarding to the areas of key interest to my research questions. The TST responses were not analysed in and of their own right, rather they were used only as an interview primer in this study. This priming, however, worked both collectively and individually. Looking at the TST statements collected provided prompts both generically across all interviews as well as with the individual who provided the response. Further, it provided some insight into specific issues within the organization that I had not previously been aware of, again enabling me to consider in advance how to approach certain topics. At an individual level the TST not only acted as a primer from a topic perspective but also as an ice-breaker at an interpersonal level, particularly when participants provided unexpected or witty responses (e.g. one participant's response to the question 'I believe an HR professional should be' was 'paid a fortune'). However, it does raise the issue that the TST (here removed from a specific theoretical consideration of the self-concept) also acted to prime my perceptions of the participant, which in turn shaped the interaction that took place. As a researcher it is therefore important to be aware that different methods (and different combinations of methods) will influence the construction of researcher and participant subjectivities (Cassell, 2005). While the primary use of the TST in this instance was as an interview primer, looking back through my notes I am reminded that I also completed the TST myself. Initially, I used the same prompt question as the participants just to test the process, but subsequently revised and revisited these lists to reflect on my personal construction of the research topic, particularly considering how my assumptions and perceptions had changed over time. This was a particularly useful aid to reflexivity when positioned alongside my use of template analysis (see King, in this volume) to interpret the interview transcripts.

In this example there was an instrumental combination of data collection methods, with the TST facilitating the interview process rather than featuring as an independent methodological component of the research project. The combination was both relatively straightforward and successful. It also highlights the benefit of a broader consideration of the data collection process beyond an assumption, particularly by novice researchers, that a researcher-led interview is the default option.

Integrative approach: using a tracer study within the preliminary fieldwork stage of an ethnography

In this second example, combining qualitative methods emerged as a response to a challenge experienced during the research process, rather than as a planned strategy developed during the research design phase. I had planned to conduct an ethnographic study and obtained access for an initial phase of preliminary fieldwork. However, on arrival I found it difficult to understand how the organization operated or to make contact with different teams who were spread across a number of locations. Initial attempts to set up meetings and interviews in order to facilitate further access proved problematic, since the dates offered were usually after the preliminary fieldwork was scheduled to finish.

While the distinctive characteristic of ethnography is some form of participant observation, ethnographers will often utilize a wide range of data collection methods, which in turn may shape and direct the understanding of the research site (Brewer, 2004; see also Yanow, Ybema and van Hulst, in this volume). I reflected on the nature of the research site and my research project and investigated the potential of using a tracer study approach to facilitate further access. In a tracer study a specific organizational process is identified and followed via the use of 'tags', which provide the basis for identifying participants and then discussing the nature of their involvement in the activity under investigation (Hornby and Symon, 1994). There is a specific focus on the active tracking of a process through and across the research site, which may set up tensions with broader (traditional) observationalist approaches to ethnography (Brewer, 2004).

Despite these concerns, introducing the idea of a tracer study to the organization prompted a very positive response from the participants. I wrote in my field notes that the organization seemed to regard this as a more tangible research activity than 'participant observation' and it was an activity that they seemed to be able to relate to more clearly. Indeed, the participants became actively involved in the tracer study and as a result process flow diagrams were produced for the organization. This prompted a further reflexive consideration of the ways in which undertaking the tracer study had changed the nature of 'participant observation' within the broader ethnographic study; specifically that it had increased the organizational participation in the research activity and that this subsequently acted to increase my participation in the organization later on. In this respect, combining these particular methods became more than a technical issue and prompted a broader methodological consideration of both my own and the organization's construction of this research project.

In this particular tracer study the 'tags' were HR activities, the progress of which was logged and monitored on a newly implemented work management system. Different types of activities were selected including an expatriate assignment, a creativity workshop, the launch of a diversity networking group and the development of a local HR plan. For each activity, I interviewed the individual with overall responsibility and then (using activity reports generated from the work management system) followed the process both forwards and backwards, talking to the others involved and collecting related documentation. In addition to conducting these data collection interviews under the heading of the tracer study, I continued to keep detailed field logs of my research activities, and thus more broadly integrated the tracer study within an ethnographic frame. Analysis of the interviews and documents produced an annotated map or chart summarizing the activities and highlighting any issues or problems identified by participants. In parallel, I wrote ethnographic accounts that adopted a broader, descriptive perspective on the local understandings of the organization generated via the tracer study.

From this perspective, the tracer study could be viewed as an act of 'participant observation' in and of its own right. Certainly it could be seen as fitting within the broad range of activities undertaken by ethnographers, who are often depicted as adopting a 'suck it and see' approach (Bate, 1997: 1152). However, it is important to reflect that the tracer study was actively constructed (by myself) as a specific research initiative, in part in reaction to the difficulties faced during this preliminary fieldwork project. It was important not only as an act of research in its own right but also as a means of generating enhanced organizational access and support for a longer-term ethnographic study. In this respect, while this example is labelled integrative, it retains some characteristics of an instrumental combination. Combining qualitative research methods should therefore not be considered as a generic or uniform practice, but viewed from the perspective of the context within which it is conducted. It is worth noting that in the subsequent analysis and academic write-up of this research, the tracer study faded into the background in respect to the broader ethnographic study (Pritchard, 2010). As identified earlier, it perhaps does not have the 'brand identity' which qualitative researchers assume may assist with the review and publication process.

In contrast to the first example then, what emerges here is a more complex picture of combining qualitative methods, which highlights the active role of the researcher at all stages of the research process. Moreover, the ways in which methods are combined may emerge and develop during the research process rather than being clearly defined during the research design stage.

Dialogic approach: using ethnography and discourse analysis

The overall research design of this study into the construction of professional knowledge and identity by HR practitioners was planned as a combination of ethnographic and discursive approaches. This project was undertaken while in pursuit of my PhD (Pritchard, 2007), which is a particular genre of research with a specific academic framing. Indeed, given that the notion of 'originality' is central to the judgement of a PhD thesis, this perhaps acts as a direct prompt to methodological inventiveness. Certainly there was a feeling that the PhD provided both space and time to engage in methodological issues; space and time which (as I have subsequently discovered) may be harder to find in shorter, budget restricted research undertakings.

Many writers on ethnography have highlighted 'discourse' as a valid research interest (Bate, 1997; Fine et al., 2008). Further, the combination of ethnographic and discursive analysis is often suggested as a useful 'mix' within organization studies. For example, this combination has the potential to address the criticism that discourse analysis removes texts from their original, organizational context (Alvesson and Karreman, 2000). Further, Fairclough (2003) suggests that CDA offers a reflexive framing for ethnography while Hansen and colleagues (Barry et al., 2006; Hansen, 2006) suggest a 'diatextual' reading (Barry et al., 2006: 1107) in which each approach is used by different researchers who will then come together to debate their findings.

However, in common with the broader mixed-methods research literature, these suggestions tend to place one or other approach in a dominant position, with the other providing a supplementary view (Creswell et al., 2003). The focus is placed on a specific aspect of research or phase rather than looking across the whole research process. In short, there is relatively little to guide the researcher as to how discourse analysis and ethnography may be combined or what challenges may be faced along the way.

In the remainder of this section I shall therefore set out some of the challenges faced during the different stages of my research project and explain how these have shaped my understanding of combining qualitative methods. Three different phases of research are examined:

- *Research design*: as the researcher attempts to map out both a philosophical and practical path to informing a research area.

- *During fieldwork*: as the researcher is removed from the academic environment and is both actively and passively constructing data.

- *Subsequent analysis*: as the researcher returns from the field and (re)constructs the story to be told.

The approach adopted here was one of engaging in a reflexive dialogue with and between these different research approaches. As will be seen, sometimes this dialogue builds on the similarities between approaches, while at other times it will be prompted by the argument or debate caused by tensions between them. In this way the researcher engages in an ongoing (self) negotiation as the approaches are used together within a single research project.

Research design

As outlined above, at the outset of the research project I was conceptually engaging with the ideas of both ethnography and discourse analysis (see Yanow, Ybema and van Hulst, and Oswick, in this volume), although at this stage they remained somewhat separated. Issues of discourse were conceptual and theoretical, entangled with my research questions and literature review. Ontological and epistemological concerns were themselves discursive, and I was unclear as to how they related to my role as a researcher. On the other hand, issues of ethnography seemed much more practical and directly related to my role as a researcher during this time, particularly in terms of securing access to a research site. There seemed to be less need to theorize and more emphasis on experiencing.

From this perspective then, the engagement with ethnography provided a framework that allowed me to defer decisions regarding my approach to discourse analysis and enabled me to move forward with the research. At the same time adopting an ethnographic perspective encouraged me to actively engage with the research context and the individuals within it. The process of obtaining access and negotiating my role and identity as a researcher within the organization was part of the research project, not preliminary to it. In contrast, my engagement with discourse analysis prompted a consideration of the researcher's role and identity as positioned within a broader discursive frame (e.g. that of academic research), which offered alternative ways of viewing both my own and others' construction of research. My experience has been that debating these two approaches and exploring alternate means of seeing the research process aided my reflexive understanding of the project, my role and participant relationships.

During fieldwork

It was at this stage that the different timeframes of the two methodological approaches came more sharply into focus. Being there and spending time is a central part of the ethnographic approach. In contrast, accounts from discourse analysts tend to focus on identifying and obtaining the 'right' texts, sometimes to the extent of giving the impression of the researcher as a 'ram raider'; namely getting what they need and then making a quick getaway. In contrast, despite the label 'participant observation', ethnographic research may be portrayed as an almost passive approach, during which the researcher somehow obtains information through a process of osmosis. Further, there is potential tension as a result of discourse analysts' interest in 'bodies of texts' (Phillips et al., 2004: 636) in contrast to ethnographers' interest in other sorts of bodies (i.e. the research participants themselves or material objects).

However, I found this tension constructive rather than destructive. Moving from one perspective to the other (and looking at the space in-between) prompts the researcher to debate the assumptions about research practice. Shifting between the consideration of 'researcher' and 'participant' roles and relationships from both a discursive and ethnographic perspective enabled a richer, more textured understanding of these to emerge during the course of the research project. For example, I considered my own field notes as texts to be analysed rather than simply as descriptions of events. Indeed, a regular discursive consideration of my field notes provided a useful prompt to reflect on the construction of research processes throughout the fieldwork. Moreover, there is a concern here that the ethnographer may go native and lose the benefit of an outsider's perspective. In this respect, I found that having a parallel focus on discourse was particularly useful; in a sense this provided the means to get close to the individual participants and still remain detached when looking at organizational texts. I was also able to reflect on my research relationships and experience these through a discursive lens. This provided a useful prompt to reflexivity by means of engaging in questions such as: how is my position as a researcher constructed? How is the process of research constructed? What means are used to construct these and what is being ignored?

At the same time, accounts of discourse analysis concentrate on analysing various types of organizational documents, yet the processes and relationships essential to obtaining these documents may be glossed over, potentially ignoring the issue that the researcher has a relationship with the text other than via analysis. In contrast, the ethnographer's focus on participant relationships helps maintain a contextual sensitivity. Furthermore, the discourse analyst may treat collected documents as fixed or static but combining discursive and ethnographic approaches offers the opportunity to adopt a more dynamic perspective, for example following the drafting of an organizational text through its various stages of production and consumption.

However, there is also a broader concern that researchers may end up flitting between these methods in a random or haphazard manner and/or executing both approaches poorly. Combining qualitative methods requires a disciplined approach to data collection activities, ensuring that this will later enable a productive viewing of the research context through different lenses. In this research project this was managed by keeping detailed field notes along with detailed logs of the organizational texts collected and created (e.g. interview transcripts). NVivo (a qualitative data analysis software package) was also used to track the links between individuals, events and texts, with the aim of recording information that would enable rather than constrain the later analysis phase.

This is not to say, however, that combining these approaches will be trouble free. There were times when the broader tensions between deconstructive and critical tendencies of discourse analysis and a more descriptive interpretative orientation to ethnography proved to be more challenging. At these points I attempted to write down my debates about working through these issues. The aim during the fieldwork was not to resolve these tensions but rather to acknowledge and record them as a resource for later analysis (Richards, 2009).

Analysis

Various authors have written about the difficulties that ethnographers can face at this stage of the research process, commenting that the process of leaving the field is as complex as arriving (Brewer, 2004). Once again ethnography offers a useful lens by which to view the researcher's role and acts as a prompt for ongoing reflexivity; which can sometimes be lost at the boundaries between stages in the research process. The issues of combining methods also come sharply into focus here. Authors discussing both ethnography and discourse analysis have plenty to say about the processes of analysis and writing. In practical terms, this combining of methods involved a mid-range approach that requires the researcher to move backwards and forwards between a detailed consideration of the textual data and a broader awareness of both the proximal and distal context (Wetherell et al., 2001). This approach offered the best 'fit' in terms of my research questions and offered a means of working with both ethnographic and discursive perspectives.

The approach adopted continued the principle of using a single approach to reflect back on the other, and of debating the emerging tensions. For example, in the early stages of analysis I wrote specific ethnographic accounts that focused on the different groups within the organization in which the research was being conducted. This process allowed me to work through different themes and issues and to highlight where to concentrate my efforts in terms of the more detailed discursive analysis of specific organizational texts. Subsequently, at regular intervals I was then able to step back from the discourse analytic process and look at the analysis developing alongside these accounts, particularly focusing on areas of confusion or complexity where different stories might be unfolding. This process allows the researcher to play with different analytical stories, to develop different threads and then step back and see what is emerging. I did not attempt to produce an overall integrative account but rather sought to understand the range of stories (both ethnographic and discursive) that could be told.

Obviously it is not possible to say that all researchers would experience the creative tension I have outlined here in the same way; however, I suggest that combining qualitative research methods offers the opportunity to enhance the researcher's understanding of the phenomenon under investigation.

Conclusion

In this chapter I have examined the practice of combining qualitative methods within the broader context of mixed-methods research and then explored three examples (described as instrumental, integrative and dialogic) from my own research experience. Taken together, these highlight the importance of reflexivity (Alvesson and Sköldberg, 2000; see also Haynes, in this volume) and an increasing emphasis on the temporal dimensions of research practice (Cunliffe et al., 2004).

However, we can also see that notions of 'combining' and 'mixing' warrant more attention to be paid in the methodological literature. In some cases, more obviously here in the first two examples explored, the combinations may be relatively straightforward but can still exert a critical influence on the construction of the research process. In other cases, particularly where there are more significant methodological tensions between the approaches, we can see that 'combining' is an active process that continues through all the stages of the research project. It becomes a key aspect of the researchers' role and may involve a process of continual adjustment and readjustment as the project unfolds.

And yet there are risks as well. While the accounts above examine the way in which the researcher can move between different methods, this needs to be a considered and careful undertaking rather than a constant switching that could prove confusing and counterproductive. In all the examples discussed, I have noted that the practice of reflexively documenting the research process provides an essential means of examining how the practice of combining methods is unfolding. This practice, along with paying considerable attention to data management throughout, is a critical aspect of the research process. I would also recommend opening up your research practice to others, for example to participants and/or academic peers, in order to generate discussion.

I am not suggesting that we try to develop new 'super-methods' as a result of such a combination nor that we simply increase a project's method count for effect. However, I do offer the view that working through and between theoretical and practical tensions when combining qualitative methods provides opportunities to enrich both the research process and the findings that emerge. Moreover, I hope to encourage other researchers to share their experiences of 'qual-qual' mixed-methods approaches, so we can further develop and enhance our qualitative research practice.

Further Reading

Please see other relevant chapters in this book for further information regarding the individual qualitative methodologies and methods discussed.

For a critical examination of mixed-methods practice see Bryman (2008). For a comprehensive overview of the methodological and method issues encountered within a wide range of mixed-methods research contexts see Tashakkori and Teddlie (eds) (2003).

For a consideration of mixed-methods practice from a qualitative perspective see the recent special issue in *Qualitative Inquiry* (2010, volume 16, issue 6), which includes the Denzin, Morse and Hesse-Biber articles cited in this chapter.

Acknowledgements

Aspects of this chapter were first presented at the European Association of Management (EURAM) conference (with Gillian Symon, May 2009). I would like to thank all those present, and Cathy Cassell and Bill Lee in particular, for their support in developing this line of enquiry.

Funding

Aspects of this research were supported by the Economic and Social Research Council (Grant Number PTA-0302004-00095).

References

Alvesson, M. and Karreman, D. (2000) 'Varieties of discourse: on the study of organizations through discourse analysis', *Human Relations*, 53 (9): 1125–1149.

Alvesson, M. and Sköldberg, K. (2000) *Reflexive Methodology: New Vistas for Qualitative Research*. London: Sage.

Barry, D., Carroll, B. and Hansen, H. (2006) 'To text or context? Endotextual, exotextual and multi-textual approaches to narrative and discourse', *Organization Studies*, 27 (8): 1091–1110.

Bate, S.P. (1997) 'Whatever happened to organizational anthropology? A review of the field of organizational ethnography and anthropological studies', *Human Relations*, 50 (9): 1147–1175.

Brewer, J.D. (2004) 'Ethnography', in C. Cassell and G. Symon (eds), *Essential Guide to Qualitative Methods in Organizational Research*. London: Sage, pp. 312–322.

Broadfoot, K., Deetz, S. and Anderson, D. (2004) 'Multi-levelled, multi-method approaches to organizational discourse', in D. Grant, C. Hardy, C. Oswick and L. Putnam (eds), *The Sage Handbook of Organizational Discourse*. London: Sage, pp. 193–212.

Bryman, A. (1984) 'The debate about quantitative and qualitative research: a question of method or epistemology', *The British Journal of Sociology*, 35 (1): 75–92.

Bryman, A. (2008) 'Of methods and methodology', *Qualitative Research in Organizations and Management*, 3 (2): 159–168.

Buchanan, D.A. and Bryman, A. (2007) 'Contextualising methods choice in organizational research', *Organizational Research Methods*, 10 (3): 483–501.

Burke Johnson, R., Onwuegbuzie, A.J. and Turner, L.A. (2007) 'Towards a definition of mixed methods research', *Journal of Mixed Methods Research*, 1 (2): 112–133.

Cassell, C. (2005) 'Creating the interviewer: identity work in the management research process', *Qualitative Research*, 5(2): 167–179.

Cox, J. and Hassard, J. (2005) 'Triangulation in organizational research: a re-presentation', *Organization*, 12 (1): 109–133.

Creswell, J.W. (2003) *Research Design: Qualitative; Quantitative and Mixed Method Approaches* (2nd edn). London: Sage.

Creswell, J.W., Plano Clark, V.L., Gutman, M.L. and Hanson, W.E. (2003) 'Advanced mixed methods research design', in A. Tashakkori and C. Teddlie (eds), *Handbook of Mixed Methods in Social and Behavioral Research*. London: Sage, pp. 209–240.

Cunliffe, A.L., Luhman, J. and Boje, D.M. (2004) 'Narrative temporality: implications for organizational research', *Organization Studies*, 25 (2): 261–286.

Denzin, N. (2010) 'Moments, mixed methods and paradigm dialogs', *Qualitative Inquiry*, 16 (6): 419–427.

Fairclough, N. (2003) *Analyzing Discourse: Textual Analysis for Social Research*. London: Routledge.

Fine, G.A., Morrill, C. and Surianarain, S. (2008) 'Ethnography in organizational settings', in D.A. Buchanan and A. Bryman (eds), *Handbook of Organizational Research Methods*. London: Sage.

Finlay, L. (2002) 'Negotiating the swamp: the opportunity and challenge of reflexivity in research practice', *Qualitative Research*, 2 (2): 209–230.

Frost, N., Nolas, S.-M., Brooks-Gordon, B., Esin, C., Holt, A., Mehdizadeh, L. and Shinebourne, P. (2010) 'Pluralism in qualitative research: the impact of different researchers and qualitative approaches on the analysis of qualitative data', *Qualitative Research*, 10 (4): 441–460.

Giddens, A. (1990) *The Consequences of Modernity*. Cambridge: Cambridge University Press.

Greene, J.C. and Caracelli, V.J. (2003) 'Making paradigmatic sense of mixed methods', in A. Tashakkori and C. Teddlie (eds), *Handbook of Mixed Methods in Social and Behavioral Research*. London: Sage, pp. 91–110.

Hansen, H. (2006) 'The ethnonarrative approach', *Human Relations*, 59 (8): 1049–1075.

Hesse-Biber, S. (2010) 'Emerging methodologies and methods practices in the field of mixed methods research' (Introduction to the special issue), *Qualitative Inquiry*, 16 (6): 415–418.

Hornby, P. and Symon, G. (1994) 'Tracer studies', in C. Cassell and G. Symon (eds), *Qualitative Methods in Organizational Research: A Practical Guide*. London: Sage, pp. 167–188.

Kincheloe, J.L. (2005) 'On to the next level: continuing the conceptualization of the bricolage', *Qualitative Inquiry*, 11 (3): 323–350.

Knights, D. (2006) 'Authority at work: reflections and recollections', *Organization Studies*, 27 (5): 699–720.

Lewis, M. and Grimes, A. (1999) 'Metatriangulation: building theory from multiple paradigms', *Academy of Management Review*, 24 (4): 672–690.

Morse, J. (2010) 'Simultaneous and sequential qualitative mixed methods designs', *Qualitative Inquiry*, 16 (6): 483–491.

Phillips, N., Nelson, B.J., Lawerence, K.A., Thomas, B. and Hardy, C. (2004) 'Discourse and institutions', *Academy of Management Review*, 29 (4): 635–652.

Pritchard, K. (2007) 'Knowledge at work: a study of HR professionals'. Unpublished PhD Thesis, Birkbeck College, University of London, London.

Pritchard, K. (2010) 'Becoming an HR strategic partner: tales of transition', *Human Resource Management Journal*, 20 (2): 175–188.

Pritchard, K., Briner, R.B. and Symon, G. (2004) 'Talking about knowledge with human resource practitioners', paper presented at the 5th European Conference on Organizational Knowledge Learning and Capabilities, Innsbruck, April.

Pritchard, K. and Symon, G. (2009) '"Going between": insights gained from combining qualitative methods in organisational research', paper presented at the 9th EURAM Annual Conference, Liverpool, May.

Rees, A. and Nicholson, N. (1994) 'The twenty statements test', in C. Cassell and G. Symon (eds), *Qualitative Methods in Organizational Research*. London: Sage, pp. 37–54.

Richards, L. (2009) *Handling Qualitative Data: A Practical Guide* (2nd edn). London: Sage.

Shotter, J. and Lannamann, J. W. (2002) 'The situation of social constructionism: its "imprisonment" within the ritual of theory-criticism-and-debate', *Theory and Psychology*, 12 (5): 577–609.

Tashakkori, A. and Teddlie, C. (eds) (2003) *Handbook of Mixed Methods in Social and Behavioural Research*. London: Sage.

Waddington, K. (2005) 'Using diaries to explore the characteristics of work-related gossip: methodological considerations from exploratory multimethod research', *Journal of Occupational and Organizational Psychology*, 78 (2): 221–236.

Weick, K.E. (1995) *Sensemaking in Organizations*. London: Sage.

Wetherell, M., Taylor, S. and Yates, S. (2001) *Discourse as Data: A Guide for Analysis*. London: Sage.

9 Longitudinal Research and Analysis

Ann Langley and Inger Stensaker

Introduction

This chapter examines methods for doing longitudinal research, and more particularly longitudinal qualitative case studies carried out inside organizations. While the word 'longitudinal' may, strictly speaking, refer to any research that involves observations spread out over time (including historical and time series analysis), in this chapter, we discuss large-scale organizational case studies in which at least a part of the data is collected in real time. Real-time longitudinal analysis has its strengths, but also poses particular challenges that we describe and illustrate in this chapter.

A number of contributions have previously addressed issues surrounding longitudinal case studies and constitute valuable resources for this discussion. In particular, in a comprehensive overview, Pettigrew (1990) drew attention to the epistemological and pragmatic issues surrounding choice of research sites, data collection and analysis. Leonard-Barton (1990) provided an interesting comparison of the advantages and disadvantages of real-time *vs* retrospective case analysis, suggesting that the two may ideally complement each other. She argued that real-time studies are less efficient and potentially raise more questions about reactivity between researchers and ongoing events. However, they also enable a closer analysis of process and a more accurate understanding of chains of cause and effect. Dawson (1997) reflected on the pragmatics of doing longitudinal research, noting that having knowledge of how to do good process research is a tacit skill acquired through experience. More recently, Balogun et al. (2003) considered how to capture large-scale change processes across organizations in real time, proposing diary methods, periodic focus groups and collaborative research as three data collection methods for meeting this challenge. Van de Ven and Poole (1990) and Langley (1999) focused more specifically on analysis approaches for making sense of large amounts of complex temporally-embedded process data.

This chapter will illustrate some of these ideas and others, drawing on two different empirical research experiences in which we have been separately involved (see the vignettes below). Both research programmes focused on understanding the implementation of large-scale organizational change. We begin by presenting the two vignettes, and then discuss two key underlying challenges associated with doing this kind of real-time longitudinal research: *ambiguity* and *sensitivity*. We follow this with an exploration of three elements of the research process – design, data collection and data analysis – and discuss how we addressed each of these in our own studies in the light of the two key challenges. We conclude with some general observations and recommendations about doing longitudinal real-time research.

Two Research Programmes

Vignette 1: a research programme in the Scandinavian energy industry

This research programme involving Inger Stensaker and colleagues included two change projects in the energy industry in Scandinavia: (1) a re-engineering project that was studied from 1998 to 2002, and (2) a merger integration taking place in the years 2008–2010 involving the same company. Both research projects were designed to study change as it occurred in real time in its natural setting.

The first change project aimed to substantially reduce costs by re-engineering the organization to maximize the benefits of an Enterprise Resource Planning (ERP) system. Organizational changes included new work processes, a flatter organizational structure reducing the number of middle managers, management by objectives (goal-steering) replacing a previous focus on budgets, a coaching rather than controlling leadership style, and introducing multi-disciplinary teams. The second change project aimed to closely integrate two merging energy companies.

The rationale behind the merger was to create a robust organization geared towards international growth, with more efficient operations nationally, and to develop new and alternative sources of energy. Goals included a tightly integrated new organization where all employees had equal and fair opportunities. This was expected to facilitate knowledge sharing and a transfer of best practices.

The research for both these projects involved data collection at multiple organizational levels using various types of qualitative data such as interviews, observations and documents. Both projects were designed as embedded case studies, but with a selection of organizational entities at the same level in order to facilitate a comparison. Some of the organizational units were subject to data collection in both of the projects, and these can also be viewed as one longitudinal project over a 12-year time span. Re-entering the same organization to study two separate change projects revealed inter-linkages between the projects, as a number of change ideas that appeared in the first research project reappeared and were reinforced in the second project. Several academic papers were produced on the basis of the first project (Stensaker et al. 2002; Stensaker and Falkenberg, 2007; Stensaker et al., 2008; Stensaker and Langley, 2010). The second is still ongoing.

Vignette 2: a research programme on Canadian health care organizations

This research programme involved a series of studies of healthcare change in Quebec, Canada. Along with her colleagues Jean-Louis Denis, Lise Lamothe, Linda Rouleau and others, Ann Langley has been investigating changes in healthcare since the early 1990s. We will focus on two of these investigations: a study of teaching hospital mergers and a study of a more recent restructuring involving the creation of territorially-based healthcare networks.

The teaching hospital merger study was launched as several major mergers were announced. The team studied the process of integration for three of these mergers: two involving three hospitals each, and one involving five separate institutions. The purpose here was twofold: to examine how the newly formed management teams would negotiate strategic reconfigurations of their operations between the different sites, and to examine in more detail how operating units at the micro-level would combine their operations when they were forced to consolidate. Data collection continued from 1997 to 2002 on two of the sites.

The health network implementation study involved data collection from 2005 to 2007, and focused on four newly created organizations called health and social services centres (HSSCs), that had been designed to integrate all health and social services on their geographic territories. These organizations were required to merge several different previously autonomous entities (ranging from two to six different organizations), to develop contractual relationships with independent healthcare providers, and to implement a new philosophy called the 'population-based approach' in which they became responsible not only for specific patients requiring services but also for the health and wellbeing of citizens living in their territory.

Each of these studies again involved multiple levels of analysis (senior management and operating units) and multiple sources of data, including observations of meetings, interviews and the collection of documentary evidence. Multiple types of comparison were made possible by these studies: across organizations, across units within these organizations, and across time periods. The studies have given rise to a variety of publications (e.g. Denis et al., 1999; Denis et al., 2001; Denis et al., 2009; Denis et al., 2011) and data analysis is still continuing with data from both studies.

Challenges of Real-Time Longitudinal Research: Ambiguity and Sensitivity

While change processes can be studied retrospectively, there are particular advantages to examining these in real time. Most importantly, neither the researchers nor the participants will be biased by having knowledge of the outcomes. Researchers will learn along with the protagonists. The ups and downs of the everyday experience of managing change will be available for study and are less likely to be artificially smoothed out by a retrospective rationalization (Golden, 1992). This also means that researchers are more likely to have access to processes that are not perfectly successful, where issues are more sensitive because they are current, live and immediate.

On the other hand, following change in real time is particularly demanding. Uncertainty about outcomes and access to sensitive issues constitute a double-edged sword. The uncertainty and ambiguity connected with organizational change also has implications for how the researcher approaches the task. It requires flexibility in terms of the methods employed and a tolerance of ambiguity. In addition to entering a chaotic and complex situation, the researcher conducting longitudinal real-time qualitative research has limited control over what happens and must remain flexible in terms of how to approach the task of studying the change. Although often entering the field with a specific research question and focus in mind, he or she cannot know in advance which events and issues will become most important for this particular change project, nor which information and data will become valuable sources of evidence.

Because organizational changes also entail uncertainty for organizational members, such processes are delicate for managers and employees. Organizational politics and identity issues flourish during change. Longitudinal change researchers therefore need to be attentive to the sensitivity of conducting research and reporting results to organizations in the midst of a change process. For example, organizational members will sometimes ask for input and advice and some may treat academics like consultants, expecting solutions and answers and perhaps even expecting them to take sides. Researchers risk being dragged into internal politicking and research results can be 'used' in various intended and unintended ways. When reporting back to the organization, the researcher has to consider what can and cannot be said openly. Since longitudinal designs require long-term relationships with the organization, sensitivity to the internal politics of change becomes essential and must be balanced with the requirements of academic rigour and ethics. While researchers may tend to take on the role of a critical and external voice providing constructive feedback, they will also need to be conscious of their potential impact on organizational decisions and processes and carefully consider when and how results can be communicated internally as well as externally.

These twin features of real-time longitudinal case studies – *ambiguity* and *sensitivity* – will constitute key elements of our discussion as we describe the different stages of longitudinal qualitative research and analysis below. We focus on three dimensions of the research process – design, data collection and data analysis – discussing how we addressed each of these in our work, and more generally how case study researchers might think about them.

Design

The real-time researcher undertaking studies such as those we have described above embarks on a voyage of discovery where neither outcomes, nor theoretical frames, nor methodological designs can be easily pinned down a priori. This means that classic case study designs in which organizations with more and less successful outcomes are compared (e.g. Eisenhardt, 1989) cannot be established unequivocally beforehand. Outcome cannot be a criterion for the choice of cases. Moreover, the design of a longitudinal change project will need to be flexible and open to improvisation as new situations emerge. In addition, a key challenge in designing a real-time study involving data collection over time will almost always be tied to access. Research designs may have to be adjusted because of access problems. Conversely serendipitous design opportunities may appear while the research is in progress. In this section, we elaborate on three ideas related to research design for longitudinal studies, addressing the twin concerns of ambiguity and sensitivity: (1) context-driven design; (2) emergent design; and (3) design-access interdependence.

Context-driven design

In a situation of ambiguity about possible outcomes, longitudinal case studies can usefully rely on the *context* as a design criterion. Specifically, if an existing theory or the researcher's experience provides clues about contextual features that might influence how the process will play out, it can be helpful to draw on such insights when setting up the study. The researcher can still be flexible in terms of which particular organizations/divisions (or other 'case' units) to focus on, as long as these meet the contextual criteria. As with other kinds of comparative case studies it is important to consider which dimensions one expects variation on and to identify dimensions that should remain roughly constant. Typically the selection of cases will then be based on expectations of similarities or differences in the various contexts. This approach provides structure to the open-ended and often rather complex task of entering multiple sites during change.

For example, in the healthcare network study described above, each of the newly created health and social service centres had to merge three different types of organizations that had previously been operating on their geographic territories: nursing homes, community clinics (offering home care and social services) and acute-care hospitals. A major element of variety in the context concerned whether an acute-care hospital was operating on the territory or not and would thus be included in the merger. Prior to entering the field, we reasoned that those centres that did include a hospital would be faced with a much more complex integration task in which the larger size and more dynamic milieu of the hospital might tend to dominate the other components of the system. On the other hand, those centres that did not include a hospital would be faced with a more complex external environment since they would then have to negotiate for access to hospital care. We therefore took care to incorporate these contextual elements in our initial design to enable strong comparisons. Thus, of the four centres to be studied, we deliberately sought out two that included hospitals and two that did not. We were fortunate in that a large number of these organizations had been created and we were able to negotiate access with suitable candidates.

Emergent design

An emergent design implies that the researcher designs the study while it is ongoing. Typically, this means that the researcher begins the fieldwork without having fleshed out the entire design. For example, this may mean doing research within one organizational entity (case) and then, based on the data and information that emerge, choosing the next case. Hence, the criteria for design issues emerge based on the previous case – a form of progressive theoretical sampling favoured by grounded theorists (Strauss and Corbin, 1990). This allows for maximum flexibility, but may be subject to political processes, as the sites that emerge as the most interesting from a researcher's perspective might entail substantial work to gain access.

In the Scandinavian re-engineering project, the research was designed in an emergent manner. The researchers aimed to collect the data at a corporate level and in two or three business units. The comparative design was considered particularly important since all data were collected within the same corporate setting. Because the researchers had limited knowledge about the company and the various business units the first case was chosen opportunistically and based on geographical proximity, allowing for extensive interactions and observations and ensuring maximum learning at an early stage. Two subsequent business units were chosen based on information that was gathered within the first site. The research focused on how the corporate change initiative was shaped and adjusted by managers and employees in lower-level divisions as it was implemented. Through the data collection, it became clear that the first business unit had a limited influence on corporate decisions, whereas other business units were perceived as more influential. This guided the subsequent choice of two additional business units as sites for our research.

An example of a combined emergent and contextual approach to design occurred in the merger integration study in the energy industry. Here the researchers had historical data on one of the divisons from the re-engineering study. The insights that were developed about a division in the first project led the researchers to request access to this unit for the second study also. The arguments for studying this particular division were substantiated based on in-depth knowledge about the organizational context that was particularly tied to previous reactions to change within the unit. Hence emerging insights were coupled with a contextual approach to design.

Design-access interdependence

As mentioned above, one of the most interesting though potentially discon-certing aspects of doing longitudinal research in real time is that one never knows what might happen. One result of this is that the research design and access issues can become deeply intertwined. Indeed the sensitivity of longitu-dinal research critically affects the capacity to choose, gain and maintain access. Even when an initial agreement for research participation exists, there may still be issues surrounding who and what exactly researchers may have access to, as well as when and how. This demands patience and flexibility. There may be various reasons for possible access difficulties after having entered the field. The environment and context may have changed, making the change initiative less relevant. For instance, in a merger integration study con-ducted by a colleague in the telecommunications sector, the deal failed and the merger simply did not happen, simultaneously killing off the research project after it had started (Meyer and Altenborg, 2008). Other problems may arise because the change process might have taken a different turn from the one expected, leading organizations to rethink the consequences of having researchers present. Rightly or wrongly, managers may feel that researchers may have interfered with the change process and negatively affected it. Or the researchers might have reported critical findings that managers are not ready or open to hear about. For whatever reason, being denied access after entry into the field involves the risk of losing valuable data.

So what can be done if access is denied after entry into the field? One strat-egy is to try to make the best possible use of the existing data as long as per-mission to use what has been collected so far is not withdrawn. For instance, in the failed telecom merger described above, the researcher reoriented the research towards merger failures rather than integration processes (Meyer and Altenborg, 2008), basically transforming the design and even the research questions to adjust to what was possible.

Conversely, once access to relevant situations has been obtained, the unex-pected can often become the source of the richest insights and lead to seren-dipitous emergent designs. As long as the researchers have managed to gain credibility and trust early on within the setting, this may enable an understand-ing of situations about which one might have been unlikely to obtain access had it been known in advance that such events would occur.

For example, in the healthcare network study, one of the four organizations we studied experienced difficulties in the development of its reorientation plan, eventually resulting in the departure of the CEO. In one sense this upset the research programme, delaying the change implementation process and thus our observation of it. On the other hand, the researchers were fortunate to be able to collect data on the emergence of these difficulties. They were able to use their prior meeting observations to understand the genesis of the situation over time, and to interview people as they were dealing with it. It is unclear whether access to such data would have been obtainable after the fact, and if it had been, selective memories and rationalization would have simplified people's understandings of an inherently complex process. Similarly, in the Scandinavian re-engineering study, one of the units that was expected to be most successful in implementing the change and that had been selected partly for that reason actually experienced considerable conflict during the research. These phenomena could not have been predicted, but they led to richer understanding and analysis.

Data Collection

The ambiguity, open-endedness and sensitivity of real-time longitudinal research create further challenges for data collection. Where to focus an observation when there is so much going on? What are the best ways to capture both the richness and the breadth of data needed to make a contribution to understanding when the parameters of the situation are evolving and require constant adjustment? How can researchers truly make the most of a real-time experience? In this section, we review three issues associated with data collection: (1) managing a large-scale and long-term data collection; (2) enlarging the concept of data; and (3) building the capacity for flexibility.

Managing large-scale and long-term data collection

The research projects we have described here could not have been easily handled by single researchers working alone. Capturing change processes in real time seems to require being in several places at once. Paradoxically, researchers may sometimes feel that they are wasting their time as they may sit in meetings and feel that nothing much is going on. And yet, at other times, they will kick themselves for having missed a critical incident that happened while they were focusing on something else. Balogun et al. (2003) suggested the use of participant diaries and focus groups (see Kandola, in this volume) to leverage researchers' time in such efforts. Nevertheless, large-scale projects require large-scale teams and these bring with them other challenges and requirements.

For example, in the hospital merger project, the research team was comprised of three faculty members and three graduate students. There were also two on-site researchers, one of whom participated in the research design and conceptualization and co-authored papers. To manage researchers' time while ensuring that they were all benefiting from the valuable tacit knowledge that comes from direct contact with sites, they shared interviewing and meeting observations and then held intensive research meetings to discuss their learning up to that point. The need to regularly produce research outputs for feedback to the sites or for academic events was an important factor in stimulating exchanges that enabled researchers to stay in close contact with the data as they collected it. Through this experience, they also learnt the importance of a highly rigorous system for managing the emerging database. This involved timely transcriptions of meetings and interviews and the creation of a web-based data depot shared by all team members. This learning was useful in designing the approach to the even more complex health network study.

Enlarging the concept of 'data'

We have argued that one of the benefits of longitudinal real-time research is that the researcher learns in parallel with the participants in the site. Yet longitudinal real-time research can quickly turn into the equivalent of retrospective research if events and researchers' reactions to them are not recorded or reflected on at the time of their happening. In other words, if research in real time is to enable researchers to see events in a way that is closer to that experienced by the participants on the scene, where life is open-ended and endings and beginnings often flow into each other (Weick, 1999), then the data collection should involve recording not only meeting dialogues and interviews but also the researchers' experience of them.

For example, in doing longitudinal research, one may see shifts not only in the way other people construe situations, but also in one's own feelings and interpretations as events unfold. Looking at data prospectively in a systematic way requires continuous researcher documentation, preferably in a research journal, not only of the site data but also of personal theorizing over the length of a project, with more organized outputs generated over time (placed in a sealed envelope for future consultation?) and reviewed as they change (see Haynes on reflexivity, in this volume). In this vein, Bitektine (2007) has recently proposed prospective case studies as a systematic research approach. We have simulated this approach less formally in some cases by producing research outputs before projects were fully complete.

In this sense, it is important to note that researchers' recorded reflections about the site at different points in time themselves constitute *data* for later analysis. Generalizing on this thought, a variety of other elements that are often neglected in case study research could and probably should be considered as data. For example, Kisfalvi (2006) argues that researchers should become more aware of their own emotions in doing fieldwork, considering these as potential data sources. She illustrates this argument by showing how her own emotional reactions to one of the protagonists in her research site (recorded in a research journal) offered hints as to how others might also view this individual, which could then be explored with those others.

In her research on the Scandinavian re-engineering project, the second author only came to fully understand the nature of life on an oil rig when the gas alarm went off and she had to spend an evening in a lifeboat. Offshore employees are often concerned about safety issues during organizational change, and having been subject to a real emergency situation accentuated this issue for the researcher. The phrase used by many respondents during interviews about their superiors 'being in the same boat' came to life. While the safety and dependency issues had resulted in strong bonds and what is often referred to as a 'closed' culture with a low acceptance of new people, it became clear to the second author that new employees, once physically on the platform, were quickly included within the community. Hence the experiences became data indicating that the challenges related to rotating personnel and achieving social integration seemed to have been exaggerated.

Beyond their own reflections and emotions, researchers might also pay greater attention to items such as the physical arrangements, layout, body language and dress as well as changes in these when attempting to capture the experiences they are observing. Photographic evidence should not be neglected as a potential source of data supporting this type of observation (see Vince and Warren, in this volume).

Building the capacity for flexibility

We have already mentioned how doing longitudinal real-time case studies often brings researchers into unexpected situations. More significantly perhaps, ongoing work may sometimes lead to a rethink of the phenomenon being studied and of the study's theoretical focus. As data accumulate, and especially if ongoing researcher reflections are written down, something of significance in the site may attract attention, a sort of 'aha' moment, when the researcher thinks: '*This* is what is going on … I should be looking at it'. Of course, one should not change foci every day and one should be wary of 'research by wandering around', which is unfocused, disorganized and ultimately unproductive (Miles and Huberman, 1994). However, we are convinced that some of the most interesting insights do come from researchers' contact with real situations and those key opportunities should not be missed.

For example, after observing the hospital merger implementation process in one of the sites between 1997 and 2000, one thing that forcibly struck us was the constant reversal of previous decisions and the apparent difficulty the organization was experiencing in moving forward to implement its reconfiguration. Periods of enthusiasm and dynamism alternated with periods of collapse and frustration as decisions were reversed and the cycle then started all over again. The study had originally been designed to focus on collective strategic leadership and the phenomenon of 'strategic reversal' as we labelled it had not been part of our initial frame (how could we have predicted this?). However, this was clearly happening and we saw an opportunity to study it. This led us to embark on a new phase of data collection – where we considered how the already available data could help us document the process, and what additional data were needed to explore this further using the concepts from actor-network theory. A new series of interviews was conducted and ongoing observations focused more strongly on this phenomenon. Without undermining the original focus, this new orientation generated one of our favourite outputs from this research (Denis et al., 2011).

Clearly, shifting foci in real time is an important decision that should not be taken lightly. On the other hand, one of the particular advantages of real-time research is the ability to be flexible. We believe that the *capacity* for flexibility must, however, be incorporated into the data collection from the beginning. Thus, we tend to collect more data than might be needed rather than less, because we are never 100 per cent certain about what will end up being important. This may mean taking copious notes in meetings even if the topics discussed appear at first sight to be peripheral. This may mean using interview guides to focus the discussion, as well as leaving space for respondents to go beyond previously listed issues if they have something important to say. Doing so again means reflecting constantly on one's experiences of the site, the data being collected and what these might mean.

Data Analysis

The first author has previously written about approaches to analysing and theorizing from process data collected through longitudinal case studies (Langley, 1999; 2009). In this section, we draw on some of these ideas, but we also examine other issues surrounding data analysis raised by the key features of real-time longitudinal studies that we have focused on so far: ambiguity and sensitivity. The issue of ambiguity is particularly challenging, because while flexibility can be maintained throughout the previous stages, at the point of analysis, some degree of convergence must be achieved. How can this be done successfully? In this section we focus on three main themes: (1) analytical progression and narrative multiplicity; (2) leveraging temporality; and (3) thinking cumulatively.

Analytical progression and narrative multiplicity

We have argued above that longitudinal real-time case studies can benefit from ongoing interpretive reflections as the research moves forward. Looking at this same issue differently, we believe that much can be gained from a form of progressive analytical thinking, in which earlier analyses (perhaps carried out while still in the field) focus on substantive issues, and later ones gradually raise the level of abstraction and draw in more elaborate comparisons and theoretical resources. Preliminary analyses are particularly useful to make sense of ongoing data collection for feedback to sites. This feedback helps validate the analysis and may become an additional data source for further reflection. We have often published our first outputs from longitudinal research studies in more substantively oriented journals based on this first level of analysis. The thinking that this generates becomes a resource for later work that might be published in more generic management journals.

For example, the first output from the teaching hospital merger study (Denis et al., 1999) essentially described and compared a series of context, content and process indicators surrounding two mergers. We noted that the processes used to manage the mergers were very different – more conflictual in one case and more consensual in the other – and yet surprisingly, the outcomes appeared to be very similar. We used this observation to reflect on the causes of this similarity and based on this we identified the managerial implications. The article was published in a Canadian public administration journal. Subsequent outputs involved a variety of different analytical foci and theoretical frames. For example, one article contributed to the development of a theory of collective leadership and strategic change in pluralistic settings (Denis et al., 2001). The most recent contribution focuses on what we now call 'escalating indecision', the phenomenon of strategic reversal and the perpetual reconsideration of decisions that we described earlier (Denis et al., 2011). Notice that these two analyses appeared in organizational theory journals rather than dedicated healthcare or public administration journals. This is because increasing abstraction and comparison can enable the theorizing to be raised to be a more general level.

As can be seen, we have also applied multiple theoretical frames to the same dataset or to different subsets of the data. This too is typical in longitudinal case study research. For example, in the Scandinavian re-engineering study, a variety of publications have appeared discussing issues of sensemaking, identity and power. Provided the data collected are rich and some provision has been made for flexibility, this will be possible and even desirable. In most of our research, we have applied different theoretical lenses sequentially rather than simultaneously. However, Langley (1999) also notes the potential of the 'alternate templates' strategy for theorizing in which different conceptual interpretations are explicitly compared, as in Allison's (1971) classic study comparing three different interpretations of the Cuban missile crisis.

Leveraging temporality

The very purpose of doing longitudinal research is to understand how phenomena evolve over time. It therefore seems important to incorporate temporality into the analysis. This is less self-evident than it may seem to begin with. Surprisingly, many studies of change do not pay a great deal of attention to temporal evolution but rather reduce the analysis to detecting relationships between antecedents and outcomes (Van de Ven, 1992). This is not necessarily without interest of course. However, it does condense and simplify the richness of temporal experience that real-time longitudinal data provide. Researchers are often trained to think in terms of categories such as concepts and variables, and they may then have difficulty conceiving of phenomena in temporal terms. This requires a shift towards categories such as events, activities and choices, and their grouping into phases and sequential chains.

A first requirement for leveraging temporality in longitudinal analysis is to ensure that the data themselves are chronologically dated and organized. We have found it useful to give electronic data-files names that begin with the case identifier followed by dates in a year-month-date order to ensure that all the files automatically order themselves chronologically in computer storage. This facilitates chronological data-coding (starting with the earliest files and moving forward), another way to ensure that as analysis proceeds, event chains and temporal differences are encountered and understood. Of course, while observational (see Brannan and Oultram, in this volume) and documentary data (see Lee, in this volume) are usually temporally specific, interview data (see Alvesson and Ashcraft, in this volume) tend to be temporally chaotic: while the date of the encounter is known, respondents often shift backward and forward in time in their accounts of events, requiring a careful positioning of the comments within a chronology, as well as the recognition that all memory-based accounts are reconstructions. We try to code interview data using both temporal and concept or event codes so that extracts can be contextualized within relevant time periods.

At least three other devices can be useful for ensuring that temporality is taken seriously during the analysis process itself. One approach is to attempt to draw a representation of the flow of events in the data over time – a strategy that Langley (1999) called 'visual mapping'. Flow charts representing different cases can then be compared and common patterns can be identified.

A second approach, especially useful with multiple interview accounts, is to plot the narratives of different individuals (see also Maitlis, in this volume). We used this approach on the hospital merger data to examine the identity issues experienced by different groups as they confronted the various attempts at integration. Each narrative had two columns, a first column containing key event descriptions and a second column reflecting quotations from interviews that represented individuals' perceptions of these events. We found that members of the same occupational group tended to use similar narrative elements, which then enabled us to merge these and come up with a set of generic narratives reflecting different identification and integration profiles.

Finally, a third approach that we have found particularly useful in long-term studies is temporal bracketing: subdividing the data into phases separated by clear discontinuities – e.g. those involving changes in leadership or distinct shifts in the nature of change activities (Langley, 1999). This enables the comparison of successive periods taken as replicated units of analysis where actions carried out in a given period may lead to changes in the context that will influence actions in subsequent periods. We used this approach to develop a dynamic model of collective leadership and strategic change using the hospital merger data (Denis et al., 2001). It was also mobilized in the re-engineering study, where we examined successive phases in implementation across the three business units studied, showing how the choices of change agents during one period affected the political, substantive and relational concerns that would orient their activities in the following period (Stensaker and Langley, 2010).

Thinking cumulatively

In addition to analytical progression, where substantive and specific insights are formed into more abstract ideas, researchers who work longitudinally can think cumulatively in their analysis by coupling their current data sets with previous data, and by coupling their data sets with other researchers' data.

Both of the research programmes reported on here consisted of several research projects within the same organizations or industries over a long period of time. Each project was a separate study, but coupling research projects during analysis can make for an even longer time frame. Analysing the data collected in a division of the energy company during the merger integration process together with data from the previous change project provides a deep contextual understanding, and it also uncovers historical linkages, similar types of processes or mechanisms or the opposite, a lack of memory, where similar decisions are made over and over again. Conducting studies that aim for some level of replication, either in their research site or focus, will often result in an implicit accumulation occurring even if this is not planned. Researchers develop their thoughts and analytical insights, drawing on previous experiences and learning as they approach new data sets. For example, data from the healthcare merger integration study were combined with data from prior change studies to develop the theory of collective leadership and change presented by Denis et al. (2001).

Conclusion

Real-time longitudinal research raises issues of ambiguity and sensitivity, creating a number of challenges for researchers. We have described these challenges with examples from our own research and provided some suggestions about how to handle them and how to take advantage of the fluidity, open-endedness and richness of such research processes. Although real-time longitudinal research can be time consuming and challenging, the potential benefits are important. We believe that these kinds of studies are essential for developing a better understanding of the processes of change in and around organizations.

In addition to the insights that real-time longitudinal research provides, it is important to note that such methods are also compatible with a productive and rewarding career path, as the work of individuals such as Andrew Pettigrew, Jean Bartunek and Andrew Van de Ven illustrates. Warnings are sometimes heard about the difficulties of publishing qualitative and longitudinal research, and there may be concerns about its inherently time-consuming nature. However, we would argue that researchers who adopt this method will embark on a continuous learning process, where the nature of the research and the data will provide multiple opportunities for contributing, drawing on many of the strategies that we have described in this chapter (e.g. analytical progression, narrative multiplicity and cumulative thinking). We hope that this chapter will encourage others to join us in this stimulating enterprise.

Further Reading

A variety of other resources are available to those interested in qualitative longitudinal research. We recommend particularly a series of articles published in two issues of *Organization Science* (volume 1, issues 3 and 4), several of which have already been mentioned (Leonard-Barton, 1990; Pettigrew, 1990; Van de Ven and Poole, 1990), but see also Barley (1990). A 1997 special issue of *Scandinavian Journal of Management* on process research also offers useful ideas (see for example, Dawson, 1997), as does Langley's (1999; 2009) discussion of process theorizing and research design. Finally, for some exemplars of empirical longitudinal studies published in article form on a variety of different topics, see Barley (1986), Feldman (2000), Balogun and Johnson (2004), Cardinal et al. (2004) and Pratt et al. (2006).

References

Allison, G.T. (1971) *The Essence of Decision*. Boston, MA: Little-Brown.

Balogun, J., Huff, A. and Johnson, P. (2003) 'Three responses to the methodological challenges of studying strategizing', *Journal of Management Studies*, 40 (1): 197–224.

Balogun, J. and Johnson, G. (2004) 'Organizational restructuring and middle manager sensemaking', *Academy of Management Journal*, 47 (4): 523–549.

Barley, S.R. (1986) 'Technology as an occasion for structuring: evidence from observations of CT scanners and the social order of radiology departments', *Administrative Science Quarterly*, 31: 78–108.

Barley, S. (1990) 'Images of imaging: notes on doing longitudinal fieldwork', *Organization Science*, 1 (2): 220–247.

Bitektine, A. (2007) 'Prospective case study design: qualitative method for deductive theory testing', *Organizational Research Methods Journal*, 11 (1): 160–180.

Cardinal, L., Sitkin, S.B. and Long, C.P. (2004) 'Balancing and rebalancing in the creation and evolution of organizational control', *Organization Science*, 15 (4): 411–431.

Dawson, P. (1997) 'In at the deep end: conducting processual research on organizational change', *Scandinavian Journal of Management*, 13 (4): 389–405.

Denis, J.-L., Dompierre, G., Langley, A. and Rouleau, L. (2011) 'Escalating indecision: between reification and strategic ambiguity', *Organization Science*, 22 (1): 225–244.

Denis, J.-L., Lamothe, L. and Langley, A. (1999) 'The struggle to implement teaching hospital mergers', *Canadian Public Administration*, 42 (3): 285–311.

Denis, J.-L., Lamothe, L. and Langley, A. (2001) 'The dynamics of collective leadership and strategic change in pluralistic organizations', *Academy of Management Journal*, 44 (4): 809–837.

Denis, J.-L., Lamothe, L., Langley, A., Breton, M., Gervais, J., Trottier, L.-H., Contandriopoulos, D. and Dubois, C.-A. (2009) 'The reciprocal dynamics of organizing and sensemaking in the implementation of major public sector reforms', *Canadian Public Administration*, 52 (2): 225–248.

Eisenhardt, K.M. (1989) 'Making fast strategic decisions in high velocity environments', *Academy of Management Journal*, 31 (4): 543–576.

Feldman, M.S. (2000) 'Organizational routines as a source of continuous change', *Organization Science*, 11 (6): 611–629.

Golden, B.R. (1992) 'The past is the past – or is it? The use of retrospective accounts as indicators of past strategy', *Academy of Management Journal*, 35 (4): 848–860.

Kisfalvi, V. (2006) 'Subjectivity and emotions as sources of insight in an ethnographic case study: a tale of the field', *M@n@gement*, 9 (3): 109–127.

Langley, A. (1999) 'Strategies for theorizing from process data', *Academy of Management Review*, 24 (4): 691–710.

Langley, A. (2009) 'Studying processes in and around organizations', in D. Buchanan and A. Bryman (eds), *Sage Handbook of Organizational Research Methods*. London: Sage, pp. 409–429.

Leonard-Barton, D. (1990) 'A dual methodology for case studies: synergistic use of a longitudinal single site with replicated multiple sites', *Organization Science*, 1 (3): 248–266.

Meyer, C.B. and Altenborg, E. (2008) 'Incompatible strategies in international mergers: the failed merger between Telia and Telenor', *Journal of International Business Studies*, 39 (3): 508–525.

Miles, M.B. and Huberman, A.M. (1994) *Qualitative Data Analysis*. Thousand Oaks, CA: Sage.

Pettigrew, A.M. (1990) 'Longitudinal field research on change: theory and practice', *Organization Science*, 1 (3): 267–292.

Pratt, M.G., Rockmann, K.W. and Kaufmann, J.B. (2006) 'Constructing professional identity: the role of work and identity learning cycles in the customization of identity among medical residents', *Academy of Management Journal*, 49 (2): 235–262.

Stensaker, I. and Falkenberg, J. (2007) 'Making sense of different responses to corporate change', *Human Relations*, 60 (1): 137–177.

Stensaker, I., Falkenberg, J. and Grønhaug, K. (2008) 'Implementation activities and change recipient sensemaking', *Journal of Applied Behavioral Science*, 44 (2): 162–185.

Stensaker, I. and Langley, A. (2010) 'Change management choices and trajectories in a multidivisional firm', *British Journal of Management*, 21 (1): 7–27.

Stensaker, I., Meyer, C.B., Falkenberg, J. and Haueng, A.C. (2002) 'Excessive change: coping mechanisms and consequences', *Organizational Dynamics*, 31 (3): 296–312.

Strauss, A and Corbin, J. (1990) *Basics of Qualitative Research*. Newbury Park, CA: Sage.

Van de Ven, A.H. (1992) 'Suggestions for studying strategy process: a research note', *Strategic Management Journal*, 13 (summer special issue): 169–188.

Van de Ven, A.H. and Poole, M.S. (1990) 'Methods for studying innovation development in the Minnesota Innovation Research Program', *Organization Science*, 1 (3): 313–335.

Weick, K.E. (1999) 'That's moving: theories that matter', *Journal of Management Inquiry*, 8 (2): 134–142.

10 Doing Qualitative Business and Management Research in International and Intercultural Contexts

Laurie Cohen and M.N. Ravishankar

Introduction

In this chapter we provide a broad overview of the contexts and configurations of international and intercultural business and management research, highlighting some of the common issues faced by qualitative researchers working in these diverse settings. Following a general introduction in which we draw particular attention to issues of collaboration, language and the role and position of the researcher, we turn more specifically to research in multinational offshore outsourcing organizations – an employment space that has seen exponential growth in recent years and that we have both studied. In our experience, these emerging and rapidly changing forms of organization typically involve complex relationships not only between people from different national/cultural backgrounds and employment roles (e.g. customer/service provider), but also between more and less economically developed countries and their historical legacies.

We believe that researchers working from qualitative perspectives are particularly well placed to capture the dynamism, complexity and often the tensions inherent in these emergent forms of organization. But at the same time these settings create some intriguing and often vexing research challenges for qualitative researchers, which have thus far received only limited scholarly attention (Westwood, 2004; Karra and Phillips, 2008). By focusing on our experiences of doing research in these contexts, we will provide insights that resonate with international and intercultural work more generally, highlighting the complex play of power, identity and language, and drawing attention to the importance of reflexivity in the process of doing research in these emergent spaces.

Like much business and management research, international and cross-cultural research in organizational settings tends to be dominated by positivist methodologies, with qualitative approaches very much in the minority (Peterson, 2004). Reasons for this are varied and well-rehearsed, including, as Marschan-Piekkari and Welch (2004b) explain, assumptions about the greater legitimacy of natural science-type approaches and the supremacy of US models of good research, institutionalized in training regimes and publication imperatives. That said, in spite of the persistence of this trend, Marschan-Piekkari and Welch point out that scholars still make regular pleas for more qualitative research in these fields. Here again, the cries are familiar – though perhaps even more compelling in intercultural contexts – including issues such as the importance of cultural sensitivity, local knowledge rather than one-size-fits-all approaches, challenges to ethnoncentrism, the need for greater flexibility and an ability to adapt to contingencies in the course of the research process. Given the theme of this edited collection, we are assuming that readers are already well versed in these arguments and thus we are not going to discuss them in detail. Rather, we simply wanted to briefly sketch out the research landscape from which our central concerns about international and intercultural qualitative work emerge.

With regard to the contexts of qualitative international and cross-cultural research, these are many and varied, not just in terms of the empirical settings, but also with respect to the researchers themselves and the methods they use. For example, Marschan-Piekkari and Welch's comprehensive edited collection, *Handbook of Qualitative Research Methods for International Business* (2004a), includes interview-based research into multinational companies (MNCs) in single and/ or multiple sites (Marschan-Piekkari et al., 2004b); case studies of national companies investigated by people from outside of that context (Wilson, 2004); mixed-methods studies of expatriates working in different countries, researched by people from the host or home country, or from a third country (Peterson, 2004); and contextualized ethnographies into local organizations conducted by researchers from that country but living and working elsewhere (Michailova, 2004). Each of these settings, of course, raises different methodological challenges and opportunities. In what follows we focus on three of these emerging issues: collaboration, language, and the role and position of the researcher. While these issues are of course significant in qualitative research generally, they become even more pertinent in international and intercultural settings.

Collaboration

An important consideration, with respect to qualitative, intercultural research design, is that of collaboration. The studies we refer to in this chapter have used a wide spectrum of collaborative models. These range from large-scale, international research projects where collaborators located in different countries conduct parallel studies, effectively 'owning' their own data and only coming together at key phases in the process (e.g. Peterson, 2004), to small studies conducted by researchers, often with long established research relationships and friendships, who work closely together throughout the research process (e.g. Adler and Adler, 2005). Whereas the former tend to be transactional, based on formalized contracts and protocols, the latter is relational, informal, flexible and based on a high level of trust. Of course different models are appropriate for different contexts and purposes. However, what has become apparent to us is that researchers can have contrasting ideas about what this means. These ideas are partly informed by different research traditions, and here we would highlight the importance of full and frank discussions between collaborators about how they understand collaboration in general, and with respect to their particular research intentions. Without such shared understandings, it has been our experience that relationships can break down and potentially exciting studies can come to nothing.

Importantly, though, these dynamics do not exist in isolation. Rather, they are situated within a broader international research landscape in which scholars, institutions and publication regimes in certain countries appear to define the standards, while others work hard to make themselves acceptable in these terms. In these highly charged and politicized contexts, research collaborations can be seen as contested and challenging processes. For example, in studies involving collaborations between more and less economically developed countries, Wilson (2004) refers to the tendency for some researchers to '[extract and use] data in a way that assists the foreign [Western] research, and gives nothing in return. Too often Western researchers utilise material from overseas contexts to boost their own standing as "international" researchers' (2004: 436). Of course we are not suggesting that this is always or even typically the case, or that where it is the people involved simply accept or accommodate this situation. Nor do we think that the rules of this game can only be seen by certain parties. Rather, open access to information ensures that these rules are visible to everyone, and people no doubt know what they are getting into when they enter into collaborative relationships. However, this wider context can create a certain, more generalized level of mistrust and instrumentality, and we are both familiar with cases in which this has stymied the development of informal, relational collaborative projects.

Language

Language is another fundamental issue in international and intercultural research, but one that has only been discussed in a limited way in the methodological literature. Here Soderberg's (2006) narrative analysis of a merger between a Danish, Swedish, Norwegian and Finnish company is a very interesting exception. Soderberg is based in Denmark and her team was international, with researchers from each of the countries represented in the merger. Although English was the lingua franca in each of these organizations, interviews were conducted in respondents' and the researchers' native languages. Soderberg explained that this enabled all parties to express themselves openly and without constraint. She also suggested that respondents were more willing to talk about their merger partners with a compatriot. This issue of the research language and in particular the role of English as the lingua franca becomes even more interesting when we consider: (a) what happens when people are operating outside of their native languages, (b) the relative status of different languages in particular business sectors, and (c) the wider canvas in which these language choices are played out – particularly with respect to relationships between more and less economically developed countries.

While on one hand the increasing use of English as the global lingua franca has been seen as a mechanism for facilitating mutual understanding (Tietze, 2008), questions have also been raised about the extent to which this can be seen as part of the process through which Anglophone countries have achieved increasing cultural dominance on the world stage. From this perspective, it has been suggested that 'English acts as an invisible, hegemonic force which exerts strong influence over the framing and ordering of the global world and organizations constituent of it' (Tietze, 2010: 12). Of course one could also argue that this viewpoint underestimates the diversity within English itself and the extent to which multilingual people are able to draw on a whole repertoire of linguistic resources to suit particular circumstances. Indeed, scholars such as Luo and Shenkar (2006) and Steyaert et al. (2010) have highlighted the creative and often strategic ways in which people working in multicultural contexts negotiate over language choice to suit their particular purposes, interests and contexts.

Likewise, with respect to research methodology, language cannot be thought of as a 'neutral' or 'innocent' (Tietze, 2010) tool for collecting data. Rather, in international and cross-cultural research, the ways in which researchers and respondents use language provide important insights into issues of identity and competence, into the privileging of certain points of view and the subordination of others, and the ways in which individuals position themselves within these diverse meaning systems. Of course this is particularly important in qualitative research where meaning making is central and can never be taken for granted.

The Role of the Researcher: Insider and Outsider Perspectives

In their 2004 collection, Cassell and Symon emphasized the importance of reflexivity in qualitative research practice, an issue that Haynes further develops in this volume. Central here is the relationship between the researcher and their research setting (see also Tietze, in this volume). In the context of international and intercultural research, consideration of this relationship raises some particularly complex questions, as was vividly illustrated in Patricia and Peter Adler's (2005) research into the lives of workers in a Hawaiian resort. Although the Adlers are both American, culturally the Hawaiian island on which their study was based was very different from their home in Colorado, and to add to this diversity between US states, the hotel workforce was itself international. To further complicate matters, although they were transparent about their status as researchers, the Adlers first became interested in Hawaii when they went as tourists, and indeed they could have been mistaken for customers in the resort they studied. Thus their roles were at once confounded – as Americans but not quite part of this particular American cultural context, as researchers but looking a lot like customers. Considering this and the Soderberg example noted earlier, what quickly becomes apparent is how difficult it is to separate the researcher from the research context.

Turning to the researchers themselves, a key issue is whether they are 'insiders' or 'outsiders'. Sometimes these distinctions are clear-cut, as in the case of Elizabeth Wilson, noted above, an English woman who discusses her experiences of doing research in India, or in Grisar-Kasse's (2004) story about being a German researcher in Senegal. However, in other cases the distinctions are far more blurred. Taking ourselves as examples, when Ravi, who is from Bangalore but lives and works in the UK, does work in his home city, is he an insider? If so, how can he be described as doing 'international' research? On the other hand Laurie is from the USA but has lived in the UK for 28 years. The vast bulk of her work is in the UK – in this context is she an outsider or an insider? And what if she went back to conduct research in the USA? The permutations are endless, and problematic. Given the centrality of these questions in the literature (see for example Easterby-Smith and Malina, 1999; Karra and Phillips, 2008), this variation and contestation are worthy of note.

With respect to the researcher's relationship with the context, some further issues merit our consideration. A central theme running through the methodological literature in this field is that of culture: cultural sensitivity, difference, awareness. While these are undoubtedly crucial issues that we continually recognize in our own research, in our view much of the literature deals with culture in quite an unproblematic way, failing to adequately consider issues of power and the historical legacies that underpin these differences. Proposing a postcolonial reading (Prasad, 2003a) of international business and comparative management studies, Westwood draws on Ong (1987), suggesting that such a reading would conceptualize culture as:

> 'historically situated and emergent, shifting and incomplete meanings and practices generated in webs of agency and power' (Ong, 1987: 2–3). Cultures are no longer considered as if they developed in splendid isolation from one another, but dynamically as ongoing constructions through their engagements and intersections. (Westwood, 2004: 74)

Thus it is not sufficient to think of cultures as simply different from one another. Rather, they are constructed, reproduced, resisted and changed through social practice, and are played out in hierarchies of status, privilege, domination and subordination. Here we are not arguing for a kind of cultural determinism. Rather, like Ong, we would want to highlight the role of individual (and collective) agency in the ways in which culture is negotiated and played out. However, we are suggesting that we need to look critically at these historically embedded, contested, dynamic relationships as inextricable to the process of doing research in international and intercultural settings. Thus, going back to our own experiences for a moment, when the two of us do research in India we cannot simply dismiss the facts – that Ravi is Indian, Laurie is American/British, and both live in the UK – as mere cultural trifles. Instead, these differences matter substantively and methodologically, and in the course of doing our research we need to examine their significance. As noted at the outset of this chapter, we suggest that these relationships seem to be illustrated in sharp relief in the context of offshore outsourcing arrangements. In the sections that follow we will highlight key features of these arrangements and examine some issues that resounded in our own work in these contexts.

Experiences of Researching the Offshore MNC Space[1]

One particular expression of globalization, which we have focused on in our research over the last few years, is the offshore outsourcing (popularly referred to as 'offshoring') phenomenon. In the main, the huge cost savings associated with offshoring work to countries in the developing world have made it a very attractive proposition for companies (Friedman, 2005). Perhaps the country whose name is most often mentioned in this context is India, which has become one of the leading providers of offshoring services in several areas including finance, information technology (IT), life sciences and human resource administration. Having outlined the broad terrain of qualitative intercultural business and management research, in this section we turn to our own research in these contexts and examine some of the methodological challenges we faced with respect to: (1) the implications of historical legacies for the research process, and (2) the insider/outsider statuses of researchers and the use of English as the research lingua franca.

Drawing on case study and ethnography methods, Ravi has conducted longitudinal field studies in a number of research sites in India over the last eight years. His fieldwork has largely been concentrated in four offshoring MNCs operating in the IT services sector. Some of his research fieldwork at these MNCs

---

[1]Throughout this chapter we use the general term 'offshoring MNCs' to refer both to the business process outsourcing MNCs and the information technology outsourcing MNCs.

has also been published in international academic journals (e.g. Ravishankar and Pan, 2008; Ravishankar et al., 2010; Ravishankar et al., 2011). Three of these companies were headquartered in India at the time of the research while the fourth, a Europe-based MNC, operated a subsidiary unit in a number of locations across India. Relationships in these organizations were culturally complex, in the first three organizations between Indian employees and Western clients, and in the fourth between Indian employees and their European colleagues. In general, in relation to the Indian employees, the clients/European colleagues appeared to enjoy a higher status in the organizational arrangements. Here it is important to note that these status differentials would have been very difficult to observe empirically through rigorous and structured interviews, and only became apparent through more contextually sensitive ethnographic approaches, including wide-ranging qualitative interviewing, observation and immersion in the field setting (see Yanow, Ybema and van Hulst, in this volume).

A native of Bangalore and with a similar background to many of the employees, in these settings Ravi looked and sounded like a local. His insider status enabled him to draw on multiple qualitative data sources, including documents, emails, internet and field notes. In two of the MNCs, Ravi was given access to confidential company documents, including minutes of formal meetings conducted by different project teams. On a few occasions, he was also present during employee team-building sessions and at internal training seminars designed to improve the communication skills of employees. An important source of data in these studies was semi-structured interviews with employees at different levels in the organizational hierarchy. Members of top-management teams, heads of business units, project managers, project leaders, software engineers, technical analysts and sales and business development personnel took part in the interviews. The fieldwork also included both participant and non-participant based observations of people engaged in various work and non-work related activities, during which time many informal conversations ensued. These informal conversations covered many different topics, oft-times generating opinions about issues well outside the scope of the particular study.

Laurie's experience of research in this context is based on an extensive case study she and Amal El-Sawad conducted in a financial services company operating in both the United Kingdom and Mumbai.[2] At the time of the study (2005–2006) the organization operated three customer service centres in the United Kingdom and

---

[2]This research was conducted collaboratively with Amal El-Sawad, and was supported by the British Academy and the Economic and Social Research Council.

one in Mumbai. The Mumbai site was a wholly-owned subsidiary of the UK parent company and in this 'captive' unit, Indian employees worked in the same regulatory environment as their UK counterparts, within the same overall structural context, and were managed with reference to very similar human resources policies and practices, opportunities and constraints, with minor differences reflecting aspects of the local environment. Fieldwork was conducted at all four sites.

In contrast to Ravi's experience, in the Indian setting Laurie was very much an outsider. Excellent access arrangements enabled the team to conduct a wide range of in-depth interviews with employees at different hierarchical levels, ranging from entry-level agents through to the managing director. In addition to these interviews, extensive field notes were generated through non-participant observation. Because of the distance involved, the Mumbai experience was concentrated and intense. In the first instance the visit lasted for two weeks, and a year later they returned for another week, which included further fieldwork, feeding back preliminary findings and running a practitioner-academic seminar.

We have already commented on the cultural complexity of the offshoring space where cultural groupings are situated in hierarchies of status and influence. As researchers we were not immune to these dynamics, but part-and-parcel of them. Because he looked like a local, Ravi was able to blend in and move inconspicuously around his case study organizations. However, for Laurie, who looked like either headquarter staff or the client, access was certainly more formal and 'managed'. Not only did this impact on access issues, but also on her relationships with staff where she was sometimes treated with a degree of caution and deference. Interestingly, it was in encounters with other visitors, employees on secondments, trainers and consultants, that she was able to collect more informal, spontaneous data.

Historical legacies and their significance for the research process

In his postcolonial critique of the international business and comparative management field, Westwood (2004) argues that much research in this area has been conducted as if in a historical vacuum and that, as such, it proceeds without sufficient consideration of the significance of historical events and relationships for how work happens, or for people's experiences of work in these contexts (Prasad, 2003b). Earlier in the chapter we highlighted the implications of such legacies for research collaboration. Based on our own experiences of setting up collaborative projects in these settings, we would suggest that the Indian offshoring space, central to which are relationships between more and less economically developed countries often with long and complex shared histories, provides some useful insights. From a methodological perspective, in our research the importance of India and the UK's historical legacy emerged at two points in the research process: gaining research access and data analysis.

Turning first to the issue of access, a striking feature of the financial services study was Indian employees' enthusiasm for the study and willingness to participate. The researchers were in a fortunate position because they had, in principle, been given access to all four customer service centres. However, having secured senior managers' willingness to participate in the study, recruiting participants was another matter. In the UK sites this took a considerable amount of perseverance since employees were, for various reasons, reluctant to get involved. In general, people seemed to be wary and mistrustful and the researchers had to work hard to generate rapport. In Mumbai, however, employees were full of enthusiasm and expressed their desire to help. People were particularly interested in being part of a study that was being conducted by doctors from a prestigious British university. Interestingly this was a feature that in the UK context only seemed to exacerbate the suspicious, stand-offish attitude. We cannot draw any definitive conclusions about this difference. However, we would suggest that the historical relationship between Britain and India, which cast many Indians in subservient, 'helping' positions (and conversely placed the British in more powerful positions), the role of the British educational system in the development of India's educational infrastructure and the continuing symbolic power of the British system, could have been contributing factors.

Second, with regard to data analysis, we turn to some fascinating accounts of language in the offshoring space. On one hand, because of the widespread dissemination of English in its institutions and indeed in the fabric of its cultural, social and economic life, India is seen as a very desirable outsourcing partner (Dossani and Kenney, 2003; Taylor and Bain, 2005; NASSCOM, 2007). On the other hand, though, the extent of Western clients' difficulties in understanding Indian accents is a familiar complaint. For this reason, customer-facing employees are given extensive language training. Somewhat to our surprise, respondents were extremely positive about this; indeed, a UK manager explained how Mumbai employees frequently requested *extra* language and culture instruction. Interestingly, losing one's 'Indian-ness' (in terms of accent and inflection) was seen not only as a practical matter to ensure understanding, but also as something more ideological, about underpinning values and an enduring sense of British English as being of the highest quality. As one respondent explained, speaking the 'Queen's English' was still a potent symbol of success, and therefore it was entirely reasonable for employees who were to be servicing British clients to aspire to this standard. Cohen and El-Sawad (2007) have written about this substantive issue elsewhere. For our purposes here, though, we offer this example to highlight how, in analysing the accounts we generated, it was not sufficient simply to look at English language skill as one feature among many others in the Business Process Outsourcing context. Rather, it was essential to consider how people's accounts of and judgements about language use in this context drew on wider historical patterns and legacies.

Respondents' contrasting experiences of working for US and UK companies further illustrated this point. Many of the people we interviewed had previously worked for US companies and they were very keen to highlight the differences between these workplaces. Although the USA was certainly depicted as the main player in the world of offshoring, respondents had very negative things to say about their experiences of these organizations. First, it was when they worked for US companies that they were typically asked to take on American pseudonyms and identities. Although they talked about this with humour, they were extremely judgemental about many of their US clients who, through their ignorance, demanded that such games be played. In contrast, they spoke more benignly about UK outsourcing firms in general and especially the client base. Several respondents had family or friends in the UK, which seemed to create a sense of familiarity, and many had experienced an education based on the British system. Regarding their particular organization, they were extremely proud to be working for this long established, traditional UK 'badge' – and felt that being part of this gave them added kudos in the eyes of their friends and family. In addition to the rich detail that these accounts offer into what it is like to work in India's emerging sectors, at the same time they provide other insights into how people position themselves, and India, in relation to the UK and the USA, and of the continued significance of historical relationships for contemporary experiences of work. In our view, it is essential that in their analysis, qualitative researchers attend to the ways in which such relationships are played out in respondents' accounts.

The paradox of insider and outsider perspectives

It is widely believed that qualitative researchers who execute international management research projects in their own national, linguistic and socio-cultural contexts find it easier to negotiate access with gate-keepers and to establish trust and a rapport with respondents (Marschan-Piekkari and Welch, 2004b; Karra and Phillips, 2008). Such researchers have been popularly referred to in the business and management literature as insiders (Chapman et al., 2004). On the other hand, those for whom the research site is unfamiliar and foreign are often seen as outsiders. Although outsiders miss out on the obvious advantages enjoyed by insiders in the process of accessing research sites and conducting qualitative fieldwork, they are thought to be more successful than the insiders in maintaining an objective detachment from the research site and the respondents. Of course, as we noted earlier, in many cases the insider and outsider labels may not always accurately describe the complex relationships between a researcher and the research context.

One reason why insiders are seen as being better equipped in handling the challenges of qualitative data gathering is their ability to converse with the respondents in their local language. Indeed, at a number of research sites in our studies of IT services organizations, Ravi, the insider, spoke the same first language, Kannada, as many of the respondents. However, respondents refused to engage him in a conversation in Kannada and insisted that all talk should only be in English. According to some, speaking English was a sign of 'professionalism'. On the other hand, conversing in a local language with Ravi would mark them out as crude and ordinary people and they therefore sought to preempt such an interpretation by speaking English. Some also warned Ravi that if he spoke Kannada none of the respondents would take him seriously.

Interestingly, many respondents in these studies felt that they could express their 'real' feelings about issues much better in a local language. But since speaking in a local language was perceived as a sure sign of incompetence in their globally focused organizational settings, they stuck to English, which was safe and, more crucially, signalled quality. Clearly, this experience raises several issues about the perceived higher status and power attributed to the use of English in these settings. From a methodological perspective, this preferred use of English by respondents turns the notion of language-based advantages enjoyed by insiders on its head. It also underscores the difficulties of collecting rich interview data in such contexts, for both insiders and outsiders. Another key aspect within the qualitative research process relates to the differential treatment of insiders and outsiders by gate-keepers in the sponsoring organizations.

Here we turn to one of Ravi's field studies, conducted over a three-year period at an India-based global MNC. In this research, Ravi was not permitted by the gate-keepers to interview the top-management team and senior managers despite repeated requests. Around the same time, a researcher from a mid-size

US university who intended to conduct interviews for a similar research project was given unlimited and unhindered access to all key decision-makers in the organization. According to the gate-keepers, it was a matter of great pride to everyone in the organization that the US researcher was visiting them and it was therefore important that they 'work hard' to make a 'good impression' on him. In contrast, Ravi with a familiar Indian accent and appearance did not warrant serious attention. Our aim in revisiting this experience is not to offer a critical analysis of the preferential treatment given to the outsider in the data-gathering stages of the study. In any case, such an analysis is outside the scope of this chapter. Rather, we seek to emphasize the point that in these research settings, an outsider from the developed world can often be perceived as being powerful or seen as having a higher status and that this perception can have real consequences for how the qualitative research process unfolds. In this case, in relation to Ravi (the insider) the researcher from the USA (the outsider) found it much easier to access and interview senior and middle-level managers in the organizational hierarchy. But somewhat paradoxically, given his intimate access to influential people, the researcher from the USA became frustrated towards the end of his field trip at not being able to 'hit it off' with the respondents. He complained to Ravi that the 'performances' staged by the respondents were too carefully crafted and that their talk was full of politically correct opinions and jargon. Further, since he was not connected to any informal social network in the research setting, he found himself struggling to recruit a diverse group of respondents.

In comparison to the US researcher, Ravi, although very much the notional insider, found it almost impossible to access key respondents since he was seen as powerless as well as having a lower status by the gate-keepers. Yet, paradoxically, as an insider familiar with the research site he was able to draw on a large informal network of social contacts and acquaintances who assisted in recruiting respondents for the study. Also, most of the respondents recruited in this manner appeared to be unencumbered by any requirements of political correctness during interviews and thus proved to be sources of rich data. In contrast, though, discussing our research experiences and the data we generated, it became apparent that it was precisely because of Laurie's outsider status that she was able to ask questions about respondents' experiences that may have been uncomfortable for someone who was part of the same social and cultural context. Thus respondents raised their concerns about issues like caste, class, gender and religion, and how these mattered in the work setting. As with conversations between strangers on a train, quite intimate issues were discussed, with all being safe in the knowledge that Laurie's and her respondents' worlds would probably never meet.

In summary, our experience of conducting field studies in the offshoring MNC context suggests that a more nuanced appreciation of the challenges faced by insiders and outsiders at different phases of the research process is required. The significant influence of language – the choice of research language and the implications of this – and power – the researchers' status, background and position with respect to the fieldwork setting – within the data-gathering process highlights the need to carefully revisit and refine the ways in which we think about and conduct qualitative research in international settings.

Some Concluding Reflections

In this chapter we have highlighted the diverse and sometimes highly charged contexts of international and intercultural business and management research – contexts that cannot be thought of simply as benign research locations, but as contested, inextricable and inevitable dimensions of the research itself. While qualitative approaches certainly have the capacity to elucidate the complexity of such arenas, these insights cannot be taken for granted. Rather, our own experiences have convinced us that they are contingent on researchers' reflexive engagement with the process (see also Easterby-Smith and Malina, 1999; Haynes, in this volume): from the earliest decisions about project design and collaboration arrangements, to issues about access, data collection techniques, relationships between researchers and respondents and finally through to data analysis.

Focusing on our experiences of researching in India's offshoring space, we have emphasized the need for researchers to extend their gaze beyond the perimeters of their particular empirical settings, to the wider national/cultural canvases in which these organizations operate, including not only current arrangements but also the historical circumstances from which these arrangements emerged. We have argued that aspects of the research process such as negotiating access and the development of research relationships must be understood as situated within and significantly influenced by these wider concerns. The concept (and indeed the process) of reflexivity must likewise be seen as extending beyond the level of the individual researcher, their chosen methods and the roles that they establish in the conduct of their research. In particular, we need to be attentive to the fact that as researchers we are ourselves part of these wider patterns, tensions and legacies, and so must consider the implications of this for the research process.

Further Reading

Rebecca Marshan-Piekkari and Catherine Welch's (2004a) edited collection, *Handbook of Qualitative Research Methods for International Business*, provides an invaluable introduction to the field. Contributions range from coverage of wide ranging theoretical and empirical concerns, through to particular approaches, including case studies, interviewing and ethnography, and stages in the research process from research design through to data analysis and dissemination. To further develop ideas about the dissemination (and reading) of qualitative international business research, Sara McGaughey's (2006) paper, 'Reading as a method of inquiry: representations of the born global', also offers an insightful analysis. Readers interested in pursuing postcolonial lines of argument introduced here might turn to Frenkel's (2008) 'The multinational corporation as a third space: rethinking international management discourse on knowledge transfer through Homi Bhabha' and Anshuman Prasad's (2003a) collection of papers, *Postcolonial Theory and Organizational Analysis*, although the only contribution that deals explicitly with methodological issues (ethnography) is Pushkala Prasad's (2003b) 'The return of the native: organizational discourses and the legacy of the ethnographic imagination'. With respect to debates around language and in particular the use of English, Susanne Tietze (2008; 2010) has written widely, although here again her focus has not been specifically methodological. Anne-Marie Soderberg's (2006) narrative analysis of a Scandinavian merger likewise examines linguistic issues – focusing not on the use of English as the lingua franca, but on the implications of using researchers and respondents using a common language. Through her analysis Soderberg raises important issues about insider/outsider perspectives – debates further developed by Easterby-Smith and Malina in their 1999 paper, 'Cross-cultural collaborative research: toward reflexivity' and Neri Karra and Nelson Phillips (2008) in 'Researching "back home": international research as autoethnography'.

References

Adler, P. and Adler, P. (2005) *Paradise Laborers: Hotel Work in the Global Economy*. Ithaca, NY: ILR Press.

Cassell, C. and Symon, G. (eds) (2004) *Essential Guide to Qualitative Methods in Organizational Research*. London: Sage.

Chapman, M., Gajewska-de Mattos, H. and Antoniou, C. (2004) 'The ethnographic international business researcher: misfit or trailblazer?', in R. Marschan-Piekkari and C. Welch (eds), *Handbook of Qualitative Research Methods for International Business*. Cheltenham: Edward Elgar, pp. 287–305.

Cohen, L. and El-Sawad, A. (2007) 'Lived experiences of offshoring: an examination of UK and Indian financial service employees' accounts of themselves and one another', *Human Relations*, 60 (8): 1235–1262.

Dossani, R. and Kenney, M. (2003) 'Went for cost, stayed for quality? Moving the back office to India', *Asia Pacific Research Centre Working Paper*, Stanford, CA. See http://APARC.stanford.edu.

Easterby-Smith, M. and Malina, D. (1999) 'Cross-cultural collaborative research: toward reflexivity', *Academy of Management Journal*, 42 (1): 76–86.

Frenkel, M. (2008) 'The multinational corporation as a third space: rethinking international management discourse on knowledge transfer through Homi Bhabha', *Academy of Management Review*, 33 (4): 924–942.

Friedman, T. (2005) *The World Is Flat: The Globalised World of the 21st Century*. London: Penguin.

Grisar-Kasse, K. (2004) 'The role of negative personal experiences in cross-cultural case study research: failure or opportunity?', in R. Marschan-Piekkari and C. Welch (eds), *Handbook of Qualitative Research Methods for International Business*. Cheltenham: Edward Elgar, pp. 144–161.

Karra, N. and Phillips, N. (2008) 'Researching "back home": international management research as autoethnography', *Organizational Research Methods*, 11 (3): 541–561.

Luo, Y. and Shenkar, O. (2006) 'The multinational corporation as a multilingual community: language and organization in a global context', *Journal of International Business Studies*, 37: 321–339.

Marschan-Piekkari, R. and Welch, C. (eds) (2004a) *Handbook of Qualitative Research Methods for International Business*. Cheltenham: Edward Elgar.

Marschan-Piekkari, R. and Welch, C. (2004b) 'Qualitative research methods in international business: the state of the art', in R. Marschan-Piekkari and C. Welch (eds), *Handbook of Qualitative Research Methods for International Business*. Cheltenham: Edward Elgar, pp. 5–24.

Marschan-Piekkari, R., Welch, C., Penttinen, H. and Tahvanainen, M. (2004) 'Interviewing in the multinational corporation: challenges of the organizational context', in R. Marschan-Piekkari and C. Welch (eds), *Handbook of Qualitative Research Methods for International Business*. Cheltenham: Edward Elgar, pp. 244–263.

McGaughey, S. (2006) 'Reading as a method of inquiry: representations of the born global', *Management International Review*, 46 (4): 461–480.

Michailova, S. (2004) 'Contextualising fieldwork: reflections on conducting research in Eastern Europe', in R. Marschan-Piekkari and C. Welch (eds), *Handbook of Qualitative Research Methods for International Business*. Cheltenham: Edward Elgar, pp. 365–383.

NASSCOM (2007) *IT Industry Factsheet*. See www.nasscom.org.

Ong, A. (1987) *Spirits of Resistance and Capitalist Discipline: Factory Women in Malaysia*. Albany, NY: State University of New York Press.

Peterson, R. (2004) 'Empirical research in international management: a critique and future agenda', in R. Marschan-Piekkari and C. Welch (eds), *Handbook of Qualitative Research Methods for International Business*. Cheltenham: Edward Elgar, pp. 25–55.

Prasad, A. (ed.) (2003a) *Postcolonial Theory and Organizational Analysis: A Critical Engagement*. London: Palgrave.

Prasad, P. (2003b) 'The return of the native: organizational discourses and the legacy of the ethnographic imagination', in A. Prasad (ed.), *Postcolonial Theory and Organizational Analysis: A Critical Engagement*. London: Palgrave, pp. 149–170.

Ravishankar, M.N., Cohen, L. and El-Sawad, A. (2010) 'Strategies of resistance, accommodation and the pursuit of aspiration among new economy firms in India: reflections from two cases', *Industrial Relations Journal*, 41 (2): 154–167.

Ravishankar, M.N. and Pan S.L. (2008) 'The influence of organizational identification on organizational knowledge management (KM)', *Omega – The International Journal of Management Science*, 36 (2): 221–234.

Ravishankar, M.N., Pan S.L. and Leidner, D.E. (2011) 'Examining the strategic alignment and implementation success of a KMS: a subculture based multi-level analysis', *Information Systems Research*, 22: 1.

Soderberg, A. (2006) 'Narrative interviewing and narrative analysis in a study of a cross-border merger', *Management International Review*, 46 (4): 397–416.

Steyaert, C., Ostendorp, P. and Gaibrois, C. (2010) 'Multi-lingual organisations as "linguascapes": negotiating the position of English through discursive practices', *Journal of World Business*, 46 (3): 270–278.

Symon, G. and Cassell, C. (2004) 'Promoting new research practices in organizational research', in C. Cassell and G. Symon (eds), *Essential Guide to Qualitative Methods in Organizational Research*. London: Sage, pp. 1–10.

Taylor, P. and Bain, P. (2005) '"India calling to far away towns": the call centre labour process and globalisation', *Work, Employment and Society*, 19 (2): 261–282.

Tietze, S. (2008) *International Management and Language*. London: Routledge.

Tietze, S. (2010) 'We speak worlds: English, language diversity and international management'. Inaugural Lecture, Nottingham Business School, Nottingham Trent University.

Westwood, R. (2004) 'Towards a postcolonial research paradigm in international business and comparative management', in R. Marschan-Piekkari and C. Welch (eds), *Handbook of Qualitative Research Methods for International Business*. Cheltenham: Edward Elgar, pp. 56–83.

Wilson, E. (2004) 'An outsider in India', in R. Marschan-Piekkari and C. Welch (eds), *Handbook of Qualitative Research Methods for International Business*. Cheltenham: Edward Elgar, pp. 421–438.

11 Writing Up as a Legitimacy Seeking Process: Alternative Publishing Recipes for Qualitative Research

Joep Cornelissen, Hanna Gajewska-De Mattos, Rebecca Piekkari and Catherine Welch

Introduction

There has been growing interest among qualitative researchers in understanding and scrutinizing the processes of writing up and publishing qualitative research as journal articles. Obtaining insight into these aspects of qualitative research is not straightforward, however. While the outcome – the published article – is readily available, decisions about how to write up qualitative data for publication typically are not. In this chapter, we set out to explore those aspects of publishing qualitative research that are largely hidden and whose conventions and rules are not often made explicit.

When embarking on writing this chapter we expected to find a stark contrast between North American and European journals regarding the ways in which qualitative research is reported (Collin et al., 1996; Bengtsson et al., 1997). In particular, we anticipated finding a contrast between a predominantly positivist and 'nomothetic' tradition prevailing in the USA and various European traditions that are more knowledgeable about qualitative, 'idiographic' research. Indeed, some writers have drawn on this contrast to advise authors that in order to have an idiographic paper published by a major North American journal 'the paper should not diverge from a conventional [nomothetic] design more than is absolutely called for' (Bengtsson et al., 1997: 488).

Given this background, we decided to compare and contrast papers by the same authors and involving the same research project, but published in different outlets. We consulted a previously compiled database and selected qualitative articles written by the same author(s): for each author or set of authors, we compared one of their articles published in a top North American journal in management (e.g. *Academy of Management Journal*) with one published in the highest ranking European journal in management (*Journal of Management Studies*). By focusing on these 'matched pairs'[1] of articles, we were able to investigate a range of pressures and influences on the way a single author or team of authors writes up their work for publication.

It is clear that guides to writing and publishing qualitative research have accumulated in recent years. The topic has been approached from multiple angles: qualitative researchers publishing helpful 'how to' guides, typically aimed at PhD students and junior researchers (see e.g. Woods, 1999; Golden-Biddle and Locke, 2007; Holliday, 2007; Wolcott, 2009); reviewers and editors providing 'insider' advice (e.g. Gephart, 2004; Suddaby, 2006; Pratt, 2008; Bansal and Corley, 2011); 'confessional tales' by successful authors (e.g. Birkinshaw, 2004); and traditions that emphasize the literary, performative nature of scholarly research, such as postmodernism, literary criticism and rhetoric, the sociology of science and narrative research (e.g. Czarniawska, 1999; Johnson et al., 2006)

Yet at the same time, Pratt (2009) argues that qualitative researchers – and their reviewers – lack a 'boilerplate' for writing up their qualitative research for publication. He observes that 'as a profession, we tend to be more forthcoming about how to conduct studies than we are about publishing them' (Pratt, 2008: 482). Three reasons can be put forward for this lack of clear guidelines or recipes (see also Symon and Cassell, in this volume). The first is the mistaken application of quantitative conventions for reporting research findings. In a survey of qualitative authors, Pratt (2008) found that a common experience was for qualitative research to be judged by reviewers and editors according to quantitative standards. The application of 'inappropriate standards' to their research is, we suspect, a common experience for qualitative researchers, and

---

[1]Although in the case of one author we analysed three articles instead of two.

not just the respondents to Pratt's survey. Our own experiences of reviewing and writing for publication confirm this. Qualitative researchers may be forced to conform to dominant conventions or indeed may risk rejection.

A second issue is the division among qualitative researchers over appropriate conventions for writing up a study. Holliday (2007), for example, contrasts the 'naturalist' approach to reporting with 'the postmodern liberation'. While the former, he argues, adopts a realist stance and accepts conventional, positivist standards of reporting, the latter

> enable[s] a far greater variety in procedure and scope in which data is presented more creatively and [with] openness about who the researcher is and how she spins validity through argument. (Holliday, 2007: 20)

This lack of consensus among qualitative researchers means that a 'boilerplate' is not just unachievable, but also undesirable, given that it would obscure the fundamental philosophical differences underlying various and in some senses opposing traditions. Johnson et al. (2006) therefore argue for a set of recipes that are contingent and dependent on the philosophical assumptions underlying the qualitative research.

A third factor complicating the topic of writing and publishing qualitative research is that the conventions for academic writing are often taken for granted rather than explicitly debated. These conventions are probably best seen as tacit rules of the publishing game that are implicit to the process and largely learnt through experience. Increasingly, however – and even in management research, despite the conservatism of the mainstream – these rules of the game are being scrutinized and even challenged (Bansal and Corley, 2011). Of note here is the rise of postmodernism, which has questioned assumptions about representation in the academy. Reporting is no longer seen as the 'straightforward reporting of observed phenomena' (Golden-Biddle and Locke, 2007: 11), but as the author's imaginative construction (see for example McGaughey, 2004; Alvesson and Kärreman, 2007). These acts of imagination and creativity are, however, constrained by power and hegemony (Meriläinen et al., 2008): the institutions of the academy prescribe what can be written, and how, and therefore also imply what must remain silent.

All these factors – the continued dominance of quantitative standards and the positivist milieu surrounding management research (see for example *Journal of Management Studies*, 2011), the philosophical divisions among qualitative researchers and the lack of an open discussion on the writing and publishing process – make publishing a challenging journey for the qualitative researcher. The journey metaphor is probably an apt one for many qualitative researchers; it emphasizes the ongoing movement and learning that is required, with the end destination (i.e. the final output of having your article published) not always certain. There can be many false starts and disappointments along the way, and equally as travellers on this journey we need to make the choices and the reasons for them explicit (i.e. which journals we would like to publish in and who the audiences are for our research) and ultimately also the choices about what kind of researcher we aspire to be.

In keeping with the metaphor of a journey, we have structured this chapter according to the process that we underwent in researching and writing it. Our starting point was to analyse 'matched pair' case studies, which were part of an existing dataset. Accordingly, in the next section we shall turn to our analysis of these articles. Given that our expectation of a stark transatlantic divide was not upheld, we will then position the articles within broader conventions or recipes for writing up qualitative research – some of which are codified but others are more tacit. Identifying and contrasting these diverse recipes provides a richer understanding of the trends we found in the matched pairs.

Experiences from the Field

This chapter has its origins in an extensive review undertaken for another study (Welch et al., 2011), which covered the *Academy of Management Journal (AMJ)*, *Journal of International Business Studies (JIBS)* and *Journal of Management Studies (JMS)* in the period 1999–2008. Every article published in these three journals during this period was analysed and coded according to whether it was non-empirical, quantitative, qualitative or case study based. The review by Welch et al. (2011) shows that the three journals are still dominated by quantitative studies.

Within this dataset, we identified five sets of case studies published in both European and North American journals by the same author(s). To aid comparison, we decided to focus on the case study method as the method of qualitative inquiry that was used across these studies. Importantly, across these five matched pairs, it is worth noting that the same case study design or even the same data were used and published (albeit with a different set of research questions and theoretical angle) for both a North American and a European journal. As such, it allows us to put conventions for publication associated with journals across each side of the pond in perspective.

We subsequently contacted the authors directly, asking them for their own reflections on the publishing process associated with different journals. Our questions centred on the differences between the initial submission and final version, how the paper was shaped by the editors and reviewers involved, and how the authors themselves compared their own 'matched pair' articles. In particular, we were probing for insights on whether they had anticipated certain conventions and expectations in relation to writing their papers for these journals in advance, and also whether the respective review processes influenced the way in which they revised the paper (including their method section and data analysis) for publication. We also asked the authors to comment on our own interpretation of the publishing process based on an analysis of their papers, which was presented to them in the form of a table.

For the five initially identified matched pairs, we received responses and input from four of the five lead authors, and their papers are listed in Table 11.1 below. We also compared these published case studies ourselves using the following aspects of the research and data analysis: the structure of the article (deductive or inductive); the methodological references (what type of literature was cited); any overlap of data between the matched pairs (complete or partial); the explicit use of propositions; the description of data analysis; case narrative or cross-case comparisons; and the overall rhetoric of the paper (positivist or constructivist).

Analysis of Matched Pairs

We originally expected to find a persistent transatlantic divide between the US and European articles for each matched pair. Our analysis, however, did not find this to be as significant an influence across all the matched pairs as we had anticipated. We shall proceed by first providing an overview of each matched pair. We will then consider the evidence for transatlantic differences within each matched pair.

Table 11.1   Sets of reviewed European and North American academic articles

	JMS	AMJ/JIBS
Matched pair 1	Chreim (2005)	Chreim, Williams and Hinings (2007)
Matched pair 2	Maitlis and Lawrence (2003)	Maitlis (2005)
Matched pair 3	Ferner (2000)	Ferner, Almond and Colling (2005)
Matched pair 4	Jarzabkowski and Wilson (2002) Jarzabkowski (2003)	Jarzabkowski (2008)

Matched pair 1

From the articles we have analysed, Chreim (2005) and Chreim et al. (2007) seem the most divergent. Chreim et al. (2007) label their study a form of 'naturalistic inquiry' and, unlike many qualitative contributions in the *Academy of Management Journal*, they do not provide propositions. However, they do use a very traditional theoretical model as the centrepiece for their empirical findings, and their longitudinal case study is structured and reported in a 'mainstream' manner. Chreim (2005) takes a very different approach in terms of the philosophical position (constructivist), method (narrative analysis) and data sources (document analysis, without any supporting interviews). Here, there may be some evidence of transatlantic differences at play: the less traditional study has been published in a European journal that is open to new forms of analysis and presentation.

Matched pair 2

The two articles with Maitlis as the lead author show far less divergence. The Maitlis and Lawrence (2003) article is based on one of the three cases published in Maitlis (2005). As a single case study, it includes a detailed case narrative, which is absent in the multiple case study write-up in the 2005 article. However, closer examination reveals that despite the fact that the *JMS* paper is a single case study with a strong narrative element, the case study approach and philosophical assumptions underpinning the two articles are in fact very similar. Thus, the narrative in Maitlis and Lawrence (2003) is followed by a section setting out a theoretical framework and accompanying propositions. While the authors position themselves in the tradition of process-oriented strategy research, they gently criticize process studies for being too focused on 'rich descriptions', at the expense of developing a 'set of core concepts and relationships that can be used … across a wide variety of organizational contexts' (Maitlis and Lawrence, 2003: 123). The North American version of the study, Maitlis (2005), is very consistent with this approach, and likewise produces a theoretical framework together with propositions.

Matched pair 3

Ferner (2000) and Ferner et al. (2005) are also similar in many ways, although it should be noted that the *Journal of International Business Studies* paper provides more detail on the study's methodology, compares the multiple cases more systematically and structures the findings section more tightly. The *JIBS* paper makes reference to quantitative standards and expectations, acknowledging that the 'small-*n*' nature of the research means that any conclusions are 'tentative' (Ferner et al., 2005: 317). They also 'translate' their analytical approach into quantitative terms, referring to the 'dependent variable' in their study – but putting this term in quotation marks as though to stress that this is only a loose translation. However, the articles are similar in that they are written in an essayistic, reflective style, according to which the forcefulness of the argument rather than tight structuring carries the paper. This suits the main theoretical contribution of the paper, which rather than offering a new model, framework or set of propositions, makes the argument for an alternative lens on the multinational corporation. In other words, the contribution lies in looking at a well-known phenomenon in a new and more critical light. The paper therefore does not claim to be building theory, providing a platform for hypothesis testing or examining a new empirical phenomenon – rather, Ferner and colleagues are persuading their readers to view interactions within the multinational corporation through a different theoretical lens.

Matched pair 4

In the case of Jarzabkowski's work, it is interesting to see how she has made use of the same cases, varying the theoretical lenses and writing it up in different ways. The *Academy of Management Journal* article in 2008 demonstrates the prototypical use of an inductive theory-building protocol (leading to propositions) whereas the *Journal of Management Studies* articles provide a model without formal propositions. Furthermore, the 2002 *Journal of Management Studies* article contains very little detail on the actual data analysis. The three articles thus hint at differences in expectations between US and European journals, in terms of the detail required on data collection and analysis (including representations of data) and the (explicit) links between data and any theorizing. Such differences may have become more marked since the early 2000s, but equally one could argue that European journals have started to emphasize greater rigour in qualitative research. Additionally, there is a further observation around theoretical representation; from a meta-perspective, the articles develop similar arguments (i.e. strategizing activities are influenced by the institutional environment) but employ different theoretical lenses and vocabularies. Hence, changes and variation in the theoretical language used may thus imply changes in audiences and thus also different contributions. A final interesting point is the inductive nature of the case studies but the somewhat deductive way in which the *Academy of Management Journal* and *Journal of Management Studies* (2003) papers are written up, primarily to position the study in line with a theoretical tradition or theorizing objective.

North American versus European: How Different?

To put these general observations in perspective, we asked the lead authors of these four matched pairs for their reflections on the highlighted differences, as well as more directly for their reflections on these studies and the respective review and editorial processes involved. We also explicitly asked the authors to contrast their experiences with North American and European journals.

When we approached the authors, they provided us with insights concerning both the nature of the changes they had made to conform to journal standards and at what point in the research process these had taken place. On the whole, all four authors discerned notable differences in expectations between North American and European journals, although they did not 'reverse engineer' their studies or even explicitly design them with a particular journal in mind. In other words, they formulated questions and designed studies in line with more general standards of good qualitative research, whether that was more inductive or deductive and more emic versus etic in orientation. Only once the studies were completed did they consider options for publication and start to write up their papers for submissions. In the write-up stage, the authors tried to anticipate what would be expected by the reviewers and editors of the journals in question.

Our correspondence with the authors reveals that there can be a disconnection between the actual conduct of qualitative research and the way the study is framed, written up and represented in published articles. The issues that came through most strongly in our communication with the authors were associated with North American quality criteria regarding reliability and external validity. These quality criteria have been imported from quantitative, positivist research and directly applied to evaluate qualitative research (e.g. by Yin, 2009). The authors were divided in their responses to the reviewers' demands to adopt these quality criteria. Some of them took a stand against these demands because they regarded them as a violation of good qualitative research. Others accepted them as an expectation or convention that pragmatically needed to be heeded.

The North American emphasis on reliability translates into concerns about the transparency and rigour of analytical processes in qualitative research. Bluhm et al. (2011) argue that transparency is highly valued by North American journals because it allows for the replication of a study. They find a statistically significant difference between North American and European journals in terms of transparency in published articles. US journals had a higher ratio of transparent articles with a higher rate of increase in transparency over the ten-year period investigated than their European counterparts did (Bluhm et al., 2011). Bansal and Corley (2011) examined qualitative articles published in *AMJ* from 2001 to 2010 and observed a trend towards the increasing use of coding in data analysis. They interpreted this as a response to the demands for transparency. Through coding, authors of qualitative articles can establish an explicit connection between raw data and theoretical conclusions. Bansal and Corley (2011), however, express a concern that coding has become the standard for all types of qualitative research even when it may not fit the approach taken in the study.

In our correspondence with the authors, inter-rater reliability was mentioned as an instance of robustness checks in the context of coding qualitative data. Both Chreim and Jarzabkowski referred to it as a perennial concern with *AMJ* submissions. Both authors also questioned the value of such measures as part of coding protocols and the objectivity of the mechanics. Such an assessment – if involving outside coders with less familiarity with the case or if the second-order categorization could legitimately be said to consist of fuzzy sets of categories (as opposed to mutually exclusive options) – may reify the nature of qualitative data and as such also provide a false sense of security.

Nonetheless, inter-rater reliability measures, such as the kappa statistic (Cohen, 1960), are in fact being increasingly suggested, it seems, by reviewers as part of grounded theory or interpretive methodologies. Nag, Corley and Gioia in their (2007) *AMJ* paper similarly mentioned (in a footnote) how they considered inter-rater reliability assessments as outside of their interpretive tradition of research, but also said that they did it anyway in order to comply with reviewer expectations. Among our matched pairs, only Jarzabkowski had measures for inter-rater reliability both in her *AMJ* and in one of her *JMS* papers. Chreim (2005: 589) takes the opposite approach and explicitly rejects the need for replicability: 'My study provides one of different readings of the narratives … I now leave my research narrative for the reader to interpret'.

What is interesting about this development is that it not only signals the perceived importance of robustness checks, apparently to shore up confidence in the theoretical inferences made, but that it also implies the need for qualitative studies to be geared towards a structure where instances of raw, first-order data can be categorized in terms of neatly contained sets (second-order codes), over which the agreement (or lack of agreement) between coders can be computed. In other words, even with interpretive methodologies, the bias seems to be towards a form of analysis and theorizing that favours analytical reduction over phenomenological richness, narrative representation and grounding, where the credibility of the analysis stems from the author's (demonstrated) knowledge of the case. The Maitlis studies are a case in point: the narratives of the change processes in the three orchestras studies feature in the *JMS* article, but are mentioned only as a methodological step as part of the *AMJ* article.

A second issue mentioned by all four authors in our communication with them is external validity and how concerns for generalizability featured much more prominently in North American journals than in European journals. Chreim and Ferner mentioned this expectation explicitly as one associated with *AMJ* and *JIBS*. Like reliability, external validity as a quality criterion stems from positivistic assumptions and the importance attached to generalizability (Numagami, 1998; *Journal of Management Studies*, 2011). Among our matched pairs, two of the authors (Chreim and Ferner) did not discuss generalizability in their *JMS* article but did so for their *AMJ* piece. The other two authors (Jarzabkowski and Maitlis) addressed generalizability in their articles for both journals.

Among those authors who discuss generalizability at all, we found two distinct approaches: the first was simply to state that the small-n nature of the study 'does not allow broad generalizations to be drawn about the patterns of occurrence of the dependent variable' (Ferner et al., 2005: 311; see also Jarzabkowski, 2003). The second approach was to discuss the basis for generalizability or transferability in a detailed way. In her study of symphony orchestras, Maitlis (2005) identifies common characteristics between orchestras and medium-sized private enterprises. She therefore states that 'orchestras … provide a surprisingly high level of generalizability to a broader population of organizations' (2005: 24). Similarly, Jarzabkowski (2008: 643), in her study of strategy processes in universities, expects that the findings 'may have relevance to many organizations that share characteristics with universities' such as 'hospitals and cultural and professional service organizations'. Both approaches represent a conciliatory response to positivist norms of generalizability as they do not reject the goal of generalizability altogether.

The comments we received from the authors conform to expectations: the North American journals insist on the standards of 'normal science', while European journals are more eclectic. However, as well as these isomorphic pressures at work, we can also see that the authors of the matched pairs draw on and adapt different templates or 'recipes' for writing up qualitative research. We use the term 'recipe' here because instead of hard and fast rules writing up seems to involve rather normative guidelines that have been provided to maximize the chances of a qualitative study being published. We turn now to our categorization of the main publishing recipes that have been provided in recent years as a way of making the standards and criteria for publication transparent.

Publishing Recipes for Qualitative Researchers

Advice to qualitative researchers on how to write up and publish their work ranges from, at one extreme, downplaying and even denying the qualitative component of the study to, at the other extreme, experimenting with novel representational forms, such as poetry. We shall commence with the recipes that have been codified in the existing methodological literature and then proceed to discuss the more tacit practices that were identified in the journal analysis conducted by Welch et al. (2011). We shall also add in some insights from our own editorial, reviewing and writing experiences.

Hiding qualitative research

The first recipe, that of concealment, has been described as 'closet' qualitative research (Sutton, 1997). In this approach, the qualitative component of the study is minimized or even not reported at all. Sutton (1997) outlines a number of situations where it might be advisable to conceal the role of qualitative research in the study: when the insights generated from qualitative data are stronger than the data themselves; when the qualitative data distract from rather than add to the key storyline of the paper; when the journal only publishes conceptual papers; and when the target audience is biased against qualitative research. Examples of each recipe are of course difficult to identify because of their invisibility. Instead, we must rely on authors' own 'confessional tales'. For example, Birkinshaw (2004) relates how he has fallen back on concealing or downplaying the qualitative component when seeking to publish research based on mixed methods. Our own experiences suggest that the pressures that Birkinshaw was reacting to were not isolated ones. One of us was recently part of a review process in which a reviewer recommended a qualitative paper be turned into a conceptual paper because the reviewer was not comfortable with the 'small-n'

and exploratory design of the study. We have also attended 'meet the editors' sessions at international conferences where editors have equated qualitative research with conceptual, non-empirical research.

The drive to conceal qualitative dimensions of a study is not just fuelled by the dominance of quantitative research and positivist doubts about the scientific value of qualitative research. The strong bias these days towards a theoretical contribution as a price of entry for publication may also push the empirical detail of the research to the background, at times reducing the richness of the phenomenon or case to an analytical structure or storyline (see for example Hambrick (2007) for a critique of this development).

Mimicking the deductive reporting of qualitative data

A recipe we found in the dataset (although not among our matched pairs) can be termed 'mimicking' (Pratt, 2008), in that the qualitative researcher writes up the study as if it were a deductive, quantitative study. At its extreme, a mimicking reporting style means placing the literature review up front, posing hypotheses or propositions at the beginning of the paper and using the language of hypothesis testing throughout the article. In such an article, a casual reader might actually miss the qualitative data on which it is based – especially as the data may be quantified where possible, using frequency counts and descriptive statistics.

The emergence of the mimicking reporting style can be traced back to attempts to make qualitative research appear more conventional, or in Pratt's words (2008: 496), 'making "oval" pegs seem "round(er)"'. Bengtsson et al. (1997) report the pressures that may encourage or even force qualitative researchers to conform to deductive norms of reporting. If qualitative studies were true to their theoretical objectives in terms of theory generation and development they would position a less extensive literature review upfront than is the case in traditional articles. However, Bengtsson et al. encountered considerable resistance among North American reviewers to such a reporting structure. As a result of their experiences, they recommend qualitative researchers be more explicit in explaining the format of a paper or following deductive norms. As a result, the structure of the published paper is the reverse of the research process and, more importantly, of the original theoretical objective (Bengtsson et al., 1997: 484): 'Even though the research process is significantly different from the one applied in a nomothetic study, this does not necessarily mean that it has to be fully reflected in the actual presentation of the findings'.

Factor-analytic reporting

The third recipe can be labelled factor-analytic reporting, following Lee (1999) and Bluhm et al. (2011). It reduces large amounts of qualitative data into meaningful 'factors' that are theoretically derived from the data but can also be generalized to include other similar contexts. A paper concludes with validated constructs and propositions that can form the basis for further (quantitative) measurement and extension of the study to other settings. This recipe is based on an 'inverted' logic, in that the standards and expectations of 'mainstream deductive' research are maintained but the traditional structure of an academic article is reversed. Many papers subscribing to grounded theory or using grounded theory techniques (Corbin and Strauss, 2008) would write up according to this reverse structure.

In case-based research, Eisenhardt (1989; Eisenhardt and Graebner, 2007) is perhaps the most prominent as well as the most coherent advocate of this approach. She advises researchers to make theory and propositions not the 'rich story' but the centrepiece of their write-up. Data are summarized in a table to support each proposition and to make the link between theory and data explicit. In our own efforts to publish qualitative research we have often been advised by reviewers to add propositions at the end of a paper. Bengtsson et al. (1997) also encountered reviewers' preferences to present findings in the form of propositions.

Of the matched pairs we reviewed, this recipe was the most common. It was applied in Maitlis and Lawrence (2003), Maitlis (2005) and Jarzabkowski (2008). Bansal and Corley (2011) confirm that the combination of the inductive generation of propositions and coding has become a discernable trend in papers published in *AMJ* from 2001 to 2010. We also found articles that, while they did not formally develop propositions, nevertheless presented a model that brought together the factors identified in the analysis: Jarzabkowski and Wilson (2002: 360), for example, suggest that in their approach 'themes [from the data] are used to derive an explanatory framework'. It is noteworthy that in this analytical process, authors did not necessarily see model development as an outcome of pure induction as Eisenhardt (1989) does. Rather, for example, Jarzabkowski and Wilson (2002) identify both inductive and deductive steps in their analytical process.

Non-traditional reporting

The fourth recipe can be termed 'non-traditional', in that it challenges nomothetic assumptions about how research should be presented for publication. A multitude of novel techniques can be employed in the space of a journal article (see for example Golden-Biddle and Locke, 2007). For example, the author can reject the use of the passive voice and instead assert his or her authorship and role(s) in the study. The researcher may experiment with alternatives to the traditional 'sandwich' structure of an academic text, in which theory is positioned on either side of the data (Golden-Biddle and Locke, 2007). Or the author may even adopt a postmodern approach and challenge traditional forms of representation by using poetry, storytelling and narratives or visual forms (e.g. McGaughey, 2004).

Of the articles in our matched pair dataset, Chreim (2005) has been closest to a non-traditional piece. She is very sensitive to the limitations of any form of interpretation in knowledge production and rejects the notion that her account is anything more than one interpretation among many possible ones. Inevitably, she writes, 'the narrative research enterprise … falls short of providing comprehensive and incontrovertible accounts of the voices that constitute organizations' (Chreim, 2005: 589). However, it is noteworthy that overall we did not find much innovation in the matched pairs.

Essayistic reporting

This is an induced recipe, which we identified from the matched pair analysis (Ferner, 2000, Ferner et al., 2005). As such, we have not found it discussed in the methodological literature on qualitative reporting. The focus in this style of reporting is on the exposition of the argument. The measure of quality is therefore the forcefulness of the argument developed, not the methodological rigour on which the other reporting styles rely. It breaks what is now becoming the expectation regarding scientific reporting, namely that there is a detailed discussion and transparency to the analytical steps taken by the author. Such papers tend to be loosely structured and may not have the kind of headings and sections a reader expects to see in an academic paper. What is interesting is that historically journals such as *AMJ* and *JMS* used to consist primarily of papers written in essayistic styles and in which observations were blended with thoughtful arguments in a largely free-flowing text. In the early volumes of both journals, an essayistic style was shared by both qualitative and quantitative studies. From the 1990s onwards, however, the general style of writing for most papers, qualitative studies included, has become more formal-analytical. In one sense, with the overall genre of academic writing for these journals changing and moving away from an essayistic style, it has also meant as a consequence that qualitative research became bereft of a legitimate mode of reporting.

Conclusion

Our analysis of the four matched pair articles revealed that the diversity of reporting styles that we found cannot be explained by the transatlantic divide alone. Rather, we have suggested a more complex and nuanced view of how qualitative research is written up for publication in top management journals. While each recipe can be traced to specific philosophical assumptions – positivism and its opposing traditions, interpretivism and constructivism – the final reporting style is also affected by pragmatic considerations in terms of the pressure to get published. In this chapter we have argued that authors engage in a balancing act: seeking to gain legitimacy through a particular way of writing up their qualitative data while at the same time trying to stay true to their own philosophical approach and the original integrity of their research projects.

The potential danger in legitimacy seeking is converging on a particular reporting style regardless of whether or not this fits with the purpose of the study. Our own comparisons between the matched pairs and the responses from the authors indicate that North American journals increasingly converge on the factor-analytic approach. This significant use of the factor-analytic style in writing up qualitative research is probably best understood in the context of positivism and its direct and indirect influence on the design of qualitative research. That is, qualitative research is designed, written up and assessed in the context of an intellectual milieu dominated by positivism (see Pratt, 2008). What is important to recognize is that within the factor-analytic perspective on qualitative research, the description of particular management situations or organizational settings is seen as instrumental to the end of theoretical 'objectification' and generalization. As in any form of generalizing science, the activity of qualitatively describing the particular is meant to serve the process of abstracting a set of theoretical factors and highlighting the generalization of these factors across settings.

Bansal and Corley (2011) express concern about the evidence they found for the emergence of what they term 'an *AMJ* style'. They summarize the key features of this style as being an increasing reliance on coding data; the use of tables and diagrams to display findings; and the use of propositions to demonstrate the theoretical contribution of a study. In other words, the factor-analytic style has established itself in the journal. While we can only speculate on the reasons for this preference, clearly the factor-analytic style is a response to the isomorphic and mimetic pressures stemming from the positivist tradition. In future years, if this trend continues, one may expect qualitative scholars to bring their studies that are already *ex ante* into line with journal expectations. As qualitative researchers ourselves we would be concerned about such a development, as it may seriously affect the variety of qualitative research conducted and the integrity of the research.

Our analysis shows that the factor-analytic style is also increasingly being followed in European journals, rendering the North American and European journals more similar to each other. For example, purely essayistic contributions are rare these days in European journals. Although European journals are relatively more inclusive and allow for much more variety in contributions, increasingly these journals also demonstrate a convergence on certain types of contributions. Indeed, as Ferner commented to us, reviewers for these journals are also increasingly occupied with notions of reliability and external validity in the same vein that we have discussed in this chapter.

The future challenge for European journals therefore may be to uphold their much greater diversity and to ensure that research projects are judged by reviewers and editors with the appropriate set of quality criteria in mind (i.e. criteria that would be apt and justifiable in the light of the research conducted: see Johnson et al., 2006). There is also a real opportunity here, following Bluhm et al. (2011), in that European journals may take a leaf out of the book of North American journals and heed the call for rigour and detail in data analysis. Doing so may help in validating, standardizing and mainstreaming new and emerging qualitative methods, such as discourse and narrative analysis and visual methods. Similarly, North American journals may follow the lead of European journals in being open to various forms of qualitative research and data analysis (which obviously may also require a less strict focus on a factor-analytic structure across all qualitative studies). This would bring benefits in that it would broaden the reach and diversity of qualitative research presented in these journals. It would also be important for signalling appropriate ways of doing qualitative research to the next generation of scholars in our field.

While there will always be pragmatic and institutional pressures on an author's reporting style, we identified that authors in our dataset made their own choices even if doing so meant that they followed the same reporting style for both the North American and European outlets. Qualitative research encompasses many philosophical traditions (Piekkari and Welch, 2011) and a single 'boiler-plate' (Pratt, 2009) for reporting would be limiting. We therefore conclude our own publishing journey by advocating that journals need to be more tolerant and inclusive of the innovations and differences in reporting styles.

Acknowledgements

We wish to thank Emmanuella Plakoyiannaki and Eriikka Paavilainen-Mäntymäki for their contribution to the original data analysis of *AMJ*, *JIBS* and *JMS*, on which this chapter is based. We would also like thank all the authors whose work served as a basis for analysis in this chapter and who kindly shared their own reflections on the publishing process associated with different journals. We would also thank Cathy Cassell and Gillian Symon for their editorial comments.

Further Reading

The following readings provide useful practical insights into publishing qualitative research: Birkinshaw (2004), Bluhm et al. (2011), McGaughey (2004), Pratt (2008; 2009), Welch and Welch (2004) and Zalan and Lewis (2004).

References

Alvesson, M. and Kärreman, D. (2007) 'Constructing mystery: empirical matters in theory development', *Academy of Management Review*, 32 (4): 1265–1281.

Bansal, P. and Corley, K. (2011) 'From the editors: the coming of age for qualitative research: embracing the diversity of qualitative methods', *Academy of Management Journal*, 54 (2), 233–237.

Bengtsson, L., Elg, U. and Lind, J.-I. (1997) 'Bridging the transatlantic publishing gap: how North American reviewers evaluate European idiographic research', *Scandinavian Journal of Management*, 13 (4): 473–492.

Birkinshaw, J. (2004) 'Publishing qualitative research in international business', in R. Marschan-Piekkari and C. Welch (eds), *Handbook of Qualitative Research Methods for International Business*. Cheltenham: Edward Elgar, pp. 570–584.

Bluhm, D.J., Harman, W., Lee, T.W. and Mitchell, T.R. (2011) 'Qualitative research in management: a decade of progress', *Journal of Management Studies*, 48(8): 1866–1891.

Chreim, S. (2005) 'The continuity-change duality in narrative texts of organizational identity', *Journal of Management Studies*, 42 (3): 567–593.

Chreim, S., Williams, B.E. and Hinings, C.R. (2007) 'Interlevel influences on the reconstruction of professional role identity', *Academy of Management Journal*, 50 (6): 1515–1539.

Cohen, J. (1960) 'A coefficient of agreement for nominal scales', *Educational and Psychological Measurement*, 20 (1): 37–46.

Collin, S.-U., Johansson, U., Svensson, K. and Ulvenblad, P.-O. (1996) 'Market segmentation in scientific publications: research patterns in American vs European management journals', *British Journal of Management*, 7 (2): 141–154.

Corbin, J. and Strauss, A. (2008) *Basics of Qualitative Research: Techniques and Procedures for Developing Grounded Theory* (3rd edn). Thousand Oaks, CA: Sage.

Czarniawska, B. (1999) *Writing Management: Organization Theory as a Literary Genre.* Oxford: Oxford University Press.

Eisenhardt, K.M. (1989) 'Building theories from case study research', *Academy of Management Review*, 14 (4): 532–550.

Eisenhardt, K.M. and Graebner, M.E. (2007) 'Theory building from cases: opportunities and challenges', *Academy of Management Journal*, 50 (1): 25–32.

Ferner, A. (2000) 'The underpinnings of bureaucratic control systems: HRM in European multinationals', *Journal of Management Studies*, 37 (4): 521–539.

Ferner, A., Almond, P. and Colling, T. (2005) 'Institutional theory and the cross-national transfer of employment policy: the case of 'workforce diversity' in US multinationals', *Journal of International Business Studies*, 36 (3): 304–321.

Gephart, R.P. (2004) 'From the editors: qualitative research and the *Academy of Management Journal*', *Academy of Management Journal*, 47 (4): 454–462.

Golden-Biddle, K. and Locke, K. (2007) *Composing Qualitative Research* (2nd edn). Thousand Oaks, CA: Sage.

Hambrick, D.C. (2007) 'The field of management's devotion to theory: too much of a good thing?', *Academy of Management Journal*, 50 (6): 1346–1352.

Holliday, A. (2007) *Doing and Writing Qualitative Research* (2nd edn). London: Sage.

Jarzabkowski, P. (2003) 'Strategic practices: an activity theory perspective on continuity and change', *Journal of Management Studies*, 40 (1): 23–55.

Jarzabkowski, P. (2008) 'Shaping strategy as a structuration process', *Academy of Management Journal*, 51 (4): 621–650.

Jarzabkowski, P. and Wilson, D.C. (2002) 'Top teams and strategy in a UK university', *Journal of Management Studies*, 39 (3): 355–381.

Johnson, P., Buehring, A., Cassell C. and Symon, G. (2006) 'Evaluating qualitative research: towards a contingent criteriology', *International Journal of Management Reviews*, 8 (3): 131–156.

Journal of Management Studies (from the Editors) (2011) 'Ethnography in the context of management and organizational research: its scope and methods, and why we need more of it', *Journal of Management Studies*, 48 (1): 198–201.

Lee, T.W. (1999) *Using Qualitative Methods in Organizational Research.* Thousand Oaks, CA: Sage.

Maitlis, S. (2005) 'The social processes of organizational sensemaking', *Academy of Management Journal*, 48 (1): 21–49.

Maitlis, S. and Lawrence, T.B. (2003) 'Orchestral manoeuvres in the dark: understanding failure in organizational strategising', *Journal of Management Studies*, 40 (1): 109–139.

McGaughey, S. (2004) '"Writing it up": the challenges of representation in qualitative research', in R. Marschan-Piekkari and C. Welch (eds), *Handbook of Qualitative Research Methods for International Business*. Cheltenham: Edward Elgar, pp. 529–550.

Meriläinen, S., Tienari, J., Thomas, R. and Davies, A. (2008) 'Hegemonic academic practices: experiences of publishing from the periphery', *Organization*, 15 (4): 584–597.

Nag, R., Corley, K.G. and Gioia, D.A. (2007) 'The intersection of organizational identity, knowledge, and practice: attempting strategic change via knowledge grafting', *Academy of Management Journal*, 50 (4): 821–847.

Numagami, T. (1998) 'The infeasibility of invariant laws in management studies: a reflective dialogue in defense of case studies', *Organization Science*, 9 (1): 2–15.

Piekkari, R. and Welch, C. (eds) (2011) *Rethinking the Case Study in International Business and Management Research*. Cheltenham: Edward Elgar.

Pratt, M.G. (2008) 'Fitting oval pegs into round holes: tensions in evaluating and publishing qualitative research in top-tier North American journals', *Organizational Research Methods*, 11 (3): 481–509.

Pratt, M.G. (2009) 'For the lack of a boilerplate: tips on writing up (and reviewing) qualitative research', *Academy of Management Journal*, 52 (5): 856–862.

Suddaby, R. (2006) 'From the editors: what grounded theory is not', *Academy of Management Journal*, 49 (4): 633–642.

Sutton, R.I. (1997) 'The virtues of closet qualitative research', *Organization Science*, 8 (1): 97–106.

Welch, C., Piekkari, R., Plakoyiannaki, E. and Paavilainen-Mantymaki, E. (2011) 'Theorising from case studies: towards a pluralist future for international business research', *Journal of International Business Studies*, 42 (5): 740–762.

Welch, D. E. and Welch, L. S. (2004) 'Getting published: the last great hurdle?' in R. Marschan-Piekkari and C. Welch (eds), *Handbook of Qualitative Research Methods for International Business*. Cheltenham: Edward Elgar.

Wolcott, H.F. (2009) *Writing Up Qualitative Research* (3rd edn). Thousand Oaks, CA: Sage.

Woods, P. (1999) *Successful Writing for Qualitative Researchers*. London: Routledge.

Yin, R.K. (2009) *Case Study Research: Design and Methods* (4th edn). Thousand Oaks, CA: Sage.

Zalan, T. and Lewis, G. (2004) 'Writing about methods in qualitative research: towards a more transparent approach', in R. Marschan-Piekkari and C. Welch (eds), *Handbook of Qualitative Research Methods for International Business*. Cheltenham: Edward Elgar.

Assessing Qualitative Research

Gillian Symon and Catherine Cassell

Introduction

What constitutes good qualitative research? Given that they outline aspects of good practice in applying qualitative research in the field, all the authors in this volume address this question, slanted to their own particular methodological interests. However, there is a stream of research that has directly sought to identify those characteristics that could be said to define 'quality' in qualitative research. In this chapter, we will review this research and illustrate it through our own theoretical and empirical work. However, not all qualitative researchers agree with this line of investigation, arguing that any derivation of qualitative criteria enacts power relations that tend to subjugate qualitative research. In this chapter, we will also present the 'criteriology debate' that rages in the area (e.g. Smith and Hodkinson, 2005).

Many authors have argued that qualitative research cannot be assessed by the same criteria as those applied to quantitative research (e.g. Morgan, 1983; Denzin, 1988; Seale, 1999; Easterby-Smith et al., 2008), given that the methodologies utilized by researchers in each area are so different. In quantitative research, criteria such as reliability and validity are well known and upheld as elements that have to be 'proved' by the researcher as part of the research process in order for the research itself to be accepted as worthy of consideration. In this research, researcher attention to the methodological means of achieving objectivity produces a 'scientifically rigorous', and hence, 'believable' study. In qualitative research, where objectivity is not the goal – indeed where subjectivity, interpretation and emancipation may be key elements (see Duberley, Johnson and Cassell, in this volume) – such criteria as construct validity make little sense. However, they may still be being applied inappropriately, with the result that potentially good quality qualitative research never reaches the public arena. Such misguided assessment may arise because of deeply held beliefs about what should constitute 'good' research on the part of the assessor – based on philosophical, or even political, commitments to positivist research (e.g. see Pfeffer, 1993) – or simply because they are unaware of other criteria that may be used (Pratt, 2008; Cassell and Symon, 2011). In either case, it seems incumbent on qualitative researchers to take issue with this state of affairs if we are to see more qualitative research being published. Tracy (2010) gives three main reasons for the development of specific assessment criteria for qualitative research:

- *Pedagogical*. Having guidelines helps us to learn how to practise, and also how to develop our practice. As we have said previously, having a 'recipe' in the early stages of our research careers helps us to learn even while such learning may then encourage us to later question and improvise (Symon and Cassell, 1998).

- *Developmental*. Producing such guidelines encourages researchers from different areas of qualitative research to debate and learn from each other.

- *Political*. Having guidelines enables us to persuade other groups of scholars that our work is valuable. A common language of generally systematic evaluation may encourage others to credit and support our work.

We should note that much of the work in this area is not confined to organizational research. Although management and organizational researchers have been active in considering this issue (e.g. see the special issue of *Organizational Research Methods*, volume 11, issue 3, 2008), much of this debate has gone on in the wider social science arena (e.g. see various editions of *The Handbook of Qualitative Research*, edited by Denzin and Lincoln, and the journal *Qualitative Inquiry*). Therefore we must draw here on work from within the qualitative research arena more broadly.

In this chapter, we will first consider some 'alternative' lists of quality criteria that have been produced to assess qualitative research, encompassing those derived from methodological or epistemological principles and those derived from an empirical analysis of reported practices. We will then outline the arguments made against the derivation of explicit assessment criteria for qualitative research, concluding with some comments on the possible future for such criteria in qualitative management and organizational research.

Assessment Criteria for Qualitative Research

As above, a number of lists of criteria for judging qualitative research have been produced and it is not possible to review all of these in this chapter: instead we will give examples of 'universal' criteria and of more 'contingent' criteria. We will also distinguish between lists in terms of whether they are derived from methodological or epistemological principles, or whether they are derived from researchers' claimed practice. We will illustrate the latter through our own research, specifically with management and organization researchers.

Methodologically and theoretically derived lists: universal criteria

Perhaps the best known and earliest formulation of a list of criteria for assessing qualitative research is that formulated by Guba and Lincoln (1989). Their motivation to do this came from a recognition that positivist criteria were inappropriate for the assessment of what they termed 'Naturalistic Inquiry' and that it was necessary to devise and publicize alternative criteria so that qualitative research was not judged by quantitative evaluation standards by default. The derivations of these alternative criteria were informed by the very criteria Lincoln and Guba wanted to replace and were essentially a substitution for these, but adjusted for a constructivist epistemology. Table 12.1 summarizes these criteria against the positivist criteria they are meant to mimic.

In the parallel criterion of *credibility*, rather than trying to find a best fit between interpretation and reality, the researcher tries to demonstrate a good fit between 'constructed realities of respondents and the reconstructions attributed to them' (Guba and Lincoln, 1989: 237), with the achievement of this to be demonstrated through a variety of methodological means such as:

* *Prolonged engagement.* Spending enough time at the research site or with the participants to be able to claim going beyond superficial observation and to have established a rapport and immersion.

Table 12.1   Guba and Lincoln's (1989) Parallel Quality Criteria

Positivist term	Naturalistic term
Internal validity	Credibility
Generalizability	Transferability
Reliability	Dependability
Objectivity	Confirmability

- *Peer debriefing*. Discussing ongoing research practice in the field with a colleague who encourages reflexivity on the part of the researcher by challenging assumptions and making tacit understandings explicit and acts as a sounding board for the development of the research.

- *Negative case analysis*. Refining analysis through a consideration of those cases that do not fit the original interpretation until the researcher has arrived at the most inclusive explanation possible (and has demonstrated that other explanations have been fully considered).

- *Progressive subjectivity*. Keeping a record (perhaps in a research diary) of initial constructions of the research and the researcher's developing understanding, with the aim of checking that original constructions have been challenged and changed through a consideration of the research participants' constructions.

- *Member checking*. Testing the researcher interpretation of the data with the research participants throughout the research process (e.g. by discussing emerging results with various interest groups within the research) to check that the participants' views have been accurately captured and to add additional material.

With reference to *transferability*, rather than trying to demonstrate that the results generalize to all other contexts, the researcher provides enough detail about the specific research case (e.g. through thick description) that the reader can judge what other (similar) contexts – and particularly whether their own situation – might be informed by the findings.

The criterion of *dependability* refers to demonstrating how 'methodological changes and shifts in constructions' (Guba and Lincoln, 1989: 242) – unacceptable in a positivist approach but essential in a research process that seeks to refine understanding as part of the research – have been captured and made available for evaluation. Guba and Lincoln describe this as an audit process, and again, it could be achieved through keeping a research diary and detailing this emergent process in any account of the research. The reader is then able to judge why certain decisions were made and how the eventual understanding of the research situation was achieved.

Similarly, a *confirmability* audit seeks to make clear where the data came from (e.g. interview, document, observation, etc.) and how such data were transformed into the presented findings. In other words, it provides a detailed account of the data collection and analysis processes such that the reader is assured that 'data, interpretations, and outcomes of inquiries are rooted in contexts and persons apart from the [researcher] and are not simply figments of the [researcher's] imagination' (Guba and Lincoln, 1989: 243).

The criteria outlined above appear to be very thorough and many qualitative researchers could find helpful methodological tips here for constructing a story of their research that is convincing and credible to readers from a range of epistemological positions. However, these initial criteria have been subject to criticism (Smith, 1990) not least from Lincoln and Guba themselves, who claimed their own criteria were limited, not just because they have their basis in positivist assumptions, but also because they focus too much on method as the means by which quality can be ensured, i.e. the more thorough the method, the more we can guarantee the quality of the research and the credibility of the claimed findings. However, 'outcome, product and negotiation criteria are equally important in judging a given criteria' (Lincoln and Guba, 1985: 245). As a consequence Lincoln and Guba then voiced a set of ('truly') alternative criteria, that they termed 'authenticity' criteria, which were meant to supplement their original list. These criteria focused on issues such as the fairness of the research process, the extent to which all stakeholders' views are explicitly considered and represented in the data, that the research has been a learning experience for the participants and that it has in some way changed the research situation (for the better). Since then, both separately and together, Lincoln and Guba have continued to add to and modify their criteria. For example, in 1995, Lincoln specified eight standards for qualitative research, encompassing:

- The standards set by the relevant inquiry community (e.g. publication guidelines).

- The standard of positionality, wherein the stance of the researcher is explicitly acknowledged.

- The standard of community, wherein the research addresses and serves the community in which it was carried out.

- The standard of voice, wherein the research gives voice to the participants, including multiple and conflicting views.

- The standard of critical subjectivity, wherein the researcher engages in reflexivity and seeks self-transformation through the research.

- The standard of reciprocity, wherein there is mutuality between the researcher and the research participants.

- The standard of relationship, wherein the research respects the collaborativeness of the research.

- The standard of sharing, wherein the researcher shares the rewards of the research with the participants.

These additional criteria show much more of a concern with the nature of the relationship with the research participants and ethical considerations than previous lists.

In a similar bid to produce a set of universal quality criteria but specifically driven by a concern that UK government policy-makers may not know how to judge the worth and implications of qualitative research, Spencer et al. (2003) were funded by the UK's Cabinet Office to produce as comprehensive a list of assessment criteria as possible while still being accessible to a range of users. Because of its practical nature, we might consider Spencer et al.'s framework to be particularly relevant to research in management and organizations. Drawing on existing lists and other writings in the area, plus some interviews with relevant researchers, Spencer et al. produced a framework based on 18 different questions pertinent to the various sections of a research report, with suggestions about the features that would be expected in any high quality example. Given its antecedents, this list is deliberately accessible, explicit, thorough and practical, with the report even containing a template to use when judging any particular report.

Many of the questions they suggest are asked of the qualitative research report are questions that would be equally valid for quantitative research and could be considered hallmarks of general scientific practice – in particular reproducing cultural assumptions and norms about how scientific reports are written up and presented (e.g. as represented in the labelling of the sections of the report being considered, the concentration on providing rationales for research design decisions, the concerns over providing an overall logical and coherent narrative). This all-encompassing consideration may be becau[se they were essentially writing for an audience of laypeople (government officials and policy-makers); however, it does tend to prejudice against any creativity or idiosyncrasy of presentation, and, overall, to be conservative in orientation.

In a more recent version of such lists, Tracy (2010) argues that, despite the paradigmatic and methodological diversity of the field, it is possible to distinguish 'universal' criteria for the assessment of qualitative research if we focus on 'common end goals' rather than 'variant mean methods':

> The conceptual discrimination of qualitative *ends* from *means* provides an expansive or 'big tent' (Denzin, 2008) structure for qualitative quality while still celebrating the complex differences amongst various paradigms [...] we can create a conceptualization in which qualitative researchers can agree on common markers of goodness without tying these markers to specific paradigmatic practices or crafts. (Tracy, 2010: 839)

Tracy believes that we can identify a number of criteria that are common to qualitative research despite paradigmatic differences (e.g. reflexivity) or that might be common to different approaches but executed differently depending on the underlying paradigm (e.g. member *checking*, suggesting some underlying 'truth' or member *reflection*, suggesting acceptance of different interpretations and the importance of critical appraisal). These criteria are summarized in Table 12.2.

Methodologically and theoretically derived lists: contingent criteria

The lists described above were specifically conceptualized to have general applicability. However, various researchers (e.g. Johnson et al., 2006; Amis and Silk, 2008) argue against such a broadbrush approach, insisting that the criteria are paradigm specific. Thus, Johnson et al. aim to develop 'a criteriology that enables different sets of evaluation criteria to be *contingently* deployed so that they fit the researcher's mode of engagement' (Johnson et al., 2006: 134, emphasis in original). Johnson et al. develop a priori four sets of assessment criteria from the ontological and epistemological commitments of four research paradigms (see Duberley, Johnson and Cassell, in this volume) pertinent to the management and organization field (see Table 12.3).

Going further, some authors have devised lists that are discipline specific (e.g. psychology, Salmon, 2003; information systems, Klein and Myers, 1999; health research, Whittemore et al., 2001) or method specific (e.g. interviews, Kvale, 1996; ethnography, Golden-Biddle and Locke, 1993; grounded theory, Fendt and Sachs, 2008; document analysis, Platt, 1981; case studies, Cepeda and Martin, 2005; action research, Reason, 2006). Creswell (2007), for example, derives different sets of criteria for narrative research, phenomenological,

Table 12.2   Tracy's (2010) list of universal qualitative assessment criteria

Criterion (end goal)	Description
Worthy topic	A topic that, for example, is of theoretical interest or contemporary societal or personal interest, or that challenges assumptions
Rich rigour	A research project that acknowledges complexity by including, for example, rich descriptions and a variety of relevant theoretical and methodological concepts, and has clearly involved researcher effort, reflection and meticulous practice
Sincerity	A research project that evidences reflexivity (see Haynes, in this volume), honesty and transparency in its execution
Credibility	A research report that appears trustworthy and morally actionable through the use of thick description, a multiplicity of sources/methods/researchers, multivocality (representation of a range of participant voices) and participant feedback
Resonance	Research outputs and conclusions that are meaningful to their audiences through an evocative presentation, 'transferability' (see Guba and Lincoln, 1989) and 'vicarious experience' (Tracy, 2010: 845)
Significant contribution	Research outputs and conclusions that develop current theoretical and methodological understanding, encourage further development and inform practice
Ethical	A research process that has encompassed ethical practices: procedural (institutional rules, e.g. informed consent), situational (contextually specific ethical actions), relational (personal actions in the field) and exiting (the manner in which research is completed)
Meaningful coherence	A research report that 'eloquently interconnect[s] ... research design, data collection and analysis with [the] theoretical framework and situational goals' (Tracy, 2010: 848). It is important to note here that Tracy's avoidance of paradigm incommensurability or ontological oscillation does not exclude 'borrowing' concepts from a variety of paradigms or methodologies but does suggest researchers have to be explicit about and explain the rationale for doing this

grounded theory, ethnographic and case study research. While these are specific to each method, it is possible to extract a more abstract list of criteria from across these. Thus there is an expectation that researchers using the methods will adopt and explain/describe the appropriate focus of analysis (e.g. for narrative analysis, the stories of a few individuals; for ethnography, a culture-sharing group); that, in the majority of cases, themes will be identified that connect to an overall story; and that the researcher will adopt a reflexive stance. So it is possible that looking across discipline- or method-specific criteria, one would find very similar overarching criteria to those identified in the lists reviewed above. Having said that, there is no doubting the utility of criteria that are specific to the method one is currently using and which can provide quite detailed advice. The debate over whether abstract, universal criteria can or should be derived may boil down to a pragmatic argument concerning the

Table 12.3   Adapted from Johnson et al.'s (2006) contingent criteriology

Epistemology	Assessment criteria	Questions to ask of the text
Positivism	• Internal validity • External validity • Construct validity • Reliability	Is the data collection and analysis sufficiently rigorous? Are the phenomena of interest adequately operationalized? Is the process described in sufficient detail to be replicable? Is the sampling sufficiently random/extensive and the analysis sufficiently rigorous for the results to also pertain to other samples?
Neo-empiricism (Interpretivism)	Internally reflexive audit trail demonstrating • Credibility • Dependability • Confirmability • Ecological validity • Transferability/logical inference	Is evidence provided that this is an authentic representation of what happened? Are the findings free from researcher bias, and the effects of bias minimized or otherwise accounted for? Have alternative explanations been considered and negative cases analysed? Do the findings speak to real life events and contexts? Has the extent of the findings' applicability elsewhere been considered and is this feasible?
Critical theory	• Accommodation • Catalytic validity • Epistemically reflexive dialogue • Discursive democracy	Have the findings been related to established theory? Has the researcher engaged in a reflexive consideration of their own position? (Are their beliefs and commitments clear?) Have hegemonic regimes of truth been identified, unsettled and challenged? Are the readers and participants encouraged to see the world in new ways? Does the research lead to possibilities for change? Have participants in the research confirmed the credibility of the analysis?
(Affirmative) Postmodernism	• Giving voice to previously silenced textual domains • Unsettling the hegemonic • Articulating the incommensurable plurality of discourses etc. • De-centring the author through multivocality	Have assumptions and commitments been deconstructed? (e.g. have boundaries been challenged? Have the accepted/assumed concepts been problematized? Are the persuasive strategies revealed?) Is the analysis and argument subjectively credible (to the reader)? Has the author reflexively considered their own narrative and elements of its production? (e.g. how does the paper 'work' as a convincing narrative?)

uses to which they may be put. More specific lists may be useful for informing research practice, while more universal criteria may be proposed to inform assessment activities (such as reviewing journal articles) where it is more efficient to have one list to consult.

Empirically derived lists: an example

Taking the unwieldiness of the criteria lists together with the acknowledgement that researchers may have to work creatively within such lists to produce honest yet appropriately structured accounts of their research practice suggests that exploring 'assessment-criteria-in-use' with researchers themselves would be illuminating. Whether reporting their own research or assessing others' work, do researchers actively apply these existing criteria? And how do they manage the complex process of weighing flexibility of practice against the apprehension of later judgement by (unknown) peers? What tacit judgements are being made? Which criteria really seem to matter?

Together with our colleagues, Prof Phil Johnson, Anna Buehring and Dr Vicky Bishop, we investigated management researchers' general perceptions of qualitative research, to identify their training needs with respect to qualitative research and to derive a set of criteria for assessing the quality of qualitative research.[1] We interviewed 45 academics falling within four different stakeholder groups: academic disseminators (e.g. journal editors, assessors from funding agencies), qualitative researchers, directors of PhD programmes and practitioners (e.g. consultants and public sector employees concerned with practice- or policy-oriented research). Among the questions we asked this panel of experts were probes to uncover the explicit and implicit criteria they adopted in assessing qualitative management research.

Through a process of template analysis (see King, in this volume), we inductively generated a set of descriptors from the transcripts, which encapsulated all the criteria on which the sample seemed to base their judgements of quality. Looking across these detailed criteria, and in an iterative process among the research team, we then grouped these into second-order descriptors and into three main areas of concern for quality (see Table 12.4). We can see that in making their judgements researchers do not just focus on outputs, but also the process of achieving those outputs and the credibility of the final presentation. Overall, it was notable that most of the informants we spoke to claimed that they did not draw on any of the sets of criteria we outlined earlier. In discussing how they made their judgements, they suggested they relied more on their personal judgement than any existing standards.

It is interesting that, despite claiming not to use specific alternative lists of assessment criteria, some of the criteria outlined above do find an echo in

[1]ESRC research grant, H333250006; for the full report of this research see Cassell et al., 2005.

Table 12.4   Summary of derived criteria from management scholars and practitioners

Quality output	Making a contribution	New insights
		Practical outcomes
		Creating new problems
		Beyond the specific
	Interesting	Addresses the 'so what' issue
		Matter of personal taste
Quality process	Technical accomplishment	Rigour
		Detective work
	Not linear	Flexible
		Responsive
	Transparent	Systematic
		Theoretically informed
		Epistemologically congruent
	Reflexive	Considering own influence
		Giving a balanced account
Quality performance	Logical argument	Logics of discovery
		Consistency
	Recognize limitations	Not going beyond the data
		Crafting a believable account
	Convincing	Rhetorical skills
		Reader's role
		Telling a story

existing lists. This could indicate that the research community does share certain beliefs about what constitutes good quality qualitative research, or it could instead indicate that the research participants have unknowingly been influenced by the lists already produced. In briefly exploring Table 12.4 further, we specifically highlight those criteria that develop previous lists, where qualitative practice may deviate most explicitly from quantitative practice, and areas of ambivalence.

Quality output

Our sample partly judged qualitative research in terms of the extent to which the research made a contribution to our understanding of a particular research topic: both in terms of new insights into that topic and formulating practical outcomes on the basis of those insights. So far, these criteria seem pertinent to any kind of scientific endeavour. However, what may be different and specific to qualitative criteria is the idea of 'creating new problems' – in other words that empirical research should not only provide theoretical understandings of phenomena but should also 'problematize' the research area, calling into question assumptions, definitions and accepted frameworks (Alvesson and Sandberg, 2011). In addition, participants thought the research output should be 'interesting' but it was clear that what was considered 'interesting' might vary considerably – one participant commented that 'So much qualitative research is just not interesting enough to keep me engaged' (academic disseminator panel), while another concluded, 'Quantitative studies are a way of telling stories … they're just not as interesting' (academic disseminator panel). Such an observation draws attention to the role of subjective judgement in assessing research that cannot be 'controlled' by lists of criteria, and also the possibility that the criteria themselves are open to interpretation.

Quality process

Another important element to the panels' assessments was the extent to which the research appeared to have followed a high quality process. That the work should be 'technically accomplished' would again be indicative of any scientific endeavour, but the participants were generally ambivalent about what this might mean, as this seemed to come close to giving credence to concerns usually associated with quantitative research. Thus:

> It's kind of dressing up qualitative research in quantitative clothes, isn't it? That you're making a big deal out of the procedures and steps that you go through … in the same way you would if you were reporting … 'I did this T test' and 'I found R Squared' … But having said that I think it's a good thing. It's got to be a good thing to be more systematic and at least force people to think more about why they're doing things. (practitioner panel)

This kind of statement echoes the general ambivalence qualitative researchers may have about assessment criteria. Qualitative researchers themselves want some limits to a completely open field of research conduct that would be so unrestricted as to have no meaning, but realize that this is something of a double-edged sword that leaves the research open to inappropriate judgements. In more obvious opposition to quantitative approaches is the celebration of flexible and responsive research: 'To me a marker of good qualitative research conduct is that something changes between the original plan and how you end up doing it' (qualitative researcher panel). Reflexivity can be considered another distinctive component of qualitative research but a specific limitation put on this by the panels was that a proper balance had to be found between giving enough detail to inform the reader's interpretation and being self-indulgent or over-elaborating.

Quality performance

The third main area of quality assessment addressed by our research panels concerned the ways in which the researcher created and presented a credible story of the research. Again, as with quantitative research, a logical and internally consistent story was expected where it was clear how the initial theorizing had led to specific research strategies and where theoretical conclusions were clearly implied by relevant data. However, given the philosophical diversity of qualitative research, there was a greater concern with the epistemological consistency throughout (e.g. that a social constructionist account is social constructionist throughout and does not stray into some form of qualitative positivism). While a certain form of rhetorical skill is endemic in the traditional presentation of quantitative research (to the point where it is accepted practice rather than viewed as a particular cultural form), our panels recognized that qualitative research may have to form new kinds of rhetorical skills to make the qualitative form of presentation convincing and credible. For example, the use of metaphor:

> you're trying to sort of like [in] one ... 'take', if I may use the photographical analogy, to get this complexity. Many details are lost ... but if you're lucky ... if your metaphor grasps it ... if your picture sort of gets a good angle, the reader or the audience gets a much better picture ... – or at least believes to have a better understanding – than those small dead fragments ... added to one another. (qualitative researcher panel)

The members of our interview panels were also more aware of the role of the reader as an integral part of the research process. While the researcher is always trying to convince the reader, some qualitative researchers may attribute a much more active role to the reader in this process:

> the idea of most researchers is that it's not dependent on the reader, so the truth is in the text itself, but you know and I know that the truth is between the text and the reader of course. (academic disseminator panel)

Overall, the research report was thought to be convincing and of a high quality if it told some sort of 'compelling story' (practitioner panel).

What emerges from our consideration of the criteria various assessors claim to be using is that the idea of 'criteria' is not unproblematic: that assessors may feel ambivalent about their own application of particular criteria and that they may disagree about the meaning of these criteria. When we actually ask people about their assessment practices and allow them to discuss these in some detail, we also see that they pay quite a lot of attention to the overall (subjective) 'feel' of a piece rather than solely its ability to tick boxes on a list of (fragmented) elements of good practice: is the research interesting? Is the story told engaging? Is the argument compelling? So qualitative researchers should learn from this that producing good qualitative research is not just about getting the process 'right' but also about the 'art of rhetoric' and telling a 'good' story.

It is of particular interest to note at this point that the quality criteria seem to shift and change in importance over time. We have noted this already in the work of Lincoln and Guba, which may be explained by their developing understanding of the field. Savall et al. (2008) analysed reviewer practices at one specific European management journal over a period of 28 years and concluded that while issues of 'internal validity' were prominent in the first ten years, issues of 'external validity' seemed to grow in importance in the following ten years. These changes in criteria over time may reflect both a wider acceptance of qualitative research and a growing diversity within the field as new approaches gain credence (e.g. postcolonialism, see Duberley, Johnson and Cassell, and Cohen and Ravishankar, both in this volume) and new methods come to the fore (e.g. autoethnography, see Humphreys and Learmonth, in this volume; visual methods, see Vince and Warren, in this volume).

Against Assessment Criteria

The proliferation of lists acknowledges the diversity of qualitative research, and empirical research suggests that qualitative researchers may not have a shared view on assessment criteria. However, Tracy argues that this position stands in stark contrast to the parsimony and consensus of quantitative criteria and therefore may be confusing and have less political force. We would question the implied comparison Tracy is making here, giving the appearance of qualitative researchers trying to mimic quantitative research in our practice (even if this is politically motivated). However, on a pragmatic level, we may argue that the range of criteria produced is so extensive that it would be difficult for any research to cover all of these. In this way, qualitative research may disadvantage itself with respect to quantitative research by trying too hard to justify itself. Paying attention to each of these aspects would mean such lengthy research reports they could not be published other than in book form (Pratt, 2008).

Indeed, in recognition of this problem, Easterby-Smith et al. (2008: 422) argue against detailed lists of criteria, although they also suggest that 'there are still features that we expect to see in research conducted by ourselves and others', which include: an understanding of existing perspectives on the issue; thorough methodological practices; the production of evidence to support views; an elucidation of the non-trivial contribution made by the research; and reflexivity on the part of the researcher. Other than the last aspect (which is substituted by a concern with objectivity), these criteria also pertain to the reporting of positivist, quantitative research. Reducing such lists to essentials appears, in this case at least, to also lose the distinctiveness of the qualitative assessment problem. What we may see here is an attempt to persuade qualitative researchers to conform to the basic tenets of 'scientific' practice (e.g. having a literature review, reporting the methodology in detail), common across both quantitative and qualitative research, rather than an attempt to create unique criteria for qualitative research.

More fundamentally, Smith and Hodkinson (2005: 922), as proponents of relativism, argue that as there is no absolute 'truth' or objectivity against which articles and proposals can be judged, all 'criteria must be thought of not as abstract standards but rather as socially constructed lists of characteristics'. As such, all these lists are infinitely contestable. Indeed, the anti-foundationalism of qualitative research would suggest that any form of assessment criteria is simply inappropriate for qualitative research because no criteria could be regarded as certain or privileged. If we view knowledge as socially constructed then how can we have rigid criteria for assessing how that knowledge is produced?

In addition and similarly, we might argue that criteria are inappropriate because there is little 'methodological orthodoxy in qualitative research yet criteria are usually procedural' (Spencer et al., 2003: 42). As qualitative methods are generally flexible in nature, an over-emphasis on rigorous methods is simply too constraining for qualitative researchers' practice. Individual qualitative researchers can find themselves caught between the desire to creatively follow the path of their research exploration and the desire to produce an account of this path that fits the constraints of accepted report structures (e.g. journal articles) and will be found credible by a range of evaluators. This may partly account for some attempts to focus on criteria other than methodological ones (e.g. the orientation to consequences we see in

Lincoln and Guba's authenticity criteria and critical management's concern with encouraging emancipation as an outcome).

What commentators seem to object to here is not that a judgement is made (because we all make judgements all the time) but rather that, as a community of qualitative researchers, we could delimit some sort of universal criteria that would hold in any context, for any (qualitative) work and for any assessor. Even if we were to agree on a list, we would all interpret the criteria differently, and indeed some criteria may be in conflict with each other (as we have seen in the empirical example) so individual, context-specific judgements are always paramount. The problem is that by devising lists we set up an expectation that we will all conform to such lists and this restricts the flexibility, subjectivity and (to some extent) relativity that are at the heart of qualitative research as practice (Bochner, 2000). Smith and Hodkinson (2005) draw attention to the fact that evaluation is about the allocation of scarce resources. Many researchers want to be published in well-respected journals and so papers are assessed in order to see which can be deemed of a high enough quality. Many researchers want to be funded but there is a finite pot of research monies and so proposals are assessed to see which are most credible in their claims of providing answers to important questions. The use of assessment criteria is thus always a political act, determining what will succeed and what will fail. Thus, they argue, we should eschew formalized and accepted lists as tools of oppression.

Schwandt (1996: 70) concludes that what should be at issue is not devising a set of criteria but addressing 'how to cultivate practical reasoning. And for tentative answers to this refined problem, we do not look to following procedures or defining or specifying the right criteria but to the practices, consequences and outcomes of our ways of deliberating'. He continues that, rather than seeking to emulate particular criteria, our work should be informed by 'guiding ideals' and that the process of achieving these ideals should be thought of as 'enabling conditions', including 'aesthetic, prudential and moral considerations', rather than a set of research procedures. Such guiding ideals encompass:

- Generating knowledge that complements (rather than replacing) practice, and aims to understand practice from a variety of perspectives.

- Seeking to 'enhance or cultivate critical intelligence' in stakeholders within the research project.

- Aiming for a research report that enables learning and the 'capacity for practical wisdom' (Schwandt, 1996: 70).

Research can be evaluated on the extent to which it achieves these social, moral and educative aims.

Smith and Deemer (2000) also suggest an alternative to a focus on assessment criteria, arguing we should think in terms of 'characteristics'. Based on their own relativist commitments, such characteristics would be: open-ended; partly unarticulated; rooted in the researcher's own standpoint; and subject to constant reinterpretation.

Conclusion

The attentive reader will have noticed that we have not come up with one overarching list nor suggested which of the lists presented is 'best'. Indeed, as debated above, we might ask ourselves, can we have a general list of quality criteria for all forms of qualitative research? As Tracy herself, despite producing a comprehensive list of criteria, argues:

> the creative brilliance of qualitative methods, like any interpretive art, is learned through practice and apprenticeship. While rules and guidelines are helpful, if it were really as straightforward as 'eight simple criteria', there would be no magic, no surprises, and therefore no genius. (Tracy, 2010: 849)

We have outlined above where some commentators have disagreed altogether with the idea of assessment criteria for qualitative research – on philosophical and political grounds – but also raised our own points of concern in this respect, including:

- Many of the 'lists' of criteria in existence are very comprehensive but as a guide to good practice seem overwhelming, and possibly actually detrimental to the practice of qualitative research because they create unachievable expectations for any one report of qualitative research. In producing such lists it seems as if qualitative researchers are anxious to prove to sceptics that their work is completely transparent in order to prove trustworthy, and yet elements of quantitative research are taken on trust. Do reviewers and readers have to take on trust some of the qualitative research activity, in the same way as they do the correct generation of numbers by quantitative researchers?

- Both these long lists and even shorter heuristics repeat many criteria that are characteristic of any form of research, quantitative or qualitative. This raises the issue of whether there is some form of academic practice that is just 'research', common to both qualitative and quantitative forms (e.g. embedding the current research in an understanding of previous research)? Or whether we can have a form of research (that might be qualitative but not necessarily so) that also challenges some of these basic tenets and requires quite different forms of expression and composition (e.g. autoethnography, see Humphreys and Learmonth, in this volume, and some forms of dramaturgical research may look and sound quite different from the accepted norm).

- It is clear from empirical work examining what criteria stakeholders draw on themselves that such criteria could never be pinned down so comprehensively that there was no room for subjective interpretation – indeed, many qualitative approaches would argue for this to be impossible. So some flexibility around the use of criteria is required.

As qualitative research is so diverse, our overall view is that qualitative researchers should draw on those elements of quality that they think are most relevant to their own research and be careful in their writings to indicate to potential assessors what the aims of the research were and therefore how it should be judged. Pratt (2008) notes that qualitative researchers may set themselves up for failure by including *implicit* indicators in their papers of how their research should be judged. Here he is particularly highlighting the problem of including some indicators of quantity (e.g. number of hours of interviews transcribed) that then might trigger a positivist set of assessment criteria from a reviewer. What we might want to argue more strongly is that in our writings we are quite *explicit* about where we stand in the assessment criteria debate and on what basis we think our work should be judged – perhaps explicitly demonstrating how we have fulfilled the particular goals we set ourselves as qualitative researchers. The least reviewers can do, in their turn, is be quite explicit about the criteria by which they judged any report or proposal and why these criteria seemed justifiable to them. The onus then is not just on the researcher but also on the assessor to be candid about their own practices. This is also the case for journals. Some commentators argue that raising qualitative researchers' and reviewers' awareness of what constitutes high quality qualitative research is insufficient to increase the number of qualitative papers we might see published in research journals and suggest that journals themselves need to change their own practices to more effectively accommodate qualitative work (e.g. Easterby-Smith et al., 2008; Pratt, 2008).

While qualitative researchers continue to be ambivalent about attempts to delineate quality criteria for qualitative research, we should, at the very least, be aware of what criteria may exist and what the arguments about their use would be, so that we can either apply these criteria to our own work or argue for not applying them in a persuasive way. The problem would be if we continued as if we were just unaware of any of these debates.

Further Reading

Spencer et al.'s (2003) report for the UK's Cabinet Office, *Quality in Qualitative Evaluation: A Framework for Assessing Research Evidence*, provides a helpful overview of a range of published qualitative research assessment frameworks and a review of the debates in the area (see especially Chapter 3). The special issue of *Organizational Research Methods*, volume 11, issue 3, published in 2008, provides some interesting empirical work and an overview of some of the issues currently facing the field. Seale (1999) in his *The Quality of Qualitative Research* provides a comprehensive overview of a variety of perspectives and issues in the area and is of practical utility.

References

Alvesson, M. and Sandberg, J. (2011) 'Generating research questions through problematization', *Academy of Management Review*, 36 (2): 247–271.

Amis, J. and Silk, M. (2008) 'The philosophy and politics of quality in qualitative organizational research', *Organizational Research Methods*, 11 (3): 456–480.

Bochner, P. (2000) 'Criteria against ourselves', *Qualitative Inquiry*, 6 (2): 266–272.

Cassell, C., Buehring, A., Symon, G., Johnson, P. and Bishop, V. (2005) *Benchmarking Good Practice in Qualitative Management Research*. ESRC Research Report.

Cassell, C. and Symon, G. (2011) 'Assessing "good" qualitative research in the work psychology field: a narrative analysis', *Journal of Occupational and Organizational Psychology*, 84 (4).

Cepeda, G., and Martin, D. (2005) 'A review of case studies publishing in *Management Decision* 2003–2004: guides and criteria for achieving quality in qualitative research', *Management Decision*, 43 (6): 851–876.

Creswell, J. (2007) *Qualitative Inquiry and Research Design* (2nd edn). Thousand Oaks, CA: Sage.

Denzin, N. (1988) 'Qualitative analysis for social scientists', *Contemporary Sociology*, 17 (3): 430–432.

Easterby-Smith, M., Golden-Biddle, K. and Locke, K. (2008) 'Working with pluralism: determining quality in qualitative research', *Organizational Research Methods*, 11 (3): 419–429.

Fendt, J. and Sachs, W. (2008) 'Grounded theory method in management research: users' perspectives', *Organizational Research Methods*, 11 (3): 430–455.

Golden-Biddle, K. and Locke, K. (1993) 'Appealing work: an investigation of how ethnographic texts convince', *Organization Science*, 4 (4): 595–616.

Guba, E.G. and Lincoln, Y.S. (1989) *Fourth Generation Evaluation*. Newbury Park, CA: Sage.

Johnson, P., Buehring, A., Cassell, C. and Symon, G. (2006) 'Evaluating qualitative management research: towards a contingent criteriology', *International Journal of Management Reviews*, 8 (3): 131–156.

Klein, H. K., and Myers, M. D. (1999) 'A set of principles for conducting and evaluating interpretive field studies in information systems', *MIS Quarterly*, 23 (1): 67–93.

Kvale, S. (1996) *InterViews: An Introduction to Qualitative Research Interviewing*. Thousand Oaks, CA: Sage.

Lincoln, Y. (1995) 'Emerging criteria for quality in qualitative and interpretive research', *Qualitative Inquiry*, 1: 275–289.

Lincoln, Y.S. and Guba, E.G. (1985) *Naturalistic Inquiry*. Beverley Hills, CA: Sage.

Madill, A., Jordan, A. and Shirley, C. (2000) 'Objectivity and reliability in qualitative analysis: realist, contextualist and radical constructionist epistemologies', *British Journal of Psychology*, 91: 1–20.

Morgan, G. (1983) *Beyond Method*. Beverley Hills, CA: Sage.

Pfeffer, J. (1993) 'Barriers to the advancement of organization science: paradigm development as a dependent variable', *Academy of Management Review*, 18 (4), 599–620.

Platt, J. (1981) 'Evidence and proof in documentary research I: some specific problems of documentary research', *Sociological Review*, 29 (1): 31–52.

Pratt, M. (2008) 'Fitting oval pegs into round holes: tensions in evaluating and publishing qualitative research in top-tier north American journals', *Organizational Research Methods*, 11 (3): 481–509.

Reason, P. (2006) 'Choice and quality in action research practice', *Journal of Management Inquiry*, 15 (2): 187–203.

Salmon, P. (2003) 'How do we recognise good research?', *The Psychologist*, 16: 24–27.

Savall, H., Zardet, V., Bonnet, M. and Peron, M. (2008) 'The emergence of implicit criteria actually used by the reviewers of qualitative research articles: the case of a European journal', *Organizational Research Methods*, 11 (3): 510–540.

Schwandt, T. (1996) 'Farewell to criteriology', *Qualitative Inquiry*, 2 (1): 58–72.

Seale, C. (1999) *The Quality of Qualitative Research*. London: Sage.

Smith, J.K. (1990) 'Goodness criteria: alternative research paradigms and the problem of criteria', in E.G. Guba (ed.), *The Paradigm Dialogue*. London: Sage.

Smith, J.K. and Deemer, D. (2000) 'The problem of criteria in the age of relativism', in N. Denzin and Y. Lincoln (eds), *Handbook of Qualitative Research* (2nd edn). Thousand Oaks, CA: Sage.

Smith, J.K. and Hodkinson, P. (2005) 'Relativism, criteria and politics', in N. Denzin and Y. Lincoln (eds), *The Sage Handbook of Qualitative Research* (3rd edn). Thousand Oaks, CA: Sage.

Spencer, L., Ritchie, J., Lewis, J. and Dillon, L. (2003) *Quality in Qualitative Evaluation: A Framework for Assessing Research Evidence*. Report from the Cabinet Office, UK.

Symon, G. and Cassell, C. (eds) (1998) *Qualitative Methods and Analysis in Organizational Research*. London: Sage.

Tracy, S. (2010) 'Qualitative quality: eight "big tent" criteria for excellent qualitative research', *Qualitative Inquiry*, 16 (10): 837–851.

Whittemore, R., Chase, S. and Mandle, C. (2001) 'Validity in qualitative research. *Qualitative Health Research*, 11 (4): 522–537.

13 Teaching Qualitative Research in the Business School

Mark Learmonth and
Michael Humphreys

Introduction

Anecdotally at least, we get the impression that being asked to teach qualitative research methods is something of a poisoned chalice for many academics in business schools. The subject is generally perceived as dry and boring, perhaps because it appears to be content-free, mechanical and rather abstract. Indeed we both got 'landed' with teaching qualitative methods as our first teaching responsibilities when we first became lecturers ourselves – perhaps because it was difficult to say no! Although there is a wealth of textbooks on qualitative research – both the conceptual ideas underpinning it as well as 'how to do it' in terms of methodologies (e.g. Bryman and Bell, 2007; Seale et al., 2007; Hammersley, 2008; Saunders et al., 2009; Silverman, 2010) – there seems to be very little guidance on 'how to teach it'. In our experience, although textbooks are useful, most of us actually learn the skills of qualitative research by doing it (and making mistakes on the way!) Similarly, we learned (and continue to learn) how to teach qualitative research by actually teaching it – and by making mistakes in the classroom.

What we seek to do in this chapter, therefore, is to reflect upon our experiences of teaching qualitative research methods in the context of our own business school. Every year, since 2004, we have taught large classes of Master's students (up to 300) in standard lecture theatres – doing so (out of choice) as a double-act. Though not without its problems and frustrations, as the years have gone by we have gradually improved our teaching evaluation scores and increasingly come to enjoy teaching these classes.[1]

The chapter proceeds as follows. First we set out some ideas about teaching and learning, focusing on teaching as improvisation and some analogies between teaching and musical performance – analogies we ourselves have found helpful in guiding and developing our practice. We then present specific examples of how we operate – i.e. some of the things we *do* in our classes. These are examples of activities that have not only worked well for us in the classroom; but more importantly, student feedback also suggests that our approach has proved valuable in developing their dissertations and other research projects. It is important to stress that we are not being prescriptive – we are describing what works for us. The point is to find ways of playing to your own strengths and interests. You may not play a musical instrument, but what we are suggesting is that you bring some aspect of your 'self' and your personal enthusiasms to the classroom. We find it remarkable how enthusiastic the students' response can be when, from time to time at least, we remove the mask of teacher/expert.

Teaching as an Improvisational Art

> While pedagogical expertise and technical knowledge are essential to it, ultimately teaching is a creative act; it makes something fresh from existing knowledge in spontaneous, improvised efforts of mind and spirit, disciplined by education and experience. (Banner and Cannon, 1997: 3)

Drawing on the work of Jamous and Peloille (1970), Delamont (1995: 7) examines teaching in terms of its 'location in a two-dimensional space of indeterminacy and technicality'. For Delamont, technical skills and knowledge are the explicit, rule governed, codified part of any job or occupation, whereas on the other hand 'indeterminacy is the hidden curriculum of the job performance: all the tacit, implicit, unexamined facets of any job' (Delamont, 1995: 7). We argue that it is important to insist – however much tension exists between technicality and indeterminacy in occupational performance – that *both* should be included in all teaching practice. Gage (1978: 15), in the aptly titled book *The Scientific Basis of the Art of Teaching*, recommends that:

---

[1] Indeed, we recently won a 'Lord Dearing Award' (the University of Nottingham's recognition of teaching excellence) for teaching these classes.

> As a practical art, teaching must be recognised as a process that calls for intuition, creativity, improvisation, and expressiveness – a process that leaves room for departures from what is implied by rules, formulas and algorithms.

For us in this chapter, it is the intuitive and improvisatory elements of teaching that are the main focus of attention. This is not to say, however, that the technical elements are unimportant; it is more the case that the scientific models that stress these elements have had more than their fair share of attention. In redressing the balance, however, we would agree with Delamont's point that the 'invocation of teaching as artistry is a vague one' and that:

> those who use the metaphor rarely specify what kind of performer or creator they have in mind. Is the teacher an actor, a painter, a sculptor, a poet, a ballet dancer, a musician, a composer, a chef, a playwright, a novelist, a choreographer, a quiltmaker, a fashion designer, or a singer? (Delamont, 1995: 7)

Teachers in general, conceivably, could be all or any of these but what about those who teach qualitative research methods? As we said earlier, many might assume it must be taught mechanically and scientifically. However, the approach we use and wish to recommend is one where teachers in performance might be more like jazz musicians or improvisational actors. For us, it is improvisation that is the key concept.

Hatch (1999: 78), in her paper on the value of the jazz metaphor in the study of organizations, argues that improvisation 'constitutes the distinguishing feature of Jazz'. She goes on to describe a typical performance as:

> structured around the playing of tunes which themselves are loosely structured via partial musical arrangements called heads. The head of a tune defines, at a minimum, a chord sequence, a basic melodic idea, and usually an approximate tempo … Improvisation centres around the head, which is usually played through 'straight' (without much improvisational embellishment) at the beginning of the tune, then improvised upon, and finally returned to and played again as the ending. The head gets a tune started by suggesting a particular rhythm, harmony and melody. The tune is then built from this starting point via improvisation within which different interpretations of the initial idea are offered and new ideas and further interpretations can be explored.

We believe that there is much of value to be learned from working creatively as a teacher who improvises within a rule-bound framework. To say that teaching involves improvised performances is to suggest that it involves skills such as flexibility, intuition, spontaneity and creativity (Miner et al., 1996; Weick, 1998). Just as improvisation in jazz requires a familiarity with certain social norms and musical customs (Berliner, 1994), effective teaching needs the prior absorption of considerable knowledge, skills and conventions. As Crossan and Sorrenti (1997: 165) make clear, 'good improvisation relies on the traditional technical skills gained through practice'. The point here is that teachers, like jazz musicians, will react to circumstances on the spur of the moment: 'When I start off, I don't know what the punch line is going to be' (Buster Williams, cited in Berliner, 1994: 218).

In other words, we argue that good teachers must be willing, creatively and imaginatively, to improvise – not only as regards subject matter but also in the face of unexpected events: late students, awkward questions, strange answers and different levels of understanding within one session. Such effective improvisation is crucially dependent, therefore, on intuition; a quality that has been defined as 'an unconscious process based on distilled experience' (Crossan and Sorrenti, 1997: 57), or an 'analysis frozen into habit and into the capacity for rapid response through recognition' (Simon, 1989; see also Agor, 1986; Atkinson and Claxton, 2000).

The development of intuitive improvisational skills may be a gradual one, arising from the

> experiences of the teacher. Effective teaching, just like a successful jazz session, arises from an intuitive, improvisational, dynamic performance within a planned and mutually understood framework. We think that the best teachers are not only well prepared but also practised and skilful improvisers. The art of teaching, just like the art of jazz, is revealed only in 'live' performance and involves the creativity of spontaneous, intuitive improvisation in the lecture theatre. Thus, our depiction of the teacher as an improvisational performer is an attempt to grasp some of the subtleties and complexities in our working lives as academics. Teachers, just like creative artists, should seek to create 'a richness, immediacy and a graphic quality which engages the mind and imagination'. (Hartley, 1994: 210)

Thus, there is an intangible quality to good teaching. This quality arises from the synergistic combination of planning and improvisational performance involving subject matter, student–teacher dialogue, practical work and demonstration. In Berliner's (1994: 243–244) account of the learning processes of jazz musicians, he notes that:

> By observing critical discussions and participating in them, learners become sensitive to wide-ranging criteria appropriate for the evaluation ... and they gain a deep respect for the refined listening abilities that attune seasoned artists to every nuance and detail of improvised performance.

In our teaching of qualitative research, we attempt to create such a critical dialogue between lecturers and students in an environment that includes ideas such as demonstration, rehearsal and practice. In other words, we are arguing for teaching research methods via the performance and improvisatory aspects of the art of teaching.

All the above points are particularly pertinent for us – in a sense our teaching double-act is like being in a small jazz band – we have to react and respond to the other's improvisations in real time. This is not something one can rehearse,[2] though we do feel we have improved over the last six years of teaching together. We can prepare, to a certain extent, by planning the framework and broad activities ('the head' in jazz terms); but we also need to be able to 'jam' (i.e. respond to each other's improvisations on the theme). Good improvisation, after all, involves trying hard not to try too hard – which is to say that it calls for us to be both active and passive. Preparedness is absolutely necessary, yet it is also the case that, for it to be successful, improvisation is a collective activity which requires that the performers are (at least sometimes) surprised by what emerges. Good improvisation has two paradoxically necessary conditions – it can occur only if we have prepared for it and yet it will work only if the event of the improvisation exceeds our preparations and takes us unawares. As the jazz musician Ornette Coleman told Jacques Derrida:

> What's really shocking in improvised music is that despite its name, most musicians use a 'framework' … as a basis for improvising. I've just recorded a CD with a European musician, Joachim Kühn, and the music I wrote to play with him, that we recorded in August 1996, has two characteristics: it's totally improvised, but at the same time it follows the laws and rules of European structure. And yet, when you hear it, it has a completely improvised feel. (Coleman and Derrida, 2004: 321)

This means, of course that there is always a risk of failure – what Hatch (1999: 83) calls a 'trainwreck': 'where the musicians so interfere with one another that they cannot go on playing the tune'. Furthermore, it is not just the performers who are important to whether an improvisation works – the 'audience' are also crucial. Indeed, in our teaching experience, there have been times when things that worked one year fall flat the next. But we think it is these kinds of risks that give an exciting edge to both jazz and this kind of teaching. The risks of improvisation and collaboration are vividly evoked by Misha Mengelberg:

---

[2]Miles Davis, the jazz trumpeter and band leader, was notorious for telling his musicians not to practise and not to rehearse, but to save all their ideas for live performance in his band.

> Part of improvisation, of the act of improvising, playing with other people, has very much to do with survival strategy. You have, of course, all your expectations and plans destroyed the moment you play with other people. They all have their own ideas of how the musical world at that moment should be. So there are two, three, five, six composers there at the same time destroying each other's ideas, pieces. (in Corbett, 1995: 236)

Having extolled the value of improvisation in teaching, we should acknowledge that it is a scary thing to do – it is after all inherently risky. So, to return to a musical analogy, musical beginners will usually need to bring along a score and only play the written notes. However, as confidence and experience increases, improvisation is something that starts to become possible – you can move away from the written notes – at least from time to time. We certainly did not try to improvise during our first lectures in 2004, but it was an ideal we aimed for. Even today, we still use a written 'score' i.e. a teaching plan and a set of notes that we regularly refer to. So, if you're new to teaching qualitative research, we'd suggest that you start with a solid teaching plan and slowly introduce elements of improvisation in response to students' questions and your own interests. After all, as we emphasised above, it is only possible to improvise when you are thoroughly prepared.

So, now we turn to what these sorts of ideas can mean in practice for us.

A Musical Brief Encounter with Qualitative Research Methods

Our aim as a teaching duo is to generate and nurture an enthusiasm among our students for qualitative research methods. Ours is a module that many Master's students in business think will probably be uninteresting and irrelevant to their future managerial practice – though it is compulsory. Our overall approach, therefore, is one founded upon interaction, participation and improvisation. In the end, we are trying to get students involved with research at a deeper level than that which is required merely to pass the module. Although we aim to help all students, in particular with their dissertation, we hope that some, at least, will be inspired to move on to further study, and as we also teach qualitative research on the PhD programme, we know that this can happen.

We typically have three separate weekly two-hour classes of Master's students in groups of up to 300. Many have not studied in the UK before (they come from almost 50 different countries); they're usually unfamiliar with qualitative research and often arrive sceptical of its value to their future careers in corporate and financial management. These are not easy groups to teach, particularly in formal lecture theatres. But we have worked together since 2004/2005 and have continuously reflected on what has worked well and less well (indeed, some of these specific experiences and ideas have been pub- lished, e.g. Humphreys, 2006). So the teaching approach set out below has evolved – an approach that has also been enriched by developing a mutual trust that enables us to take risks and experiment with different content and styles of delivery. And although we have the option of sharing out the load between us and halving our student contact time, we have chosen to teach all these sessions as a team because of the synergy we get from working together.

A typical session

Mini-lecture

Before the module starts, every student receives a pack containing the module outline and copies of a research paper for each session (which we ask them to read prior to the class), along with three questions linked to the academic paper, for discussion in groups. We start each session with a 30-minute lecture on a foundational aspect of qualitative methods that is closely related to the pre- reading (for example, research interviews, ethnographic approaches, participant observation, grounded theory, coding and other methods of data collection or analysis). Although we take it in turns to deliver the lectures, we also interject or interrupt one another, improvising to present alternative views, clarify argu- ments, emphasise particularly important points, and so on. In other words, we operate self-consciously as a double-act – students have likened us to figures such as Laurel and Hardy, good cop/bad cop, and even Jekyll and Hyde. This way, students are exposed to our different personalities, experiences and styles of research practice. We also seek deliberately to reflect something of the nature of academic debate (at conferences and seminars) and we encourage student participation throughout the session. In other words, we try to communicate our own enthusiasm for, and enjoyment of, our work as academics. The aim is to inspire students to think creatively about research, and to demonstrate what it can do for their current studies and future working lives.

Group discussions

The next phase is a 30-minute group discussion, which focuses on the three set questions about the pre-reading. In this part of the session we start by giving supplementary guidance about the kind of issues the students could consider in their groups. (The groups, made up of around eight students in each, are pre-arranged to be representative of different nationalities and main degree subject.) During the group work, we circulate and join in with the students' debates to give them guidance, stimulate ideas and challenge them to think through issues in greater depth. In this way, we get the chance to learn at least some of the students' names and they can also get to know us on a less intimidating level. Towards the end of this part of the session, we tell three groups that they need to prepare a short presentation on one of the questions in plenary, in order to initiate a whole-class discussion. Although in the early weeks we can find that some students have not read the set article, the group work and the possibility of having to present seem to exert enough peer pressure to encourage the majority to get into the habit of doing the necessary reading. Indeed, one of our aims is to push students into reading scholarly articles that they might find challenging – and to see such reading as an integral part of their whole degree.

Plenary

We then convene 30 minutes of plenary discussion in which we encourage as many students as possible to make a contribution to answering the set questions and to raising wider issues about research processes. The aim is to encourage interactions between student/student and student/lecturers, creating an atmosphere of constructive, critical debate about scholarly endeavour. This is hard work, especially at the beginning of the module, but we find that having two lecturers running and taking part in the debate makes it easier to stimulate student participation. In the inevitable silences, our team approach to teaching allows us to continue the debate and try to rouse students with self-consciously provocative and controversial statements. Over the weeks, many students become comfortable with this way of working and therefore are also more willing to contribute. In addition we try very hard to use as many of their names as possible when inviting particular students to respond to specific questions so that they feel their contribution is being noticed and valued.

Summary phase

Finally, there is 20 minutes of summary and suggestions about how *we* might have answered the questions. This is a semi-formal lecture, but again, we improvise in our presentation, incorporating the themes and ideas that the students have brought to the discussions. Often, we genuinely learn from students' comments in the plenary, and so this part of the session ends up as a three-way conversation – between us as the two lecturers and many of the students.

Overall, then, working together as a team in running a session in this way, especially given the large numbers, means that interaction and group learning are much more achievable. Not only that, it's more fun for the students (and for us) and makes the challenging content more accessible.

The First and Last Sessions

To illustrate what happens in class more specifically, we now describe the approaches we take in the first and last sessions of the module.

In the first session we aim to introduce our subject in ways that will grab students' attention and make them think that there might be some value in attending further lectures (remember, many students turn up thinking it's going to be dull and irrelevant). A particular problem here is that some will not have read any of the module materials (though they would have been asked to do so) and still will be in the throes of culture shock, arriving at a new university (not to mention a new country). And, by an accident of timetabling, ours is usually the first lecture that students will attend.

However, we don't want to dumb-down the contents to give the impression that qualitative research is a soft option simply to make it more palatable. So, after necessary preliminaries about the structure and content of the module, followed by an introductory lecture on the nature of qualitative research in organizations, we show a short clip from the 1946 British film *Brief Encounter*. In introducing the clip we suggest that watching it represents an opportunity to do a simplified version of cultural anthropology i.e. observing a strange culture that no one in the lecture theatre has been part of. A key point during our introductory lecture is the importance of *inference* in the practice of qualitative research. In order to guide their 'observations' as they watch the clip, therefore, we suggest some sociological issues that might be inferred from it – such as the nature of the British class system, gender roles and British attitudes to other nations at that time.

The rest of the session is a plenary discussion in which we encourage students to share their views and ideas about the clip. The intent here is to give them an accessible way to see that qualitative research can be complex, nuanced and interesting – and thus, worthy of further study. Not only do the students seem to enjoy the film clip (they laugh at the jokes and some of them tell us that they subsequently buy the DVD), many are also able to provide interesting and perceptive responses to our questions. If the interactions in this first session go well (and they always have so far) this encourages both us and the students to look forward to subsequent classes.

In the module's final session, most students are, by now, accustomed to our participative and interactive ways of working so we feel able to use potentially riskier approaches. This last session needs to bring together themes from previous classes concerned with analysing and interpreting qualitative material. Earlier, we dealt with some of the more routine aspects of analysis, so the final session emphasises the creative and imaginative approaches to interpretation.

One of us has helped to write a paper called 'Is ethnography jazz?' (Humphreys et al., 2003), which is also the set paper for the session, and the opening 30-minute lecture is about how an analogy with jazz can help us make sense of qualitative material. In order to give these ideas more impact, before the group discussion we illustrate our point through some actual jazz. Each student is supplied with a single sheet of music ('Cantaloupe Island' by Herbie Hancock) and we tell them that this music could be thought of as similar to some qualitative material needing interpretation. We are both amateur musicians (Mike, saxophone, Mark, flute) and, together with student-musician volunteers, we play the basic melody, each improvising on the theme in a rudimentary manner.

We then contrast *our* novice attempts to play jazz with a film clip of Herbie Hancock's quintet playing the same tune, but with (let us say) rather more sophistication and complexity in their improvised interpretation. The aim here is to illustrate the creativity demanded by good qualitative research. The approach also functions to reassure students that, as novice researchers, they should not expect to be able to do sophisticated analysis from Day One, but that with practice and application they can improve, produce work good enough for a dissertation and, should they wish to do so, progress further still. The group and plenary discussions are enhanced by both the fun of our faltering attempts and the contrast with impressive jazz musicianship. We understand that many students find this session particularly memorable and we hope that this helps to fix the whole module in their minds. As one student put it in feedback on the module: 'the jazz concert in the last lecture was brilliant and helpful to approach the subject in a different way'.

Coda

We acknowledge that our approach doesn't work for everyone – some students would clearly prefer merely to be given 'the answers'. Our view is that to accede to such demands would contradict the ethos of qualitative research, as we can hardly claim that our subject is complex and nuanced, and then provide ostensibly simple recipes and prescriptions. We agree with Rebecca Attwood (2009: 35) who recently commented that some 'students who just want to be told what they need to know to pass exams give good teachers low ratings … but other students love it because their other classes aren't challenging enough'. We work on the premise that Master's students should welcome a challenge and reactions from students suggest that many do indeed 'love it'. In summary then we are 'not recommending that all teachers take up the saxophone' (Humphreys, 2006: 184), but we are commending the ideas surrounding improvisation as an approach to teaching. After all, in the immortal words of Duke Ellington:

It don't mean a thing (if it ain't got that swing)!

Further Reading

More detail regarding improvisation can be found in Nachmanovitch (1990). See also, 'Cantaloupe Island' – (Hubbard, Henderson, Hancock, Carter, Williams) – NYC 1985: www.youtube.com/watch?v=J5GEZD4GMOs.

References

Agor, W. (1986) 'The logic of intuition: how top executives make important decisions', *Organizational Dynamics*, Winter: 5–18.

Atkinson, T. and Claxton, G. (eds) (2000) *The Intuitive Practitioner*. Buckingham: Open University Press.

Attwood, R. (2009) 'No apples for teachers', *Times Higher Education Supplement*, 19–25 February, pp. 30–35.

Banner J.M and Cannon, H.C. (1997) *The Elements of Teaching*. Newhaven, CT: Yale University Press.

Berliner, P.F. (1994) *Thinking in Jazz: The Infinite Art of Improvisation*. Chicago: University of Chicago Press.

Bryman, A. and Bell, E. (2007) *Business Research Methods* (2nd edn). Oxford: Oxford University Press.

Coleman, O. and Derrida, J. (2004) 'The other's language: Jacques Derrida interviews Ornette Coleman, 23 June 1997', *Genre*, 36 (2): 319–328.

Corbett, J. (1995) 'Ephemera underscored: writing around free improvization', in K. Gabbard (ed.), *Jazz Among the Discourses*. Durham, NC: Duke University Press, pp. 217–224.

Crossan, M. and Sorrenti, M. (1997) 'Making sense of improvisation', *Advances in Strategic Management*, 14: 155–180.

Delamont, S. (1995) 'Teachers as artists', in L.W. Anderson (ed.), *International Encyclopaedia of Teaching and Teacher Education*. London: Pergamon Press.

Gage, N.L. (1978) *The Scientific Basis of the Art of Teaching*. New York: Teachers College Press.

Hammersley, M. (2008) *Questioning Qualitative Inquiry: Critical Essays*. London: Sage.

Hartley, J.F. (1994) 'Case studies in organizational research', in C. Cassell and G. Symon (eds), *Qualitative Methods in Organizational Research: A Practical Guide*. London: Sage.

Hatch, M.J. (1999) 'Exploring the empty spaces of organizing: how improvisational jazz helps redescribe organizational structure', *Organization Studies*, 20 (1): 75–100.

Humphreys, M. (2006) 'Teaching qualitative research methods: I'm beginning to see the light', *Qualitative Research in Organization and Management*, 1: 173–188.

Humphreys, M., Brown, A.D. and Hatch, M.J. (2003) 'Is ethnography jazz?', *Organization*, 10 (1): 5–31.

Jamous, H. and Peloille, B. (1970) 'Professions or self-perpetuating system: changes in the French University-Hospital system. In J. Jackson (ed.), *Professions and Professionalisation*. Cambridge: Cambridge University Press, p. 109–152.

Miner, A.J., Moorman, C. and Bassoff, C. (1996) 'Organizational improvisation in new product development'. Unpublished manuscript: University of Wisconsin.

Nachmanovitch, S. (1990) *Free Play: Improvisation in Life and Art*. New York: Penguin Putnam.

Saunders, M., Lewis, P. and Thornhill, A. (2009) *Research Methods for Business Students*, (5th edn). Edinburgh: Pearson Education.

Seale, C., Gobo, G., Gubrium, J.F. and Silverman, D. (2007) *Qualitative Research Practice*. London: Sage.

Silverman, D. (2010) *Doing Qualitative Research: A Practical Handbook* (3rd edn). London: Sage.

Simon, H.A. (1989) 'Making management decisions: the role of intuition and emotion', in W.H. Agor (ed.), *Intuition in Organizations*. Newbury Park: Sage.

Weick, K.E (1998) 'Improvisation as a mind set for organizational analysis', *Organization Science*, 9 (5): 543–555.

PART II

CORE METHODS OF QUALITATIVE INQUIRY IN ORGANIZATIONAL RESEARCH

14 Interviews

Mats Alvesson and Karen Lee Ashcraft

Introduction

In contemporary Western society, interviews are routinely done as a way of seeking knowledge about all kinds of phenomena. This society can with some justice be referred to as an interview society. Across a wide array of cultural arenas, interviews have become a primary way of gathering information and getting to know people. Common interview subjects include far more than public figures, organizational spokespersons, celebrities, experts or job candidates. These days, even the most intimate of relationships can enlist the interview genre, as in the case of commodified exchanges such as 'speed dating' as well as many online social networks. In this sense, interviews can be said to have assumed an economy and politics of their own, complete with various constituencies competing for the 'exclusive interview' that promises to reveal the 'inside scoop straight from the source', and with various subjects strategizing how to spin favourable identities towards a competitive advantage.

In the social sciences, interviews have long been a central technique of knowing, and organization studies is no exception. It is typically said that 'scientific' interviews are a mode apart and that they yield higher quality knowledge – systematic rather than haphazard, more objective than partial, comprehensive instead of selective, standardized and methodical as opposed to journalistic and sensational, and so the list of contrasts goes on. Among most organization scholars, research interviews are deemed reliable gateways into what goes on in organizations: how leadership is conducted, what values and beliefs people hold, how decisions are made, or the story behind a successful innovation or change effort. In an ideal world, 'good' researchers plan and conduct interview sessions such that 'good' interviewees feel compelled to share openly their considerable knowledge.

It is a tempting portrait, to be sure, that demarcates and idealizes the research interview as a principal way to know organizational life. After all, interviewing tends to be more convenient, accessible and economical than other qualitative methods, such as participant observation. But there is also much cause to challenge this easy portrait – to reflect on the fuzzy boundaries and muted politics that often characterize research interviewing, to question common reliance on interviews as transparent windows into the truths of organizational life.

In this chapter, we focus on interviewing in the context of qualitative organizational research, acknowledging that quantitative scholarship can also utilize interviews and that much interview-based research reflects quantitative logics and leanings. We aim to interrogate common assumptions about qualitative interviewing while simultaneously offering useful guidance for those undertaking the method. In this sense, we advocate what might be called a 'reflexive pragmatics' of interviewing, at once concerned with cultivating a conscious reflection on deeper epistemological, political and technical problems as well as expanding the repertoire through which these problems can be managed in practice.

Stepping back a level of abstraction from most accounts of interview 'types', we begin by identifying four of the most prevalent orientations to interviewing in organization studies. We then utilize these orientations to frame and organize our discussion of technique, which (re)considers the most commonly referenced 'stages' of interviewing: selecting participants, constructing an interview guide, negotiating the session and analysing the conversation. We conclude by identifying the key challenges encountered in contemporary interviewing and we propose some possibilities for addressing these.

Positions on Interview Research

There are many ways of structuring available approaches to interviewing. Lindlof and Taylor (2002), for example, distinguish among a) ethnographic (i.e. informal and impromptu questions posed in the field), b) informant (i.e. repeated conversations with an expert whose particular knowledge helps the researcher make sense of what is happening in the field), c) respondent (i.e. the most common, wherein participants are asked to share their own perspectives and experiences), d) narrative (i.e. oriented towards storytelling or plot lines) and e) focus group (i.e. questions designed to provoke interactive answers, even debate, among multiple participants) interviews. Their list highlights several axes along which interviews may differ, such as location, degree of formal structure, kind of participant and conversation purpose. Similarly, other lists imply continua through which interviews can be characterized – for example, structured to unstructured, dyad to group, and so forth (Fontana and Frey, 1994). Although such typologies (see also Cassell, 2008) are helpful in illuminating the complex range of practical choices that researchers make in the interviewing process, they say less about the epistemological and ontological premises researchers bring to the table – consciously or unconsciously – as they go about making those decisions. We thus zoom the lens outwards in order to identify four radically different orientations to the question: what is an interview, and what kinds of knowledge claims does it enable (Alvesson, 2011)?

Neo-positivism: the interview as a modified oral survey instrument through which 'softer' forms of objective and generalizable knowledge can be discovered

A traditionally dominant stance is that of *neo-positivism*. If published research is any indicator, it remains common for researchers to report interview statements as evidence, where the value is guaranteed or at least supported by standardized means, such as interview schedules, data processing procedures and codifications of data. Practitioners of this approach typically claim to capture what is really 'out there' by following a research protocol and gathering relevant responses, while minimizing researcher influence and other sources of 'bias'. The interest is in 'facts' about behaviour, practice, attitude, value and so on; and it is deemed crucial to compile 'undistorted' data that can be aggregated and compared. Hence, interviews in this vein tend to be carefully planned and tightly structured, with minimal explanation of the study to participants and little variation or deviation from protocol. The ideal is a fully transparent research process, marked by 'objectivity' and 'neutrality' and rendered accessible to reader assessment.

Scholars increasingly recognize, however, that respondents may produce only superficial and cautious responses under such circumstances. Deeper understandings that stem from the richness of context are hardly possible. Because meaning and sensemaking are complex, follow-up questions become crucial to understanding; yet these incur deviations from protocol and often spark additional ambiguity, as talk is often incoherent (Potter and Wetherell, 1987). Data thus become too thin and their interpretation uncertain.

Romanticism: the interview as an authentic dialogue that can draw out (inter)subjective knowledge through attempting a relationship

A second position on interviews can be called *romanticism*. By this, Dingwall (1997) means that the nearer we come to the respondent, the closer we are to apprehending the real self. Through closeness and depth, we can find the authentic and true expressed in talk. The romantic interviewer, advocating a more 'genuine' human interaction, seeks to cultivate interpersonal relations founded on a rapport, trust, commitment and 'warmth' between researcher and interviewee, such that the latter feels free to express the self openly. The typical ambition of such interviews is to accomplish 'deeper, fuller conceptualisations of those aspects of our subjects' lives we are most interested in understanding' (Miller and Glassner, 1997: 103). Researchers rely on interviewees' narrations about their lives as a way to understand them, since 'story-telling stays closer to actual life-events than methods that elicit explanations' (Hollway and Jefferson, 2000: 32).

Romantics take seriously the risk that interviewees may be guided by social desirability, anticipating what the interviewer wants to hear or the cultural norms for preferred expressions. They also believe, however, that establishing close relations with respondents – who become 'participants' rather than ' subjects' – can minimize this problem. Some identify 'active interviewing' as an ideal form (Ellis et al., 1997; Holstein and Gubrium, 1997; Holstein and Gubrium, 2003), in which the researcher transforms the participant 'from a repository of opinions and reasons or a wellspring of emotions into a productive source of knowledge' (Holstein and Gubrium, 1997: 121) by acting on an awareness that 'the subject's interpretative capabilities must be activated, stimulated and cultivated' (1997: 122). The interviewer and the interviewee collaborate in the 'co-construction of knowledge' and the enterprise 'works against asymmetry, emphasizing a more fundamental sense of the shared task at hand, which now becomes a form of "collaboration" in the production of meaning' (Holstein and Gubrium, 2003: 19).

In contrast to neo-positivist interviews, romantic interviews can be difficult to assess precisely because they are so context-bound and, specifically, dependent on the dynamics of a particular research relationship and interaction. Establishing the 'right' relational conditions can be time-consuming, while comparing and structuring the resulting material can be difficult. Moreover, the researcher may erroneously presume an 'authentic' exchange and lose the counterbalance of analytic distance in the process.

Localism: the interview as a situated social accomplishment that deserves study in its own right, not for what it says about social life elsewhere

A comparatively small but growing branch of interviewing breaks with the assumptions and goals of the first two orientations. We refer to this third position as *localism*. Whereas both neo-positivists and romantics treat interviews as a natural way to access organizational realities beyond the interview, localists emphasize that interview statements must be understood in context, specific to the situation in which they are produced (Silverman, 2006). An interview is a genre of conversation that should be studied as such, not treated as a tool for data collection on something outside of itself. In other words, localists do not assign interviews an ontological status that is distinct from other social situations. People talk with their friends and neighbours, serve customers at work, go to the gym and rear children. Likewise, they participate in interviews. Interview talk is akin to these other phenomena – a social encounter rather than some sort of meta-encounter that illuminates 'regular' social encounters. Interviewees are therefore not reporting external events but producing situated accounts, drawing on cultural resources to yield morally adequate justifications. As expressed by Potter (1997: 147), 'social structure becomes part of interaction as it is worked up, invoked and reworked'. Sources of inspiration for localism include ethnomethodology, conversation analysis and certain forms of discourse analysis (Silverman, 2006).

Localism can be said to entail a relatively narrow research agenda that tends to trade relevance to organizational life for intense rigour. More extreme versions encourage a myopic focus on the interview situation such that any contextual information 'external' to the immediate interaction cannot be legitimately considered. Hence, inferring claims that yield knowledge about broader phenomena becomes difficult.

Reflexivism: the interview process and not merely the content, as a vital form of evidence

A fourth approach grants the localist claim that interviews are a social practice unto themselves, but researchers in this newer and growing vein – which we call *reflexivism* (recognizing that there are other uses of this term; Alvesson and Sköldberg, 2009) – do not maintain that anything beyond the interview situation is irrelevant. Instead, reflexivists comb the process and not merely the content of interviews precisely for how that process informs the phenomena under investigation. In this way, reflexivism shares with the first two orientations the premise that interviews are a way to generate knowledge about the organizational world. Yet it rejects the neo-positivist notion that interviewing is a scientific practice hovering above and beyond culture, and it replaces the romantic quest for authenticity with an interest in the tactics both parties employ to navigate the interview. Reflexivism therefore challenges the humanist underpinnings of romanticism in favour of interrogating the politics of interviewing.

Interviewers in this emerging tradition take seriously their own status as situated cultural subjects who are negotiating with other cultural subjects (i.e. participants). Instead of attempting to eliminate bias (like neo-positivists) or distance (like romantics), or surrendering altogether the capacity of interviews to inform other social phenomena (like localists), they glean insights from admitting and then probing the inevitable partiality that is always part of research relations. In other words, rather than try to find an 'appropriate' place to stand, they try to grapple with the fact that knowledge is invariably produced from where they *already* stand. Reflexivists thus reclaim scholarly interviewing as a meta-practice by simultaneously treating it as a relational, cultural and political practice – or as Kauffman (1992: 187) summarizes, 'The researcher-researched relationship, as it develops and is expressed in negotiations over the research process, is a map *for* the analysis more than a qualifier of it'.

Potential problems with this version of reflexivism include a tendency to engage in confessional analysis that leans towards self-absorption, where researchers dissect their own positionality and performance in ways that obscure rather than inform the broader phenomena at hand. It remains difficult to establish clear connections between the politics of interviews and organization theory (for a successful example, however, see Kondo, 1990).

Interviewing – More Than a Technical Issue

Three of the four positions (localism being somewhat of an exception) share a sense that research interviews can be carried out in better and worse ways (i.e. evaluations of technical quality are possible and useful), though their prescriptions for good interviewing vary. Indeed, most authors on interviews are occupied with such technical matters as study design, participant selection and access, the conduct of the conversation, the use of technology, modes of transcription and the management and analysis of copious amounts of text. There is a broadly shared concern for good practice in the service of knowledge generation, though – as shown above – the four approaches reflect divergent views of scientific practice, how one does it well and what kinds of knowledge claims it enables.

Interview practice has, to some extent, developed from neo-positivist advice to an increased awareness of the complexity of the interview situation. Still, the literature on interviewing overwhelmingly stresses tool and technique and, specifically, how to elicit the most productive talk from participants. Although they often signal an awareness of complications, most writers seem to assume that interviewing skills can be developed to manage problems and minimize errors on the road to quality empirical material (see, for example, Fontana and Frey, 1994; Charmaz, 2003; Fontana and Frey, 2005). In this sense, the neo-positivist 'pipeline' or romanticist 'dialogue' metaphor of interviewing – in which interviewing is a portal or gateway to organizational life – continues to dominate.

Yet this persistent view of interviews as transparent windows through which to observe organizational behaviour – and the attendant concern for a 'right' technique – minimizes precisely what the localists and reflexivists are at pains to show: that the interview situation is a socially and linguistically complicated situation. Interview accounts may just as well be seen, for example, as political representations of the favourable 'truth' one wants to communicate (i.e. impression management) (Alvesson, 2011). Even as such considerations typify organizational life, most research reports continue to assume that they are somehow absent or minimized in the interview situation, particularly if the researcher is adept. Our point is that it is vital not to oversimplify and idealize the interview situation – to avoid assuming that interviewees are primarily competent and moral truth tellers who will act in the service of science, serving up data that will reveal their 'interiors' or the realities of their social institutions. Following the insights of localists and reflexivists, it is equally important not to dismiss the social and linguistic complexities of interviews as sources of bias.

We argue that the interview, as a complex social and cultural event, calls for a theoretical understanding, or rather a reflexive approach in which a set of various theoretical viewpoints can be considered and, when there are reasons for doing so, applied (Alvesson and Sköldberg, 2009). Without a theoretical understanding supporting critical judgement, any use of interview material risks naivety and leaves interpretations poorly grounded. Simply put, technique is important but cannot stand alone; discussions of good practice are best framed in terms of the deeper epistemological orientations at hand. Hence, we advocate approaching interview practice in a more reflective way than is often suggested. Rather than prioritizing technique or offering 'best practice' recipes that sever technique from epistemology, we suggest that interviewers conceive of good technique within the larger philosophical position that guides their research.

Kvale (1996) proposes the metaphor of craft as a way to move talk of technique away from the customary 'tips and recipes' model. For Kvale, the craftsmanship metaphor offers a path beyond the dualism of all-method (i.e. scientific rigour is achieved by following a set of prescribed rules and techniques) *vs* no-method (i.e. once interviews are deconstructed as complex social practices, all efforts at scientific rigour become pointless). 'Craft' helps us leave the criteriology of the former without surrendering to the relativism of the latter. It does so, first, by casting the researcher as capable of developing increasingly sophisticated knowledge, skills and tools (of a practical *and* epistemological nature) – capable, in other words, of transitioning from novice to expert through apprenticeship. Equally important, however, 'craft' reminds us that such knowledge, skills and tools (i.e. technical and theoretical proficiency) never guarantee good practice or desirable products. Quality, in our view, is an important consideration, cultivated yet not guaranteed by the development of one's interview craft, which invariably requires a situational adaptation as well as accountability for emergent problems and choices.

Who to ask: participant selection

A common practical question is who should be interviewed. While the answer may appear to be obvious based on the research purpose (e.g. studying accountants found guilty of fraud), in most cases, it will be far from self-evident. When selecting participants and deciding on how to utilize their accounts, two guiding principles can assist with this. The first is *representativeness* in a loose sense. It is generally deemed important to have some breadth and variation among interviewees such that they allow coverage of the social category one seeks to explore. That said, what *sort* of representation and to what extent this matters will likely depend on one's epistemological orientation and specific research purpose. A second principle entails aiming for *quality* in the interview responses. What quality means, exactly, will also vary by research orientation and goal. One who sees interviewees as 'informants', for example, might pay considerable attention to participants who will render rich (e.g. intricate, perceptive, insightful) accounts. Less anxious about reducing bias through comprehensive representation, this researcher would be eager to use the resources (e.g. intellectual, verbal, emotional, moral) of qualified people with the 'right' experiences and an ability and willingness to communicate these. Sometimes key informants will emerge and the researcher will cultivate close relations with these participants, more in line with romanticist leanings. They may be targeted for repeat interviews, for advice on who to interview, for help in getting additional background material and for analytical support (e.g. understanding the cultural context).

Well-selected interviewees can be quite helpful, but sometimes researchers will become inclined to rely heavily on those to whom they have ready access or who are similar to themselves in terms of values and other identity features. Worse yet, researchers may be tempted to overemphasize, or represent as 'universal', the voices of those with whom they share a common prejudice. To these habits, the scepticism of the localists and the process scrutiny of the reflexivists can provide an essential counter. Also, in recognition of these temptations, it can be a wise general rule to balance the principles of representativeness and quality, seeking both a breadth of representation and participants with much to offer in depth.

What to ask: interview guide

As hinted earlier, interview conversations can range from the highly structured, complete with detailed interview guides (so-called speaking questionnaires), to the loosely or even un- structured. Here again, one's epistemological position (see Duberley, Johnson and Cassell, in this volume) and the specific research purpose will be the decisive factors. Neo-positivism typically involves a high degree of structure, while romanticism favours openness and relational flow over rigidity. Localists and reflexivists are less concerned about best degrees of structure, though they are (differently) interested in the significance of the structures adopted and the variations that emerge in response.

An intensified structure tends to amplify the probability that interviewees will respond to parameters set by the researcher rather than pursuing themes they regard as interesting or important (thereby minimizing richness and novelty); but it also facilitates an easier sorting, comparison and analysis of the material. Low degrees of structure can facilitate encounters with surprise, with new perspectives and questions, as interviewees become free enough to develop tangents of interest. The risk, of course, is that interviewees may move in directions that will be of little or peripheral relevance to the research; and wide variations among accounts can make it especially difficult to sort, compare and analyse material. Given the publication conventions regarding methods sections, large variations in the interview protocol may also be difficult to explain and justify. Semi- or loosely structured qualitative research often relies on a good deal of intuition and hermeneutic readings, which cannot easily be translated into traditional procedural language. As noted earlier, extreme romanticist studies may suffer the most in these respects.

It is also possible to combine different design elements, employing varied degrees of structure in a single project. One option is to start with a set of open-ended interviews in order to refine the focus and conduct of the study. After an exploratory phase, the researcher might then produce a more specific set of questions. A reverse logic could also work, beginning with standardized questions to get an overall 'lay of the land' and, later, selecting some themes for a fuller exploration in more open, in-depth interviews. While these conversations would be guided by a clear theme, within that limited focus, they could proceed quite freely. Specific to case studies, interviewers may wish to vary considerably the questions asked in order to access different dimensions of the case. Such a tactic can elicit different viewpoints and deeper insights, especially when incorporated as part of a 'detective' orientation, where the researcher follows new 'leads' and tests her or his evolving understanding of the context.

How to ask, as well as listen and tell: interview practice

In highly structured neo-positivist interviews, the idea is that the carefully formulated interview guide performs most of the work, reducing the interviewer's burden in the actual interview. As with questionnaire studies, then, the bulk of the conceptualizing work must be done before the 'data collection' begins. In

romanticist and reflexivist interviewing, much of the 'heavy lifting' of interviewing is focused on the actual interaction. For romantics, this entails savvied
on-the-spot interpretations about the feelings and expectations of interviewees
and judgements about what to do next: how are the trust and rapport evolving?
How are participants reading and responding to questions? Do they appear to
be sharing the 'authentic' inside story? Are their responses sufficiently clear and
should unanticipated themes be pursued? For reflexivists, the 'heavy lifting'
takes the form of a dual consciousness about the process and content: monitoring one's own participation as well as how the research relationship is being
negotiated while simultaneously tracking the content of the conversation.
From either orientation, it is misleading to speak of 'data collection', as if interviewing is simply a matter of applying pre-formed questions in order to tap
people for information. It is not surprising, then, that some researchers become
exhausted after even a few hours of loosely structured interviewing.

As with many narratives, interviews can be punctuated into a beginning,
middle and end. Initially, the interviewer tries to 'break the ice' and establish a
collaborative relation or rapport. Romanticist researchers are likely to devote
much energy to this phase, whereas the neo-positivist usually assumes a lesser
burden in this respect. Reflexivists devote attention to if, when, how and why a
rapport is established. For instance, how do the cultural identities of researcher
and researched affect their relationship as well as the kind of knowledge communicated and the manner in which it is shared? For researchers in this vein,
such reflexive tasks will continue throughout the interview, no matter how one
punctuates the time.

Especially for interviewers hailing from the other three perspectives, the
middle section of an interview is typically the longest; and it is also when interviewee responses to interviewer questions are most expected. The latter may
start with a clearly demarcated theme, posing follow-up questions in search of
clarification, increased depth, precision, illustrative examples and/or verifica-
tion/support for (or a contradiction with) the interviewee's initial claims. When
interviewees say relatively little and the interviewer seeks more, a number of
helpful tactics may come into play: the interviewer can simply pause (indicating that further interviewee talk is welcome), ask for more information ('that's
very interesting; can you elaborate a bit more …?'), ask for counter-examples
('is it always like that or are there variations …?'), point out contradictions or
introduce doubts ('help me reconcile that with what you said earlier …' or 'I've
heard other people say the opposite … why do you think they would?').

Towards the conclusion, many interviewers will ask if the interviewees wish to add something else, either to supplement earlier talk or introduce anything that they deem relevant that was not solicited earlier. It sometimes happens that, when the audio- or video-recorder (if used) is switched off, the interviewee begins to speak differently (e.g. less cautiously or performatively). This does not necessarily mean that their talk is more 'real' or honest, and this effect can stem from many other factors as well (e.g. the freedom to introduce any last-minute thoughts they wish; the comfort, relaxation or relief that may come towards the end of a session). Localists and reflexivists, albeit for different reasons, will take a particular interest in tracing variations here. For localists, a key question might be: how is interview talk influenced by and/or acting upon the immediate surrounding (technological) environment (e.g. recorded talk or discourse 'off the record')? For reflexivists, the question shifts toward how does technology (or other objects) play into the relational and cultural politics of the interview and how does it affect the knowledge produced?

Knowing what's been said: analysis

Across the four positions, analysing – or comparing, categorizing, interpreting and creatively deploying – interview material is widely regarded as among the most demanding activities of interview research. Even authors on qualitative method will typically emphasize the systematic and iterative work required to codify interview accounts. The resulting impression is that, through the diligent application of any number of sorting techniques, orderly patterns will 'emerge'. Popular approaches like grounded theory (see Kenealy, in this volume) maintain that such techniques generate results that are more reliable, in that they are rigorously supported by the empirical material (Glaser and Strauss, 1967: Strauss and Corbin, 1994). We are somewhat less optimistic, however, about the capacity of methodical codification to produce the most interesting research results. It is our sense that the usual procedure emphasis fosters faith in interviews as a solid source of knowledge that can be sifted through dependable tools. In this way a careful, critical assessment of the interview material – in all of its messy human variation, contradiction and incoherence – is often minimized. In other words, meticulously following steps can lead to a fixation on or romance with method at the ironic expense of creative and critical thinking (Alvesson and Sköldberg, 2009). For us, then, a sustained reflective pause is as much or more a part of rigour as any formulaic procedure. There are strong reasons to take seriously questions regarding what interview material really means and for what purposes it can be used. For localists who draw strict boundaries around the social practice of research interviews, these may be less pressing matters. But for those who take inter- viewing as any sort of meta-practice that implicates larger social and organi- zational phenomena, such questions – we would argue – should be among the first and most persistent in the analytic process.

Illustrations of Interviews

Examples from our own research interviews can help to illuminate some of the points made above. For instance, one of the authors, Karen (referred to in first person in this section), learned much about the relation between interviewing orientation and technique from the contrast between two projects. The first was a study of a non-profit organization that dealt with domestic violence (e.g. Ashcraft, 2000, 2001, 2006); the second was a study of occupational identity among com- mercial airline pilots (e.g. Ashcraft, 2005, 2007; Ashcraft and Mumby, 2004).

In the first, I sought to the understand the dynamics of participation and power in a self-proclaimed feminist organization, which pursued egalitarian relations amid a conventional bureaucratic form. The guiding research question was how do participants perform equality in the face of hierarchy? The interview compo- nent of the project was designed to balance the extensive participant observation conducted by providing an opportunity for explicit reflection on participant understandings as well as specific observations derived from the field. I devel- oped a standardized interview guide that corresponded with my research inter- ests and observations thus far. Note the neo-positivist stance implied here, where interviewing is another window on organizational reality, a validity check of sorts. That this tacit stance was paired with critical, feminist interests suggests the sort of ironic hybrids that often emerge in actual interview practice.

During initial conversations with the staff, I noticed that members were extremely guarded, particularly when asked about power relations and chal- lenges within the organization. From these early sessions, I gleaned that 'trust through participation' was essential to participants speaking freely in inter- views. Oddly, the members seemed to find my presence as an observer of their practice unproblematic, yet they did not believe it was appropriate to openly discuss internal challenges with an outsider, who might use the information to discredit feminist practice. I thus decided to become a member, establishing trust by completing volunteer training and serving as a regular worker in the shelter and on the crisis hotline. From a neo-positivist stance, this decision might be seen to complicate analytical objectivity (e.g. 'going native'); conversely, it could be interpreted to enhance it by affording access to members' 'true' or 'real' perspectives. From a romanticist stance, the decision can be seen as a crucial gesture of authentic relating – a move that enabled participant sharing by demonstrating the researcher's commitment to genuine understanding through 'walking in their shoes.' Somewhere between these positions is where I stood (albeit semi-consciously) at the time.

I soon discovered, however, that this insider status carried with it certain dilemmas. Interview participants began to presume my alignment with their own views and the simple question 'Why?' became difficult to ask without jeopardizing my status as a competent member and feminist. Here, we can see that interviewee *and* interviewer are engaged in impression management (i.e. 'Are we good feminists?') and invoking ideologically correct scripts in order to perform identity work that manages this pressure. In this sense, the interview serves the political function of enacting and justifying the very phenomenon under investigation: feminist organizing. From a reflexivist stance, these are critical pieces of evidence towards answering the research question. How members (including the interviewer) used the interviews to perform and regulate feminist identity and to assuage political 'hotspots' yields insight into the repertoire of ways by which they experienced and coped with tensions of power and participation. At the time, however, I saw these primarily as technical and relational dilemmas to be managed in the pursuit of insight (i.e. more in line with neo-positivist and romanticist than reflexivist stances).

However, the airline pilot study shifted my understanding. Like the feminist organization study, a standardized interview guide organized the pilot sessions, although interviewees could take these wherever they wished. In contrast to the earlier study, the interview component of this project stood alone, not in support of participant observation, and most participants did not know one another or even work for the same airline. The guiding research question was how do factors such as gender and race play into participant accounts of their work and professional identity? Pilots spoke of their professional lives openly and at great length. In sharp contrast with the challenge of stimulating the domestic violence staff to talk *enough*, every pilot interviewed seemed to find their work lives inherently interesting and worthy of research. Not only that, I was surprised to find myself enacting my own identity as an airline pilot's daughter, not only by mentioning the family's flying credentials, but also by performing as both researcher and complicit, adoring woman who hangs on his every word. Without fail, the interviewees insisted on paying for any food or drink consumed during the session (despite reminders of research funding) and walking me to my car. Several interviewees shed tears during the interview, explaining that it was a relief to share with a sympathetic ear the emotional demands of flying.

At first, as a self-identified feminist, I found these dynamics difficult to manage; each session was a delicate balance of honouring participant perspectives while also holding onto my own (i.e. the research interview as a local accomplishment in its own right). Soon, however, I came to see the link between the interview identity work and the 'dependable, protect-and-provide father' image that was so pivotal to pilots' professional identity. In this sense, the negotiation of the interview relationship *became* the storyline, revealing the precise character of gender relations in the profession, such as the implicit relational contract between professional and client (i.e. trading fatherly protection for romantic adoration). It is in this sense that the reflexivist position can take the interviewer–interview relation as a useful source of information without becoming unduly distracted from the central research question.

Some Further Problems in Interview Research

As should be clear by now, qualitative interview research is hardly easy. In addition to the complexities already considered, we conclude with three further problematics for scholarly interviewing, which stem from our contemporary 'interview society' (mentioned at the outset) and dominant norms for presenting research results in publication (alluded to in the previous discussion – e.g. the about methodology sections).

A call for critical readings: asking why instead of why not?

Most published research reports based on interview data convey a strong faith in interview accounts as a reliable source of evidence, and we suspect that scholarly faith is buttressed by the status of interviews as a pervasive cultural genre. The relation between interview accounts and organizational realities is often largely taken-for-granted, as if the question is 'why would we *not* take what participants say at face value'? We see merit in countering, or at least seriously balancing, this relatively uncritical unidirectional faith. Specifically, we propose a reverse interpretive logic, wherein researchers should present good reasons as to *why* readers should take interview accounts as credible representations of organizational realities (whatever the claim – e.g. objective, subjective or intersubjective) beyond themselves before granting their status as valid evidentiary material. That they appear 'naturally' trustworthy and 'clearly' linked to organizational practice does not mean we need receive them so readily as such.

Exacerbated by the interview society?

Because we live in an 'interview society' in which the interview genre dominates mass media, entertainment and other settings, people are accustomed to its form and practice and to accept its means of gathering and generating knowledge as straightforward and valid (Dingwall, 1997; Silverman, 2006). As noted earlier, however, interview talk may say more about performing and adapting to social, cultural and political norms – including codes about the desirability of appearing 'authentic' – than it says about other social and organizational realities. It is not self-evident that ambitious social scientists can afford to be uncritically confident that they exceed talk show hosts – say, Oprah Winfrey or Dr Phil – in providing the public with 'true' and 'useful' knowledge about social life. Critics increasingly raise concerns about the sloppiness of interview standards as the genre becomes another 'fact of life': 'Interviews are carried out time and again with little hesitation and hardly an afterthought. The individual interview has become a ubiquitous feature of everyday life' (Holstein and Gubrium, 2003: 4). Relatedly, some claim that interviewing is over-utilized in social science research because it affords 'quick and dirty' data, circumventing the more demanding ethnographic work of 'being there' through immersion for an extended period. We have endeavoured here to underscore the point that doing research interviews well does not mean doing them quickly or from a preoccupation with technique. At the very least, doing interviews well entails careful, critical and self-conscious epistemological reflection among researchers, as well as a healthy scepticism among readers and consumers.

Expectation to report interview studies as linear, rational and objective

Academic journal publication conventions have a tendency to domesticate scholarly writing, such that many qualitative authors will learn or experience pressure to contradict their espoused anti-positivist theoretical orientations in their methodological accounts and analytic representations (Briggs, 2003: 500). The standard journal format and perhaps the conditioned reflexes (including impatience?) of readers seem to fuel the residual presence of neo-positivism. In reports of empirical research, readers have come to expect (or have been 'disciplined' to expect) a concise yet precise and convincing methods section. How the researcher produced the empirical material (the so-called data collection) as well as the ensuing analysis of findings (e.g. how and why were excerpts selected and interpreted?) and conclusions (e.g. how and why were larger inferences made?) – such questions are supposed to be answered in a clear and transparent fashion. Because a great deal of qualitative research does not (and should not) proceed in such a neat and clean linear mode, this sort of accounting mandate arguably demands retrospective sensemaking (in this case, a generous term for creative reconstruction, if not fabrication) from many qualitative scholars. Little room – literally and figuratively – is allowed for the kinds of cautions, caveats and considerations advocated here, such as paying attention to epistemological matters like the kinds of truth claims warranted and why, attempts to do justice to the unruly character of talk, or efforts to link the interview process to interpretations of content. In sum, the norms of academic writing and reporting empirical material tend to reinforce an approach to interviews aligned with neo-positivism or perhaps a constrained version of romanticism.

Conclusion

In this chapter, we have offered a brief overview of the interview as a qualitative method for organization researchers. We identified four positions – neo-positivism, romanticism, localism and reflexivism – that represent quite different ideals of what interviews are, the (im)possibilities of their relation to knowledge about other sites and forms of reality, what the relationship between interviewer and interviewee should look like, and what designs and techniques are preferable. Ultimately, we would contend that interviewing is a complex social activity that calls for careful, intensive and sceptical reflection.

We would thus urge a greater emphasis on theoretical considerations, particularly as a way to contextualize and temper the prevailing focus on methodical procedure and faith in personal accounts as a mirror on organizational life.

Further Reading

For a thorough critique of interviews see the following: Alvesson (2011); Fontana and Frey (2005); and Kvale and Brinkman (2009).

References

Alvesson, M. (2011) *Interpreting Interviews*. London: Sage.

Alvesson, M. and Sköldberg, K. (2009) *Reflexive Methodology* (2nd edn). London: Sage.

Ashcraft, K.L. (2000) 'Empowering "professional" relationships: organizational communication meets feminist practice', *Management Communication Quarterly*, 13: 347–392.

Ashcraft, K.L. (2001) 'Organized dissonance: feminist bureaucracy as hybrid organization', *Academy of Management Journal*, 44: 1301–1322.

Ashcraft, K.L. (2005) 'Resistance through consent? Occupational identity, organizational form, and the maintenance of masculinity among commercial airline pilots', *Management Communication Quarterly*, 19: 67–90.

Ashcraft, K.L. (2006) 'Feminist-bureaucratic control and other adversarial allies: how hybrid organization subverts anti-bureaucratic discourse', *Communication Monographs*, 73: 55–86.

Ashcraft, K.L. (2007) 'Appreciating the "work" of discourse: occupational identity and difference as organizing mechanisms in the case of commercial airline pilots', *Discourse & Communication*, 1: 9–36.

Ashcraft, K.L. and Mumby, D.K. (2004) 'Organizing a critical communicology of gender and work', *International Journal for the Sociology of Language*, 166: 19–43.

Briggs, C. (2003) 'Interviewing, power/knowledge and social inequality', in J. Holstein and J. Gubrium (eds), *Inside Interviewing*. Thousand Oaks, CA: Sage.

Cassell, C. (2008) 'Interviews in organizational research', in D. Buchanan and A. Bryman (eds), *The Sage Handbook of Organizational Research Methods*. London: Sage.

Charmaz, K. (2003) 'Qualitative interviewing and grounded theory analysis', in J. Holstein and J. Gubrium (eds), *Inside Interviewing*. Thousand Oaks, CA: Sage.

Dingwall, R. (1997) 'Accounts, interviews and observations', in G. Miller and R. Dingwall (eds), *Context and Method in Qualitative Research*. London: Sage.

Ellis, C., Kiesinger, C. and Tillmann-Healy, L. (1997) 'Interactive interviewing', in R. Hertz (ed.), *Reflexivity and Voice*. Thousand Oaks, CA: Sage.

Fontana, A. and Frey, J. (1994) 'Interviewing: the art of science', in N. Denzin and Y. Lincoln (eds), *Handbook of Qualitative Research*. Thousand Oaks, CA: Sage.

Fontana, A. and Frey, J. (2005) 'The interview: from neutral stance to political involvement', in N. Denzin and Y. Lincoln (eds), *The Sage Handbook of Qualitative Research* (3rd edn). Thousand Oaks, CA: Sage.

Glaser, B.G. and Strauss, A.L. (1967) The *Discovery of Grounded Theory: Strategies for Qualitative Research*. Chicago, IL: Aldine.

Hollway, W. and Jefferson, T. (2000) *Doing Qualitative Research Differently*. London: Sage.

Holstein, J.A. and Gubrium, J. (1997) 'Active interviewing', in D. Silverman (ed.), *Qualitative Research*. London: Sage.

Holstein, J.A. and Gubrium, J. (2003) 'Inside interviewing: new lenses, new concerns', in J. Holstein and J. Gubrium (eds), *Inside Interviewing*. Thousand Oaks, CA: Sage.

Kauffman, B. (1992) '"Feminist facts": interview strategies and political subjects in ethnography', *Communication Theory*, 3: 187–206.

Kondo, D. (1990) *Crafting Selves: Power, Gender, and Discourses of Identity in a Japanese Workplace*. Chicago: University of Chicago Press.

Kvale, S. (1996) *InterViews: An Introduction to Qualitative Research Interviewing*. London: Sage.

Kvale, S. and Brinkman, S. (2009) *Inter-Views*. Thousand Oaks, CA: Sage.

Lindlof, T.R., and Taylor, B.C. (2002) *Qualitative Communication Research Methods* (2nd edn). Thousand Oaks, CA: Sage.

Miller, J. and Glassner, B. (1997) 'The "inside" and the "outside": finding realities in interviews', in D. Silverman (ed.), *Qualitative Research*. London: Sage.

Potter, J. (1997) 'Discourse analysis as a way of analysing naturally occuring talk', in D. Silverman (ed.), *Qualitative Research*. London: Sage.

Potter, J. and Wetherell, M. (1987) *Discourse and Social Psychology: Beyond Attitudes and Behaviour*. London: Sage.

Silverman, D. (2006) *Interpreting Qualitative Data* (3rd edn). London: Sage.

Strauss, A. and Corbin, J. (1994) 'Grounded theory', in N. Denzin and Y. Lincoln (eds), *Handbook of Qualitative Research*. Thousand Oaks, CA: Sage.

15 Focus Groups

Binna Kandola

Introduction

The use of focus groups in the social sciences waxes and wanes depending on the prevailing attitude towards them and the popularity of alternative approaches. Although the last 20 years have seen an increase in their use for research purposes, they have been used as a research tool for nearly a century. Stewart et al. (2007) identify three influences on focus group methodology:

- Sociology and social psychology.

- Clinical psychology.

- Market research.

Researchers with a sociology or social psychology background tended to use the method to gain insights into group-related topics such as social interaction and cohesion. These applications broadened out in the 1940s with the advent of radio. Broadcasters and researchers were interested in finding out why some programmes were more popular than others. Technology was created that enabled group participants to press buttons while listening to a programme indicating whether they liked or disliked something. Modern versions of these devices are still in use today. There was, in other words, a focus on the research, as all data were obtained from groups of people. The clinical psychology approach was less direct, preferring people to discuss whatever it was they wanted to give expression to. This type of approach was more influenced by psychotherapy and facilitators tended to have a psychotherapeutic background. Market researchers, however, tended to be less concerned about the theoretical background and would use whatever technique and methodology they felt was appropriate. This might sometimes be less rigorous but it shows us that the focus group is a versatile and adaptable method, which can be fun as well as informative. Following these traditions, the roots of focus groups can be traced back to the early twentieth century.

However, if you look beyond the social sciences to other disciplines you will find methods that appear remarkably like focus groups but are called something else. In design, architecture and engineering circles there is a technique called the charette. This enables stakeholders to have their say in, for example, the design of a building. This approach has its roots in the nineteenth century and possibly earlier. So focus groups, or other variations, have a long history.

Now before going any further it is important to recognize here that my own approach to focus groups owes more to the sociological and social psychological tradition than to the others. And while not being a market researcher I do believe that we can apply different formats to focus group discussions and data gathering.

Projects using focus groups as the primary source of information can run into a number of difficulties. These include:

- Clarifying what the project is about and how focus groups can help.

- Identifying who you would like to have attending the groups in the first place.

- Communicating the purpose of the group to ensure people turn up.

- Ensuring that everyone participates in the meeting.

- Having a clear methodology.

- Analysing the results.

- Having facilitator skills.

In other words, running focus groups successfully requires much more than just facilitating sessions: there is a lot of planning, communication and persuasion involved. So unless these factors are considered, no matter how good the facilitation itself is, the overall result will not be a good one. In the remainder of this chapter each of these issues is addressed in turn.

Clarity of Purpose: Why Would You Use Focus Groups?

Focus groups are almost an everyday tool in marketing and political circles, typically being used to provide in-depth insights into, for example, products, brands and policies. When skilfully handled, they can tease out how people feel about a given topic and these data are clearly useful in advertising, presenting and generally communicating information to the general public. There are also many other uses for focus groups (Schafer, 1990).

Focus groups work particularly well when researchers are trying to explore people's feelings and experiences in more depth than can be obtained from a survey, for example. They can help to determine the mood or climate regarding a particular topic and can also help in providing ideas for future actions that an organization can take.

The first step towards having focus groups requires researchers to know why they are being used. It also means they must think through the alternatives to using them. It then requires that they be clear about what the purposes of the study are and how the data are going to be used.

Sampling

This can be a tricky area. Occasionally there will be few or no restrictions about the number of focus groups that are to be carried out but this is rare. Usually there will be restrictions on time and budget, which means thinking carefully about the number of focus groups to be conducted, where they will be held, and the number of people that will need to be involved. As with a lot of things regarding focus group these questions will be answered more through art than science. Political considerations will often come into play, e.g. all functions will expect to be involved; all the regions will need to be covered.

Apart from that the numbers to be seen will really depend upon the nature and complexity of the topic being investigated. If, for example, this is the experiences of women in non-stereotypical roles, it may be necessary to carry out focus groups with women at different levels in the organization – those in general management positions as well as those in specialist positions – and at different office locations. Such analysis, however, will require increasing the number of groups. Mixing the focus groups in terms of levels, geography, etc. is also an option but this requires the facilitator or moderator to be able to dissect the opinions of the different people involved rather skilfully. It needs to be acknowledged, however, that such fine-grain analyses are very difficult to achieve a high degree of reliability from focus groups. Ideally what researchers really want to achieve is to be able to call a halt when they think they are gaining no new insights or information from the focus groups they are conducting.

This of course means that they are analysing the focus groups as they are being conducted rather than waiting for all the data collection to be completed before examining them.

Communication

The focus groups obviously need sufficient numbers of people to attend them to make them effective. This means not having so many that people feel intimidated or unable to contribute because of the sheer numbers involved. But it also means not having so few so that researchers become concerned that their opinions and views do not reflect those of the wider population.

Communication therefore is of great importance. People need to be aware of:

- The purpose of the meeting.

- The outputs of the study.

- The reason why they have been chosen.

- The practicalities and logistics of the session, e.g. where it is being held, timings, etc..

Sometimes inducements may be necessary and even when not needed, these may be offered. This could be as straightforward as offering a nice lunch, inclusion in a prize draw or even some financial reward, e.g. money or vouchers. The idea behind doing so is, of course, to ensure people turn up rather than to persuade them to reflect a particular point of view (which of course would be bribery!).

Communicating the project to the intended participants needs to be done in good time so that they can put the dates in their diaries. Four to six weeks notice is typically about what is needed, with a reminder closer to the event. There should be a contact point for participants to get in touch regarding confirmation of attendance and to answer any queries that people may have.

If researchers are conducting focus groups for research purposes within an organization it is always helpful that they get the support and sponsorship of someone senior. Ideally the communication should then come from both individuals, i.e. the researcher and the sponsor, but not necessarily jointly. A message from the senior sponsor could say, for example, that a piece of research is going to be carried out by an independent academic. It could also say why the research is important to the organization and that people's participation would be welcome. At a not too distant point later, say a few days maximum, a message from the researcher would build on the sponsor's comments, providing more detail on the method and reinforcing the confidential nature of the project. Separating this communication helps to establish this independence of the research.

It is not uncommon at the start of a session to find that people will complain that they have no idea what the focus group is about and that they were told by their line manager that they needed to attend. In other words, this is not the ideal start. Clear, timely information will therefore help to create the right impression before the session itself starts. Once people are in the room it is important that the facilitator establishes their credibility, confidence and confidentiality.

Credibility is partly about sharing relevant experiences with the participants and it is also partly about communicating with confidence. This sharing of experience, in my view, needs to be done relatively briskly – namely walking the fine line between conveying expertise and bragging. On the one hand, the participants need to feel they are in capable hands in this session, with someone who knows what they are doing and will guide them expertly through the next few hours or so. This helps to allay any potential anxieties the participants may have. On the other hand, they must not come across as someone who considers themselves superior to the people in the room, which will only serve to create a gulf between facilitator and participant and this will mean that people will feel too inhibited to participate. This may sound a little harsh but academic researchers can sometimes let themselves down by not appearing professional enough early enough.

By confidence I mean that people should feel able to speak up. This is dependent on the skills of the facilitator, the process that is being operated and the general behaviour of the other participants. In short it is about the environment in which the discussion takes place. The facilitator needs to ensure that everyone understands that all views related to the topic are welcome. This will mean that early on in the discussion it is established that all views and opinions are going to be taken seriously and that nothing will be considered frivolous or silly: there will be no value judgements made about their comments. Clearly, this is partly connected to the process being followed and we will come to this shortly. However, it is mainly due to the skills and style of the facilitator. A dismissive style, misrepresenting what people are saying or allowing people to criticize the comments from others are just some of the things that can inhibit discussions.

Having said this, it is important that the discussion is not dominated by one or two people, which if researchers are not careful can be a fairly typical occurrence. In such situations the facilitator will need to ensure that they remain in charge of the discussion, encouraging the talkative members to rein themselves in for a moment in order for other people to have their voices heard. The facilitator will need to make it clear that while the individuals' contributions are welcome it would be good to hear from others in the room. It requires a degree of firmness to carry this out while at the same time ensuring that the vocal person is still encouraged to participate.

Confidentiality is part of the way in which the facilitator can create a confidence in others to talk freely but it is also of such importance that specific reference needs to be made to it. It sounds like a straightforward topic: everything that is said in the room will be treated in confidence. As with most things though it is not necessarily as simple as it may seem. For example, the rules of confidentiality should not apply if the facilitator hears of any illegal activity or action that could be a hazard to health and safety. Outside of these circumstances though it is difficult to think of a situation where the facilitator would have to break the confidentiality rule: indeed it is most important that they abide by it.

Sometimes the organization may ask for information about what happened in a focus group, who said what and what is emerging from the research. Through conversations like this, especially if it is with someone researchers trust, it would be easy to let their guard drop and divulge information that was given in good faith by participants. Researchers may sometimes feel the pressure because it is the sponsor who is asking the question and the research is dependent on their continued support. Despite this it is critical that the desire to please does not override their better judgement. In a meeting recently, the contact, a very rigorous and scrupulous individual, asked me whether it might be possible to have the transcripts of the things people had said in the groups. He wanted these so that he and his team could analyse them further. He also wanted to see whether they could identify any differences between ethnic groups, gender, etc. When we said he would be unable to do this because we had promised the participants that the material would be handled in confidence he immediately recognized the error he had made and apologized.

Confidentiality among the participants, however, is a different matter altogether. Facilitators can only ask participants to agree to keep things in confidence, but they cannot ensure that this will be the case.

On one occasion a colleague conducted a focus group and gained participants' support for the need to maintain confidentiality. During the discussion a member of staff, who was not present in the room, was referred to. Although no names had been shared another participant was able to recognize who was being discussed and on leaving the focus group told her friend what had been said about her. This person, unhappy at what had been discussed, then issued a grievance against the person making the remarks. This was subsequently not upheld on investigation, but it does show firstly the importance of laying down the ground rules and secondly the difficulties of ensuring participants do not divulge confidences themselves. It also highlights the fine line that one needs to tread between encouraging a discussion but not allowing other people to be criticized, particularly those who are not present.

Ensuring Everyone Participates

The whole point of a focus group is to hear the views of a number of people, not just one or two of them. If the discussion is dominated by a small group of individuals this clearly defeats the object of the exercise. It is important therefore that a good process is employed, which ensures that everyone feels able to participate and their views are considered to be valued and legitimate.

A simple process, introduced to me by Sylvia Downs, a former colleague, has proved to be enormously effective. The focus group participants should be asked to work in pairs (this is usually done by working with the person next to them, but does not have to be). Questions that need to be responded to are then introduced one at a time. Participants are given time to discuss and record their responses on paper or flipcharts. Once the question has been considered the facilitator asks for each pair in turn to give one of their ideas, observations or comments. The facilitator writes down what they say onto a flipchart before asking the next pair for their comments. This process continues until all the pairs have exhausted their comments. At this point, the facilitator can ask for an elaboration of some of the remarks made or specific examples to illustrate what was said.

So that is an overview for what the process is, but the thing that makes it effective is the micro behaviour of the facilitator and an understanding of why things must be done in a certain way.

Pairs

People work in twos for the simple reason that a conversation needs to take place. In small groups with even as few as three people, one person could take a back seat and not participate at all. In a pair, even if one person does all the talking the other at the very least has to listen. So working in pairs is an effective way of getting people involved without feeling exposed. Allowing them to discuss their thoughts and ideas first also enables people to get their voices heard and to rehearse what they are going to say before sharing it with the wider group.

Asking each pair in turn

This is important and each pair must be given the opportunity to speak without being interrupted by others. Giving them this space establishes the ethos that everyone is going to be heard. Furthermore, as it is a response from a two-member team, no person is necessarily personally exposed.

Writing comments onto a flipchart

The idea here is that the participants can see how their comments are being recorded publicly. As far as possible the facilitator must always use the words that the participants use. Too often facilitators can summarize, or see what they do as summarizing, but in doing so can subtly alter the meaning of what is said. If views are to be condensed it is important that the facilitator first checks with the participants to ensure that they are happy with the paraphrasing. Not only does this maintain the integrity of the data collection it also helps to create an atmosphere of openness and transparency.

Moving onto the next pair

Researchers should always ask people for a comment. They must be careful when people say, 'Our idea is already up there' as this may indicate a reluctance to speak up. If they say this then they should ask them to share their thoughts anyway as sometimes these can be subtly but distinctively different even though superficially they appear to be the same.

Continuing until all the points are collected

Often we will find that we must do two more rounds of the room to get all the ideas and comments out. After a couple of rounds we may just ask if there are any other points people want to make that haven't been captured already.

Asking for examples or further elaboration

Once the ideas have been collected researchers can ask people to provide a clarification of anything that appears unclear. They could also ask for examples to illustrate what is meant by a particular comment. It is important that these examples are specific and have been witnessed by the people themselves, i.e. not based on hearsay (I will discuss below how such examples can be collected using the Critical Incident Technique).

Having a colleague to act as a scribe

In order to record the examples correctly it is useful to have a colleague present who can act as a scribe. They should note down what the person says in their own words as far as possible. The facilitator and scribe should repeat back the example to ensure that they have understood and recorded the example in a way that the participant understands and agrees with.

Moving on to the next question

The above process can be followed for all subsequent questions; however, facilitators should start with a new flip chart page when getting the feedback.

The above process is deceptively simple but it enables:

- A climate of openness to be established.

- Trust to be conveyed by and developed with the facilitators.

- Everyone to participate.

- Views to be aired.

- The recording of comments and views to be correct.

Methodology

The above process and principles can be applied to almost any focus group methodology. In this section I would like to discuss some different approaches that can be used in focus groups: keys to understanding; the critical incident technique (CIT); the repertory grid; and appreciative inquiry.

Keys to understanding

The 'keys to understanding' (Pearn and Mulrooney, 1995) are essentially a framework for asking questions, which has been shown to be highly effective. Designed to be used to help people learn new concepts, the keys can be usefully applied to focus groups settings. There are five keys:

1 *Purpose* – exploring the possible purposes of something.

2 *Comparison* – how it compares and contrasts with something already familiar to the participants.

3 *Viewpoints* – how it is seen from different people's perspectives.

4 *Problems* – what problems will or might arise?

5 *Checks* – how can we check or evaluate our understanding?

So, for example, if the focus group concerned employee wellbeing, the keys could be used to shape the questions to be asked.

1 What purposes do you think are served by focusing on the wellbeing of our employees? (Purpose).

2 How does our approach to wellbeing compare with other organizations' approaches? (Comparison).

3 How is the wellbeing programme viewed by different groups of people, e.g. front-line staff, management, senior management? (Viewpoints).

4   What problems have arisen in the implementation of the programme? (Problems).

5   How could you tell if the programme was working effectively? (Checks).

A final question could be: 'What actions would you suggest we take to make the programme truly effective?'

This is an example but it shows how the keys to understanding can be used to set both breadth and depth around a specific topic. When used in conjunction with the process for facilitation outlined earlier, it can prove to be very effective.

Critical incident technique

This methodology was designed shortly after the Second World War by John C. Flanagan (1954). The focus of this method uses specific examples relevant to the topic that the participant is directly involved in or observes first hand. The example or incident has to be *critical*, i.e. the outcomes are either very successful or unsuccessful.

The key steps involve describing:

- The background to the incident, e.g. when and where.

- What exactly happened in the situation and why it was so critical.

- The feelings of different people and the actions taken.

- The outcomes.

Again the sequence of steps makes this easy to follow in focus group settings. Using the wellbeing study, the question asked of the group could be: 'Think of an example where something occurred in the organization that you witnessed which had a significant impact either positively or negatively on your own personal wellbeing or someone you work with'.

Participants are then asked to share the example or examples with their partner and focus on:

- What action was taken.

- How people felt about it.

- The outcomes and effect it had on the participant and the people around them.

This technique differs from the others in that it provides detailed examples rather than pithier observations, which can be more easily bullet pointed on a flip chart. It also requires the facilitator, while the incident is being recalled, to be thinking about what further information is required to ensure that the example is as full and complete as it can be.

When CIT is used in interview situations it is dependent on the interviewee's perception of the incident. A benefit and potential drawback of the group discussion is that others may chip in with their views on what happened and why. This is acceptable and to be encouraged only insofar as the original contributor agrees with the others' view. The advantage of this method is that it involves real situations and as a consequence can provide a genuine insight into actual behaviours that are either effective or ineffective. The storytelling approach also means that it is inherently interesting.

In group settings of course extra effort has be taken to ensure anonymity and confidentiality. However, the nature of some critical incidents will mean that other people, who are not directly involved, may either have heard of what happened and/or know the principal characters involved. The rules around confidentiality therefore need to be stressed. It can also suffer from the recency effect, i.e. people remembering events that occurred more recently. If incidents are recalled from longer ago, however, some information may be forgotten and may be mis-remembered and distorted.

Repertory grid technique

The repertory grid (RG) technique is the methodology devised as part of George Kelly's (1991) personal construct theory (PCT). In essence the theory says that we all make sense of the world in different ways. The way we analyse events, perceive people, etc. is determined by our schema, or constructs, and these are individual and personal. The theory is of less relevance here but the method of eliciting the constructs is important and this is known as the repertory grid technique.

The facilitator has a number of elements related to the topic being discussed. Elements are examples of what is being examined and they should be as concrete as possible. There could be eight to twelve of these (it is likely that some preparatory work will have been needed to establish which elements would be the most relevant).

In the focus group three elements will be chosen, either by the facilitator or one of the participants. The participants must then identify the way in which two of the elements are similar and different from the third. As the process is personal, different combinations of elements will be made and different constructs will emerge. This is all fine, fun and interesting. It is the role of the facilitator to explore the constructs in more detail to find out what exactly is meant. A scribe is also of great use here. It is not suprising if only three or four iterations of the process are all that can be carried out in a three-hour session.

The elements for a wellbeing study could include different types of initiatives or benefits, e.g. head massages, gym memberships, home working.

A final step could include creating a grid with the elements across the top and the constructs down the side. Each element would then be rated against each comment. Every person would do this and the grid would be analysed using specialist software designed for this purpose. In practice this can often be very time consuming and may not be possible in time constrained consultancy assignments, but the academic researchers may find this a worthwhile exercise.

The RG is a good technique to enable a discussion around specific elements of the topic in question, which other methods do not do. It can, with the right group, produce a wealth of information, which can of course then create problems of its own in terms of getting this analysed. It requires strong facilitation to get the best out of it and to ensure that the group stays on track.

Appreciative inquiry

The basic tenet of 'appreciative inquiry' (Watkins and Mohr, 2001) is to focus on what is good and effective about an organization and use this as the starting point for any future change. The approach is based on what is known as the four Ds:

- *Discover*: trying to find out what works well currently.

- *Dream*: visioning what perfection would be like.

- *Design*: creating the perfect process.

- *Destiny*: what we are going to do next to ensure that the design is delivered.

As with the keys of understanding, the four Ds are readily translatable into focus group formats. So, using the same wellbeing topic as earlier, the questions would be:

- In terms of employee wellbeing, what works well currently? (Discover).

- What would your vision be of an organization that is the best at looking after the wellbeing of its employees? (Dream).

- What processes would we need to have to ensure we improve the wellbeing of all employees? (Design).

- What do we need to do next to put these processes into place? (Destiny).

The appreciative inquiry approach quite deliberately and consciously makes people think very positively about the organization and, as it says in the title, appreciate the good things that are happening. It is used as a starting point for further investigation and exploration. In contrast to the keys of understanding, there is no real discussion about the problems, which could lead to a somewhat overly optimistic view of what is achievable. On the other hand, it may also prevent the disgruntlement that can occur when problems are being discussed. It fits in with the current thinking on positive psychology and its emphasis on upsides and making the most of them.

Analysing the Data

Whatever method is employed there is still the difficulty of analysing qualitative data. Content analysis is the most straightforward way of doing this, identifying, classifying and categorizing themes. This could be done by hand or by using specific software designed to be used with qualitative data, such as NVivo (see Sinkovics and Alfoldi, in this volume).

Ideally each focus group would be analysed separately rather than combining all of the data together. Separate analysis will be more laborious but it pays dividends in the end as it will enable a comparison of the groups to take place so that researchers can see if different locations have different priorities, problems or situations. Care needs to be taken not to over-interpret these differences.

With many of the methods we can end up with lists of ideas and observations and it can be difficult to identify priorities. This can be particularly galling when looking at the actions people think an organization should take. A simple way around this is to give each person five self-adhesive dots. These represent five votes and they must apply these to the actions (or whatever question is being considered) in whatever way the participant sees fit. If, for example, there are five actions of equal importance they can cast one vote for each of these. At the other extreme they may see one action that is, for them, the greatest priority, in which case it will receive all five votes. This is not an exact science but it is surprising how quickly priorities can emerge for a group. This can help academics and consultants alike to determine what employee priorities are.

Facilitator Skills

We can have a clear purpose, a great method, and a good turnout, but still have a poor outcome from a focus group, i.e. little or no information, poor participation. This highlights the importance of good facilitation. It is an exercise that requires some skill and we can really notice how important this is when we are able to compare poor and expert facilitation. A good facilitator will exert a subtle, unobtrusive yet firm control of the group, enabling individuals to feel they have a valued part to play in the process.

In the main, the facilitator will be non-judgemental and welcoming.

Table 15.1 shows the various things, both verbal and non-verbal, that a good facilitator will do, while Table 15.2 shows the things they need to avoid.

Table 15.1   Things a focus group facilitator should do

Verbal	Non-verbal
• Acknowledgement – e.g. 'yes', 'uh huh' • Open questions – e.g. 'who', 'how', 'what', 'when', 'where' and 'why' • Summarizing and reflecting – e.g. 'So what you're saying is …' • Allowing time for people to respond • Referring to people by name	• Smiling • Nodding • Eye contact

Table 15.2   Things a focus group facilitator should avoid doing

Verbal	Non-verbal
• Criticizing or disagreeing – e.g. 'I disagree', 'You're wrong' • Agreeing – e.g. 'That is correct' • Owning personal opinions • Making recommendations – e.g. 'You should …' • Using 'closed', 'leading' or 'double-headed' questions • Interrupting	• Frowning • Looking bored • Shaking head • Gazing away from the group • Fidgeting • Pointing at people

Over and above this, however, the facilitator needs to ensure that the process remains on track and that the information being obtained is relevant. So while there is a need for them to be listening, and to be seen to be listening, the facilitator also has to be thinking, for example, about:

- *Relevance*: is this contribution relevant for this study?

- *Timing*: how much time do we have left?

- *Clarity*: am I getting the point this person is making?

- *Detail*: is there sufficient detail here which will be helpful in the analysis?

- *Participation*: is everyone taking part? Are some people dominating?

In short a good facilitator, while actively listening to each participant, also needs to be thinking about these other broader considerations all of the time.

Conclusion

Focus groups can be a very effective way of gathering data about people's views and for generating ideas about future action. In order to work effectively care needs to be taken in being clear about the purposes for which they are being used. There are many other factors that need to be considered in setting up and running groups, including communication, facilitation and analysis. Having a clear process to encourage discussion is important as well as a method that is appropriate to the aims and objectives of the project. A constant factor in all focus groups is the skills of the facilitator. Hopefully this chapter will be of assistance in helping to avoid the sorts of problems described in the first section.

The future of focus groups is fascinating given the advent of social networking media. To date the use of technology for obtaining information from groups has been somewhat limited and uninspiring, e.g. the use of moderated forums and discussion boards. However, an interesting exercise in public engagement is being conducted by the US State Department with the support of the head of that department, Hillary Clinton. It utilizes a new social media technology called Opinion Space, developed by Berkeley's Centre for New Media. Anyone can participate in this exercise. Each person responds to five questions and their results are mapped in relation to everyone else who has participated. In addition, everyone can view these comments, or a sample of the comments, made by others and they can rate each of these. The system then shows the comments that people most agree with. It may be too early to say how successful this approach is, but there can be little doubt that the gathering, sharing and evaluation of qualitative data could be revolutionized by the advent of methods such as this.

Further Reading

For an excellent background to focus groups as well as providing sound practical advice, take a look at one of the following three books: Stewart, Shamdasani and Rook (2007); Morgan (1997); and Kreuger and Casey (2000).

References

Flanagan, J.C. (1954) 'The Critical Incident Techniques', *Psychological Bulletin*, 51: 4.

Kelly, G.A. (1991) *The Psychology of Personal Constructs*. New York: Norton.

Kreuger, R.A. and Casey, M.A. (2000) *Focus Groups: A Practical Guide for Applied Research* (3rd edn). Thousand Oaks, CA: Sage.

Morgan D.L. (1997) *Focus Groups as Qualitative Research* (2nd edn). Thousand Oaks, CA: Sage.

Pearn, M.A and Mulrooney, C. (1995) *Tools for a Learning Organisation*. London: IPD.

Schafer, M. (1990) 'Data collection in the UK and how it differs from the US', *Applied Marketing Research*, Second Quarter, 30: 2.

Stewart, D.W., Shamdasani, P.N. and Rook, D.W. (2007) *Focus Groups: Theory and Practice* (2nd edn). Thousand Oaks, CA: Sage.

Watkins, J.M. and Mohr, B. (2001) *Appreciative Inquiry*. San Francisco, CA: Jossey-Bass/Pfeiffer.

Participatory Visual Methods

Russ Vince and Samantha Warren

Introduction

This chapter discusses drawing and participant-led photography as approaches
that explicitly involve research respondents in the co-creation of qualitative
data. Through these examples we demonstrate the utility of employing visual
methodologies in the investigation of organizational life. We begin with a brief
overview of the development of visual studies in organizational research
before discussing ways in which drawings and participant-led photography
have been used in the field. This sets the scene for two examples from our own
research. The first outlines how Russ used drawing as a method to generate
emotional data about organizational change (Vince and Broussine, 1996) and
the second describes Samantha's use of participant-led photography to
produce data about the importance of personal space in 'hot-desk' workplace
environments (Warren, 2006). We then extend this discussion by addressing
what we see as two of the key challenges in participatory visual research methodology: ethics and the analysis of visual data. We conclude with some personal reflections on the use of participatory visual methods in our research.

We focus on participatory visual methods for two reasons. First, in our
opinion, involving research participants in the generation of data about their
organizational lives – beyond traditional 'question and answer' techniques – is
of growing importance given an increasing sensitivity to the ethics of the qualitative research process as it matures as an established methodological paradigm
(Gottlib-Conn, 2008, and see Holt, in this volume). As academic researchers, we
gain from understanding the experiences of those we research, but in comparison

these people may receive relatively little in return. The people who are kind enough to help us with our research receive little or no 'right of reply' to what we say about their worlds (Wray-Bliss, 2003; Brewis and Wray-Bliss, 2008). Given the rise in scrutiny by institutional research ethics committees (Gottlib-Conn, 2008), and greater demands by research funding councils to demonstrate the 'impact' of our research on stakeholder communities beyond academia, we believe that involving research participants remains a high priority for qualitative research and that visual methods offer excellent opportunities for this.

Second, the methodological commentary on the analysis of 'pre-existing' visual materials is far more developed than that concerned with generating visual material as part of the research process (see, for example, van Leeuwen and Jewitt, 2001; Kress and van Leeuwen, 2006). However, in this chapter we are making a distinction between methods that enable research participants to express themselves visually – such as asking them to create an artefact, draw, recount their dreams or take photographs – and the researcher's analysis of 'found' organizational images, such as brochures, advertisements, websites, films, etc., which does not usually overtly involve participants (Warren, 2009). It is the former variant of visual methodology that we are concerned with in the following discussions.

Overview: Visual Organization Studies

The inclusion of this chapter in the 'core methods of qualitative inquiry' section of this volume is an indication of the rising interest in visual methods shown by organizational researchers. Long established in anthropology and sociology, visual methods either utilize processes of visualization to generate data, or take visual artefacts as their unit of analysis (Warren, 2009). Despite a provenance of several decades in the social sciences, visual studies of organizational life have been slow to appear (Strangleman, 2004), and those that have, have been largely undertaken by sociologists of work or from within the fields of education and healthcare research (Prosser, 1998; Morgan et al., 2009), rather than by organization or management scholars (e.g. Harper, 1984; Halford, 2004; Strangleman, 2008). In recent years there has been a steady growth in interest in the visual within organization and management studies itself, as evidenced by the formation in 2007 of *in*Visio, the International Network for Visual Studies of Organization, the first journal special issue on 'Visual Perspectives on Accounting' (*AAAJ*, 2009), the 28th Standing Conference on Organizational Symbolism's 2010 conference theme of 'Vision' (*SCOS*, 2010) and the commissioning of a special issue on visual qualitative research by the journal *Qualitative Research in Organizations and Management* due to be published in 2012. Elsewhere, in her commentaries on the current state of the field, Samantha gives a variety of reasons for this surge in interest (Warren, 2008; 2009). These include a cultural predisposition towards 'the aesthetic' in contemporary advanced consumer society that generates an image-saturated society; an epistemological turn towards the material and aesthetic in organization studies; and the practical fact that digital technologies have made the collection, storage, manipulation and display of images a routine affair, which has democratized photography and increased its reach both as a social practice and accessible research method.

In organization studies, examples of visual research include semiotic and critical visual analysis of organizationally produced images, such as annual reports (Davison, 2009; Davison and Skerratt, 2007; and see Lee, in this volume), advertisements (Borgerson and Schroeder, 2002; Schroeder, 2002; and more classically Williamson, 1978), websites (Kivinen, 2006; Cho et al., 2009), promotional literature (Belova, 2004; Hancock, 2005) and representations of work and organization in popular media (Guthey and Jackson, 2005; Bell, 2008; Hancock, 2008; McDonald, 2009). Other research has considered the impor- tance of architecture and the aesthetico-symbolic dimension of corporate life (Gagliardi, 1990; Jackson and Carter, 2000; Dale and Burrell, 2003) and indeed the visual manifestations of organizational death (Strangleman, 2009; Bell, forthcoming). A further branch of research has employed visually oriented methods to generate data about organizational phenomena, including employee identities (Warren and Parker, 2009; Shortt, 2010), fun at work (Warren and Fineman, 2007), leadership (Wood and Ladkin, 2007), strategy (Meyer, 1991), child and immigrant workers (Bolton et al., 2001, Gallo, 2002), change (Vince and Broussine, 1996) and process re-engineering (Buchanan, 2001).

It is this last variant of visual methodology that specifically concerns us in this chapter. As noted above, we consider two participatory visual methods – drawing and participant-led photography – and it is to these discussions that we now turn.

Two Worked Examples

Example one: drawings

The use of drawings in management and organization studies can be traced back to the late 1980s. One of the key early examples is Shoshana Zuboff's (1988) book

In the Age of the Smart Machine: The Future of Work and Power. Professor Zuboff asked clerical workers to draw pictures showing how they felt about their jobs before and after the installation of a new computer system. These drawings helped staff to articulate feelings that had been implicit and were hard to define. In terms of understanding and developing the method, a key paper was published in *Organization Science* (Meyer, 1991) called 'Visual data in organizational research'. Meyer acknowledges that 'visual instruments seem uniquely suited to … efforts to build theory and research focusing on human awareness, interpretation and consciousness' (Meyer, 1991: 232). There are a number of published papers that can provide the researcher with discussions and/or examples of this method in organization studies (Vince, 1995a; Holliday, 2000; Kearney and Hyle, 2004; Stiles, 2004; Strangleman, 2004; Bryans and Mavin, 2006; Bagnoli, 2009). The method has been used by researchers interested in revealing the links between individuals' real and imagined idea of 'the organization' they work in (Hutton et al., 1997) and the organizing dynamics and forces that shape and are shaped by their interpretations and actions. Drawings can provide 'a succinct presentation of participant experiences'; they offer opportunities to engage overtly with researcher bias; and the approach triangulates well with other qualitative data generation methods (Kearney and Hyle, 2004).

   Here, we discuss an example of Russ's research that used drawings as a method to study emotions, relations and politics associated with change processes in public sector organizations (Vince and Broussine, 1996). The starting point of this research 'was the belief that change depends as much on comprehending and managing emotional relatedness as it does on employing rationality and logic to solve problems' (Vince and Broussine, 1996: 4). In other words, asking individuals to produce drawings to generate visual data (in much the same way as individual interviews generate verbal data) allowed Russ and his colleague to look at the intersection between the emotional and the rational in processes of change.

   The usefulness of this research approach is that drawings tend to portray individual emotions effortlessly, since there are often unexpected and enigmatic aspects to an image. This assumption rests on a conceptual grounding in psychoanalysis whereby the emotional or 'pre-rational' contents of the mind are revealed through images, including dreams as well as drawings (see Rose, 2007, Chapter 6 and Broussine, 2008; for an introduction to these ideas). However, their real value in research is in the way they can reveal aspects of *collective* emotional experience and knowledge about a specific work context. Asking a group of participants to draw their team or organization is an invitation to generate multiple interpretations and to promote dialogue over the collective and contested meaning of individuals' images. This inevitably raises questions about the power relations that shape both experience and interpretation (Sievers, 2008).

The research by Vince and Broussine (1996) involved a total of 86 managers (49 middle managers/37 senior managers) from six organizations (four local government/two health service). Each participant produced a drawing, some of which are reproduced below (Figure 16.1).

The research process for this study was in five stages:

1   The generation of visual data concerning individual feelings about change: participants were asked to 'draw a picture that expresses your feelings about change at work in your organization'.

2   Individuals' verbal interpretation of their own drawings: participants were invited to write on the back of their drawing 'five to ten words or phrases which come to mind when you look at your picture'.

3   Team-based reflections on the visual data and the individuals' chosen words: participants showed their own drawings to the other team members, who then said what meanings they drew from the images. Different layers of data were collected. The team members' interpretations of the images were recorded by the researcher in a field diary. This information was then reviewed by the team to satisfy accuracy. Some overall reflections on the process of the research were collected by the researcher at this stage. The data were collated and reduced in order to provide a focal point for the next stage in the research process.

4   A few weeks after the initial data gathering, inter-group reflections took place involving different hierarchical groups from the same organization. These were between the middle managers and the senior managers involved in the research. Participants in this broader focus group shared the drawings, the individuals' own reflections and the original team reflections. These meetings were recorded.

5   Using techniques to promote dialogue, the middle and senior managers undertook a joint synthesis of the data in order to make sense of these for themselves, as well as discussing implications for the organization.

This approach to qualitative research is complicated, multi-layered and risky (much like the change processes and dynamics it was trying to research). The method revealed and captured those aspects of change that rarely surface, but are invariably present. For example, the drawings drew out the complexities and uncertainties involved in change processes. They also helped to identify the dualities of feelings involved – the optimism and pessimism about change, the 'hope' and the 'hatred' of change that sat side by side in these managers'

Figure 16.1   Examples of the managers' drawings from Vince and Broussine's (1996) study

experience. The managers themselves were surprised by the strength of emotions that surfaced from the drawings. They were both perplexed by and attracted to the perceptions that emerged. Through the drawings they were able to see some of the key factors in the emotional and political relations that undermined change, in particular poor inter-personal communication and difficulties generated around boundary relations.

The emotional and political dynamics underlying change are often the very things that will undermine change initiatives in organizations. However, there are also good reasons for making careful decisions about when and where to use such a method as part of a research design. The use of drawings to generate data on emotions in organizations poses ethical questions for the researcher about the depth of engagement being asked of participants (see our discussion below). It is important therefore to make sure that the method is well-explained and well-contained. The method has its risks, both in terms of the fears and anxieties that are generated for the researcher and those that are generated for participants. In addition, 'the reliability of drawings in a qualitative research process depends initially on the acceptance that there is such a thing as underlying or unconscious process and that it can be expressed and contained within an image' (Vince and Broussine, 1996: 9). In other words, the method is a leap of faith. However, we contend that all interpretive methods are to some extent a leap of faith, as they are connected to the expectation that interesting personal, interpersonal and social dynamics are likely to emerge from a qualitative approach.

Example two: participant-led photography

Participant-led photography (PLP) has less of a lineage in organization studies than the use of drawing, although it has firm foundations in health and social care studies through the work of Wang and Burris (1994; 1997) who pioneered the term 'photo-*voice*'. As this name suggests, the basic premise is that research participants are provided with a camera and asked to make a set of photographs that literally represents their view of the issue being researched. These photographs then set the agenda for a later qualitative interview with a researcher, where the participants will explain why they took the pictures and the meaning and significance they hold. There are two key benefits to this, firstly, it is the participants' subjective perspective that is foregrounded, rather than the researcher's assumptions about what might be important; and secondly, using images reduces the reliance on words, meaning the method is particularly suitable for research with people who have language difficulties, children or disadvantaged groups where perceived power differentials might preclude respondents from feeling that they are able to express themselves freely. To our mind, it is this last characteristic that distinguishes photo-voice from PLP. Photo-voice always has an emancipatory agenda whereas PLP does not – although it may do, particularly if utilized from a critical management studies position (Warren, 2005b).

The following example is drawn from Samantha's investigation into the meaning and significance of people's personal space at work through an exploration of their 'desk clutter' (Warren, 2006). Photography is an ideal medium through which to analyse the importance of space since the camera indiscriminately records everything within its 'gaze' when the shutter is pressed, capturing not only the intended subject of the photograph, but also a great deal of contextual information about the scene with it (Collier and Collier, 1986; Shortt and Warren, 2012). In Samantha's study, 31 individuals working in a 'hot desking' office within the web design department of a global IT firm were asked to take pictures of their desks and later 'talk through' the photographs. The study was part of a larger ethnographic investigation into workplace aesthetics (Warren, 2005a) and in particular, motivated by Samantha's curiosity as to why, in an office where no one was supposed to have personal desks, there was such an apparent proliferation of personal effects on display (Figure 16.2). Stages in the research process were as follows:

1   Participants were issued with digital cameras and asked to take one or two photographs of their immediate workspace.

2   The images were downloaded to a laptop for later viewing.

3   The participants were invited to 'talk through' the items depicted in the photographs with the researcher during qualitative interviews. Typical questions included asking about the history and significance of the objects in the photograph and why certain items were displayed on desks and not others.

4   Data were thus generated *through* the image in the form of the conversations that centred on it, rather than contained *in* the image itself (Belova, 2006).

5   These data were analysed thematically to ascertain the role personalization played for these participants, which included a 'material anchoring' of emotional and aesthetic ties; a mode of self-expression sometimes used to resist the perceived colonization of the individual self by the organization; and collectively to foster a sense of belonging (Warren, 2006).

6   The study concluded that efficiency-motivated moves towards hot-desking environments may damage employee wellbeing at work.

Figure 16.2   The supposed 'hot-desking' space of Dept. X

The first advantage of using photography was that of 'removed observation'. This research could have been conducted by Samantha physically sitting with the participants at their desks, asking them to talk about the objects apparent there. However, doing this in a busy office was difficult for two reasons: the absence of privacy, which would potentially compromise the richness of the data; and noise in the environment, which made audio recording the interview difficult.

It also would be very difficult to do this if the research context was such that employees did not have their own personal space at work, e.g. hospitality, estates and retail workers (Betts, 2009; Shortt, 2010), or were working remotely, such as sales people (Nathan and Doyle, 2002). One of the frustrations of handing the camera to the participants, however, was a loss of control of the process. Some participants forgot to do the task or were late which, on occasion, resulted in frustrating wasted trips to the research site.

The second advantage relates to the 'inventory' function of the camera noted above in that items within the photograph deemed unimportant to the

participant can be queried by the researcher. In the following example
(Figure 16.3), Samantha notices something in the photograph under Simon's
desk that he hasn't mentioned, so she asks him about it:

Samantha: Is that a Scalextric under there? (pointing to the red
             and black pieces of 'track' in the bottom left of the
             photograph).
Simon: No, unfortunately not! That's err, more of my mess ...
             as I said I was involved in setting up the [department]
             and at the last moment when we moved in there was a

Figure 16.3   Simon's desk

	lot of signage to be put up ... which we now don't have storage for, so its behind my desk.
Samantha:	Is storage a problem then?
Simon:	God yes, we have nowhere to put anything but we're supposed to have a, hot-desk ... clear desk policy. How's that gonna work?

As the above dialogue shows, important data about the poor practicality of the hot-desking office design would have been lost if Samantha had not been able to see an intriguing object captured in the 'inventory' recorded by the camera. The importance of these 'unintended traces' cuts to the heart of the co-creation of data we suggest is a feature of participatory visual methods – the data here were generated *by the object* rather than by the participant, and probed by the researcher in what Belova (2006) calls 'the event of seeing'. This stimulated a further process of reflection by the participant leading to unanticipated threads of discussion.

This leads to the third noteworthy dimension of this method, that quite simply, it generates talk. It speeds rapport and in the study outlined here was reported by participants as being fun to do, securing greater engagement with the project than perhaps might otherwise have been the case. Warren and Parker (2009) refer to this as the 'third party effect' to explain how a discussion is always easier when there is some*thing* to talk about. It also diffuses potentially uncomfortable personal talk since researcher and participant are not speaking directly to one another. Instead, the conversation flows through the image where attention is focused. Scarles (2010) expands on the significance of this effect by suggesting that the image can act as a point of embodied 'ignition' that unites participant and researcher in contemplation of that which is impossible to put into words (see also Warren, 2005b; 2008).

Finally, photography brings the material world into the equation. Although this was an explicit aim of Samantha's study outlined above, the addition of a material context in ethnographic research especially is vital to retain some semblance of the richness of how it felt to 'be there' in an aesthetic sense. As Dale and Burrell (2008) argue, the linguistic turn in social research of the 1960s has led to a dematerialization of social research, effectively ignoring how organizational things, objects, places and spaces shape and are shaped by social action. We contend that photography may go some way in addressing this.

Discussion: Implications for Ethics and Analysis in Qualitative Research

We have presented two vignettes of participatory visual methods in action and highlighted their respective benefits and drawbacks. Here we consider some of the common issues raised in these examples in relation to what we regard as current challenges within the field of visual organization studies. Firstly, we address the issue of ethics and consider how participatory methods are conducive to robust research ethics practice as well as drawing attention to the ongoing difficulties that the use of 'the visual' throws up. Secondly, we consider how data generated by the methods outlined above might be analysed in a way that contributes to furthering good practice in rigorous qualitative research, avoiding charges of superficial 'impressionism' that might otherwise be levelled at the interpretation of visual images.

Ethics

A key ethical issue is the extent to which participants *continue* to consent to take part in the research beyond an initial stage of 'signing the form'. In the case of PLP, this situation is not such a problem since participants retain *advance* control over what they photograph and choose to reveal to the researcher. More challenging is obtaining the consent of those who are photographed. How can informed consent be obtained from everyone who inadvertently appears in a picture taken of a busy street scene or retail store for example? Public events tend to display 'disclaimers' asking anyone who is not willing to have their photograph taken to identify themselves to the organizers – although we are unsure how exactly the organizers would actually make certain this happened.

In the case of drawing, the researcher is not always aware of the emotions that are going to be generated in participant groups (see Vince, 1995b for an example of this). Consent has to be sought from the group or groups that are being engaged in the research, but it is not possible to fully explain what the experience itself may reveal. The act of visualization may trigger unexpected emotional responses. Key to using this approach is for the researcher to be clear that there is an important boundary between drawings that are used in therapeutic interventions (see, for example, Case and Dalley, 2006; Broussine, 2008), and drawings used as a research approach to generate data. In the latter, the focal point of the research is not the individual's image, as with art therapy, but the ways in which imagery from a group depicts underlying emotions and assumptions concerning 'the way we do things here'.

Photography produces an image that is iconographic in its resemblance to the reality it was intended to represent. Consequently, it is important that line managers or other gatekeepers consent to the taking of photographs and care should be taken not to capture iconic identifying features if the organization wishes to remain anonymous. Although no formal guidelines have yet emerged from the visual research community (although see Prosser et al., 2008), Samantha's research has always been granted institutional ethical approval by asking participants to sign up to undertake 'responsible photography' (see the Appendix to this chapter). The visual image is a site for complex copyright laws, governing the right to reproduce an artwork, an image already published even when it is seemingly in the public domain (e.g. an advertisement) or one that has been legitimately purchased. This poses challenges for visual researchers who are using organizationally produced images as their data and wish to reproduce them in published work.

Analysis

How should participant-made images (whether drawn or photographed) be interpreted for the purposes of analysis in qualitative research? As Prosser and Loxley (2008) note, modes of analysing visual data need further and more detailed attention – a view with which we would concur, although structural approaches to the analysis of 'found' images that rest on similar principles to linguistic deconstruction are much more well developed. These date back to Panofsky, Pierce and Barthes who have contributed to our modern understanding of the semiotic analysis of images (see Davison, 2009 for a good overview and Schroeder, 2002 for a more critically motivated method of visual analysis). More recently, these ideas have been further developed by contemporary authors, for example contributors to van Leeuwen and Jewitt (2001) and Kress and van Leuwen (2006).

There is a dearth of methodological advice on the analysis of *participant generated* images within the visual studies field. The studies we have presented above show how images can be used to generate textual data from participants, although both approaches begin with a visual method, and they also end with a very traditional interview transcript as the participants and researcher discuss the image in words. The relationship between words and images is incredibly complex – photographs and drawings are usually used as illustrative evidence (such as in newspapers or drawings by court reporters) and, where these are the sole focus of attention, will rarely appear without a caption that (in part at least) anchors their meanings through text. Indeed, the extent to which we can ever make sense of anything, whether visual or through any other sensory mode, *without* language is a moot point (see Mitchell, 1994; Scott, 1999).

While we do not have space to do justice to these debates here, we nonetheless wish to raise the issue of analysis as a fruitful area for future development by visual organizational scholars. With the above in mind, we briefly outline three possibilities for the development of analytical techniques in participatory visual methods.

Content analysis

What small commentary there is on analysing participant made images can be found in social psychology literature and this utilizes content analysis to investigate the frequency – and by extension the significance – of certain representational features of images. For example, Ziller's (1990) notion of 'orientations' involves counting the number and types of objects depicted in his participants' images and matching them to personality dispositions as measured by psychological tests. Clarke and Holt (2010) categorize the images entrepreneurs used to symbolize their goals broadly on a content analysis basis. The utility of this last example rests less on recording observations to demonstrate their significance, and more on the occurrence of patterns as a way to generate themes.

Traditional thematic analysis

It is possible to analyse the verbal discussions generated by PLP and drawing methods using conventional transcripts of their audio recordings, according to any one of a now burgeoning array of coding procedures (see Saldana, 2009; and see King, in this volume). In this approach, the visual is useful at the beginning of the research design, but recedes in importance in the later stages. While there is clearly nothing wrong in this, it does seem to us that it is a pity that the images disappear from the analytical frame once they have 'done their job' of generating words. We would advocate that some of the images should, if possible, be published alongside the textual data in order not to lose the very richness that image-based research seeks to generate and capture. In Samantha's study (and elsewhere, see Warren, 2002; 2005a), and following Mitchell (1994), she has adopted an 'image-text' approach to the presentation of data where the interview quotes used as data are accompanied by the image they relate to. This goes some way to mediating the reliance on one or the other medium, given the complexity of the image-text nexus we allude to above. However, even this does not really involve *analysis* of the images as data in their own right as we discuss further below.

A hybrid mode of analysis?

While recognizing that images should not stand alone from the participants' explanations of them, the fact remains that the participants *chose* particular scenes, images or objects to depict from a plethora of possibilities and we speculatively suggest that this might be instructive. Are there cultural, gendered or occupational patterns that consciously or unconsciously led the participants towards certain things in their environment more than others for example? Collier (2001: 39) comes closest to fleshing out this idea with his concept of 'open viewing'. He puts forward a four step process for viewing a set of photographs together (one imagines spread out on a table in front of the researcher) in order to 'look at, "listen" to its overtones and subtleties, [and] to discover contrasting patterns' and then goes on to suggest that involving the respondent in this process can only help to verify the interpretation. While this still renders the ultimate analysis a textual one, the idea of building 'photo-sets' for participants to compare and contrast the images they use is an intriguing one and may help to integrate the visual and the verbal in a more holistic and forceful manner.

Conclusion

In this chapter we have introduced two participatory visual methods and given an overview of their use in organizational research. We have connected these methods to contemporary challenges in visual methodology and qualitative research more generally. We consider the issues of ethics and analysis to be at the centre of this approach to the practice of qualitative research. Research participants involved in this method are far more concerned with the generation of qualitative data than those who take part in more 'scientific' studies that generate quantitative data. Because of this, we believe that they are owed a particular ethical responsibility. In addition, since the validity of the findings we generate through qualitative research is measured on the basis of its plausibility and not against some external measure, we also believe qualitative researchers should be as reflexive about the way we generate those data as possible – both in terms of collecting *and* analysing these (see Haynes, in this volume). Through these two challenges we hope to have provided other researchers with an interesting set of ideas and, perhaps, inspiration for their own practice.

In keeping with this volume's desire to provide reflexive, experiential accounts of 'real' qualitative research practice, we would like to end the chapter by summarizing some of our personal experiences of using visual methods in organizational research.

Firstly, there is always a risk of style over substance. Ask yourself, 'What data does this visual method help me to obtain that I couldn't otherwise access?' Visual research needs to establish its credibility on soundly argued method-ological justification, as our concerns about the lack of analytical reflexivity demonstrate. This said, both of us are eager to see more research in management and organization studies that utilizes this approach. Publishing your own or participant produced images in academic journals is becoming easier – although obtaining permission to use images you do not own the copyright for (especially if they are already published) is not – and journal editors are likely to insist that the author traces and secures permissions for all images he or she wants to reproduce. This can be expensive, time-consuming or, indeed, impossible.

While explaining to participants that no artistic ability is required to produce a drawing, the use of images in research may nonetheless produce resistance (individual and organizational). It is not unusual to hear 'But I can't draw!' or 'I can't take good photos', so it is important to utilize what is produced, however it looks. For example, Russ had a participant who put no marks on her paper, yet the blank page was nonetheless a powerful image to express the individual and collective emotions at work. As this example shows, it is likely that you will also lose some control over the process. You will have no idea what your participant is going to draw or photograph; no idea of how it might be interpreted in context; and little idea if it will be relevant to your research objectives. This is unnerving, but also important if we are trying to do research within the complexities of organizations.

Finally, there are always technical problems, from procuring suitable equip-ment and instructing participants on how to use it, to having enough file storage in the case of scanned images or digital photographs, right through to accidentally deleting whole folders of pictures (as Samantha has learned to her chagrin!). However, we think that it is always better to do research that we will enjoy doing. The creative use of images can be fun both for the researcher and the participant. Images add interest and a depth of mutual interpretation to what can sometimes be a rather detached process.

Further Reading

Broussine (2008), Chapter 4, offers an overview of the conceptual underpinnings and ethical dilemmas in using drawing in research. Rose (2007), in our opinion, provides the best all-round introduction to visual methods in the social sciences. Warren (2009) gives an overview of the particular choices available to and challenges faced by visual researchers in the field of organization studies. Finally, see *in* Visio: International Network of Visual Studies in Organizations (www.in-visio.org). This is the interactive online hub of the network including resources, links and blog on all matters related to visual studies in organization.

References

Bagnoli, A. (2009) 'Beyond the standard interview: the use of graphic elicitation and arts-based methods', *Qualitative Research*, 9 (5): 547–570.

Bell, E. (2008) *Reading Management and Organization in Film*. London: Palgrave Macmillan

Bell, E. (2012) 'Ways of seeing organizational death: a critical semiotic analysis of organizational memorialization', *Visual Studies* (forthcoming).

Belova, O. (2004) 'Organisations and their images: an empirical exploration into the phenomenology of visual experience'. Unpublished PhD thesis, University of Essex.

Belova, O. (2006) 'The event of seeing: a phenomenological perspective on visual sense-making', *Culture and Organization*, 12 (2): 93–107.

Betts, J. (2009) 'Visual adaptation of repertory grids', presented at the ESRC 'in Visio' Seminar, 'Visual Analysis and Interpretive Methods', University of Exeter, 29 May. Available at http://in-visio.org/activities/visualanalysis/visual-adaptation-of-repertory-grids/ (last accessed 29 September 2011).

Bolton, A., Pole, C. and Mizen, P. (2001) 'Picture this: researching child workers', *Sociology*, 35 (2): 501–18.

Borgerson, J. and Schroeder, J. (2002) 'Ethical issues of global marketing: avoiding bad faith in visual representation', *European Journal of Marketing*, 36 (5/6): 570–594.

Brewis, J. and Wray-Bliss, E. (2008) 'Re-searching ethics: towards a more reflexive critical management studies', *Organization Studies*, 29 (12): 1521–1540.

Broussine, M. (2008) *Creative Methods in Organizational Research*. London: Sage.

Bryans, P. and Mavin, S. (2006) 'Visual images: a technique to surface conceptions of research and researchers', *Qualitative Research in Organizations and Management: An International Journal*, 1 (2): 113–128.

Buchanan, D. (2001) 'The role of photography in organization research: a reengineering case illustration', *Journal of Management Inquiry*, 10 (2): 151–164.

Case, C. and Dalley, T. (2006) *The Handbook of Art Therapy*. London: Routledge.

Cho, C.H., Phillips, J.R., Hageman, A.M. and Patten, D.M. (2009) 'Media richness, user trust and perceptions of corporate social responsibility', *Accounting, Auditing and Accountability Journal*, 22 (6): 933–952.

Clarke, J. and Holt, R. (2010) 'The mature entrepreneur: a narrative approach to entrepreneurial goals', *Journal of Management Inquiry*, 19 (1): 69–83.

Collier, J. and Collier, M. (1986) *Visual Anthropology: Photography as Research Method*. Albequerque: University of New Mexico Press.

Collier, M. (2001) 'Approaches to analysis in visual anthropology', in T. van Leeuwen and C. Jewitt (eds), *Handbook of Visual Analysis*. London: Sage, pp. 35–60.

Dale, K. and Burrell, G. (2003) 'An-aesthetics and architecture', in A. Carr and P. Hancock (eds), *Art and Aesthetics at Work*. London: Palgrave, pp. 155–173.

Dale, K. and Burrell, G. (2008) *The Spaces of Organisation and the Organisation of Space: Power, Identity and Materiality at Work*. Basingstoke: Palgrave.

Davison, J. (2009) 'Icon, iconography, iconology: visual branding, banking and the case of the bowler hat', *Accounting, Auditing and Accountability Journal*, 22 (6): 883–906.

Davison, J. and Skerratt, L. (2007) 'Words, pictures and intangibles in the corporate report'. Edinburgh: The Institute of Chartered Accountants of Scotland.

Gagliardi, P. (1990) *Symbols and Artifacts: Views of the Corporate Landscape*. Berlin and New York: de Gruyter.

Gallo, M. (2002) 'Picture this: immigrant workers use photography for communication and change', *Journal of Workplace Learning*, 14 (2): 49–57.

Gottlib-Conn, L. (2008) 'Ethics policy as audit in Canadian clinical settings', *Qualitative Research*, 8 (4): 499–514.

Guthey, E. and Jackson, B. (2005) 'CEO portraits and the authenticity paradox', *Journal of Management Studies*, 42 (5), 1057–1082.

Halford, S. (2004) 'Towards a sociology of organizational space', *Sociological Research Online*, 9 (1). Available at www.socresonline.org.uk/9/1/halford.html (last accessed 29 September 2011).

Hancock, P. (2005) 'Uncovering the semiotic in organizational aesthetics', *Organization*, 12 (1): 29–50.

Hancock, P. (2008) 'Fear and (self)loathing in Coleridge Close: management in crisis in the 1970's sitcom', *Organization*, 15 (5): 685–703.

Harper, D. (1984) 'Meaning and work: a study in photo elicitation', *International Journal of Visual Sociology*, 2 (1): 20–43.

Holliday, R. (2000) 'We've been framed: visualising methodology', *Sociological Review*, 504–521

Hutton, J., Bazalgette, J. and Reed, B. (1997) 'Organization-in-the-mind', in J. Neumann, K. Kellner and A. Dawson-Shepherd (eds), *Developing Organizational Consultancy*. London: Routledge.

Jackson, J. (2006) 'Ethnographic preparation for short-term study and residence in the target culture', *International Journal of Intercultural Relations*, 30 (1): 77–98.

Jackson, N. and Carter, P. (2000) 'An-aesthetics', in S. Linstead and H. Höpfl (eds), *The Aesthetics of Organization*. London: Sage, pp. 180–196.

Kearney, K.S. and Hyle, A.E. (2004) 'Drawing out emotions: the use of participant-produced drawings in qualitative research', *Qualitative Research*, 4 (3): 361–382.

Kivinen, N. (2006) *Entering Organizations: Essays on Image, Space and Difference*. Finland: Abo Akademi Turku.

Kress, G. and T. van Leeuwen (2006) *Reading Images: The Grammar of Visual Design*. London: Routledge.

McDonald, P. (2009) 'We just make the pictures…? How work is portrayed in children's feature length films', *Culture and Organization*, 15 (1): 21–38.

Meyer, A.D (1991) 'Visual data in organizational research', *Organization Science*, 2 (2): 218–236.

Mitchell, J. (1994) *Picture Theory*. Chicago: University of Chicago Press.

Morgan, M., McInerney, F., Rumbold, J., and Liamputtong, P. (2009) 'Drawing the experience of chronic vaginal thrush and complementary and alternative medicine', *International Journal of Social Research Methodology*, 12 (2): 127–146.

Nathan, M. and Doyle, J. (2002) *The State of the Office: The Politics and Geography of Working Space*. London: The Industrial Society.

Prosser, J. (ed.) (1998) *Image -Based Research: A Sourcebook for Qualitative Researchers*. London: Falmer Press.

Prosser, J., Clark, A. and Wiles, R. (2008) 'Visual research ethics at the crossroads', *Realities Working Paper Series No. 10*. Available at www.socialsciences.manchester.ac.uk/realities/publications/workingpapers/10-2008-11-realities-prosseretal.pdf (last accessed 23 April 2010).

Prosser, J. and Loxley, A. (2008) 'Introducing visual methods', *National Centre for Research Methods Review Paper No. 10*. Available at http://eprints.ncrm.ac.uk/420/ (last accessed 23 April 2010).

Rose, G. (2007) *Visual Methodologies*. London: Sage.

Saldana, J. (2009) *The Coding Manual for Qualitative Researchers*. London: Sage.

Scarles, C. (2010) 'Where words fail, visuals ignite: opportunities for visual auto-ethnography in tourism research', *Annals of Tourism* 37 (4): 905–926. DOI: 10.1016/j.annals.2010.02.001.

Schroeder, J. (2002) *Visual Consumption*. London: Routledge.

Scott, C. (1999) *The Spoken Image: Photography and Language*. London: Reaktion Books.

Shortt, H. (2010) 'The hair salon – constructions of space and identity'. Unpublished PhD thesis, University of Bath.

Shortt, H. and Warren, S. (2012) 'Hairdressers: visual narratives of identity in an iconic profession', *Visual Studies* (forthcoming).

Sievers, B. (2008) 'Perhaps it is the role of pictures to get in contact with the uncanny: the social photo-matrix as a method to promote understanding of the unconscious in organizations', *Organization and Social Dynamics*, 8 (2): 234–254.

Stiles, D.R. (2004) 'Pictorial representation', in C. Cassell and G. Symon (eds), *Essential Guide to Qualitative Methods in Organizational Research*. London: Sage.

Strangleman, T. (2004) 'Ways of (not) seeing work: the visual as a blind spot in WES?', *Work, Employment and Society*, 18 (1): 179–192.

Strangleman, T. (2008) 'Representations of labour: visual sociology and work', *Sociology Compass*, 2 (5): 1491–1505.

Strangleman, T. (2009) 'Negotiating organizational power: the politics of visual research', paper presented to the ESRC inVisio Seminar Series, University of Bath, October.

Van Leeuwen, T. and Jewitt, C. (eds) (2001) *Handbook of Visual Analysis*. London: Sage.

Vince, R. (1995a) 'Working with emotions in the change process: using drawings for team diagnosis and development', *Organisations and People*, 2 (1): 11–17.

Vince, R. (1995b) 'Emphasizing learning in management research', *Management Learning*, 26 (1): 55–71.

Vince, R. and Broussine, M. (1996) 'Paradox, defence and attachment: accessing and working with emotions and relations underlying organizational change', *Organization Studies*, 17 (1): 1–21.

Wang, C. and Burris, M.A. (1994) 'Empowerment through photo novella: portraits of participation', *Health Education Quarterly*, 21 (2): 171–186.

Wang, C. and Burris, M.A. (1997) 'Photovoice: concept, methodology and use for participatory needs assessment', *Health and Behaviour*, 24 (3): 369–387.

Warren, S. (2002) 'Show me how it feels to work here: using photography to research organizational aesthetics', *Ephemera: Theory and Politics in Organizations*, 2 (3): 224–245.

Warren, S. (2005a) 'Consuming work: an exploration of organizational aestheticization'. Unpublished PhD thesis, University of Portsmouth.

Warren, S. (2005b) 'Photography and voice in critical qualitative management research', *Accounting, Auditing and Accountability Journal*, 18 (6): 861–882.

Warren, S. (2006) 'Hot nesting? A visual exploration of personalised workspaces in a "hot-desk" office environment', in P. Case, S. Lilley and T. Owens (eds), *The Speed of Organization*. Copenhagen: Copenhagen Business School Press, pp. 119–146.

Warren, S. (2008) 'Empirical challenges in organizational aesthetics research: towards a sensual methodology', *Organization Studies*, 19 (4): 559–580.

Warren, S. (2009) 'Visual methods in organizational research', in A. Bryman and D. Buchanan (eds), *Handbook of Organizational Research Methods*. London: Sage, pp. 566–582.

Warren, S. and Fineman, S. (2007) 'Don't get me wrong but ... ambivalence and paradox in a "fun" work environment', in C. Rhodes and B. Westwood (eds), *Humour, Organization and Work*. London: Routledge, pp. 92–112.

Warren, S. and Parker, L. (2009) 'Beancounters or bright young things? Towards the visual study of identity construction among professional accountants', *Qualitative Research in Accounting and Management*, 6 (4): 205–223.

Williamson, J. (1978) *Decoding Advertisements: Ideology and Meaning in Advertising*. London: Boyars.

Wood, M. and Ladkin, D. (2007) 'The event's the thing: encounters with the leaderful moment', paper presented to 25th Standing Conference on Organizational Symbolism, Ljubljana, Slovenia.

Wray-Bliss, E. (2003), 'A right to respond? Monopolisation of "voice" in CMS', *Ephemera: Theory and Politics in Organizations*, 4 (2): 101–120.

Ziller, R. (1990) *Photographing the Self: Methods for Observing Personal Orientations*. Newbury Park, CA: Sage.

Zuboff, S. (1988) *In the Age of the Smart Machine: The Future of Work and Power*. New York: Basic Books.

Appendix: Example of a Brief given to Research Participants taking Photographs

Responsible photography

Taking pictures can be a personal thing – please ask any people who are the subjects of your photographs for permission to show them to us (either before or after you take the picture).

You might also need to take care not to photograph anything that invades another person's privacy or contravenes your organization's confidentiality policy (for example, the visible contents of documents or computer screens). Rest assured that we can digitally obscure any identifying features of people or the company (e.g. faces, company logos, etc.) and you will be given full opportunity to have any of the pictures we discuss deleted. In fact we will ask you for permission to use each individual picture in any articles or books resulting from the research during our 'interview' meeting, so you will be in full control at every stage.

Other than these commonsense precautions, feel free to take the camera anywhere and everywhere for a few days to help you remember to use it. We hope you will enjoy taking part in the research and look forward to seeing the pictures you take.

Once again, we'd like to thank you for agreeing to help us with this important study, if you have any questions at all about the research at any stage, please do not hesitate to contact us on XXX.

Kind regards,
Sam Warren

17 Participant Observation

Matthew J. Brannan and Teresa Oultram

Introduction

Participant observation (PO) is a specific approach to the gaining of knowledge, based upon direct contact between the researcher and the social objects of interest. The *experiential* core of PO means that, to an extent, we are all participant observers, whether consciously or otherwise, as participation is a feature of all social interaction. Thus Hammersley and Atkinson see PO not so much as a particular research technique but rather as a 'mode of being-in-the-world' (1994: 249). From this perspective, unlike many other research techniques and methods, the elementary rules of participation essentially are learned forms of human socialization. At its most basic level, PO works as a mode of inquiry through the direct experience of circumstances and events; the researcher *becomes* the research instrument. Whereas other forms of investigation will produce text, speech and numerical forms of information, PO, in the first instance, produces sensuous bodily experience, which is then encoded into other communicable forms. PO demands that the researcher consciously places him- or herself into the social milieu in which he or she is interested, thus 'getting one's hands dirty' (Hobbs and May, 1993: xviii). This *placing* is both conceptually and practically significant by determining the experience, and thus the inquiry, more generally. Social situations, or research settings, that emerge rather than those that are artificial contrivances are favoured and, in this respect, recurring social rituals such as initiation, celebration and departure are all frequently recurring motifs in PO research.

Closely related to, but not to be confused with, the practice of ethnography (see Yanow, Ybema and van Hulst, in this volume), PO is often the preferred, or chosen, technique in terms of the operationalization of ethnographic study. The distinction between the two is to be found in the way that PO invokes the act of participatory fieldwork itself, rather than a wider research process. Further, if, as is claimed, ethnography consists of two moments (Willis and Trondman, 2000: 5), then PO is often the first moment, or the moment of being, that brings the researcher into contact with the objects of research interest.

This chapter is organized as follows. First we consider variations in the application of PO, a variety of possibilities are noted, and the key themes, issues and challenges for those deploying PO are considered. The chapter in turn seeks to explore some of the problematic features and controversies that are associated with the use of participant observational techniques. In an attempt to illustrate the realities of PO in action, the chapter then presents a dialogue between the authors in the form of an interview, where the use of PO in a specific context is discussed.

Variations in Participation

PO has been deployed in a number of settings and a review of the utilization of PO reveals a range of practice. A useful framework has developed from an influential article by Raymond Gold (1958). Gold identified four idealized PO roles and provided a useful foundational classificatory framework, although some further comments and refinements are necessary here. His approach differentiated between the *degree* of participation of the researcher in the social setting and is, therefore, a researcher-centric mode of classification.

Complete participation (also sometimes known as covert PO): in effect this seeks to disguise the role of observer to the extent that the observational objectives are undisclosed to other research participants. Complete participation gives the researcher sufficient 'cover' to conduct an observation while providing an explanation (the researcher adopts a relevant group membership role) for their location in the social context. However, this is to a large extent dependant upon the maintenance of the narrative and, therefore, the role demands a degree of duplicity.

Participant as observer: this is characterized by the researcher openly adopting *both* the participant and observer roles. While the researcher fully participates in the social situation they also disclose the observational objectives to the other participants, making it known that the development and cultivation of relationships with participants is for the purposes of research. As the adoption of both participant and observer is disclosed, a key challenge for the researcher is to negotiate and establish the specific dimensions of these roles.

Observer as participant: this is characterized by a brief engagement in the research setting, where the role of the researcher is known but they may not have sufficient exposure to develop a full under-standing of the meaning and culture of the setting. The title of this category reflects the secondary role of participation and has led some to term this 'quick and dirty' (Hughes et al., 1994) or 'micro' research (Heath and Luff, 1992). In most social situations, full participation, even in elementary forms of social engagement, requires extensive learning and socialization. In the absence of full participation, research of this type is likely to be facilitated by existing full participants allowing or facilitating a partial participation.

Complete observer (disinterested spectator): while classified by Gold as a PO classification, the complete observer does not engage with other participants and therefore it can be questioned whether this style of research belongs within PO. In this mode of engagement, the researcher plays no active role in the social situation, merely observing events as they unfold. It is assumed that the observational role and intent of the observer are communicated to research participants.

Adler and Adler (1987) offer a slightly different typology, focusing on member-ship roles. This recognizes the extent to which the researcher accepts being and is accepted as a fellow member and, therefore, offers a less researcher-centric classification. Dividing Gold's 'participant as observer' into two categories:

Peripheral membership allows for a close and frequent interaction with the group, with the aim of gaining acceptance as an 'insider' by members, but without taking on a core role within the group. The observational role is seen as the primary role, with participation used as a means to gain a 'better observational point' (Adler and Adler, 1987: 48).

Active membership, in contrast, for Adler and Adler, can fit into either Gold's category of 'participant as observer' or that of 'complete participant', dependent upon whether the researcher adopts an overt or covert position.

Common to both categories, the researcher interacts with participants as a colleague focusing on the group's tasks, with the observational role taking a secondary focus. Finally, they offer a further category, which they claim, goes beyond Gold's 'complete observer' role.

Complete membership allows the researcher to immerse themselves fully in the group and shows a genuine commitment to the group and its goals. For some, this amounts to 'going native' or losing their supposed objectivity, but Adler and Adler believe that the depth of data gathered and the degree of the researcher's own subjective insight make this a valid PO approach.

While these frameworks are useful, it is clear that forms of PO have diversified, that tensions exist between the classifications, and that PO in practice might, in the course of one research project, span several classifications. Renée Fox (2004: 213), for example, claims that at the core of PO is a 'dynamic equilibrium between participation and observation – a continuous balancing and rebalancing of involvement and detachment', and this reminds us that caution is needed when reading PO classifications as ideal types; these act as guides and should not be allowed to become fixed and immutable.

Debates and Controversies in Participant Observation

Having outlined the frameworks for thinking about PO, the next section seeks to explore some of the current major points of debate and controversy in relation to the use of PO. We consider ethical practice, managing field relations and political dimensions to the PO research process.

Ethical practice: the covertness or openness of a PO research

A key decision for researchers in designing and implementing PO is the degree of disclosure they are willing or able to provide in situ. However, irrespective of circumstances and constraints, covert forms of PO, which fail to inform participants of the true intention of the researcher, have been criticized for being unethical, dishonest, failing to respect human rights and potentially putting the participants' interests at risk (Jorgensen, 1989; Hammersley and Atkinson, 1995). Bulmer (1982), for example, questions how covert techniques can be justified when the research relationship should be based on trust and honesty.

Adler and Adler (1987) point out that duplicity is potentially problematic not only for participants but also for researchers. The maintenance of multiple roles for prolonged periods while conducting their research can become confusing and overwhelming. In contrast, Berreman (2007) challenges the idea that the pretence is problematic for the researcher, arguing that social interaction often involves impression management and some form of secrecy. Similarly, Reinharz (1997) points out that we adopt many different identities during fieldwork, and the key to successful research is through reflexive writing practice (see Haynes, in this volume).

Others (Douglas, 1976; Van Maanen, 1988; Ferdinand et al., 2007) have defended the covert approach by arguing that the benefits can outweigh the potential risks. These justifications centre on the minimization of disruption to the field through non-disclosure, which is considered important for the integrity of the observations. Politically it may also be important to document participants acting without any knowledge of the researcher. According to Douglas (1970, as cited in Bulmer, 1982) the use of covert methods is necessary for 'good' research as, he believes, the social order rests on deceitfulness and secrecy and to penetrate this requires researchers, as outsiders, trying to get in by using deception. From this perspective there may be important 'public interest' issues at stake in the pursuit of covert PO and this is especially the case where PO seeks to document social activity which perpetuates division, inequality and repression.

Brewer (2000) challenges the distinction between overt and covert PO, arguing that this may instead be re-conceptualized as a continuum with varying degrees of openness within the types of PO adopted. This is especially significant given that the duration of most PO projects is likely to mean that research aims and objectives change over time. Questions may be raised over the extent of consent, even following full disclosure. It is likely, for example, that consent is given on behalf of group members by a spokesperson or gate-keeper and, although this may be expedient for the researcher, it cannot be assumed that this implicates consent for all participants. In many cases of PO, in fact, permission will not, or could not, be negotiated with every member of the group, where research sites are large or dynamic for example. A further dilemma is that the researcher often does not, or cannot, completely define all research interests to the participants (Fine, 2001; Ferdinand et al., 2007). The dynamic nature of PO implies an iterative process, refining and re-defining its interests and terms of reference. Given this, the completeness of initial disclosure, and therefore consent, is likely to be highly constrained. Hammersley and Atkinson (1995), for example, claim that, unless constantly reminded, participants will quickly forget about the research interests and are likely to make comments they may not wish to have expressed openly.

In summary, therefore, it seems that, although a commonsense consensus emerges for the necessity for PO to be grounded in clear disclosure, for a number of practical and pragmatic reasons it may be impossible for the PO researcher to comply fully with the demands of being an ethical researcher (see Holt, in this volume, for a further discussion of ethics in qualitative research).

The research relationship: understanding the meaning and logic of human cultures

The techniques of PO have arisen out of the wider humanist tradition in the social sciences that seeks to position the researcher 'close' to the research participants in spatial, economic, political, cultural and emotional terms. This proximity fosters a sensitivity to the *'lived experience'* of the social situation in an effort to gain an insight into the 'insiders' world of meaning' (Jorgensen, 1989: 8). Watson (2011), while championing PO, challenges the legitimacy to claims of revealing people's 'lived experience' (see also Jones, 2000). Instead, he claims that the focus should be on 'the connection between the actions and utterances of people in social settings with the culture, discourses, narratives, and social, economic and political structures within which those actions and utterances occur' (Watson, 2011: 213). Seen from this perspective, the focus of PO should be on 'how things work' in field settings (Watson, 2011). PO's purpose thus becomes to understand specific cultures, in particular exploring human experience and relating how participants make sense of their own social situations. PO is therefore often characterized by its sensitivity to the language used by participants as a way of apprehending this point of view. Cultures are considered to have a logic and practice, which makes sense to the participants but may, from the outside, appear illogical, unordered or random. Moreover, culture is learnt and cannot be observed directly (Clifford, 1990; Grills, 1998). PO, and more precisely the researcher's participation in a particular culture, may allow the researcher to experience the culture for him or herself and, through a process of immersion and participation, begin to experience and come to understand the logic and the meanings that lie behind social practice, as these may be tacit or difficult to communicate through verbal interaction or description alone.

Participating in the daily lives of participants allows observation and interaction, by personally experiencing and sharing the daily routines and practices of those being studied (Brewer, 2000: 59). It is through this participation that the researcher may begin to understand the meaning and logic of social practice; thus what was initially experienced as different and alien starts to become more familiar. This has led some writers to claim that PO must involve a level of sustained time commitment (see for example Adler and Adler, 1987; Bate, 1997; Watson, 2011), challenging the validity and rigour of those who have adopted a 'quick and dirty' or 'jet-plane' (Agar, 1980) approach. Nonetheless, the process of familiarization with the strange is a basic human capacity and, in essence, a process of learning. PO, therefore, might usefully be considered as both exposure to the unfamiliar and an inherent process of learning. The articulation of how learning is accomplished through participation (see Lave and Wenger, 1991) is an apt description of the essential mechanics of PO.

The pursuit of objectivity remains a central concern with, for example, calls for researchers to suspend their emotional attachment and maintain an 'objective' detachment, thereby becoming a 'professional stranger' and 'detached participant' to ensure the maintenance of a critical perspective (Malinowski, 1922). In contrast, feminist researchers often argue for a 'total immersion' of the researcher in the field (see Reinharz, 1992), accepting the emotional and subjective nature of research and pointing towards what they see as the politics of the research act. Similarly, postmodernist and poststructuralist writers tend to reject claims that PO can produce an authoritative and objective account, instead favouring a recognition of the privileged position of the researcher and the impact this has upon their always partial account. Work within this tradition draws attention to the fact that all accounts are constructions (Hertz, 1997: viii) and, as such, these reflect the, often implicit, assumptions of the researcher and the social, historical and political circumstances of their production (Agrosion et al., 2000).

The dichotomy of insider/outsider has been challenged as being too crude a polarization (Woodward, 2008). For Naples (1997: 70), for example, 'insiderness' and 'outsiderness' are permeable social locations that are experienced not just by the researcher but also by community members, and are invariably tied into social interactions.

Political nature of PO

Some authors argue that PO has an essentially political nature (Punch, 1994; Fine, 2001), reflecting the privileged position of the researcher in terms of 'doing' the research and disseminating the results (Agrosion et al., 2000). Wray-Bliss (as cited in Ferdinand et al., 2007) asserts that participant observers act within the field in ways that reflect their own personal moral views and behaviours. This opens up important questions in relation to the extent that research can ever be 'value free' and whether researchers can ever remain 'objective and impartial'. Ferdinand et al. (2007) argue that participant observers do not enter into the research field passively; instead, they do so with particular research agendas and questions that they wish to answer.

Alvesson and Deetz (2000), from a critical management perspective, go further here, suggesting researchers have an ethical responsibility to expose unjust or unethical practices observed during fieldwork. Indeed critical theorists enter the field deliberately to seek out and examine the ways in which 'powerful groups oppress and dominate those less powerful' (Rossman and Rallis, 2003) and, in doing so, aim to privilege the voices of those less powerful groups.

Tensions are inherent in the practice of PO in terms of its initial goals and objectives of study and the use to which PO research might be put. Here the historical connection that PO has to forms of anthropology and ethnography cannot be ignored. Seen from this vantage point, critical scholars have noted that the central concern of PO remains an attempt to understand 'the other' and, for a variety of reasons, this might be considered politically problematic. In particular, anthropology has long been associated with political and economic interests, in securing a 'cultural grasp of the "natives"' (Prasad, 2005: 77) in the furtherance of colonization. This debate finds a contemporary articulation in the controversy over the use of anthropological techniques, expertise and knowledge by the United States military during combat operations. McFate (2005: 25), for example, advocates such practice, claiming that 'cultural knowledge' is needed to wage the 'war on terror'. In contrast, González (2007) and Price (2007) question the ethics and academic validity of such actions.

Applying Participant Observation in Practice

In an attempt to highlight some of the challenges of implementing PO in organizational research, we now draw upon an example of the technique in use. In order to do this we use the format of an interview to offer a dialogue between the first and the second authors of this chapter. The interview draws upon the experience of a PO investigation of a call centre located in the West Midlands, United Kingdom, where the first author spent 13 months employed as a customer service representative (CSR).

TO   Would you like to give us some background as to why you chose this study?

MB   I have always been interested in work and employment issues and under-standing how work was changing, which made me want to look at call centres, as they became an increasingly important form of employment.

TO   You adopted a PO approach. Had you prior experience of this, how did you know this was the right approach to adopt?

MB   I remember reading Paul Thompson and Stephen Ackroyd's 'All Quiet on the Workplace Front' [1995]. This alerted me to the fact that you could take a very detailed single case study as a way of exploring much wider sets of social relations and that there had been a drift away from this kind of detailed empirical work and I started to explore the rich tradition of industrial sociology, including authors like James Ditton [1972; 1977], Huw Beynon [1973], Donald Roy [1958], and Michael Burawoy [1979; 1985]. Shortly after, Sue Fernie and David Metcalf [1997] famously described the call centre as an '*electronic panopticon*' where management surveillance is rendered perfect, foreclosing the possibility of resistance. This set up the basis of my research and, very quickly and clearly, the aim became to get into the call centre and empirically see for myself if the call centre made management control perfect.

TO   What were the unique features of PO and why was this the method you adopted?

MB   If I wanted to understand workplace resistance, how was it best to do it? I did consider other approaches but I was led by my research question. It seemed counter-intuitive that I would ask management's permission to talk to workers about resisting management. I therefore adopted a dual role – I disclosed my research interest but took a full role as a paid employee, as this seemed to me to be the best way to get close to the action that I wanted to explore. I didn't really think about or theorize this to a massive extent, it just became what I considered to be an effective way for me to experience the social relations of production.

TO   What were the limitations or potential dangers of your approach?

MB   One of the issues many researchers face is undertaking an extensive field-work project when you are intellectually least equipped. So, in my case, I was undertaking fieldwork with no sociological or research methods training – terrifying and exhilarating all at the same time. I was trying to be a call centre worker, while in the evenings and weekends trying to come to terms with sociological concepts and ideas at the same time as writing up my field notes.

TO   How concrete were your ideas and concepts before you started your research?

MB   I'd read quite a lot of orthodox labour process work, which was like a theoretical backpack that I took into the field with me. But this was quite limited, as I'd gone straight from a degree to a Master's degree to a PhD. I

(Continued)

(Continued)

knew I was looking for empirical examples of how workers thwart mana-gerial ambitions and control strategies and I thought I knew how I could relate this to wider sets of social relations. I also knew that this could take a variety of forms; so I'd read work about pilfering, the re-appropriation of time and more sophisticated ideas around notions of identity.

TO   What are your memories and thoughts about actually becoming an employee while still being a researcher and operating this dual role? Having to learn the job while still being a researcher, was this a difficult task?

MB   Very challenging, and this was a key research finding. Call centre work at that time was portrayed as being mundane and routine with high levels of labour turnover. In the popular press, for example, I remember call centre workers being presented as battery hens and other animals; and it was considered a job that anyone or 'anything' could do. My first couple of weeks in the call centre were almost a case of shock and awe! Total sensory bombardment, with a cacophony of noise making it really difficult to con-centrate on customers' conversations. I also found it difficult to get up to speed with the computer interface and to learn to do this while I was talking to a customer, trying to do what felt like a hundred and one things at once. So, actually, the demands of the job were incredibly high. My difficulty learn-ing the job surprised me and felt like something that needed an explanation in the context of such a negative public perception. That process of just 'becoming', what the call centre managers would refer to as a 'competent CSR', was actually very difficult, so why wasn't this job valued in society?

As a participant observer, the initial entry and shock of the working envi-ronment, having not really experienced anything like that before, the sensory feeling of 'overload' and sense of dislocation and confusion, are important in terms of understanding what it means to be a call centre worker and became important sensory data. Making the most of this data is hard, especially when you are trying to learn how to become competent at a particular job and all that this entails. In many ways it's a form of extreme ethnography, and I remember often leaving work with a thump-ing headache and just having to lie in a dark room with a flannel over my head to recover! You are very much pushed to the limits in terms of your ability to adapt and your capacity to deal with the situation.

TO   How did you start to fit into the organization and how did you develop relationships with your colleagues?

MB   Like many call centres, the call centre where I worked divided work func-tionally into teams. A team consisted of between 5 and 12 members of

(Continued)

(Continued)

staff. I went through a period of initial induction of about a month before I was assigned to a team and that became the location for the duration of the fieldwork, so I formed very close bonds with that team. It wasn't unusual, because of the nature of call centre turnover, to have new start-ers and the group was used to dealing with new employees, having a repertoire of rituals and initiations for new recruits. For example, new team members were referred to in the third person as 'the temp' rather than by name, clearly a status divide which drew attention to the 'newness' of employees and the temporary nature of their employment contracts, despite the fact that not all new employees were temporary. Also, as a rec-ognition I think that the work was quite difficult and tough, not a lot was done to ameliorate this and therefore new employees were very much *temporary* until they proved they were competent to management and also proved their mettle to other CSRs. During that time, as well as taking calls, as 'the temp' I was required to provide 'tea and toast' functions (fetching tea and toast from the canteen for other CSRs). This taught me a lot about PO because it's unlikely that, if I was conducting interviews for example, I would have been asked to make the tea and toast, but this experience gave me the sense of what it is really like to work in the call centre, and more than that, to know the value of what it means to become, or to move beyond, being 'the temp' and to have your colleagues call you by your name, because that suggests that you're actually okay at your job.

TO   So would your colleagues and managers have seen you as an employee rather than a researcher who was also employed?

MB   Very much so, that was one of the things that struck me. If you were a Foucauldian you might say that there was a dominant discourse about answering calls on time. Other identities really seemed less relevant, you're there to answer calls and, if you are not able to do that, problems arise. But if you are able to do that then you can really be whoever you want to be. It was almost like my secondary identity was as a researcher. It didn't really make sense to the rest of the team, they made fun of my role as a researcher, they saw it as a hobby, but it didn't really matter and they would identify me not as a researcher but as a colleague, someone there to answer the phone. This is also quite similar to the managerial perspective I encountered. When I spoke to the HR manager about my research she quite clearly said, 'I don't mind what you do, as long as it doesn't interfere with you taking calls'.

TO   Can you say a little bit about how you gained consent for this research?

MB   I started with a top-down approach. I first asked for permission from the HR manager and made clear what I was doing and how I might use my

(Continued)

(Continued)

observations. Soon after I joined my team the call centre manager spoke to the team leader and she was happy also, then it was left to me to frame my research how I wanted with my colleagues. During the period of the fieldwork people came and left the team and I was careful to make sure that I told everyone within the team about my research. But how do you really know when you have consent? I relied on having conversations with those I was working with and talking through what I was doing and what I wanted to achieve. I think the issue of consent is a very vexed and dynamic question for PO. I knew that my colleagues knew about my research because they frequently mocked it – so, for example, when one of the CSRs came in late to work, another colleague stood up with a clipboard and pretended to make a note saying that I should do the same. So quite clearly there was knowledge of what I was doing. On other occasions, however, what I was doing, especially in management circles, would be misinterpreted. My focus on resistance, for instance, became reframed as an interest in knowledge management or performance management. Although I tried to be clear about what I was doing, it struck me that, often, it was almost as if it didn't register, or perhaps those I was working with had different views about what I was doing or what I should be doing. Yet even within these restricted parameters there are limits to consent, thus it was impracticable to prefix every conversation (with customers for example) with a disclosure about my research, or for that matter with the other 400 employees that worked for the call centre but not within my team.

TO   What were the practicalities of doing the research? How did you manage a full-time job and conduct your research?

MB   I was quite lucky to be on a PhD programme that placed very few demands on me in terms of teaching, so I had quite a lot of liberty to work full time but initially found it difficult to make notes in situ. I ended up making notes on my workstation while at work, and that worked well because it didn't draw unwarranted attention, it wasn't unusual for people to be using the keyboard and making notes. It wasn't that I was being duplicitous but I didn't want to draw massive amounts of attention through note taking.

TO   What should PO focus on, key events or the mundane and routine?

MB   The beauty and power of PO is its ability to find the extraordinary in the ordinary, and it is going through that process of participation that helps to capture that. Paul Willis talks about the 'dialectics of surprise' and I think that is incredibly important, to try where possible to move away from preconceived ideas, like my focus on resistance, and to be driven by surprise.

(Continued)

(Continued)

> Then to try and account for the surprise by, for example, following Burawoy to find and understand events and situations as local manifestations of broader global structures and relations.

TO How did you go about leaving the field?

MB I was really unsure about when I should leave the field and I think that this was an anxiety about having sufficient material for a PhD. I didn't really feel like I had a story to tell and I felt if I hung around more I might find a better story. I always had in my mind that I would do a discrete period of time and then I would leave the field and start a process of analysis. In reality I was constantly evaluating what I came across, and being driven by surprise moves the research focus further on and makes it even more difficult to know when to leave the field.

TO Given your difficulty leaving the field, how much was this an attachment to the call centre and your role there?

MB It took me a while to become known as a competent CSR. I was very aware that I was indebted to my colleagues for helping me through the process – not that that was unusual, new CSRs were helped, although there was a kind of 'tough love' in the call centre. As a competent CSR you know that your presence, not as a researcher, but as a worker, is going to be missed. I felt a loyalty to my team to minimize the impact of my departure and that's quite apart from my anxiety over the value of the research. I also noticed that I had started to come up against what methodologists might call 'theoretical saturation', not really coming across anything new. On reflection, I feel like I misjudged the duration of my fieldwork and stayed too long, probably because I was actually enjoying it!

TO How did you make the transition from PO within the call centre back to researcher?

MB An academic post came up where I could combine my PhD and some tutorial work and this gave me a way out of the field. It seems incredible to me now that I would need an alibi, or reason, to leave the field but I felt that I did and I knew that it would be impossible to combine the PO with the academic role. So I'm lucky the post came when it did or I might still be working within the call centre! I don't recall thinking about an exit strategy before I started my fieldwork, but clearly I should have. I suspect that the portrayal of 'exit' in methodology text books, for example, is rather too straightforward and simplistic, but I think that the practicalities of PO, and certainly my experience, are far more messy and it's very difficult to know when to leave.

TO Did you use any other forms of data collection?

(Continued)

(Continued)

MB   I was really keen to conduct follow-up interviews, to test my ideas on colleagues and to see what they thought about what I found. I thought this would give me the chance to reflect on my time in the call centre and ask some pretty direct questions. I think it's a sign of the strength of the research that management was willing to let me come back to the call centre to conduct interviews and, more importantly, that people would be let off the phones to come and talk to me because that was incredibly unusual.

TO   Do you think there was a different relationship during the follow-up interviews?

MB   Looking at the text of the interviews reveals a formality in the way that my former colleagues were talking to me, which is, I think, interesting. The interviews were conducted between four and six months after I had left the field but with people that I'd worked with for a year, and yet it was like they didn't know me at all. I asked for permission to record the interviews and that became a symbol, it was remarked on and interviewees became coy about talking to me where, in contrast, they were enthusiastic and effusive during the fieldwork. In talking about resistance, for example, things that we had engaged in together became a discussion that was off limits; at least as far as a tape recorded interview was concerned. Very clearly there was a different relationship at play and this is incredible when thinking about the start of this conversation, where I said that it seemed counter-intuitive to interview on a subject like resistance where I would need managerial consent to hold the interviews. If, having spent a year with these workers, they were still coy about talking on tape – can you imagine what sort of response I would have received, what sort of dynamics would be at play if I had only conducted interviews? The strangeness and awkwardness of these interviews really told me something interesting about PO and its strengths as a research method.

TO   What would your advice be to someone who is considering PO and other techniques?

MB   PO needs to be designed in from the research question stage. I think, as researchers, we always face a set of limitations and compromises but what is crucial to PO is the sensuousness of the experience of putting yourself on the line. Feeling what it is like to be in a given situation transforms the way in which you interpret other people's actions in that same situation. But this is incredibly difficult to achieve, the maintenance of relationships, together with physical, emotional and intellectual work, all place a huge burden on the researcher. I also think it has become more difficult to conduct PO more generally; institutional pressures to publish, the impact

(Continued)

(Continued)

agenda and trends in research ethics have all moved in directions which I think makes PO more difficult. PO makes high demands and it's difficult to take a full role in any in-group and meaningfully inhabit other worlds at the same time. In the workplace, for example, the work that is done *matters* – in the call centre the amount of calls that you take, and the way that you take them, *matter.* If you are not pulling your weight this has real implications for those around you. You can very quickly find yourself having to choose between participation and observation and I certainly went through periods where I wasn't taking notes because I was solely concentrating on trying to 'cut it' on the call centre floor. But this, in itself, is a research finding that tells us something very important and dramatic about 'what it means to be a call centre worker.'

Conclusion

This chapter provides a brief introduction to the practice and theory of PO, as characterized as a process of sustained contact between the researcher and research participant. The chapter highlights the experiential core of PO as a mode of being in the world and this is illustrated with the example drawn from call centre research. The *placing* of the researcher, and the collection of data through a bodily sensuous experience, as seen in the example discussed, are a defining characteristic of the approach and present unique potentials and equally pose many problematic issues. The strength of PO is its ability to place the researcher close to the issues of interest: in the case above this was working within the call centre to gain a sense of the dynamics of employment within the organization first hand. Participation allows the exploration of domains of human experience, such as informal, emotional or cultural aspects of life, which may not be revealed through other more distant methods. Yet these strengths are also problematic features of PO, as they place significant burdens on the researcher in a broad sense and raise complex and difficult issues in relation to ethical research practice. The chapter highlights the problematic nature of conducting ethical PO, the issues that start with, rather than are resolved by, informed consent. Moreover, the management of the research relationship, especially where field relations are fostered for the purpose of research, provides an inherently political dimension to PO research. Yet despite these difficulties, and an institutional context that seems increasingly hostile to long duration PO work, the interest in and development of PO remains healthy. The depth and sophistication of understanding that PO potentially fosters are likely to ensure that this long remains the case.

Further Reading

For more details on participant observation, we suggest you read Spradley (1980), Jorgensen (1989) and DeWalt (2010), which provide comprehensive guides to conducting PO. Czarniawska (1998) offers insights into the experiences of being a PO researcher, focusing, in particular, on narrative and the identity of the researcher. More details on the case study featured in this chapter can be found in Brannan (2005a; 2005b; and 2007), Brannan and Hawkins (2007) and Brannan and Priola (2010).

References

Adler, P. and Adler, P.A. (1987) *Membership Roles in Field Research*. Newbury Park, CA: Sage.

Agar, M. (1980) *The Professional Stranger: An Informal Introduction to Ethnography*. New York: Academic Press.

Agrosion, M., Perez, A. and Mays, K. (2000) 'Rethinking observation: from method to context,' in N.K. Denzin and Y.S. Lincoln (eds), *Handbook of Qualitative Research* (2nd edn). Thousand Oaks, CA: Sage, pp. 673–702.

Alvesson, M. and Deetz, S. (2000) *Doing Critical Management Research*. London: Sage.

Bate, S.P. (1997) 'Whatever happened to organizational anthropology? A review of the field of organizational ethnography and anthropological studies', *Human Relations*, 50 (9): 1147–1174.

Becker, H. and Geer, G. (1957) 'Participant observation and interviewing: a comparison', *Human Organization*, 16 (3): 28–32.

Berreman, G. (2007) 'Behind many masks: ethnography and impression management', in A. Robben and J. Stuka (eds), *Ethnographic Fieldwork: An Anthropological Reader*. Oxford: Wiley-Blackwell, pp. 135–158.

Beynon, H. (1973) *Working For Ford*. London: Penguin.

Brannan, M.J. (2005a) 'Workplace resistance in a call centre environment', unpublished PhD thesis, University of Wolverhampton.

Brannan, M.J. (2005b) '"Once more with feeling": ethnographic reflections on the mediation of tension in a small team of call centre workers', *Gender, Work and Organization*, 12 (5): 420–439.

Brannan, M. J. (2007) 'Sexuality, gender and legitimate peripheral participation: an ethnographic study of a call centre', in J. Hughes, N. Jewson and L. Unwin (eds), *Communities of Practice: Critical Perspectives*. London: Routledge, pp. 120–130.

Brannan, M.J. and Hawkins, B. (2007) '"London calling": selection as pre-emptive strategy for cultural control', *Employee Relations*, 29 (2): 178–191.

Brannan, M.J. and Priola, V. (2010) '"Girls who do boys like they're girls'? Exploring the role of gender in the junior management of contemporary service work', *Gender, Work and Organization*. DOI: 10.1111/j.1468-0432.2009.00493.x.

Brewer, J.D. (2000) *Ethnography*. Buckingham: Open University Press.

Bulmer, M. (1982) 'Merits and demerits of covert observation', in M. Bulmer (ed.), *Social Research Ethics*. New York: Homes and Meier Publishers Inc., pp. 217–251.

Burawoy, M. (1979) *Manufacturing Consent*. London: University of Chicago Press.

Burawoy, M. (1985) *The Politics of Production: Factory Regimes under Capitalism and Socialism*. London: Verso.

Clifford, J. (1990) 'Notes on (field)notes', in R. Sanjek (ed.), *Fieldnotes: The Makings of Anthropology*. New York: Cornell University Press.

Czarniawska, B. (1998) 'A narrative approach to organization studies', *Qualitative Research Methods, Volume 43*. Thousand Oaks, CA: Sage.

DeWalt, K. (2010) *Participant Observation: A Guide for Fieldworkers*. California: Altamira Press.

Ditton, J. (1972) 'Absent at work: how to manage monotony', *New Society*, 21: 697–681.

Ditton, J. (1977) *Part-time Crime: An Ethnography of Fiddling and Pilferage*. London: Macmillan.

Douglas, J. (1976) *Investigative Social Research: Individual and Team Field Research*. Beverly Hills, CA: Sage.

Ferdinand, J., Pearson, G., Rowe, M. and Worthington, F. (2007) 'A different kind of ethics', *Ethnography*, 8 (4): 519–543.

Fernie, S. and Metcalf, D. (1997) '(Not) hanging on the telephone: payment systems in the new sweatshops', *Centre for Economic Performance, Discussion Paper No. 390*. London: London School of Economics.

Fine, G.A. (2001) 'Ten lies of ethnography: moral dilemmas of field research', in A. Bryman (ed.), *Ethnography, Volume III*. London: Sage, pp. 370–383.

Fox, R. (2004) 'Observations and reflections of a perpetual fieldworker', *The Annals of the American Academy of Political and Social Science*, 595 (1): 309–326.

Gold, R. (1958) 'Roles in sociological field observation', *Social Forces*, 36: 217–233.

González, R. (2007) 'Towards mercenary anthropology?', *Anthropology Today*, 23 (3): 14–28.

Grills, S. (1998) 'An invitation to the field: fieldwork and the pragmatist's lesson' in S. Grills (ed.), *Doing Ethnography: Fieldwork Settings*. Thousand Oaks, CA: Sage.

Hammersley, M. and Atkinson, P. (1994) 'Ethnography and participant observation', in N.K. and Y.S. Lincoln (eds), *Handbook of Qualitative Research*. Thousand Oaks, CA: Sage, pp. 88–98.

Hammersley, M. and Atkinson, P. (1995) *Ethnography: Principles in Practice*. London: Routledge.

Heath, D. and Luff, P. (1992) 'Collaboration and control: crisis management and multimedia technology in London Undergound line control rooms', *CSCW*, 1 (1): 69–94.

Hertz, R. (1997) 'Introduction: reflexivity and voice', in R. Hertz (ed.), *Reflexivity & Voice*. London: Sage, pp. vii–xviii.

Hobbs, D. and May, T. (1993) *Interpreting the Field: Accounts of Ethnography*. Oxford: Clarendon Press.

Hughes, J., King, V., Rodden, T. and Andersen, H. (1994) 'Moving out from the control room: ethnography in system design', *CSCW '94 Proceedings of the 1994 ACM Conference on Computer Supported Cooperative Work*, pp. 429–439.

Jones, T.E. (2000) 'Ethnography, belief ascription, and epistemological barriers', *Human Relations*, 53 (1): 117–152.

Jorgensen, D.L. (1989) *Participant Observation*. London: Sage.

Lave, J. and Wenger, E. (1991) *Situated Learning – Legitimate Peripheral Participation*. Cambridge: Cambridge University Press.

Malinowski, B. (1922) *Argonauts of the Western Pacific*. London: Routledge.

McFate, M. (2005) 'Anthropology and counterinsurgency: the strange story of their curious relationship', *Military Review*, March–April: 24–38.

Naples, N.A. (1997) 'A feminist revisiting of the insider/outsider debate: the "outsider phenomenon" in rural Iowa,' in R. Hertz (ed.), *Reflexivity & Voice*. London: Sage, 70–9

Prasad, P. (2005) *Crafting Qualitative Research: Working in the Postpositivist Traditions*. New York: M.E. Sharpe.

Price, D. (2007) 'Buying a piece of anthropology?', *Anthropology Today*, 23 (3): 8–13.

Punch, M. (1994) 'Politics and ethics in qualitative research,' in N.K. Denzin and Y.S. Lincoln (eds), *Handbook of Qualitative Research*. Thousand Oaks, CA: Sage, pp. 88–98.

Reinharz, S. (1992) *Feminist Methods in Social Research*. New York: Oxford University Press.

Reinharz, S. (1997) 'Who am I? The need for a variety of selves in the field', in R. Hertz (ed.), *Reflexivity & Voice*. London: Sage, pp. 3–20.

Rossman, G. and Rallis, S. (2003) *Learning in the Field: An Introduction to Qualitative Research* (2nd edn). Thousand Oaks, CA: Sage.

Roy, D. (1958) '"Banana time": job satisfaction and informal interaction', *Human Organization*, 18: 58–68.

Spradley, J. (1980) *Participant Observation*. New York: Rinehart and Wilson.

Thompson, P. and Ackroyd, S. (1995) 'All quiet on the workplace front? A critique of recent trends in British industrial sociology', *Sociology*, 29 (4): 610–633.

Van Maanen, J. (1988) *Tales of the Field*. Chicago: University of Chicago Press.

Watson, T.J. (2011) 'Ethnography, reality, and truth: the vital need for studies of "how things work"', *Journal of Management Studies*, 48 (1): 202–217.

Willis, P. and Trondman, M. (2000) 'Manifesto for ethnography', *Ethnography*, 1 (1): 5–15.

Woodward, K. (2008) 'Hanging out and hanging about: insider/outsider research in the sport of boxing', *Ethnography*, 9 (4): 536–560.

18 Autoethnography in Organizational Research: Two Tales of Two Cities

Michael Humphreys and Mark Learmonth

Introduction

In this chapter we aim to explore some of the ideas and debates that have come to surround the term 'autoethnography' in social sciences, and in organization studies more particularly. We shall do this primarily by exemplification: we offer personal stories of our experiences at two very different academic conferences – the Academy of Management Conference (AoM), New Orleans in 2004, and the Congress of Qualitative Inquiry (CQI), Urbana-Champaign in 2005. In doing so, we join an emergent practice concerned with writing about the self in the context of organizational studies (e.g. Watson, 1995; Reedy, 2003; Parker, 2004; Brewis, 2005; Humphreys, 2005; Clark/Keefe, 2006; Grey and Sinclair, 2006; Haynes, 2006; Learmonth, 2007; Ford and Harding, 2008; Karra and Phillips, 2008; Doloriert and Sambrook, 2009; Humphreys and Learmonth, 2010; Pilegaard et al., 2010).

Writing ethnographically on the self is what has recently attracted the label 'autoethnography'; a genre of work that has made significant strides as a research strategy in recent years, but not without conceptual controversies and practical difficulties – some of which we consider – prior to offering our own version of autoethnography. Our chapter, then, affirms Fine's (1994: 30–31) claim that 'intellectual questions are saturated in biography and politics and that they should be'.

Autoethnography: Analytic and Evocative?

Autoethnographic subject matter has become eclectic, to say the least. (For a review of the topics covered by autoethnographers see Holman Jones, 2005; for a review of similar work, specifically in an organizational context, see Parry and Boyle, 2009.) Nevertheless, the outcome of all autoethnographic work is that, in some way or other, 'the self and the field become one' (Coffey, 2002: 320). However, because of autoethnography's concern with the self, one of the central debates is around the possible relationship(s) between theories of the self and identity, and methods for representing the self. Indeed, the currency and intensity of the debate was illustrated by a 2006 special issue of the *Journal of Contemporary Ethnography*. This was devoted entirely to discussing the proposals of the special issue's first essay: Anderson's (2006: 392) elaboration of what he calls *analytic* autoethnography, which he offered out of a concern for 'reclaiming and refining autoethnography as part of the analytic ethnographic tradition'.

For Anderson, the currently dominant mode of autoethnography (which he refers to as *evocative* autoethnography) is problematic, in that it typically refrains from – indeed, refuses to engage with – conventional sociological analysis (even though it is often associated with scholars who are institutionally located within sociology departments). He cites the well-known work of Ellis and Bochner, who assert that 'the mode of story-telling [in autoethnography] is akin to the novel or biography and thus fractures the boundaries that normally separate social science from literature ... the narrative text [of autoethnography] refuses to abstract and explain' (Ellis and Bochner, 2000; in Anderson, 2006: 377). In part, Anderson objects to evocative autoethnography on grounds that it is modelled more upon novelistic lines than the received conventions of social science writing: as Denzin (2006: 422) puts it, evocative autoethnographers 'want to change the world by writing from the heart'. It seems to us, then, that evocative autoethnographers typically reject the inclusion of formal analysis, because they believe that to do so would compromise their autoethnographic stories' power to evoke – evocation being their key contribution.

Of course, there is an aesthetic element to this debate: which style of writing is most compelling? But Anderson's objections also have epistemological and political implications. We ourselves would temper his (2006: 378) exhortation to be 'consistent within traditional symbolic interactionist epistemological assumptions and goals', but we feel it is important, nevertheless, to retain his 'commitment to theoretical analysis'. One of the major reasons to be committed to analysis is that an insistence on stories being allowed to speak for themselves can dim the ethnographer's appreciation of the multiple ways in which their stories might 'speak'. We think that the following story, which comes right at the end of *The Ethnographic I: A Methodological Novel about Autoethnography*, is a good illustration of such dangers. It concerns the author, Ellis, talking with her partner, Art, about celebrating the near-completion of her book:

> 'I think I'm ready to buy that new car now,' I say, referring to the silver SLK-320 Mercedes sports car we've looked at and test driven several times.
>
> 'That would be wonderful,' Art says. 'What made you decide?'
>
> 'Mom's dying,' I respond. '... Mom loved new cars. It would be a tribute to her.'...
>
> Art nods. 'Why do you think she loved new cars so much?'
>
> 'They symbolized freedom and independence, adventure and escape, frivolity and treating oneself ...'
>
> 'Okay, tomorrow let's go get it,' I say. ...
>
> We toast the decision with our champagne....
>
> The talk finished for now, feelings and bodies take over. We bask in the warmth of our love for each other, and finally, the immediacy of the relational moment. (Ellis, 2004: 349)

For some, this story may well evoke the emotions surrounding the events of that occasion. However, in its (apparently unexamined) celebration of conspicuous wealth, personal freedom and traditional family values, the story also seems to us to naturalize some of the ideologies associated with the American political Right. And though attempts at formal analysis do not guarantee that our stories will lose their capacity to be read in divergent ways, we submit that had there been a concern to link this text with social theory, the author may have become more aware of its possible ideological dimensions. After all, if her story is open to the kind of political reading we have offered, the Left-leaning objectives often claimed for evocative autoethnography – which Denzin and Giardina (2005: xv) see as an important challenge to what they call 'Bush science' – risk being damaged.

On the other hand, however, an over-riding concern with analysis might risk the opposite problem – losing the evocative power of autoethnography. Denzin (2006: 419) illustrates how this could occur, with a juxtaposition of Anderson's ambitions for analytic autoethnography against a statement from Neumann, a leading proponent of the evocative tradition:

Autoethnographic texts ...

Democratize the representational sphere

of culture by locating the particular experiences of

individuals in tension with dominant expressions of

discursive power. ([Neumann] 1996, 189)

[compared with Anderson's:]

Analytic autoethnography has five key features. It is ethnographic work in which the researcher (a) is a full member in a research group or setting; (b) uses analytic reflexivity; (c) has a visible narrative presence in the written text; (c) [sic] engages in dialogue with informants beyond the self; (d) is committed to an analytical research agenda focused on improving theoretical understandings of broader social phenomena. (Anderson, 2006: 375)

Thus, while a refusal to abstract and explain may be politically dangerous, we would still seek to retain those aspects of evocative autoethnography which represent a powerful means (albeit among other means) to 'move ethnography away from the gaze of the distanced and detached observer and toward the embrace of intimate involvement, engagement, and embodied participation' (Ellis and Bochner, 2006: 433–434).

In this chapter, then, we are also attempting to produce work that is evocative, but that also has an analytic purchase and engagement with social theory. In other words, we seek to engage with a more traditional sociologically *analytic* concern: that is, analysing some of the tensions we experience between what might be seen as one's '"internal" self-identities and the "external" social-identities to which they relate' (Watson, 2008: 123). But we do so by using *evocative*, personal accounts. In this way, we are attempting to communicate what it is like to be involved, engaged and embodied participants in the academic world.

Autoethnographic Introduction

We worked together at Nottingham University Business School between 2004 and 2010, and soon discovered we had things in common – other than our broadly similar intellectual orientations. Neither of us regarded himself as an established academic – we were both late starters (receiving our PhDs aged 41 (Mark) and 52 (Mike)), and so we carry the baggage of long-term careers outside academia. And we share similar understandings of our former jobs, in the sense that we now see them as arenas in which we were often very uncomfortable with who we were. For example, Mark still recalls the time when he falsified health statistics to make them politically acceptable. Mike's discomfort was crystallized when he realized that the cost of his business-class flight to Upper Egypt (for a consultancy in technical education) cost more than the Egyptian college principal's annual salary. In other words, we were becoming the kind of people we wished we were not.

These experiences led us both to try to change career through pursuing Master's degrees. As mature students we could peer into the world and work of university academics. They appeared to deal (more or less exclusively) with what was interesting. And, what's more, these academics apparently worked without the complications of career progression; as Ruth (2008: 106) puts it, they seemed to have lives 'devoted to inquiry and education'. These, in retrospect, naive observations encouraged us to undertake PhDs and move, eventually, into academic careers – in part, with the hope of becoming 'different' people.

Nevertheless, Mark thought he could throw off his managerial suit, and Mike his consultant's briefcase to adopt identities within which they both hoped they would be much happier. Unfortunately (if, in retrospect perhaps, rather unsurprisingly) things did not quite turn out this way. It wasn't, after all, just about casting off our *jobs* – it was about remaking our *selves* within what we imagined would be a purer intellectual environment. We each still like to think of our selves as people who want to write and teach in ways that reflect our moral, political and aesthetic concerns. However, we have also become increasingly fearful that another, more disturbing self is simultaneously trying to pursue with 'skill and courage … the [career] game' (MacDonald and Kam, 2007: 641) often played in academia. The anxiety then is that this 'other' self will end up only producing what Grey and Sinclair (2006: 452) call 'routinized, professionalised "publication"', and similarly, that this other self will teach merely to get good student evaluations (Burrell, 1997).

AoM and CQI

We move now to telling tales of our duplicity. First, we shall set the scene – conferences in New Orleans (AoM) and Urbana-Champaign (CQI). The annual AoM conference is the world's biggest academic meeting in management and organization. In New Orleans there were about 6,000 delegates and while there was a relative heterogeneity to the intellectual content of the papers presented these were overwhelmingly concerned with established managerial themes. But *we* tended to notice more the activities outside the formal events of paper presentations. For example, it was striking how all the proceedings were conducted in expensive hotels; the way these were dominated (numerically at least – and probably *not* least) by men – who often wore business suits; how the drinks parties and similar events (provided free by publishers under the auspices of leading journals or by wealthy business schools) were an important part of the conference. Also, one could hardly escape noticing that an official aim of the conference was to provide a significant venue in which (especially young, immediately post-PhD) management academics were formally interviewed for jobs in US universities. All of which provoked considerable anxiety. It was not just that the business suits were a reminder of our former selves, it was also the pervasive managerial ethos of the event. So, it is unsurprising to find that Burrell has described the AoM in almost nightmare-like terms. For him it 'drips power, bureaucratic hierarchy and patriarchy … it is the modern fair in which we and our relationships are all commodified. It is a three day market in which we are all likely to be bought and sold unless we are very, very careful' (Burrell, 1993: 76).

If the AoM was a nightmare, then the CQI seemed equally dream-like, but much less frightening. For example, it was a smaller meeting, with about 600 delegates, the majority of whom were women. There was also a much greater range of lifestyle choices evident among the participants – which is to say (among other things) that no one wore a business suit. Indeed, the convenor,

Norman Denzin, always seemed to be wearing shorts and sandals. At the CQI, ordinary university classrooms (rather than plush hotels) were used to present papers; there were no publishers' parties and, as far as we were aware, no recruitment was carried out – certainly not in the overt, officially sanctioned manner that was practised at the AoM.

Each of us became fascinated by the evident contrasts between the two events and, thinking there might be something of interest to pursue, decided to start writing about these contrasts. Thus in June 2005, shortly after getting back from the CQI, we produced our first tales. Mark wrote the initial version of the tale of CQI (Urbana-Champaign) and Mike the first draft of the tale of AoM (New Orleans) from which the first tales (below) were eventually derived. From a methods point of view, it is worth making explicit that these texts of our stories were not derived from any kind of ethnographic field notes – none were taken because the significance of the events only became evident to us later on. Thus the tales were initially constructed, from memory and subsequently evolved through discussions with one another and also from presentations of proto-versions at various conferences.

First tales

For a time after the initial versions were written, these tales felt like they represented how each of us *really* thought about aspects of our own jobs. Mark's tale of Urbana-Champaign was a reminder of the utopian ideals that inspired his move into an academic career in the first place. The careerism and rather stultifying academic environment Mike constructed (and escaped from) through the New Orleans tale came to encapsulate many of his fears about the sort of academic work that is institutionally approved in business schools. Mark certainly liked himself much better when he acted in the sort of ways encouraged at the CQI. Mike also liked himself much better when he was able simply to ignore the sorts of things one is supposed to do – both at the AoM and in our faculty.

Were we working in the tradition of evocative autoethnography, we should perhaps have stopped at this point and left the stories to speak for themselves. Indeed, in his tale of academic life, Sparkes evocatively suggests that the current ways in which UK academics are judged has polarized faculty staff into 'weasels' and 'scholars' (2007: 522). For him, weasels are 'only interested in themselves and getting promotion' (2007: 531); while in contrast, his preferred

Table 18.1 First tales

Mark in Urbana-Champaign	Mike in New Orleans
I loved this conference: such a change from your average management event! The first afternoon consisted of special workshops – I went to one on performance ethnography. During the session we were split into groups and asked to prepare a performance on our first experiences of racism. We decided to start by telling one another our own particular story – a fascinating experience – especially as the group was made up of people from all over the world. For instance, someone had grown up in a black township in 1960s South Africa: what, he wondered, was his *first* experience of racism? Another group member had spent her childhood in a privileged family in the southern states of America, waited on by African-American servants: she too wondered about her first experience of racism. Needless to say, the session was more than merely interesting – it was also challenging and personally involving. And it set the tone for the rest of the conference. Many subsequent presentations, like this first session, explored the political through the personal. The focus was very much on autoethnography and performance ethnography, though with room for more conventional papers (like mine). And my most enduring memories are of the effective performances. I particularly remember the almost unbearable accounts of child prostitutes in South America; reliving a father's funeral brought me close to tears; and hearing about someone else's adolescent angst helped me to understand a surprising amount about my own current relationships as an adult. There were very few papers on my putative interest, but then that hardly mattered because of the rich experiences many of the other presentations provided. In fact, it wasn't just the content, but the atmosphere and overall feel of the conference that was refreshingly different from any management conference I'd been to. The apparent absence of people 'networking' was novel (as was the absence of publishers' drinks parties and people job hunting). Here I felt I could appreciate the people I met for who they were, in themselves – without an eye on the position they held or what they'd written.	I had been looking forward to this conference: the attraction was New Orleans and the prospect of music in the birthplace of jazz! Although I had a large group of colleagues travelling with me there were only two or three who shared my musical interests so the conversations in airports and on the plane leaned towards issues of academic life, papers, reviews and career moves. The overly academic tone of the conversation was apparent in the stretch limousine that took us from the airport to our hotel. As we set off, the driver, an African-American man in his 50s, asked in his languid southern drawl, 'You guys all been to New Orleans before?' and one of my colleagues sitting nearest to him replied, 'No we're neophytes!' The driver didn't say another word. Although the August humid heat was oppressive I was soon wandering the French Quarter, sipping cold beer in bars with incredibly eclectic juke boxes. There were buskers on the street that would have been gigging session musicians at home. There were record stores where you could lose days just browsing the shelves. We found the brilliant PBS radio station: WWOZ with its output of jazz, blues, Cajun, Zydeco and gospel music. We rode the street cars and took cab rides to the live music venues. We embraced the Satchmo Summerfest and saw Aaron Neville, Ellis Marsalis, Irving Mayfield and the New Orleans Jazz Orchestra all in one evening at the Mahalia Jackson Theater. Eating gumbo and jambalaya, we marvelled at Jason Marsalis and Kermit Ruffins on percussion and bass at the Café Brasil and we ate red beans and rice watching second-line bands competing with each other outside the Louisiana State Museum's Old U.S. Mint. Oh yes, there was also a conference to go to: 6000 delegates attending sessions in vast corporate hotels. There were suits and ties everywhere in the icy air-conditioned rooms as young scholars vied with each other for the best faculty posts. We attended our own sessions to find that we had been given a 20-minute slot alongside a strange mix of disparate papers. So the good parts of the New Orleans experience were about the place. I felt comfortable, involved and immersed in things that really interested me: music, people, culture, food and drink.

scholars produce 'insightful work [that] comes from investigations that have never been near a ... research grant application' (2007: 564). Using Sparkes's typology, these stories might suggest that we are scholars – pure and simple.

However, both of us have spent a fair proportion of the subsequent years writing conference papers and talking to other academics about these issues. The sorts of selves implicit in the above accounts are attractive, but each of us has slowly come to admit that these are not the only accounts that could be written. Frighteningly, the growing realization is that each of us has not only deceived others – but also deceived himself. After all, having both (successfully) prepared cases for promotion in the period that this chapter has been under preparation, publishing it would clearly assist us in our further ambitions. Perhaps each of us is again becoming that which he fears most – even as we write this chapter. Indeed, it is entirely possible to read this chapter – at least up to this point – as an attempt to carve out a career by ostensibly writing about *not* wanting a career.

More recently, in an acknowledgement of these anxieties – but also with an analytic concern – we have individually written rather different tales of the same conferences. In comparison, the first tales might be seen as a naively evocative representation. The following second pair of tales is offered, therefore, as a way to examine and problematize our first thoughts; in other words, we are offering the sort of problematization and analysis that we have criticized evocative autoethnography for avoiding. Our second tales illustrate that an alternative interpretation of apparent purity is equally available – a reading that has made each of us afraid for the stability of our individual identities.

Second tales

These tales have proved painful to read: surely they're neither Mike nor Mark! On the other hand, however, for both of us they were disturbingly easy to write. Seeing our reflections in the mirrors of these different tales is embarrassing, and given the anxiety they generate, they each seem to represent a self we want to conceal from others. As part of the project of self, both of us would rather think of himself – and present himself – as untainted by careerism, instrumentalism and so on. Which raises the question: why expose our selves now? Is it for self-knowledge and advancing the cause of research? Or perhaps part of the price to be paid to get something else published and on our respective *curricula vitae*? Or both motives simultaneously?

Table 18.2 Second tales

Mike in New Orleans	Mark in Urbana-Champaign
In 1999, my PhD supervisor told me that 'presenting a paper at the AoM is always a good line on your CV'. The AoM in Washington in August 2001 was my first management conference and although I was amazed by the opportunities it gave me to meet and network with 'useful' people I was scared of presenting myself on such a stage. The most beneficial meetings were with my future colleagues at Nottingham where I had just netted a faculty position to start in the November. I was so delighted by the career enhancement of the Washington experience that I'm pleased to say I wrote an influential article based on its effects (Humphreys, 2005). Once in post at Nottingham, I made sure that the AoM was an annual event. And it worked! I arrived in the 'Big Easy' as a newly promoted Associate Professor, I had several publications on the go (take a look at Humphreys and Brown, 2002a and 2002b) – now I was a 'real' academic! And I knew that my jazz interests and expertise would be very useful. I found myself at the hub of a network of musically enthusiastic academics and I was able to make some very positive connections with senior colleagues, many of whom were on the editorial boards of 'good' journals. (Indeed, it was because of this conference that I was invited on to one such editorial board.) Conversations that started with jazz morphed easily into discussions of current research and potential publication. Some of the best networking opportunities were at the various drinks receptions, and the finest of these was held in a huge room with a balcony overlooking Bourbon Street. Using the conference catalogue it was easy to construct an individual timetable to maximize my presence, seeing the 'stars' and chatting to the 'up-and-coming' about current and future projects, exchanging business cards and setting up visits, seminars and possible collaborations. The AoM is a great example of the maxim 'it's not *what* you know but *who* you know that counts'. Its 6000 delegates present the best opportunity to get access to the maximum number of the powerful and prominent, some of whom I subsequently used as referees in promotion applications.	Why bother with this conference? Well, admittedly it's an unconventional, somewhat scary thing to do (after all, attending it could have damaged my career in a business school) but the risks have paid off. I guessed – rightly – that it could help me develop a niche to make a name for myself in organization studies. After all, at the time of the 2005 conference I was writing a critique of evidence-based management (Learmonth, 2006; 2008; 2009) – and criticizing the evidence-based movement was a major theme of the conference. Also, very few people in business schools are doing autoethnography; performance ethnography and other work in that kind of tradition – things I reckon I can use to get ahead of the game in organizational analysis. And I did (see Learmonth, 2007)! The feeling at the time that this conference would be very useful in career terms turned out to be right. For example, I sent Norman Denzin, the conference convenor, my paper on evidence-based management; he liked it and used it in a high-profile way – he made it the White Paper for the 2007 conference. Attendance at the conference also highlighted some references that I probably wouldn't have seen otherwise, references that ended up in a paper I wrote for *Academy of Management Review* (Learmonth, 2006). (And, as everyone in business schools knows, if you get a paper in *AMR* then you're really cooking with gas!) The 2005 conference also gave me an opportunity to network with the small number of people from business schools who were there – two of whom turned out to be editors of a management journal. In fact, they asked me and Mike to write a short paper about the 2005 CQI (Learmonth and Humphreys, 2006). It was a new journal (i.e. it doesn't count much in the career stakes), but because it was a new journal it tried to sell itself at the 2007 CQI. So, on arrival in 2007, we noticed that our paper was in the conference pack that all delegates received. It's all about getting your name known, after all! This same networking that started in 2005 also resulted in my being invited to contribute a chapter to a book, as well as to speak at two high-profile seminars – both of which are now on my CV – naturally!

No doubt it is impossible for us to answer this question entirely satisfactorily. We are reminded of the words of Joseph Conrad: 'no man ever understands quite his own artful dodges to escape from the grim shadow of self-knowledge' (2007 [1900]: 63). Nevertheless whatever our motives, they are most likely self-serving, at least in part. As the Nobel prize-winning novelist J.M. Coetzee (who has written several successful autobiographical novels) comments about similar kinds of public confessions:

> the possibility we face is of a confession made via a process of relentless self-un-masking ... [that] might yet be [concerned with] not the truth but a self-serving fiction, because the unexamined, unexaminable principle behind it may not be a desire for the truth but a desire to *be a particular way*. (1992: 280; emphasis in original)

Indeed, Coetzee goes on to claim that confession 'is only a special form of bragging' (1992: 283) even though 'in the economy of confession ... the only appetites that constitute confessable currency, are shameful appetites' (1992: 272). Perhaps this is a rather more sophisticated version of the type of attacks autoethnography sometimes attracts: for example, that it is self-indulgence (Coffey, 1999), narcissism (Keith, 1992), an 'academic wank' (Sparkes, 2002: 212) and so on. The best we can do, then, is to hope that in the discourse between our unreliable selves that we have created in this chapter, we may start to perceive some truth (Meek, 2009) – about our academic selves and our lives more generally.

Some Final Thoughts on Writing and Publishing Autoethnography

In olden days a glimpse of stocking
Was looked on as something shocking,
But now, God knows,
Anything Goes.

Good authors too who once knew better words,
Now only use four letter words
Writing prose, Anything Goes.

(Cole Porter, 1934)

Although the range of autoethnographic work is already vast, there have yet to be established 'rules' for what counts as 'good' autoethnographic research. Currently, then, it could be argued that, as Cole Porter (almost) put it, in writing autoethnography, 'anything goes'! Thus, we are probably as far away from the sort of traditional 'scientific' organizational research (with its rules and formulae) as it is possible to be.

This has its advantages, of course, in terms of freedom of expression, creativity, saying something new, etc., etc. Indeed, the autoethnographic label is often deployed in many ethnographic contexts. While, as Anderson (2006: 377) notes, self-declared autoethnographers typically publish 'especially (although not exclusively) on topics related to emotionally wrenching experiences, such as illness, death, victimization, and divorce', there are plenty of examples of other subjects as well as forms including performance ethnography (Spry, 2001) and approaches inspired by literature and poetry, music, art and so on (Weems, 2000; Maréchal and Linstead, 2010). It is perhaps unsurprising, then, that Charmaz (2006: 397) comments: '[w]hat stands as autoethnography remains unclear and contested. This term lumps [together] interesting, boring and revealing memoirs, recollections, personal journals, stories and ethnographic accounts under the same name'. So, in doing and writing autoethnography you are free to experiment – perhaps you *should be* experimental in order to do something that is evocative and interesting. We agree with Cole Porter – anything *does* go! But autoethnographic work requires a literary kind of writing skill, in order to avoid being boring, unimaginative and unreadable. Otherwise, it could easily become a self-serving exercise – what the editor of *Sociological Quarterly* referred to as 'Sociology's narcissistic turn' (Ellis, 2004: 263).

But, practically speaking, how do you start? As autoethnography is about your own lived experience, you do need to have lived and had some experiences! Of course, you wouldn't expect us to tell you how to have had experiences, but don't forget – autoethnography can be about the mundane as well as the extraordinary! However you also have to recall your lived experiences. In this regard, diaries and other forms of records (email threads, files on previous papers, old CVs, as well as more personal stuff – letters, photographs, scrapbooks, etc.) are all invaluable sources for your stories – as are your own imagination and your ability to make sense through theoretical lenses.

Don't forget, though, that the key to (any kind of) writing is reading. And we don't just mean reading other autoethnographies – novels, poetry and other forms of creative writing (such as songs, plays and films) will stimulate your imagination, illustrate different ways to tell a good story and provide examples of literary forms and possible frameworks for your own work. There is no 'blue-print' for ethnography (fortunately). But it does mean that in order to write a tale that other people will find interesting you will need to have a wide awareness of the almost infinite variety of ways in which stories can be told successfully.

And that reminds us of another point – we don't think autoethnographies are something that can be knocked off over night. For us, the tales in this chapter have taken years to appear in a form that we are happy with. In other words, we're not just recommending lots of reading we're also recommending lots of writing! The stories we tell in this chapter, for example, have undergone a number of iterations over a period of several years. Versions of our stories have been presented and published in other forms (Humphreys and Learmonth, 2010; Learmonth and Humphreys, 2011), albeit after lots of conference papers and frustrations with reviewers and editors rejecting our work. The point is that these multiple iterations have been valuable: they have helped to improve and refine our writing and the way we reflect on our own life and experiences. Although rejection is never easy to take in the end it is worth it! In other words, autoethnography is not an easy option – just writing down your thoughts may be the start, but will be most unlikely to interest anyone (other than your mum). The story needs to be told well, has to have a (theoretical/analytical) point, and you will need to be persistent.

If writing can be fun, publishing may be a different story because of the restricted range of publication possibilities in management and organization studies. It also seems that autoethnography may be (at the moment) a rather risky route to a PhD because of the lack of established evaluative criteria.[1] Currently, it is rare for the 'big' US management journals to publish anything calling itself autoethnography (though see Pilegaard et al., 2010 in *Academy of Management Perspectives,* and Karra and Phillips, 2008 in *Organizational Research Methods* for exceptions). In our own experience, one of us submitted a paper to *Academy of Management Learning & Education* that originally had autoethnog-raphy in the title (Learmonth, 2007). Although it was eventually published, the term 'autoethnography' did not survive the reviewing process! At the moment, however, sympathetic homes for management autoethnography include *Qualitative Research in Organization and Management: An International Journal*

---

[1]That said, according to Kazmi (2010: 21), '[t]he Proquest PhD dissertation index suggests that in the last 10 years ... 206 scholars have used personalised accounts for the purposes of their PhD. Among these, over 20 ... researched management issues'.

(e.g. Doloriet and Sambrook, 2009) and *Culture and Organization* (which recently published a special edition on autoethnography; Boyle and Parry, 2007). Others that we know have published autoethnography include *Organization* (e.g. Keenoy and Seijo, 2010); *Management Learning* (e.g. Bell and King, 2010); *Critical Perspectives on Accounting* (e.g. Haynes, 2006) or *Journal of Business Ethics* (e.g. Boje and Tyler, 2009). However, if you are interested in publishing outside management and organization journals, the prospects are probably better. These prospects are discussed in Ellis (2004: 261–264), where she includes a list of potential journals and book publishers that have accepted autoethnographic work.

Our recommendation for publishing autoethnography, then, is that sometimes you might need to be cunning! For example, do you have to call what you are doing 'autoethnography'? Terms such as insider accounts, personal case studies, personal ethnography, autobiographical vignettes etc., may not be as offensive to certain editors and reviewers! But we think that management studies is crying out for a definitive and authoritative article on the value of autoethnography to academics and practitioners – published in a journal of high international repute. Perhaps we'll give it a go sometime!

Further Reading

For further reading we recommend the whole of the 2006 special issue on autoethnography in *Journal of Contemporary Ethnography* because it is a critical introduction to the genre. But, for us, reading material that is 'different' sometimes works to fire our imagination in new ways. For example, Mike is a jazz fan and used David Sudnow's *Ways of the Hand* (Sudnow, 1978) to develop some of his ideas – as well as being immersed in biographies of the jazz greats such as *Bird Lives!* (Russell, 1973), *Bird's Diary* (Vail, 1996) or *Hard Bop Academy* (Goldsher, 2002). The point is to bring an informed passion and enthusiasm to your writing.

References

Academy of Management (AoM) (2004) *Creating Actionable Knowledge*, Conference Program.
Anderson, L. (2006) 'Analytic autoethnography', *Journal of Contemporary Ethnography*, 35 (4): 373–395.

Bell, E. and King, D. (2010) 'The elephant in the room: critical management studies conferences as a site of body pedagogics', *Management Learning*, 41 (4): 429–442.

Boje, D. and Tyler, J.A. (2009) 'Story and narrative noticing: workaholism autoethnographies', *Journal of Business Ethics*, 84: 173–194.

Boyle M. and Parry, K. (2007) 'Telling the whole story: the case for organizational autoethnography', *Culture and Organization*, 13 (3): 185–190.

Brewis, J. (2005) 'Signing my life away? Researching sex and organization', *Organization*, 12 (4): 493–510.

Burrell, G. (1993) 'Eco and the Bunnymen', in J. Hassard and M. Parker (eds), *Postmodernism and Organizations*. London: Sage, pp. 71–82.

Burrell, G. (1997) *Pandemonium: Towards a Retro-Organization Theory*. London: Sage.

Charmaz, K. (2006) 'The power of names', *Journal of Contemporary Ethnography*, 35 (4): 396–399.

Clark/Keefe, K. (2006) 'Degrees of separation: an ourstory about working-class and poverty-class academic identity', *Qualitative Inquiry*, 12 (6): 1180–1197.

Coetzee, J.M. (1992) 'Confession and double thoughts: Tolstoy, Rousseau, Dostoevsky', in D. Attwell (ed.), *Doubling the Point: Essays and Interviews*. Cambridge, MA: Harvard University Press, pp. 251–293.

Coffey, A. (1999) *The Ethnographic Self: Fieldwork and the Representation of Identity*. London: Sage.

Coffey, A. (2002) 'Ethnography and self: reflections and representations', in T. May (ed.), *Qualitative Research in Action*. London: Sage, pp. 313–331.

Conrad, J. (2007 [1900]) *Lord Jim: A Tale*. London: Penguin.

Denzin, N.K. (2005) *First International Congress of Qualitative Inquiry: Official Programme*, Urbana-Champaign.

Denzin, N.K. (2006) 'Analytic autoethnography or déjà vu all over again', *Journal of Contemporary Ethnography*, 35 (4): 419–428.

Denzin, N.K and Giardina, M.D. (2005) 'Introduction: qualitative inquiry and the conservative challenge', in N.K. Denzin and M.D. Giardina (eds), *Qualitative Inquiry and the Conservative Challenge*. Walnut Creek, CA: Left Coast Press, pp. ix–xxxi.

Doloriert, C. and Sambrook, S. (2009) 'Ethical confessions of the "I" of autoethnography: the student's dilemma', *Qualitative Research in Organization and Management: An International Journal*, 4 (1): 27–45.

Ellis, C.S. (2004) *The Ethnographic I: A Methodological Novel about Autoethnography*. Walnut Creek, CA: Altamira Press.

Ellis, C.S. and Bochner, A.P. (2006) 'Analyzing analytic autoethnography', *Journal of Contemporary Ethnography*, 35 (4): 429–449.

Fine, M. (1994) 'Dis-stance and other stances: negotiations of power inside feminist research', in A. Gitlin (ed.), *Power and Method: Political Activism and Educational Research*. New York: Routledge, pp. 13–35.

Ford, J. and Harding, N. (2008) 'Fear and loathing in Harrogate or a study of a conference', *Organization*, 15 (2): 233–250.

Goldsher, A. (2002) *Hard Bop Academy: The Sidemen of Art Blakey and the Jazz Messengers*. Milwaukee: Hal Leonard Corp.

Grey, C. and Sinclair, A. (2006) 'Writing differently', *Organization*, 13: 443–453.

Haynes, K. (2006) 'Linking narrative and identity construction: using autobiography in accounting research', *Critical Perspectives on Accounting*, 17: 399–418.

Holman Jones, S. (2005) 'Autoethnography: making the personal political', in N.K. Denzin and Y.S. Lincoln (eds), *The Sage Handbook of Qualitative Research* (3rd edn). Thousand Oaks, CA: Sage, pp. 763–791.

Humphreys, M. (2005) 'Getting personal: reflexivity and autoethnographic vignettes', *Qualitative Inquiry*, 11: 840–860.

Humphreys, M. and Brown, A.D. (2002a) 'Dress and identity: a Turkish case study', *Journal of Management Studies*, 39 (7): 927–952.

Humphreys, M. and Brown, A.D. (2002b) 'Narratives of organizational identity and identification: a case study of hegemony and resistance', *Organization Studies*, 23: 421–447.

Humphreys M. and Learmonth, M. (2010) 'Public sector management? But we're academics, we don't do that sort of thing!', in G. Currie, J. Ford, N. Harding and M. Learmonth (eds), *Making Public Services Management Critical*. New York: Routledge, pp. 55–67.

Karra, N. and Phillips, N. (2008) 'Researching 'back home": international management research as autoethnography', *Organizational Research Methods*, 11 (3): 541–561.

Kazmi, B.A. (2010) 'Universalizing human rights in transnational business networks: a personal account of the making of the Atlanta Agreement and its moral logics'. Unpublished PhD thesis: University of Nottingham.

Keenoy, T. and Seijo, G. (2010) 'Re-imagining e-mail: academics in *The Castle*', *Organization*, 17 (2): 177–198.

Keith, M. (1992) 'Angry writing: (re)presenting the unethical world of the ethnographer', *Environment and Planning D: Society and Space*, 10: 551–568.

Learmonth, M. (2006) 'Is there such a thing as "evidence-based management"? A commentary on Rousseau's 2005 presidential address', *Academy of Management Review*, 31 (4): 1089–1091.

Learmonth, M. (2007) 'Critical management education in action: personal tales of management unlearning', *Academy of Management Learning & Education*, 6 (1): 109–113.

Learmonth, M. (2008) 'Evidence-based management: a backlash against pluralism in organizational studies?', *Organization*, 15 (2): 283–291.

Learmonth, M. (2009) 'Rhetoric and evidence: the case of evidence-based management', in D. Buchanan, and A. Bryman, (eds), *Handbook of Organizational Research Methods*. London: Sage, pp. 93–109.

Learmonth, M. and Humphreys, M. (2006) 'The 2nd International Congress of Qualitative Inquiry: reflections on the value for organization and management scholars', *Qualitative Research in Organization and Management*, 1 (2): 135–137.

Learmonth, M. and Humphreys, M. (2011) 'Autoethnography and academic identity: glimpsing business school doppelgangers', *Organization*, forthcoming.

MacDonald, S. and Kam, J. (2007) 'Ring a Ring o' Roses: quality journals and gamesmanship in management studies', *Journal of Management Studies*, 44: 640–655.

Maréchal, G. and Linstead, S. (2010) 'Metropoems: poetic method and ethnographic experience' *Qualitative Inquiry*, 16 (1): 66–77.

Meek, J. (2009). 'The many faces of J.M. Cotzee', *Guardian Review*, 5 September: 2–4.

Murgia, A. and Poggio, B. (2009) 'Challenging hegemonic masculinities: men's stories on gender culture in organizations', *Organization*, 16 (3): 407–423.

Neuman, M. (1996) 'Collecting ourselves at the end of the century', in C. Ellis and A. Bochner (eds), *Composing Ethnography: Alternative Forms of Qualitative Writing*. London: Alta Mira Press.

Parker, M. (2004) 'Becoming a manager: or, the werewolf looks anxiously in the mirror, checking for unusual facial hair', *Management Learning*, 35 (1): 45–59.

Parry, K. and Boyle, M. (2009) 'Organizational autoethnography', in D.A. Buchanan and A. Bryman (eds), *The Sage Handbook of Organizational Research Methods*. London: Sage, pp. 690–702.

Pilegaard, M., Moroz, P.W. and Neergaard, H. (2010) 'An auto-ethnographic perspective on academic entrepreneurship: implications for research in the social sciences and humanities', *Academy of Management Perspectives*, 24 (1): 46–61.

Reedy, P. (2003) 'Together we stand? An investigation into the concept of solidarity in management education', *Management Learning*, 34 (1): 91–109.

Russell, R. (1973) *Bird Lives!* London: Quartet Books.

Ruth, D. (2008) 'Being an academic: authorship, authenticity and authority', *London Review of Education*, 6 (2): 99–109.

Sparkes, A. C. (2002) 'Autoethnography: self-indulgence or something more?', in A.P. Bochner and C. Ellis (eds), *Ethnographically Speaking: Autoethnography, Literature and Aesthetic*. Walnut Creek, CA: Altamira Press, pp. 209–232.

Sparkes, A.C. (2007) 'Embodiment, academics, and the audit culture: a story seeking consideration', *Qualitative Research*, 7 (4): 521–550.

Spry, T. (2001) 'Performing autoethnography: an embodied methodological praxis', *Qualitative Inquiry*, 7 (6): 706–732.

Sudnow, D. (1978) *Ways of the Hand: The Organization of Improvised Conduct*. London: Routledge.

Vail, K. (1996) *Bird's Diary: The Life of Charlie Parker 1945–1955.* Chessington: Castle Communications.

Watson T.J. (1995) 'Rhetoric, discourse and argument in organizational sense making: a reflexive tale', *Organization Studies*, 16 (5): 805–821.

Watson, T.J. (2008) 'Managing identity: identity work, personal predicaments and structural circumstances', *Organization*, 15 (1): 121–143.

Weems, M. (2000) 'Windows', *Qualitative Inquiry*, 6 (1): 152–163.

Practising Organizational Ethnography

Dvora Yanow, Sierk Ybema, and Merlijn van Hulst

On Ethnography and Organizational Ethnography: An Overview

'Ethnography' is typically used to mean three things. Its literal meaning, from the Greek, refers to a particular kind of writing: a written account (*graphein*) of a people (*ethnos*). This meaning has been eclipsed by two others, especially as ethnography has been taken up in some disciplines outside of anthropology. Its second and more common usage refers to a set of methods or a research strategy, also called field research or fieldwork: some combination of observation, with whatever degree of participation (see Brannan and Oultram, in this volume); talking to people (often called 'interviewing' when the formalities of setting up appointments are involved; see Alvesson and Ashcraft, in this volume); and the study of material artefacts, to understand their meanings for situational actors. In organizational settings, material artefacts will typically include research question-relevant texts (e.g. annual reports, correspondence, internal memos, cartoons/jokes/photos on office doors and bulletin boards, webpages, etc.; see Lee, in this volume). In a third sense of the term, methodologists are increasingly pointing to ethnography's distinctive 'sensibility': an orientation towards the social world – actors, (inter-)actions, settings – and the material objects in it, which focuses on the centrality of meaning and meaning-making to research practices (see also Pader, 2006).

In our view, ethnography entails all three of these: a research process involving *fieldwork methods* engaging the extraordinary-in-the-ordinary with a particular sensibility towards often more hidden or concealed meaning-making processes, reported in *a particular form of writing* that places both author and reader at the scene, in the thick of things, through actor-centred and context-sensitive analysis and theorizing grounded in layered data (Ybema et al., 2009, Chapter 1). As its purpose is to give readers a sense of what 'life' is like in the setting under study, ethnography commonly rests on an in-dwelling in that place, typically in a situation-specific role. This usually requires prolonged observation over time (and perhaps over different spatial locations; discussed below). Such in-dwelling requires ethnographers to be *there*, in the setting, long enough to be able to understand the common sense, everyday, unwritten and unspoken, tacitly known 'rules of engagement' used by situational 'natives', moving from being more of a stranger to that setting to being more of a 'familiar' in and with it (while rendering it 'strange' again in the writing). Much as 'being there' in everyday life involves engaging with those one encounters (family members, co-workers, bus drivers, shopkeepers, etc.), ethnography itself is more than a set of interviews, entailing a degree of 'living with and living like those who are studied' (Van Maanen, 1988: 2). Ethnographic fieldwork can be done in a variety of ways and with differing intensities (we therefore see little use in specifying a minimal field period), but it typically involves more than flying in and out of the field for a brief, tourist-like visit. Hence, we would join with Bate (1997) in decrying the use of 'airplane' (quick, short-duration) ethnography, whether by consultants or by academics (see also Brannan and Oultram, in this volume). Ethnographic 'being there' becomes a characteristic not only of the field research but also of the writing as well: layered descriptions of objects, events, actors and inter-actions help to create a non-fictional (albeit necessarily fabricated) account of organizational life, which places both author and reader at the scene.

Methodologically speaking, ethnographic research can be informed by either realist-objectivist or constructivist-interpretivist approaches (see Duberley, Johnson and Cassell, in this volume). Ethnographers can seek to discover 'how things are really done' or 'what really happened' in a particular organizational situation, in an ontologically realist fashion, seeing themselves as objective observers and sensemakers. Or they can proceed from the perspective that social realities are intersubjectively constructed, seeing themselves as co-constructors and co-interpreters of the meaning(s) of organizational events along with situational members, reflecting on their own roles in shaping those interpretations.

Lastly, although ethnography is thought by many to have originated in anthropology, an historical account of its academic origins shows that they lie in administrative practices, specifically in empires' need to manage far-flung and distant outposts. Hence, it might be 'better to regard academic anthropology as a specific instance of ethnographic practice than the other way around' (Salemink, 2003: 9). Those organizational ethnographers not trained in anthropology departments who are anxious about their methods training manqué and bona fides can, then, relinquish these concerns and get to work on developing and articulating what *organizational* ethnography is or should be, drawing on a rich heritage of organizational ethnographic research, ranging from government bureaucracies to schools, from hospitals to coal mines.

In what follows we discuss the uses of ethnography in organizational research, after which we present three examples of ethnographic research to illustrate the particular problematics of organizational ethnography. These examples inform our subsequent discussion of the multi-sited, reflexive and relational character of ethnographic research.

Uses in Organizational Research: Historical to the Present

Organizational ethnography enjoys a long heritage, across a wide range of organizational types and disciplinary homes. Elton Mayo's 1920s–1930s Hawthorne studies are a case in point (e.g. Mayo, 1933), as are the classic, late 1940s to early 1960s in-depth analyses of the 'informal organization', such as Whyte (1948), Selznick (1949), Gouldner (1954), Blau (1955), Dalton (1959), Goffman (1959), Kaufman (1960), Roy (1960) and Crozier (1964). These detailed accounts of organizational life based on field research communicate the sense of 'being there' amid the social aspects of organizations, their backstage politics, power games and other unintended, non-rational and at times dysfunctional consequences. These studies, as organizational ethnography *avant la lettre*, upended the purportedly 'rational' organizing that Max Weber's ideal type bureaucracy theories, depicting formal organizations as efficiently functioning machines, had led researchers to expect.

The development from the 1950s onwards of mainframe computers, survey research, statistical science and behaviouralist theories eclipsed ethnographic approaches, as research aiming to measure organizational structures, contingencies and behaviours by quantitative means came to dominate organizational studies. Towards the end of the 1970s, a growing unease with such quantification and the concomitant neglect of social actors' everyday practices, lived experiences and processes of meaning-making generated a renewed interest in qualitative methods. Theoretical developments across the social sciences, among them the interpretive and linguistic turns (e.g., Geertz, 1973; Rabinow and Sullivan, 1979/1985), also drove these methodological changes. Notable among the theorists leading this 'methodological renewal' in organizational studies is John Van Maanen (e.g. 1979; 1988; 1995), whose empirical and methodological work both demonstrated and theorized the place of *organizational* ethnography.

First manifested in studies of organizational symbolism and culture, the renewed attention to ethnography also invigorated older fields of study, from strategy to leadership, organizational design and change to workplace practices, cross-cultural communication to ethics and normative behaviour (see, e.g. Barley, 1983; Dubinskas, 1988; Kondo, 1990; Collinson, 1992; Ingersoll and Adams, 1992; Watson, 1994; Orr, 1996; Yanow, 1996; Delbridge, 1998; Rosen, 2000). Ethnographic (and other qualitative) research strategies have increasingly been coming back into organizational studies, in various theoretical contexts (see, e.g. Morey and Luthans, 1987; Schwartzman, 1993; Bate, 1997; and more recently, Prasad and Prasad, 2002; Neyland, 2008; Fine et al., 2009; Ybema et al., 2009). Ethnographies of public sector organizations are also returning, joining the earlier bureaucracy and public administration work of Blau, Crozier, Kaufman and Selznick cited above (e.g. Stein, 2004; Dubois, 2010), along with others in educational studies, healthcare studies and other fields.

The intertwining of ethnographic methods with a growing interpretive methodological awareness might be seen as having moved the study of particular organizational studies topics toward more 'collective', meaning-focused perspectives, among them organizational culture, identity formation and organizational learning (e.g. Kunda, 1992; Cook and Yanow, 2006 [1993] ; Nicolini et al., 2003; Brown and Humphreys, 2006), arenas erstwhile dominated by more positivist psychological and social-psychological approaches. From there, it was not a big leap to narrative or discursive approaches (e.g. Ybema, 2010) or to the practice studies (e.g. Orr, 1996; Miettinen et al., 2009) that join activity theory and actor-network theory, both drawing on ethnographic methods. Apart from its ability to depict the liveliness of organizational life, organizational ethnography promises to elucidate two aspects for which other methods, such as surveys, are less suitable: (1) its 'hidden' dimensions, and (2) its actor-context relations.

Sensitivity to hidden dimensions of organizational life

In drawing close to subjects and situations, organizational ethnographers can potentially make explicit often overlooked, tacitly known and/or concealed dimensions of meaning-making, among them emotional and political aspects. In noting the relative power of organizational actors, their interests and their strategies, ethnographies can have a direct, critical, even shocking quality, laying bare otherwise hidden and even harsh social realities and exposing the entanglements of culture with power. For organizational members, such explicit descriptions of routine, taken-for-granted ways of thinking and acting can be both familiar and surprising as they see themselves through the ethnographer's eyes. In revealing these aspects of organizational life, such ethnographies may at times challenge what organizational actors would like to hear or read about themselves and their organizations. While offering a much needed critical voice, such ethnographies also, however, require ethnographers to consider their own position, their positionality (discussed below) and the ethical implications of their work.

Sensitivity to the interplay between actors and context

Secondly, organizational ethnography can contribute to current structure-agency debates in the social sciences that continue to carve up organizational studies (Reed, 2006), as it combines an orientation towards subjective experience and individual agency with a sensitivity to the broader social settings and the historical and institutional dynamics in which these are embedded. Alternating close-ups of actors, situations and interactions with broader views that sketch wider social and historical contexts, power relations and meta-discourses, ethnography 'sees the world in a grain of sand' (slightly paraphrasing William Blake), exploring and exemplifying the general through the local and the particular. The combination of contextual analysis with an actor-centred approach promises to remedy the 'ahistorical, acontextual and aprocessual' qualities of much of organizational studies (Pettigrew, quoted in Bate, 1997: 1155).

Ethnography's research techniques take on a particular form in meeting the specific demands of management and other organizational settings. For one, researchers cannot count on walking in on an executive unannounced, and so ethnographic 'talk' often includes formal interviews. Mintzberg's (1970) 'structured observation', an alternative to the diary studies used at the time, added direct observation to the study of managers. Wolcott's (2003 [1973]) 'shadowing' (of a school principal) is yet another way to observe organizational leaders ethnographically.

The variety of ethnographic studies of organizations and organizing is reflected in our own fieldwork. We draw on three examples, conducted in different periods and in different contexts, to illustrate the attributes of organizational ethnography discussed above, its range and its sensitivity to the hidden dimensions of organizational life as well as to the interplay between contexts and actors. These studies also lay the empirical groundwork for our subsequent discussion of three current issues relevant to organizational ethnography: (1) multi-sited research in which fieldworkers follow actions, actors and artefacts; (2) highly reflexive research with respect to knowledge claims; and (3) highly relational research that treats participants as co-researchers.

Three Examples

Collective identity formation among newspaper editors (Sierk Ybema)

The very first day of my 1997 and 1998 fieldwork in the editorial rooms of two Dutch national newspapers started with the daily meeting of *Trouw*'s editorial staff at the end of the morning (Ybema, 2003). Later, I learned that these meetings usually took less than 30 minutes and were frequented by no more than 10 editors. This time, however, the room was stuffed, all 25 seats taken, at least another 25 editors sitting on tables on the sides or leaning against the walls. A prolonged debate ensued about a front-page article in that morning's newspaper that had outraged a large number of editors. If I was truly interested in identity I had found my bread buttered on both sides, the editors assured me afterwards. Following these discussions gave me a beeline right into the middle of the newspaper's internal debates about its identity and thus into the more or less concealed power- and emotion-ridden dimensions of meaning-making. Detailed descriptions of ritual gatherings in organizational settings, such as Christmas celebrations (Rosen, 2000) or informational meetings (Alvesson, 1996; see also Schwartzman, 1993), were in the back of my mind when I decided to focus my research on the heated discussion in this editorial meeting and, subsequently, to follow the forming of opinion on that day's opening article in conversations, on the intranet and in formal and informal get-togethers.

Processes of de-ideologization in Dutch society, along with the professionalization of journalism, from the 1960s onwards and the slow but gradual decrease of newspaper readership in the 1990s had created a problem of identity and image for those newspapers that had drawn inspiration from their religious or political roots. This ideological and 'reputational' crisis challenged editors of the originally Protestant newspaper *Trouw* and the politically left-wing *de Volkskrant* to rethink their overall direction, refashion the papers' profiles and thereby fundamentally reconsider the organizational identity of each. I was interested in this intense process of renewed meaning-making, asking how that collective identity came to be represented in the everyday discourse of newspaper editors now that these institutions had been cut loose from their ideological moorings.

Throughout the research I 'followed' particular issues, events, persons and texts. Shadowing the Day Chief and, subsequently, the Night Chief in the early weeks of my fieldwork, for instance, provided an excellent, 16-hour-long introduction to the editorial process and the time-pressures, groups of professionals and content demands it involved. Identity discourse was commonly present in everyday discussions about actual practices and newspaper contents, and I closely followed debates about particular identity-sensitive (and heavily discussed) issues, such as that front-page article at *Trouw* or the journalistic 'profile' of the new weekly *Volkskrant-magazine.* Using the discursive interactions over these issues as *tableaux vivant* in my writing and treating them as a 'total social fact' (Mauss, 1990 [1925]) – a comprehensive social event that opens up windows on a range of related micro-events and broader contingencies – allowed me to trace the different threads – professional, political, ideological, commercial – of the process of identity formation knotted together in these issues or incidents. Following issues, events, persons and texts on the move allowed me in my research narrative to provide a view of 'the inside' or, more accurately, the multiple insides of identity formation processes, while simultaneously sketching the wider contexts in which these 'insides' were embedded (the second aspect of organizational ethnography described above). In Sergio Leone filmic fashion, I alternated 'extreme close-ups' that 'zoomed in' on persons-in-(inter)action, with their detailed facial expressions, gestures, talk and intonation, with 'wide-angle' or 'long shots' that 'zoomed out' and showed panoramic views of institutional contexts, historical backgrounds, power relations and societal discourses (see also Nicolini, 2009).

Influenced by the 'linguistic turn' in the social sciences and organizational studies' growing interest in identity issues, I adopted a discourse analytical approach (see also Oswick, in this volume). Having read literature that theorizes social, ethnic and organizational identities in terms of continuity, distinctiveness and cohesion, including describing organizational members' firm positioning of a shared and stable collective self vis-à-vis competitors or clients, I was surprised to notice that editors did not try to restore or shore up their precarious, non-cohesive, collective selves. Instead, they claimed that neither the ideological content of their newspaper nor the symbolic boundaries between different newspapers could define their collective identity in a clear, unifying, historically consistent way. Rather than impress an outside world of competitors, readers or the general public by making self-praising comparisons with 'others' (as is usually described in the identity literature), the editors emphasized historical discontinuities, the increasing *in*distinctiveness of the newspaper vis-à-vis its competitors and the looming danger of losing the competition to those 'others'. A condensed explanation for why the editors engaged in this unexpected rhetoric rests on their felt need to stress the drama of the situation, to express their hopes and fears and to sell a change process or to resist it (Ybema, 2010).

Sensemaking in local government (Merlijn van Hulst)

Between the end of 2003 and the beginning of 2006, I conducted ethnographic fieldwork in two Dutch municipalities (van Hulst, 2008a). I had no formal position in the local governments under study, but my research role and work were supported by the administrators and announced in a letter to municipal employees and council members. Each municipality provided a desk and access to almost all meetings and archives. After a while I began to sit in on the weekly meetings of each board of aldermen with their respective mayors. This gave me, on the one hand, an overview of things happening in each place and, on the other, a sort of fieldwork rhythm. In each municipality I decided to zoom in on two political and administrative processes that people I spoke to regarded as highly relevant to that municipality.

Although the fieldwork was hosted by formal organizations, the local bureaucracies of the two towns, my focus on sensemaking processes took me beyond the boundaries of these organizations. I observed meetings of the municipalities' management teams, most of the town council meetings and many meetings of the various council committees. In addition to those taking place within the town halls, I became interested in presentations of plans to members of the public outside of them. I also visited the meetings of political parties, sounding boards and a neighbourhood committee to find out how different groups and individuals made their own interpretations of events.

Being in the field opened doors to all kinds of data and data sources that would otherwise have been hard to access. These included meetings that were closed to the general public, informal documents, such as leaflets or handwritten speeches, and unplanned casual conversations at the photocopy machine. In both municipalities I obtained copies of a large number and variety of documents: agendas and minutes of meetings, policy documents, politicians' speeches, local and regional newspaper articles, texts on municipality webpages, materials on political parties' websites, political pamphlets and political programmes. In addition, I had many conversations with actors involved in or knowledgeable about the issues under study. The character, duration, time and location of these conversations differed. Most typical were the short chats in the hallways of the town halls before or after meetings and during breaks, longer conversations during lunches and dinners, and formal, open-ended interviews in offices and at people's homes. Requiring many hours in the field, ethnographic fieldwork places demands on the researcher's social and improvisational skills. Overall, ethnographic fieldwork offered the possibility of personally experiencing the events taking place and processes unfolding (see also van Hulst, 2008b), and observation made it possible to generate data that would have been impossible to find in documents and hard to gather through interviewing alone.

On a theoretical level, the fieldwork enabled me to move from 'culture' to 'narrative'. My initial research puzzle had concerned culture in local government. When I studied organizational anthropology in the second half of the 1990s, the concept of culture as something shared and stable was no longer the only view in organizational studies. However, explaining this to public administration researchers and political scientists especially was not always easy, due to their disciplines' different orientations. Following organizational scientists such as Linda Smircich (1983), I defined organizational culture as a process of sensemaking. While writing about the issues I studied in the first town, however, I stumbled upon a concept that was even more helpful in 'seeing' what was going on there: storytelling. As I entered my second fieldwork period, that concept helped me understand more clearly how the experiences I encountered during various forms of observation, conversation and reading connected people in the field to each other, as well as connecting myself as a researcher to the field.

Implementing public policies through organizations (Dvora Yanow)

Between 1972 and 1975 I worked in a series of roles in two community centres, as part of a government corporation in Israel, in two different towns, returning in 1980–1981 for six months' follow-up observation, interviewing and document analysis from a base adjacent to the national headquarters (Yanow, 1996). Both towns were immigrant towns remote from urban centres, and the agency's raison d'être was to provide non-formal educational and cultural activities – language, cooking and photography courses, folkdancing, tennis, etc. – leading to residents' integration into the state and the adoption of its national cultural ethos. As a Community Organizer, my first role, a position funded by the Housing Ministry, my supervisor in each centre had me map each town and its neighbourhoods, noting the type and condition of housing and infrastructure (poor lighting, bad sewerage, uncollected garbage), the locations of services (the town hall and its departments; banks, grocery stores, markets, synagogues; youth, sports, union and other kinds of clubs and social halls; and so on), and residents' demographic characteristics (year of immigration, ethnic group, family size, ages, etc.). At one point I became Acting Director of the second centre, subsequently becoming the Director of two departments. I also became a member of the corporation's national advisory group, giving me an overview of the larger operation. When I returned for the follow-up study, it was as a non-participating observer.

My research question grew out of the initial experience: why was it so difficult for my community organizer colleagues and myself to accomplish in the field what we thought we had a clear national mandate for? My undergraduate background in political science led me to frame my research as a policy implementation study, as the community centres were implementing national public policy. To understand this implementation, I needed to know something about organizations, the entities charged with putting policy into practice. Yet existing implementation and organizational theories, emphasizing rational-technical decision-making and instrumental goal-setting, did not help me understand my own lived experience. US social sciences were then opening up to science studies, hermeneutics and phenomenology, and what came to be called 'the interpretive turn', and these readings (e.g. Kuhn, 1970 [1962]; Berger and Luckmann, 1966; Geertz, 1973) led me to others in symbolic-cultural anthropology and the philosophy of (social) science. I came to see the events and circumstances I was studying as entailing the communication of policy and organizational meanings through language (especially the organization's name and an organizational metaphor), material objects (the centres' buildings and their design and pro-grammes) and acts (organizational rituals and their myth-like components). Implementation, I saw, was enabled or confounded by overlaps or differences between policy and organizational founders' and leaders' intended meanings, embedded in and communicated through those elements, and town residents' and others' own 'readings' of those elements and their meanings.

Given the research focus on meaning, I cannot imagine conducting the study in any other way. My theorizing grew out of the observations, experiences, read-ings and conversations that I had on site, informed by knowledge of the orga-nization's history and sociopolitical context and by the theoretical literature's debates. Experience in two centres added a comparative angle. Without 'being there', experiencing the organization, the towns, their physical layout and problems, and their residents' ways of life, I would not have understood the founder's statement that the 'community centre would be a functional supermarket' – I needed to know what 'supermarket' meant to people there at that time to understand its meaning in community centre terms. As I was interested in present-day problems, historical-archival analysis, while engaging, would have been insufficient, even with interviews; nor would a survey have enabled me to explore the meaning-focused questions I was interested in.

The disadvantages were personal, rather than methods-related in the narrow sense. Being on location in remote settings, let alone 'foreign' ones, for extended periods of time, separated from family and friends and one's famil-iar way of living, is not easy. The literature has not spoken much of the emo-tional strain of prolonged field research (but see Ortbals and Rincker, 2009), let alone of the sexual and other physical aspects that can pose challenges – relationships between researchers and researched; harassment of female researchers; being 'out' in the field (see Lewin and Leap, 1996); mobility and other problems of 'wheelchairedness' (Mike Duijn, personal communication, 2009); the aging field researcher; and other bodily, emotional, mental or social limitations (Schwartz-Shea and Yanow, 2011).

Contemporary Issues in Organizational Ethnography: Multi-sited, Reflexive and Relational

These research examples illuminate three issues on the methodological table today: ethnography's 'multi-sitedness'; reflexivity (see also Haynes, in this

volume), including on the researcher's positionality; and the intrinsically relational character of ethnographic fieldwork.

Multi-sited ethnography

The settings of traditional ethnography had a distinctive character: the locations were relatively bounded – or appeared that way. More recently, anthropologists have started speaking of 'multi-sited' ethnography, its marking
underscoring the difference in this conceptualization. Our examples
suggest, however, that in organizational ethnography, multi-sitedness is the
norm; it may even be one of its distinctive characteristics, as organizational
ethnographers typically follow actors, actions, artefacts and the ideas they
embody and reflect. Following these travelling ideas, persons and so forth
leads researchers to different organization-related sites, especially when conceiving of organizations as loosely coupled systems, inter-organizational fields
or networks. We see this in Ybema's following of the newspaper editors' work,
decisions, rituals, rumours, discussions and the report, new logo, front page,
product, etc.; in van Hulst's following of actors and acts both inside and
outside of the town halls; and in Yanow's trailing of self-contained centres and
the parent organization, as well as of oversight ministries, funding agencies
and overseas donors and ideas. Orr (1996), in another example, followed
copier technicians visiting clients and meeting colleagues in multiple locations
far from the corporation's central office. Indeed, such 'following' can make the
research process seem to meander, challenging the researcher to travel with or
trail issues, persons and/or texts to various locations. Even if one remains
within the walls of a single organization, 'mapping' across its departments and
hierarchical levels, one is perforce engaged in a multi-sited study.

Reflexivity and positionality

Reflexivity, including on the researcher's positionality, is increasingly central to
ethnographic research, in particular that which is informed by a constructivist-
interpretivist methodology in which researcher objectivity is not (assumed to
be) present. This casts in heightened relief the matter of 'truth claims' and what
positivist-informed research calls their 'validity' and 'reliability'. As those
terms encapsulate the notion that research can mirror the world being
observed, they are less appropriate for assessing research that proceeds from

a constructivist-interpretivist perspective. Rather than seeing data as existing independent of the researcher, waiting in 'the field' to be discovered, interpretive ethnographers look at how happenstance shaped their access to various organizational parts, persons, documents, etc. The truth claims question pivots on how both data and analyses were generated and developed, requiring reflective transparency on researchers' positionality in two senses: their 'geographic' location within the organization and their demographic characteristics, either of which might shape access and sight, enabling some things while limiting others. Rather than seeing themselves as objective, uninvolved discoverers of pre-existing data, interpretive ethnographers see themselves as actively involved in the (co-)construction of those data, and they also see their narratives as constructing the organizational 'realities' they report. While reflecting on these matters could certainly be part of the field research itself, such reflexivity is primarily marshalled on the written page.

Location-based positionality is a matter of particular concern in organizational ethnography, given the links between hierarchy, knowledge and power. Researchers who immerse themselves in 'being there' make themselves more likely to be associated with or drawn into a particular perspective. The community centre study's second phase illustrates one dimension of this problematic: perceiving Yanow as 'coming from agency headquarters' because she was located nearby, local centre staff at times treated the research visit as an opportunity to put a particular spin on what was said and shown, thinking it a way to convey messages to the CEO (despite the fact that she had no such access to him). In the newspaper case, positionality was interpreted in professional terms: some journalists seemed highly suspicious that Ybema would want to make headlines with his research, in a journalistic fashion. To overcome this, he positioned himself as someone who was not interested in headlines and scoops, whose (academic) book would not be out for at least another year (which made them more cooperative, albeit puzzled at the value of such 'outdated' data). For van Hulst, a kind of locational positionality emerged in one board meeting when civil servants were asked to leave the room so that board members could have a private conversation. As he packed his ethnographer's gear to leave too, one of the board members announced: 'Researcher-of-the-administration stays'. While experiencing this as both a surprise and honour, van Hulst noted the trickiness of such a positioning, which might affect his ability to take a critical stance towards those in power. Geographic positionality can also be a matter of the (in-)sight afforded by different locations, as Pachirat (2011) documents with his promotion from slaughterhouse floor to Quality Control.

In its demographic sense, positionality entails the gender, race-ethnic, class, age, sexuality and other characteristics that can affect a researcher's access to certain situations and/or (categories of) persons, others' sensemaking of the researcher and the researcher's ability to understand others' experiences. Shehata (2006), for instance, documents how his birthplace, educational attainment, socio-economic background, gender and religious affiliation shaped how he was perceived on the shopfloor, what he was allowed to do and kept from doing, and the kinds of settings he could and could not enter. Interpretive ethnographers are increasingly expected to provide greater transparency concerning their methods and their positionality, in all senses of the term, as a way of supporting the truth claims they advance.

'But I thought we were friends?!' and other issues in the relational character of research

Explicit recognition of the relational character of fieldwork is increasing, and along with it both the ethical and methodological implications. To begin with, ethnographers must negotiate 'access' to their research sites; but whereas this traditionally was seen as a kind of 'knocking on the administrative and/or chief's door', today it is increasingly seen as a matter of establishing and sustaining relationships over time. This makes access more than a one-shot permissional activity, as the essays in Feldman et al. (2003) make clear. Moreover, fieldwork 'friendships' require care, including making decisions about how instrumentally to treat those whom researchers encounter or seek out in the conduct of the research: there is a difference between conceiving of situational actors as properties of the researcher ('my' informants) and treating them in a Buberian 'I-Thou' fashion. What will happen to fieldwork relationships when the researcher concludes his/her time in the field? And what slights or betrayals might bring a situational member to exclaim, in anger and/or anguish, 'But I thought we were friends?!' (Beech et al., 2009).

A second aspect of the relational character of ethnographic research links to epistemological concerns: the researcher's need to become as familiar as possible with the local culture in order to understand its workings, while maintaining enough epistemological 'stranger-ness' that a recognition of the common sense, the everyday, the unspoken/unwritten and the tacit retains its analytic purchase (see, e.g. Ybema and Kamsteeg, 2009). The ways of knowing and kinds of knowledge entailed in this balancing have been called emic/etic (see Headland et al., 1990), insider/outsider (e.g. Bartunek and Louis, 1996), experience-near/experience-distant (Geertz, 1973). For Ybema, for instance, working to remain a relative 'outsider' to the newspaper and to preserve some of the initial surprise was as important as working to become an 'insider' and to achieve immersion. The long time it took him to understand the implications of his observations was frustrating, but it was only through taking seriously his own bewilderment that new insights emerged.

Some confusion has developed, however, particularly in organizational studies, concerning what it means as a researcher to be an 'insider'. Is the aim truly to lose one's 'outsider' status? Is that even conceivable? The ontological possibility of organizational 'outsiders' becoming 'insiders' as they seek to add local, emic knowledge to theory-rooted etic knowledge is far more fraught than has been acknowledged to date. Insider/outsider objectifies local 'informants', treating them as a means toward the researcher's ends in ways that nullify the relational character of field research. On the epistemological side of things, emic/etic reifies the notion that 'local' knowledge and 'theoretical' knowledge are separate kinds. In interaction, the two term pairs negate the hermeneutic-phenomenological notion that knowledge, or understanding, is co-created in the interaction between researchers and their situational partners, neither of whom can become the other (with the possible exception of 'native anthropologists'; see Narayan, 1993; see Nencel and Yanow, 2008). On this, further theorizing is called for.

Why Organizational Ethnography?

To conclude, we must engage with the matter of what might lead an organizational researcher to undertake an ethnographic study. Current methodological debates often stipulate that the choice of method should be driven by the research question, rather than vice versa. Although in sympathy with this argument, we think it shortchanges the matter by implying that methods are chosen in an entirely rational fashion. Our own research and teaching experiences suggest, instead, that research questions and methods are much more mutually constituted – and at times are so intricately bound up with each other as to be inseparable. Our sense of this links strongly to the third understanding of ethnography named in the opening section.

An ethnographic sensibility is not something that a researcher just sets aside; neither is it something that one picks up as one would select a method from a 'toolbox', a common metaphor in methods textbooks. At least one of us would want to say that her question-methods packet chose her, rather than vice versa – meaning that their development was intertwined, as well as being linked to, her (unspoken) proclivities. For another of us, training in survey research and statistical analyses had provided little knowledge of other research traditions; still, he was strongly drawn to processes of meaning-making and organizational power games, believing these notions would help him understand what was 'actually' going on in the organization he was studying. This predilection for meaning-focused research and qualitative methods was also inspired by opportunity (good access to inner decision-making circles) and situation (strong disagreements surfacing in the field, which were hard to ignore).

Although this position may be in keeping with a hermeneutic-phenomenological stance, it is driven not by our philosophical presuppositions but by our lived experiences, as both researchers and teachers, in which we have seen people, ourselves included, drawn towards framing research questions in particular ways that will call on particular methods because of ways of seeing and knowing that preceded the research project, reflecting something much deeper than the rational-instrumental choosing of a tool.

Ethnographic research is a complex practice. Although reading about organizational ethnography as well as reading well-written organizational ethnographies can definitely help researchers become good ethnographers, its practice is largely learned through the doing – in the field – as one experiences and develops a certain sensibility for organizational ethnography itself. This suggests that a discussion of ethnography's advantages and disadvantages is misplaced to the extent that it rests on those very rational considerations and choices that we think do not well describe the research experience. Organizational and other scholars need, instead, to know what ethnographic methods do well and less well and perhaps to focus more on enabling students and colleagues to recognize their own personal strengths and limitations and how these might play out in the conduct of ethnographic research.

Further Reading

Interest in organizational ethnography has recently taken off, garnering attention through workshops, conferences, journal special issues and methods-focused books, leading us to anticipate a surge in monographs. Kunda (1992) and Orr (1996) remain the most cited as leading exemplars of the genre. For introductions to organizational ethnographic methods and methodological concerns, see Neyland (2008), Kostera (2007) and Ybema et al. (2009). The first two of these focus more on methods, conveying something of the 'how to' of ethnographic research, with introductory chapters on culture, ethnography and organizations (Kostera) and treatments of the whole research process illustrated by various organizational ethnographies (Neyland). The third is more methodological in orientation; it both introduces and critically discusses various practices in organizational ethnography, tackling the key challenges and methodological, analytical, (re)presentational, ethical and social problematics that arise in the doing and writing of organizational ethnography. For an overview of ethnography's past and potential contributions to organizational studies, see Fine et al. (2009). And while not specific to organizational studies, Atkinson et al. (2001) offer an outstanding collection of essays on methodological issues of concern to organizational ethnographers.

References

Alvesson, M. (1996) *Communication, Power and Organization*. Berlin: De Gruyter.

Atkinson, P., Coffey, A., Delamont, S., Lofland, J. and Lofland, L. (eds) (2001) *Handbook of Ethnography*. London: Sage.

Barley, S. (1983) 'Semiotics and the study of occupational and organizational cultures', *Administrative Science Quarterly*, 28 (3): 393–413.

Bartunek, J.M. and Louis, M.R. (1996) *Insider/Outsider Team Research*. Thousand Oaks, CA: Sage.

Bate, S.P. (1997) 'Whatever happened to organizational anthropology?', *Human Relations*, 50 (9): 1147–1171.

Beech, N., Hibbert, P., MacIntosh, R. and McInnes, P. (2009) 'But I thought we were friends?', in S. Ybema, D. Yanow, H. Wels and F. Kamsteeg (eds), *Organizational Ethnography*. London: Sage, pp. 196–214.

Berger, P.L. and Luckmann, T. (1966) *The Social Construction of Reality*. New York: Anchor Books.

Blau, P. (1955) *The Dynamics of Bureaucracy*. Chicago: University of Chicago Press.

Brown, A.D. and Humphreys, M. (2006) 'Epic and tragic tales: making sense of change', *Journal of Applied Behavioral Science*, 39 (22): 121–144.

Collinson, D.L. (1992) *Managing the Shopfloor*. Berlin: De Gruyter.

Cook, S.D. and Yanow, D. (2006 [1993]) 'Culture and organizational learning', in B. Czarniawska (ed.), *Organization Theory*, vol. 1. Cheltenham: Edward Elgar, pp. 259–276.

Crozier, M. (1964) *The Bureaucratic Phenomenon*. Chicago: University of Chicago Press.

Dalton, M. (1959) *Men who Manage*. New York: Wiley.

Delbridge, R. (1998) *Life on the Line in Contemporary Manufacturing*. Oxford: Oxford University Press.

Dubinskas, F.A. (ed.) (1988) *Making Time: Ethnographies of High Technology Organizations*. Philadelphia, PA: Temple University Press.

Dubois, V. (2010) *The Bureaucrat and the Poor*. Aldershot: Ashgate.

Feldman, M.S., Bell, J. and Berger, M.T. (eds) (2003) *Gaining Access*. Walnut Creek, CA: Altamira.

Fine, G.A., Morrill, C. and Surianarain, S. (2009) 'Ethnography in organizational settings', in D.A. Buchanan and A. Bryman (eds), *The Sage Handbook of Organizational Research Methods*. London: Sage, pp. 602–619.

Geertz, C. (1973) *The Interpretation of Cultures*. New York: Basic Books.

Goffman, E. (1959) *The Presentation of Self in Everyday Life*. Garden City, NY: Anchor Books.

Gouldner, A.W. (1954) *Patterns of Industrial Bureaucracy*. New York: Free Press.

Headland, T.N., Pike, K.L. and Harris, M. (eds) (1990) *Emics and Etics: The Insider/ Outsider Debate*. Newbury Park, CA: Sage.

Ingersoll, V.H. and Adams, G. (1992) *The Tacit Organization*. Greenwich, CT: JAI Press.

Kaufman, H. (1960) *The Forest Ranger*. Baltimore, MD: Johns Hopkins Press.

Kondo, D. (1990) *Crafting Selves*. Chicago, IL: University of Chicago Press.

Kostera, M. (2007) *Organisational Ethnography*. Lund: Studentlitteratur AB.

Kuhn, T. (1970 [1962]) *The Structure of Scientific Revolutions* (2nd edn). Chicago: University of Chicago Press.

Kunda, G. (1992) *Engineering Culture*. Philadelphia, PA: Temple University Press.

Lewin, E. and Leap, W.L. (eds) (1996) *Out in the Field*. Urbana: University of Illinois Press.

Mauss, M. (1990 [1925]) *The Gift*. London: Routledge.

Mayo, E. (1933) *The Human Problems of Industrial Civilization*. New York: Macmillan.

Miettinen, R., Samra-Fredericks, D. and Yanow, D. (2009) 'Re-turn to practice', *Organization Studies*, 30 (12): 1309–1327.

Mintzberg, H. (1970) 'Structured observation as a method to study managerial work', *Journal of Management Studies*, 7 (1): 87–104.

Morey, N.C. and Luthans, F. (1987) 'Anthropology: the forgotten behavioral science in management history', in F. Hoy (ed.), *Best Papers Proceedings of the 47th Annual Meeting of the Academy of Management*. Athens, GA: University of Georgia, pp. 128–132.

Narayan, K. (1993) 'How native is a "native" anthropologist?', *American Anthropologist*, 95: 671–686.

Nencel, L. and Yanow, D. (2008) 'On methodological relics: reconsidering etic outsiders, emic insiders, and fieldwork relationships', paper presented at the European Association of Social Anthropologists, Ljubljana (26–30 August).

Neyland, D. (2008) *Organizational Ethnography*. London: Sage.

Nicolini, D. (2009) 'Zooming in and zooming out: a package of method and theory to study work practices', in S. Ybema, D. Yanow, H. Wels and F. Kamsteeg (eds), *Organizational Ethnography*. London: Sage, pp. 120–138.

Nicolini, D., Gherardi, S. and Yanow, D. (2003) 'Toward a practice-based view of knowing and learning in organizations', in D. Nicolini, S. Gherardi and D. Yanow (eds), *Knowing in Organizations: A Practice-based Approach*. Armonk, NY: M.E. Sharpe, pp. 3–31.

Orr, J. (1996) *Talking about Machines*. New York: Cornell University Press.

Ortbals, C.D. and Rincker, M.E. (eds) (2009) 'Fieldwork, identities, and intersectionality: a symposium', *PS: Political Science & Politics*, 42 (2): 287–385.

Pachirat, T. (2011) 'The *political* in political ethnography: reflections from an industrialized slaughterhouse on perspective, power, and sight', in E. Schatz (ed.), *Political Ethnography: What Immersion Contributes to the Study of Power*. Chicago: University of Chicago Press, pp. 143–162.

Pader, E. (2006) 'Seeing with an ethnographic sensibility', in D. Yanow and P. Schwartz-Shea (eds), *Interpretation and Method: Empirical Research Methods and the Interpretive Turn*. Armonk, NY: M.E. Sharpe, pp. 161–175.

Prasad, A. and Prasad, P. (2002) 'The coming of age of interpretive organizational research', *Organizational Research Methods*, 5 (1): 4–11.

Rabinow, P. and Sullivan, W.M. (eds) (1979, 1985) *Interpretive Social Science* (1st and 2nd edns). Berkeley: University of California Press.

Reed, M. (2006) 'Organizational theorizing', in S.R. Clegg, C. Hardy, T.B. Lawrence and W.R. Nord (eds), *The Sage Handbook of Organization Studies* (2nd edn). London: Sage, pp. 19–54.

Rosen, M. (2000) *Turning Words, Spinning Worlds*. Amsterdam: Harwood.

Roy, D. (1960) 'Banana time', *Human Organization*, 18: 156–68.

Salemink, O. (2003) 'Ethnography, anthropology and colonial discourse', in *The Ethnography of Vietnam's Central Highlanders*. London: Routledge Curzon, pp. 1–39.

Schwartzman, H.B. (1993) *Ethnography in Organizations*. Newbury Park, CA: Sage.

Selznick, P. (1949) *TVA and the Grass Roots*. Berkeley: University of California Press.

Shehata, S. (2006) 'Ethnography, identity, and the production of knowledge', in D. Yanow and P. Schwartz-Shea (eds), *Interpretation and Method: Empirical Research Methods and the Interpretive Turn*. Armonk, NY: M.E. Sharpe, pp. 244–263.

Smircich, L. (1983) 'Studying organizations as cultures', in G. Morgan (ed.), *Beyond Method*. London: Sage, pp. 160–172.

Stein, S.J. (2004) *The Culture of Education Policy*. New York: Teachers College Press.

van Hulst, M.J. (2008a) *Town Hall Tales*. Delft: Eburon.

van Hulst, M.J. (2008b) 'Quite an experience: using ethnography to study local government', *Critical Policy Analysis*, 2 (2): 143–159.

Van Maanen, J. (1979) 'The fact of fiction in organizational ethnography', *Administrative Science Quarterly*, 24: 539–550.

Van Maanen, J. (1988) *Tales of the Field*. Chicago: University of Chicago Press.

Van Maanen, J. (1995) 'An end to innocence: the ethnography of ethnography', in J. Van Maanen (ed.), *Representation in Ethnography*. Thousand Oaks, CA: Sage, pp. 1–35.

Watson, T. (1994) *In Search of Management*. London: Routledge.

Whyte, W.F. (1948) *Human Relations in the Restaurant Industry.* New York: McGraw-Hill.

Wolcott, H.F. (2003 [1973]) *The Man in the Principal's Office: An Ethnography.* Walnut Creek, CA: AltaMira Press.

Yanow, D. (1996) *How Does a Policy Mean?* Washington, DC: Georgetown University Press.

Ybema, S. (2003) *De Koers van de Krant: Vertogen over Identiteit bij Trouw en de Volkskrant* [*Discourses on Tradition and Transition: Conflict about the Newspaper's Identity among Editors of Trouw and de Volkskrant*]. Amsterdam: VU University Amsterdam.

Ybema, S. (2010) 'Talk of change', *Organization Studies*, 31 (4): 481–503.

Ybema, S. and Kamsteeg, F. (2009) 'Making the familiar strange', in S. Ybema et al. (eds), *Organizational Ethnography.* London: Sage, pp. 101–119.

Ybema, S., Yanow, D., Wels, H. and Kamsteeg, F. (2009) 'Studying everyday organizational life', in S. Ybema et al. (eds), *Organizational Ethnography.* London: Sage, pp. 1–20.

20 Case Studies in Organizational Research

David A. Buchanan

Personal Research Experience 1: The Case of the Polish Call-girls

You are the new professional services manager for a computer company. Margins on hardware have fallen. Revenue growth will come from selling business solutions and consulting services. Growth in your section will take staff away from the sales area. On your third day in the job, the company's most successful sales manager approaches you, unprovoked, insults you, and threatens to have you removed from the company whenever he wants. He is on the same management grade and you both report to the same company director. He generates 40 per cent of the company's turnover, and high levels of commission, from one customer whose buyer is a close personal friend of his. He is in his mid-30s, recently married, and about to start a family. He consistently tries to block your contacts with this major customer. You discover through a trick that he is capturing your email traffic, and probably that of other managers. He is undermining your credibility with your own staff with rumours and innuendo. You also know that he incurs high expenses on overseas trips that generate no new sales. On a joint business development trip to Poland, he arranges for two call-girls to come to your hotel room, apparently planning to take photographs with which to discredit you. (Buchanan and Badham, 2008: 111)

Casual conversations can have unanticipated consequences. I mentioned my interest in researching organization politics, a topic where controversy and sensitivity can inhibit frank and honest discussion. 'You should speak to my husband Brian', said Carla. 'He's dealing with an issue at work at the moment. I'm sure he'd be willing to tell you about it'. Meeting with Brian for about an hour, he explained his relationship with a senior colleague in his new organization, the devious political tactics used by this manager to interfere with Brian's new role and how Brian was responding. I recorded and transcribed the conversation and returned it to Brian out of courtesy and for an accuracy check. He called back to say thanks for the transcript, which had helped him to think through the issues; he had been placed by his colleague in an awkward interpersonal and professional position. However, he explained that 'things have moved on', so we met again, and the process was repeated. I now had over two hours of narrative concerning the use of extreme political tactics directed at Brian, the tactics that he had used in response and the outcomes of this exchange.

I had no research project plan at this point, no funding. My aim was to gather interesting information, collect anecdotes for the classroom, generate ideas for further research and perhaps develop a teaching case. While considering these options, the call for papers for the British Academy of Management's annual conference appeared. Why not develop Brian's experience into a case study? I submitted the paper to the conference expecting it to be rejected; a single case, a thin sliver of one person's experience, no information from others, poor contextualization (this had to remain anonymous), lacking methodological rigour. To my surprise, the paper was favourably reviewed and the conference presentation went well. I revised it for the *British Journal of Management*, again anticipating rejection.

The paper was accepted (Buchanan, 1999): 'The logic of political action: an experiment with the epistemology of the particular'. The last part of the subtitle concerned the single case underpinning the argument; there was no representative sample. There were two 'experiments' in the subtitle. One concerned the exploration of what could be learned from such limited evidence. The second concerned whether an academic journal would publish this. These experiments appear to have been successful.

This experience suggests that case study research based on a single individual is publishable. Not all journal editors and referees are sympathetic, however, and it is usually necessary to justify this approach, to a degree that is not expected of positivist researchers using quantitative methods, even when they are putting sophisticated parametric statistical analysis to use on ordinal-scale data.

This also illustrates how, in practice, the textbook logic of literature review, questions, research design and data collection can be subverted. I was already familiar with much, but not all, of the literature on organization politics. In this area, a positivist tradition dominates, based on surveys (e.g. Ferris et al., 2002; 2007). One focus of this work has concerned the Perceptions of Organization Politics (POPS) scale (Ferris et al., 2005), but to judge from the output of those researchers, they appear never to have spoken to managers or other employees about their perceptions of politics. I think that this is unsatisfactory. I also knew that politics was typically defined as self-serving, deviant, damaging behaviour. Brian's response to the 'dirty tricks' had been to use political tactics to benefit the organization, his department, his personal reputation and his value to the company. Challenging current definitions, here was an example of constructive political behaviour (Buchanan, 1999: 85).

In his standard text on case studies in social research, Robert Yin (2009) devotes a chapter to 'designing case studies'. He argues that, 'you need a plan or *research design*' (Yin, 2009: 25), with five components: questions, propositions, unit(s) of analysis, logic linking data to propositions and criteria for interpreting findings. This may be one way to conduct case study research, but is not the only way. With Brian's narrative, the interesting questions (beyond, 'What's happening here?') were formed after the case was documented. Case researchers may often have to consider retrospectively, 'What questions does this case study allow us to answer?', as well as the questions they originally posed.

What Makes a Case?

What constitutes a case study has been a matter for some debate. Yin's (2009: 18) definition is:

> A case study is an empirical inquiry that investigates a contemporary phenomenon in depth and within its real-life context, especially when the boundaries between phenomenon and context are not clearly evident.

While case studies can be pre-defined in focus and scope, they can also be emergent and self-defining. As well as being able to design studies as Yin prescribes, researchers must also be able to spot the interesting, the different, the unusual, the novel, the surprising – the black swan which challenges the theory that 'all swans are white' (a representative sample of black swans is unnecessary). A case study can become an example of something different from what was originally intended, as a second illustration, described later, demonstrates. The 'phenomenon' in Yin's definition thus covers a range of possibilities. There is no single correct answer to the question of, 'What makes a case?' Examples with units of analysis other than the individual include:

- *Organizations*: the longitudinal study of the chemicals manufacturing company ICI by Andrew Pettigrew (1985) is a benchmark in both methodology and the study of organizational change. Based on interviews, informal conversations, documents and observation, this study established processual-contextual perspectives on change, since developed by others, notably Patrick Dawson (2003). Pettigrew traced the experiences of five divisions of ICI, making this a 'nested' case study, of those divisions, and their interactions, in the organization.

- *Change processes*: Donde Plowman and colleagues (2007) studied an American church over a protracted period of change. This began in a minor way and was 'amplified' through several mechanisms to generate a radical shift in mission and activity, from a sedate 'silk stockings' church, to one that served a wider population, including minorities and the homeless. This study challenges the view that radical change has to be a managed, top-down process dependent on leadership. Data for this study were obtained through interviews, newspaper articles, church documents and grant applications, websites and informal observation.

- *Decision processes*: the decisions of the American president John F. Kennedy and his advisers in 1962 during the Cuban Missile Crisis, which brought the world close to nuclear holocaust, were analysed by Graham Allison (1969 and 1971). His account relies on published academic sources in international politics and policy analysis, a biography of Kennedy, government papers and the *New York Times*. He contrasts three models of decision-making: rational policy, organizational process and bureaucratic politics models. He notes that critical strategic decisions are not above politics and that 'bargaining games' influence key decisions.

- *Respondent validation mechanisms*: organizational researchers often feed back their findings to participants, to check accuracy and interpretations. Although this process can raise problems, 'respondent validation' or 'member review' mechanisms are under-researched. From personal experience, Karen Locke and Ramakrishna Velamuri (2009) present a case of respondent validation, concerning research exploring resistance to corrupt practices in an Indian organization. Their case narrative describes what happened when their findings were fed back; company managers did not like what was said and demanded changes. This analysis allows the researchers to explore the problems that respondent validation can generate, along with options for addressing these issues.

- *Events*: why in 1994, over Northern Iraq, did two US Air Force F-15 fighter jets shoot down two US Army Black Hawk Helicopters, killing all 26 passengers and crew, in perfect flying conditions, with no hostile action nearby, watched by a coordinating AWACS aircraft overhead? Scott Snook (2000) develops a multi-level case analysis, exploring individual, group, organizational and contextual explanations. He develops a theory of 'practical drift', explaining how operations depart from written procedures, thus contributing to such incidents. The work of Charles Perrow (1999) is based on case studies of different types of disasters, leading to the theory of 'interactive complexity'. The study by Diane Vaughan (1996), of the Challenger shuttle launch decision, is a study both of this tragic event and its multiple (technical and organizational) causes, and also of the fatal launch decision.

These examples of different units of analysis illustrate the potential of case studies, which is limited only by the researcher's ingenuity. We have single cases, nested cases, multiple cases – the topics and combinations are endless; this list has no closure.

The case study is a research design and not a method. The case study may rely on a single method for collecting data; interviews are popular. But case studies are more often a multi-methods design, combining quantitative and qualitative data. In his chapter on 'collecting case study evidence', Yin (2009: 102) focuses on six methods: documentation (see Lee, in this volume), archival records, interviews (see Alvesson and Ashcraft, in this volume), direct observations, participant observation (see Brannan, in this volume) and physical artefacts. He adds that films, photographs, videotapes (see Vince and Warren, in this volume), 'street' ethnography, psychological testing and life histories can also be relevant.

Yin's list is far from complete. Snook (2000: 15–16) lists the sources for his 'friendly fire' case as follows:

> [O]fficial government documents, archival records, interviews, physical artefacts, gun target footage, videotapes, audio tapes, training records, maintenance records, technical reports, trial transcripts, AWACS data tapes, internal Department of Defence (DOD) memoranda, press releases, newspaper clippings, congressional hearings, criminal investigations, conference briefings, flight records, mishap reports, personnel records, military flight plans, oil analyses, medical evaluations, psychological evaluations, human factors reports, optics reports, crash site analyses, equipment teardowns, weather observations, accident site photographs, witness statements, regulations, directives, maps, communications logs, intelligence briefings, task force airspace control

orders, pre-mission briefs, flight logs, lists of corrective actions taken, and DOD fact sheets.

As a commissioned officer in the US Army, Snook had experience of combat and had been wounded by 'friendly fire' on Grenada in 1983. For this study, he also analysed two commercial videos, one from an Iraqi news team, on the scene, and another made by the ABC news magazine *Prime Time Live* including interviews with key players. Snook (2000: 17) also reports that:

> I obtained a copy of the F-15 gun-sight-video footage of the shootdown that includes not only video, but also an audio record of the tragedy from the cockpit of the trail F-15. I also analysed a copy of video footage taken by a commercial camcorder inside the AWACS. This camera was focused on an extra controller console in the AWACS during the shoot-down and graphically captured the same radar screen available to AWACS controllers during the incident.

Snook's data concerned an event lasting only eight minutes. Case researchers often complain of 'data overload' (Dawson, 1997). While some sources are common, it is the phenomenon itself, the context in which it is set and the research aims that decide which methods and data are relevant. This includes non-traditional data such as newspapers, radio programmes and television documentaries, if these are useful, albeit partial, sources of relevant information. Sources that are partisan or biased can also be valuable, as these reflect stakeholder positions and interpretations, which influence the views and decisions of other actors in the drama and often help to shape the outcomes.

We could add data sources from personal reflection, autoethnography (see Humphreys and Learmonth, in this volume), survey questionnaires, diary studies, focus groups (see Kandola, in this volume), informal conversations and respondent validation briefings. The appropriate sources depend on the case and on the investigative skills of the researcher, seeking evidence and clues, wherever they can be found.

The Current Status of Case Research

In his foreword to the fourth edition of Yin's text (2009: viii), Donald Campbell stresses the importance of experimental control in research, observing that scientific certainty is jeopardized 'in out-of-doors social science', and carping about 'the ambiguities of non-laboratory settings'. Surely it is the desire to understand the ambiguity of the great outdoors that makes social and organizational research intriguing and worthwhile?

Donald Campbell and Julian Stanley (1966) were responsible for sowing the first seeds of suspicion regarding the status of case studies, in their seminal work on research design. They defined the 'one-shot case study' as a design in which a group is studied after having been subjected to some form of intervention that was presumed to have caused change. Suppose the outcome was successful. How do we know that it really was the intervention that caused that outcome, and not some other set of factors, such as events and conditions in the environment, a general trend occurring anyway (maturation), or chance? Unless we have a comparison group operating under the same conditions over the same period, but not subjected to the intervention, then we cannot be sure. They concluded that, 'such studies have such a total absence of control as to be of almost *no scientific value*' (Campbell and Stanley, 1966: 6), adding that, 'it seems *well-nigh unethical* at the present time to allow case studies of this nature' (1966: 7).

Thomas Cook and Donald Campbell (1979) later weakened these arguments, replacing 'case study' with the clumsier 'one-group posttest-only design'. While noting the lack of control, comparison, and observation prior to treatment, they conceded that the characteristics of case study designs in social science partially addressed those problems. These are not studies in which a single variable is measured at one point in time, and 'the case study as normally practiced should not be demeaned by identification with the one-group posttest-only design' (Cook and Campbell, 1979: 96). On the contrary, the 'posttest' phase of most case studies usually explores multiple factors, the researcher has rich contextual knowledge and 'intelligent presumptions can be made about what this group would have been like' in the absence of the intervention (1979: 96).

Today, methods texts have mandatory chapters on case studies. Robert Stake (1994 and 2000) has chapters in both editions of the *Handbook of Qualitative Research* (Denzin and Lincoln, 1994 and 2000). Jean Hartley (2004) wrote the chapter in the *Essential Guide to Qualitative Methods in Organizational Research* (Cassell and Symon, 2004). Andrea Ellinger et al. (2005) offer a dry account in *Research in Organizations: Foundations and Methods of Inquiry* (Swanson and Holton, 2005). Louise Fitzgerald and Sue Dopson (2009) explore comparative case study designs in *The Sage Handbook of Organizational Research Methods*

(Buchanan and Bryman, 2009). Here are two typical assessments: Hartley (2004: 323 and 332) states 'there is growing confidence in the case study as a rigorous research strategy', and 'case study research can be engaging, rewarding, stimulating and intellectually challenging', while Fitzgerald and Dopson (2009: 481) argue 'case study research is a valuable and developing research design with significant potential to contribute to They argue organizational studies', and 'case study designs have been undervalued'.

These assessments are some distance from 'unscientific and unethical'. Contemporary commentary, however, is uneven and there are many journal editors and academic reviewers who are not impressed by case studies (or qualitative research in general). Terri Scandura and Ethlyn Williams (2000) reviewed the methods reported in studies published in the *Academy of Management Journal*, *Administrative Science Quarterly* and *Journal of Management*, from 1985 to 1997. They noted a drop in the use of surveys, laboratory experiments and simulations, and an increase in field studies (cases). They criticized this trend because field studies lacked the precision and control that ensure internal validity and generalizability. They argued that organizational researchers 'need to question whether studies with ambiguous conclusions can say much about the settings in which they occur. It may be that, without rigour, relevance in management research cannot be claimed' (Scandura and Williams, 2000: 1263). Kathleen Eisenhardt and Melissa Graebner (2007: 26) also describe case designs as a 'complement to mainstream deductive research', indicating that they are not 'mainstream'.

These debates are not about designs or methods. They arise from the conflict between positivist and constructivist epistemologies. The former are wedded to a nomothetic, variance-based, hypothetico-deductive logic, and the latter to an inductive, idiographic, interpretative agenda often linked to processual theoretical perspectives. Positivists do not like small idiosyncratic samples; constructivists have a different approach to developing understanding of social and organizational phenomena. We will revisit these issues in the discussion of generalizing from case study evidence.

The researcher considering a case study approach, however inventive in technique and relevant to the project, is by no means guaranteed a safe passage through the stages of funding body appraisal, ethical approval and journal peer review. This does not mean that we should abandon case designs. We need to develop compelling justifications for their use, detailed descriptions of the design in practice and novel, interesting and important findings.

Personal Research Experience 2:
The Case of the Missing Project Leads

> Distributed change agency typically involves small teams and senior groups. In this qualitative study of service improvements in the treatment of prostate cancer at an acute hospital, Grange, change roles were distributed more widely, with responsibilities 'migrating' among a large informal cast supporting four central characters. This distribution appears to have been triggered by the change goals and substance, and by the network organization through which services were delivered. Cross-case comparisons with other hospitals, Henley and Norwood, suggest that a combination of factors contributed to the development of a distributed approach. Analytical generalization invites speculation concerning the transferability of this model, with 'nobody in charge', to other settings. (Buchanan et al., 2007: 1065).

From 2002 to 2005, I worked with a team funded by part of the UK National Health Service. Using a case study approach, this project explored the roles of managers and doctors implementing strategic changes in six hospitals and five primary care organizations. Three of the hospital case studies concerned cancer services and the other three involved maternity; the primary care cases focused on diabetes services. Data sources included website downloads, organization documents, observation at key meetings and interviews. Within-case analysis was complemented with cross-case comparisons; this account focuses on within-case analysis at one site.

The fieldwork was divided across the team, and I worked mainly at Grange, a hospital with an annual budget of £80 million, and 1,600 staff. Grange also belonged to the regional Glenelg cancer network. Each case focused on an area that had experienced change. At Grange this concerned prostate cancer services, provided by the department for general surgery and urology, which had an annual budget of £4 million, diagnosing 200 cases of prostate cancer a year, and employing five consultant surgeons and two consultant urologists.

The 21 interviews at Grange covered four themes; respondent background, role interpretation, relationships and service improvements – including the nature and objectives of changes, project management structures and outcomes. We knew that Grange had made significant improvements to their prostate cancer services. They had reduced the waiting time from referral to treatment from around six months to two weeks (the speed of treatment influences survival). Although facing the same pressures, the other two cancer service sites had not made such improvements, so Grange was a 'maverick' or an 'outlier'. Although the waiting time target of two weeks appeared simple, the changes required to meet it were complex, involving new equipment and facilities, new roles and the redesign of processes. So how had these changes been managed so successfully?

The research problems at this site began with the interview questions concerning project management structures. Who was the project manager or lead? Who were the members of the project team? We also knew from other healthcare research that complex multi-layered management structures typically accompany change initiatives like this. However, our interviewees at Grange could not answer these questions, because there were no project managers and no project team. Content analysis of the interview transcripts stalled, because the answers to those questions were missing.

I then focused the analysis on answers to the question, 'Who were involved in implementation roles?' This revealed that four individuals had been particularly influential, but at different stages in the process, and that a further 23 individuals had played major roles, along with 26 other managerial, administrative and clinical groups, including patients, patient representatives and other organizations across the cancer network. What emerged was a picture of a change process in which roles were dispersed not only across the target organization, Grange, but also across other organizations as well. Different individuals and groups had taken responsibility for different aspects of the change at different times, handing over that responsibility to others as necessary. Comparing the change management process at Grange with a conventional implementation guide (Gustafson et al., 2003) showed that they had ignored the textbook, but had been successful anyway.

I was familiar with some of the literature on 'distributed leadership' (Gronn, 2002; Bennett et al., 2003). That work was mostly conceptual and rooted in experience in education. Grange offered an empirical case study of 'distributed change agency' in healthcare. I wrote the paper with colleagues as a single case study and we submitted this to the *Human Relations* journal. Two of the three referees questioned the value of the single case. We were invited to 'revise and resubmit'. It was not possible within the journal's word limit to present the other cases in detail, so we developed a table to contrast the experience of Grange with that of the Henley and Norwood hospitals on contextual, structural, managerial, clinical, processual and substantive dimensions, and the outcomes. Those comparative dimensions were derived partly from processual-contextual perspectives on change and partly from the data. With this and other minor revisions, the paper was accepted (Buchanan et al., 2007).

The title of the paper, 'Nobody in charge', reflected the main finding. The argument was similar to that in Plowman et al. (2007), although those researchers adopted a different theoretical lens. Grange was an example of a 'nested' case study, of a clinical service within a surgical directorate within an acute hospital. This was also one of multiple case studies (Stake, 2006; Fitzgerald and Dopson, 2009) where findings could be combined and contrasted with results from other sites. The case that emerged from this study was not what was originally planned. It was not to be a study of distributed change leadership. It should instead have concerned the relationships between managers and doctors.

What's the 'So What?'

In their guidelines for authors, the editors of *Harvard Business Review* advise contributors that they are looking for the 'So what?', the 'aha' – the compelling insight. This is good advice, whatever the journal, and has implications for case selection and data analysis.

Case selection

Having established the subject of interest and the (initial) research questions, and having decided that a case study design is appropriate, how does the researcher select the appropriate case or cases? The conventional answer is that cases should be representative of the phenomenon under investigation. And that may involve a 'safe' decision rule. However, we have to consider what can be learned from further study of the typical, the commonplace. Kathleen Eisenhardt (1989) and Andrew Pettigrew (1990) both argue that researchers should consider choosing extreme situations, critical incidents, social dramas, 'polar' types, outliers and mavericks, where the experience of the phenomena under investigation is intense and visible. Case selection thus often relies on theoretical sampling: on what should we focus our attention in order to develop our understanding of this phenomenon?

As the examples in this chapter suggest, however, case studies can also be 'self-selecting', emerging from opportunities and evidence. I did not anticipate that Brian's story would produce a case study of constructive political behaviour. I did not predict that the Grange Hospital experience would produce a case study of distributed change leadership. The 'So what?' in both cases emerged during the analysis.

Data analysis

Yin (2009: 126) admits that the analysis of case study data is difficult, 'because the techniques still have not been well defined'. Eisenhardt (1989) made that observation 20 years ago. Given the variety of forms that case studies can take and the range of sources from which data can be drawn, the development of standardized analytical strategies would be challenging. There are of course established methods for analysing many of the kinds of quantitative and qualitative data that typically inform case studies. But this suggests a fragmented approach to the analysis of, say, interviews and documents, and does not deal with how data can be analysed to capture and interpret the holistic integrity of a case. While statistical methods and content or template analysis (see King, in this volume) are useful, we need to find other ways in which to analyse what is often a significant volume of case study data.

A useful first step is to develop a *case description*, without the clutter of referencing and without systematic analysis. What should be included in this case description? Everything – including details that are not (perceived to be) relevant (at this stage) and aspects of the context in which the phenomenon is embedded. What is the purpose of this description? This is a form of data reduction, crafting the information overload into a coherent account, which then becomes the platform for analysis and the basis for reports and publications. This is a 'base document' from which analyses, selective descriptions, explanations and new theories can be 'mined'. The description, which often takes the form of a narrative, will probably never be published in this form, although it may be fed back to research participants for comment. It is during this step that the 'aha' often appears, based on an anomaly, on something unusual or surprising, on the unexpected – a 'black swan'.

Yin (2009) suggests five other analytical techniques:

1 *Pattern matching*: comparing the pattern in the case or cases with one predicted in other commentary. The comparison of the approach to change implementation at Grange with the model of Gustafson et al. (2003) is an example of pattern matching (Buchanan et al., 2007: 1082).

2 *Explanation building*: generating propositions or hypotheses about causal patterns and links for further investigation. The closing section of 'Nobody in charge', identifying the conditions under which distributed change agency is appropriate, is an example of explanation building (Buchanan et al., 2007: 1083–1085).

3 *Time-series analysis*: tracking event sequences over time, comparing actual and theoretically predicted patterns, often in the form of narrative. Ann Langley (1999 and 2009) and Brian Pentland (1999) describe techniques for analysing temporally-based process data.

4 *Logic models*: this also involves matching actual with predicted outcomes, over a series of iterations, with immediate, intermediate and ultimate outcomes. This approach is often used to evaluate interventions, such as the introduction of novel classroom activities to improve academic performance.

5 *Cross-case synthesis*: comparing data from different cases across a uniform framework. 'Nobody in charge' provides an example comparing three hospitals on several factors (Buchanan et al., 2007: 1072–1073). This explains why Grange was successful and the other two hospitals were not.

These techniques are neither rigid nor exclusive. They can be used and developed in different ways, depending on the setting, and can be applied in parallel to the same data.

Theory testing

Case studies are traditionally categorized as descriptive, exploratory or explanatory (Yin, 2009). These headings capture only part of the case study potential. Cases can develop and test theory and in many instances the 'So what?' has fundamentally altered perceptions of the field. The designation of case studies as 'not mainstream' is painfully inappropriate.

The 'So what?' of the case may lie in the development of theory for further exploration. Cases have thus been described as 'pre-research' reconnaissance, generating ideas for 'real research' by conventional (rigorous, positivist, deductive) means. The use of case studies to test theory is not widely appreciated. Alex Bitektine (2008) describes prospective case study designs in which theory-based hypotheses concerning a social or organizational process are first developed, to be compared at a pre-determined time in the future with the observed process outcomes. Brian Pentland (1999) and John Hassard and David Buchanan (2009) respectively explore the use of fictional narratives and feature films, treated as case studies, to test organization theory.

The reputation of case studies as plausible research designs has probably been damaged by their association with case teaching in organization and management. Clayton Christensen and Paul Carlile (2009) argue that case studies can be used in the classroom inductively to develop, test and improve theory. The first step involves observation, description and the formulation of constructs. The second step concerns building frameworks and typologies based on the attributes of the phenomenon. The third step is to develop models expressing the relationships between attributes and observed outcomes.

Case Study Myths

Let us dispose of two myths surrounding case study research.

The myth of triangulation

Case studies involve multi-methods research, one of the advantages of which is the ability to use many sources of evidence as corroboration, to triangulate facts, to develop converging lines of inquiry, to produce more accurate accounts (Yin, 2009: 115–116). But as David Buchanan and Patrick Dawson (2007) argue, with regard to organizational change, the accounts of those involved vary and compete with each other. These divergences arise from differences in experience and because accounts can be politically inspired, and designed for specific audiences, to encourage particular decisions and behaviours. They argue that it is useful to expose the polyphonic, polysemic nature of organizations; many voices, many meanings. Many voices are silenced by prevailing power structures and relationships, and one role of the researcher is to give those voices expression. See, for example, the accounts by Hazen (1993), O'Connor (1995) and O'Leary (2003).

The myth of non-generalizability

The claim that, 'you can't generalize from a single case', displays a lack of understanding of both case study research and concepts of generalization. With a single case, or a small number of cases, one cannot rely on statistical methods to calculate whether one can extrapolate sample findings to a wider population. For most of the cases cited here, it is not even clear what that wider population comprises. Generalizability, or external validity, concerns the application of findings to settings other than the one studied. While establishing the internal validity of a study – did that cause generate this effect? – is a matter of logical deduction (Campbell and Stanley, 1966), assessing external validity is a matter of judgement. Is it reasonable to claim that these findings, this argument, those relationships, apply in other settings? Going beyond a statistical generalization, there are at least four other modes in which case study findings are generalizable.

1 *Moderatum generalizations*. This term was coined by Malcolm Williams (2000: 138) to refer to speculative associations: 'If characteristics point to particular structures in one situation, then one can hypothesize that the existence of such structures in a further situation will lead to at least some similar characteristics [. . .] Though there may be evidence of a shared reality as experienced, or shared underlying structures, the complexity of these structures and the possibility of agency to transform them, means that generalizations can be only moderate ones'. Eisenhardt (1989) and Langley (1999) also claim that it is possible to identify low-level patterns and develop generalizations with eight to ten cases.

2 *Naturalistic generalization*. Robert Stake (1994: 240) notes that, 'The reader comes to know some things told, as if he or she had experienced them. Enduring meanings come from encounter, and are modified and reinforced by repeated encounter'. The process through which we learn from case (and other) accounts and apply them to our own context, Stake defines as naturalistic generalization, which is similar to the concept of transferability (Lincoln and Guba, 1985). With a study of organization development interventions, say, or research into managerial politics, the reader naturally considers, would those methods work in my company, can I adopt those behaviours?

3 *Analytical refinement*. The findings from case research do not generalize from sample to population, but from experience and observation to theory. Suppose we have a concept of political behaviour as self-serving and damaging. Now we have a case in which politics benefit the company. Our concept may still apply to some instances, but it is inaccurate and must be revised. Suppose we have a model which says that, to be successful, change must be implemented in a certain manner. Now we have a case of an organization which departed from that model, but was nevertheless successful. We need to revise the model. Haridimos Tsoukas (2009) refers to this process as analytical refinement (also called analytical generalization). This relies on the case study being an example of the phenomenon under investigation. It is important to note that this does not involve proving or disproving theories, but does involve broadening our understanding with the accumulation of fresh observations.

4 *Isomorphic learning.* Accidents and disasters are unique, which may be why the 'lessons learned' from such incidents are often not implemented in comparable settings. Analysis of the findings of inquiries, however, shows that the same lessons and recommendations keep recurring. Technical issues (the shuttle's 'O-ring') are typically outweighed by organizational and managerial factors (training, management style, communications). Brian Toft and Simon Reynolds (2005: 66 and 72–75) thus argue that the lessons from an event can be applied in other settings. They refer to this as isomorphic learning, which includes event isomorphism (separate incidents, identical hazards), cross-organizational isomorphism (different organizations, same sector), common mode isomorphism (different sectors, similar processes) and self-isomorphism (sub-units operating in similar ways).

These forms of generalization are neither discrete nor mutually exclusive. Isomorphic learning is a form of naturalistic generalization, applied to particular incidents with regard to organization and management practice. Analytical refinement and naturalistic generalization may both apply to most organizational case studies.

Challenges and Prospects

Case study designs are well established in organizational research, but they are not universally accepted. The challenge is to ensure that the approach is seen as valid and valuable across the research community. One test will be the acceptance of case study papers by journal editors without the need for a 'boilerplate' paragraph repeating the justification for these designs. One threat to this agenda is the evidence-based management movement, which encourages a traditional positivist, variance-based approach. Another threat concerns the procedures of research ethics committees, which expect adherence to pre-specified protocols rather than the flexible departures, following lines of enquiry as they arise, which are a strength of case designs. The two key texts on case study designs are authored outside the field of organization studies. Robert Stake's interests lie with the evaluation of educational programmes. Robert Yin's background combines history and experimental psychology. While the issues that their texts address are generic, organizational research presents a different profile of opportunities, constraints and expectations (Buchanan and Bryman, 2007). Case study research designs in organization studies would benefit from having their own champions.

Further Reading

For practical and theoretical advice on the use, selection, conduct, analysis and writing of case studies in organizational research, the best starting point is still Robert Yin's (2009) text, which doctoral examiners and journal referees will probably expect to see in your list of references (but use selectively and critically).

For further methodological guidance, with regard to the use of cases to test and develop theory, and to the use of multiple and comparative case designs, refer to Bitektine (2008), Eisenhardt and Graebner (2007) and Fitzgerald and Dopson (2009).

There are many exemplary research (as opposed to teaching) case studies available. The (2007) paper by Donde Plowman and colleagues is particularly interesting as it is based on a single qualitative case, but was published in a journal that is traditionally biased towards quantitative positivist research design. The book by Scott Snook (2000) is also based on a single case, an incident lasting only eight minutes, offering an extraordinarily rich multi-level processual explanation for what went wrong. Snook's approach to his case data presentation, analysis and the development of explanation can be applied to a wide range of other less extreme organizational research settings.

References

Allison, G.T. (1969) 'Conceptual models and the Cuban missile crisis', *The American Political Science Review*, 63 (3): 689–718.

Allison, G.T. (1971) *The Essence of Decision: Explaining the Cuban Missile Crisis*. Boston, MA: Little, Brown.

Bennett, N., Wise, C. and Woods, P. (2003) *Distributed Leadership*. Nottingham: National College for School Leadership.

Bitektine, A. (2008) 'Prospective case study design: qualitative method for deductive theory testing', *Organizational Research Methods*, 11 (1): 160–180.

Buchanan, D.A. (1999) 'The logic of political action: an experiment with the epistemology of the particular', *British Journal of Management*, 10 (special conference issue): 73–88.

Buchanan, D.A., Addicott, R., Fitzgerald, L., Ferlie, E. and Baeza, J. (2007) 'Nobody in charge: distributed change agency in healthcare', *Human Relations*, 60 (7): 1065–1090.

Buchanan, D.A. and Badham, R. (2008) *Power, Politics, and Organizational Change: Winning the Turf Game* (2nd edn). London: Sage.

Buchanan, D.A. and Bryman, A. (2007) 'Contextualizing methods choice in organizational research', *Organizational Research Methods*, 10 (3): 483–501.

Buchanan, D.A. and Bryman, A. (eds) (2009) *The Sage Handbook of Organizational Research Methods*. London: Sage.

Buchanan, D.A. and Dawson, P. (2007) 'Discourse and audience: organizational change as multi-story process', *Journal of Management Studies*, 44 (5): 669–686.

Campbell, D.T. and Stanley, J.C. (1966) *Experimental and Quasi-Experimental Designs for Research*. Chicago, IL: Rand McNally and Company.

Cassell, C. and Symon, G. (eds) (2004) *Essential Guide to Qualitative Methods in Organizational Research*. London: Sage.

Christensen, C.M. and Carlile, P.R. (2009) 'Course research: using the case method to build and teach management theory', *Academy of Management Learning and Education*, 8 (2): 240–251.

Cook, T.D. and Campbell, D.T. (1979) *Quasi-Experimentation: Design and Analysis Issues for Field Settings*. Chicago, IL: Rand McNally College Publishing Company.

Dawson, P. (1997) 'In at the deep end: conducting processual research on organizational change', *Scandinavian Journal of Management*, 13 (4): 389–405.

Dawson, P. (2003) *Reshaping Change: A Processual Approach*. London: Routledge.

Denzin, N.K. and Lincoln, Y.S. (eds) (1994) *Handbook of Qualitative Research*. Thousand Oaks, CA: Sage.

Denzin, N.K. and Lincoln, Y.S. (eds) (2000) *Handbook of Qualitative Research* (2nd edn). Thousand Oaks, CA: Sage.

Eisenhardt, K.M. (1989) 'Building theories from case study research', *Academy of Management Review*, 14 (4): 532–550.

Eisenhardt, K.M. and Graebner, M.E. (2007) 'Theory building from cases: opportunities and challenges', *Academy of Management Journal*, 50 (1): 25–32.

Ellinger, A.D., Watkins, K.E. and Marsick, V.J. (2005) 'Case study research methods', in R.A. Swanson and E.F. Holton (eds), *Research in Organizations: Foundations and Methods of Inquiry*. San Francisco, CA: Berret-Koehler Publishers Inc, pp. 327–350.

Ferris, G.R., Adams, G., Kolodinsky, R.W., Hochwarter, W.A. and Ammeter, A.P. (2002) 'Perceptions of organizational politics: theory and research directions', *Research in Multi-Level Issues Volume 1: The Many Faces of Multi-Level Issues*: 179–254.

Ferris, G.R., Treadway, D.C., Kolodinsky, R.W., Hochwarter, W.A., Kacmar, C.J., Douglas, C. and Frink, D.D. (2005) 'Development and validation of the political skill inventory', *Journal of Management*, 31 (1): 126–152.

Ferris, G.R., Treadway, D.C., Perrewé, P.L., Brouer, R.L., Douglas, C. and Lux, S. (2007) 'Political skill in organizations', *Journal of Management*, 33 (3): 290–320.

Fitzgerald, L. and Dopson, S. (2009) 'Comparative case study designs: their utility and development in organizational research', in D.A. Buchanan and A. Bryman (eds), *The Sage Handbook of Organizational Research Methods*. London: Sage, pp. 465–483.

Gronn, P. (2002) 'Distributed leadership as a unit of analysis', *Leadership Quarterly*, 13 (4): 423–451.

Gustafson, D.H., Sainfort, F., Eichler, M., Adams, L., Bisognano, M. and Steudel, H. (2003) 'Developing and testing a model to predict outcomes of organizational change', *Health Services Research*, 38 (2): 751–776.

Hartley, J. (2004) 'Case study research', in C. Cassell and G. Symon (eds), *Essential Guide to Qualitative Methods in Organizational Research*. London: Sage, pp. 323–333.

Hassard, J.S. and Buchanan, D.A. (2009) 'From *Modern Times* to *Syriana*: feature films as research data', in D.A. Buchanan and A. Bryman (eds), *The Sage Handbook of Organizational Research Methods*. London: Sage, pp. 620–635.

Hazen, M.A. (1993) 'Towards polyphonic organization', *Journal of Organizational Change Management*, 6 (5): 15–26.

Langley, A. (1999) 'Strategies for theorizing from process data', *Academy of Management Review*, 24 (4): 691–710.

Langley, A. (2009) 'Studying processes in and around organizations', in D. A. Buchanan and A. Bryman (eds), *The Sage Handbook of Organizational Research Methods*. London: Sage, pp. 409–429.

Lincoln, Y.S. and Guba, E.G. (1985) *Naturalistic Inquiry*. Beverly Hills, CA: Sage.

Locke, K. and Velamuri, S.R. (2009) 'The design of member review: showing what to organization members and why', *Organizational Research Methods*, 12 (3): 488–509.

O'Connor, E.S. (1995) 'Paradoxes of participation: textual analysis and organizational change', *Organization Studies*, 16 (5): 769–803.

O'Leary, M. (2003) 'From paternalism to cynicism: narratives of a newspaper company', *Human Relations*, 56 (6): 685–704.

Pentland, B.T. (1999) 'Building process theory with narrative: from description to explanation', *Academy of Management Review*, 24 (4): 711–724.

Perrow, C. (1999) *Normal Accidents: Living With High-Risk Technologies*. New Jersey: Princeton University Press.

Pettigrew, A.M. (1985) *The Awakening Giant: Continuity and Change in ICI*. Oxford: Basil Blackwell.

Pettigrew, A.M. (1990) 'Longitudinal field research on change: theory and practice', *Organization Science*, 1 (3): 267–292.

Plowman, D.A., Baker, L.T., Beck, T.E., Kulkarni, M., Solansky, S.T. and Travis, D.V.T. (2007) 'Radical change accidentally: the emergence and amplification of small change', *Academy of Management Journal*, 50 (3): 515–543.

Scandura, T.A. and Williams, E.A. (2000) 'Research methodology in management: current practices, trends, and implications for future research', *Academy of Management Journal*, 43 (6): 1248–1264.

Snook, S.A. (2000) *Friendly Fire: The Accidental Shootdown of US Black Hawks Over Northern Iraq*. Princeton and Oxford: Princeton University Press.

Stake, R.E. (1994) 'Case studies', in N.K. Denzin and Y.S. Lincoln (eds), *Handbook of Qualitative Research*. Thousand Oaks, CA: Sage, pp. 236–247.

Stake, R.E. (2000) 'Case studies', in N.K. Denzin and Y.S. Lincoln (eds), *Handbook of Qualitative Research* (2nd edn). Thousand Oaks, CA: Sage, pp. 435–454.

Stake, R.E. (2006) *Multiple Case Study Analysis*. New York: The Guilford Press.

Swanson, R.A. and Holton, E.F. (eds) (2005) *Research in Organizations: Foundations and Methods of Inquiry*. San Francisco, CA: Berret-Koehler Publishers Inc.

Toft, B. and Reynolds, S. (2005) *Learning from Disasters: A Management Approach* (3rd edn). Houndmills, Basingstoke: Palgrave Macmillan.

Tsoukas, H. (2009) 'Craving for generality and small-N studies: a Wittgensteinian approach towards the epistemology of the particular in organization and management studies', in D.A. Buchanan and A. Bryman (eds), *The Sage Handbook of Organizational Research Methods*. London: Sage, pp. 285–301.

Vaughan, D. (1996) *The Challenger Launch Decision: Risky Technology, Culture, and Deviance at NASA*. Chicago: University of Chicago Press.

Williams, M. (2000) 'Interpretivism and generalization', *Sociology*, 34 (2): 209–224.

Yin, R.K. (2009) *Case Study Research: Design and Methods* (4th edn). Thousand Oaks, CA: Sage.

21　Action Research

Julie Wolfram Cox

Introduction

In this chapter action research (AR) is presented as an endeavour that is both liminal and hybrid in nature. It is liminal in the sense that it exists in the interstices between research, consulting, social action and reflection. It is hybrid in the sense that new forms of AR combine and supplement earlier approaches (e.g. Stebbins and Shani, 2009). The associated variety and popularity of AR in organizational studies has been the subject of much discussion and several attempts have been made to compare and contrast different emphases among AR approaches (Cassell and Johnson, 2006; Gill and Johnson, 2010). Given this variety it is important that the prospective action researcher takes time to situate AR practice within the field of study and consider carefully the nature and assumptions underlying his or her work. While such considerations are, of course, relevant to all research (Crotty, 1998), they remain of particular importance for AR given (much contested) concerns with its rigour, its heralded death (Sanford, 2005 [1970]) and even its more recent hubris (Wolfram Cox and Cooke, 2007).

This chapter aims to assist the action researcher to gain (more) familiarity with such discussions. After presenting some widely used definitions of AR, a brief introduction to its development is presented in an effort to display the sources of variety among AR approaches. Next comes a consideration of what AR is *not*. Issues to consider are highlighted, as are the author's own reflections on navigating and re-negotiating relationships over the term of a project on governance and accountability in policing.[1] Emphasis is placed on AR in organizational settings and recent reflexive efforts to display rather than sanitize or evaluate AR in absolute terms are applauded.

What is Action Research?

As defined by French and Bell (1999: 130), AR is:

> the process of systematically collecting research data about an ongoing system relative to some objective, goal, or need of that system; feeding these data back into the system; taking actions by altering selected variables within the system based both on data and on hypotheses; and evaluating the results of actions by collecting more data.

In recent times Reason and Bradbury's broader (2001: 1) definition has also gained currency. They saw AR as 'a participatory, democratic process concerned with developing practical knowing in the pursuit of worthwhile human purposes … and more generally the flourishing of individual persons and their communities'.

In recognition of the variety of perspectives on AR, some have claimed that there is neither a simple guide nor a single definition for AR (Robinson, [1993] 2005). Indeed, it has been argued that AR is best represented as a 'family' of approaches (Reason and Bradbury, 2001; Stebbins and Shani, 2009; Bradbury Huang, 2010) or perhaps a food of many flavours (Chandler and Torbert, 2003).

Within this diversity some common threads remain. Gill and Johnson (2010: 99) suggest that most action researchers (still) 'tend to follow Lewin' and use 'an iterative cycle of problem identification, diagnosis, planning, intervention and evaluation of the results of action in order to learn from experience and as a prelude to further diagnostic activity and the planning of subsequent interventions'. In many representations this process appears as a spiral (Sykes and Treleaven, 2009). Whatever the specific approach, Gill and Johnson (2010: 103) have stressed the collaborative nature of the AR relationship and the notion that 'action research is not done *upon* people, rather it is research that is done *with* those people'.

---

[1]The research discussed here was funded by an Australian Research Council Linkage Project Grant and by Victoria Police, for whose continued support I am most grateful. I would also like to thank Georgina Caillard for her assistance with and comments on this draft.

Development and Differentiation[2]

Sources and streams of action research

In an early commentary on the derivations of AR, Rapoport (2005 [1970]: 26) distinguished four 'streams of development': the Tavistock stream of experience in the United Kingdom during and after World War II, an operational research stream that also developed out of the war, a group dynamics stream attributed to Kurt Lewin and his followers in the United States and an applied anthropology stream. While Rapoport's derivation may be readily contested (e.g., Curle, 2005 [1949]; Fals-Borda, 2005 [1984]; Cooke, 2005 [2003]) it remains useful in tracing particular emphases in the practice of AR and for allowing a consideration of influences other than those of Lewin and Tavistock (e.g. Maurer and Githens, 2010).

Scope of action research

The emphasis of early AR work was on material changes assessable in the short term and usually conducted by an outside professional consultant (e.g. Lippitt, 2005 [1959]; Whyte, 2005 [1961]). In contrast, more recent models of AR practice include the use of internal researcher/consultants who lose the remoteness and the impartiality of the unfamiliar, detached 'expert' (e.g. Coghlan, 2005 [2001]; Coghlan and Brannick, 2009).

Also contrasting with the local and material locus of early AR researchers were those who depicted its purpose as broader social change. As early as 1945 Lewin supported an extension of the reach of AR on the basis that its focus on the *how* of social interventions obscured the bigger *why* questions of their purpose and legitimacy (Lewin, 2005 [1945]: 20). This interest in large societal issues is also evident in Lewin's (2005 [1946]) account, *Research on Minority Problems*, where he argued for AR's potential both for solving social problems and for extending the principles of experimental science (Greenwood and Levin, 1998; see also Cassell and Johnson, 2006).

Participation and action

After several other early papers on AR also addressed issues of racism and ethnicity, AR's social change imperative started to gather momentum. What

---

[2]Developed from Wolfram Cox and Cooke (2007).

became known as participatory research was seen to be concerned more with conflict than consensus social theory and to place more emphasis on promoting system transformation and the problems of equity, self-reliance and oppression than on promoting reform and the problems of efficiency and growth within a client system (Brown and Tandon, 2005 [1983]). Departing from Lewin, and arguing that both AR and participatory research 'explicitly reject the irrelevance [*sic*] of more traditional conceptions of social science research', Brown and Tandon ([1983] 2005: 32) examined the prospects for beneficial, but inevitably problematic interactions between the traditions.

Participatory research was also termed 'participatory action research (PAR)', a conflation itself subject to variations of meaning (see Brown, 2005 [1993]). For example, Orlando Fals-Borda (2005 [1984]; 2005 [1987]), the foremost developer and advocate of PAR, aimed to use action-research-type techniques for progressive social change. His approach to PAR can be compared with that of W.F. Whyte (Whyte et al., 2005 [1989]; Argyris and Schön, 2005 [1989]). In Whyte's version, PAR is explained as an applied research strategy, unusual in its recognition of the value and legitimacy of labour unions and affinity with traditions of industrial democracy.

Whyte and his co-authors also connected PAR to wider understandings of the nature of science in society. Lacking the societal praxis of Fals-Borda and associated more with organizational or corporate settings (Cassell and Johnson, 2006), Whyte's PAR is hard to distinguish from 'normal' AR when participation is a defining feature. By 1983, Brown and Tandon (2005 [1983]) framed this comparison as one between First World AR and the tradition of participatory research that had emerged in the Third World. They stated that the First World tradition focused on individual and group levels of analysis while that of the Third World was concerned with societal change.

Negotiating (and re-negotiating) participatory action research: an example from the field

Such categorizations assume that the nature and intent of an AR project will remain fairly static throughout its duration, a stability that is ironic given the iterative nature of the AR process and assumes that a shared concept of the research can be both attained and maintained over time. A project with which I have been involved over the last four years highlights that such stability is not always the case.

The project concerned governance and accountability with Victoria Police (VP) in the state of Victoria, Australia. The original plan was to use action research to investigate, analyse, evaluate and facilitate a shift from command and control-based governance to more collaborative and even collegiate (professional, egalitarian) structures and processes. The project was set up along traditional (First World) PAR lines: as a working collaboration between an external research team from two universities and an internal VP steering committee as the client. An assessment of the effectiveness of police research networks had called for the greater use of such participatory action research due to its emphasis on equal partnership and dialogue among participants and researchers and in this sense the methodology for the research to be undertaken for this project was to be congruent with its focus, for this collaboration was to be modelled through the research process as well as being the subject of the research. Based on a joint consultation, the original research design incorporated joint VP and research team participation ranging from the refining of the research questions and methodology through to the data collection, analysis, implementation and assessment of interventions.

The initial encouragement for what became our project had been given by an advisor (now retired) to the then Chief Commissioner of Police, Christine Nixon. Ms Nixon had introduced several changes to the structures and emphases of Victoria Police and her advisor was keen for our work to take the form of an AR project, 'so that it would not sit on the shelf'. Together we applied for additional funding from the Australian Research Council. Such funding applications are encouraged both within Australian universities, where they hold much prestige, and within Victoria Police, which has developed a good reputation as a major supporter of publicly funded collaborative research, including the involvement of police officers in data collection and analysis. After two tries and various adjustments in personnel and content to strengthen its theoretical contribution, the application was successful. While much research into the organization had been initiated during Ms Nixon's term, ours was the first such project to involve work with police management as its subject.

The news of the application's success finally arrived about seven months after its submission and the start of the project was further delayed due to the need to set up research contracts and to arrange ethics clearances across two universities and Victoria Police. Within this period (roughly a further year), an initial steering committee was formed and some internal 're-selling' of the project was required as senior personnel had changed. Soon afterwards, and in the first of several re-negotiations, I was asked to meet with VP's then Organization Development Steering Committee and to respond to suggestions about the project's emphasis. Over time the membership of our project steering committee was subject to some further changes due to the promotion and retirement of several staff, meaning that we again needed to re-negotiate the nature of what had originally been a project identified as needed from within Victoria Police, to explain the collaborative intent behind the research process and to justify our interest in qualitative research to officers and managers who were more familiar and more at ease with large quantitative data sets.

Thus the very basis for and ownership of the project was subject to several shifts. Its form also changed, for in developing the funding proposal the written project outline had had to be translated into a form that was acceptable for academic peer review and then had to be re-translated for the steering committee. Over the period since our initial meetings, organizational priorities had changed and the steering committee suggested some specific emphases for our studies based on a change in leadership at VP and an assessment of some existing experimentation in governance arrangements.

We requested union representation on the steering committee but this was declined. We were required to attend steering committee meetings every three months, much of which were devoted to meeting formal project management requirements including the submission of progress documents and a discussion of the project risks. Over time the length of the steering committee meetings was reduced and the researcher membership of all such committees was also reduced to include only the chief investigators for each project, meaning that our research assistants were unable to attend most meetings. After two such steering committee meetings we received two formal letters outlining changes to the scope of the project, including one that precluded us from continuing our ongoing observation of particular committees when all such observations (for all projects involving external researchers) were stopped in response to a senior management request.

This process of negotiation and re-negotiation meant that we needed to re-start the project several times, which also involved several re-drafts of our suggested methodology. In the meantime a series of organizational changes was already underway and the emphasis of the project moved away from implementation and towards evaluation and feedback. However, and to some extent despite formal requirements from VP, the universities, their lawyers and administrators, much goodwill remained. The formal management processes did not stifle the collaboration itself, our ability to interview far and wide or to present our findings with reference to the full diversity of opinions represented in our research and more general implications for public management. As argued by Sykes and Treleaven (2009: 226), 'effective engagement of participants require[s] a sensitive consideration of organizational contexts and power relationships'.

Action research and science

In addition to the importance of the politics of organizational collaboration, other challenges to the potential of AR reflect larger concerns about the very nature of social science. For example, while not naming AR as such, Selltiz and Cook (2005 [1948]) set out the case for AR to be brought to a wider audience. They described the need to bridge a gap between 'pure' research aimed at identifying general social principles and 'applied' research so narrowly designed as to have no relevance other than to the often artificially constructed scenarios it investigates. Required instead, they argued, was research that addresses real and immediate social problems but uses the traditional scientific method and produces actual social change. Adding to this, Rapoport (2005 [1970]: 25) wrote that: 'Action research aims to contribute both to the practical concerns of people in an immediate problematic situation and to the goals of social science by joint collaboration within a mutually acceptable ethical framework'.

Taking a more pessimistic perspective toward AR at the time, Sanford (2005 [1970]) adopted the tone of a premature and indeed mistaken obituary in his comparison of AR of the 1940s and 1950s with that of the late 1960s, by which time he argued that there had been little emphasis on the study of actions and that the separation of action from research had meant that AR had had little influence in the social sciences, except in education, his chosen context. His preference was for 'research-action' with the aim of promoting liberation and growth through the processes of research.

Such a reference – and deference – to science has proved common even from the early days (see Chein et al., 2005 [1948]) and, as suggested by Cooke (2006), scientism was embedded by Lippitt (2005 [1950]) into his constructions of the AR-derived 'change agent' identity. While the notion, tacit and explicit, of the action researcher as change agent still prevails, and some forms of AR retain a positivist epistemology and commonality with the scientific method (Aguinis, 2005 [1993]), most do not (Chandler and Torbert, 2003; Ellis and Kiely, 2005 [2000]). Action researchers have moved from the somewhat defensive claim that AR 'transcends the sterile specialization of the social sciences' (Blum, 2005 [1955]: 316) to a careful differentiation of themselves *from* positivist scientism, albeit through such (scientific) terms as validity (Ellis and Kiely, 2005 [2000]), generalization and rigour (Melrose, 2005 [2001]; see also Cassell and Johnson, 2006).

For example, Susman and Evered (2005 [1978]) located the action researcher within a 'different' science, one that also requires different criteria and methods; namely, understanding rather than explanation, making things happen rather than prediction, conjectures rather than deduction or induction, engagement rather than detachment, and action rather than contemplation. More specifically, McTaggart (2005 [1998]) put forward the view that the discourse of validity has been colonized by positivist thought and argued for validation to become, instead, a social and political process concerned with making commitments transparent to participants through appropriate communicative structures (see also Checkland and Howell, 2005 [1998]). He argued that PAR was not valid unless it met the criteria of defensibility, educative value, political efficacy and moral appropriateness. In terms of external validity, in particular, Schön (2005 [1995]) placed discussions of rigour and of relevance within the institutional context of the research university and in relation to the new scholarship advocated by Boyer, with its emphasis on integration and application. Schön argued for the need to legitimize a new type of generalization: that of 'reflective transfer', where actionable knowledge can be carried over to new practice situations through the use of models or prototypes.

Thus, points of reference and distinction have moved from the development of varieties of AR within the span of activity that bridges organizational consultation and science towards some effort to breach that span altogether and to establish broader criteria for the assessment of action. For example, and like Third World PAR, Reason's (1994; 2005 [1999]) development of the related notion of co-operative inquiry aimed for democratization and emancipation through research. It also problematized 'the positivist view of the action researcher as a detached expert who exercises a legitimate role as architect of change' (Cassell and Johnson, 2006: 800).

Action science, action inquiry and action learning

Thus, comparisons among the varieties of AR are important as they help us to understand both the scope and the type of science relevant to AR in organizations (see Bain, 2005 [1951]; Shumsky, 2005 [1958]). In a much-cited paper, Argyris and Schön (2005 [1989]) sought to locate AR by comparing it with PAR

(Whyte's version) and action science, with the latter two being 'members of the same action research family' (Argyris and Schön, 2005 [1989]: 139). As described by Cassell and Johnson (2006: 794), action science interventions are based on 'the researcher's interpretive understanding of organizational participants' practical reasoning as "theories-in-use" that occupy organizational back stages and are hidden by the evasions constituted through "espoused theories"'. Argyris and Schön (2005 [1989]) drew attention to tacit practitioner theories-in-use that serve to distort and undermine AR findings and interventions if they are not surfaced. Doing so through action science was seen to allow for learning about tacit theories-in-use through which feelings of embarrassment and threat develop.

As argued by Gustavsen, such a combination of theory and practice has long been evident in AR, even if there have been shifts in emphasis over the years: from analytic-descriptive with a strong element of systems thinking, to a theoretical foregrounding of local constructivism, and on to a renewed emphasis on theoretical generalizing from local organizational patterns to 'make a number of (initially) local projects interact with each other to constitute broader waves of change' (Gustavsen, 2008: 432). Further, Reason (1994: 49) distinguished action science from Torbert's action inquiry:

> Action *science* focuses on the ways practitioners construe their behavior, their implicit cognitive models, and their actual behavior. Action *inquiry*, while addressing these, in addition addresses outcomes … and the quality of one's attention … Further, action inquiry addresses the question of how to transform organizations and communities into collaborative, self-reflective communities of inquiry.

Raelin (2005 [1989]) has argued that action science goes deeper in such surfacing than does action learning, although both show the same 'action' perspective. Action learning, also called 'work-based learning' (Raelin, 2000; 2006) has a fairly narrow focus and usually takes place within facilitated learning sets that meet on a regular basis and reflect on members' actions in negotiating real-time work problems. (For a useful summary see Ellis and Kiely (2005 [2000]) who compare AR with PAR, action learning and action science in terms of ideology, procedure and validity criteria.)

Thus, the various and changing identities of AR and of action researchers have been represented through a series of differentiation and comparison processes, with the divisions within these showing an increasing specification while remaining highly normative.

Appreciative inquiry and transformative AR

The normative nature of AR is perhaps most evident in the now popular form of appreciative inquiry (e.g. Cooperrider and Srivastva, 2005 [1987]), which moves away from a problem-centred approach to AR on the basis that a resolution of problems can, at best, assist a system to return to the status quo rather than to progress and develop. Avoiding social frames of reference to distinguish their contributions, these authors drew instead on metaphysics, ancient inspirational archetypes (Cooperrider and Srivastva, 2005 [1987]) and ecology (see Reason and Torbert, 2005 [2001]) to argue the importance of their works. In their widely cited paper, Cooperrider and Srivastva (2005 [1987]) argued for the replacement of value-free science with the more active, invested, appreciative and transformative emphasis of 'socio-rational' science, stating their 'conviction that action-research has the potential to be to the postindustrial era what "scientific management" was to the industrial' (2005 [1987]: 52).

Like Cooperrider and Srivastva, and taking a broader perspective than Friedman and Rogers (2009), Maurer and Githens (2010: 269) have also aimed to move beyond problem-solving approaches to consider AR as a 'worldview', suggesting that 'the potential of AR lies in the creation of mutual understanding and learning in and through dialogue, critical reflection, and action'. They distinguished conventional, critical and dialogical AR, noting that these categories overlapped but also stressing the potential of dialogical AR, which encourages critical reflection on practices, for surfacing values and for a subtle exploration of critical issues. They concluded by suggesting an inquiry into the possibilities for such (democratic) dialogue even in strict hierarchical and authoritarian organizations.

Also aiming for a transformational social science, although not in a radical sense, Reason and Torbert (2005 [2001]) argued a case for the importance of practical knowledge and for 'critical inquiry in action' (2005 [2001]: 234). In contrast to the linguistic turn where the emphasis is on the role of language in constructing reality, they stated that the action turn gives an emphasis to enquiry that contributes directly to the flourishing of human persons, their communities and the ecosystems of which they are part.

In many ways, such grand statements about AR are quite understandable, for they represent one response to its provisionality and somewhat secondary status in relation to positivist science. They are certainly not new, for Shumsky (2005 [1958]) presented a manifesto in which he suggested the need for an AR 'movement'. However, such efforts are arguably conservative in the interests that they serve. For example, the paper by Cooperrider and Srivastva (2005 [1987]) accepts social arrangements as arising from agreement (unlike Rahman, 2005 [1982]; Fals-Borda, 2005 [1984]) and is exclusively organizational/managerial when it comes to intervention. Similarly, Reason and Torbert (2005 [2001]) have argued that good theory is not just descriptive, inductive or deductive, universalizable and analytic, but also normative, analogical, timely and implementable so as to sustain personal, social and community development.

What Action Research is Not

In terms of form, both Cooperrider and Srivastva (2005 [1987]) and Reason (2005 [2003]) made liberal use of antimonies in their carving out of potential futures for AR, supplementing these with persuasive illustrations to drive home their arguments. Differentiating what AR was *not* was also evident in Schein's (2005 [1995]) attempt to clarify what he saw as confusion among notions of process consultation, AR and clinical inquiry in terms of researcher and client needs and interests; joint ownership of interventions; and the recognition that entry into a diagnostic relationship is itself a major intervention. While Schein viewed both process consultation and clinical inquiry as client-centred, AR may be more consultant-driven, unlikely to surface valid data, and may even cause damage to the client. In all these narratives, though, there are at least two processes in hand – of differentiation and specification, of what is and is not required of the authentic practitioner.

In the face of such complexity, Bradbury Huang (2010) has suggested that it is still possible to articulate what AR is *not*: interacting only with formal powers and with researcher-only ownership of research data; offering insights alone; and poorly conducting conventional research. To this may be added Gill's earlier (1986) comparison of (problem-based traditional) AR with consultancy and basic research and Gill and Johnson's (2010) comparison of such AR with both true experiments and quasi-experiments.

However, in recent times the growing complexity of approaches to AR has made such clear differentiations difficult. For example, in one recent article Stebbins and Shani (2009) presented a framework of collaborative research orientations. Reflective design theory is described as a collaborative framework (Docherty et al., 2008) for large and complicated organizations; a hybrid that 'incorporates aspects of clinical inquiry, AR, appreciative inquiry, collaborative management research, sociotechnical systems, and self-design theory' (Stebbins and Shani, 2009: 60). As noted by Dick (2011: 123), '[l]abels for participative, action-oriented research methods continue to multiply'.

Conclusion

Wilson's (2005 [1947]) call for a meaningful self-awareness on the part of the action researcher launched what has become a recent emphasis in, if not type of, AR: reflexive AR. While action researchers are, by and large, no longer required to undergo psychoanalysis, as was the case for those who worked for the Tavistock Institute in its early days (Trist and Murray, 1990), the framing of reflexivity primarily as a personal and individualistic concern remains. For example, like McTaggart (2005 [1998]) and Checkland and Holwell (2005 [1998]), Regehr outlined some means by which researchers can allow greater scrutiny of their value position.

Both Regehr (2005 [2000]) and Greenwood (2005 [2002]) called for action researchers to show greater courage in these endeavours. Such courage is evident in the recent flood of reflexive writing on the limits of collaboration (Cunningham, 2008; Arieli et al., 2009; Galuppo et al., 2011) and, in particular, on PAR (David, 2005 [2002]; Smith et al. 2010), including accounts of partial successes and failures (Williams et al., 2005 [2003]) and of compromises such as within our VP project, as described above. This reflexivity is perhaps most evident in recent feminist PAR (Gatenby and Humphries, 2005 [2000]; Katila and Meriläinen, 2005 [2002]).

In combination such works present dilemmas faced by the authors as action researchers while also addressing the precarious identity of AR, an identity which is perhaps most evident in what Cassell and Johnson (2006: 805) have termed 'deconstructive AR' practices that may 'question the familiar and taken-for-granted'. Cassell and Johnson raise the possibility that a postmodern stance may inform 'interventions that unsettle hegemonic discourses, and give voice to alternatives so as to encourage heteroglossia, rather than directing substantive organizational change' (Cassell and Johnson, 2006: 804). Examples included were Barry's (1997) discussion of interventions designed to unsettle dominant organizational narratives and Treleaven's (2001) discussion of the processes and effects of destabilizing gender narratives developed by female participants in a collaborative enquiry group.

Returning to our own example, shifts in the focus of the organization and the researcher/client relationships and priorities over the course of our VP project have meant that the nature of research analysis and 'intervention' also became deconstructive and dialogical in nature. Rather than intervene in the organization's decision-making and accountability structures and processes (as we had originally planned), the focus of our work to date has shifted towards a joint articulation and dialogue about discourses of professionalism, tradition, collaboration, community responsibility and gender within the organization and their effects on the breadth and depth of organizational change. Originally aimed at reviewing what had been heralded as a most progressive, if controversial, period within Victoria Police's history, we found that the more palatable 'good news stories' were complicated by other perspectives that were sometimes discounted or individualized as unrepresentative of the (current) organization as a whole. Our challenge was to work with the steering committee over time so that these views were heard, at least in part; a process that has involved the joint planning of research and some joint analysis of data and has now developed towards the co-authorship of a paper on the doing of collaborative research. At the boundary between action and more traditional research in terms of the extent of the intervention, the building of relationships has allowed for candid exchanges and facilitated the ongoing development of a project that could have otherwise been dismissed as lacking contemporary relevance due to changes in both the internal organizational and external political environment of the organization since its initiation.

In this context it is notable that Treleaven's more recent work includes a discussion of the links between critical AR and organizational ethnography and the application of critical discourse analysis 'in order to identify and understand the production and operation of the powerful discourses driving competing political agendas within organizations' (Sykes and Treleaven, 2009: 220). This includes not only the 'possibility for the discussion of multiple interpretations, representations and discourses' but also for 'engaging with people toward participant-led change and action' (2009: 224), perhaps heralding a further research-led turn in the story of AR.

Further Reading

Many original and important review works appear in the edited collection *Fundamentals of Action Research* (Cooke and Wolfram Cox, 2005) and Gill and

Johnson (2010) have presented a comprehensive review of suggested readings. Regular updates on contemporary AR literature have been provided by Dick (2004; 2006; 2009; 2011).

References

Aguinis, H. (2005 [1993]) 'Action research and scientific method: presumed discrepancies and actual similarities', in B. Cooke and J. Wolfram Cox (eds), *Fundamentals of Action Research*, vol. 3. London: Sage, pp. 347–367.

Argyris, C. and Schön, D. A. (2005 [1989]) 'Participatory action research and action science compared: a commentary', in B. Cooke and J. Wolfram Cox (eds), *Fundamentals of Action Research*, vol. 2. London: Sage, pp. 137–147.

Arieli, D., Friedman, V. J. and Agbaria, K. (2009) 'The paradox of participation in action research', *Action Research*, 7 (3): 263–290.

Bain, R. ([1951] 2005) 'Action research and group dynamics', in B. Cooke and J. Wolfram Cox (eds), *Fundamentals of Action Research*, vol. 1. London: Sage, pp. 319–366.

Barry, D. (1997) 'Telling changes: from narrative family therapy to organizational change and development', *Journal of Organizational Change Management*, 10 (1): 30–46.

Blum, F. ([1955] 2005) 'Action research – a scientific approach?', in B. Cooke and J. Wolfram Cox (eds), *Fundamentals of Action Research*, vol. 3. London: Sage, pp. 309–317.

Bradbury Huang, H. (2010) 'What is good action research'? *Action Research*, 8 (1): 93–109.

Brown, L.D. (2005 [1993]) 'Social change through collective reflection with Asian non-governmental development organizations', in B. Cooke and J. Wolfram Cox (eds), *Fundamentals of Action Research*, vol. 3. London: Sage, pp. 57–83.

Brown, L.D. and Tandon, R. (2005 [1983]) 'Ideology and political economy in inquiry: action research and participatory research', in B. Cooke and J. Wolfram Cox (eds), *Fundamentals of Action Research*, vol. 2. London: Sage, pp. 25–49.

Cassell, C. and Johnson, P. (2006) 'Action research: explaining the diversity', *Human Relations*, 59 (6): 783–814.

Chandler, D. and Torbert, B. (2003) 'Transforming inquiry and action: interweaving 27 flavors of action research', *Action Research*, 1 (2): 133–152.

Checkland, P. and Howell, S. (2005 [1998]) 'Action research: its nature and validity', in B. Cooke and J. Wolfram Cox (eds), *Fundamentals of Action Research*, vol. 3, London: Sage, pp. 423–437.

Chein, I., Cook, S. and Harding, J. (2005 [1948]) 'The field of action research', in B. Cooke and J. Wolfram Cox (eds), *Fundamentals of Action Research*, vol. 1. London: Sage, pp. 151–164.

Coghlan, D. (2005 [2001]) 'Insider action research projects: implications for practising managers', in B. Cooke and J. Wolfram Cox (eds), *Fundamentals of Action Research*, vol. 3. London: Sage, pp. 229–244.

Coghlan, D. and Brannick, T. (2009) *Doing Action Research in your own Organization* (3rd edn). London: Sage.

Cooke, B. (2005 [2003]) 'A new continuity with colonial administration: participation in development management', in B. Cooke and J. Wolfram Cox (eds), *Fundamentals of Action Research*, vol. 4. London: Sage, pp. 207–225.

Cooke, B. (2006) 'The Cold War origin of action research as managerial cooptation', *Human Relations*, 59 (5): 655–693.

Cooke, B. and Wolfram Cox, J. (eds) (2005) *Fundamentals of Action Research*. London: Sage.

Cooperrider, D. and Srivastva, S. (2005 [1987]) 'Appreciative inquiry in organizational life', in B. Cooke and J. Wolfram Cox (eds), *Fundamentals of Action Research*, vol. 2. London: Sage, pp. 51–97.

Crotty, M. (1998) *The Foundations of Social Research: Meaning and Perspective in the Research Process*. St. Leonards, Australia: Allen and Unwin.

Cunningham, W. S. (2008) 'Voices from the field', *Action Research*, 6 (4): 373–390.

Curle, A. (2005 [1949]) 'A theoretical approach to action research', in B. Cooke and J. Wolfram Cox (eds), *Fundamentals of Action Research*, vol. 1. London: Sage, pp. 263–277.

David, M. (2005 [2002]) 'Problems of participation: the limits of action research', in B. Cooke and J. Wolfram Cox (eds), *Fundamentals of Action Research*, vol. 4. London: Sage, pp. 107–205.

Dick, B. (2004) 'Action research literature: themes and trends', *Action Research*, 2 (4): 425–444.

Dick, B. (2006) 'Action research literature 2004–2006', *Action Research*, 4 (4): 439–458.

Dick, B. (2009) 'Action research literature 2006–2008', *Action Research*, 7 (4): 423–441.

Dick, B. (2011) 'Action research literature 2008–2010: themes and trends', *Action Research*, 9 (2): 122–143.

Docherty, P., Kira, M, and Shani, A.B. (eds) (2008) *Creating Sustainable Work Systems: Emerging Perspectives and Practice* (2nd edn). London: Routledge.

Ellis, J. and Kiely, J. (2005 [2000]) 'Action inquiry strategies: taking stock and moving forward', in B. Cooke and J. Wolfram Cox (eds), *Fundamentals of Action Research*, vol. 4. London: Sage, pp. 85–119.

Fals-Borda, O. (2005 [1984]) 'Participatory action research', in B. Cooke and J. Wolfram Cox (eds), *Fundamentals of Action Research*, vol. 2. London: Sage, pp. 3–24.

Fals-Borda, O. (2005 [1987]) 'The application of participatory action-research in Latin America, in B. Cooke and J. Wolfram Cox (eds), *Fundamentals of Action Research*, vol. 3. London: Sage, pp. 33–55.

French, W.L. and Bell, C.H. (1999) *Organization Development* (6th edn). Upper Saddle River, NJ: Prentice-Hall.

Friedman, V.J. and Rogers, T. (2009) 'There is nothing so theoretical as good action research', *Action Research*, 7 (1): pp. 31–47.

Galuppo, L., Gorli, M. and Ripamonti, S. (2011) 'Playing dissymmetry in action research: the role of power and differences in promoting participative knowledge and change', *Systemic Practice and Action Research*, 24 (2): 147–164.

Gatenby, B. and Humphries, M. (2005 [2000]) 'Feminist participatory action research: methodological and ethical issues', in B. Cooke and J. Wolfram Cox (eds), *Fundamentals of Action Research*, vol. 2. London: Sage, pp. 261–288.

Gill, J. (1986) 'Research as action: an experiment utilising the social sciences', in F. Heller (ed.), *The Use and Abuse of Social Science*. London: Sage.

Gill, J. and Johnson, P. (2010) *Research Methods for Managers* (4th edn). Los Angeles, CA: Sage.

Greenwood, D.J. (2005 [2002]) 'Action research: unfulfilled promises and unmet challenges', in B. Cooke and J. Wolfram Cox (eds), *Fundamentals of Action Research*, vol. 4. London: Sage, pp. 173–195.

Greenwood, D.J. and Levin, M. (1998) *Introduction to Action Research: Social Research for Social Change*. Thousand Oaks, CA: Sage.

Gustavsen, B. (2008) 'Action research, practical challenges and the formation of theory', *Action Research*, 6 (4): 421–437.

Katila, S. and Meriläinen, S. ([2002] 2005) 'Metamorphosis: from "nice girls" to "nice bitches": resisting patriarchal articulations of professional identity', in B. Cooke and J. Wolfram Cox (eds), *Fundamentals of Action Research*, vol. 4. London: Sage, pp. 275–296.

Lewin, K. (2005 [1945]) 'Action research and minority problems', in B. Cooke and J. Wolfram Cox (eds), *Fundamentals of Action Research*, vol. 1. London: Sage, pp. 19–31.

Lewin, K. (2005 [1946]) 'Research on minority problems', in B. Cooke and J. Wolfram Cox (eds), *Fundamentals of Action Research*, vol. 1. London: Sage, pp. 32–42.

Lippitt, R. (2005 [1950]) 'Action-research and the values of the social scientist', in B. Cooke and J. Wolfram Cox (eds), *Fundamentals of Action Research*, vol. 3. London: Sage, pp. 301–307.

Lippitt, R. (2005 [1959]) 'Dimensions of the consultant's job', in B. Cooke and J. Wolfram Cox (eds), *Fundamentals of Action Research*, vol. 3. London: Sage, pp. 191–199.

Maurer, M. and Githens, R. P. (2010) 'Toward a reframing of action research for human resource and organization development: moving beyond problem solving and toward dialogue', *Action Research*, 8 (3): 267–292.

McTaggart, R. (2005 [1998]) 'Is validity really an issue for participatory action research?', in B. Cooke and J. Wolfram Cox (eds), *Fundamentals of Action Research*, vol. 3. London: Sage, pp. 395–421.

Melrose, M.J. (2005 [2001]) 'Maximizing the rigor of action research: why would you want to? How could you?', in B. Cooke and J. Wolfram Cox (eds), *Fundamentals of Action Research*, vol. 3. London: Sage, pp. 439–461.

Raelin, J.A. (2005 [1989]) 'Action learning and action science: are they different?', in B Cooke and J. Wolfram Cox (eds), *Fundamentals of Action Research*, vol. 2. London: Sage, pp. 159–180.

Raelin, J.A. (2000) *Work-based Learning: The New Frontier of Management Development*. Upper Saddle, NJ: Prentice-Hall.

Raelin, J.A. (2006) 'Does action learning promote collaborative leadership?', *Academy of Management Learning and Education*, 5 (2): 152–168.

Rahman, M.A. (2005 [1982]) 'The theory and practice of participatory action research', in B. Cooke and J. Wolfram Cox (eds), *Fundamentals of Action Research*, vol. 2. London: Sage, pp. 11–24.

Rapoport, R.N. (2005 [1970]) 'Three dilemmas in action research with special reference to the Tavistock experience', in B. Cooke and J. Wolfram Cox (eds), *Fundamentals of Action Research*, vol. 4. London: Sage, pp. 25–44.

Reason, P. (1994) 'Human inquiry as discipline and practice', in P. Reason (ed.), *Participation in Human Inquiry*. London: Sage, pp. 40–56.

Reason, P. (2005 [1999]) 'Integrating action and reflection through co-operative inquiry', in B. Cooke and J. Wolfram Cox (eds), *Fundamentals of Action Research*, vol. 2. London: Sage, pp. 235–259.

Reason, P. (2005 [2003]) 'Pragmatist philosophy and action research: readings and conversation with Richard Rorty', in B. Cooke and J. Wolfram Cox (eds), *Fundamentals of Action Research*, vol. 4. London: Sage, pp. 297–319.

Reason, P. and Bradbury, H. (eds) (2001) 'Introduction: inquiry and participation in search of a world worthy of human aspiration', *Handbook of Action Research*. London: Sage, pp. 1–14.

Reason, P. and Torbert, W. (2005 [2001]) 'The action turn: towards a transformational social science', in B. Cooke and J. Wolfram Cox (eds), *Fundamentals of Action Research*, vol. 4. London: Sage, pp. 229–266.

Regehr, A. (2005 [2000]) 'Action research: underlying or undermining the cause?', in B. Cooke and J. Wolfram Cox (eds), *Fundamentals of Action Research*, vol. 4. London: Sage, pp. 157–172.

Robinson, V.M.J. (2005 [1993]) 'Current controversies in action research', in B. Cooke and J. Wolfram Cox (eds), *Fundamentals of Action Research*, vol. 4. London: Sage, pp. 59–84.

Sanford, N. (2005 [1970]) 'Whatever happened to action research?', in B. Cooke and J. Wolfram Cox (eds), *Fundamentals of Action Research*, vol. 4. London: Sage, pp. 3–23.

Schein, E.H. (2005 [1995]) 'Process consultation, action research and clinical inquiry: are they the same?', in B. Cooke and J. Wolfram Cox (eds), *Fundamentals of Action Research*, vol. 2. London: Sage, pp. 149–158.

Schön, D. (2005 [1995]) 'Knowing-in-action: the new scholarship requires a new epistemology' in B. Cooke and J. Wolfram Cox (eds), *Fundamentals of Action Research*, vol. 3. London: Sage, pp. 377–394.

Selltiz, C. and Cook, S.W. (2005 [1948]) 'Can research in social science be both socially useful and scientifically meaningful?', in B. Cooke and J. Wolfram Cox (eds), *Fundamentals of Action Research*, vol. 1. London: Sage, pp. 165–173.

Shumsky, A. (2005 [1958]) 'Action research and modern man', in B. Cooke and J. Wolfram Cox (eds), *Fundamentals of Action Research*, vol. 3. London: Sage, pp. 3–13.

Smith, L., Bratini, L., Chambers, D.-A., Jensen, R. V. and Romero, L. (2010) 'Between idealism and reality: meeting the challenges of participatory action research', *Action Research*, 8 (4): 407–425.

Stebbins, M. W. and Shani, A.B. (2009) 'Clinical inquiry and reflective design in a secrecy-based organization', *Journal of Applied Behavioral Science*, 45 (1): 59–89.

Susman, G., and Evered, R. (2005 [1978]) 'An assessment of the scientific merits of action research', in B. Cooke and J. Wolfram Cox (eds), *Fundamentals of Action Research*, vol. 3. London: Sage, pp. 319–345.

Sykes, C. and Treleaven, L. (2009) Critical action research and organizational ethnography', in S. Ybema, D. Yanow, H. Wels and F. Kamsteeg (eds), *Organizational Ethnography: Studying the Complexities of Everyday Life*. Los Angeles, CA: Sage, pp. 215–230.

Treleaven, L. (2001) 'The turn to action and the linguistic turn: towards an integrated methodology', in P. Reason and H. Bradbury (eds), *Handbook of Action Research: Participative Inquiry and Practice*. London: Sage, pp. 261–272.

Trist, E. and Murray, H. (1990) 'Historical overview: the foundation and development of the Tavistock Institute to 1989', in E. Trist and H. Murray (eds), *The Social Engagement of Social Science, A Tavistock Anthology*, vol. 1: *The Socio-Psychological Perspective*. Philadelphia: University of Pennsylvania Press, pp. 1–34.

Whyte, W. F. (2005 [1961]) 'An action research program for the personnel man', in B. Cooke and J. Wolfram Cox (eds), *Fundamentals of Action Research*, vol. 2. London: Sage, pp. 291–315.

Whyte, W. F., Greenwood, D. and Lazes, P. (2005 [1989]) 'Participatory action research: through practice to science in social research', in B. Cooke and J. Wolfram Cox (eds), *Fundamentals of Action Research*, vol. 2. London: Sage, pp. 99–136.

Williams, G., Srivastava, M., Corbridge, S. and Véron, R. (2005 [2003]) 'Enhancing pro-poor governance in eastern India: participation, politics and action research', in B. Cooke and J. Wolfram Cox (eds), *Fundamentals of Action Research*, vol. 3. London: Sage, pp. 321–346.

Wilson, A.T.M. (2005 [1947]) 'Some implications of medical practice and social casework for action research', in B. Cooke and J. Wolfram Cox (eds), *Fundamentals of Action Research*, vol. 1. London: Sage, pp. 131–149.

Wolfram Cox, J. and Cooke, B. (2007) 'Action research and identity', in A. Pullen, N. Beech and D. Sims, *Exploring Identity: Concepts and Methods*. Houndmills: Palgrave, pp. 221–236.

Using Documents in Organizational Research

Bill Lee

Introduction

Qualitative research involving fieldwork is often costly. Documentary analysis by contrast may involve few costs apart from the researcher's time (c.f. Rapley, 2007: 12). Moreover, documents are manifold, playing an important role in organizational life, providing details of policies, procedures, prospective plans such as investment appraisals and records of events such as minutes of meetings. There are many additional documentary sources about organizations, including newspaper reports, government abstracts, tribunal records of misdemeanours and pressure groups' objections to developments. It is, thus, possible to use documents to address a broad range of research questions. As many documents are readily available and endure over time, the research questions and answers may cover a much longer period than may be possible when other research methods are used.

Yet documents have often been under-utilized in research into organizations, vis-à-vis their availability. This may be related in part to a belief that documents are too readily available to be of any real use; either the really interesting questions have already been asked of the documents or the number of documents available is now so great that it has become almost impossible to organize an enquiry to make a sufficiently succinct and meaningful statement on the basis of an analysis of documents about an organization. The ready availability of documents – especially given the materials that are now digitized for collection through the internet – obviously causes problems. But documents also offer numerous opportunities for research and obstacles to their use may reside in not knowing how to source, verify and analyse them to answer research questions.

This chapter aims to consider how questions may be formulated and answered by the systematic collection and analysis of documents. The remainder of the chapter proceeds in the following way. First, the question of what is a document will be considered. Thought will then be given to how to scope research by defining relevant research questions and how to gather the documents to help provide answers to those questions. Attention will then be turned to how to conduct different types of analysis of documents depending on one's epistemology and illustrations of studies involving documents will be drawn from the author's work.

Defining a Document

Hodder (2003: 703) has described a document as 'mute evidence … [which] unlike the spoken word, endures physically and thus can be separated across space and time from its author, producer and user'. Hodder's definition captures the way in which documents allow information to be transposed across time and geographical distance. However, it is questionable whether all documentary records should be considered as 'mute'. There has been an increasing variety of forms of records that have been kept over the past 150 years that do not store only the written word, but are able to project both sound and vision, including film, digital versatile discs, compact discs, pages in cyberspace, etc. Many are not mute in the sense of giving off no sound, although they may be unheard and unseen unless the researcher includes their manifest qualities in the research design.

It is important to consider whether any message either represented in – or symbolized by – a document may be universally understood, or subject to different interpretations. Prior (2003: 2) argues documents involve 'creators (agents, writers, publishers, publicists and so on), users (readers, or receivers) and settings. All three realms are implicated in the emergence of documentation'. Prior's definition introduces the potential for an author's intended meaning, when creating a document, to vary from the understanding that users derive from the document, which could be influenced by the regulatory and institutional setting including language, belief systems and legal requirements. Prior (2008) subsequently highlights how documents may take on the role of actants – i.e. hybrids of objects and actors. When seen in this way, documents have relational properties with other actors, helping to structure relationships both between the documents and the actors and between different actors where the documents are employed. Thus, Prior (2008: 824) says, 'documents serve not merely as containers of content, but as active agents in episodes of interaction and schemes of social organization'.

It may, thus, be argued that a document is a durable repository for textual, visual and audio representations that may be retained and used in different times and spaces, creating the possibility that the meanings of the representations may be interpreted differently – and employed accordingly – by the user, partly because of variations between the regulatory and institutional setting of the producer and user of the document. The user may either be the researcher or another actor in a setting where the documents are employed and the employment of those documents may – or may not – advantage some parties or disadvantage others.

Scoping Research with Documents

The choice of research question will depend in part on the researcher's epistemological position – see below – and whether that position puts greater emphasis on documents' properties as repositories, or also recognizes their potential constitutive capabilities. Different authors (Bricknell, 2008; Prior, 2008) have identified different types of research question that may be considered using documents. Examples include:

- For what purpose were the chosen documents designed?

- How effectively have the chosen documents been designed to realize the purpose for which they were intended?

- Do all documents of a particular genre cover the same issues in the same way?

- Are people interpreting the documents in ways intended by the authors and what are the consequences if they are not doing so?

- How do the contents of documents – such as regulations and policies – help to structure relationships between those parties affected?

- How are people constructing and using documents to project a particular view of themselves or others?

- What insights might documents provide about broader processes on the phenomena in which we are interested?

The different types of research questions require that the researcher conducts either a survey of a population of a particular type of document, a case study of a particular phenomenon using documents, or considers individual cases of different types of documents. As the collection of documents can be inexpensive, a study involving documents is most likely to be useful if documents can provide a pertinent way of addressing the research question when (a) other sources are not sufficient in number or adequate *per se* and (b) documents are available in an ample enough number to provide a sensible answer. Subsidiary considerations depending on the research question include the following:

- If a survey of particular types of documents is being considered, is the total population involved in a particular phenomenon – such as the companies adopting a particular human resource policy of interest – known?

- Are the documents in that population easily accessible?

- If case studies are being considered, either of particular documents or of a particular event or phenomenon using documentary evidence, would the documents that are studied be recognized as sufficiently credible to provide a commentary?

- If one is studying the potential constitutive qualities of documents, is there evidence available to show the impact of the documents?

If documents are an appropriate and ample source to provide a credible answer to the research question, the investigation may go ahead. Of course, the answer to the questions may be 'only partly'. If, however, there are other sources of evidence available to address the parts of research questions that documents are unable to address satisfactorily, a research strategy may be devised in which documents are used in conjunction with other methods.

Collecting Documents

The collection of documents will depend in part on whether the chosen research question addresses the whole population that has to be surveyed, or considers a particular event, organization or phenomenon that requires the study of one or more cases. In both situations, the development of the internet has helped to transform the document collection process. If a survey of organizations is to be conducted and the full composition of that population is known, it may be possible to visit those organizations' websites to download the documents. For example, lists of the top 100 and 250 FTSE companies are widely available. Such organizations' websites are located easily by simply entering their names into a search engine. Many documents such as annual accounts and financial reports, corporate social responsibility reports, product range and historical details are generally available through corporate websites. Internal documentation such as employment policies, collective agreements with trade unions, market intelligence and accounting practices may not be so easily accessible. Nevertheless, documents that are not considered to be commercially sensitive may be made available by a corporation on request if the researcher writes to them, specifying in concise detail what he or she is looking for.

A lot of material may also be available via the internet when the research question requires the conduct of one or more case studies of a particular event, organization or phenomenon. General search engines such as Google facilitate drawing on global resources and an inestimable number of documents. There are two major problems with this approach. First, there will not be a catalogue for all of the information that is available and an initial search using a single term relating to the phenomenon of interest may yield hundreds of thousands of references. Thus, it may be necessary to focus the search more and more narrowly by combining the original search term with others that are related to the research questions until the number of references becomes more manageable. Secondly, although it may be possible to attribute some data to original sources, the validity and origins of some other web pages may be indeterminate, requiring that the information that is reported be authenticated by reference to another source. Useful sources *per se* – that could also help authenticate information in sources that cannot be attributed – are newspapers.

An extensive set of newspapers may be accessed through the Newspaper Subset of the British Library's catalogue (see http://catalogue.bl.uk). Many academic libraries subscribe to *NewsBank*, which provides access to electronic copies of the majority of the UK's daily and Sunday newspapers. *NewsBank* has a search facility that allows the retrieval of all articles on a chosen topic that appeared in any of the newspapers during a period specified by the researcher. Individual newspapers may also have their own indexes – including overseas ones such as the *New York Times* – that may be searched on-line for articles on particular events or organizations. Other important sources of documentation that could help with research are available through government-sponsored websites in the UK. Documents on current government policies may be found at www.direct.gov.uk. Details of documents about historic events, companies and phenomena may be found at www.nationalarchives. gov.uk. Information on parliamentary debates and the emergence of legislation is available through Hansard (see www.publications.parliament.uk/pa/pahansard.htm). There are also important academic sources of documents that are either available, or there is a catalogue of information, through the internet. This includes research conducted by others that is stored at the UK data archive at Essex (see: www.data-archive.ac.uk). Additionally, there is Archives Hub, which provides descriptions of around 200 archives held in UK universities and colleges and a number of research institutes and museums (see: www. archiveshub.ac.uk/). An important emergent facility is the British Library's Management and Business Portal, which provides access to a broad range of sources including the British Library's digital collection. This can be accessed via www.mbsportal.bl.uk/index. A guide to digital datasets relevant to management and business studies may be found on the site at www.mbsportal. bl.uk/taster/subjareas/resmethods/bl/116166datasets_MBS_SA.pdf.

Not all catalogues have been digitized, so a visit to an archive will sometimes be necessary. When visiting archives, it is important to go prepared. Having identified the relevant archive, check:

- The times that the archive is open to the public.

- What proofs of identity will be required for membership of the archive or for access to its records.

- Whether the documents that are required are kept at the archive where there is public access or at a remote location that will necessitate the items being ordered several days in advance of the planned visit.

- How many documents may be accessed at any one time.

Some documents are extremely precious, so many personal belongings such as portable computers, books, ink pens, food and drink may not be permitted in the reading rooms. There are also likely to be restrictions on what items may be photocopied and so it is essential to take writing materials. If information is noted from a source, an extremely clear record of where the information was obtained should be kept in order to provide references when using those data in subsequent work. (For a more extensive discussion of preparations for – and the problems of – conducting research in archives, see Walker, 2004.)

Analysing Documents and Some Illustrations

Once the documents have been collected, a preliminary form of analysis may be necessary to establish whether they should be considered reliable and authentic in the sense of remaining in the form produced by the original author. With contemporary documents, it may be possible to check with the original author whether these have been altered in any way. If the document is sourced from an archive, the archive may have records of provenance that will indicate the article's authenticity. If, however, the document has been obtained from another source and it is not possible to check with the original author that the document is authentic, it may be necessary to consider a number of questions to assess its usefulness. These should include:

- Can the source from which the document was obtained be seen as reliable?

- What was the history of the document before it was obtained?

- Was the document complete as originally constructed or had some of it been partially destroyed, edited or tampered with?

- Is it plausible that the person who produced the document may have wanted to produce a document for the designated purpose?

- Are there other documents that might help to verify the authenticity – and enhance an understanding – of the original document?

- Are those other documents accessible and – if so – through which channels?

Once the authenticity of the documents has been considered, further analysis is likely to be necessary in order to formulate answers to the research questions. There are many different ways of analysing documents (see, for example, Lincoln, 1980; Prior, 2008). The taxonomy of documentary analyses used below will be based around four epistemological positions in qualitative research, adapted broadly from Johnson et al. (2006). These will each be linked to particular methods of documentary analysis, with

Table 22.1   Epistemological position and form of documentary analysis

Epistemology	Form of analysis
Positivism	Objective content analysis that may be quantitative or qualitative. Survey or case study
Interpretive approaches including phenomenology	Ethnographic content analysis of cases
Critical theory	Chronological case study that recognizes a dialectical relationship between text and outcome
Constructivism	Discourse analysis of text

illustrations from the author's work. However, neither the epistemological positions, nor the forms of analysis associated with them here, should be viewed as mutually exclusive of each other. It is possible for the different epistemological positions to inform the same project at different stages, just as it is possible for someone working from one epistemological position to use a method associated with another position in a different way. Table 22.1 provides a summary of the different types of epistemological position and associated forms of documentary analysis. Each will be considered in turn.

Positivist approach

Positivists view a reality that exists independent of observers. An objective, observational language parallels that reality and allows an understanding of the meaning of that reality by analysing what is said. Content analysis provides a tool for understanding meanings that are reported in documents. Those meanings are not considered to be contestable if systematically derived. Thus, Berelson (1952: 18) says: 'Content analysis is a research technique for the objective, systematic ... description of the manifest content of communication'. A logical corollary is that the meaning may be measured in some form. This may be by quantifiable measures such as the *frequency* with which something appears that may indicate the *importance* of a topic afforded by the document and the *balance of favourable and unfavourable references* which may provide a measurement of the *bias* or *direction* of the document (Krippendorff, 2004: 59). However, it might also involve a more qualitative analysis in terms of gradations such as *qualifications* or *provisos*, which will give an indication of the *intensity* or *strength* of the concerns (see Krippendorff, 2004).

The process of applying content analysis is likely to be a sequential one involving a unilinear progression from document collection, analysis and interpretation (Altheide, 1987: 67). A positivist approach may involve a case study of a document or a survey of a population of documents. Where a survey is conducted, sampling techniques may be used to 'answer the research question with sufficient confidence' (Krippendorff, 2004: 121). Content analysis requires the development of a framework to code and help transform the evidence from documents into answers to specified research questions. Holsti (1969) suggests five principles to create a reliable taxonomy for coding. First, the categories used to classify text should be derived from variables in the research questions or hypotheses of the researcher. Second, the categories that are created must be exhaustive, at least along the important criteria, so that each unit of text – such as a sentence, paragraph or article – may be put into one category or another. Third, categories should be mutually exclusive, so that each unit of text will be placed in only one cell in the process of categorization. Fourth, categories will be independent of one another, so the assignment of one unit of text will not lead to the immediate assignment of another. Fifth, the categories should be derived from a single classification principle, so that levels of analysis that are conceptually different should be kept so.

An example here is Lee and Cassell's (2004) content analysis of information for union learning representatives (ULRs) on trade union websites. This was conducted because Catherine Cassell and I were planning an interview study (see Alvesson and Ashcraft, in this volume) to explore the introduction of ULRs and their facilitation of workplace learning opportunities. That study emerged within a programme of research that led to numerous publications (e.g. Cassell and Lee, 2007; 2009; Lee and Cassell 2008), so this case shows how documentary research can fit into a broader research strategy. In preparing for interviews, we wanted to find out how trade unions supported ULRs. As the most readily available form of support was trade union websites, we surveyed these in preparation for our later research. We decided to conduct a systematic content analysis of UK trade union websites to address the following two research questions: 1) how easy would it be for ULRs to access information to carry out their role from their union's website? And 2) what information would ULRs be able to obtain from this source?

We obtained a list of TUC-affiliated trade unions and conducted a Google search to identify whether each had a website. This allowed us to make our research questions more concise by considering only TUC-affiliated trade unions with websites and we conducted a full census of those trade unions. Consistent with a positivist approach, we assumed a single definition of ease of access to information that was related simply to the design of the website. Thus, we ignored other factors that might have affected whether individual ULRs could obtain that information, such as whether: lay officials had personal computers; they were sufficiently confident in their use of those computers; those computers were linked to the internet; the internet connection was made through an exchange that provided a strong uninterrupted connection; and the personal computer had a sufficiently large hard drive to download information quickly. Consistent with Holsti's guidance, we derived the categories for classifying the content of trade union websites from our research questions above, formulated criteria relating to ease of access and defined a full range of information that could help ULRs conduct their role.

To confirm some notion of objectivity for the framework and the validity of its use, we each analysed the same small set of websites initially. The level of consistency between our analyses suggested a confirmation of these issues. This exercise also allowed us to iterate our framework to ensure it was exhaustive for our purposes, i.e. that all issues relevant to the research questions were listed under appropriate categories, with the default options for the respective research questions being that access to a site required a membership number or no useful information could be found anywhere on the site. These categories were ultimately mutually exclusive, so that websites either had pages dedicated to ULRs or they did not. Similarly, they either had other pages that contained information that were useful to ULRs or they did not. The categories were kept independent of one another, so – for example – the absence of a page dedicated to ULRs did not presuppose that there would be no information of use to ULRs elsewhere on the site. Our categories were organized along a single classification principle, so that levels of analysis that were conceptually different – such as the ease with which information could be obtained and the types of information available – were kept separate. Although the information could be measured quantitatively, such as by the number of topics on which ULRs could gather information, we were also able to provide a more qualitative understanding by describing the process that ULRs would have to undertake in order to access the information and the type of information that they might be able to obtain, be it learning materials, guidance on workplace organization for learning, legal rights, etc.

Interpretive approaches

Interpretive approaches – such as phenomenology – are concerned with the ways in which people experience their world in the specific contexts that they occupy. By implication, social meanings are at the centre of any analysis. Thus, documents contain signs and symbols that have to be interpreted. Moreover, the ways in which the signs and symbols are formatted will be subjected to the conventions that prevail in a particular culture. Any interpretation of what those signs are intended to symbolize, or how they are received, must be linked to the culture in which the author prepares the document and the reader digests its contents. Such an understanding is derived from an 'ethnographic content analysis' (Altheide, 1987) and involves reading the text and focusing on 'situations, settings, styles, images, meanings and nuances presumed to be recognizable by the human actors/speakers involved' (Krippendorff, 2004: 16; see also Altheide, 1987: 68). An ethnographic content analysis will involve taking cases of documents and making constant comparisons between them to 'check, supplement, and supplant prior theoretical claims by simultaneously obtaining categorical and unique data for every case studied in order to develop analytical constructs' (Altheide, 1987: 68). Thus, unlike the unilinear process in positivist forms of content analysis, ethnographic content analysis is both reflexive and circular with data being used to develop concepts throughout the process of analysis.

A method akin to ethnographic content analysis was adopted for a study of the alleged damaging effects of accounting on new technology (Lee, 1996; Jones and Lee, 1998). Throughout the late twentieth century, there were suggestions that accounting practices embodied high productivity assumptions, so investment appraisals only allowed new systems that could be justified by increases in volume of output and reductions in labour input, while ongoing cost control measures assumed high levels of output vis-à-vis low levels of labour input with any variance from the low input-high output measure being viewed disparagingly. It was assumed that the high productivity assumptions in accounting techniques either discouraged an introduction of the innovative flexible manufacturing system (FMS) that could manufacture a wide variety rather than large volumes of products, or would lead to inappropriate high-volume manufacturing by any FMS that was introduced.

To assess the validity of these claims, cases concerning companies that had introduced FMS were identified from the trade press and visited. At this time, investment justification documents of FMS and flexible budgets from the departments in which the FMS were deployed were collected to investigate whether accounting methods either discouraged the introduction of FMS or led to their misuse once they were introduced. A form of ethnographic content analysis of documents was an important part of the case studies of the companies. This example thus illustrates how documents can be used as part of case study research (see Buchanan, in this volume). Other methods revealed that, when engineers proposed FMS, they would prepare a document that: described the configuration of FMS; outlined its strengths; detailed the range of products that it was going to manufacture in specified batch sizes at desired levels of system utilization; and conducted a financial appraisal based on the monetary benefits that the specified use of the system would bring against its relative costs. An accountant would check the financial aspects of the proposal and then forward it to a decision-maker. If the FMS was introduced, the assumptions in the initial proposal would be embodied in the flexible budget against which the performance of the system was judged.

The ethnographic content analysis involved, first, drawing a matrix to compare how the initial proposals of FMS had envisaged the performance of each system in quantitative terms of range, batch sizes and machine utilization, to see whether all systems were assumed to have comparable strengths. This revealed three broad motives for FMS. The majority of configurations were introduced to machine a limited range of parts in large batch sizes to realize high levels of system utilization. Another group of systems was introduced to machine a wide range of parts in small batch sizes and assumed lower levels of system utilization. The third group of configurations was introduced to machine a limited range of parts in small batch sizes and also did not emphasize high levels of system utilization. The description of the systems in each document was then compared with all others to establish whether each had been designed to realize particular forms of output. This confirmed that only one of the three different uses above had been embodied in the design of each FMS. The narratives in the documents that described the deployment and strengths of each system were read and variations between them were used to develop the concept of a production strategy embodied in the design and management of the FMS to explain the variations in expected levels of performance between them. These were summarized as 'volume production', 'flexible manufacturing' and the 'just-in-time production' of high value parts. In this way, documents were used iteratively to develop concepts that allowed the understanding that configurations of FMS were not uniform but instead had been constructed to realize different objectives and that accounting techniques had been varied to reflect each configuration's different strengths.

Critical theory

There are many genres of 'critical' theory: Marx's ideas will be drawn on here. Like many subsequent critical theorists, Marx saw the access to power in organizations as unequal. For Marx, a key source of power was control over economic resources. Moreover, access to power is likely to result in an ability to disseminate one's ideas and to persuade others of the value of those ideas, reconstituting the relationship between those with more or less power. Thus, there is a dialectical relationship between power and the ideas expressed in documents. This position is consistent with a view of documents as being both a repository of information and constitutive of relationships involving people affected by those documents' contents. A range of techniques could be used to analyse documents' constitutive role.[1] A case study method is used here (see Buchanan, in this volume). If a case study is organized chronologically, it is possible to envisage a sequence of events involving the composition and use of the documents and an assessment of their impact in the reconstitution of relationships. It is useful to have a set of rules to guide the composition of the case. Various authors (e.g. Lincoln, 1980: 34–35) have provided suggestions for what these rules might cover. These include:

- Clear criteria for the selection of case studies to ensure that the cases chosen are the appropriate ones for addressing the research questions, rather than being ones that will simply produce the answers that the researcher wants. Of course, the universe of possible cases may be one if the phenomenon investigated is unique.

- A checklist or a clear set of themes intended to ascertain information about certain outcomes of interest. These themes will emerge from the research problem.

- A set of decision rules to help ensure consistency in what is classified as part of each theme.

As the method is being applied to appraise the constitutive quality of documents, one might also ask 'What if?' questions of whether outcomes following the publication or use of documents would have occurred without the intervention of the document.

Lee's (2010) document-based case study investigated how the UK government's experiment with Individual Learning Accounts (ILAs) was evaluated by regulators and the impact that those regulators had on the demise and

---

[1]For example, Prior (2008) uses social network analysis as part of actor-network theory.

abandonment of ILAs. Gramsci's interpretation of Marx was used to explain how the Conservative administrations of 1979–1997 had introduced policies of purchasing state-financed services from independent bodies through markets. These markets were overseen by state-appointed regulators that had the authority to produce reports about the provision of those services. ILAs were introduced by the Labour government that replaced the Conservative administrations. The Labour government continued to use markets to deliver services, but also sought to facilitate lifelong learning by creating ILAs that offered everyone state monies to purchase learning. Registration for ILAs occurred faster than anticipated, so the scheme soon ran out of funds. There were suggestions that the scheme had been defrauded by unscrupulous learning providers and members of parliament asked regulators to investigate. Although the government promised to reintroduce ILAs, it took several years before a more limited, targeted scheme of financial assistance for learning was introduced. This suggested the question: what role did the regulators who reported on the demise of ILAs play in this scenario?

Four sets of regulators produced formal reports about ILAs. These were the Education and Skills Select Committee (E&SSC), the National Audit Office, the Public Accounts Committee and the Parliamentary Ombudsman. The reports were read initially to get a sense of their contents and to identify relevant themes to help extrapolate information that could answer subsidiary questions of the above general research question. These subsidiary questions were: 1) how had the different regulators perceived the ILA experiment? And 2) what had been the impact of their pronouncements? The first question was addressed by asking: did the reports provided a bias of strengths over weaknesses in references to ILAs? In what areas did references to strengths and weaknesses appear – such as education and learning or financial management? What were the perceived outcomes of those strengths and weaknesses? And what were the suggested solutions to any weaknesses? Through a further reading of the reports, an entire checklist of terms relating to education and learning, financial management, problems with the scheme and solutions to problems were listed. For example, terms relating to problems included abuse, fraud, financial loss, poor quality learning and unscrupulous providers, while terms relating to solutions included audit, registration of providers, accreditation of providers, etc.

A set of decision rules was formulated to guide the subsequent analysis of the reports. This included the following:

- Count each reference to any of the specified terms.

- Read each sentence and paragraph in which the term appears and document the reference as either: an education and learning strength or weakness; a positive or negative financial management facet; a positive or negative outcome; a financial management, educational quality or some other type of solution to a negative outcome.

- Note any quantification of the financial value of any alleged fraud and abuse and of the number of people that are claimed to be involved.

- Make note of whether the reference appears in witness statements or whether the information has appeared in the formal report and so can be seen to have the regulators' approval.

- Read through reports in their entirety to ensure that the bias of references reflects the full content of the report and no important issues have been omitted.

This analysis was performed for each report so that a chronology could be mapped which showed that while the first report by the E&SSC questioned the evidence of fraud and called for a re-introduction of ILAs, the latter reports blamed the government department that oversaw the scheme for insufficient financial controls, which allowed several hundred fraudsters to pose as learning providers and defraud the scheme by £97 million. These reports also accepted a later government decision to replace universal ILAs by a smaller targeted scheme. The question was asked 'what if' the regulators had not made their interventions. A newspaper search of prosecutions revealed that the risk of financial abuse had been vastly overstated. A newspaper search also revealed that the relevant government department was wary of ambitious universal schemes because of the regulators' criticisms. In this way, it was possible to highlight the potential constitutive nature of the regulators' reports.

Constructivist approaches

Constructivists[2] see social reality as constructed and sustained in the course of social interactions. Language plays an important role in these social interactions and should be perceived as constitutive of relationships and of the identities of people involved in those relationships. Constructivists may use

---

[2]See Cunliffe (2008) for an easy-to-understand distinction between the way in which postmodernists and constructivists may use discourse analysis differently.

discourse analysis (see Oswick, in this volume) to understand how language represented by text in documents has mediated in – and helped to constitute – social actions. It is not easy to outline a clear set of rules for conducting discourse analysis. Phillips and Di Domenico (2009: 560) argue: 'The breadth of textual analysis that could be used ... and the diversity of the phenomenon under investigation means that ... researchers need to develop an approach that makes sense in the light of their particular study *and* establish a set of arguments to justify the particular approach they adopt'. Although different authors will adopt different ways of conducting discourse analysis and use different terms to describe what they are doing, analyses are often conducted at one or more of the following levels. First, there is the context in which the interaction involving the discourse takes place and how that interaction gives rise to a specific social order. Second, there is the general direction of the account in the discourse and its implicit morality and assumptions. Third, there are the particular techniques that are used in the discourse to convey impressions of scale, importance, insignificance or to bring the discourse to an end. Here, I will apply discourse analysis to an interpretation of the regulators' reports that were discussed above.

Regulators' reports are composed by a committee after they have collected evidence from a range of sources, including 'expert' witnesses. Texts of reports will contain the narrative of regulators and statements from witnesses. The text involving the collection of evidence could be divided up into exchanges to identify who said what to whom and the role of each of those participants as either witnesses or members of the committee. By analysing how members of the committee asked questions, pressed for answers and reprimanded witnesses for taking too long to answer a question, an understanding could be achieved of how those members helped to construct the nature of a committee and its investigations. Similarly, analysis of responses from witnesses into such categories as 'refinement' (through a response that states conditions under which assumptions in a question hold), 'over-compliance' (through unqualified answers directed only to the terms of the question), 'evasion' (by providing a response that does not address a question), or 'denial' (of any knowledge, etc.), could be used to understand how witnesses helped construct the order of the committee.

Alternatively, the accounts of individual witnesses could be read. The view of each witness could be constructed around a conceptual pro forma derived from a reading of the types of questions and evidence provided in the report. This could include what the ILA monies were for, how actual use varied from the prescription for the use of monies, who was responsible for the variations, how did those people achieve such a variation and what were the consequences of that variation? By analysing the text of individual witnesses or the narrative of a report in this way, it would be possible to see how one or more accounts were constructed to suggest some individuals were responsible for a subversion of the aims of the ILA scheme. An analysis could be conducted on each component sentence of the text to identify the devices used by different witnesses to help construct their respective accounts. Thus, some witnesses offered anecdotes, others made comparisons with past initiatives and still others drew analogies between their situation and others in different contexts. For example, one witness to the E&SSC suggested that he stood alongside '*bona fide* trainers [that] had to fight arrivistes whose only interest in training was its ability to earn them quick money for no effort'. Although there was no physical combat involved, the image portrayed is one of 'good' providers having to struggle against 'bad' ones. The relative success of different witnesses in getting their viewpoint accepted could be assessed by investigating the extent to which the regulators endorsed opinions akin to those of different witnesses.

Conclusion

This chapter has explained what constitutes a document and shown how to scope research involving documents, gather relevant documents and analyse those documents once they have been collected. Attention has been given to how particular types of analysis complement different epistemological approaches. However, the framework provided is a heuristic device and it is important to realize that authors will use different types of epistemological approach according to the research question that they are asking and the reason why they are asking that question. Indeed, illustrations of documentary analysis where different epistemological assumptions are apparent have been drawn from the author's work. Nor should it be assumed that studies will contain only one form of documentary analysis. While a different body of the author's research has been used to illustrate one corresponding form of analysis, several forms of analysis – and epistemological position – could feature in the same body of work. For example, the study of the influence of accounting on the introduction and deployment of FMS was presented as an interpretive study that required an ethnographic content analysis. However, the investment appraisal documents had a constitutive dimension as their assumptions were embodied in the cost control mechanisms that guided the operation of the FMS. The studies do illustrate that documentary analysis is a rule-guided process, so it is important to compose, apply and report procedures and selection criteria for the inclusion and exclusion of information when seeking answers to research questions. Formulation and a systematic application of rules can help to justify the approach adopted.

Further Reading

When read in conjunction with each other, Krippendorff (2004) and Prior (2003) provide useful overviews of different approaches to the analysis of documents from different epistemological positions. A useful source for understanding the underlying methodologies and related epistemologies informing the organization of the wide range of documents that are available is the long-standing *Journal of Documentation*. Many excellent studies of organizations that draw on the use of documents may also be found in *Discourse and Communication*. Documents do take on a variety of forms and there are numerous useful readings that are dedicated to different types or uses of documents. Walker (2004) provides an informative and entertaining discussion of the trials, tribulations and joys of conducting archival research. Alazewski (2006) also provides a useful introduction to diaries as a research method. Documents may contain visual representations as well. Vince and Warren's chapter in this collection provides some insights into methods for analysing visual representations.

References

Alazewski, A. (2006) *Using Diaries for Social Research*. London: Sage.
Altheide, D.L. (1987) 'Ethnographic content analysis', *Qualitative Sociology*, 10 (1): 65–77.
Berelson, B. (1952) *Content Analysis in Communicative Research*. New York: Free Press.
Bricknell, D. (2008) 'Historical analysis', in R. Thorpe and R. Holt (eds), *The Sage Dictionary of Qualitative Management Research*. London: Sage, 108–109.
Cassell, C. and Lee, B. (2007) 'Re-vitalising learning and development? Exploring the role of the trade union learning representative', *Personnel Review*, 36 (5/6): 781–799.

Cassell, C. and Lee, B. (2009) 'Trade union learning representatives: progressing partnership?', *Work, Employment & Society*, 23 (2): 213–230.

Cunliffe, A.L. (2008) 'Discourse analysis', in R. Thorpe and R. Holt (eds), *The Sage Dictionary of Qualitative Management Research*. London: Sage, pp. 81–82.

Hodder, I. (2003) 'The interpretation of documents and material culture', in N.K. Denzin and Y.S. Lincoln (eds), *Handbook of Qualitative Research*. London: Sage. pp. 703–716.

Holsti, O.M. (1969) *Content Analysis for the Social Sciences and Humanities*. Reading, MA: Addison-Wesley.

Johnson, P., Buerhring, A., Cassell, C. and Symon, G (2006) 'Evaluating qualitative management research: towards a contingent criteriology', *International Journal of Management Reviews*, 8 (3): 131–156.

Jones, T.C. and Lee, B. (1998) 'Accounting, strategy and AMT investment', *Omega*, 26 (6): 769–783.

Krippendorff, K. (2004) *Content Analysis: An Introduction to Its Methodology* (2nd edn). Thousand Oaks, CA: Sage.

Lee, B. (1996) 'The justification and monitoring of AMT: an empirical study of 21 installations of FMS', *Management Accounting Research*, 7 (1): 95–118.

Lee, B. (2010) 'The Individual Learning Account experiment in the UK: a conjunctural crisis?' *Critical Perspectives on Accounting*, 21 (1): 18–30.

Lee, B. and Cassell, C. (2004) 'Electronic routes to change? A survey of website support for trade union learning representatives', *International Journal of Knowledge, Culture and Change Management*, 4: 701–711.

Lee, B. and Cassell, C. (2008) 'Employee and social reporting as a war of position and the union learning representative initiative in the UK', *Accounting Forum*, 32 (4): 276–287.

Lincoln, Y.S. (1980) 'Documentary analysis and record utilization: new uses for old methods', paper presented at the Annual Meeting of the American Educational Research Association, Boston, April.

Phillips, N. and Di Domenico, M. (2009) 'Discourse analysis in organizational research: methods and debates', in D.A. Buchanan and A. Bryman (eds), *The Sage Handbook of Organizational Research Methods*. London: Sage.

Prior, L. (2003) *Using Documents in Social Research*. London: Sage.

Prior, L. (2008) 'Repositioning documents in social research', *Sociology*, 42 (5): 821–836.

Rapley, T. (2007) *Doing Conversation, Discourse and Document Analysis*. London: Sage.

Walker, S. (2004) 'The search for clues in accounting history', in C. Humphrey and B. Lee (eds), *The Real Life Guide to Accounting Research*. Oxford: Elsevier, pp. 5–21.

Grounded Theory: A Theory Building Approach

Graham J.J. Kenealy

Grounded Theory and Organizational Research

Grounded theory is a systematic approach to data collection and analysis that was discovered by Glaser and Strauss in the 1960s. The discovery of this method was first presented to the academic community in their book *The Discovery of Grounded Theory* (1967), which still remains the primary point of reference for those undertaking grounded theory research. While already very popular in many fields of research, this very powerful method is rapidly increasing in popularity in the field of organizational and management research and for many this means reverting back to grounded theory in its original form, adopting the idea that the method only produces scientifically valid and robust results when used as a complete package rather than remodelled in the various forms.

Unlike most other research methods, grounded theory does not start with a detailed review of the literature. The underlying logic of grounded theory and that which differentiates it from other research methods is that it is explicitly emergent. Its focus is not hypothesis testing, rather the aim is to find out which theory accounts for the research situation; ultimately the aim is to discover the theory implicit in the data. The point here is that there is a distinction between hypothesis-testing research and emergent research in respect of how and when the literature contributes to the research process.

There are two important points to be made about the literature. The first is that in an emergent study the researcher will not know at the beginning of the project which literature will later turn out to be relevant. This has implications as to what point in the research process the researcher starts the literature search. The second is that the literature is not given a position of privilege when compared to other data; rather it is treated simply as data with the same status as all the other data (Dick, 2002).

Most researchers will first examine the relevant literature well in advance of starting the data collection process. In a grounded theory study, data collection starts as soon as the research arena has been identified. Constant comparison and theoretical sampling remain the core processes of the grounded theory building approach. Constant comparison is the process by which data are collected and analysed simultaneously, comparing incident with incident while looking for distinguishable differences and/or similarities that will explain what is happening. Theoretical sampling (see also Saunders, in this volume) is the process of deciding which data should be collected and where, directed and determined by the emerging theory. The aim is to compare the literature with the emerging theory in the same way that any other data sources are compared with the emerging theory. Therefore the format of grounded theory is such that there is a continual interplay between the literature, other data and the emerging theory so that sense can be made of both the data from the study and the data derived from the literature.

Since its inception in sociology in 1967 and its subsequent migration to the field of organizational and management research in the 1970s, grounded theory has slowly developed to become what is now considered a respected methodology in the organizational researcher's armoury. This grounded theory methodology is based on the belief that, as individuals within group environments comprehend events personally, common patterns of behaviour are revealed (Glaser, 1998). As a group interacts together people do in fact make sense of their own environment despite the apparent chaos. Grounded theory is well suited to understanding the social processes and the consequential psychological effects inherent in organizational management dynamics in what is seemingly a chaotic environment. Grounded theorists working closely with the data can very quickly move away from description to work at a conceptual level; its strengths lie in the process of theorizing thereby explaining what is actually going on rather than describing what is happening. It helps to develop perspectives and to learn about how participants manage their lives in the context of existing and future organizational challenges; it is there-fore well suited to organizational sociology and psychology and time dependent behavioural inquiry. It is particularly useful for research in areas that have not previously been studied, where there is an obvious gap, and where new perspectives could benefit areas for management involvement and organizational improvement.

This method is particularly suited to looking at rarely explored phenomena where an extant theory would not be appropriate. In such situations, a grounded theory building approach is more likely to generate novel and accurate insights into the phenomenon under study rather than a reliance on either past research or office bound thought experiments (Glaser and Strauss, 1967).

Irrespective of whether the analyst adopts the classical grounded theory methods developed by Glaser and Strauss (1967) or the more regimented approach advocated by Strauss and Corbin (1990; 1998), the method is increasingly being adopted by organizational and managerial researchers across the globe. Most commentators (Lincoln and Guba, 1985; Robson, 2001; Huberman and Miles, 2002; Denzin and Lincoln, 2005) writing on the subject of qualitative research methods discuss the merits of grounded theory and increasingly papers are being published in the management arena based on research developed using this methodology. To the experienced grounded theorist it is plain to see that quite often manuscripts claiming to be grounded theory analysis are presented in such a way that this would be more consistent with other methodological frameworks (Goulding, 2002).

It is difficult to find examples of research in the organizational and management field that follow the exact tenets of classical grounded theory such as that by Raffanti (2005), Holton (2007), Kenealy and Cartwright (2007) and Thulesius and Grahn (2007); indeed most appear to be an adaptation of the method. This view is underpinned by Locke's (2001) perspectives; she points out that there is an inclination to adapt and adopt grounded theory methods within the management research field; a direction to which Glaser (1998) is strongly opposed. Glaser calls this adaptation 'remodelling' (Glaser and Holton, 2004). Remodelling includes the integration of other qualitative research methods into the grounded theory model.

A closer inspection of the language used in the grounded theory based management research publications (Sutton and Callahan, 1987; Eisenhardt, 1989) demonstrates the use of remodelled versions of the original grounded theory within this domain. There is a propensity among some organizational and management researchers to favour more rigid structured research methods.

This can in part be attributed to the strong influences of the positivist paradigm within this field and the regimented processes that positivist methods invariably attract. Without labouring the point too much, the process of 'constant comparison' and 'theoretical sampling' violates longstanding positivist assumptions about how the research process should work; that is, constant comparison contradicts the requirements of a clean separation between data collection and analysis while theoretical sampling violates the ideal of hypothesis testing in that the direction of new data collection is determined not by a priori hypotheses, but by an ongoing interpretation of the data and emerging conceptual categories (Suddaby, 2006). Grounded theory research should be conducted systematically and rigorously, utilizing the full package, and not tackled in part with a casual or ad hoc approach that is continually mixed up with the dictums of other methods. 'Systematically' and 'rigorously' here should not be confused with rigidity and structure, which are not usually appropriate with qualitative research (Mason, 2006), let alone grounded theory.

Fundamentals of Classic Grounded Theory

In an attempt to present the reader with a greater understanding of the method, in this section I move away from generalized perspectives and discussions to focus more on the application of classic grounded theory.

It is appropriate at this stage of the chapter to mention the importance of starting your study without preconceived ideas. Glaser's (1992; 1998) approach to grounded theory starts by looking at the particular area of study, with this being either a process or a specific activity where the relevant issues are allowed to emerge during the course of the research process, based entirely upon the participant perceptions.

Unlike most other research methods it is unnecessary for grounded theorists to immerse themselves in the setting or to become part of the group under study in order to understand the meaning and significance that people place upon the behaviour of themselves and others. Grounded theory is an inductive approach, which also uses an element of deduction to allow theoretical sampling to take place. Glaser's teachings – and indeed the experience of the author of this chapter – are that concepts emerge quickly without the researcher needing to spend too much time in the field, thereby running the risk of their influencing the research participants (Glaser, 2007).

The data – collection and analysis

Grounded methodology differs from other methodologies in so far as it does not follow the regime of data collection and data analyses and ultimately presenting the findings. Not only is the approach noticeably different from other methodologies but as you progress through this chapter you will also become aware of how the language differs from that used in other approaches. With this methodology the theory evolves during the research process itself and is the product of a continuous interplay between the analysis and data collection. In simple terms the prescribed stages of grounded theory – namely, data collection, coding, interpretation, literature searches, memo writing and conceptualizing – are all progressed simultaneously as codes and categories evolve (Glaser and Strauss, 1967).

There is no need to start a grounded theory study with weeks and weeks of literature searches. The starting point for any grounded theorist is data collection and the primary instrument of data collection is the unstructured interview, which is designed to elicit open-ended discussions of what is happening in the research setting. The researcher starts conducting interviews the moment participants are identified; these are normally individuals who have lived the experience under study. After the initial interviews the theorist relies on theoretical sampling to focus on the data that are relevant to the study. Theoretical sampling therefore directs the researcher to 'where next' to head for data collection. The grounded theorist also quickly becomes sensitized to observational data: informal observations, impressions and comments. The author's own experience is that a wealth of data can be found away from the interview room; data can be obtained from informal discussions at informal meeting points such as lunchtimes and coffee breaks. Either way discussions or interviews should not be recorded on electronic media of any form; the interviewee becomes too guarded when electronic wizardry is placed on the table before them and fails to relate their stories and experiences fully. Glaser (1998) recommends the use of unobtrusive contemporaneous notes during the interview discussion itself followed by accurate field notes immediately after each interview. The follow-up notes will serve to underpin the basic notes generated in the interview itself allowing for coding later on.

The focus during the early stages will be to generate substantive codes that will reflect the events encountered – all from the participant's own perspective.

Coding

Substantive coding is the umbrella heading for 'open' and 'selective' coding; it is the start of the theory development process, which commences with the open coding of the data as these are collected. The goal is to generate an emergent set of categories and their properties, which will fit and integrate with the theory. Integration in this sense means that it fits and is relevant to the theory (Glaser, 1998).

Open coding attempts to faithfully reflect and explain the events that occurred through the participants' own eyes. In practice this entails a careful examination of the collected data, drawing out single events or components of the event. These events are categorized under conceptual labels or headings that reflect its single entity meaning. The data are coded in every possible way; Glaser (1978) calls this 'running the data open', coding anything and everything that might fit, initially to generate as many codes as possible. This process continues until new incidents do not warrant new codes (as new categories), because they fit into existing coded categories. The level of importance is determined by their originality (identifying new and novel phenomena) combined with the relative frequency at which each incident is expressed by the informants. Open coding allows the researcher to see the direction in which to take the study before becoming selective and focused on a particular problem. Thus when they do begin to focus, relevance is assured.

From the start, the analyst asks questions of the data: what are these data a study of? What category does this incident indicate? What is actually going on in the data? What are the main concerns being faced by the participants? And what accounts are there of resolving these concerns? These questions keep the analyst theoretically sensitive and transcending when analysing, collecting and coding data. They force them to focus on patterns among the incidents that will yield codes in order to rise conceptually above the detailed description of incidents, while coding into as many categories as possible (Glaser, 1978).

As time progresses the data collected and the subsequent coding will become more selective; selective coding will be the next step on from open coding, which allows integration and abstraction to develop freely without the incumbency of non-relevance. The cessation of open coding refocuses attention more on coding those variables that relate to the core variable (how participants are resolving the problem). Selective coding also ultimately conceptualizes the empirical substance of the area under study, grouped under conceptual (explanatory) headings rather than descriptive headings (Glaser, 1978); it moves the process onto a higher conceptual level and it begins the instant that similarities in the codes have been identified. This stage of the process entails examining and collapsing codes into higher level categories. The researcher constantly compares the open codes with existing and new (incoming) data, moving from specific incidents to abstraction (Schreiber and Stern, 2001) in sufficiently significant ways so as to produce a parsimonious theory.

Using open-ended questions enables respondents to relate their stories and establish each actor's main concerns, thereby providing a direction for subsequent interviews. It is the response from a participant that will allow the interviewer to probe them further to collect as much relevant information as possible. Initial interviews allow the researcher to direct attention towards category refinement. Selective coding and category refinement provide more depth in specific areas, thus allowing the theoretical sampling process to take over.

Theorizing at a conceptual level is the ultimate goal. *Theoretical coding* is the final step in the theoretical development process and conceptualizes how the substantive codes relate to each other as a hypothesis to be integrated into the theory. The term 'hypothesis' is the one used by Glaser and Strauss (1967) to mean that there is merely a suggestion in the data (not that there are facts); however Whetten (1989) felt the term 'proposition' was more appropriate. He argued that 'propositions' involve conceptual relationships whereas 'hypotheses' require measurable relationships. Both terminologies are used in this chapter in the same context as described here.

Memoing and theoretical sampling

Memos facilitate the theorizing and writing-up of ideas around the substantive codes and their theoretical relationships as they emerge during the data collection, coding and analysis (Glaser, 1998). There are no set rules as to how many memos should be generated; the point here is that the process requires the emerging conceptual ideas to be recorded in the form of memos. While the field notes and coding are essential stages of the whole process, the conceptual and theoretical memos are the key reference documents that are generated over the entire investigatory process. They provide a trustworthy and credible step-by-step record of the theory building process.

Subsequent data collection and coding is thereby refocused on that which is relevant to the emergent conceptual framework. The selective data collection continues until the researcher has sufficiently elaborated and integrated the core variable, its properties and its theoretical connections to other relevant categories.

Novice researchers constantly ask about the format and layout of field notes and memos. The way the researcher generates field notes is non-prescriptive and is considered a personal choice. Experience will allow the novice to develop methods of taking interview notes quickly with the least amount of distraction to the interviewee. More importantly, field notes should be generated immediately after each interview to underpin the basic notes generated in the interview itself, which are subsequently coded. Many researchers prefer to do these by hand while others will type them directly using electronic media.

Theoretical coding considers concepts that are the essential relationship between data and theory. The code allocated by the researcher (the conceptual code) conceptualizes the underlying pattern of the empirical indicators within the data. By developing hypothetical relationships between conceptual codes, the researcher then begins to see the kind of categories (and their properties) that can handle the data theoretically, and so knows how to code all the data, ensuring the emergent theory fits and works. Several images and patterns of the substantive area are linked together with the skilful use of theoretical coding to form the conceptual categories and properties of the theory (Glaser, 1978). *Theoretical sampling* is the prime mover of coding, collecting and analysing. It is both directed by the emerging theory and it directs its further emergence. It is the 'where next' in collecting data, 'for what' according to the codes, and the 'why' from the analysis of the memos. The general procedure of theoretical sampling is to elicit codes from raw data from the start of the data collection through to constant comparative analysis, then to use the codes to direct further data collection (Glaser, 1978).

Theoretical sampling continues the process of abstraction and integration to the point of saturation.[1] It constantly focuses the collection and analysis of data, so that the researcher is not collecting the same data over and over based on the same questions (as other research methods do, which ignores the interchangeability of indices). It keeps the data collection to a minimum, instead of allowing too much data to accumulate. It responds to the need for more data that are relevant for the emergence of new categories and properties (Glaser, 1998).

As the process of coding, sampling and sorting continues (that is the sorting of memos into categories) invariably one category will repeatedly emerge as being related to more than the other categories and their properties:

---

[1]'Saturation' is the term used to identify the point in the research when no new categories are emerging from the new data collected. It is at the point when all new data merely slot into existing categories and properties.

the *core category*. This is generally identified as the category that continually resolves the main concerns of the participants (Glaser, 1998).

Writing-up the manuscript

The accepted norm in organizational and management research is to present papers in a traditionally structured way by presenting the theory, along with where and how it sits within the chosen domain against previous research in the field, with all of this supported by a detailed account of the data collection, analysis, results and discussion. Indeed it has always been important that the researcher recognizes the limitations of the research and the research findings at the end of the manuscript/paper.

It has been suggested (Suddaby, 2006) that grounded theory manuscripts quite often appear to be presented as a jumble of literature consultation, data collection and analysis in an ongoing iteration that produces many relatively fuzzy categories that over time reduce to fewer, clearer conceptual structures, presenting the theory at the end. Suddaby also suggests that presenting grounded theory in this way for organizational and management research only serves to distance the majority of researchers, particularly those normally working in the positivist paradigm.

Despite the over generalized belief that grounded theory manuscripts appear to be presented as a jumble of literature consultation, data collection and analysis there are good examples of well-structured grounded theory manuscripts such as those presented by Raffanti (2005), Holton (2007) and Kenealy and Cartwright (2007). The careful development of memos described earlier allows the theorist to deliver the story to the audience with relative ease irrespective of the structure. The obvious difference is the use of literature and how this is written into the final version of the manuscript.

Scientific rigour

The stumbling block here and therefore the area of greatest debate has been the perceived inability of qualitative based research, particularly grounded theory, to demonstrate scientific rigour (Lincoln and Guba, 1987; Corbin and Strauss, 1990). Easterby-Smith et al.'s (2003) view is that grounded theory has been criticized as being suspect because of its lack of clarity and standardization of methods, citing positivist perspectives in respect of the importance of 'finding the truth' as the culprit. The adaptation of positivist cannons such as reliability, validity, generalizability, and objectivity to judge the processes of qualitative research is ill founded (see also Symon and Cassell, in this volume). Goulding (2002) goes a long way to construct parallels between grounded theory and other qualitative approaches, suggesting that all too often qualitative research is wrongly assessed as being valid according to quasi-positivistic criteria. Given the paradigm dominance within the field of organizational and management research this is hardly surprising. Goulding (2002) cites Lincoln and Guba's (1985) criteria for assessing the trustworthiness of qualitative insight as the more realistic model when working in the area of grounded theory. Their four criteria – credibility, transferability, dependability and confirmability – are seen as the key to assessing trustworthiness. Here the goal is to demonstrate that the enquiry was carried out in a way which ensures that the subject of the enquiry was accurately identified and explained.

Glaser (1998) is quite specific on the criteria for judging and carrying out grounded theory and offers a four-point checklist: fit, workability, relevance and modifiability.

Fit according to Glaser (1998) is another word for validity. Does the concept adequately express the pattern in the data that it purports to conceptualize? *Workability* also refers to the concept. Are the concepts and the way they are related to the hypotheses sufficiently accounted for? How are the main concerns of participants in a substantive area continually resolved? *Relevance* makes the research important because it deals with the main concerns of the participants involved. To study something that interests no one except a few is probably to focus on non-relevance or even trivia. Relevance, like good concepts, evokes an instant grab. Glaser (1998) also places great importance on *modifiability*. He suggests that the theory is not being verified as in verification studies and thus can never be described as being right or wrong. It simply gets modified when new data are available to compare it with.

Application: A Lived Example

A recent research project involving the author explored how a large UK government organization coped with radical structural change over time, providing insights into the temporal effects of 'enforced accelerated work pace' on behaviour and receptivity, all within an organizational context.

Presenting the whole research project here would not be practical nor indeed would it be beneficial to demonstrating application; with this in mind only the first part of the emergent theory is presented.

The temporal effects of an enforced accelerated work pace

In this research the primary instrument of data collection was the unstructured interview, designed to elicit an open-ended description of what is happening in terms of change behaviour, all supported by the interviewer's own observations.

As this was a study focusing on organizational change behaviour it made sense to select participants who had been identified as being subjected to the greatest levels of change. The researcher conducted 24 interviews (during several site visits at four area offices) with each interview lasting between 40 and 80 minutes. Towards the end of the initial interviews, the researcher started to focus on category refinement. Selective coding and category refinement provided more depth in specific areas allowing the theoretical sampling process to take over. Theoretical sampling triggered a further 40 face-to-face interviews continuing the process of abstraction and integration to the point of saturation. The second round of 40 interviews were shorter than the initial 24, varying in length between 10 minutes for the shortest interview and 45 minutes for the longest.

Using open-ended questions that enabled respondents to relate their stories, these early interviews served as the basis for identifying and establishing the actors' main concerns and for providing a direction for subsequent interviews. The open-ended questioning was initially non-directive, specifically designed to relax the interviewee thus allowing them to talk freely. It was the response from the participant that allowed the interviewer to then probe them more to collect as much relevant information as possible. Care was taken to avoid leading interviewees and introducing interviewer bias. The interviews were not taped but unobtrusive contemporaneous notes were taken. Field notes were generated immediately after each interview to underpin the basic notes generated in the interview itself. These notes were subsequently coded. This time the data collected and the subsequent coding were more selective, allowing integration and abstraction to develop freely without the incumbency of non-relevance.

The main principles and guidelines for conducting open coding were carefully adhered to, including labelling themes with codes to preserve their conceptual meanings. Starting with the basic open coding, 109 labels were subsequently rearranged into concepts under specific categories and integrated into the theory. The level of importance was determined by their originality (identifying new and novel phenomena) combined with the relative frequency with which each theme was expressed by the informants.

Theoretical sampling directed the interviews back to some of the original respondents for a second interview and again three months after that. Focusing on the main themes that had emerged in their first interviews, constant comparisons allowed the researcher to consider the dimension of time on the respondents' perception of the change process. The process required the emerging conceptual ideas to be recorded in the form of memos.

The most striking category that emerged from this initial phase of interviews was that of 'input sensitivity'. This was the term used by the researcher to identify the actors who became acutely sensitized to the actual hours they were forced to work (irrespective of their contractual obligations). Working extra hours emerged as a contributing factor to their anxiety and therefore it made sense to look for other participants who had been forced to work extra hours because of the change, rather than those individuals who were working the extra hours voluntarily.

Because of the frequency with which worked hours was mentioned and the consistency of 'input sensitivity' across the organization (judged by the similarity in their statements in this category) theoretical sampling very quickly focused on those individuals who worked more than their contracted hours as a result of the change initiative. Apart from the interview data and the researcher's real-time observation notes, other secondary data used to ground the theory included data derived from past research that had been conducted at the subject organization prior to this project. Returning to data in this way is not unusual given the iterative nature of the grounded theory methodology (Glaser, 1978; Strauss and Corbin, 1990).

The next section brings together the ordered details of the research codes and memos. The formulated hypothesis identified a temporal sequence between a number of categories. Suffice to say time played a significant role in shaping the theory. Theoretical sampling took the researcher back to individuals who had already been interviewed for more comparative data in relation to the effect of time on their resolving behaviour. It has already been said that a number of the respondents were interviewed again approximately three months after their first interview and again approximately three months after that. The purpose was to see if time had affected the respondents' perceptions of the change process, focusing on the main themes that had emerged in their first interviews, namely: how did they feel they were coping with and managing change; how did they feel about working longer hours (were they contributing the extra hours by choice or was it still, as some perceive it, forced upon them); and finally how would they categorize their own psychological wellbeing (were they still up for the challenge or did they feel that there was a reduction in their enthusiasm; and if so why?).

The initial focus was to identify the behavioural responses emerging from the radical change initiative at the subject organization, particularly behavioural patterns relating to change receptivity along with those affecting or effected by work pace. This led to the discovery of the coping reflex stages of enforced accelerated work pace which was the theoretical contribution of this work (see Kenealy and Cartwright, 2007).

Grounded Theory and the Novice Researcher

It would be unfair to close this chapter without first considering the problems normally encountered by the novice researcher entering the field of organizational and management research and in particular grounded theory research for the first time.

Grounded theory training

It is no surprise that research methods used and indeed honed as a trainee will invariably form the backbone of future research projects. Most organizational and management research training, particularly in UK universities, until recent times focused heavily on quantitative techniques, to the detriment of qualitative-based methods (Easterby-Smith et al., 2003) and especially grounded theory. While there has been an increase in qualitative research and qualitative research training, until recently there has still been a lack of experienced grounded theorists and grounded theory training.

Training is important to help the novice decipher the inconsistency of the methods literature, which is partly caused by the two schools of thought (Glasserian and Straussian) and is further exacerbated by the tendency of organizational and management researchers to adapt and adopt (Locke, 2001). At the end of this chapter there are some useful contacts and details of appropriate support material for those who are working 'minus mentor'[2] and wishing to undertake a classic grounded theory study.

Overcoming the problems of access

Another concern expressed by a number of commentators (Locke, 2001; Easterby-Smith et al., 2003) writing on the subject of grounded theory is the question of access. They see access to managed organizations as difficult and problematic, suggesting that some assumptions of grounded theory have to be amended to deal with difficult situations. Most business managers, if they are willing to allow access (irrespective of the research methodology), need to plan the research activity around the normal operational activity in such a way as to limit the impact to the business. With this in mind the researcher seeking access has to demonstrate how they intend to conduct their research in the form of an access proposal. The structure of the proposal should, among other things, present the reader with information such as the envisaged interview dates, interview durations and participant groups, i.e. gender, age, department, job role, job grade and/or location. This sort of detail may be difficult for the grounded theorist to present before data collection starts. The very nature of the method, more specifically 'theoretical sampling', means that the parallel process of data collection and analysis itself determines how and where to find more data as the process progresses. It is not practical for researchers to access participants in organizational environments on an ad hoc basis nor would business managers be able to accept this practice in their organizations.

There is no doubt that access poses difficulties for any researcher. For many the deciding factor will be the duration of access. The uphill battle to gain access could be swayed by the duration of access the researcher requests. Obviously the shorter the access the more chance one has of persuading business managers to allow the project to go ahead. Grounded theory does not start with a preconceived idea of sample size or a fixed duration for interviews. Each interview continues until the participant has exhausted their story and these interviews will proceed until 'saturation' is reached. Yet it is difficult to persuade a business leader to give access without first furnishing them with details of the sample size and how long the interviews will be. That said the

---

[2]'Minus mentor' is a phrase coined by Stern (1994) to describe a grounded theorist working without structured training and direction.

grounded theory method tends to yield results far quicker than most other methods, so the advice here is clear: anyone undertaking a grounded theory study should use these advantages as their selling point to gain access.

If the researcher has reached the stage where he or she is generating an access proposal one would assume that they have already got through the initial approach or even the initial meetings and discussions. Their next aim will be to make sure the door that has now been opened is firmly wedged open. Gaining access is a critical juncture of any empirical research project and without the guidance of colleagues or, in the case of PhD students, supervisors the novice could fall at a very important hurdle. For the experienced grounded theorist an assessment can be made based on previous experience. Experience can help to provide an approximation of the number of interviews required, along with an approximation of the duration of each interview. Identifying exactly which group of participants the researcher would like to interview is a little more difficult. One solution, as with any other research project, would be to identify the group that the researcher feels (at the planning stage) would make a valuable contribution. Once access has been established it is always easier to renegotiate a change in direction or a short extension later should this become necessary. With grounded theory it is always much easier to finalize access requirements after the theoretical sampling is well advanced. Saturation, the point at which the researcher considers stopping data collection, emerges well before the novice actually takes heed of this and stops.

For those who do manage to gain access, limiting disruption and access time is important. For most novices there will be an inclination to follow the hermeneutics practices of tape recording and then transcribing interviews in their entirety. If this process had to be completed for each and every interview before deciding who to interview next (theoretical sampling) then the access problem will only be exacerbated. According to Glaser (1998) this is a very time-consuming and fruitless exercise whereas contemporaneous notes can help to determine the next step quickly thereby reducing the access time.

Conclusion

There has been a great deal of confusion caused by the rhetorical discourse between the two contradicting views of Glaser (1992) and that of Strauss and Corbin (1990). This chapter has avoided the rhetorical wrestling of these two schools of thought to focus on offering advice to those who have little experience of using grounded theory. It is difficult for the novice researcher to accept that there are quite different research methods all of which purport to be grounded theory yet have contradicting principles of application. That said, apart from the terminologies, the basic tenets of grounded theory from both perspectives remain the same; both stick to the basic premise that grounded theory serves to generate theory that is grounded in the data; both agree on the importance of getting out into the field and of making a constant comparison of incidents related to participant stories; both agree with coding, memoing, conceptualizing and theorizing. However there are differing views of reliability and validity, which will invariably confuse those who are new to the method.

The novice theorist is well advised to consider following the guidance of one method over the others, taking care not to adapt the method too much. This will allow the development of a greater level of understanding of the skills required to conduct a grounded theory study without the incumbency of deciphering the 'rhetorical wrestle'.

On a final note, grounded theory research demands particular qualities of the researcher that have to be learned before they gain confidence. For one, it requires the strength of character to rely on the data; that theory will emerge without forcing the data. It also requires creativity; creative in the sense that the researcher must focus on generating ideas that fit and work, and the data take considerable thought (Glaser, 1978). Most important of all, it requires experience; the experience of understanding what the research is meant to achieve and the experience of applying grounded theory tools. This does not mean the novice is excluded from using grounded theory, quite the opposite, it simply means that a greater understanding can only be reached by practising and using the method.

Further Reading

The message in this chapter is quite clear. Many texts written around the method can be confusing and may cause many budding grounded theorists to refocus on other methods. The advice here is to approach the method with the attitude of either adopting classic grounded theory, that is grounded theory in its purist form, or one of the remodelled versions, and avoid mixing all the methods together. This will allow a greater understanding of the method, thus making it easier to study other versions later on. There is an abundance of help for the grounded theorist wishing to conduct research in its purist form ranging from websites, workshops, journals and texts. As a novice some years ago I was advised to read Glaser (1998) and Glaser (1978). The advice was quite specific; read these texts in the order that I have presented them above as they are good first reference points. Once you have given enough time to those presented above other valuable texts include Glaser and Strauss (1967), Glaser (1992), Glaser (2001), Glaser (2003), Glaser (2005), Glaser and Holton (2007) and Stern (1994).

A very useful website for those wishing to study classic grounded theory is www.groundedtheoryonline.com.

References

Corbin, J. and Strauss, A. (1990) 'Grounded theory research: procedures, cannons and evaluative criteria', *Qualitative Sociology*, 13 (11): 3–21.

Denzin, N.K. and Lincoln, Y.S. (2005) *The Sage Handbook of Qualitative Research* (3rd edn). London: Sage.

Dick, B. (2002) *Grounded Theory: A Thumbnail Sketch*. Available at www.scu.edu.au/schools/gcm/ar/arp/grounded.html (last accessed 6 October 2011).

Easterby-Smith, M., Thorpe, R. and Lowe, L. (2003) *Management Research: An Introduction*. London: Sage.

Eisenhardt, K. (1989) 'Making fast strategic decisions in high-velocity environments', *Academy of Management Journal*, 32 (3): 543–576.

Glaser, B. (1978) *Theoretical Sensitivity: Advances in the Methodology of Grounded Theory*. Mill Valley, CA: The Sociology Press.

Glaser, B. (1992) *Basics of Grounded Theory Analysis*. Mill Valley, CA: The Sociology Press.

Glaser, B. (1998) *Doing Grounded Theory: Issues and Discussion*. Mill Valley, CA: The Sociology Press.

Glaser, B. (2001) *The Grounded Theory Perspective: Conceptualization Contrasted with Description*. Mill Valley, CA: The Sociology Press.

Glaser, B. (2003) *The Grounded Theory Perspective II: Description's Remodelling of Grounded Theory Methodology*. Mill Valley, CA: The Sociology Press.

Glaser, B. (2005) *The Grounded Theory Perspective III: Theoretical Coding*. Mill Valley, CA: The Sociology Press.

Glaser, B. (2007) *Grounded Theory Institute: 2007 Forum*. London.

Glaser, B. and Holton, J. (2004) *Remodelling Grounded Theory*. Forum Qualitative Sozialforschung/Forum: Qualitative Social Research. Available at www.qualitative-research.net/fqs-texte/2-04/2-04glaser-e.htm (last accessed April 2007).

Glaser, B. and Holton, J. (2007). *The Grounded Theory Seminar Reader*. Mill Valley, CA: The Sociology Press.

Glaser, B. and Strauss, A.L. (1967) *The Discovery of Grounded Theory*. New York: Aldine Publications.

Goulding, C. (2002) *Grounded Theory: A Practical Guide for Management, Business and Market Researchers*. London: Sage.

Holton, J. A. (2007) 'Rehumanising knowledge work through fluctuating support networks: a grounded theory', *The Grounded Theory Review: An International Journal*, 6 (2): 23–45.

Huberman, A.M. and Miles, M.B. (2002) *The Qualitative Researcher's Companion*. London: Sage.

Kenealy, G.J.J. and Cartwright, S. (2007) 'The temporal sensitivity of enforced accelerated work pace: a grounded theory building approach', *The Grounded Theory Review: An International Journal*, 6 (2): 117–145.

Lincoln, Y.S. and Guba, E.G. (1985) *Naturalistic Enquiry*. Beverly Hills, CA: Sage.

Lincoln, Y.S. and Guba, E.G. (1987) *But Is it Rigorous? Trustworthiness and Authenticity in Naturalistic Evaluation*. Newbury Park, CA: Sage.

Locke, K. (2001) *Grounded Theory in Management Research*. London: Sage.

Mason, J. (2006) *Qualitative Researching* (2nd edn). London: Sage.

Raffanti, M.A. (2005) 'Weathering change: coping in a context of pervasive organisational change', *The Grounded Theory Review*, 5 (1): 53–77.

Robson, C. (2001) *Real World Research*. Oxford: Blackwell Publishers.

Schreiber, R. and Stern, P. (2001) *Using Grounded Theory in Nursing*. New York: Springer Publishing Company.

Stern, P.N. (1994) 'Eroding grounded theory', in J. M. Morse (ed.), *Critical Issues in Qualitative Research Methods*. Thousand Oaks, CA: Sage, pp. 212–223.

Strauss, A. and Corbin, J. (1990) *Basics of Qualitative Research: Grounded Theory Procedures and Techniques*. Thousand Oaks, CA: Sage.

Strauss, A. and Corbin, J. (1998) *Basics of Qualitative Research: Techniques and Procedures for Developing Grounded Theory* (2nd edn). Thousand Oaks, CA: Sage.

Suddaby, R. (2006) 'From the editors: what grounded theory is not', *Academy of Management Journal*, 49 (4): 633–642.

Sutton, R.I. and Callahan, A.L. (1987) 'The stigma of bankruptcy: spoiled organisational image and its management', *Academy of Management Journal*, 30: 405–436.

Thulesius, H.O. and Grahn, B.E. (2007) 'Reincentivizing work: a grounded theory of work and sick leave', *The Grounded Theory Review: An International Journal*, 6 (2): 47–66.

Whetten, D.A. (1989) 'What constitutes a theoretical contribution?', *Academy of Management Review*, 14: 490–495.

Doing Template Analysis

Nigel King

What is Template Analysis?

One common feature of the many different types of qualitative research described in this and other books is that it produces extensive and complex textual data (and occasionally also visual data: see Vince and Warren, in this volume). How the researcher moves on from this to produce an understanding of the experiences captured in the texts depends on their choice of data analytical techniques. In this chapter, I will describe one such technique: template analysis (TA). I will outline the principles behind it and consider the circumstances in which it might be preferred to other well-known forms of qualitative data analysis. Through the use of an extended example from a real research project I will go through the key steps required to utilize the technique.

Template analysis is a style of thematic analysis that balances a relatively high degree of structure in the process of analysing textual data with the flexibility to adapt it to the needs of a particular study. It has mostly been used to analyse data from individual interviews (see Alvesson and Ashcraft, in this volume, for more on qualitative interviewing), but it can be applied to other forms too. The example used in this chapter employed focus group interviews (see also Kandola, in this volume), while Kent (2000) used it to analyse free response items on a questionnaire, and it could certainly be applied to data from diaries or to observational field notes (see Yanow, Ybema and van Hulst on ethnography and Brennan on participant observation, in this volume). Central to the technique is the development of a coding template, usually on the basis of a subset of the data, which is then applied to further data, revised and reapplied. The approach is very flexible regarding the style and format of the template that is produced and unlike some other thematic approaches does not suggest in advance a set sequence of coding levels.

Template analysis revisited

The first version of this chapter appeared more than ten years ago (Symon and Cassell, 1998). Since then, the number of publications describing studies that have used TA has grown considerably. An ongoing literature review I am compiling with Jane Melvin has identified well over 200 such articles. In terms of broad area, organizational research (including business and management) is clearly the largest (e.g. Kenny and Briner, 2010), followed by health (Howard et al., 2008). Beyond these, TA is used in a wide range of other settings, including education (Au, 2007), clinical psychology/psychotherapy (Stratton et al., 2006) and sports science (Nash and Sproule, 2009). TA studies vary considerably in size, from a single autobiographical case (King, 2008) to studies that in qualitative terms may be considered very large (Donnelly, 2008, for instance included 81 interviews).

Definitional and epistemological issues

Template analysis is not a complete and distinct methodology, but rather is a technique that may be used within a range of epistemological positions (see Duberley, Johnson and Cassell, in this volume). On the one hand, it can be employed in the kind of realist qualitative work that accepts much of the conventional positivistic position of mainstream quantitative social science. By this I mean research that is concerned with 'discovering' the underlying causes of human action and which seeks to achieve researcher objectivity and to demonstrate coding reliability (Kidd, 2008). On the other hand, template analysis can be used within what Madill et al. (2000) call a 'contextual constructivist' position. Here, the researcher assumes that there are always multiple interpretations to be made of any phenomenon, which will depend upon the position of the researcher and the context of the research. Concern with coding reliability is therefore irrelevant; instead the emphasis is on the reflexivity of the researcher (see Haynes, in this volume), the attempt to approach the topic from differing perspectives and the richness of the description produced (Wimalasiri et al., 2008). Phenomenological, interactionist and some narrative approaches (see Maitlis, in this volume) fall within this category.

Template analysis is generally not used in methodologies that take a radical relativist approach to examining how language is used in interaction to construct versions of our world – as in various forms of discourse and conversation analysis (see Oswick, and Greatbatch and Clark respectively, in this volume). There are, however, examples of social constructionist studies that are concerned with broad patterns of discourse use rather than the close analysis of interactions, and that have used a thematic style of analysis (e.g. Taylor and Ussher, 2001). In principle, such studies could use a template style for their thematic analysis.

Why use template analysis?

Why should anyone about to embark on a qualitative research project choose to use template analysis? In particular, why should they choose it over other approaches that resemble it, such as grounded theory (for example, Corbin and Strauss, 2008, and see Kenealy, in this volume), interpretative phenomenological analysis (IPA; for example, Smith et al., 2009) or more generic forms of thematic analysis (e.g. Braun and Clarke, 2006)? In this section I will consider the advantages that template analysis may offer in relation to these alternatives.

Focusing first on grounded theory, for some researchers a preference for template analysis may be based on their philosophical position. Since its inception by Glaser and Strauss in *The Discovery of Grounded Theory* (1967), grounded theory has developed in a number of different directions, including a divergence between the original authors (Strauss and Corbin, 1990; Glaser, 1992) and a social constructionist version proposed by Charmaz (1995). The Strauss and Corbin approach is probably the best known and most widely used, and both it and Glaser's version retain a realist orientation. That is to say, its users have mostly claimed to be discovering the 'real' beliefs, attitudes, values and so on of the participants in their research. Those qualitative researchers taking a contextual constructivist stance that is sceptical of the existence of 'real' internal states to be discovered through empirical research may therefore feel that template analysis is more conducive to their position.

Template analysis may also be preferred by those who are not inimical to the assumptions of grounded theory but find it too prescriptive (especially in the Strauss and Corbin version), in that it specifies procedures for data gathering and analysis that *must* be followed (Corbin and Strauss, 2008). By contrast, template analysis is, on the whole, a more flexible technique with fewer specified procedures, permitting researchers to tailor it to match their own requirements.

When employed within a broadly phenomenological approach, template analysis is in practice very similar to IPA. The main differences between approaches are the use of a priori codes in template analysis and the balance between, within and across case analysis. IPA tends to analyse individual cases in greater depth before attempting any integration of a full set of cases. The net effect of these differences is that template analysis is generally somewhat less time-consuming than IPA and can handle rather larger data sets more comfortably. IPA studies are commonly based on samples of 10 or fewer; template analysis studies usually have rather more participants, with 15 to 30 being common.

Some writers – notably Braun and Clarke (2006) – argue for the use of a generic form of thematic analysis, one that is not wedded to a particular methodological and theoretical position. This is in effect the same position that I would take in stating that template analysis is a technique rather than a methodology, which can be used from varying philosophical positions. It is worthwhile considering why one might choose template analysis rather than the kind of thematic analysis Braun and Clarke describe. I would suggest that there are three features that vary between the techniques and that might influence a researcher's choice: the flexibility of the coding structure, the use of a priori themes, and use of the initial template.

Flexibility of the coding structure

Some approaches specify in advance how the coding should be structured, typically moving from descriptive themes that are close to the data, to feeding into a smaller number of interpretive themes and then in turn into a few major (or 'overarching') themes (see Langdridge, 2004; King and Horrocks, 2010). By requiring a step-by-step move from the more concrete and data-grounded to the more abstract and interpretive, such techniques can be useful in discouraging inexperienced qualitative researchers from rushing to impose strong interpretations on the data at an early stage. However, it is debatable whether there is ever such a clear distinction between descriptive and interpretive coding. Furthermore, the norm of a three-level hierarchy may restrict analysts from exploring the richest aspects of the data in any real depth. Template analysis does not insist on a fixed number of levels of coding hierarchy – instead it encourages the analyst to develop themes more extensively where the richest data (in relation to the research question) are found. Equally, template analysis does not insist on an explicit distinction between descriptive and interpretive themes, nor on a particular position for each type in the structure.

Use of a priori themes

Types of thematic analysis can be considered in terms of the extent to which they take a 'bottom up' or 'top down' approach. In the former, existing theoretical or practical commitments are actively avoided, to allow themes to be developed inductively from the data. This is the case in the thematic analysis used in IPA and grounded theory. By contrast, top down approaches seek to define and apply themes that are informed by theory or practice ('practice' here could mean, for example, basing the coding structure around evaluation criteria). Matrix analysis (Nadin and Cassell, 2004) and framework analysis (Pope et al., 2000) generally adopt this kind of approach. Template analysis can be positioned in the middle ground between top down and bottom up styles of analysis. It allows the researcher to define some themes in advance (a priori themes), but usually only a limited number that correspond to key concepts or perspectives for the study. It also insists that these are used tentatively, with the possibility always considered that any a priori theme may need to be redefined or discarded.

Use of the initial template

Most thematic approaches will require the researcher to carry out each step of the analysis on each transcript (or other piece of textual data). In template analysis, the use of an initial template based on a sub-set of the data changes the process. Following the construction of the initial template, the researcher does not need to begin with preliminary coding for the next and subsequent transcripts. As will be seen in the example later in this chapter, analysis progresses instead through an iterative process of applying, modifying and re-applying the initial template. This style of analysis can be more efficient than those that require all the steps to be carried out on all the data. Crucially, using the initial template does not, in my experience, seriously risk reducing the depth of the analysis if this is carried out properly.

Key Features of Template Analysis

Defining themes and codes

Themes in qualitative analysis may be defined as the recurrent and distinctive features of participants' accounts (in interviews, diaries, blogs and so on) that characterize perceptions and/or experiences, seen by the researcher as relevant to the research question of a particular study. The issues involved in defining the concept of 'theme' are explored further in Braun and Clarke (2006) and King and Horrocks (2010). For the purposes of the present chapter, there are three points related to this definition that require some comment:

1   The term 'theme' implies repetition. It should not be applied to a single isolated instance where a view is expressed or an experience described. While themes are usually identified across several cases, something important that is identified several times within a single case could still be defined as a theme.

2   Themes are not independent of the researcher who defines them. They do not lie waiting to be discovered, like a fossil in a rock. Even the most realist-oriented qualitative research recognizes that themes are not objective 'facts'.

3   To be useful, themes must be relatively distinct from each other. Some overlap is inevitable, but an extensive blurring of boundaries between themes is to be avoided.

Coding is the process of attaching a label (code) to a section of text to index it as relating to a theme. Within a template there may also be some codes that strictly speaking do not index themes but rather serve as 'placeholders' (Gibbs, 2002) to help organize associated themes. For instance, in a study of staff views on a new IT system, we might use staff groups as placeholder codes under which themes relating to each group are organized.

Hierarchical coding

A key feature of template analysis is the hierarchical organization of codes, with groups of similar codes clustered together to produce more general higher order codes. Hierarchical coding allows the researcher to analyse texts at varying levels of specificity and there can be as many levels of themes as the researcher finds useful. Importantly, the extent to which main (i.e. top level) themes are elaborated – in terms of the number and levels of sub-themes – should reflect how rich they prove to be in terms of offering insights into the topic area of a particular study. It is worth bearing in mind, though, that too many levels can be counter productive to the goal of attaining clarity in organizing and interpreting the data.

As well as being organized hierarchically, the template can present lateral links between themes. This may be in the form of a small number of integrative themes that cut across many of the main themes or it may involve more complex links between individual themes. Using and depicting such lateral links on the template is discussed below.

Parallel coding

Template analysis usually permits a parallel coding of segments of text, whereby the same segment is classified within two (or more) different codes at the same level. Parallel coding is only likely to be problematic in research that is located strongly towards the positivist end of the qualitative research spectrum, where researchers may wish to combine template analysis with elements of quantitative content analysis.

Integrative themes

Sometimes as the template develops it will become clear that there are certain themes that seem to pervade much of the data, cross-cutting many or all of the other thematic clusters. For example, in a study of experiences of diabetic renal disease (King et al., 2002), we found that 'uncertainty' permeated much of the data. To have simply treated this as a top-level theme in itself would not have drawn sufficient attention to the way it related to all the other thematic clusters. Equally, adding 'uncertainty' as a sub-theme to each top-level theme would not in our view have made its importance apparent enough. We therefore identified it as an integrative theme, shown on the template as connecting the other themes laterally.

One way to conceptualize integrative themes is as undercurrents running through participants' accounts; often, perhaps, not addressed explicitly but very apparent to the careful reader. In the diabetic renal disease study we identified a second integrative theme of 'stoicism' to indicate the typical stance towards their illness taken by almost all participants. They did not explicitly describe themselves as 'stoical' but demonstrated it in many different aspects of their accounts of their illness experience. The integrative theme of 'stoicism' was of interest because it appeared to contradict claims in the literature that people no longer felt the need to maintain a 'stiff upper-lip' towards personal suffering.

Displaying the template: lists and mind-maps

The template itself has an important communicative function; it is therefore worthwhile to think carefully about how best to present it. There are two main styles that can be used. First, themes can be presented in a list, with levels indicated by indentation, typography (e.g. font size and style) and/or a numbering system. Second, themes can be laid out in a format similar to a 'mind-map', which might also use typographic details as well as connecting arrows to indicate hierarchical levels. The mind-map version allows lateral links between thematic clusters to be shown more clearly than in the list style. It is, however, more complex and for the full template would take up considerably more space in its display than the list version. Although most published studies using template analysis present the template in list form, it is useful to think about using the mind-map style when the lateral links between thematic clusters are important. It is always possible to convert this to a list format if that works better in a written account of the study.

Quality checks

The issue of quality in qualitative research is dealt with in detail by Symon and Cassell in this volume. Here I will highlight specific points relating to template analysis. Some of the commonly used strategies for enhancing the quality of data analysis include: independent coding and critical comparison among researchers and by expert panels; respondent feedback; and the provision of audit trails. All of these are assisted by the systematic nature of template analysis and the possibility it offers to document emerging thinking through the modification of the template. The compiling of an audit trail, in particular, fits very well with this approach. An audit trail in qualitative research is a record of the steps the researcher has gone through in carrying out an analysis and the way his or her thinking has developed. I would always recommend that a full record is kept of how the template develops over the course of the analysis, numbering and dating successive versions and keeping notes as to the reasons for any major changes made to it.

Developing the Template: An Example

Having described the approach in general terms, I will present here the steps involved in using it for the analysis of data from a quite recent study carried out by members of my team at the University of Huddersfield. Some background to the project is necessary here in order to understand the material that we were working with.

Background: the community group participation study

As part of their wider health strategy (Department of Health, 1999) from 2002 the UK government set up 350 Health Living Centres (HLCs) . These served as a focus for community-based initiatives and activities to improve health and wellbeing in areas of significant deprivation. The Centre for Applied Psychological Research (CAPR) at the University of Huddersfield was commissioned to carry out a series of evaluation studies for an HLC in a deprived urban area in northern England, which I will refer to as the Broomville Health Partnership (BHP). The project team of myself, Emma Kirkby-Geddes and Alison Bravington carried out focus groups (see Kandola, in this volume) with members of three community groups supported by the BHP. Details of the groups are given in Table 24.1 below.

Table 24.1 Focus group participants

Group	Number of participants	Characteristics of participants
Coffee Morning	4 (+ leader)	1 female, 3 male Approx. age range: 58–82 All white
Craft Group	10 (+ leader) Volunteer helpers: 1 Carers: 1	8 female, 2 male Approx. age range 42–86 8 white, 2 SE Asian
Exercise Group	6 (+ leader)	5 female, 1 male: Approx. age range: 68–88 All white

The focus groups were audio-recorded, transcribed verbatim and analysed using template analysis. The stages of this analytical process are described below. The transcripts were laid out double spaced with wide margins, and line numbered, to facilitate analysis – especially in the early stages.

The overall aim of this part of the evaluation programme was:

- To examine how those participating in group activities supported by BHP experience their involvement with the Healthy Living Partnership, in the context of their views of Broomville as a community.

By 'involvement' we meant both participation in their own group and their wider engagement with the BHP and the activities and facilities it supported.

A priori themes and preliminary coding

Before beginning preliminary coding, it is essential to read through the transcripts for familiarization and to check for any possible errors in transcription.

The first transcript should be taken and every section of text that seems to offer something of relevance to answering the research question marked, noting in the margin a preliminary code title that sums up what is of interest here. If using a priori themes, it is best to have a sheet beside the transcript listing and defining these; should a section of text emerge that can be encompassed by one of the a priori themes, make a note of this in the margin. At this stage if there is doubt as to whether a particular issue is relevant, it is best to err on the side of inclusivity and code it. It can always be set aside later if it transpires that it does not add to the interpretation.

In the BHP community group participation study we began our analysis with the focus groups, listening to the recordings and then focusing particularly on the Coffee Morning group transcript. Before commencing preliminary coding we identified six a priori themes, based on the BHP's evaluation priorities and on our initial reading and discussion of the transcripts. These are described in Table 24.2.

Next we each independently read through the selected transcript and added preliminary codes in the margins and/or above the text wherever any section of the discussion appeared to relate to matters relevant to the study aims. If such sections could be encapsulated by one of the a priori themes we noted this on the transcript too.

Initial template

A key decision in template analysis is when to begin to develop an initial template. As noted above, this is normally based on a sub-set of the data, but there can be no fixed rule as to how soon it should be attempted. In general, the

Table 24.2   A priori themes in the community group participation study

A priori theme	Description
Perception of self	Includes: physical insecurity, social isolation, personal effects of ageing
Quality of group	Includes: atmosphere, values of the group
Practicalities	Includes: practical aspects of the groups, such as rooming, scheduling sessions
Who we are as a group	Includes: issues of group identity and how these relate to personal identity
Perceptions of Broomville	Includes: physical space and resources, local people
World gone down the plughole	Includes: all references to a general sense of quality of life and values deteriorating over time

more diverse the accounts provided by participants within a study, the more transcripts will need to be analysed to produce a workable initial template.

Developing the initial template begins with the clustering of preliminary codes, to bring them into meaningful groups within which hierarchical and lateral relations between themes can be defined. This should be a very fluid and exploratory process, in which many different ways of organizing themes are attempted. In the clustering process, it should not be assumed that a priori themes are necessarily going to be at the top levels of clusters; they can be moved around anywhere in the emerging structure until a place is found where they seem to function best.

In our study we produced an initial version of the template on the basis of the preliminary coding of the first focus group. We began by looking at each other's coding, discussing the similarities and differences and agreeing on a provisional set of themes to organize. We wrote each potential theme on a Post-it note and placed the notes on large sheets of paper in what seemed to be meaningful clusters. The advantage of using Post-its is that they can easily be moved around to explore alternative ways of organizing the template, but of course other methods could be used. After a lengthy process of trying out different versions of the structure we agreed on the initial template shown in Figure 24.1.

Two of the a priori themes were not included in the initial template – Perception of Self and Practicalities. In both cases, we found there was little that would 'fit' under the a priori theme title that did not also fit elsewhere on the template. Further, Perception of Self seemed overly individualistic when the data showed that issues such as ageing and physical insecurity were almost always raised in the context of relationships in the group, the community and society more widely. There were also a number of preliminary themes that we could not include comfortably on the template. At this stage we simply left these as Uncategorized.

The initial template included one integrative theme: Shrinkage. This captured the way that many participants seemed to describe a sense of their world shrinking – personally through such things as the effects of ageing and collectively through the loss of local amenities and facilities.

Modifying the template

Once an initial template is constructed, the researcher must work systematically through the full set of transcripts, identifying those sections of text that are relevant to the project's aims and marking them with one or more appropriate code(s). In the

1.   WHO WE ARE AS GROUP

1.1   Our purpose as a group
1.1.1   Doing specific activities
1.1.2   Vehicle for activity *vs* End in itself
1.1.3   Being a presence in Broomville (Church)

1.2   Inward *vs* outward looking
1.2.1   Exclusivity

      1.2.1.1   Not too much growth
      1.2.1.2   Existing relationships

1.2.2   Inclusivity

      1.2.2.1   Seeking growth

1.2.3   Fundraising
1.2.4   Connection with other church activities

2. QUALITY OF GROUP

2.1   Caring for each other
2.1.1   Practical help
2.1.2   Ethos of caring
2.1.3   Christian fellowship

2.2   Intra-group dynamics
2.2.1   Leader telling group what they (should) think
2.2.2   Resisting leader

      2.2.2.1   Re. faith/ethnic diversity
      2.2.2.2   Re. children = vibrancy

2.2.3   Humour
2.2.4   Reassurance

3. PERCEPTIONS OF BROOMVILLE

3.1   Physical geography of Broomville
3.1.1   Proximity of Village Hall

3.2   Diversity
3.2.1   +ve re diversity of people
3.2.2   Diversity of worship
3.2.3   Diversity of activities

      3.2.3.1   Plenty
      3.2.3.2   Not enough

3.3 Green environment
3.3.1   Improvements to environment
3.3.2   Better than other similar (multi-cultural) areas
3.3.3   Ownership of environmental improvements (children)

(Continued)

(Continued)

3.4   **'Broomville don't care'**
3.4.1   Involvement from outside Broomville
3.4.2   People won't get involved
3.4.3   Excuses (or not) for lack of involvement

3.5   **Intergenerational issues**
3.5.1   Children as constructive

      3.5.1.1   In organized contexts
      3.5.1.2   Schools' involvement in community

            3.5.1.2.1   Flower beds
            3.5.1.2.2   Pensioner dinners

3.5.2   Children as destructive

      3.5.2.1   Wild
      3.5.2.2   Environmental damage
      3.5.2.3   Litter

3.5.3   Children as future/sign of life
3.5.4   General negativity (nothing to like about Broomville)

3.6   **World down plughole**
3.6.1   Night-time dangerous

A. SHRINKAGE
(INTEGRATIVE THEME)
A1 Churches going/moving to fringes
A2 People not going out at night

[Uncategorized]
Activities outside the group
Involvement in/understanding of wider PPH activities
Finding out about PPH activities
Getting older
Impact of lottery funding

Figure 24.1   Initial template from the community group participation study

course of this, inadequacies in the initial template will be revealed, requiring changes of various kinds. It is through these that the template develops to its final form.

Having developed the initial template in the community group participation study, we again went through the first focus group transcript to check that it had succeeded in capturing everything we felt to be important in the data in relation to our research aims. As a result we made several changes:

- We added a new top-level theme: Understanding and Perception of BHP.

- We added a new integrative theme: Getting Older.

- We divided the top-level theme Perceptions of Broomville into two second-level themes: People and Physical Space and Facilities.

We then applied this revised initial template to the remaining two focus groups, noting where relevant material in these could not be readily covered by any theme on the template and where necessary revising the template accordingly. Finally we read through the individual interview transcripts to identify any further revisions needed. This resulted in the final version of the template shown in Figure 24.2.

Throughout this process we reorganized the template in various ways. Examples of these are given below.

Insertion

After producing the initial template we added a new third-level theme of Inter-racial Issues, under Perceptions of Broomville/People. While some issues relating to ethnicity did appear on the first version of the initial template, and more were added subsequently, it was only at this point that we recognized that the importance of the area in general was best reflected by pulling together such a theme. The theme included both an explicit discussion of 'race' (mostly regarding the South Asian community) in the Coffee Morning Group and more implicit allusions in the other two groups.

> I've lived with Asians, they've been there 10 to 12 years, and they, it's taken that long for them to start speaking to you. They just ignore you, and even now, they'll turn their nose up at you and look the other way when they walk past you. (Roger, Coffee Morning Group)

> Well, if you can speak the truth and speak out, we were pushed out [of our usual room] for the Asian ladies; if I shouldn't have said that, I don't know, but we were – so. (Joyce, Exercise Group)

> [Member next to Joyce makes exaggerated gesture of holding her head in her hands; others look embarrassed.]

1. US AS A GROUP

1.1   Looking inward
1.1.1   Exclusivity

        1.1.1.1   Restricting growth
        1.1.1.2   Existing relationships

1.1.2   Ethos of group

        1.1.2.1   Caring
        1.1.2.2   Practical help
        1.1.2.3   Christian fellowship

1.1.3   Intra-group dynamics
        1.1.3.1   Leader telling group what they (should) think
        1.1.3.2   Resisting dominant voice

                1.1.3.2.1 Re. faith/ethnic diversity
                1.1.3.2.1 Re. children = vibrancy
                1.1.3.2.2 Re. takeaways

        1.1.3.3   Humour
        1.1.3.4   Leader supporting members

1.1.4   Value of activity

        1.1.4.1   Activity as ends or means
        1.1.4.2   Sharing food/drink
        1.1.4.3   Importance of talk/sociability
        1.1.4.4   An excuse to get out
        1.1.4.5   Direct health benefits
        1.1.4.6   Meanings related to specific activities

1.2   Looking outward
1.2.1   Seeking growth
1.2.2   Taking group activity home
1.2.3   Spreading/sharing the ethos

        1.2.3.1   Being a presence in Broomville
        1.2.3.2   Wider Christian/faith activities
        1.2.3.3   Fundraising for charities

2.   PERCEPTIONS OF BROOMVILLE

2.1   People
2.1.1   Intergenerational issues

        2.1.1.1   Children as constructive

                2.1.1.1.1   In organized contexts
                2.1.1.1.2   Schools' involvement in community

(Continued)

(Continued)

2.1.1.1.2.1	Flower beds
2.1.1.1.2.2	Pensioner dinners

2.1.1.2   Children as destructive

2.1.1.2.1   Wild
2.1.1.2.2   Environmental damage
2.1.1.2.3   Litter

2.1.1.3   Children as future/sign of life
2.1.1.4   Young people don't get involved
2.1.1.5   Generations want different things

2.1.2   Inter-racial issues

2.1.2.1   'Us and them'

2.1.2.1.1 Asians unfriendly
2.1.2.1.2 Asians keep to their own comfort zone
2.1.2.1.3 Asians changing nature of community
2.1.2.1.4 Competition for resources

2.1.2.2   Coming together

2.1.2.2.1 Cooking/eating together
2.1.2.2.2 Coming out of comfort zones
2.1.2.2.3 Diversity a good thing
2.1.2.2.4 Asians participating in Broomville activities

2.1.2.3   Difficult/taboo topic

2.1.3   'Broomville don't care'

2.1.3.1   Involvement from outside Broomville
2.1.3.2   People won't get involved

2.1.3.2.1   Asians

2.1.3.3   Excuses (or not) for lack of involvement

2.1.3.3.1   Not lack of information

2.1.4   Contesting the 'Broomville don't care' attitude

2.1.4.1   (Local) Government initiatives cf bottom up community activity
2.1.4.2   Local government has good ideas. But…
2.1.4.3   Doing it from own heart, and pocket
2.1.4.4   Roots of voluntary community action in Christianity

2.2   Physical space and facilities
2.2.1   Physical geography of Broomville

2.2.1.1   Proximity of Village Hall
2.2.1.2   Top and Bottom

(Continued)

(Continued)

2.2.1.2.1   Long way to walk
2.2.1.2.2   Two communities in one

2.2.2   Green environment

2.2.2.1   Improvements to environment
2.2.2.2   Better than other similar (multi-cultural) areas
2.2.2.3   Ownership of environmental improvements (children)

2.2.3   Urban mess

2.2.3.1   Too many takeaways

2.2.3.1.1   Destroying community

2.2.3.2   Lack of cleanliness

2.2.4   Facilities

2.2.4.1   Good bus service
2.2.4.2   Poor main road
2.2.4.3   Other venues for activities

2.2.5   Diversity

2.2.5.1   +ve re diversity of people
2.2.5.2   Diversity of worship
2.2.5.3   Diversity of activities

2.2.5.2.1   Plenty
2.2.5.2.2   Not enough

3.   UNDERSTANDING AND PERCEPTION OF BHP
3.1   Understanding of wider BHP activities

3.1.1   Involvement in BHP planning

3.2   Finding out about BHP activities
3.3   Impact of lottery funding

3.3.1   On Broomville in general
3.3.2   On specific services at BHP

3.4   Facilities at Village Hall

3.4.1   Issues re rooms
3.4.2   Access to Village Hall

A. WORLD GONE DOWN THE PLUGHOLE
(INTEGRATIVE THEME)

B. GETTING OLDER
(INTEGRATIVE THEME)

Figure 24.2   Final template from the community group participation study

Deletion

The top-level theme Quality of Group was deleted at version four of the template and the second-level theme Our Purpose as a Group (under Us as a Group) was removed in the final version. This was because, as the analysis progressed, we increasingly observed that, in terms of our research aims, the most important aspect of how people saw their groups was the balance (and at times tension) between a tendency to 'look inwards' at processes and relationships and a willingness to 'look outwards' to how the group related to lives beyond the meetings and to the wider community.

Merging

On the initial template under Perceptions of Broomville we included as a second-level theme World Gone Down the Plughole. This captured the view that the world in general was a less safe, friendly and comfortable place to live in than it had been in the past. We distinguished such views from specific comments about how Broomville had declined, which we captured under the integrative theme Shrinkage. The quotes below illustrate the two themes:

World Gone Down the Plughole

But where is nice to live these days? Where do, do you feel safe, any, any of you, well I can't go out at night. (Maureen, Exercise Group)

Shrinkage

I mean the shops up there are frankly not worth bothering, they're very expensive and they haven't got the variety ... You've got to leave Broomville, get out of Broomville to get your stuff, now. (Roger, Coffee Morning Group)

As we developed the template further we became increasingly uncertain as to whether the distinction made above was a meaningful one. Eventually we decided to merge the two themes together, using the World Gone Down the Plughole title as we felt it better encapsulated the tone of participants' comments.

Changing the scope

Having deleted the top-level theme Quality of Group (see above), we made changes in scope to the subsidiary theme Caring for Each Other and its sub-themes.

We concluded that the notion of 'caring' in the groups was best seen as an aspect of their ethos and therefore reversed the hierarchical order here on the final template. This enabled us to get a clearer understanding of the differences in ethos between the groups than was the case when ethos was subsumed under the notion of 'caring'.

Changing the higher order classification

The previous example involved a change in the higher order classification as well as a change in the scope for the themes, since Ethos of Group moved into the second-level theme Looking Inward. This created a potential difficulty in that aspects of ethos that concerned how groups related to the world beyond them could have been neglected. We addressed this by constructing a third-level theme under Looking Outwards entitled Spreading/Sharing the Ethos.

The 'final' template

One of the most difficult decisions to make when constructing an analytical template is where to stop the process of development. It is possible to go on modifying and refining definitions of codes almost ad infinitum, but research projects inevitably face external constraints which will mean that there is not unlimited time to produce an 'ideal' template. The decision about when a template is 'good enough' is always going to be unique to a particular project. However, no template can be considered 'final' if there remain any sections of text that are clearly relevant to the research question but stay uncoded.

Interpreting and Presenting Template Analysis

Interpretation

Developing a template and using it to code a set of transcripts does not represent the end of the process of analysing and interpreting the data. If the themes are simply listed and the main findings summarized under each this will result in a very flat description of the data. Exactly how to go about drawing together an interpretation of the coded data depends on the aims and content of the particular study. I will offer some guidelines and examples that may serve as a useful starting point.

Listing codes

I usually find it useful at an early stage to compile a list of all codes occurring in each transcript, with some indication of their frequency. The distribution of codes within and across transcripts can help to draw attention to aspects of the data that warrant further examination. For example, if a theme occurs prominently in all but one of a set of interview transcripts, it may be revealing to look closely at the one exception. Or if certain themes occur frequently in the transcripts of one sub-set of the sample but hardly ever in another, whether this may exemplify a meaningful difference in views or experiences between the two should be considered. Note, though, that while frequencies of themes and the patterns of their distribution may suggest areas for closer examination, they cannot in and of themselves tell us anything meaningful.

Selectivity

There is always the need to be selective in identifying which themes to examine in depth. It is important not to rush to a decision about which key themes should be the focus, and it should not automatically be assumed that any a priori themes retained in the final template should be included among these. Equally, prioritizing themes to focus on should not be based on mere frequency, as explained above. Rather the task is to consider carefully how each theme (or cluster of themes) sheds light on the topic of interest.

Openness

The need to be selective in analysing and interpreting data must be balanced against the need to retain openness towards it. The researcher must not be so strongly guided by the initial research questions that all themes that are not obviously of direct relevance are disregarded. Themes that are judged to be of marginal relevance can play a useful role in adding to the background detail of the study, without requiring a lengthy explication. More problematic are those themes that are clearly of great importance to participants, but which seem to lie well outside the scope of the study. In such cases, there should be a careful consideration of whether the investigation of the 'excluded' theme casts any significant light on the understanding of central themes in the study. If it does, then it should be included in the interpretation.

Relationships between themes

Whether or not the template has been designed to incorporate integrative themes and/or other lateral links, as the interpretation proceeds consideration should be given to whether there are relationships between themes that need to be highlighted. In the community group participation study, for instance, we recognized that some of the intergenerational and inter-racial issues (themes 2.1.1 and 2.1.2 on the final template, Figure 24.2) were manifest in the intra-group dynamics (theme 1.1.3) and reflected this in our report (King et al., 2009). Sometimes it will be sufficient to draw out such connections in the findings and discussion of the write-up. Alternatively, as Crabtree and Miller (1999) suggest, maps, matrices and other diagrams can be used to explore and display template analysis findings.

Presentation

The final task is to present an account of the interpretation of the data. As with other stages of template analysis, it would be wrong to try to define one single 'correct' way to do this. The nature of the data, the type of document to be produced (including its word length) and, critically, the intended readership need to be considered. All the same, it is possible to identify three approaches to presentation, any one of which might prove useful.

1   *A set of individual case studies, followed by a discussion of the differences and similarities between cases.* This gives the reader a good grasp of the perspectives of individual participants. However, where there are a relatively large number of participants, this format can be confusing for the reader and repetitive, and it does rely on there being sufficient space to provide an adequate description of each case.

2   *An account structured around the main themes identified, drawing illustrative examples from each transcript (or other text) as required.* This tends to be the approach that most readily produces a clear and succinct thematic discussion. The danger is one of over-generalization, and losing sight of individual experiences.

3   *A thematic presentation of the findings, using a different individual case study to illustrate each of the main themes.* This can be a useful synthesis of approaches (1) and (2) above; the key challenge is to select the cases in a way that fairly represents the themes in the data as a whole.

Whatever approach is taken, the use of direct quotes from the participants is essential. These should normally include both short quotes to aid the understanding of specific points of interpretation and more extensive passages, giving readers a flavour of the original texts.

Advantages and Disadvantages of the Technique

Arguably, the greatest advantage of template analysis is that it is a highly flexible approach that can be modified for the needs of any study. It does not come with the heavy baggage of prescriptions and procedures and, as such, is especially welcome to those who want to take a phenomenological and experiential approach to organizational research. At the same time, the principles behind the technique are easily grasped by those relatively unfamiliar with qualitative methods and so it can be a valuable introduction to the whole field. Template analysis works very well in studies that seek to examine the perspectives of different groups within an organizational context – for example, different professions working in a collaborative setting or different grades of staff affected by a particular organizational change. Finally, the discipline of producing the template forces the researcher to take a systematic and well-structured approach to handling the data.

The strong emphasis on the coding structure in template analysis may be seen as a disadvantage by some researchers, for two rather contrasting reasons. On the one hand, this emphasis may seem potentially to stand in the way of a personal engagement with the data for those whose preferred style is a very open, unstructured engagement with texts. On the other hand, some may be too easily seduced into focusing excessively on the details of template construction, neglecting the crucial point made earlier that developing the template is a means to an end (making sense of the data) and not the purpose of the analysis in itself. In response to both these positions I would argue that the flexibility of template analysis should allow researchers to tailor it to suit their own style and stance towards qualitative data analysis, though in the end as with any analytical technique this will not suit everyone.

Conclusion

Template analysis has become a widely used technique for the thematic analysis of qualitative data, in organizational studies and beyond. The main reasons for its popularity, I would suggest, are its combination of a clear, structured and systematic approach with the flexibility to adapt it to specific needs – both in terms of the content of particular studies and the epistemological positions used. I hope this chapter has given a sense of how researchers new to the technique might go about employing it in their own research; and that those already familiar with the technique may have garnered some new ideas for how to creatively develop their analytical practice.

Further Reading

Examples of research using template analysis include: Gollop, Whitby, Buchanan and Ketley (2004), King, Bell, and Thomas (2004), Poppleton, Briner, and Kiefer (2008) and Waring and Wainwright (2008).

General texts on thematic analysis include: Braun and Clarke (2006), King and Horrocks (2010) Chapter 9: 'An introduction to interview data analysis', and Nadin and Cassell (2004).

References

Au, W. (2007) 'High-stakes testing and curricular control: a qualitative metasynthesis', *Educational Researcher*, 36 (5): 258–267.

Braun, V. and Clarke, V. (2006) 'Using thematic analysis in psychology', *Qualitative Research in Psychology*, 3: 77–101.

Charmaz, K. (1995) 'Grounded theory', in J.A. Smith, R. Harré and L. van Langenhove (eds), *Rethinking Methods in Psychology*. London: Sage.

Corbin, J. and Strauss, A. (2008) *Basics of Qualitative Research: Techniques and Procedures for Developing Grounded Theory* (3rd edn). London: Sage.

Crabtree, B.F. and Miller, W.L. (1999) 'Using codes and code manuals: a template organizing style of interpretation', in B.F. Crabtree and W.L. Miller (eds), *Doing Qualitative Research* (2nd edn). Newbury Park, CA: Sage.

Department of Health (1999) *Saving Lives: Our Healthier Nation*. London: HMSO.

Donnelly, R. (2008) 'Careers and temporal flexibility in the new economy: an Anglo-Dutch comparison of the organisation of consultancy work', *Human Resource Management Journal*, 18 (3): 197–215.

Gibbs, G. (2002) *Qualitative Data Analysis: Explorations with NVivo*. Buckingham: Open University Press.

Glaser, B. (1992) *Emergence vs Forcing: Basics of Grounded Analysis*. Mill Valley, CA: The Sociology Press.

Glaser, B. and Strauss, A.L. (1967) *The Discovery of Grounded Theory*. New York: Aldine Publications.

Gollop, R., Whitby, E., Buchanan, D. and Ketley, D. (2004) 'Influencing sceptical staff to become supporters of service improvement: A qualitative study of doctors' and managers' views', *Quality and Safety in Health Care*, 13: 108–114.

Howard, R., Avery, A. and Bissell, P. (2008) 'Causes of preventable drug-related hospital admissions: a qualitative study', *Quality and Safety in Health Care*, 17: 109–116.

Kenny, E.J. and Briner, R.B. (2010) 'Exploring ethnicity in organisations', *Equality, Diversity and Inclusion: An International Journal*, 29 (4): 348–363.

Kent, G. (2000) 'Understanding the experiences of people with disfigurements: an integration of four models of social and psychological functioning', *Psychology, Health and Medicine*, 5 (2): 117–129.

Kidd, J.M. (2008) 'Exploring the components of career well-being and the emotions associated with significant career experiences', *Journal of Career Development*, 35 (2): 166–186.

King, N. (2008) 'What will hatch? A constructivist autobiographical account of writing poetry', *Journal of Constructivist Psychology*, 21 (4): 274–287.

King, N., Bell, D. and Thomas, K. (2004) 'Family carers' experiences of out-of-hours community palliative care: a qualitative study', *International Journal of Palliative Nursing*, 10 (2): 76–83.

King, N., Carroll, C., Newton, P. and Dornan, T. (2002) '"You can't cure it so you have to endure it": the experience of adaptation to diabetic renal disease', *Qualitative Health Research*, 12 (3): 329–346.

King, N. and Horrocks, C. (2010) *Interviews in Qualitative Research*. London: Sage.

King, N., Kirkby-Geddes, E. and Bravington, A. (2009) *Evaluation of the Impact of Paddock Pathways to Health Membership on Beneficiaries' Health, Well-being and Social Functioning*. Centre for Applied Psychological Research, University of Huddersfield.

Langdridge, D. (2004) *Introduction to Research Methods and Data Analysis in Psychology*. Harlow: Pearson Education.

Madill, A., Jordan, A. and Shirley, C. (2000) 'Objectivity and reliability in qualitative analysis: realist, contextualist and radical constructionist epistemologies', *British Journal of Psychology*, 91: 1–20.

Nadin, S. and Cassell, C. (2004) 'Using data matrices', in C. Cassell and G. Symon (eds), *Essential Guide to Qualitative Methods in Organizational Research*. London: Sage.

Nash, C.S. and Sproule, J. (2009) 'Career development of expert coaches', *International Journal of Sports Science & Coaching*, 4 (1), 121–138.

Pope, C., Ziebland, S. and Mays, N. (2000) 'Qualitative research in healthcare: analysing qualitative data', *British Medical Journal*, 320: 114–116.

Poppleton, S., Briner, R.B. and Kiefer, T. (2008) 'The roles of context and everyday experience in understanding work–non-work relationships: A qualitative diary study of white- and blue-collar workers', *Journal of Occupational and Organizational Psychology*, 81 (3): 481–502.

Smith, J.A., Flowers, P. and Larkin, M. (2009) *Interpretative Phenomenological Analysis: Theory, Method, Research*. London: Sage.

Stratton, P., McGovern, M., Wetherell, A. and Farrington, C. (2006) 'Family therapy practitioners researching the reactions of practitioners to an outcome measure', *Australian and New Zealand Journal of Family Therapy*, 27 (4): 199–207.

Strauss, A. and Corbin, J. (1990) *Basics of Qualitative Research: Grounded Theory Procedures and Techniques*. London: Sage.

Symon, G. and Cassell, C. (eds) (1998) *Qualitative Methods and Analysis in Organizational Research*. London: Sage.

Taylor, G.W. and Ussher, J.M. (2001) 'Making sense of S&M: a discourse analytic account', *Sexualities*, 4: 293–314.

Waring, T. and Wainwright, D. (2008) 'Issues and challenges in the use of template analysis: Two comparative case studies from the field', *The Electronic Journal of Business Research Methods*, 6 (1): 85–94, available online at www.ejbrm.com.

Wimalasiri, V., Beesley, N., Cheyne, A. and Daniels, K. (2008) 'Social construction of the aetiology of designer error in the UK oil and gas industry: a stakeholder perspective', *Journal of Engineering Design*, 21 (1): 49–73.

25 Conversation Analysis in Management Research

David Greatbatch and Timothy Clark

Introduction

Talk is central to the accomplishment of a range of management activities, including strategizing, selling, interviewing, chairing meetings, negotiating and presenting. Despite this, organizational talk has attracted relatively little consideration in the management research literature. Recently, however, a number of scholars have begun to consider how various approaches to the analysis of talk, developed in a range of disciplines, can be used to offer distinctive and important insights into the accomplishment and coordination of management activities. One approach that has attracted considerable interest is conversation analysis (CA) (e.g. see Boden, 1994; Silverman, 1997; Woodilla, 1999; Forray and Woodilla, 2002; Greatbatch and Clark, 2003; Putnam, 2003; Samra-Fredericks, 2003; Cooren and Fairhurst, 2004; Fairhurst, 2004; Llewellyn, 2004; Samra-Fredericks, 2004, Greatbatch and Clark, 2005; Clifton, 2006; Hindmarsh and Pilnick, 2007; Llewellyn, 2008; Greatbatch and Clark, 2010; Llewellyn and Hindmarsh, 2010a; 2010b; Samra-Fredericks, 2010).

CA emerged in the 1960s as part of the broader programme of research known as ethnomethodology, which developed from Harold Garfinkel's (1967) seminal studies of the social organization of everyday social actions and activities. Drawing on this initiative and ordinary language philosophy (Wittgenstein, 1953; Austin, 1962; Searle, 1969), which recognized that talk is a primary vehicle for the accomplishment of social action, Harvey Sacks and his colleagues, Emanuel Schegloff and Gail Jefferson, launched a radically distinct programme of research which recognized that the analysis of tape recordings of naturally occurring talk-in-interaction provided the possibility of developing a 'naturalistic observation discipline which could deal with the details of social action(s) rigorously, empirically, and formally' (Schegloff and Sacks, 1973: 233). Their ground-breaking research has inspired an array of empirical studies of the accomplishment of social actions and activities in talk-in-interaction in a wide range of settings.

   Below, we introduce CA and then illustrate how it can be used to explicate the ways in which management tasks and activities, in this case presenting, are accomplished as they emerge in real-time interaction and to 'respecify' key themes in management research.

Conversation Analysis

By analysing audio and/or video recordings of naturally occurring talk-in-interaction, CA researchers are able to reveal and analyse fine-grained aspects of human conduct that are unavailable for systematic study via more traditional modes of inquiry such as the analysis of field notes, interviews, responses to questionnaires or experimentally produced data. The use of these audiovisual data also establishes important constraints on the quality and rigour of research by enabling social scientists to independently evaluate the strength of each other's findings by reference to the original data. Thus, as Atkinson and Heritage (1984: 4) suggest:

   In sum, the use of recorded data serves as a control on the limitations and fallibilities of intuition and recollection; it exposes the observer to a wide range of interactional materials and circumstances and also provides some guarantee that analytic considerations will not arise as artefacts of intuitive idiosyncrasy, selective attention or recollection, or experimental design.

In contrast to some theories of language use and linguistic analysis (e.g. speech act theory), CA recognizes that utterances and the actions they accomplish are inseparable from the context in which they occur. This is because each utterance is produced with respect to the immediately preceding utterances, while simultaneously contributing to the framework to which subsequent utterances will be addressed; in other words each utterance is both 'context shaped and context renewing' (Heritage, 1984: 242). As a result, the character of an utterance/action can only be determined with reference to the local configuration of conduct in which it is produced and rendered intelligible (Schegloff and Sacks, 1973). CA therefore focuses on the sequential organization of utterances in talk-in-interaction.

In contrast to cognitive perspectives (in the fields of psycholinguistics, cognitive psychology, cognitive anthropology, etc.), which explain face-to-face interaction in terms of the participants' cognitive states (their plans, intentions, goals) and/or which treat talk as a passive medium through which information is transmitted from one mind to another, CA focuses on the generic practices through which specific actions (and activities) are systematically accomplished in talk-in-interaction. This involves identifying patterns of verbal and/or non-verbal interaction through the use of analytic induction. Previous research has identified such patterns in relation to a wide range of phenomena in everyday conversational interaction, including: how encounters are opened and closed; how turns at talk are allocated; how disagreements are initiated, managed and exited; how topics are introduced and changed; and how bad news is broached and received. A central aspect of CA research is that once a pattern of interaction has been identified, researchers undertake 'deviant case analysis' by focusing on cases in which participants depart from the pattern and establishing whether departures are treated as accountable. As Heritage (1995: 399) observes:

> Used in this way, deviant case analysis is an important resource for determining whether the basic pattern simply embodies an empirical regularity that happens to occur, or whether it involves something that is oriented to as a normative interactional procedure.

In undertaking this form of 'pattern and deviant case' analysis (Heritage, 1995: 399), CA researchers repeatedly replay audio or video recordings of naturally occurring interaction, carefully transcribing the events. The transcripts capture not only what is said, but also a variety of details of speech production, such as overlapping talk, pauses within and between utterances, stress, pitch and volume. They may also track visual conduct such as gaze direction and gesture. These transcripts facilitate the fine-grained analysis of the recordings, enabling researchers to reveal and analyse tacit, 'seen but unnoticed' (Garfinkel, 1967) aspects of human conduct, which would otherwise be unavailable for systematic study. Extracts from the transcripts are included in research reports as exemplars of the interactional phenomena under investigation.

CA places rigorous constraints on the use of 'wider' social and organizational contexts and identities to explain features of talk in interaction. Participants in talk-in-interaction can be accurately categorized in terms of numerous social identities, including those related to age, race, sex, social class, occupation and rank in an organizational setting (Sacks, 1995). This poses the question of how professional analysts can determine which, if any, of the array of social identities that can be applied to participants are relevant to understanding their conduct at any point in time (Schegloff, 1991; 1992). In response to this question CA distinguishes between discourse identities, such as 'questioner-answerer' and 'inviter-invitee', which are intrinsic to talk-in-interaction, and larger social/organizational identities (Goodwin, 1987), such as sex, ethnicity and occupational role, which derive from wider societal and institutional formations and thus reach beyond the talk itself. Some CA studies restrict their focus to discourse identities, explicating sequentially organized aspects of talk-in-interaction that are relatively autonomous of other aspects of social organization. However, others explore how participants make larger social and organizational identities relevant within their talk and how the invocation of such identities can constitute both a constraint on and a resource for the accomplishment of the activities in which the participants are engaged. Thus, for example, Goodwin (1987) shows how a speaker at a family gathering makes relevant his spousal relationship with a co-participant by producing a display of uncertainty about household affairs, which positions the latter as a 'knowing recipient' and the other participants as 'unknowing recipients'. Similarly, research on the news interview shows how discourse identities (and the activities in which they are embedded) invoke the institutional identities news interviewer and news interviewee by positioning the broadcast journalists as formally neutral (neutralistic) 'questioners', the guests as 'answerers' and the television or radio audience as 'primary recipients' of the talk (Heritage and Greatbatch, 1991; Clayman and Heritage, 2003). Thus, rather than viewing context as 'encompassing' social interaction, CA focuses on those aspects of context that can be shown to be relevant to the participants themselves as their interactions unfold.

CA and the Analysis of Talk and Organizations

As noted above, CA has been increasingly used to analyse interactions in which participants undertake organizational task or role-based activities. Thus, for example, CA studies have focused on interactions in medical consultations, broadcast interviews, emergency call centres, business meetings, classroom lessons, divorce mediation sessions, small claims courts and psychiatric intake interviews (see, for example, Atkinson and Heritage, 1984; Button and Lee, 1987; Boden and Zimmerman, 1991; Drew and Heritage, 1992; Boden 1994; Heritage and Maynard, 2006; Heritage and Clayman, 2010; Llewellyn and Hindmarsh, 2010a). These studies examine how participants orient to social institutions and their associated identities within their talk, and how this constitutes both a constraint on and a resource for the accomplishment of the activities in which they are engaged. It is the development of CA studies of organizational talk that has led a number of scholars to advocate bringing CA into management research.

One limitation of CA in the context of management research is that it does not encompass management activities that are not primarily accomplished through talk-in-interaction. However, in recent years a range of video-based studies of naturally occurring work and interaction has emerged, which, while drawing on CA, adopt a broader focus by also analysing how various artefacts (tools, texts and technologies) feature in the accomplishment and coordination of organizational activities. These studies have been undertaken in a variety of workplace settings, including offices (Suchman, 1987; 1992), airport operation rooms (Goodwin and Goodwin, 1996), urban transport control rooms (Heath and Luff, 2000), City trading rooms (Heath et al., 1994–95) and emergency dispatch centres (Whalen, 1995). In contrast to mainstream CA research, these often rely on information gathered through non-participant observation and qualitative interviews. This has proved necessary because the patterns of interaction, and the organization of activities, in complex organizational settings often cannot be discerned or understood solely from the analysis of video recordings. The use of such 'ethnographic' information remains highly contentious because it may be used to warrant claims which are not grounded in the understandings and orientations that interactants display to each other in situ (Hopper, 1991; Clayman and Maynard, 1995). Nonetheless, this body of research has demonstrated that, although the approach of CA cannot be simply 'applied' to activities in such settings, since those activities are rarely accomplished wholly through talk, it nonetheless provides the foundation for the explication of the social interactional organization of work, interaction and technology (Luff et al., 1994; Heath and Luff, 2000).

Using the CA Approach

We illustrate the CA approach by reference to our study of how management ideas are disseminated and received in real-time speaker/audience interaction on the international management lecture circuit. In so doing, we draw on and adapt previously published material to show how CA can lead to distinctive and important insights into issues that are studied by management researchers. Specifically, we focus on the use of humour, an issue that has attracted a considerable amount of attention in organization and management studies (Collinson, 1988; Linstead, 1985; Rodrigues and Collinson, 1995; Collinson, 2002; Greatbatch and Clark, 2003; 2005; Sturdy et al., 2007; 2009).

Our study focused on the public performances of so-called management gurus. Management gurus are purveyors of influential management ideas such as excellence, culture change, learning organization and business process re-engineering. In addition to writing best-selling management books they disseminate their ideas in live presentations on the international management lecture circuit (Huczynski, 1993; Jackson, 2001). As perhaps the highest profile group of management speakers in the world, they use their lectures to build their personal reputations with audiences of managers. Many gain reputations as powerful orators and subsequently market recordings of their talks as parts of management training packages.

The data for our original study comprised video recordings of the gurus' public lectures, which were drawn from commercially produced the training packages. The videos analysed in the study featured Tom Peters, Rosabeth Moss Kanter, Gary Hamel and Peter Senge. Those involving Peters and Moss Kanter combined footage of the two gurus lecturing with case studies and interviews concerning organizations that are mentioned in the gurus' lectures. The videos involving Senge and Hamel included complete performances.

The 20 hours of video material contain approximately 15 hours of the gurus lecturing to audiences of managers.

Previous research on humour and laughter

Empirical studies of humour in organizational and workplace contexts indicate that it serves five primary functions: (1) to create and maintain social cohesion and group solidarity (e.g. Bradney, 1957; Roy, 1958; Coser, 1959; 1960; Sykes, 1966; LaFave and Mennell, 1976; Fine, 1979; Boland and Hoffman, 1986; Fine, 1987; Dwyer, 1991; Fine, 1996; Meyer, 1997; 2000); (2) to attack others in socially acceptable ways and/or to enhance self-esteem at the expense of others (e.g. Collinson, 1988; Perry, 1992; Rodrigues and Collinson, 1995); (3) to gain the approval of others (Fine, 1996; Meyer, 1997; 2000); (4) to manage embarrassment, fear or stress in threatening situations (e.g. Coser, 1960; Fine, 1977; Linstead, 1985; Dandridge, 1986; Ott, 1989; Vinton, 1989); and (5) to express opposition, resistance and dissent (e.g. Collinson, 1988; Mulkay, 1988; Rodrigues and Collinson, 1995; Collinson, 2002). As Giles et al. (1976) emphasize, people may use humour to achieve any combination of these objectives in any given situation.

Humour researchers have also sought to account for the fact that humour is situationally dependent and subjective (Winick, 1976; Raskin, 1985; Carrell, 1992). People's ability to perceive humour in a given message has been shown to be dependent on their familiarity with social scripts and patterns of communication, which enable them to recognize humorous deviations from expected patterns of behaviour. The success of humour has also been shown to depend on the willingness of specific audiences to appreciate humour and not to regard it as irrelevant, unacceptable or inane (Raskin, 1985). Thus, as Meyer (2000: 316) observes, 'attempts at humour that meet with success depend directly on the specific audience and the situation in question'.

These studies powerfully demonstrate that people will use humour to accomplish important objectives. However, although they will adopt a variety of theoretical and methodological perspectives and have been conducted by researchers based within a range of disciplines, including management, they all neglect one crucial aspect of humour and laughter; they do not attend to the practices through which humour-related actions such as jokes, quips, laughter, smiles and grins are produced, interpreted and coordinated in naturally occurring encounters (Norrick, 1993). The significance of this is underlined by CA findings of jocular talk and laughter. These studies, which are based on detailed analysis of audio and video recordings of naturally occurring interactions, reveal that people rely upon a range of tacit, seen-but-unnoticed practices and procedures in order to produce, recognize and manage humour-related actions. Thus, for example, although laughter is often depicted as a spontaneous response to 'humorous' talk, in practice it is routinely invited by prior speakers through the use of a range of techniques, which enable them to indicate that, and when, it is appropriate for others to laugh. Moreover, respondents have at their disposal an array of practices through which they can produce, or decline to produce, laughter and other humour-related responses (e.g. Jefferson, 1979; Jefferson et al., 1987; Glenn, 1989; 1991/1992; Gavioli, 1995; Rutter, 1997).

It is perhaps not surprising that CA studies have had little, if any, impact on humour research. With notable exceptions (Glenn, 1989; Rutter, 1997), CA researchers have not drawn attention to the relevance of their findings for theories and issues in the field of humour research and more generally.

The interactional organization of humour and laughter during management guru lectures

While the management guru lectures do not contain any disaffiliative responses such as booing and heckling, the audience members do regularly produce displays of affiliation with the gurus by, inter alia, clapping, laughing supportively, nodding their heads and smiling. In some cases, these affiliative responses are produced by one or two individuals. In others, however, they involve numerous audience members acting in concert with each other. When audience members collectively display their affiliation with the gurus, they do so predominantly by laughing in response to purportedly humorous messages.

Having observed this we decided to focus our attention on the 88 cases of collective audience laughter, with a view to understanding how collective audience laughter is evoked and coordinated and how it features in the communication of the gurus' management ideas. We began by transcribing all the instances of collective audience laughter, using transcription symbols drawn from the CA transcription notation developed by Gail Jefferson and additional symbols devised by Max Atkinson in his CA studies of political oratory (see the Appendix to this chapter, and for details on this notation see Atkinson and Heritage, 1984). These symbols enabled us to capture fine-grained details of the delivery of the segments of the lectures that give rise to laughter, the positioning of audience laughter in relation to these messages and the timing and delivery of the gurus' subsequent talk. We also described aspects of the gurus visual conduct in italics, using left hand brackets to indicate where this is positioned in relation to the gurus' speech and/or audience laughter [e.g. see Extract 1 on p. 489, Lines 5, 7, 10].

By repeatedly viewing and analysing the 88 episodes of collective audience laughter and refining the transcripts as we did so, we identified three important (and interrelated) patterns of conduct. The first concerns the timing and coordination of episodes of audience laughter. As Clayman (1992; 1993) observed, collective audience responses during speeches and presentations (including laughter and applause) may be facilitated by two methods: independent decision-making (which involves audience members independently recognizing that and when some form of response is relevant); and mutual monitoring (which involves audience members reacting to the aural and visual actions of a few of their counterparts). Responses that are mainly facilitated by independent decision-making begin with a 'burst' and quickly grow in intensity as numerous audience members respond in concert. The ability of individual audience members to respond in concert at or near to message completion points depends upon speakers supplying their messages with emphasis and clearly projectable completion points around which audience members can coordinate their actions. Responses that are primarily organized by mutual monitoring are characterized by 'staggered' onsets as the reactions of a handful of audience members prompts others to respond. In the case of the gurus' lectures, independent decision-making plays a predominant role in the genesis of audience laughter: most episodes of audience laughter will begin with a burst, either just before or immediately after message completion.

Second, most cases of audience laughter are not simply spontaneous reactions to messages whose content is self-evidently humorous. Usually audience laughter is 'invited' by the gurus through the use of a range of verbal and non-verbal practices. Thus the gurus 'highlight' their messages in relation to the surrounding speech through volume, pitch or stress variation; marked speeding up or other rhythmic shifts; and/or facial, hand and/or body gestures. They also supply the messages with clearly projectable completion points, around which audience members can coordinate their responses. And, rather than relying on audience members to recognize their humorous intent from the content of their messages alone, they establish the relevance of audience laughter by, for example: (1) announcing that they are about to say something humorous, (2) smiling or laughing, and/or (3) using 'comedic' facial expressions, gestures and prosody – including, for example, displays of emotions such as disgust, disbelief, anger, horror and amazement by themselves or others to the actions, practices or issues that are being discussed. This is not to say that these non-verbal actions are inherently 'comedic'. Their possible status as such derives from their use with particular verbal messages and devices, whose 'comedic' status in turn derives in part from their use with such non-verbal actions. In other words, the speakers' verbal and non-verbal actions are reflexively related – the comedic status of each resting in part on their use in conjunction with the other.

Third, messages that precipitate laughter are constructed in ways which mean that subsequent audience laughter is not open to interpretation as an unequivocal and unvarnished expression of support for the management gurus' core ideas. This is because the gurus invest their messages with multiple sources of humour and/or invite displays of affiliation with values that do not derive directly from their core management ideas and visions. This enables the gurus to elicit collective displays of affiliation, regardless of whether or not audience members agree with their core ideas and visions.

Extract 1

1	TP:	My favourite <u>Perroism</u> of all was his description, <u>right</u> before
2		leaving GM, of what he sa:w as the difference between
3		Electronic Data Systems and GM. (0.6) He said,
4		['At <u>EDS</u> (.) WHEN YOU SEE A SNAKE (.) YOU <u>KILL</u> IT'.
5		[*Leans forward, glares, uses angry tone of voice*
6	Audience:-->	[LLLLLLLLLL LLLLLLLLLL LLLLLL-L-L[-L
7		[*Turns and walks* [
8	Peters:	[He said, 'At GM when
9		you see a snake, [you search the world for the <u>top</u>
10		[*Leans forward/smile face*
11		consultant on snakes'.
12	Audience:-->	LLLLLLLLLL LLLLLLLLLL
13	Peters:	Then you appoint a committee on snakes and you <u>study</u>
14		snakes for the next two years. (1.0) <<u>Flat</u> (.) <u>fluid</u> (.) and get on with it
15		(.) that':s the creature

Extract 1 above from a lecture by Tom Peters, which is drawn from Greatbatch and Clark (2003; 2005), illustrates these three phenomena and the level of detail involved in CA research. In this extract Peters supports his argument that organizations should adopt 'flat and fluid' structures by quoting Ross Perot. The quotation praises one company, Electronic Data Systems (EDS), for purportedly adopting a 'flat and fluid' structure, and disparages another company, General Motors (GM), for purportedly retaining a cumbersome bureaucratic structure. Both the commendation of EDS and the criticism of GM are followed by audience laughter.

First, Peters provides the messages that evoke laughter with both emphasis and clearly projectable completion points by, inter alia, using a puzzle-solution format (Atkinson, 1984a; 1984b; Heritage and Greatbatch, 1986). Thus he begins by establishing a puzzle in the minds of the audience members (lines 1–3): what did Ross Perot see as the difference between EDS and GM? He then offers a two-part solution, which is formed as a contrast (Lines 3–4 and 8–9 and 11). In this way, he highlights the contents of the messages against a background of surrounding speech materials. He also provides the audience members with resources to anticipate the completion of the two messages, for they can match each part of the emerging solution to the puzzle in order to infer what it will take for it to be complete. In the case of the second part of the solution/contrast, they can also match it against the first part. In both instances, Peters confirms the relevance of laughter by ceding the floor until the audiences' laughter ends (lines 6 and 12) and then, when he resumes speaking, neither asserting nor otherwise indicating that the audience's laughter was inappropriate or unexpected (lines 13–15).

Second, Peters does not rely solely on the 'humorous' content of his remarks to establish the relevance of audience laughter; he also 'invites' audience laughter through the use of a range of non-verbal techniques. In the first case of laughter (line 6), which follows Peters' depiction of Perot's commendation of EDS, Peters uses comedic gestures, facial expressions and prosody. As he quotes Perot on EDS, he suddenly leans forward, glares at a section of the audience and speaks louder as he adopts a 'mock angry' tone (lines 4–5). Then, as he completes the quotation ('you kill it'), he bares his teeth as he 'spits' out the words. Together with Perot's incongruous metaphorical imagery – seeing and killing snakes in a corporate context – Peters' non-verbal actions establish the possible relevance of audience laughter. In the second case of audience laughter (line 12), which follows Peters' depiction of Perot's disparagement of GM (Lines 8–9 and 11), Peters, reverting to a 'low key' form of speech delivery, establishes the possible relevance of laughter by leaning forward and smiling at the audience as he completes the quotation (line 10). Thus Peters does not solely rely on the content of his message to indicate to the audience members that his message is humorous and that laughter is an appropriate response.

Third, Peters evokes laughter in response to his (and Perot's) praise of the supposedly rapid reaction of one organization and criticism of the purportedly slow reactions of another. However, there are several other potential sources of humour in addition to the critique of big 'bureaucratic' organizations per se. These include Perot's metaphorical imagery and style of speaking, and Peters' mimicry of these. Consequently, individual audience members may be displaying their appreciation of the humour in these features, as opposed to (or in addition to) Perot's evaluation of the corporations' actions and, by extension, Peters' core ideas on management practice. This means that while audience members' engage in collective displays of affiliation with Peters, their laughter does not represent *unvarnished* expressions of support for the position he is using the Perot quotation to substantiate. Thus, by offering multiple sources of humour Peters is able to invest their remarks with considerable affiliative potential by permitting participants to hold multiple understandings of the situation but display these as a unified response.

The analysis above illustrates a range of features of CA, including: CA's concern with the sequential organization of social actions accomplished in and through naturally occurring social interaction; CA's treatment of *all* linguistic, paralinguistic and visual actions as potentially relevant to the analysis of the accomplishment and coordination of social actions; and CA's insistence on grounding social scientific analysis in the understandings that participants negotiate and display to each other during their interactions. In the next section we briefly illustrate how CA research considers wider social and organizational contexts, in this case genres of public speaking.

Wider social contexts

Management gurus' lectures are akin to various other forms of public speaking, including business presentations, training seminars and university lectures, in which applause rarely occurs *either* on its own *or* in conjunction with laughter (other than at the beginning and end). The gurus' lectures therefore stand in contrast to genres of public speaking in which audiences use applause either as a standalone response to affiliate with speakers' messages (e.g. during political speeches) or, more commonly, in conjunction with laughter in order to register their appreciation of speakers' wit or originality and/or to display agreement with the underlying messages that speakers are using humour to convey (e.g. after-dinner speeches, stand-up comedy routines, as well as political speeches).

From a CA perspective, these regularities do not arise because genres of public speaking, once established, constitute 'external' contexts or 'frames' (Goffman, 1983) that encompass and determine participants' conduct; rather the participants themselves orient to and make relevant specific genres of public speaking within their interactions on a moment-by-moment basis. This means that participants may shift, if only momentarily, from one genre to another as a lecture or speech unfolds.

In the case of the management guru lectures this becomes especially apparent when one examines deviant cases in which audience members clap. Consider the following example from a Tom Peters' lecture in which a handful of people start to clap following the onset of collective audience laughter.

Extract 2 – 'Paperless toilet' [TOC1: 35.20]

1	TP:	Two weeks later I got back to the United States, reading the Wall Street
2		Journal there's an article, (.) 'Japanese takes to hi-tech <u>bathrooms</u>' is the title.
3		(0.4) <u>Ten</u> percent of American- of the market place in Japan is this kind of
4		toilet and it's a growing activity. (0.2) He says- I'll read you a sentence (0.2)
5		'A paperless toilet that sprays <u>warm water</u> like a <u>b</u>idet except it comes from
6		several directions. (0.6) Blows warm air to dry and even sprays scent.
7	AUD:	lll[lllll llll [lllll llllllllll l-l-[l-l-l-l-l-l-l-l-l-l=
8	TP:	[*TP smiles* [[And that's not all.
9	AUD	[x-x-x-x-x
10	AUD:	=l-[l-l
11	TP:	[Machine keeps the [seat warm in the Winter.
12		[*TP smiles*
13	AUD:	llllllllll lllllllllll [lllllllll
14	AUD:	[x-x-x-x
15	TP:	But that's the world. (0.3) That's the world in which people with
16		exotic degrees and no degrees have gotta find employment. (0.4)
17		That's the world in which companies have got (.) to compete

In this case, audience laughter (lines 7 and 13) in response to Peters' descriptions of a paperless toilet twice prompts a small number of audience members to clap (lines 9 and 14). This raises two interrelated questions. Why do some audience members (but not others) start to clap? And why doesn't their conduct prompt a larger number of audience members to applaud? With regard to the first question, it is noticeable that by engaging in humour concerning bodily functions as he describes the hi-tech toilet, Peters' conduct is perhaps more akin to an observational comedy routine (in which it is appropriate to use applause in conjunction with laughter in order to register appreciation of a speaker's wit) than educational management lecturing (in which it is not). This may be what prompts some audience members to clap, amid the widespread laughter. As to why others do not clap – although many, if not all, of them do laugh – by refraining from applauding they continue to treat laughter-without-applause as the appropriate response. In this example, then, individual audience members display competing understandings of whether or not applause is relevant. By clapping some propose that Peters has, if only momentarily, adopted a stance associated with genres of public speaking in which the co-occurrence of laughter and applause is appropriate; whereas the conduct of the other audience members is consistent with the conventions associated with guru lectures.

Theoretical implications

The CA study discussed here offers a distinctive perspective on two interrelated issues that have attracted widespread attention in management research, namely humour and group cohesiveness. Previous research into the functions of humour suggests that it can promote the emergence and maintenance of group cohesiveness by, inter alia, clarifying and reinforcing shared values and social norms; disciplining those who violate the rules of a social group and unifying other group members against them; and dividing group members from other groups (those who would be expected to adopt a different perspective, e.g. see Meyer, 2000). It is unclear whether the gurus and their audiences can be classified as members of distinctive social groups. Indeed, part of the management gurus' mission is to recruit managers to such groups, whose boundaries are defined by reference to their members' affiliation with the gurus' theories. Nonetheless, by evoking and producing laughter, the gurus and their audience members engage in public displays of consensus and 'like-mindedness' (Glenn, 1989) and thereby *constitute* themselves as 'in-groups' that share a common perspective in relation to the circumstances and events that the gurus describe. When gurus attack/disparage others (e.g. Peters' attack on GM in the example above), the gurus and those audience members who laugh also publicly differentiate themselves from individuals or groups who purportedly do not share the values or perspectives they are expressing. In these cases, then, humour and laughter serves to delineate group boundaries by acting as both a unifier and divider (Meyer, 2000). Whether these publicly displayed group affiliations actually reflect audience members' commitment to the gurus' views and thus may extend beyond the lifetime of the gurus' lectures is, of course, open to question. Nonetheless, even those cases of laughter that are not open to interpretation as unvarnished expressions of support for the gurus' core ideas indicate a shared perspective and – like affiliative interactional practices in general (Goffman, 1983; Heritage, 1984) – contribute to a sense of cohesion and intimacy, which might make audiences more receptive to the gurus' recommendations.

The processes involved here have been largely overlooked in previous research due to the lack of systematic studies of the verbal and non-verbal practices that inform both the production and recognition of jocular talk and the coordination and interpretation of responses by hearers. Our CA study of management guru oratory shows that analysis of these practices provides insights into both the situational dependency and the functions of humour in management and other settings. This is not to deny the importance of other contextual factors such as people's emotional states, and their familiarity or unfamiliarity with social scripts, cultural norms or institutional conventions. Nevertheless, detailed scrutiny of the verbal and non-verbal practices through which humorous talk and responses are organized provides unique insights into why people laugh, when they do so, and what social functions their laughter performs.

Conclusion

CA researchers use inductive search procedures in order to locate recurring patterns of social action and interaction in everyday contexts. In so doing, they focus on aspects of human conduct that can only be systematically examined through repeated scrutiny of audio and/or video recordings of naturally occurring encounters. They also ground analytic and theoretical claims in the moment-to-moment understandings of their circumstances that participants unavoidably display to one another as their interactions emerge in real time.

Some CA researchers have brought this approach into management research and are already generating distinctive and important insights into the real-time accomplishment of organizational tasks and activities. Their work clearly demonstrates that CA offers a unique approach to the analysis of organizational conduct, which can lead to the respecification of core concepts in management research literatures. Now that this foundation has been laid, CA has the potential to enrich and make significant theoretical contributions to a range of debates and literatures within management research.

Further Reading

Woofit (2005) in his *Conversation Analysis and Discourse Analysis* provides a very useful introduction to CA, which highlights the similarities and differences between conversation analysis and discourse analysis, critical discourse analysis and discursive psychology. Heritage and Clayman's (2010) book *Talk in Action: Interactions, Identities and Institutions* is a comprehensive introduction to the conversation analytic approach to institutional talk. Llewellyn and Hindmarsh's (2010a) edited book *Organisation, Interaction and Practice* includes both theoretical and empirical chapters, which discuss and exemplify how conversation analysis and ethnomethodology can be used to study organizations.

References

Atkinson, J.M. (1984a) *Our Masters' Voices: The Language and Body Language of Politics*. London: Routledge.

Atkinson, J.M. (1984b) 'Public speaking and audience response: some techniques for inviting applause', in J.M. Atkinson and J. Heritage (eds), *Structures of Social Action: Studies in Conversation Analysis*. Cambridge: Cambridge University Press, pp. 370–409.

Atkinson, J.M. and Heritage, J. (1984) *Structures of Social Action: Studies in Conversation Analysis*. Cambridge: Cambridge University Press.

Austin, J.L. (1962) *How to Do Things with Words*. Oxford: Oxford University Press.

Barley, S. and Kunda, G. (2001) 'Bringing the work back in', *Organization Science*, 12 (1): 76–95.

Boden, D. (1994) *The Business of Talk: Organizations in Action*. Cambridge: Cambridge University Press.

Boden, D. and Zimmerman, D.H. (1991) *Talk and Social Structure: Studies in Ethnomethodology and Conversation Analysis*. Cambridge: Polity Press.

Boland, R.J. and Hoffman, R. (1986) 'Humor in a machine shop: an interpretation of symbolic action', in P. Frost, V. Mitchell and W. Nord (eds), *Organizational Reality: Reports from the Firing Line*. Glenview, IL: Scott Foresman, pp. 371–376.

Bradney, P. (1957) 'The joking relationship in industry', *Human Relations*, 10: 179–187.

Button, G. and Lee, J.R.E (eds) (1987) *Talk and Social Organisation*. Clevedon and Philadelphia: Multilingual Matters.

Carrell, A. (1992) 'The need to incorporate audience and situation into a theory of humor', paper presented at the Speech Communication Association annual convention, Chicago, IL.

Clayman, S.E. (1992) 'Caveat orator: audience disaffiliation in the 1988 presidential debates', *Quarterly Journal of Speech*, 78: 33–60.

Clayman, S.E. (1993) 'Booing: the anatomy of a disaffiliative response', *American Sociological Review*, 58: 110–30.

Clayman, S. and Heritage, J. (2003) *The News Interview: Journalists and Public Figures on the Air*. Cambridge: Cambridge University Press.

Clayman, S. and Maynard, D. (1995) 'Ethnomethodology and conversation analysis', n P. ten Have and G. Psathas (eds), *Situated Order: Studies in the Social Organization of Talk and Embodied Activities*. Washington: University Press America, pp. 1–30.

Clifton, J. (2006) 'A conversation analytical approach to business communication', *Journal of Business Communication*, 43 (3): 202–219.

Collinson, D.L. (1988) 'Engineering humour: masculinity, joking and conflict in shop-floor relations', *Organisation Studies*, 9 (2): 181–199.

Collinson, D.L. (2002) 'Managing humour', *Journal of Management Studies*, 39 (3): 269–288.

Cooren, F. and Fairhurst, G.T. (2004) 'Speech timing and spacing: the phenomenon of organizational closure', *Organization*, 11 (6): 793–824.

Coser, R.L. (1951) 'Some social functions of laughter', *Human Relations*, 12: 171–181.

Coser, R.L. (1960) 'Laughter among colleagues: a study of the social functions of humour among the staff of a mental hospital', *Psychiatry*, 23: 81–95.

Dandridge, T.C. (1986) 'Ceremony as an integration of work and play', *Organizational Studies*, 7 (2): 159–170.

Drew, P. and Heritage, J. (1992) *Talk at Work: Interaction in Institutional Settings*. Cambridge: Cambridge University Press.

Dwyer, T. (1991) 'Humour, power and change in organisations', *Human Relations*, 44 (1): 1–19.

Fairhurst, G.T. (2004) 'Textuality and agency in interaction analysis', *Organization*, 11 (3): 335–353.

Fine, G.A. (1977) 'Humour in situ: the role of humour in small group culture', in A.J. Chapman and H.C. Foot (eds), *It's a Funny Thing, Humour*. New York: Pergamon.

Fine, G.A. (1979) 'Small groups and culture creation: the idioculture of little league baseball culture', *American Journal of Sociology*, 44: 733–745.

Fine, G.A. (1987) *With the Boys: Little League Baseball and Preadolescent Culture*. Chicago: University of Chicago Press.

Fine, G.A. (1996) *Kitchens: The Culture of Restaurant Work*. Berkeley: University of California Press.

Forray, J.M. and Woodilla, J. (2002) 'Temporal spans in talk: doing consistency to construct fair organization', *Organization Studies*, 22 (6): 899–917.

Garfinkel, E. (1967) *Studies in Ethnomethodology*. Cambridge: Polity Press.

Gavioli, L. (1995) 'Turn-initial versus turn-final laughter: two techniques for initiating remedy in English/Italian bookshop service encounters', *Discourse Processes*, 19: 369–384.

Giles, H., Bourhis, R., Gadfield, N.J., Davies, G.J. and Davies, A.P. (1976) 'Cognitive aspects of humour in social interaction', in T. Chapman and H. Foot (eds), *Humour and Laughter: Theory, Research and Applications*. London: Wiley.

Glenn, P.J. (1989) 'Initiating shared laughter in multi-party conversations', *Western Journal of Speech Communication*, 53: 127–149.

Glenn, P.J. (1991/1992) 'Current speaker initiation of two-party shared laughter', *Research on Language and Social Interaction*, 25: 139–162.

Goffman, E. (1983) 'The interaction order', *American Sociological Review*, 48 (1): 1–17.

Goodwin, C. (1987) 'Forgetfulness as an interactive resource', *Social Psychology Quarterly*, 50 (2): 115–130.

Goodwin, C. and Goodwin, M. (1996) 'Seeing as a situated activity: formulating planes', in Y. Engestrom and D. Middleton (eds), *Cognition and Communication at Work*. Cambridge: Cambridge University press, pp. 61–95.

Greatbatch, D. and Clark, T. (2003) 'Displaying group cohesiveness: humour and laughter in the public lectures of management gurus', *Human Relations*, 56 (12): 1515–1544.

Greatbatch, D. and Clark, T. (2005) *Management Speak: Why We Listen to What Management Gurus Tell Us*. London: Routledge.

Greatbatch, D. and Clark, T. (2010) 'The situated production of stories', in N. Llewllyn and J. Hindmarsh (eds), *Organisations, Interaction and Practice: Studies in Real Time Work and Organising*. Cambridge: Cambridge University Press, pp. 96–118.

Heath, C., Jirotka, M., Luff, P. and Hindmarsh, J. (1994–95) 'Unpacking collaboration: the interactional organisation of trading in a City dealing room', *Computer Supported Coorperative Work: Journal of Collaborative Computing*, 3 (2): 147–165.

Heath, C. and Luff, P. (2000) *Technology in Action*. Cambridge: Cambridge University Press.

Heritage, J. (1984) *Garfinkel and Ethnomethodology*. Cambridge: Polity Press.

Heritage, J. (1995) 'Conversation analysis: methodological aspects', in U.M. Quasthoff (ed.), *Aspects of Oral Communication*. Berlin: De Gruyter, pp. 391–418.

Heritage, J. and Clayman, S. (2010) *Talk in Action: Interactions, Identities and Institutions*. Oxford: Wiley-Blackwell.

Heritage, J. and Greatbatch, D. (1986) 'Generating applause: a study of rhetoric and response at party political conferences', *American Journal of Sociology*, 92: 110–57.

Heritage, J. and Greatbatch, D. (1991) 'On the institutional character of institutional talk: the case of news interviews', in D. Boden and D.H. Zimmerman (eds), *Talk and*

Social Structure: Studies in Ethnomethodology and Conversation Analysis. Cambridge: Polity Press, pp. 93–137.

Heritage, J. and Maynard, D. (eds) (2006) *Practicing Medicine: Structure and Process in Primary Care Encounters*. Cambridge: Cambridge University Press, pp. 313–339.

Hindmarsh, J. and Pilnick, A. (2007) 'Knowing bodies at work: embodiment and ephemeral teamwork in anaesthesia', *Organizational Studies*, 28 (9): 1395–1416.

Hopper, R. (ed.) (1991) *Conversation Analysis and Ethnography*. Special Issue of *Research on Language and Social Interaction*.

Huczynski, A. (1993) *Management Gurus: What Makes Them and How to Become One*. London: Routledge.

Jackson, B.G. (2001) 'Re-engineering the sense of self: the manager and the management guru', *Journal of Management Studies*, 33 (5): 571–590.

Jefferson, G. (1979) 'A technique for inviting laughter and its subsequent acceptance declination', in G. Psathas (ed.), *Everyday Language: Studies in Ethnomethodology*. New York: Irvington.

Jefferson, G., Sacks, H. and Schegloff, E.A. (1987) 'Notes on laughter in the pursuit of intimacy', in G. Button and J.R.E. Lee (eds), *Talk and Social Organisation*. Clevedon, UK: Multilingual Matters.

LaFave, L. and Mennell, R. (1976) 'Does ethnic humour serve prejudice?' *Journal of Communication*, 26: 116–123.

Linstead, S. (1985) 'Jokers wild: the importance of humour in the maintenance of organizational culture', *The Sociological Review*, 33 (4): 741–767.

Llewellyn, N. (2004) 'In search of modernisation: the negotiation of social identity in organisational reform', *Organization Studies*, 25: 947–968.

Llewellyn, N. (2008) 'Identifying with the audience: a study of community police work', *International Journal of Public Administration*, 31: 971–987.

Llewellyn, N. and Hindmarsh, J. (eds) (2010a) *Organisations, Interaction and Practice: Studies in Real Time Work and Organising*. Cambridge: Cambridge University Press.

Llewellyn, N. and Hindmarsh, J. (eds) (2010b) 'Work and organisation in real time: an introduction', in N. Llewellyn and J. Hindmarsh (eds), *Organisations, Interaction and Practice: Studies in Real Time Work and Organising*. Cambridge: Cambridge University Press.

Luff, P., Heath, C.C. and Greatbatch, D. (1994) 'Work, interaction and technology: the naturalistic analysis of human conduct and requirements analysis', in M. Jirotka and J. Goguen (eds), *Requirements Engineering: Social and Technical Issues*. London: Academic Press, pp. 259–288.

Meyer, J.C. (1997) 'Humour in members' narratives: uniting and dividing at work', *Western Journal of Communication*, 61 (2): 188–208.

Meyer, J.C. (2000) 'Humor as a double-edged sword: four functions of humor in communication', *Communication Theory*, 10 (3): 310–331.

Mulkay, M. (1988) *On Humour: Its Nature and its Place in Modern Society*. Oxford: Blackwell.

Norrick, N.R. (1993) *Conversational Joking: Humor in Everyday Talk*. Indianapolis: Indiana University Press.

Ott, J.S. (1989) *The Organizational Culture Perspective*. Chicago: Dorsey Press.

Perry, N. (1992) 'Putting theory in it's place: the social organisation of organizational theorizing', in M. Reed and M. Hughes (eds), *Rethinking Organization*. London: Sage.

Putnam, L. (2003) 'Dialectical tensions and rhetorical tropes in negotiations', *Organization Studies*, 25 (1): 35–53.

Raskin, V. (1985) *Semantic Mechanisms of Humor*. Boston, MA: Reidel.

Rodrigues, S.B. and Collinson, D.L. (1995) 'Having fun: humour as resistance in Brazil', *Organisation Studies*, 16 (5): 739–768.

Roy, D.F. (1958) 'Banana time: job satisfaction and informal interaction', *Human Organisation*, 18: 158–168.

Rutter, J. (1997) 'Stand-up as interaction: performance and audience in comedy venues'. Unpublished PhD thesis, University of Salford.

Sacks, H. (1995) *Lectures on Conversation*. Oxford: Blackwell.

Samra-Fredericks, D. (2003) 'Strategizing as lived experience and strategists' everyday efforts to shape strategic decisions', *Journal of Management Studies*, 40 (1): 141–174.

Samra-Fredericks, D. (2004) 'Managerial elites making rhetorical and linguistic "moves" for a moving (emotional) display', *Human Relations*, 57 (9): 1103–1143.

Samra-Fredericks, D. (2010) 'The interactional accomplishment of a strategic plan', in N. Llewellyn and J. Hindmarsh (eds), *Organisation, Interaction and Practice*. Cambridge: Cambridge University Press, pp. 198–217.

Schegloff, E.A. (1992) 'On talk and its institutional occasions', in P. Drew and J. Heritage (eds), *Talk at Work: Interaction in Institutional Settings*. Cambridge: Cambridge University Press, pp. 101–134.

Schegloff, E.A. (1997) 'Whose text? Whose context?', *Discourse and Society*, 8: 165–187.

Schegloff, E.A. and Sacks, H. (1973) 'Opening up closings', *Semiotica*, 7: 289–327.

Searle, J.R. (1969) *Speech Acts*. Cambridge: Cambridge University Press.

Silverman, D. (1997) 'Studying organizational interaction: ethomethodology's contribution to the "new institutionalism"', *Administrative Theory & Praxis*, 19 (2): 178–195.

Sturdy, A.J., Clark, T., Fincham, R. and Handley, K. (2007) 'Management consultancy and emotion: humour in action and contexts', in S. Fineman (ed.), *The Emotional Organization*. Oxford: Blackwell, pp. 134–152.

Sturdy, A.J., Clark, T., Fincham, R. and Handley, K. (2009) *Management Consultancy: Boundaries and Knowledge in Action*. Oxford: Oxford University Press.

Suchman, L. (1987) *Plans and Situated Actions*. Cambridge: Cambridge University Press

Suchman, L. (1992) 'Technologies of accountability: on lizards and aeroplanes', in G. Button (ed.), *Technology in Working Order*. London: Routledge, pp. 113–126.

Sykes, A.J.M. (1966) 'Joking relationships in an industrial setting', *American Anthropologist*, 68 (1): 189–193.

Vinton, K.E. (1989) 'Humor in the workplace: it's more than telling jokes', *Small Group Behaviour*, 20 (2): 151–166.

Whalen, J. (1995) 'A technology of order production: computer aided dispatch in public safety communications', in P. ten Have and G. Psathas (eds), *Situated Order: Studies in the Social Organization of Talk and Embodied Activities*. Washington: University Press America, pp. 187–230.

Winick, C. (1976) 'The social context of humor', *Journal of Communication*, 26 (3): 124–228.

Wittgenstein, L. (1953) *Philosophical Investigations*. Oxford: Blackwell.

Woodilla, J. (1999) 'Workplace conversations: the text of organising', in D. Grant, T. Keenoy and C. Oswick (eds), *Discourse and Organisation*. London: Sage, pp. 31–50.

Woofitt, R. (2005) *Conversation Analysis and Discourse Analysis: A Comparative and Critical Introduction*. London: Sage.

Appendix

Conversation analysis transcription notation

- The points at which overlaps between the gurus speech and audience laughter begin (a left hand bracket, [ ) and end (a right hand bracket,]), e.g. see Extract 1, Lines 6 and 8.

- Where there is no interval between adjacent actions (equals sign =).[1]

- The lengths of silences within and between the gurus' speech and the audience responses in tenths of a second (numbers in parentheses, e.g. (0.5)), e.g. see Extract 1, Lines 3 and 14.

- Gaps of less than two-tenths of a second (a dot in parenthesis (.)), e.g. see Extract 1, Line 14.

- Cut of sounds like a guttural stop (a dash –).

- Some form of stress via pitch and/or amplitude (underlining, Word), e.g. see Extract 1, Lines 1, 4, 13, 15.

- Talk that is spoken louder than surrounding talk (capital letters, WORD), e.g. see Extract 1, Line 4.

- Prolongation of the immediately preceding sound (colons, Wo::rd), e.g. see Extract 1, Line 15.

- Falling, non-terminal and rising intonation (periods, commas and question marks respectively), e.g. see Extract 1, Line 11.

- Discernible inhalations (h's preceded by a period, .hhh).

- Discernible aspirations (h's without a preceding period, hhh).

- Laughter (a string of L's, LLLL), e.g. see Extract 1, Lines 6, 12.

- Spasmodic laughter (a chain of L's punctuated by dashes, L-L-L-L), e.g. see Extract 1, end of Line 6.

---

[1]The equal signs are also used to link different parts of a single action/utterance when those parts are carried over to another line, by transcript design, to accommodate an overlapping action/utterance.

- Actions that are being discussed in the commentary (-->), e.g. see Extract 1, Line 12.

- Speeding up of talk (<), e.g. see Extract 1, Line 14.

- Isolated clapping ([x-x-x-x-x), e.g. see Extract 3, Line 10.

Discourse Analysis and Discursive Research

Cliff Oswick

Introduction

It has been suggested that 'discourse is a process of meaning-making through talk and text' (Oswick, forthcoming) and that discourse analysis is 'the study of how meanings are produced, and of which meanings prevail in society' (Iedema, 2008: 389). Cunliffe (2008: 81) goes further and suggests that: 'Discourse analysts study the structures of meaning, expressions, themes, routine ways of talking, and rhetorical devices used in constructing reality'. The overarching inference that can be derived from these assertions is that discourse analysis is concerned with processes of social construction (i.e. meaning-making) through the study of language and language-use.

Discourse analysis cannot easily be reduced down to a single technique. Instead, it should be regarded as constituted through a bundle of methods that can be used to analyse talk and text. On this basis, it is better to think in terms of 'discursive analyses' rather than 'discourse analysis'. Although there might be varieties of discourse analysis, there are two overriding features that distinguish it from other language-based approaches. First, with discursive research the interest in language-use extends beyond a narrow focus on the use of a specific word or words. Hence, approaches such as 'content analysis' (Neuendorf, 2002; Krippendorff, 2004) and 'corpus linguistics' (McEnery and Wilson, 1996; Biber et al., 1998), which typically focus on an aggregated analysis of word frequency, fall outside of the scope of discourse analysis. The common feature of discourse-based approaches is that they consider language at the level of a statement or series of statements rather than simply considering the pattern and prevalence of usage of an individual word (or sample of words) as the unit of analysis. Put differently, discursive approaches privilege the consideration of words in combination (i.e. as a string of words that convey meaning) as opposed to more micro-oriented language-based approaches, which consider words in isolation.

The second, and related, generic feature of discursive approaches that distinguishes them from cognate methods is that they are attuned to aspects of context when examining an extract of written text or an episode of verbal interaction (Keenoy et al., 1997). The process of contextualizing discursive events can take various guises depending on the particular form of discourse analysis undertaken. So, for example, an 'intertextual analysis' (Allen, 2000) would be likely to concentrate on the historical context within which a particular text can be located while a 'critical discourse analysis' (Fairclough, 1992; 1995) might foreground the socio-political context of a particular discursive event. Notwithstanding different points of contextual emphasis, the overarching feature of discursive approaches is that they move beyond the text (whether verbal or written) and consider aspects of the wider context. In effect, this differentiates discursive analyses from forms of 'conversation analysis' (Silverman, 1993; Psathos, 1995; and see Greatbatch and Clark, in this volume) where the focus of inquiry is more narrowly defined and attention is firmly fixed on the text itself and contextualization is often limited to a description of the immediate physical locale in which the focal episode of interaction is taking place (Oswick and Richards, 2004).

There are five main parts to the remainder of this chapter. First, some of the epistemological and ontological issues that prefigure and inform the decision to employ a discursive research design are outlined. Second, several discourse-based methods, applicable to organizational research, are explored. The third section considers some of the practical issues around choosing a sample of discursive material as a basis for analysis. Fourth, a brief example of a study is offered to provide a grounded illustration of how discursive research can be undertaken. Finally, some concluding remarks are offered and some suggested further reading is provided.

Research Design Issues

Prior to selecting a particular discursive method it is important to consider some wider aspects of research design (Boje et al., 2004). These issues include: the primary point of emphasis of the analysis (i.e. the focus of engagement); the limits of the scope of discourse analysis to be undertaken (i.e. the level of engagement); and, the epistemological commitments of the researcher (i.e. the mode of engagement). It may be helpful to consider each of these issues separately.

The focus of discursive engagement

In keeping with other research methods, discourse analysis can be regarded as a means (i.e. a vehicle) to arrive at specified research ends (i.e. a destination). However, the desired research outcomes of discourse analysis can vary. For some, discourse analysis is a means to organizational research ends, but for others it is a means to discursive research ends. Put differently, some researchers are primarily interested in understanding language-use and, as such, organizations are merely the sites at which discourse analysis takes place. By contrast, other researchers are interested in utilizing discourse analysis as a means to better understand organizational phenomena (i.e. leadership processes, organizational culture, power relationships and so on). In effect, we can think in terms of organizational scholars who do discourse and discursive scholars who do organizations.

For our purposes, the content of this chapter is primarily aimed at organizational scholars who wish to use discourse analysis as part of the repertoire of methods available to interrogate organizing processes and organizational practices. That said, discourse analysis is not amenable to studying all organizational phenomena. In particular, discourse analysis does not lend itself to the study of aspects of organizations and organizing that are not easily gathered or represented through language. Hence, discourse analysis is often not the best means for capturing attitudinal data. It is also not well equipped to address spatial and visual data that are not already pre-defined and prescribed in verbal terms. Discourse analysis is, however, suited to research situations where there is a process of social interaction or social engagement (Phillips and Hardy, 2002). In some instances this engagement manifests itself as verbal communication (e.g. conversations, briefings, interviews, meetings, presentations, announcements). In others, it occurs either in a written form *within* organizations (e.g. reports, manuals, newsletters, corporate websites, press releases, e-mail correspondence, advertisements) or in a written form *outside* of organizations (e.g. academic journals and books, media coverage, activist and protest leaflets and websites, public blogs, government-produced material and so on).

Levels of discursive engagement

We can conceive of discourse analysis as operating at different, but non-competing, levels ranging from a micro-focus on the 'fine grain' use of language (e.g. situated talk or a close reading of a single text) through to a macro-emphasis on the 'big picture' of perspectives and ideologies (i.e. grand narratives and meta-discourses such as feminism and neo-liberalism). This categorization is consistent with Potter and Wetherell's (1987) identification of four versions of discourse analysis: (1) the micro-discourse approach; (2) the meso-discourse approach; (3) the grand discourse approach; and (4) the mega-discourse approach. The notion of levels of analysis is also discernible in Alvesson and Karreman's (2000) distinction between discourse analysis with a small 'd' and discourse with a big 'D' where 'discourse' (with a lower case 'd') is characterized as being 'myopic' (i.e. a close-range interest in a local-situated context) and 'Discourse' (with a capital 'D') is described as 'grandiose' (i.e. long-range interest in a macro-systemic context). Discursive work that is more macro-oriented tends to draw upon philosophy, politics, history and social theory. By contrast, the interest in micro-oriented discourse analysis has developed out of the sociolinguistic tradition and, in particular, ethnomethodology (Garfinkel, 1967).

In addition to the extremes of micro and macro levels of discourse, there are intermediate or meso-levels of discursive inquiry. Meso-level discourse analysis falls between the fine grain and the big picture. As such, it typically involves a process of extrapolating from a cluster of situated texts or discerning patterns of emergent themes. The study of workplace stories and narratives would be an example of meso-level discursive analysis insofar as this type of approach occupies a middle position, which is somewhat removed from the immediacy of a single, focal text, yet it does not go so far as to seek to offer a more abstract and distanced macro-systemic perspective (Boje, 2001).

Having indicated that discourse analysis can occur at a number of levels, it is important to highlight that the delineation of levels is not absolute. Indeed, as will be demonstrated later, some approaches simultaneously operate at more than one level. It is also possible to combine different discursive approaches that have an emphasis on different levels in order to undertake forms of cross-level analysis.

Modes of discursive engagement

Discursive approaches can be used towards different epistemological and ontological ends (i.e. positivistic, critical and poststructuralist). When used in a positivist way, discourse analysis seeks to establish a coherent reality or an uncontested truth (i.e. a single meaning). Here discourse analysis is positioned as a means of establishing the definitive or unequivocal reading of a particular text or social situation (Keenoy et al., 1997). It is fair to say that this mode of discursive engagement is not prevalent in organizational research. This is largely because positivistically oriented scholars often find discourse analysis to be inherently ambiguous and therefore it is difficult to pin down meaning to a single account. In short, discourse analysis does not readily lend itself to positivist purposes.

Arguably, discourse analysis is far more suited to research that is critically orientated. Critical forms of discourse analysis draw attention to the contested nature of meaning and the discursive exercise of power (Grant et al., 2004b). Nested within a critical management agenda, this perspective explores the existence of a hegemonic struggle between a privileged discourse and a marginalized discourse (Mumby and Stohl, 1991). In effect, this orientation foregrounds the study of how and why certain views and accounts dominate while others are suppressed or silenced (Grant et al., 2010). As opposed to the single meaning resulting from positivist research, a critical approach to discourse analysis tends to reveal a bi-vocal contestation arising from opposing readings of a discourse or discourses (i.e. contested meanings). Within the critical community, organizational researchers have utilized discourse as a means of questioning dominant interests (e.g. to raise issues of race and gender, governance, corporate social responsibility, business ethics, and workers' rights as well as to challenge corporate capitalism).

Finally, a poststructuralist approach to discourse engages with multiple interpretations of reality and the indeterminacy of meaning. In contrast to a positivist approach, which concentrates on a unified account of a text(s), or a critical approach, which reveals competing discourses (i.e. bi-vocal opposition), a poststructural approach is far more plurivocal in orientation and it highlights multiple discourses (Boje et al., 2004). In effect, poststructuralist forms of discourse analysis are relativistic in orientation and, as such, they tend to reveal a repertoire of interpretations (i.e. multiple co-existing meanings).

Discursive Approaches

Having discussed some of the precursory aspects of discourse analysis (i.e. varying levels of discursive engagement and different epistemological orientations), we now consider the actual methods available to undertake forms of discourse analysis. There is a wide range of techniques that can be used as part of discourse-based research. However, this chapter will not offer a detailed treatment of either conversation analysis, narrative analysis or document analysis – three approaches that are closely related to discourse analysis – as these can be found in other chapters in this volume. That said, it is worth briefly mentioning that conversation analysis and detailed forms of documentary analysis can sometimes be utilized as sub-components of discursive research in instances where the analysis extends beyond an interactional episode or an individual text in order to generalize about issues of social context, processes of meaning-making and the nature of power relations. So, for example, 'critical discourse analysis' (Fairclough, 1992) – which will be discussed more fully below – typically integrates aspects of conversation analysis as part of a wider and more encompassing approach. Equally, narrative analysis (Reissman, 1993; Boje, 2001; and see Maitlis, in this volume) can cross over into the realms of discourse analysis in instances where the data used are gathered via naturally occurring talk or pre-existing written texts rather than through other mechanisms, such as interviews, observation or autoethnography.

Notwithstanding the wide variety of methods that can be captured under the umbrella of discourse analysis, we will primarily focus our attention on four approaches. Treatments of the less prominent discursive approaches, which have been excluded from this chapter (such as rhetorical analysis, dialogic analysis, tropological analysis, analysis of the coordinated management of meaning and interaction analysis), can be found in the *Sage Handbook of Organizational Discourse* (Grant et al., 2004a). The approaches to be discussed in this section can be summarized as deconstruction, Foucauldian-inspired analysis, critical discourse analysis and intertextual analysis.

Deconstruction

Deconstruction is a philosophical approach originally developed by Jacques Derrida. It can be described as micro-level discursive technique insofar as it involves a 'close reading' of a single text (Derrida, 1976; 1978). Currie (1998: 45) has observed that: 'Rather than seeking to stabilize, reduce or close down discourse, a deconstructive reading opens up complexity and uses it to problematize previous attempts at oversimplification'. In this regard, deconstruction is antithetical to positivist forms of discourse analysis and is instead predisposed to critical and/or poststructural modes of engagement.

It is difficult to be absolutely prescriptive about processes of deconstruction. As Kilduff and Keleman (2004: 261) have pointed out: 'The deconstructive process is adaptable to the exigencies of the text in question and deconstruction, therefore, cannot be boiled down to a formula or a method'. There are, however, some points of common or typical focus for the deconstructive process. These foci include: identifying binary oppositions (e.g. points of contradiction or opposition); a consideration of the examples used (e.g. in terms of partiality or representativeness); issues of absence and presence within the text (e.g. what is included and what is excluded); aspects of hierarchical ordering; and discrepancies within the text. For a comprehensive discussion of how to apply deconstruction to organizational research, readers should consult *Deconstructing Organizations* (Kilduff, 1993).

Foucauldian-inspired analysis

Michel Foucault's contribution to discourse analysis has been seen as highly influential (see, for example, Alvesson and Karreman, 2000; Fairclough, 2003; Dick, 2004; Cunliffe, 2008; Iedema, 2008). Like deconstruction, Foucauldian-inspired forms of discourse analysis have their roots in philosophy (Foucault, 1972; 1980; 1984). However, in terms of the level, this form of analysis operates at the other end of the spectrum to the close reading approach of deconstruction.

Cunliffe (2008: 81) has highlighted that Foucauldian-informed analysis explores 'how discursive practices constitute both objectivities (social institutions, knowledge) and subjectivities (identities and actions)'. Although concentrating on discursive practices, this form of engagement nevertheless remains relatively broad and abstract insofar as it is not aimed at a detailed analysis of texts. Rather, as Fairclough (2003: 123) points out: 'the concern is more a matter of discerning the rules which "govern" bodies of texts and utterances'.

In effect, Foucauldian-style discourse analysis centres on the study of 'discursive formations'. The analysis of these formations involves the identification, contemplation and articulation of the abstract semantic features of a discourse (or discourses) and/or sets of abstract linguistic themes (Iedema, 2008).

Critical discourse analysis

Critical discourse analysis (CDA) has been developed by Norman Fairclough (see Fairclough, 1992; 1995; 2003). It explicitly embraces a 'critical' epistemology and it challenges the delineation of macro-, meso- and micro-levels of discursive engagement. As Fairclough (1995: 97) explains:

> It [CDA] facilitates the integration of 'micro' analysis and 'macro' analysis. It is moreover a critical approach to discourse analysis in the sense that it sets out to make visible through analysis, and to criticise, connections between properties of texts and social processes and relations (ideologies, power relations) which are generally not obvious to people who produce and interpret those texts.

CDA is positioned as an approach in which a discursive event is seen as being three dimensional insofar as it is 'simultaneously a piece text, an instance of discursive practice, and an instance of social practice' (Fairclough, 1992: 4). As a result, the analysis of discourse requires: (1) an examination of the language in use (*the text dimension*); (2) an identification of the processes of textual production and consumption (*the discursive practice dimension*); and (3) a consideration of the institutional factors surrounding the event and how they shape the discourse (*the social practice dimension*).

CDA seeks to establish connections between different levels of discursive aggregation and different levels of analysis. Hence, we can envisage that:

> a piece of discourse is embedded within sociocultural practice at a number of levels; in the immediate situation, in the wider institution or organization, and at a societal level. For example, one can read an interaction between marital partners in terms of their particular relationship, relationships between partners within the family as an institution, or gender relationships in the larger society. (Fairclough, 1995: 97).

Typically the analysis of the 'text dimension' in CDA encompasses the use of 'fine grain' situated approaches such as conversation analysis or ethnomethodology (e.g. an episode of interaction between marital partners). The 'discursive practice dimension' involves moving beyond the immediate situation to consider the 'who', 'when' and 'where' of text production and consumption (including aspects of genre, issues of authorship, the positioning of stakeholders within the text and the intended audience). Finally, the 'social practice dimension' considers the wider institutional and political landscape in which a discursive event is located in terms of issues of power and hegemony (e.g. the way in which the gendered nature of society might constrain and configure both the situation-specific interaction between marital partners and processes of marital interaction more generally). Ultimately, CDA is concerned with issues of power and ideology and it is particularly suited to forms of discursive inquiry that seek to address how local texts are influenced by wider contextual factors and vice versa.

Intertextual analysis

Intertextuality can been described as being concerned with the extent to which a given text has embedded within it elements of other texts. Allen (2000: 5) points out: 'Intertextuality seems such a useful term because it foregrounds notions of relationality, interconnectedness and interdependence in modern cultural life'. Intertextual analysis focuses upon identifying, analysing and synthesizing from parts of a focal text in terms of the earlier sources and other voices, which are either implicitly or explicitly incorporated and presented within that text (Keenoy and Oswick, 2004). Given that intertextual analysis initially focuses on the actual content of a text, it could be described as a micro-level approach to discourse analysis. However, because it is concerned with the interpenetration and/or interrelationship of a text with other texts, it is perhaps more appropriate to think of intertextual analysis as a meso-level approach.

Although originally developed as a technique among literary scholars (Kristeva, 1980; Bakhtin, 1981), it has also proved to be an effective approach to studying non-fictional texts. Indeed, in extolling the virtues of applying intertextual analysis to organizational research, Keenoy and Oswick (2004: 136) suggest: 'It provides a means of, at least tentatively, apprehending the embedded, interwoven, and multivocal nature of discursive events and enables us to develop more complex and context-sensitive understandings of the episodes of discourse we choose to analyze'.

Intertextual analysis has historical overtones insofar as it has a temporal and retrospective emphasis by exploring the nature of a contemporary text in relation to a previous text (or texts). This approach can be utilized to establish the patterns of continuity or discontinuity of discursive themes and perspectives over time. Equally, it can be used to establish connections between previously unconnected texts. There are a number of ways of doing intertextual analysis. Drawing upon and extending the work of Gerard Genette (1992; 1997), it is possible to identify two different forms of intertextual analysis. First, there is what might be described as 'overt intertextuality' via the examination of 'the actual presence of one text within another' (Genette, 1997: 1–2). This involves the explicit incorporation of another text(s) within the focal text through direct quotation and/or reference. On this basis, it is often possible to draw interesting inferences regarding the influences, positioning and genealogy of a text by locating it in relation to a body of work.

Second, there are forms of 'covert intertextuality' that can be meaningfully investigated. Here the analysis focuses on more implicit connections or resonances with other texts. The practice of textual borrowing and importation can take the form of either content similarities (e.g. adopting comparable positions, using similar phrases or terminology) or genre replication, including: style of exposition, the actual layout of text (fonts size, use of headings, etc.) and the media employed (e.g. a report, general announcement or podcast). Analysing processes of 'covert intertextuality' can be usefully employed in a variety of ways. For example, it is possible to interrogate a company's espoused aims and goals by comparing them to those contained within other corporate mission statements in terms of content and style of presentation.

Choosing a Text (or Texts)

There is a danger in being too prescriptive about how to go about selecting suitable discursive material. There are, however, some important issues to consider when choosing a sample, or samples, of spoken or written text. To begin with, there is the question of what constitutes a text. For our purposes, a text is a pre-existing extract of written discourse or episode of spoken discourse. The keyword here is 'pre-existing' because discourse analysis involves the scrutiny of a language-based artifact (e.g. a company document, a promotional video, a tape-recording of a presentation or transcribed data). Moreover, the established convention in discourse analysis is that the researcher is not an active participant in the production of the discourse that he or she then seeks to analyse. So with regard to written material it should be a document that has not been authored or co-authored by the researcher and spoken material should be 'naturally occurring talk' in which the analyst is not directly involved (Potter and Wetherell, 1987). Hence, for example, transcribed material that is gathered by a researcher through semi-interviews can obviously be explored in terms of language use. However, purists would argue that it should not be regarded as 'discourse analysis' (Johnstone, 2002; Fairclough, 2003). Whether or not we subscribe to this demarcation of discourse, involvement in the discourse one seeks to then analyse is potentially problematic. Not least because, if discourse is about meaning-making it is difficult to step back and analyse meaning (and indeed infer meaning) from a conversation where the analyst has co-constructed the meaning as an interlocutor (e.g. would a topic have arisen had the researcher not raised it? Did the researcher's involvement intentionally or unintentionally steer the direction of the conversation? Is the process tautological?) The overriding implication is that data that are to be analysed through discourse analysis should be gathered in a non-participatory way (i.e. as texts that exist independently of the researcher).

A further consideration, in terms of text selection, is the need to ensure that there is an alignment between the sample of discursive material, the discursive method employed and the epistemological position taken. So, for example, if one adopted a critical epistemological stance and used deconstruction as a method, this combination would have two significant implications for the selection of discursive material. First, the need for a 'close reading', which is central to deconstruction, would mean that the analysis is likely to focus on a single text. Second, in order to accommodate critical interrogation, it is likely that the selected text is inherently partial in nature and/or represents dominant interests and a deconstruction is therefore likely to focus on the existence of privileged voices and the marginalization or subordination of alternative accounts. An overview of the connection between issues of sample and the other various aspects of discursive engagement is provided in Table 26.1.

Doing Discourse Analysis: An Example

In this section we provide an illustration of how discourse analysis can be undertaken. The example used is a study of the discursive construction of

Table 26.1   A summary of discursive approaches, orientations and emphases

Discursive approach	Level of analysis	Mode of discursive engagement	Typical form of sample and textual emphasis
Deconstruction	*Micro-level*: a detailed and text-focused close reading	Critical	A single written text – focusing on points of contradiction (and inclusions *vs* exclusions)
		Post-structural	A single written text – focusing on discrepancies, ambiguities and multiple readings
Foucauldian analysis	*Macro-level*: a broad and abstract engagement with discursive formations	Critical and post-structural	A range of texts – a focus on discerning the rules that govern bodies of texts and a consideration of the abstract semantic features of a discourse(s)
Critical discourse analysis	*Multi-level*: links the detailed use of language with wider social and political practices	Critical	A single discursive event (either spoken or written) – problematical connections between the properties of a text and the social processes and institutional practices in terms of issues of ideology and power
Intertextual analysis	*Meso-level*: considers a focal text in relation to other preceding texts	Positivist	A longitudinal chain of texts – revealing continuity, progress and/or coherence over time
		Critical	Juxtaposing a text with another text – revealing contradictions and oppositions
		Post-structural	A web or weave of texts – revealing multiple accounts and interpretations

equality, diversity and inclusion (Oswick, 2010). The primary aim of research was to identify and analyse the respective emphasis upon, and popularity of, equality, diversity and inclusion as subtly different approaches to tackling discrimination in employment. The study adopted a critical orientation and it incorporated two main strands of inquiry. It involved both the broad analysis of published work on equality, diversity and inclusion (i.e. an academic discourse) and the detailed scrutiny of a small sample of corporate videos appearing on the YouTube website (i.e. a corporate discourse). The rationale for this approach was explained as follows:

> The two sources used have been chosen because they facilitate different discursive levels of analysis (i.e. macro-level patterns and micro-level interaction). This is important insofar as it enables connections to be made, and

inferences to be drawn, between the everyday, situated use of language (written or spoken) and the more generalized, abstract meta-discursive perspectives which are informed and reinforced through these localized interactions and texts. (Oswick, 2010)

In effect, the research combined some elements of Foucauldian analysis (i.e. a macro-level analysis involving an abstract engagement with a range of texts) with CDA (i.e. using video clips as specific discursive events and seeking to understand the wider social and institutional practices within which these were embedded).

The identification of meta-discursive trends

The analysis of academic work involved a broad interrogation of the Social Science Citation Index (SSCI) over four decades in order to identify the general pattern of usage of the concepts of equality, diversity and inclusion. This broad interrogation involved keyword, topic and thematic searches of the SSCI database.

The results showed that a discernible pattern of publication was evident. First, equality was the most popular area of enquiry in the period from 1970 through to 1990. Second, the general level of interest in equality had remained more or less constant since 1990, but at that point an interest in diversity overtook equality and started to climb steeply as well as increase throughout the period between 1990 and 2010 (albeit that such interest began to flatten out during the past decade). Finally, inclusion was the least popular of the three areas of academic interest, but interest in this had increased in a significant and enduring way since the late 1990s. So, in summary, we can say that equality was initially the most popular anti-discrimination discourse, but one that has been increasingly overshadowed by a burgeoning interest in diversity, with some signs that inclusion is starting to emerge as a popular discursive formation.

Uncovering micro-discursive patterns

The focus of the analysis of detailed discursive events was video clips uploaded on YouTube in 2008 and 2009. The sample comprised of 18 videos in which company representatives talked about their organization's approach to equality, diversity and/or inclusion. The content of the videos was transcribed and the data were analysed in terms of their general narrative theme (e.g. a discernible emphasis on either equality, diversity or inclusion), discursive patterns (e.g. language-use aimed at differentiating, privileging and/or downplaying particular anti-discriminatory approaches) and aggregated content (e.g. how frequently the terms equality, diversity and inclusion were used).

The discursive analysis of the spoken discourse revealed several interesting findings. Of particular note was the absence of talk about 'equality' and 'equal opportunities'. Only three out of the 18 videos contained any discussion of equality with the remaining 15 videos all focusing on issues of diversity and inclusion. Beyond this, the discourse of the corporate representatives revealed a significant pattern to their respective positioning of diversity and inclusion. More specifically, inclusion was generally presented as more relevant, critical and/or important to organizations than diversity (i.e. ten videos presented it as more relevant/important, four videos presented it as equally relevant/important and only one presented diversity as more relevant/important). Within the specific articulations of corporate representatives it was apparent that diversity was presented in a taken-for-granted way while inclusion was portrayed as a strategic imperative. This can be seen in the assertion made by Mr H (the CEO of a community organization):

> Inclusion is important because it is really about how we as local [company name] reflect the diversity of our community. It's about our ability to be able to bring people to our mutual table.

The purchase of inclusion is similarly reinforced, and further extended, in the comments of Ms L (the Director of Global Inclusion and Diversity at a large software company). She observed:

> Diversity is what you see when you get a group of people together. Whenever there is a different person in the room from you, you got [sic] a diverse group going on. But what do we do with it? So, it's how we leverage the fact we bring different perspectives, that we bring different cultures and backgrounds together and what we do when we get those folks together, how that promotes innovation and helps us work as a better multicultural global organization … I think that's the inclusion part of the equation.

Ms L's observations are typical of those presented by a number of the videos. The pro-inclusion discourse positions diversity as inevitable and unavoidable (i.e. as a given). This is implied in Ms L's suggestion that: 'Whenever there is a different person in the room from you, you got [*sic*] a diverse group going on'. However, inclusion is not an ever-present phenomenon and it involves making a choice. In effect, it is the means by which the latent potential of diversity can be operationalized and utilized (or as Ms L frames it in corporate-speak: 'Leveraged'). Hence, in terms of anti-discrimination initiatives, the discourse of diversity becomes subtly marginalized and the discourse of inclusion becomes privileged as the primary means of facilitating the achievement of corporate goals and socially desirable outcomes.

Discursive conclusions

The overriding conclusion that can be derived from the macro-discursive study of academic texts and the micro-discursive study of the public accounts of practitioners is relatively consistent. There is a discernible shift in discursive prominence from equality to diversity and an emerging movement towards inclusion. Moreover, the temporal formation of anti-discrimination discourses exhibits a pattern which is similar to that found in the literature on management fads and fashions. As Abrahamson and Eisenman (2008: 719) have observed: 'Lexical shifts over time serve to differentiate a fashion from its predecessor, creating a sense of novelty and progress from the earlier to the later fashions'. Arguably, it is perhaps the sense of progress, newness and leverage offered by successive discursive transitions from equality to diversity to inclusion that makes them so attractive to both management academics and practitioners.

Implications for discursive research

There are two main inferences that can be drawn from the study presented. First, it provides a two-pronged illustration of the importance of aligning discursive methods with a specific level of engagement and a desired mode of engagement. We can see that the study used a more micro-oriented approach (i.e. CDA) to capture the detail of the interaction and a more macro-oriented approach (i.e. Foucauldian-inspired analysis) to explore wider trends and broader discursive formations.

Second, the study demonstrates the scope for combining discursive methods (i.e. CDA and Foucauldian-inspired analysis). The concurrent deployment of different discursive techniques can, as in the case of the above example, be utilized to capture data pertaining to different levels of analysis. Equally, discursive methods used in combination can offer either contrasting or complimentary insights when applied to discursive material gathered at the same level of analysis (e.g. deconstruction in combination with conversation analysis).

Conclusion

Discourse analysis is more than just a simplistic focus on organizational communication (i.e. the study of communication media or how organizational stakeholders interact). It is also more than a prescriptive means of scrutinizing secondary data sources (i.e. organizational documents and artifacts) as an obligatory, but necessarily supplementary, element of a wider research project(s). Discourse analysis comprises a range of language-oriented approaches that can be meaningfully deployed to study organizations and organizational phenomena. In particular, discursive approaches are especially valuable mechanisms for studying the more subjective and intangible parts of organizational and social life (e.g. aspects of power, affiliation, identity, conflict, culture and ideology).

Finally, having previously identified the potential for combining discursive approaches, it is also important to highlight that there is considerable scope for using discourse analytic methods in combination with other qualitative approaches (e.g. interviews, observational techniques, sociograms and so on). So, for example, the study of the enduring pattern of relationships between individuals revealed by social network analysis (Scott, 1992) can be enhanced by considering the actual dynamics of interaction that can be apprehended through discourse analysis. This, in turn, leads to richer and more sophisticated insights into a given social situation. Beyond the benefits of understanding relationships through discourse and vice versa, we can also derive fresh insights into agency and positionality by simultaneously deploying discursive techniques and stakeholder analysis (Burgoyne, 1994). In summary, there are many creative ways in which a rich array of discursive approaches can be triangulated with other qualitative research methods.

Further Reading

For a comprehensive treatment of discourse and discourse analysis readers should consult Jaworski and Coupland (1999) or Schriffin et al. (2001). Texts that specifically focus on discourse analysis from an organizational perspective are provided by Grant et al. (2004a) and Phillips and Hardy (2002). More information on the question of contrasting levels of discursive engagement can be found in Alvesson and Karreman's (2000) article in *Human Relations*. Finally, the following sources offer an elaboration on the main discursive approaches discussed in this chapter: deconstruction (Kilduff, 1993); intertextual analysis (Allen, 2000); Foucauldian discourse analysis (Arribas-Ayllon and Walkerdine, 2008); and critical discourse analysis (Fairclough, 1995).

References

Abrahamson, E. and Eisenman, M. (2008) 'Employee management techniques: transient fads or trending fashions?', *Administrative Science Quarterly*, 53 (4): 719–744.

Allen, G. (2000) *Intertextuality*. London: Routledge.

Alvesson, M. and Karreman, D. (2000) 'Varieties of discourse: on the study of organizations through discourse analysis', *Human Relations*, 53 (9): 1125–1149.

Arribas-Ayllon, M. and Walkerdine, V. (2008) 'Foucauldian discourse analysis', in C. Willig and W. Stainton-Rogers (eds), *The Sage Handbook of Qualitative Research in Psychology*. London: Sage.

Bakhtin, M. (1981) *The Dialogic Imagination: Four Essays*, trans. C. Emerson and M. Holquist. Austin, TX: University of Texas Press.

Biber, D., Conrad, S. and Reppen, R. (1998) *Corpus Linguistics: Investigating Language Structure and Use*. Cambridge: Cambridge University Press.

Boje, D. M. (2001) *Narrative Methods for Organizational and Communications Research*. London: Sage.

Boje, D.M., Oswick, C. and Ford, J.D. (2004) 'Language and organization: the doing of discourse', *Academy of Management Review*, 29 (4): 571–577.

Burgoyne, J.G. (1994) 'Stakeholder analysis', in C. Cassell and G. Symon (eds), *Qualitative Methods in Organizational Research: A Practical Guide*. New Delhi: Sage.

Cunliffe, A.L. (2008) 'Discourse analysis', in R. Thorpe and R. Holt (eds), *The Sage Dictionary of Qualitative Management Research, Handbook of Organizational Discourse*. London: Sage.

Currie, M. (1998) *Postmodern Narrative Theory*. New York: St Martin's Press.

Derrida, J. (1976) *Of Grammatology*. Baltimore, MD: Johns Hopkins University Press.

Derrida, J. (1978) *Writing and Difference*. Chicago, IL: University of Chicago Press.

Dick, P. (2004) 'Discourse analysis', in C. Cassell and G. Symon (eds), *Essential Guide to Qualitative Methods in Organizational Research.* London: Sage.

Fairclough, N. (1992) *Discourse and Social Change.* Cambridge: Polity Press.

Fairclough, N. (1995) *Critical Discourse Analysis: The Critical Study of Language.* London: Longman.

Fairclough, N. (2003) *Analysing Discourse: Textual Analysis for Social Research.* London: Routledge.

Foucault, M. (1972) *The Archaeology of Knowledge.* New York: Pantheon.

Foucault, M. (1980) *Power/Knowledge: Selected Interviews and Other Writings 1972–1977.* New York: Pantheon.

Foucault, M. (1984) 'The order of discourse', in M. Shapiro (ed.), *The Language of Politics.* Oxford: Blackwell.

Garfinkel, H. (1967) *Studies in Ethnomethodology.* Englewood-Cliffs, NJ: Prentice-Hall.

Genette, G. (1992) *The Architext: An Introduction*, trans. J. Lewin. Berkeley, CA: University of California Press.

Genette, G. (1997) *Palimpsests: Literature in the Second Degree*, trans. C. Newman and C. Doubinsky. Lincoln: University of Nebraska Press.

Grant, D., Hardy, C., Oswick, C. and Putnam, L. (eds) (2004a) *Sage Handbook of Organizational Discourse.* London: Sage.

Grant, D., Hardy, C., Oswick, C. and Putnam, L. (2004b) 'Organizational discourse: exploring the field', in D. Grant, C. Hardy, C. Oswick and L. Putnam (eds), *Sage Handbook of Organizational Discourse.* London: Sage.

Grant, D. Iedema, R. and Oswick, C. (2010) 'Discourse and critical management studies', in M. Alvesson, T. Bridgman and H. Willmott (eds), *The Oxford Handbook of Critical Management Studies.* Oxford: Oxford University Press.

Iedema, R. (2008) 'Discourse analysis', in S.R. Clegg and J.R. Bailey (eds), *International Encyclopedia of Organization Stuidies.* Thousand Oaks, CA: Sage.

Jaworski, A. and Coupland, N. (eds) (1999) *The Discourse Reader.* London: Routledge.

Johnstone, B. (2002) *Discourse Analysis.* Malden, MA: Blackwell Publishing.

Keenoy, T. and Oswick, C. (2004) 'Organizing textscapes', *Organization Studies*, 25 (1): 135–142.

Keenoy, T., Oswick, C. and Grant, D. (1997) 'Organizational discourses: text and context', *Organization*, 4 (2): 147–157.

Kilduff, M. (1993) 'Deconstructing organizations', *Academy of Management Review*, 18: 13–31.

Kilduff, M. and Kelemen, M. (2004) 'Deconstructing discourse', in D. Grant, C. Hardy, C. Oswick and L. Putnam (eds), *Handbook of Organizational Discourse.* London: Sage.

Krippendorff, K. (2004) *Content Analysis: An Introduction to its Methodology* (2nd edn). London: Sage.

Kristeva, J. (1980) *Desire in Language: A Semiotic Approach to Literature and Art*, trans. T. Gora, A. Jardine and L. Roudiez. New York: Columbia University Press.

McEnery, T. and Wilson, A. (1996) *Corpus Linguistics: An Introduction.* Edinburgh: Edinburgh University Press.

Mumby, D. and Stohl, C. (1991) 'Power and discourse in organization studies: absence and the dialectics of control', *Discourse and Society*, 2 (3): 313–332.

Neuendorf, K.A. (2002) *The Content Analysis Guidebook*. Beverley Hills, CA: Sage.

Oswick, C. (2010) 'The social construction of diversity, equality and inclusion: an exploration of academic and public discourses', in G. Healy, G. Kirton and M. Noon (eds), *Equality, Inequalities and Diversity: From Global to Local*. London: Palgrave, pp. 18–36.

Oswick, C. (forthcoming) 'Discourse', in M. Tadajewski, P. Maclaran, E. Parsons and M. Parker (eds), *Key Concepts in Critical Management Studies*. London: Sage.

Oswick, C. and Richards, D. (2004) 'Talk in organizations: local conversations, wider perspectives', *Culture and Organization*, 10 (2): 107–123.

Phillips, N. and Hardy, C. (2002) *Discourse Analysis: Investigating Processes of Social Construction*. Newbury Park, CA: Sage.

Potter, J. and Wetherell, M. (1987) *Discourse and Social Psychology*. London: Sage.

Psathos, G. (1995) *Conversation Analysis: The Study of Talk-in-Interaction*. Beverley Hills, CA: Sage.

Reissman, C.K. (1993) *Narrative Analysis*. Newbury Park, CA: Sage.

Schriffin, D., Tannen, D. and Hamilton, H.E. (eds) (2001) *The Handbook of Discourse Analysis*. Oxford: Blackwell Publishing.

Scott, J. (1992) *Social Network Analysis*. Newbury Park, CA: Sage.

Silverman, D. (1993) *Interpreting Qualitative Data: Methods for Analysing Talk, Text and Interaction*. London: Sage.

27 Narrative Analysis

Sally Maitlis

We live immersed in narrative, recounting and reassessing the meaning of our past actions, anticipating the outcome of our future projects, situating ourselves at the intersection of several stories not yet completed. (Brooks, 1992: 3)

What Is Narrative?

The concept of narrative describes a spoken or written text that involves temporal sequences of events and actions. Narratives need a 'valued endpoint' (e.g. capturing the heart of the princess) and a set of events and characters that make the endpoint more or less probable, accessible or vivid (e.g. rival knights, fire-breathing dragons) (Gergen, 1999). Narratives play a critical role in the structuring of human experience and identity (Bruner, 1986; Gabriel, 2000, 2004; Ibarra and Barbulescu, 2010). Indeed, as the opening quote suggests, they are often regarded as the central means through which people construct, describe and understand their experiences (McAdams, 1993). Narrative is thus not simply a way of describing reality, but a way of socially constructing reality, establishing what the connections are, were or might be among events, feelings, thoughts and actions (Gergen, 1999).

People cannot, however, simply create any preferred reality by telling a story. The social construction of reality through narrative is constrained, as it is through other means, by the social structures and cultures within which individuals live and by the material resources and skills at their disposal (Berger and Luckmann, 1967). For a story to have force as a means of social construction, it must be perceived as legitimate and meaningful by both teller and audience (Barry and Elmes, 1997). Although some writers distinguish between 'narratives' and 'stories' (e.g. Gabriel, 2004), in this chapter, I use the terms interchangeably, as is common in the organizational literature on narrative (Riessman, 2008; Hardy and Maguire, 2010; Sonenshein, 2010).

How is narrative studied?

Narrative research comes in a great many forms, differing in the researcher's central focus, the role that narrative plays and the kind of narratives under consideration. In organizational research, narrative inquiry is used to explore questions as wide-ranging as how individuals construct occupational identities (e.g. Kreiner et al., 2006; Maitlis, 2009), how meaning is made, shared and contested among organizational members (e.g. Boje, 1991; Sonenshein, 2010), and how groups of organizational constituents draw on, resist and legitimate broader institutional narratives (e.g. Brown, 2004; Boudes and Laroche, 2009; Hardy and Maguire, 2010). Thus some studies treat narrative as a form of 'verbal action', accomplishing the construction of individual and organizational identities, while others regard it as a sensemaking device, organizing actions and events into a meaningful whole that conveys emotions and interpretations and reveals the consequences of actions over time (Chase, 2005). In other research that attends to the co-creation of narratives between teller and researcher, narratives are understood as socially situated performances that will vary depending on the audience, time and location (Bauman, 1986). Less common in organizational research, but probably the dominant form of narrative analysis in psychology, is the analysis of 'life stories' to investigate identity or personality development over the life course (e.g. Lieblich and Josselson, 1997; McAdams, 1993; McAdams et al., 2006). Some of these researchers extend the concept of narrative as verbal action to explore the formative effects of narratives, examining the relationship between how individuals tell their stories and how they live their lives (McAdams and Bowman, 2001; Chase, 2005).

Narrative research draws on different kinds of narratives, including stories that are 'out there' and those that are created by researchers from pieces or sets of narratives that they collect. Narratives can vary in length from a few lines that outline a basic plot, to long and intricate stories that describe significant parts (or the entirety) of a person's life or organization's history. In organizational research, narratives have many sources, including responses to interview questions and open-ended survey questions, organizational documentation and naturally occurring social exchanges, such as meetings and company presentations. In short, organizations are full of narratives and it is almost impossible for a qualitative researcher to study an organization without encountering them in one form or another. Moreover, narratives are an important research output, since we construct meaning through the narratives we tell about our data. Because of this, our research narratives (in the form of presentations, articles and books) can be regarded as meaning-making devices through which we construct our own and others' identities (Chase, 2005).

What is narrative analysis?

Narrative analysis is the central analytic task of narrative inquiry and comes in several forms. For example, Lieblich et al. (1998) present a typology organized along two dimensions, holistic-categorical and content-form, which produce four modes of narrative analysis. These vary in their focus on the whole or part of a narrative (holistic *vs* categorical), and on what is said or how it is said (content *vs* form). Boje, in his discussion of narrative and 'antenarrative' analysis, identifies several postmodern approaches to analysing stories that he argues are 'too unconstructed and fragmented to be analyzed in traditional approaches' (2001: 1), including deconstruction, microstoria and intertextuality. Czarniawska (2004) offers many different ways of reading narratives, including structural analyses and poststructuralist 'close readings'. In the present chapter, and with the aim of providing a practical guide for organizational research, I draw on Riessman's (1993; 2008) classic texts to explore three of the most common kinds of narrative analysis: thematic, structural and dialogic/performance. While Riessman's discussion centres on individual's narratives, below I draw on examples from the organizational literature to illustrate applications of these approaches to organization studies.

Thematic Analysis

Thematic analysis is probably the most common kind of narrative analysis, exploring the content of a story and focusing on what is said rather than the way it is said. The aim of a thematic analysis is to identify key themes within a narrative or, if working with a set of narratives, to identify themes that are common to all stories within the set. This approach can be used with diverse kinds of narrative data, including stories gathered in research interviews, shared between two individuals in meetings or captured in documents. In organizational research the narrative under investigation is often a 'composite': that is, a narrative composed by the researcher from multiple data sources (e.g. Brown and Humphreys, 2003; Sonenshein, 2010). For example, in my ethnographic study of sensemaking in symphony orchestras, I created narratives of sensemaking processes that occurred around 27 different issues that arose in the orchestras during my fieldwork. I produced each narrative by tracing through the chronologically ordered raw data on each organization to identify each time a particular issue (such as decisions about repertoire) arose, and then described the sensemaking process through quotations from a combination of interviews, meeting transcripts, organizational documents and field notes (Maitlis, 2005). My thematic analysis entailed working with the 27 narratives to identify two core dimensions – animation and control – on which the sensemaking processes they described varied. From these came further themes that described the social qualities of four forms of sensemaking and their outcomes.

In their study of institutional change, Hardy and Maguire (2010) conducted a thematic analysis of narratives generated in talk and texts in and around the Stockholm Convention on Persistent Organic Pollutants (POPs). They focused on narratives about the insecticide DDT, the only chemical treated as an exception in the new global regulations that came out of the meetings. The analysis began by grouping narratives by author and 'discursive space' (i.e. where a narrative was promulgated, for example, in plenary meetings or in external communications), and each narrative was then coded for three themes: the coherent identities constructed in the narrative (e.g. what threats exist, who the victims are), the valued endpoint (e.g. the elimination of POPs, control of malaria) and the forces that enabled movement towards this endpoint (e.g. financial and technical assistance from developed countries). From here, the authors identified three prevailing narratives about DDT: 'DDT as evil threat', 'DDT as hero' and 'DDT as necessary evil', each differing in the coherent identities, valued endpoints and enabling forces they constructed and together describing the dominant narratives in circulation. The authors then linked each narrative to a different mechanism – domination, interpretation and translation – leading to change in the institutional field and in organizations.

Although thematic analysis can be conducted on a single person's narrative, it is more common in organizational research to work with multiple narratives, searching for themes that are consistent across all or within sub-groups of stories. When working in this way, thematic analysis often involves constant comparison (Strauss and Corbin, 1998), a method common to many kinds of qualitative research. Here the researcher moves repeatedly through and across the data, creating categories that allow one set of narratives to be distinguished from another on the basis of the themes these contain. This enables valuable comparisons across stories, but also typically involves 'breaking up' narratives, as themes are separated from the contexts in which they were embedded and grouped together by theme. Although narrative scholars seek to preserve the inherent sequencing and contextual richness of each story, research differs considerably in the extent to which it does this. This tension, explored in Bryant and Lasky (2007), is more acute in some analyses than others. For example, Hardy and Maguire's (2010) output of narratives allowed the portrayal of their thematic analysis to happen in a rich narrative form. This is harder to do in research that uses thematic analysis to identify the characteristics of a more abstracted output, as in the case of my sensemaking study (Maitlis, 2005), where specific narratives were left behind in my efforts to identify generalizable forms of organizational sensemaking. Thus we can see the trade-offs that come as a result of the kind of questions asked in a thematic analysis, the form of answers provided and also the quantity of data under consideration.

Thematic analysis is an especially valuable approach when a researcher wants to understand the content conveyed in a narrative, and particularly when they wish to highlight the key content elements that give the narrative its power. Thematic analyses are often used to explore core dimensions around which meanings are constructed, for example, answering questions such as, 'How do members construct their organizational identity?' and 'How do managers' understandings of change differ from those of employees?'. Thematic analyses can be either theory-led or more inductively derived. For example, Hardy and Maguire (2010) drew on previous studies that had identified 'identity', 'valued endpoint' and 'enabling forces' as important narrative themes (Martens et al., 2007; Zilber, 2007). In other research, such as Brown and Humphreys' (2003) study of epic tales of organizational change, themes of hopelessness and betrayal were induced from the data to provide core narrative plots.

In sum, thematic analysis offers a powerful and flexible way to explore central elements in the narratives constructed by individuals and groups and those circulating in the discourse of wider institutional fields. Such analyses provide valuable insights into how narratives produced among organizational members are shaped by the contexts in which they are shared, as well as how these narratives in turn produce changes in the prevailing cultural and societal discourses.

Structural Analysis

Where thematic analysis focuses on the content of a narrative, structural analysis prioritizes the way in which a story is told. Structural analyses attend to how language is used to persuade, and especially to the story's internal organization. Probably the best known approach comes from sociolinguistics (Labov and Waletsky, 1967; Labov, 1972) and identifies six components of narrative structure: an abstract (summarizing the main point of the story), an orientation (revealing the actors, time, place and situation), a complication (the sequence of events), an evaluation (commenting on the meaning of the narrative), a resolution (the outcome) and a coda (an ending and return to the present time). Although not all stories contain every element, and the order can vary, most narratives are organized in this way. Structural analyses using Labov's model can provide insights into each element's function in constructing the story and show how elements can be combined in different ways to create different kinds of meanings (Riessman, 2008). Examining the same combinations of elements across different stories can also be revealing. For example, Gersick et al. (2000), in their analysis of relationships in academia, began with a structural analysis of stories gathered from business school faculty members. They first identified 123 pairs of complications (actions) and outcomes (responses) in the stories and then turned to the content of each action-response pair to reveal four basic types of plots in academic relationships: a helping plot, a harming plot, an emotional support plot and a joint working plot.

Structural analysis can also be used to reveal the same simple structure that underlies many seemingly different stories. For example, Lamberg and Pajunen (2005) drew on Propp's (1968 [1928]) theory of folktale structure to examine a story of organizational decline and turnaround. Propp argues that although different folktales have many different characters, the number of functions they play is very small. For example, a dragon, a witch and a step-mother can each equally serve to provide 'villainy' in a story. Using Propp's set of functions, Lamberg and Pajunen (2005) showed how organizational decline and turnaround could be emplotted as a 'quest' folktale, and challenged leader-centric models of turnaround by identifying several narrative elaborations that revealed mechanisms external to the leader that would drive the organization from one state to another.

Sonenshein's (2010) study of strategic change implementation also explores core structures underlying members' narratives. He finds three narrative forms: progressive, regressive and stability narratives (Gergen and Gergen, 1997) that characterize how change is understood by different groups of employees. Progressive narratives tell a positive story of change that leads to good outcomes for the organization and its members, while regressive narratives link events to construct a story in which organizational change produces negative outcomes. The stability narrative is a 'no-change' story, a construction that emphasizes continuity and lacks an inherently evaluative component. In this study, narratives construct meaning through the overall trajectory they carve, organizing events in ways that produce positive, negative or neutral outcomes over time.

Structural analysis is especially valuable when a researcher wants to understand how the way in which a story is told makes it convincing and persuasive. Structural analyses can therefore be used to address questions such as, 'How do entrepreneurs convince investors of their credibility?' and 'How is a legitimate account of corporate social responsibility produced?'. As with thematic analyses, there is no single way of analysing narratives from a structural perspective. Yet common to all such studies is a focus not on who does what, but on how events are organized in ways that will differentially shape the meaning of a narrative. As the examples above demonstrate, while such analyses direct attention to the structural make-up of individual stories, these can also be conducted across multiple narratives to show how structural variations produce different meanings. Further, as seen in Gersick et al. (2000) and Sonenshein (2010), a structural analysis can be used as a window into differences in narrative plots.

To conclude, structural analysis provides a potent way to examine a story's internal organization, directing attention to how different components of a narrative are ordered and connected to give it plausibility and durability. Such analyses reveal fundamental similarities in what a thematic analysis might suggest are quite different stories and the important variation in narratives whose differential impact cannot adequately be explained by their content alone. As such, structural analysis allows an understanding of why some narratives command more attention than others and succeed in accomplishing change where others fail.

Dialogic/Performance Analysis

This form of narrative analysis incorporates both thematic and structural elements, but adds to them by exploring how narratives are co-constructed between teller and listener. Attention is paid not only to the dialogic relationship between narrator and audience, but also to the social, historical and cultural context in which the exchange takes place. This means that a dialogic narrative analysis, and therefore the transcripts on which it is based, should capture the roles of both narrator and researcher, allowing an exploration of how stories are produced in social interaction. When this exchange is understood as a performance, in which one party involves and persuades another, the analysis is often conducted through a dramaturgical lens. This enables an insight into how identities and other narrative accomplishments are produced through certain actors, and in particular settings, performed with and for an audience.

Riessman (2008) describes an interview she conducted with Burt, a working-class man with advanced multiple sclerosis, who tells a story about his last day on the job – the day his identity as a worker ended. Her analysis explores how he constructs his identity through his narrative, enacting a masculine and motivated person who is keen to work as he has always done. Riessman notes his performance in the heroic drama that he unfolds as he describes a physical and very personal difficulty he encounters on his last day – an inability to urinate because of his medical condition. But she also reflects on her part in it, as his audience, considering how her presence may have provided Burt with a valued opportunity to connect and be intimate with a woman who showed interest in him. She focuses on how he tells his story, using direct speech to create a performative quality, and also his use of 'asides' when he steps out of the action to explain something to his audience. Riessman also explores his use of repetition and expressive sounds to signal key points in his story. The point is not that he consciously chooses to use these devices to add drama, but that this is their effect in the narrative he performs. She continues her analysis with a consideration of how she and her interviewee co-constructed meanings of disability and identity that were located in a particular social and historical context, something she saw only in subsequent readings of the text.

This type of analysis is less common in organizational research, perhaps because of the challenges of conducting dialogic analyses on multiple members' narratives. Yet it is both possible and revealing, especially when working with transcripts of meetings and other collective activities in organizations (e.g. Mangham and Overington, 1987; Oswick et al., 2000). Riessman's example above highlights the rich and multi-layered insights that dialogic/performance narrative analysis can offer, through its close attention to the relationship between narrator, audience and context. It is an approach particularly relevant to exploring the socially situated nature of narrative and its collaborative construction, allowing us to address questions such as, 'How do team members contest new work practices?' and 'How is an organization's strategy negotiated at its annual retreat?' By including the researcher's role in such analyses, we acknowledge not only the performative quality of team meetings and annual retreats, but also the part played by the observing researcher in shaping the narrative she collects.

In sum, dialogic/performance analysis permits an examination of the different voices through which any single narrative is constructed, showing their inherently interactive, collaborative nature. This approach thus adds a powerful dimension to the analysis of narratives, providing an insight into the oft-hidden struggles for control that permeate this negotiated enterprise, and revealing how narrative authority is asserted and relinquished both among organizational members and between participant and researcher.

Identity Construction Following a Work-related Trauma: A Worked Example of Thematic Narrative Analysis

In this section, I draw from my current research with performing artists who have experienced an injury that affects their ability to do their work and which thereby presents a major challenge to their identities (Maitlis, 2010). My analysis is of life narrative interviews with these musicians and dancers, which would typically last two to three hours and lead to transcripts of about 40–50 pages. My interest is in the experience and impact of injury on identity for each individual, but I also seek to understand general patterns of identity construction across and within sub-groups of the 40 artist group and to identify kinds of identity work that are common across individuals.

The example below comes from an analysis of musicians who told narratives of post-injury growth and whose identity work led them to construct positive, agential identities as they moved forward in their lives (Maitlis, 2009). My focus here was on identifying how these individuals' identities shifted during and after the trauma and the kinds of identity work they did that allowed them to construct themselves in new positive ways. First, I analysed each interview transcript, looking for ways in which the individual talked about him- or herself before, during and after the injury occurred. I was particularly interested in how their identity as a musician was challenged by the injury that stopped them from doing work that had long been a focal part of their lives. In each transcript, I sought out ways that interviewees made sense of themselves and their choices over time. I was especially interested in how they narrated themselves at the present time and their ways of relating to their former identity of musician.

When writing this up for publication, I included very short summary narratives that I created from each interview transcript. These summary narratives were made up from quotations taken from the transcript, woven together with prose through which I could more succinctly describe periods of the interviewees' lives. Although these stories were therefore *my* narratives of their lives, this seemed to be the best way to help the reader appreciate the kind of narrative with which I was working, and to allow me to more meaningfully convey my analytic process.

For the purposes of the present chapter, I have room to provide only an abbreviated version of one of these summary narratives, that of Brian, a horn player. I have italicized key statements in the narrative, which I felt were important in Brian's construction of himself before, during and after the injury. Following the narrative, I provide a brief analysis of how he constructs his shifting identity through his account of his life. In Maitlis (2009), I worked across the analyses of several narratives to develop a model of positive identity construction following a trauma and to identify the different kinds of identity work in which musicians engaged to accomplish positive self-understandings. For the sake of illustration in the present chapter, I conclude by indicating some of the kinds of identity work that Brian carried out, supported by example quotations from the interview transcript.

Brian the Horn Player

Brian began playing piano at about age four, subsequently moving to the trumpet and then to the French horn. He played part time with the local symphony orchestra while doing his music degree and, although his first job after graduating was as a high school music teacher, he quite *soon felt the pull back to performing*, applying for and winning a permanent orchestral position. He described how full and fulfilling his professional life was then:

> You couldn't put the instrument down, you couldn't get enough of it …
> I really did define my whole life by this piece of metal and what I could
> do with it.

After playing for several years with the orchestra, Brian noticed something was wrong with one of his fingers, which would not always respond when he tried to move it. This was at first disconcerting and, as the condition worsened, very disturbing.

> It felt like, at that time, I was really coming to an end of being able to do anything.

Physiotherapy helped to extend his career, but it could not solve the neurological condition. Over the last few years, he has eased himself out of his role, playing part-time in a different position and is soon to take early retirement. He explained how he felt he had reached his 'best before' date:

> It's sort of like you go to the refrigerator and you see a tub of sour cream or salsa, and you look at the 'best before' date on it … You open it up, you may have to scrape a little something off the top, but you stir it up and you still use it for a while. It doesn't mean that it's no good anymore. It's still usable. But *there's also something else called an 'expiry date' and I think I want to get out of here before I reach that. I feel like I'm at my 'best before'.*

While this was not a choice he would have made without the injury, he did not feel negative about leaving. Using the metaphor of an *'albatross'* to describe his orchestral work, he explained:

> *It's a constant in your life that you can't turn off* … If I have a particularly onerous concert coming up, I know for several days before it I can't turn off the muzak going in my head of the problem spots. Once the concert's over, usually it's gone. But up *until that point it really is such a horrible – horrible, there I said it – a horrible constant in your life.* Playing the concert is almost a relief. So in terms of a lifelong thing, *knowing that I'm retiring from it and I can turn off that level of constant preparation, of being at a standard that you can't let slide too much, yeah, I can let go of that.*

He reflected on how it is to know he will never play certain pieces of music again:

> It's a bit of a *bittersweet feeling*, but it's good to … *say good bye to some of these pieces*, and I sometimes do that when we stand up for the bow and the piece is there and I just sort of *wave 'bye'* to it and then close the book.

Saying goodbye to his colleagues would not feel difficult. He *feels much less connected* to them than he did earlier in his career, *seeing himself as a father or grandfather figure* in an orchestra that is now made up of mostly much younger players. He has begun thinking about his retirement and what he will – and won't – do.

> I think *I don't want to play the horn at all anymore* ... They're asking me to play in the community amateur orchestra because they know I'm a professional and they want me to play. I'm not going to do that. *I don't want to play horn at that level* ... *In my head I have a concept of what I want to do,* how I want to be able to play this instrument, and *if I can't do that* ... *then I don't want to make those sounds.*

Instead, he says:

> I started out on trumpet, so I think I'll play in a community band on trumpet ... I'm not going to play horn. I'd love to go back to playing trumpet.

His other plans include doing more *teaching, and spending more time travelling and visiting family*, especially his grandchildren. Brian sees this partly as creating a distraction, saying of himself and his wife, who will also be retiring as a professional musician:

> both of us are sort of distracting ourselves from our performance – and seeing what else there is for us.

Overall, he expresses appreciation for how the injury has broadened the way he thinks of himself:

> It has allowed me to move to a better mental idea of what I am or who am I, and I'm not necessarily that horn player. I'm Brian, who has other opportunities, other things that I can do.

Exploring Brian's identities

Music was a calling for Brian, an occupation that completely consumed and defined him. The injury significantly challenged his identity, leaving him feeling unable to do what mattered most. Gradually, however, he found ways to manage his condition and continued to play, revising his self-understanding to that of a musician with an injury. Now aware of the fragility of this identity, he sought to pre-empt it spoiling this in his own mind or his colleagues' minds, not wanting to be seen as an 'expired' musician who had gone past his best. In contemplating alternative futures, he began to dis-identify with his former self, rehearsing the benefits of leaving professional musical life – shedding the

Table 27.1   Examples of Brian's identity work

Forms of identity work	Example quotations from Brian's narrative
Leaving old identities	
Making salient the costs of old identities	'it really is such a horrible – horrible, there I said it – a horrible constant in your life'
Dis-identifying with the role and colleagues	'There's very little in the way of camaraderie in what I'm doing now. Everybody is so much younger'
Creating distractions	'both of us are sort of distracting ourselves from our performance'
Drawing clear boundaries	'I don't want to play trumpet in an *orchestra* because that's, again, been my professional life. I want to make a real change from it'
Saying goodbyes	'I sometimes do that when we stand up for the bow and the piece is there and I just sort of wave "bye" to it and then close the book'
Pre-empting negative identities	'there's also something else called an "expiry date" and I think I want to get out of here before I reach that'
Exploring new identities	
Investing more in side identities	'I wanted to do a little more teaching. I haven't done any teaching in several years'
Expanding awareness of new possibilities	'I'm not necessarily that horn player. I'm Brian, who has other opportunities, other things that I can do'
Returning to former identities	'I started out on trumpet, so I think I'll play in a community band on trumpet … I'd love to go back to playing trumpet'
Experimenting with new identities	'when you retire from the orchestra they give you a pass for two tickets for any concerts … so you start being a member of the audience'

albatross of perpetual high standards, experiencing relief at not having to play the hard parts and leaving colleagues who no longer felt like friends. Preferring not to maintain a 'performing horn player' identity in a casual or amateur way, he plans to experiment with new identities, some connected to music and others not: horn teacher, community band trumpeter and grandfather. He positively anticipates constructing a broader self in future years, taking pleasure in no longer being 'that horn player', but 'Brian, who has other opportunities, other things that I can do' (from Maitlis, 2009: 53–57).

Reflections on the Analytic Process

Type of narrative analysis conducted

In this study of individuals' identity construction following a work-related trauma, I carried out a thematic analysis, focusing on the content of the narratives rather than the structure. I approached the narratives with an interest in identity and attended closely to the identity-related material of individuals' stories.

While examining thematic content, however, I was working with narratives of a pre-selected form: life stories interrupted by a specific 'complication', a complication that I expected to have a powerful role in shaping my interviewees' narratives. In keeping with much of the literature on life narratives (Lieblich and Josselson, 1997; McAdams, 1993; McAdams et al., 2006), my analysis thus unfolded around a key 'turning point', exploring individuals' identities before, during and after this point, and examining the work that they did to move between different parts of their self-narratives. Thus, I undertook a thematic analysis of a specific narrative form. Extending this to a structural analysis might involve investigating the commonalities and differences in how individuals organize events in their lives before and after an identity-disrupting turning point and how different ways of organizing the narrative construct their identity.

One could also consider these narratives through a dialogic/performance lens. Although I do not explicitly analyse my role as interviewer and audience in the above study, the dialogic nature of the narratives is clear to me and evident in the transcripts, if not in the summary narrative provided above. This is despite my efforts to shape the interview as little as possible, using a very open structure that enabled interviewees to tell their story as they chose and interrupting their flow with questions as little as possible. Yet clearly they were telling *me* their stories, doing so at a particular time in their lives and in a way that they understood as appropriate to a research interview for a study of the impact of injury on musicians' lives. These narratives, then, like any, were co-constructed performances and could be analysed as such. In addition, however, the interviews for this study have particular qualities that lend themselves to dialogic analysis. Without exception, and despite the 'research frame' of the conversation context, interviewees told very personal stories, revealing dreams, triumphs, failures and pain, and often expressing powerful emotions. I experienced the interviews as intense interactions and was repeatedly moved by what participants shared with me, as well as by the fact that they were doing so. My empathic reactions doubtless shaped the narratives, as did my unconcealed interest in how their self-understandings developed and changed over time. For all these reasons, conducting a dialogic/performance analysis of the narratives would likely uncover new and significant layers of meaning.

Pleasures and pains of the analytic process

Conducting this narrative analysis was a powerful and largely enjoyable experience for me. Yet with these joys came tensions that I have come to recognize as inherent to this kind of research. I outline here the central pleasures and pains of the process as I experienced it.

Initial readings: the process/endpoint tension

It was exciting to read and re-read each interview transcript, reliving the conversation we had had, but now with the luxury to ponder over the meanings of each utterance. With each reading, I saw new things and was reminded of points that had struck me during the interview but had since slipped from my memory. I enjoyed identifying statements that individually and together conveyed so much and I was often struck by the beautiful ways my participants described their experiences. And I felt honoured anew at what people had shared with me. Simply, I found it a great pleasure to engage in this kind of careful reading. Yet because of the length of each transcript and the relatively open coding process I adopted this was a very slow process, taking several hours per transcript. It was also a process that I knew, if rushed, would cause me to miss the very thing I was trying to understand.

Summarizing narratives: the holism/reduction tension

Producing the summary narratives was enjoyable because it gave me a chance to put down in writing what I understood as each person's story. Working to include as many of the participants' words as possible, I liked the challenge of selecting quotations that conveyed each story's essence. As my narrative developed, I appreciated having a version in a form that was so much more digestible than a 40-page transcript. And creating the narrative helped me see the sense I was making of each individual's story, in the way that telling a story so often does (Bruner, 1990; Weick, 1995). However, for all these satisfactions, summarizing the narratives was also challenging and frustrating. Qualitative analysis is always about data reduction, paring away data to allow the central themes, relationships or stories to emerge. And so, as I created each concise, coherent summary narrative, I worried about the choices I was making and the parts of the story that were getting lost. Asking interviewees to read and comment on my summaries alleviated some concerns, but their assurances of 'accuracy' could not change every story's inherent partiality and the knowledge that no story can fully capture the richness of a person's experiences.

Analysing for a core theme: the coherence/complexity tension

Narratives lend themselves to analyses of identity, especially life narratives of the kind I gathered. So, in some sense, coding these transcripts for 'identity work' and 'identity constructions' was easy – these were everywhere! But as I coded, I increasingly wondered when *isn't* a person conducting identity work in an interview? Then, as I began to partly resolve some of this issue by focusing on key segments, I started questioning what my identity lens was causing me to miss. I repeatedly found myself drawn back to powerful statements that were not directly about the person's identity, but that felt critical to his or her story. Should I follow my instinct, or should I curtail it so as not to get distracted and lose the plot I am trying to create? And again, going back to the challenge of partial stories, where should I draw lines and how would I live with my decisions?

Cross-case analysis: the breadth/richness tension

Looking for recurrent themes across individuals was satisfying. I was encouraged to see how seemingly idiosyncratic categories appeared in the context of another person's life and to discover how broadening or shifting a category a little allowed for the creation of a code that captured more of the narrative data. But this task became harder and harder as more cases were added into the analysis. It was a conceptual challenge simply to hold this much data, especially because I did not want themes to become decontextualized, as is common in cross-case comparative analyses in other forms of qualitative research. Yet retaining the narrative quality of the data grew increasingly difficult with the growing quantity of cases. This issue lies at the centre of what, for me, is perhaps the greatest challenge of narrative analysis conducted across a relatively large group. Much of a narrative's power lies in the complex story it tells and in the relationships between different parts of the story to each other and to the overall arc of the narrative. Breaking a narrative into themes and then grouping sets of similar themes together across multiple narratives makes it extremely difficult to retain the sequence, or the interrelatedness, of events and themes. But this sequencing and interrelatedness are what give narratives their distinctive richness and allow them to convey so much, so persuasively.

The four tensions captured above are all underpinned by my struggle to accept that every analytic choice I made meant giving something up: some narrative richness, some complexity, each story's 'wholeness' and, of course, much time. In the same way, while doing a thematic analysis was satisfying and rendered what I felt were valuable insights, it also meant that I paid less attention to the structural characteristics of each narrative and to its dialogic qualities. As a result, I missed many opportunities for additional and alternative understandings. As I note above, I did not entirely ignore these lenses and it would still be possible to layer them over my thematic analysis. But, as ever, we are working with trade-offs – of time, of coherence and of the story which we, as researchers, want to tell about those we have collected. My thematic analysis provided a compelling story, but I am aware that it is just one of the many that could be told.

Conclusion

Narrative analysis is an important method in many of the disciplines that underlie organization studies, including psychology, sociology and anthropology. Offering not only a valuable way of working with qualitative data, but also, and critically, a different way of thinking about our data, it includes several analytic approaches, as discussed above. These may be used individually or in combination and applied to narratives collected or constructed in a great variety of ways, with each lens providing unique understandings. In this chapter, I have tried to convey something of the intense excitement that working deeply with narrative can generate, while also sharing the tensions and struggles inherent in the process. Start small and see where it takes you! Our field has gained important insights from narrative research, but also has the potential to achieve a great deal more.

Further Reading

There are several excellent books on narrative analysis, and on narrative inquiry, the broader discipline of which analysis is a key part. Riessman (1993; 2008) explains the core narrative analysis approaches clearly and with compelling examples, as do Lieblich and her colleagues (1998). Gubrium and Holstein (2009) offer a powerful discussion of how to work with narrative that is collected 'in vivo', often through ethnographic studies. Czarniawska (1998; 2004) has written classic texts on narrative inquiry, addressing not only different analytic approaches, but also the production, collection and writing of narratives. With a focus on narrative in organizations, Boje (2001) provides a unique exploration of several postmodern approaches, while Gabriel (2000) builds a theory of storytelling through his analysis of myths, stories and folklore in organizations. Other valuable sources for narrative inquiry are Clandinin (2007) and the richly explored cases of Ochs and Capps (2001), and McAdams (1993) as well as edited volumes from the Narrative Study of Lives study (e.g. Lieblich and Josselson, 1997; McAdams et al., 2001; 2006).

References

Barry, D. and Elmes, M. (1997) 'Strategy retold: toward a narrative view of strategic discourse', *Academy of Management Review*, 22 (2): 429–452.

Bauman, R. (1986) *Story, Performance, and Event: Contextual Studies in Oral Narrative*. Cambridge: Cambridge University Press.

Berger, P.L. and Luckmann, T. (1967) *The Social Construction of Reality: A Treatise in the Sociology of Knowledge*. Harmondsworth: Penguin Books.

Boje, D.M. (1991) 'The storytelling organization: a study of story performance in an office-supply firm', *Administrative Science Quarterly*, 36 (1): 106–126.

Boje, D.M. (2001) *Narrative Methods for Organizational and Communication Research*. Thousand Oaks, CA: Sage.

Boudes, T. and Laroche, H. (2009) 'Taking off the heat: narrative sensemaking in post-crisis inquiry reports', *Organization Studies*, 30 (4): 377–396.

Brooks, P. (1992) *Reading for the Plot*. Cambridge, MA: Harvard University Press.

Brown, A.D. (2004) 'Authoritative sensemaking in a public inquiry report', *Organization Studies*, 25 (1): 95–112.

Brown, A.D. and Humphreys, M. (2003) 'Epic and tragic tales: making sense of change', *Journal of Applied Behavioral Science*, 39 (2): 121–144.

Bruner, J. S. (1986) *Actual Minds, Possible Worlds*. Cambridge, MA: Harvard University Press.

Bruner, J.S. (1990) *Acts of Meaning*. Cambridge, MA: Harvard University Press.

Bryant, J. and Lasky, B. (2007) 'A researcher's tale: dealing with epistemological divergence', *Qualitative Research in Organizations and Management: An International Journal*, 2 (3): 179–193.

Chase, S.E. (2005) 'Narrative inquiry: multiple lenses, approaches, voices', in N.K. Denzin and Y.S. Lincoln (eds), *The Sage Handbook of Qualitative Research* (3rd end). Thousand Oaks, CA: Sage, pp. 651–679.

Clandinin, D.J. (2007) *Handbook of Narrative Inquiry: Mapping a Methodology*. Thousand Oaks, CA: Sage.

Czarniawska, B. (1998) *A Narrative Approach to Organization Studies*. Thousand Oaks, CA: Sage.

Czarniawska, B. (2004) *Narratives in Social Science Research*. Thousand Oaks, CA: Sage.

Gabriel, Y. (2000) *Storytelling in Organizations: Facts, Fictions, and Fantasies*. Oxford: Oxford University Press.

Gabriel, Y. (2004) *Myths, Stories, and Organizations: Premodern Narratives for our Times*. Oxford: Oxford University Press.

Gergen, K.J. (1999) *An Invitation to Social Construction*. Thousand Oaks, CA: Sage.

Gergen, K.J. and Gergen, M.M. (1997) 'Narratives of the self', in L.P. Hinchman (ed.), *Memory, Identity, Community: The Idea of Narrative in the Human Sciences*. Buffalo, CO: SUNY Press, pp. 161–184.

Gersick, C.J.G., Bartunek, J.M. and Dutton, J.E. (2000) 'Learning from academia: the importance of relationships in professional life', *Academy of Management Journal*, 43 (6): 1026–1044.

Gubrium, J.F. and Holstein, J.A. (2009) *Analyzing Narrative Reality*. Thousand Oaks, CA: Sage.

Hardy, C. and Maguire, S. (2010) 'Organizations: discourse, field-configuring events, and change in organizations and institutional fields: narratives of DDT and the Stockholm Convention', *Academy of Management* Journal, 53 (6): 1365–1392.

Ibarra, H. and Barbulescu, R. (2010) 'Identity as narrative: prevalence, effectiveness, and consequences of narrative identity work in macro work role transitions', *Academy of Management Review*, 35 (1): 135–154.

Kreiner, G.E., Hollensbe, E.C. and Sheep, M.L. (2006) 'Where is the "me" among the "we"? Identity work and the search for optimal balance', *Academy of Management Journal*, 49 (5): 1031–1057.

Labov, W. (1972) *Language in the Inner City: Studies in the Black English Vernacular*. Philadelphia: University of Pennsylvania Press.

Labov, W. and Waletzky, J. (1967) 'Narrative analysis: oral versions of personal experience', in J. Helm (ed.), *Essays on the Verbal and Visual Arts*. Seattle, WA: University of Washington Press, pp. 12–44.

Lamberg, J. and Pajunen, K. (2005) 'Beyond the metaphor: the morphology of organizational decline and turnaround', *Human Relations*, 58 (8): 947–980.

Lieblich, A. and Josselson, R. (1997) *The Narrative Study of Lives*, volume 5. Thousand Oaks, CA: Sage.

Lieblich, A., Tuval-Mashiach, R. and Zilber, T. (1998) *Narrative Research: Reading, Analysis and Interpretation*. Thousand Oaks, CA: Sage.

Maitlis, S. (2005) 'The social processes of organizational sensemaking', *Academy of Management Journal*, 48 (1): 21–49.

Maitlis, S. (2009) 'Who am I now? Sensemaking and identity in posttraumatic growth', in L.M. Roberts and J.E. Dutton (eds), *Exploring Positive Identities and Organizations: Building a Theoretical and Research Foundation*. New York: Psychology Press, pp. 47–76.

Maitlis, S. (2010) 'Posttraumatic growth at work: reconstructing identity after a work-related trauma', paper presented at the Second International Symposium on Process Organization Studies, Rhodes, Greece.

Mangham, I.L. and Overington, M.A. (1987) *Organizations as Theatre: A Social Psychology of Dramatic Appearances.* Chichester: John Wiley and Sons.

Martens, M.L., Jennings, J.E. and Jennings, P.D. (2007) 'Do the stories they tell get them the money they need? The role of entrepreneurial narratives in resource acquisition', *Academy of Management Journal*, 50 (5): 1107–1132.

McAdams, D.P. (1993) *The Stories We Live By: Personal Myths and the Making of The Self.* New York: William Morrow and Co.

McAdams, D.P. and Bowman, P.J. (2001) 'Narrating life's turning points: redemption and contamination', in D. P. McAdams, R. Josselson and A. Lieblich (eds), *Turns in the Road: Narrative Studies of Lives in Transition*. Washington, DC: American Psychological Association, pp. 3–34.

McAdams, D.P., Josselson, R. and Lieblich, A. (2001) *Turns in the Road: Narrative Studies of Lives in Transition*. Washington, DC: American Psychological Association.

McAdams, D.P., Josselson, R. and Lieblich, A. (2006) *Identity and Story: Creating Self in Narrative*. Washington: American Psychological Association.

Ochs, E. and Capps, L. (2001) *Living Narrative: Creating Lives in Everyday Storytelling.* Cambridge: Harvard University Press.

Oswick, C., Anthony, P., Keenoy, T., Mangham, I. L. and Grant, D. (2000) 'A dialogic analysis of organizational learning', *Journal of Management Studies*, 37 (6): 887–902.

Propp, V. (1968 [1928]) *Morphology of the Folktale* (2nd edn), trans. S. Pirkova-Jakobson. Austin: University of Texas Press.

Riessman, C.K. (1993) *Narrative Analysis*. Thousand Oaks, CA: Sage.

Riessman, C.K. (2008) *Narrative Methods for the Human Sciences*. Thousand Oaks, CA: Sage.

Sonenshein, S. (2010) 'We're changing or are we? Untangling the role of progressive, regressive and stability narratives during strategic change implementation', *Academy of Management Journal*, 53 (3): 477–512.

Strauss, A. and Corbin, J. (1998) *Basics of Qualitative Research: Techniques and Procedures for Developing Grounded Theory.* Thousand Oaks, CA: Sage.

Weick, K.E. (1995) *Sensemaking in Organizations*. Thousand Oaks, CA: Sage.

Zilber, T.B. (2007) 'Stories and the discursive dynamics of institutional entrepreneurship: the case of Israeli high-tech after the bubble', *Organization Studies*, 28 (7): 1035–1054.

Index

Figure and Tables are indicated by page numbers in bold.

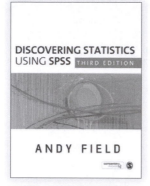
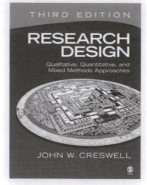
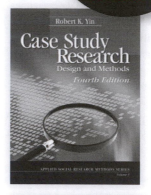

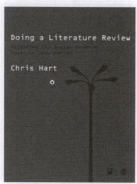
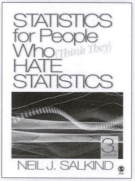

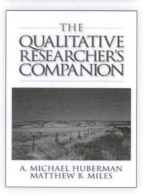

Research Methods
Books from SAGE

INTERPRETING QUALITATIVE DATA THIRD EDITION

DAVID SILVERMAN

Qualitative Research & Evaluation Methods

3 EDITION

Michael Quinn Patton

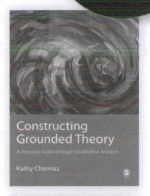

Constructing Grounded Theory

A Practical Guide through Qualitative Analysis

Kathy Charmaz

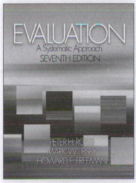

EVALUATION A Systematic Approach SEVENTH EDITION

PETER H ROSSI MARK W LIPSEY HOWARD E FREEMAN

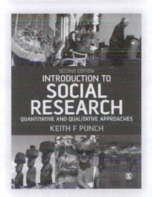

SECOND EDITION INTRODUCTION TO SOCIAL RESEARCH QUANTITATIVE AND QUALITATIVE APPROACHES KEITH F PUNCH

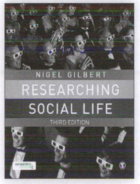

NIGEL GILBERT RESEARCHING SOCIAL LIFE THIRD EDITION

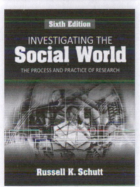

Sixth Edition INVESTIGATING THE Social World THE PROCESS AND PRACTICE OF RESEARCH

Russell K. Schutt

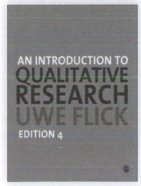

AN INTRODUCTION TO QUALITATIVE RESEARCH UWE FLICK EDITION 4

DEVELOPING EFFECTIVE RESEARCH PROPOSALS Keith F Punch SECOND EDITION

www.sagepub.co.uk

SAGE

The Qualitative Research Kit

Edited by Uwe Flick

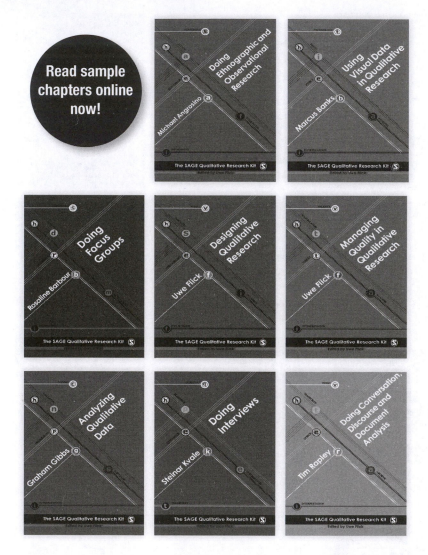

Read sample chapters online now!

- Doing Ethnographic and Observational Research — Michael Angrosino — The SAGE Qualitative Research Kit — Edited by Uwe Flick
- Using Visual Data in Qualitative Research — Marcus Banks — The SAGE Qualitative Research Kit — Edited by Uwe Flick
- Doing Focus Groups — Rosaline Barbour — The SAGE Qualitative Research Kit
- Designing Qualitative Research — Uwe Flick — The SAGE Qualitative Research Kit — Edited by Uwe Flick
- Managing Quality in Qualitative Research — Uwe Flick — The SAGE Qualitative Research Kit — Edited by Uwe Flick
- Analyzing Qualitative Data — Graham Gibbs — The SAGE Qualitative Research Kit — Edited by Uwe Flick
- Doing Interviews — Steinar Kvale — The SAGE Qualitative Research Kit
- Doing Conversation, Discourse and Document Analysis — Tim Rapley — The SAGE Qualitative Research Kit — Edited by Uwe Flick

www.sagepub.co.uk

SAGE